The Consumer Credit and Sales Legal Practice Series

DECEPTION **Y0-AAC-379**

CONSUMER WARRANTY LAW

Lemon Law, Magnuson-Moss, UCC, Mobile Home, and Other Warranty Statutes

2004 Supplement

 With CD-Rom

Carolyn L. Carter

Contributing Authors: Jonathan Sheldon, Anthony Rodriguez for Chapter 16a, Richard Rubin, Elizabeth De Armond

National Consumer Law Center

77 Summer Street, 10th Floor   Boston, MA 02110   www.consumerlaw.org

About NCLC

The National Consumer Law Center, a nonprofit corporation founded in 1969, assists consumers, advocates, and public policy makers nationwide who use the powerful and complex tools of consumer law to ensure justice and fair treatment for all, particularly those whose poverty renders them powerless to demand accountability from the economic marketplace. For more information, go to www.consumerlaw.org.

Ordering NCLC Publications

Order securely online at www.consumerlaw.org, or contact Publications Department, National Consumer Law Center, 77 Summer Street, Boston, MA 02110, (617) 542-9595 x1, FAX: (617) 542-8028, e-mail: publications@nclc.org.

Training and Conferences

NCLC participates in numerous national, regional, and local consumer law trainings. Its annual fall conference is a forum for consumer rights attorneys from legal services programs, private practice, government, and nonprofit organizations to share insights into common problems and explore novel and tested approaches that promote consumer justice in the marketplace. Contact NCLC for more information or see our web site.

Case Consulting

Case analysis, consulting and co-counseling for lawyers representing vulnerable consumers are among NCLC's important activities. Administration on Aging funds allow us to provide free consulting to legal services advocates representing elderly consumers on many types of cases. Massachusetts Legal Assistance Corporation funds permit case assistance to advocates representing low-income Massachusetts consumers. Other funding may allow NCLC to provide very brief consultations to other advocates without charge. More comprehensive case analysis and research is available for a reasonable fee. See our web site for more information at www.consumerlaw.org.

Charitable Donations and Cy Pres Awards

NCLC's work depends in part on the support of private donors. Tax-deductible donations should be made payable to National Consumer Law Center, Inc. For more information, contact Suzanne Cutler of NCLC's Development Office at (617) 542-8010 or scutler@nclc.org. NCLC has also received generous court-approved *cy pres* awards arising from consumer class actions to advance the interests of class members. For more information, contact Robert Hobbs (rhobbs@nclc.org) or Rich Dubois (rdubois@nclc.org) at (617) 542-8010.

Comments and Corrections

Write to the above address to the attention of the Editorial Department or e-mail consumerlaw@nclc.org.

About This Volume

This is the 2004 Supplement to *Consumer Warranty Law* (2d ed. 2001) with a 2004 CD-Rom. Retain the 2001 Second Edition, this Supplement, and the 2004 CD-Rom. Discard all other volumes, supplements, and CDs. Continuing developments can be found in periodic supplements to this volume and in NCLC REPORTS, *Deceptive Practices & Warranties Edition*.

Cite This Volume As

National Consumer Law Center, Consumer Warranty Law (2d ed. 2001 and Supp.).

Attention

Copyright

© 2004 by National Consumer Law Center, Inc.
All Rights Reserved

Printed in Canada

ISBN 1-931697-56-6 (this Supplement)
ISBN 1-931697-00-0 (main volume)
ISBN 0-943116-10-4 (Series)

Library of Congress Control Number 2001091815

About the Authors

Carolyn L. Carter is of counsel with NCLC, and was formerly co-director of Legal Services, Inc., in Gettysburg, Pennsylvania, and director of the Law Reform Office of the Cleveland Legal Aid Society. She is the editor of *Pennsylvania Consumer Law*, editor of the First Edition of *Ohio Consumer Law*, co-author of *Consumer Warranty Law* (2d ed. 2001), *Unfair and Deceptive Acts and Practices* (5th ed. 2001), *Repossessions and Foreclosures* (5th ed. 2002), *Automobile Fraud* (2d ed. 2003), and *Fair Credit Reporting* (5th ed. 2002), contributing author to *Fair Debt Collection* (5th ed. 2004), *Truth in Lending* (5th ed. 2003) and *The Cost of Credit* (2d ed. 2000), and the 1992 recipient of the Vern Countryman Consumer Award.

Jonathan Sheldon has been an NCLC staff attorney writing on warranty law, deceptive practices, leasing, automobile issues, and other consumer law topics since 1976. From 1973 to 1976 he was a staff attorney with the Bureau of Consumer Protection, Federal Trade Commission. His publications include co-authorship of *Consumer Warranty Law* (1997, 2001), *Unfair and Deceptive Acts and Practices* (1982, 1988, 1991, 1997, 2001), *Repossessions and Foreclosures* (1982, 1988, 1995, 1999), *Automobile Fraud* (1998, 2003), *Consumer Class Actions* (1999), and *Consumer Arbitration Agreements* (2001, 2002, 2003).

Anthony Rodriguez is an NCLC staff attorney who previously served as the Director of the Massachusetts Attorney General's Disability Rights Project, and also worked as an Assistant Attorney General in the Consumer Protection and Civil Rights Divisions. Before that, he was a legal services attorney in Los Angeles. He is co-author of *Fair Credit Reporting* (5th ed. 2002) and a contributing author to *Credit Discrimination* (3d ed. 2002).

Richard Rubin is a private attorney in Santa Fe, New Mexico, whose practice is limited to representing consumers in federal appeals and consulting for other consumer rights advocates. He is chair emeritus of the National Association of Consumer Advocates, has taught consumer law at the University of New Mexico School of Law, and presents continuing legal education and attorney training programs throughout the country. He is the 2000 recipient of the Vern Countryman Consumer Award.

Elizabeth De Armond is on the faculty of the Chicago-Kent College of Law. She is a frequent contributor to NCLC publications and is a contributing author to *Consumer Warranty Law* (2d ed. 2001), *Automobile Fraud* (2d ed. 2003), and *Fair Credit Reporting* (5th ed. 2002). Previously, she was in private practice in Texas and a clerk for the Hon. Cornelia Kennedy of the United States Court of Appeals for the Sixth Circuit. She is a member of the Illinois, Massachusetts, and Texas bars.

Acknowledgments: We want to thank the following for their contributions to this supplement: Elizabeth Ryan, Allen Agnitti, Elizabeth De Armond, Kurt Terwilliger, and Rebecca Pressman for legal research and writing; T. Michael Flinn, a private attorney in Georgia, Dani Liblang, a private attorney in Michigan, and Ron Burdge, a private attorney in Ohio, for contributing pleadings; Ron Burdge and Kan Tung Donohoe, an attorney with Kemnitzer, Anderson, Barron and Oglivie in San Francisco, for their assistance with motor home issues; Bernard Brown, a private attorney in Missouri, Dmitry Feofanov, a private attorney in Illinois, and Richard Diklich, an automotive expert in Missouri, for substantive contributions to the text. We would also like to thank the American Law Institute, the National Conference of Commissioners on Uniform State Laws, and the Permanent Editorial Board for the Uniform Commercial Code for granting permission to reprint sections of revised UCC Articles 1, 2 and 2A.

We are especially grateful to Eric Secoy for editorial supervision; Emilio Englade for editorial assistance; Shirlron Williams for assistance checking citations and web links; Shannon Halbrook for production assistance; Xylutions for typesetting services; and Neil Fogarty of Law Disks for preparing the CD-Rom.

What Your Library Should Contain

The Consumer Credit and Sales Legal Practice Series contains 16 titles, updated annually, arranged into four libraries, and designed to be an attorney's primary practice guide and legal resource in all 50 states. Each manual includes a CD-Rom allowing information to be copied into a word processor.

Debtor Rights Library

2000 Sixth Edition, 2003 Supplement, and 2003 CD-Rom, Including Law Disks' Bankruptcy Forms

Consumer Bankruptcy Law and Practice: the definitive personal bankruptcy manual, with step-by-step instructions from initial interview to final discharge, and including consumers' rights as creditors when a merchant or landlord files for bankruptcy. Appendices and CD-Rom contain over 130 annotated pleadings, bankruptcy statutes, rules and fee schedules, an interview questionnaire, a client handout, and software to complete the latest versions of petitions and schedules.

2004 Fifth Edition and 2004 CD-Rom

Fair Debt Collection: the basic reference in the field, covering the Fair Debt Collection Practices Act and common law, state statutory and other federal debt collection protections. Appendices and companion CD-Rom contain sample pleadings and discovery, the FTC's Official Staff Commentary, *all* FTC staff opinion letters, and summaries of reported and unreported cases.

2002 Fifth Edition, 2003 Supplement, and 2003 CD-Rom

Repossessions and Foreclosures: unique guide to VA, FHA and other types of home foreclosures, servicer obligations, car and mobile home repossessions, threatened seizures of household goods, tax and other statutory liens, and automobile lease and rent-to-own default remedies. The CD-Rom reprints relevant UCC provisions and numerous key federal statutes, regulations, and agency letters, summarizes hundreds of state laws, and includes over 150 pleadings covering a wide variety of cases.

2002 Second Edition, 2003 Supplement, and 2003 CD-Rom

Student Loan Law: student loan debt collection and collection fees; discharges based on closed school, false certification, failure to refund, disability, and bankruptcy; tax intercepts, wage garnishment, and offset of social security benefits; repayment plans, consolidation loans, deferments, and non-payment of loan based on school fraud. CD-Rom and appendices contain numerous forms, pleadings, interpretation letters and regulations.

2001 Second Edition, 2003 Supplement, and 2003 CD-Rom

Access to Utility Service: the only examination of consumer rights when dealing with regulated, de-regulated, and unregulated utilities, including telecommunications, terminations, billing errors, low-income payment plans, fuel allowances in subsidized housing, LIHEAP, and weatherization. Includes summaries of state utility regulations.

Credit and Banking Library

2003 Fifth Edition with CD-Rom

Truth in Lending: detailed analysis of *all* aspects of TILA, the Consumer Leasing Act, and the Home Ownership and Equity Protection Act (HOEPA). Appendices and the CD-Rom contain the Acts, Reg. Z, Reg. M, and their Official Staff Commentaries, numerous sample pleadings, rescission notices, and two programs to compute APRs.

National Consumer Law Center ■ 77 Summer Street ■ 10th Floor ■ Boston MA ■ 02110
(617) 542-9595 ■ FAX (617) 542-8028 ■ publications@nclc.org
Order securely online at www.consumerlaw.org

2002 Fifth Edition, 2004 Supplement, and 2004 CD-Rom

Fair Credit Reporting: the key resource for handling any type of credit reporting issue, from cleaning up blemished credit records to suing reporting agencies and creditors for inaccurate reports. Covers credit scoring, privacy issues, identity theft, the FCRA, the new FACT Act, the Credit Repair Organizations Act, state credit reporting and repair statutes, and common law claims.

2002 Second Edition, 2004 Supplement, and 2004 CD-Rom

Consumer Banking and Payments Law: unique analysis of consumer law (and NACHA rules) as to checks, money orders, credit, debit, and stored value cards, and banker's right of setoff. Also extensive treatment of electronic records and signatures, electronic transfer of food stamps, and direct deposits of federal payments. The CD-Rom and appendices reprint relevant agency interpretations and pleadings.

2000 Second Edition, 2004 Supplement, and 2004 CD-Rom

The Cost of Credit: Regulation and Legal Challenges: a one-of-a-kind resource detailing state and federal regulation of consumer credit in all fifty states, federal usury preemption, explaining credit math, and how to challenge excessive credit charges and credit insurance. The CD-Rom includes a credit math program and hard-to-find agency interpretations.

2002 Third Edition, 2004 Supplement, and 2004 CD-Rom

Credit Discrimination: analysis of the Equal Credit Opportunity Act, Fair Housing Act, Civil Rights Acts, and state credit discrimination statutes, including reprints of all relevant federal interpretations, government enforcement actions, and numerous sample pleadings.

Consumer Litigation Library

2003 Third Edition with CD-Rom

Consumer Arbitration Agreements: numerous successful approaches to challenge the enforceability of a binding arbitration agreement, the interrelation of the Federal Arbitration Act and state law, class actions in arbitration, the right to discovery, and other topics. Appendices and CD-Rom include sample discovery, numerous briefs, arbitration service provider rules and affidavits as to arbitrator costs.

2002 Fifth Edition, 2004 Supplement, and 2004 CD-Rom

Consumer Class Actions: A Practical Litigation Guide: makes class action litigation manageable even for small offices, including numerous sample pleadings, class certification memoranda, discovery, class notices, settlement materials, and much more. Includes contributions from seven of the most experienced consumer class action litigators around the country.

2003 CD-Rom with Index Guide: ALL pleadings from ALL NCLC Manuals, including Consumer Law Pleadings Numbers One through Nine

Consumer Law Pleadings on CD-Rom: over 700 notable recent pleadings from all types of consumer cases, including predatory lending, foreclosures, automobile fraud, lemon laws, debt collection, fair credit reporting, home improvement fraud, rent to own, student loans, and lender liability. Finding aids pinpoint the desired pleading in seconds, ready to paste into a word processing program.

Deception and Warranties Library

2001 Fifth Edition, 2003 Supplement, and 2003 CD-Rom

Unfair and Deceptive Acts and Practices: the only practice manual covering all aspects of a deceptive practices case in every state. Special sections on automobile sales, the federal racketeering (RICO) statute, unfair insurance practices, and the FTC Holder Rule.

2003 Second Edition, 2004 Supplement, and 2004 CD-Rom

Automobile Fraud: examination of title law, odometer tampering, lemon laundering, sale of salvage and wrecked cars, undisclosed prior use, prior damage to new cars, numerous sample pleadings, and title search techniques.

2001 Second Edition, 2004 Supplement, and 2004 CD-Rom

Consumer Warranty Law: comprehensive treatment of new and used car lemon laws, the Magnuson-Moss Warranty Act, UCC Articles 2 and 2A, mobile home, new home, and assistive device warranty laws, FTC Used Car Rule, tort theories, car repair and home improvement statutes, service contract and lease laws, with numerous sample pleadings.

National Consumer Law Center ■ **77 Summer Street** ■ **10ᵗʰ Floor** ■ **Boston MA** ■ **02110**
(617) 542-9595 ■ **FAX (617) 542-8028** ■ **publications@nclc.org**
Order securely online at www.consumerlaw.org

NCLC's CD-Roms

Every NCLC manual comes with a companion CD-Rom featuring pop-up menus, PDF format, Internet-style navigation of appendices, indices, and bonus pleadings, hard-to-find agency interpretations and other practice aids. Documents can be copied into a word processing program. Of special note is *Consumer Law in a Box*:

July 2004 CD-Rom

Consumer Law in a Box: a CD-Rom combining *all* documents and software from 16 other NCLC CD-Roms. Quickly pinpoint a document from thousands found on the CD through keyword searches and Internet-style navigation, links, bookmarks, and other finding aids.

Other NCLC Publications for Lawyers

issued 24 times a year

NCLC REPORTS covers the latest developments and ideas in the practice of consumer law.

2003 First Edition with CD-Rom

The Practice of Consumer Law: Seeking Economic Justice: contains an essential overview to consumer law and explains how to get started in a private or legal services consumer practice. Packed with invaluable sample pleadings and practice pointers for even experienced consumer attorneys.

2002 First Edition with CD-Rom

STOP Predatory Lending: A Guide for Legal Advocates: provides a roadmap and practical legal strategy for litigating predatory lending abuses, from small loans to mortgage loans. The CD-Rom contains a credit math program, pleadings, legislative and administrative materials, and underwriting guidelines.

National Consumer Law Center Guide Series are books designed for consumers, counselors, and attorneys new to consumer law:

2002 Edition

NCLC Guide to Surviving Debt: a great overview of consumer law. Everything a paralegal, new attorney, or client needs to know about debt collectors, managing credit card debt, whether to refinance, credit card problems, home foreclosures, evictions, repossessions, credit reporting, utility terminations, student loans, budgeting, and bankruptcy.

2002 Edition

NCLC Guide to Mobile Homes: what consumers and their advocates need to know about mobile home dealer sales practices and an in-depth look at mobile home quality and defects, with 35 photographs and construction details.

2002 Edition

NCLC Guide to Consumer Rights for Immigrants: an introduction to many of the most critical consumer issues faced by immigrants, including international wires, check cashing and banking, *notario* and immigration consultant fraud, affidavits of support, telephones, utilities, credit history discrimination, high-cost credit, used car fraud, student loans and more.

2000 Edition

Return to Sender: Getting a Refund or Replacement for Your Lemon Car: Find how lemon laws work, what consumers and their lawyers should know to evaluate each other, investigative techniques and discovery tips, how to handle both informal dispute resolution and trials, and more.

Visit **www.consumerlaw.org** to order securely online or for more information on all NCLC manuals and CD-Roms, including the full tables of contents, indices, and listings of CD-Rom contents.

National Consumer Law Center ■ **77 Summer Street** ■ **10th Floor** ■ **Boston MA** ■ **02110**
(617) 542-9595 ■ FAX (617) 542-8028 ■ publications@nclc.org
Order securely online at www.consumerlaw.org

Finding Aids and Search Tips

The Consumer Credit and Sales Legal Practice Series presently contains sixteen volumes, eleven supplements, and sixteen companion CD-Roms—all constantly being updated. The Series includes over 10,000 pages, over 100 chapters, over 100 appendices, and almost 1000 pleadings, as well as hundreds of documents found on the CD-Roms, but not found in the books. Here are a number of ways to pinpoint in seconds what you need from this array of materials.

Internet-Based Searches

www.consumerlaw.org

Electronically search every chapter and appendix of all sixteen manuals and their supplements: go to www.consumerlaw.org/keyword and enter a case name, regulation cite, or other search term. You are instantly given the book names, page numbers, and number of hits on each page in any of the NCLC manuals containing that term.

www.consumerlaw.org

Current indexes, tables of contents, and CD-Rom contents for all sixteen volumes are found at www.consumerlaw.org. Just click on *The Consumer Credit and Sales Legal Practice Series* and scroll down to the book you want. Then click on that volume's index, contents, or CD-Rom contents.

Finding Material on NCLC's CD-Roms

Consumer Law in a Box CD-Rom

Electronically search all sixteen NCLC CD-Roms, including thousands of agency interpretations, all NCLC appendices and almost 1000 pleadings: use Acrobat's search button* in NCLC's *Consumer Law in a Box CD-Rom* (this CD-Rom is free to set subscribers) to find every instance that a keyword appears on any of our 16 CD-Roms. Then with one click, go to that location to see the full text of the document.

CD-Rom accompanying this volume

Electronically search the CD-Rom accompanying this volume, including pleadings, agency interpretations, and regulations. Use Acrobat's search button* to find every instance that a keyword appears on the CD-Rom, and then with one click, go to that location on the CD-Rom. Or just click on subject buttons until you navigate to the document you need.

Finding Pleadings

Consumer Law Pleadings on CD-Rom and Index Guide

Search five different ways for the right pleading from almost 1000 choices: use the *Index Guide* accompanying *Consumer Law Pleadings on CD-Rom* to search for pleadings by type, subject, publication title, name of contributor, or contributor's jurisdiction. The guide also provides a summary of the pleading once the right pleading is located. *Consumer Law Pleadings on CD-Rom* and the *Consumer Law in a Box CD-Rom* also let you search for all pleadings electronically by subject, type of pleading, and by publication title, giving you instant access to the full pleading in Word and/or PDF format once you find the pleading you need.

Using This Volume to Find Material in All Sixteen Volumes

This volume

The Quick Reference at the back of this volume lets you pinpoint manual sections or appendices where over a 1000 different subject areas are covered.

---

* Users of NCLC CD-Roms should become familiar with "search," a powerful Acrobat tool, distinguished from "find," another Acrobat feature that is far slower and less powerful than "search." The Acrobat 5 "search" icon is a pair of binoculars with paper in the background, while the "find" icon is a pair of binoculars without the paper. Acrobat 6 uses one icon, a pair of binoculars, that brings you to a menu with several search options.

Contents

new section

replacement subsection

Chapter 2   The Magnuson-Moss Warranty Act

Chapter 3

Express Warranties

replacement subsection

replacement heading

Chapter 5

Fourteen Ways to Defeat Warranty Disclaimers

replacement heading

replacement section

replacement heading

Chapter 6

Avoiding Vertical and Horizontal Privity Requirements

Chapter 7

Establishing Breach of Warranty: Notice, Standards, Proof and Defenses

Chapter 8

UCC Self-Help Remedies: Cancellation of the Sale; Deducting Damages from the Outstanding Balance

Chapter 11   Deception, Unfairness, Unconscionability, Lack of Good Faith and Fraud

Chapter 12   Negligence and Strict Liability in Tort

Chapter 13   New Cars

Chapter 16   New Home Sales

Chapter 16a
new chapter

Laws for Assistive Technological Devices

Chapter 17

Automobile Repair, Home Improvements, and Other Services

Chapter 18   Service Contracts, Extended Warranties and Mechanical Breakdown Insurance

Chapter 19   Leases

CD-Rom Contents

How to Use/Help

Federal Statutes/History

FTC Regulations and Statements

Cumulative Index

Quick Reference to the Consumer Credit and Sales Legal Practice Series

What Your Library Should Contain

Word Files on CD-Rom

Contents of NCLC Publications

Printer-Friendly Order Form for All NCLC Publications
Secure On-line Order Form

Consumer Education Brochures, Books

Legal and General Audience Books Available to Order from NCLC
The Practice of Consumer Law, Seeking Economic Justice
STOP Predatory Lending: A Guide for Legal Advocates with CD-Rom
Return to Sender: Getting a Refund or Replacement for Your Lemon Car
The NCLC Guide to Surviving Debt (2002 Ed.)
The NCLC Guide to Consumer Rights for Immigrants
The NCLC Guide to Mobile Homes
Printer-Friendly Order Form
Secure On-line Order Form

Brochures for Consumers on This CD-Rom
General Consumer Education Brochures
Consumer Concerns for Older Americans
Immigrant Justice in the Consumer Marketplace

Order NCLC Publications, CD-Roms

NCLC Manuals and CD-Roms
Order Publications On-line
Printer-Friendly Order Form
Consumer Law in a Box CD-Rom
Credit Math, Bankruptcy Software
Printer-Friendly Publications Brochure
NCLC Newsletters
Case Assistance
Conferences, Training
Books for Lawyers, Consumers
Consumer Education Pamphlets
Consumer Weblinks

About NCLC, About This CD-Rom

National Consumer Law Center
Mission Statement
Contact Information: Boston, Washington offices
Go to NCLC Website
What Your Library Should Contain
Order NCLC Publications On-line
Learn More About NCLC Manuals, CD-Roms,
Order Form: Order NCLC Publications Via Mail, Phone, Fax

About this CD-Rom
What is Contained on this CD-Rom
Finding Aids for NCLC Manuals: What Is Available in the Books?
Disclaimers—Need to Adapt Pleadings; Unauthorized Practice of Law
License Agreement, Copyrights, Trademarks: Please Read
Law Disks: CD-Rom Producer, Publisher of Bankruptcy Forms Software

Acrobat 6.0 Problem

Acrobat Reader 5

Chapter 1

Introductory Materials

Page 1

1.1 About This Volume

Replace last sentence of subsection's ninth paragraph with:

For more information contact Publications Department, National Consumer Law Center, 77 Summer St., Boston MA 02110, (617) 542-9595.

1.2 Overview of Consumer Warranty Laws

Page 2

1.2.2 UCC Article 2

Add to text at end of subsection:

In 2003, the National Conference of Commissioners on Uniform State Laws (NCCUSL) approved a revised version of Articles 2 and 2A for consideration by state legislatures. These revisions are summarized in § 1.2aS, *infra*.

Page 3

1.2.3 UCC Article 2A

Add to text at end of subsection:

In 2003, the National Conference of Commissioners on Uniform State Laws (NCCUSL) approved a revised version of Articles 2 and 2A for consideration by state legislatures. These revisions are summarized in § 1.2aS, *infra*.

1.2.5 Unfair and Deceptive Acts and Practices (UDAP) and Fraud

Replace NCLC citation in subsection's second paragraph with:

Unfair and Deceptive Acts and Practices (5th ed. 2001 and Supp.)

Page 4

Add new subsection to text after § 1.2.7.

1.2a 2003 Revisions to UCC Articles 2 and 2A

1.2a.1 History of Revisions

For a number of years, the National Conference of Commissioners on Uniform State Laws (NCCUSL) has been engaged in a project, often controversial, to rewrite UCC Articles 2 and 2A.[11.1] There is great disagreement about the extent to which computer information transactions should be excluded from the revised Articles, as many products today contain such information. Final approval by NCCUSL and the American Law Institute (ALI) in mid-2003 has not weakened the opposition from many groups, who are concerned by the exclusion of computer information transactions. The revisions have not yet been introduced in any state legislature, and a rocky reception can be predicted when the changes are introduced.[11.2]

1.2a.2 Revised Article 2

The revised version of Article 2 would make a number of significant changes to warranty law. It would:

- Exclude "information," an undefined term, from the Article 2 definition of goods.[11.3] Revised Article 2 would leave it up to the courts to determine whether a product that includes a computer chip is governed by Article 2, thus creating a great deal of uncertainty and potentially undercutting Article 2's role as the basic law of sales.
- Provide for electronic signatures, documents, and notices, setting rules with even fewer consumer protections than provided by the Uniform Electronic Transactions Act.[11.4]
- Raise the threshold for the statute of frauds to $5000.[11.5]
- Significantly revise the law regarding the "battle of the forms."[11.6]
- Encourage sellers' imposition of post-acceptance terms by using a broad standard of whether the parties agree to such changes, and by treating clicking on an Internet button as assent to terms.[11.7]
- Separate out obligations created by the remote seller's advertisements or when the remote seller furnishes, along with the goods, a description of the goods, an affirmation of fact about the goods, or a promise of repair, replacement, or refund. Under revised Article 2, these obligations would not be warranties. They would run to the remote buyer but would apply only to goods that are new, or that are sold or leased as new.[11.8]
- Treat "remedial promises"—promises to repair or replace goods, or to refund the purchase price—separately from warranties, and measure the statute of limitations from the date of breach of the promise rather than from the date of delivery of the goods.[11.9]
- Require that a disclaimer of the implied warranty of merchantability in a consumer contract be set forth conspicuously in a written or electronic document (termed a "record" in revised Article 2).[11.10] Instead of mentioning merchantability, the disclaimer must state: "The seller undertakes no responsibility for the quality of goods except as otherwise provided in this contract."[11.11] In the alternative, the seller can use a term such as "as is."[11.12] If "as is" or a similar term is used in a consumer contract evidenced by a written or electronic document, then the disclaimer must be set forth conspicuously in the document, but otherwise it can be oral.[11.13]
- Require that a disclaimer of the implied warranty of fitness for a particular purpose in a consumer transaction be set forth conspicuously in a written or electronic document. The disclaimer must state: "The seller assumes no responsibility that the goods will be fit for any particular purpose for which you may be buying these goods, except as otherwise provided in the contract."[11.14] In the alternative, as is true of a disclaimer of the implied warranty of merchantability, the seller can use a term such as "as is."[11.15] If "as is" or a similar term is used in a consumer contract evidenced by a written or electronic document, then the disclaimer must be set forth conspicuously in the document, but otherwise it can be oral.[11.16]
- Adopt a new definition of "conspicuous," identical to that in revised Article 1, but with additional standards for electronic transactions.[11.17]
- Provide that failure to give notice of breach bars the buyer from a remedy only to the extent that the seller is prejudiced thereby.[11.18]
- Require not only buyers who reject goods but also buyers who revoke acceptance in non-consumer contracts to specify the defects on which they are relying.[11.19]
- Allow a good faith seller an opportunity to cure by tendering conforming goods not only after rejection but also, in non-consumer contracts, after revocation of acceptance.[11.20]
- Allow post-revocation or post-rejection use of the product if reasonable under the circumstances, but provide that in appropriate cases the buyer may be obligated to pay the seller for the value of such use.[11.21]
- Prohibit contractual reduction of the statute of limitations in consumer transactions.[11.22]
- Adopt a discovery rule even for warranties that do not extend to future performance, by

allowing suit up to four years after accrual of the cause of action or one year after the defect was or should have been discovered, whichever is longer, but no later than five years after accrual of the cause of action. Revised Article 2 also specifies when the cause of action accrues for various types of warranty claims.[11.23]

The revised version also incorporates an expanded definition of "good faith" that encompasses not only honesty in fact but also the observance of reasonable commercial standards of fair dealing, whether or not the seller is a merchant.[11.24] Revised Article 1, which NCCUSL approved in 2001 for consideration by state legislatures, adopts the same definition and makes it applicable to Article 2,[11.25] so this change will have no effect in jurisdictions that have already adopted revised Article 1.

1.2a.3 Revised Article 2A

The changes made by revised Article 2A generally track the changes made to Article 2. The most significant changes in Articles 2A and 2 for consumer leases are:

- The four year limitation period can not be shortened by agreement.[11.26]
- The disclaimer of the implied warranty of merchantability, instead of mentioning "merchantability," must state for consumer leases that: "The lessor undertakes no responsibility for the quality of the goods except as otherwise provided in this contract."[11.27]
- If continued use of goods after revocation is reasonable, then the use is not acceptance, but the lessee in appropriate cases will be liable for the value of the use to the lessee. Use that is unreasonable is acceptance only if ratified by the lessor or supplier.[11.28]
- Failure to provide notice after revocation bars the lessee from a remedy only to the extent that the lessor or supplier is prejudiced by that failure.[11.29]
- Lessees have warranty rights as to promises that the manufacturer or other remote seller puts in writing inside or accompanying the product, or disseminates in advertising.[11.30]

11.1   The most significant provisions of revised Articles 2 and 2A are reproduced in Appx. E.7S, E.8S, *infra*, and on the CD-Rom accompanying this volume. Drafts of the revisions are available on the NCCUSL website, www.nccusl.org.

11.2   See materials posted by Americans for Fair Electronic Commerce Transactions at www.affect.ucita.com.

11.3   Revised U.C.C. § 2-103(1)(k); *see* § 1.4.1, *infra*.

11.4   *See* U.C.C. §§ 2-103(1)(b), (f), (g), (h), (m), (p) (definitions), 2-203 (contract formation), 2-211 (legal recognition of electronic contracts, records, and signatures), 2-212 (attribution of electronic signatures), 2-213 (receipt of electronic communications). Consumer advocates and others have expressed significant concerns about many of these provisions. See materials posted by Americans for Fair Electronic Commerce Transactions at www.affect.ucita.com.

11.5   Revised U.C.C. § 2-201.

11.6   Revised U.C.C. § 2-207.

11.7   Revised U.C.C. §§ 2-207, 2-204.

11.8   Revised U.C.C. §§ 2-313A, 2-313B; *see also* Revised U.C.C. 2-103(1)(n) (definition of "remedial promise"). *See generally* § 3.1, *infra*.

11.9   Revised U.C.C. §§ 2-103(h), 2-725(2)(c); *see* § 3.1, *infra*.

11.10   *See* Revised U.C.C. § 2-103(m); *see also* Revised U.C.C. § 1-203(a)(31).

11.11   Revised U.C.C. § 2-316(2).

11.12   Revised U.C.C. § 2-316(3).

11.13   Revised U.C.C. § 2-316(3); *see* §§ 5.5, 5.8.1, *infra*.

11.14   Revised U.C.C. § 2-316(2), (3); *see* §§ 5.5, 5.8.1, *infra*.

11.15   Revised U.C.C. § 2-316(3).

11.16   Revised U.C.C. § 2-316(3).

11.17   Revised U.C.C. § 2-103(1)(b); *see* § 5.8.1, *infra*.

11.18   Revised U.C.C. § 2-607(3)(a).

11.19   Revised U.C.C. § 2-605.

11.20   Revised U.C.C. § 2-508.

11.21   Revised U.C.C. § 2-608(4); *see* §§ 8.4.6.1, 10.4.6, *infra*.

11.22   Revised U.C.C. § 2-725(1).

11.23   Revised U.C.C. § 2-715; *see* § 10.3.3aS, *infra*.

11.24   Revised U.C.C. § 2-103(1)(j). Compare to current U.C.C. § 2-103(1)(b). *See* § 11.3.2, *infra*.

11.25   *See* Revised U.C.C. § 1-201(b)(2).
11.26   Revised U.C.C. § 2A-506(1).
11.27   Revised U.C.C. § 2A-214(2).
11.28   Revised U.C.C. § 2A-517(6).
11.29   Revised U.C.C. § 2A-516(3)(a).
11.30   Revised U.C.C. §§ 2-313A, 2-313B.

1.3 Resources for Understanding and Interpreting Consumer Warranty Law

1.3.1 UCC Case Law

Addition to notes 13, 14.

13   *Add to end of note*: [*Revised Article 1, which the National Conference of Commissioners on Uniform State Laws (NCCUSL) approved in 2001 for adoption by the states, redesignates this provision as U.C.C. § 1-103(a)(3)*].

14   *See also* Gem Diamond Co. v. Klein, 43 U.C.C. Rep. Serv. 2d 568 (S.D.N.Y. 1995); Tropical Jewelers, Inc. v. Nationsbank, 781 So. 2d 392, 43 U.C.C. Rep. Serv. 2d 497 (Fla. Dist. Ct. App. 2000); Dean Mach. Co. v. Union Bank, 106 S.W.3d 510, 50 U.C.C. Rep. Serv. 2d 431 (Mo. Ct. App. 2003).

Add to text at end of subsection's second paragraph:

The goal of uniformity also may make a court more willing to find that a UCC provision prevails over an inconsistent state statute.[14.1]

14.1   Int'l Periodical Distributors v. Bizmart, Inc., 95 Ohio St. 3d 452, 768 N.E.2d 1167, 47 U.C.C. Rep. Serv. 2d 1227 (2002).

Page 5

1.3.2 Official Comments to the UCC

Addition to notes 18, 21, 22.

18   *Cf. In re* Kelaidis, 276 B.R. 266, 47 U.C.C. Rep. Serv. 2d 823 (B.A.P. 10th Cir. 2002) (Utah uses comments as guides even though it has not officially adopted them). *But cf.* Pedro v. Armour Swift-Eckrich, 118 F. Supp. 2d 1155 (D. Kan. 2000) (Kansas comments to U.C.C. not persuasive); Diamond Surface, Inc. v. State Cement Plant Comm'n, 583 N.W.2d 155 (S.D. 1998) (looking to comments for guidance even though state did not adopt them).

21   *See, e.g.,* Saber v. Dan Angelone Chevrolet, Inc., 811 A.2d 644 (R.I. 2002); J.R. Simplot Co. v. Sales King Int'l, Inc., 17 P.3d 1100, 43 U.C.C. Rep. Serv. 2d 710 (Utah 2000).

22   *Replace "U.C.C. § 1-102(2)" with:* U.C.C. § 1-102(2) [*redesignated as U.C.C. § 1-103(a)(3) by revised Article 1, which the National Conference of Commissioners on Uniform State Laws (NCCUSL) approved in 2001 for adoption by the states*].

Page 7

1.3.5 Magnuson-Moss, Lemon Laws, and UDAP Statutes

Replace NCLC citation in subsection's last entry with:

National Consumer Law Center, *Unfair and Deceptive Acts and Practices* (5th ed. 2001 and Supp.)

1.4 Scope Issues

1.4.1 Sale of New and Used Goods

Addition to note 34.

34   *Replace Ogden citation with*: Ogden Martin Sys., Inc. v. Whiting Corp., 179 F.3d 523, 38 U.C.C. Rep. Serv. 2d 699 (7th Cir. 1999); *add: See* Coburn Supply Co. v. Kohler Co., 342 F.3d 372, 51 U.C.C. Rep. Serv. 2d 80 (5th Cir. 2003) (distributorship contract is controlled by U.C.C.); Viking Supply v. Nat'l Cart Co., 310 F.3d 1092, 49 U.C.C. Rep. Serv. 2d 94 (8th Cir. 2002) (Minn. law) (distribution contract is goods); Son v. Coal Equity, Inc., 293 B.R. 392, 50 U.C.C. Rep. Serv. 2d 1114 (W.D. Ky. 2003) (coal is goods as long as seller is to sever it from the realty); W.R. Constr. & Consulting, Inc. v. Jeld-Wen, Inc., 2002 WL 31194870 (D. Mass. Sept. 10, 2002) (windows to be installed in a home were goods because they were movable at the time of identification to the contract); Cent. Ill. Light Co. v. Consolidation Coal Co., 235 F. Supp. 2d 916, 49 U.C.C. Rep. Serv. 2d 399 (C.D. Ill. 2002) (coal is goods); Flanagan v. Consol. Nutrition, 627 N.W.2d 573, 44 U.C.C. Rep. Serv. 2d 374 (Iowa Ct. App. 2001) (livestock); Directory Publishers Inc. v. Lake Country Hearth & Leisure, 753 N.Y.S.2d 660, 49 U.C.C. Rep. Serv. 2d 395 (City

Ct. 2002) (contract for yellow pages advertisement is a contract for services); Iwtmm, Inc. v. Forest Hills Rest Home, 577 S.E.2d 175, 50 U.C.C. Rep. Serv. 2d 88 (N.C. Ct. App. 2003) (agreement for sale of drugs by pharmacist to nursing home is governed by U.C.C.); Neugent v. Beroth Oil Co., 560 S.E.2d 829, 47 U.C.C. Rep. Serv. 2d 102 (N.C. Ct. App. 2002) (motor fuel is goods); MacConkey v. F.J. Matter Design, Inc., 54 Va. Cir. 1 (2000) (goods used for construction not covered once they are incorporated into realty); *see also* Watkins & Son Pet Supplies v. The Iams Co., 254 F.3d 607, 44 U.C.C. Rep. Serv. 2d 708 (6th Cir. 2001) (casting doubt on contrary holding in Herman Bros. Sales Corp. v. Hill's Pet Prods. Div., 875 F.2d 864, 44 U.C.C. Rep. Serv. 2d 695 (6th Cir. 1989)); Wang Laboratories, Inc. v. Lee, 44 U.C.C. Rep. Serv. 2d 470 (Del. Super. Ct. 1989) (distributorship agreement is sale of goods); Gladhart v. Or. Vineyard Supply Co., 164 Or. App. 438, 40 U.C.C. Rep. Serv. 2d 722 (1999) (grape plants are goods), *rev'd on other grounds*, 26 P.3d 817 (Or. 2001); Cont'l Casing Corp. v. Siderca Corp., 38 S.W.3d 782, 43 U.C.C. Rep. Serv. 2d 800 (Tex. App. 2001) (distributorship agreement involves sale of goods and is governed by U.C.C.); *cf.* i.LAN Sys., Inc. v. Netscout Serv. Level Corp., 183 F. Supp. 2d 328 (D. Mass. 2002) (U.C.C. may cover software sale but possibly not licensing of software). *But see* Top Rank, Inc. v. Gutierrez, 236 F. Supp. 2d 637, 50 U.C.C. Rep. Serv. 2d 76 (W.D. Tex. 2001) (transmission of cable television programming is not goods); Rayle v. Bowling Green State Univ., 739 N.E.2d 1260, 44 U.C.C. Rep. Serv. 2d 1000 (Ohio Ct. Cl. 2000) ("personal seat license" in football stadium not goods); Jones v. CGU Ins. Co., 78 S.W.3d 626, 48 U.C.C. Rep. Serv. 2d 501 (Tex. App. 2002) (insurance is not goods so buyer can not bring U.C.C. claim against seller's insurer); Baypoint Condo. Ass'n v. Dryvit Sys., 46 U.C.C. Rep. Serv. 2d 623 (Va. Cir. Ct. 2001) (materials are no longer goods once they are incorporated into realty).

Replace last sentence of subsection's second paragraph with:

Computer software is generally considered to fall within the definition of goods.[35]

In 2003, however, the National Conference of Commissioners on Uniform State Laws (NCCUSL) finalized a revised version of Article 2 that would exclude "information," an undefined term, from the definition of "goods."[35.1] The Official Comments state that, pursuant to this definition, information that is not associated with goods is excluded from Article 2, but if the transaction involves both goods and information it may be included.[35.2] According to the Comments, an automobile is goods even though it includes many computer programs, and an architect's provision of architectural plans on a computer disk is an example of non-goods.[35.3] Whether Article 2 should cover computer information transactions was highly controversial during the revision process and will probably continue to be so as states consider the revision. Consumer advocates have expressed concern that revised Article 2's approach will create widespread uncertainty about what rules apply to the enormous and growing number of goods that include software, and that over time this exclusion will eviscerate Article 2's role as the basic law of the sale of goods.[35.4]

35   Advent Sys. Ltd. v. Unisys Corp., 925 F.2d 670 (3d Cir. 1991) (Tex. law); ePresence, Inc. v. Evolve Software, Inc., 190 F. Supp. 2d 159, 47 U.C.C. Rep. Serv. 2d 132 (D. Mass. 2002) (when software programs, not related services, were essence of agreement, U.C.C. governs); Taylor Inv. Corp. v. Weil, 169 F. Supp. 2d 1046, 44 U.C.C. Rep. Serv. 2d 382 (D. Minn. 2001) (assuming, without deciding, that U.C.C. applies to software licensing agreement); Dahlmann v. Sulcus Hospitality Technologies, 63 F. Supp. 2d 772 (E.D. Mich. 1999) (package including hardware, software, installation, training, and support services is goods); Novacore Technologies v. GST Communications, 20 F. Supp. 2d 169 (D. Mass. 1998) (computer software), *aff'd*, 1999 U.S. App. LEXIS 24353 (1st Cir. Sept. 24, 1999); Confer Plastics, Inc. v. Hunkar Laboratories, Inc., 964 F. Supp. 73 (W.D.N.Y. 1997); NMP Corp. v. Parametric Tech. Corp., 958 F. Supp. 1536 (N.D. Okla. 1997) (licensing agreement for software is governed by Art. 2); Architectronics, Inc. v. Control Sys., Inc., 935 F. Supp. 425, 33 U.C.C. Rep. 2d 714 (S.D.N.Y. 1996); Colonial Life Ins. Co. v. Elec. Data Sys. Corp., 817 F. Supp. 235 (D.N.H. 1993) (software is a good); First Nationwide Bank v. First Nationwide Fin. Corp., 770 F. Supp. 1537 (M.D. Fla. 1991) (software licensing is governed by Art. 2); D.P. Tech. Corp. v. Sherwood Tool, Inc., 751 F. Supp. 1038 (D. Conn. 1990) ("computer systems, including software"); Analysts Int'l Corp. v. Recycled Paper Products, Inc., 45 U.C.C. Rep. Serv. 2d 747 (N.D. Ill. 1987) (computer program is a good even if seller provides services to create it); *In re* Amica, Inc., 135 B.R. 534, 17 U.C.C. Rep. 2d 11 (Bankr. N.D. Ill. 1992) (computer programs); Olcott Int'l & Co. v. Micro Data Base Sys., Inc., 793 N.E.2d 1063, 51 U.C.C. Rep. Serv. 2d 352 (Ind. Ct. App. 2003) (sale of pre-existing standardized software is goods); Sys. Design & Mgmt. Info., Inc. v. Kan. City Post Office Employees Credit Union, 14 Kan. App. 2d 266, 788 P.2d 878 (1990) (software is goods); Richard A. Rosenblatt & Co. v. Davidge Data Sys. Corp., 295 A.D.2d 168, 743 N.Y.S.2d 471, 47 U.C.C. Rep. Serv. 2d 1390 (2002) (sale of computer hardware and software is sale of goods even if service is included); Communications Groups, Inc. v. Warner Communications Inc., 138 Misc. 2d 80, 527 N.Y.S.2d 341, 6 U.C.C. Rep. 2d 636 (Civ. Ct. 1988) (computer software is a good under the U.C.C.); Smart Online, Inc. v. Opensite Technologies, Inc., 51 U.C.C. Rep. Serv. 2d 47 (N.C. Super. Ct. 2003) (might be sale of services if contract involved substantial development and customization, but not shown in this case); Gasbarre Products, Inc. v. Link Computer Corp., 40 U.C.C. Rep. 2d 446 (Pa. C.P. 1999); *see also* Softman Products Co. v. Adobe Sys., Inc., 171 F. Supp. 2d 1075, 45 U.C.C. Rep. Serv. 2d 945 (C.D. Cal. 2001) (licensing agreement for

software was really a sale for purposes of copyright infringement claim); Ankle & Foot Care Centers v. Infocure Sys., Inc., 164 F. Supp. 2d 953, 46 U.C.C. Rep. Serv. 2d 316 (N.D. Ohio 2001) (contract for software licensing and training involves mixed goods and services; whether U.C.C. applies depends on which predominates); M. A. Mortenson Co. v. Timberline Software Corp., 140 Wash. 2d 568, 998 P.2d 305, 41 U.C.C. Rep. 2d 357 (2000) (accepting parties' position that Art. 2 applies to licensing of software; case gives effect to terms, including remedy limitations, contained in shrinkwrap license and endorses notion of "layered contracting," in which contract terms are clarified or created over time in a rolling process); *cf.* Specht v. Netscape Communications Corp., 306 F.3d 17, 29 n.13 (2d Cir. 2002) (questioning whether downloadable software is goods); I.Lan Sys., Inc. v. Netscout Serv. Level Corp., 183 F. Supp. 2d 328, 46 U.C.C. Rep. Serv. 2d 287 (D. Mass. 2002) (questioning whether U.C.C. covers software licenses, but applying U.C.C. if only by analogy); Multi-Tech Sys., Inc. v. Floreat, Inc., 47 U.C.C. Rep. Serv. 2d 924 (D. Minn. 2002) (software may be goods, but a contract for developing software is not); Heidtman Steel Prods., Inc. v. Compuware Corp., 1999 U.S. Dist. LEXIS 21700 (N.D. Ohio Feb. 15, 1999) (computer consulting services contract was not a contract for goods even though final phase would have involved delivery of customized software); Conopco, Inc. v. McCreadie, 826 F. Supp. 855 (D.N.J. 1993) (computer consulting services not goods even though part of work involved customizing and modifying software), *aff'd*, 40 F.3d 1239 (3d Cir. 1994); Arlington Elec. Constr. v. Schindler Elevator Corp., 1992 Ohio App. LEXIS 953 (Ohio Ct. App. Mar. 6, 1992) (software not always goods, but it is here, where contract also included hardware and did not primarily involve customizing). *But see* Pearl Investments, Ltd. Liab. Co. v. Standard I/O, Inc., 257 F. Supp. 2d 325, 50 U.C.C. Rep. Serv. 2d 377 (D. Me. 2003) (development of software system from scratch is services); Wharton Mgmt. Group v. Sigma Consultants, Inc., 50 U.C.C. Rep. Serv. 2d 678 (Del. Super. Ct.) (contract for creation of custom software is services), *aff'd without opinion*, 582 A.2d 936 (Del. 1990). Note that Maryland (Md. Code Ann., Com. Law §§ 22-101 to 22-816) and Virginia (Va. Code Ann. §§ 59.1-501.1 to 59.1-509.2) (Michie)) have adopted the Uniform Computer Information Transactions Act, which has special provisions regarding software sales, including special warranty provisions and validation of terms contained in post-sale documents such as shrinkwrap licenses as long as the buyer has the option to return the product instead of accepting the terms.

35.1 Revised U.C.C. § 2-103(1)(k).

35.2 Official Comment 7 to Revised U.C.C. § 2-103.

35.3 *Id.*

35.4 See materials posted by Americans for Fair Electronic Commerce Transactions at www.affect.ucita.com.

Page 8

Addition to notes 36, 37.

36 Knipp v. Weinbaum, 351 So. 2d 1081 (Fla. Dist. Ct. App. 1977); Lipinski v. Martin J. Kelly Oldsmobile, Inc., 325 Ill. App. 3d 1139, 259 Ill. Dec. 586, 759 N.E.2d 66 (2001); Berney v. Rountree Olds-Cadillac Co., 763 So. 2d 799 (La. Ct. App. 2000) (implied warranty arises under Louisiana Civil Code that used goods will operate reasonably well for a reasonable period of time).

37 *Replace Roland citation with*: 768 So. 2d 400 (Ala. Civ. App. 2000).

Add to text at end of subsection:

Article 2 applies to "transactions in goods,"[39.1] not just sales, but many of the key warranty provisions only apply to a "sale" or "contract for sale" of goods, or only to a "seller."[39.2] A sale "consists in the passing of title from the seller to the buyer for a price."[39.3] An agreement by which a car salesman had use of a vehicle as a demonstrator was not a sale because it was clear that title would not pass to him.[39.4] Similarly, a bailment may not be a sale.[39.5]

39.1 U.C.C. § 2-102.

39.2 *See* U.C.C. §§ 2-312(a), 2-313(1), 2-314(1), 2-315.

39.3 U.C.C. § 2-106(1); *see also* U.C.C. § 2-103(1)(d) (definition of "seller"); § 14.6, *infra* (discussion of definition of seller).

39.4 Beattie v. Beattie (Boyles v. Martin Chevrolet-Buick, Inc.), 786 A.2d 549, 44 U.C.C. Rep. Serv. 2d 124 (Del. Super. Ct. 2001).

39.5 *See* Bonaccoloto v. Coca-Cola Enterprises, Inc., 1999 U.S. Dist. LEXIS 22732 (D. Mass. Feb. 11, 1999) (magistrate's recommended decision) (Article 2 warranties do not arise in bailment).

Page 9

1.4.3 Mobile Homes, Houses, and Real Property

Addition to notes 46, 48.

46 *See* Margarito v. Life Products Corp., 46 U.C.C. Rep. Serv. 2d 621 (E.D. Va. 1998) (slip and fall in hotel bathtub is not governed by U.C.C. because of real property exclusion).

48 *See* Heffernan v. Reinhold, 73 S.W.3d 659, 48 U.C.C. Rep. Serv. 2d 126 (Mo. Ct. App. 2002) (storm sewer pipe installed underground as part of site development before decedent bought home was not goods); Glass v. Trafalgar House Prop., Inc., 58 Va. Cir. 437 (2002); *see also* Palmer v. Espey Huston & Associates, 84 S.W.3d 345, 49 U.C.C. Rep. Serv. 2d 48 (Tex. App. 2002) (contract to build breakwater not goods because it was to be a permanent improvement to real estate).

Add to text after sentence containing note 49:

While building materials are goods when they are purchased,[49.1] once they are incorporated into realty they cease to be goods and are no longer covered by the UCC.[49.2] Thus, a person who purchases a completed house does not have UCC claims against a manufacturer who supplied construction materials to the builder.[49.3] But one court allowed home owners to sue the manufacturer as third party beneficiary of the supplier who purchased the construction materials.[49.4] The court reasoned that the home owners' claim related to goods because the materials were movable at the time of the *supplier's* purchase.

49.1　*See, e.g.,* W.R. Constr. & Consulting, Inc. v. Jeld-Wen, Inc., 2002 WL 31194870 (D. Mass. Sept. 10, 2002).

49.2　Keck v. Dryvit Sys., Inc., 830 So. 2d 1, 46 U.C.C. Rep. Serv. 2d 635 (Ala. 2002) (building materials are no longer goods if they can not be severed without material harm to the realty); Baypoint Condo. Ass'n v. Dryvit Sys., 46 U.C.C. Rep. Serv. 2d 623 (Va. Cir. Ct. 2001) (exterior insulation finish system); MacConkey v. F.J. Matter Design, Inc., 54 Va. Cir. 1 (2000) (goods used for construction not covered once they are incorporated into realty).

49.3　Keck v. Dryvit Sys., Inc., 830 So. 2d 1, 46 U.C.C. Rep. Serv. 2d 635 (Ala. 2002); Baypoint Condo. Ass'n v. Dryvit Sys., 46 U.C.C. Rep. Serv. 2d 623 (Va. Cir. Ct. 2001).

49.4　Loughridge v. Goodyear Tire & Rubber Co., 192 F. Supp. 2d 1175, 48 U.C.C. Rep. Serv. 2d 53 (D. Colo. 2002).

1.4.4 Utility Service

Addition to notes 53, 55.

53　Dakota Pork Indus. v. City of Huron, 638 N.W.2d 884 (S.D. 2002) (municipality's provision of water is sale of goods, but no implied warranty of fitness for particular purpose arises). *But see* Mattoon v. City of Pittsfield, 775 N.E.2d 770, 49 U.C.C. Rep. Serv. 2d 52 (Mass. App. Ct. 2002) (sale of water by municipality is rendition of services, not goods).

55　BTA Oil Producers v. MDU Res. Group, Inc., 642 N.W.2d 873, 47 U.C.C. Rep. Serv. 2d 1057 (N.D. 2002).

Page 10

1.4.6 Must Seller Be a Merchant?

Addition to note 64.

64　*Replace "U.C.C. § 1-204(1)" with*: U.C.C. § 2-104(1).

Add note 64.1 at end of sentence following sentence containing note 64.

64.1　Bobholz v. Banaszak, 655 N.W.2d 547, 49 U.C.C. Rep. Serv. 2d 25 (Wis. Ct. App. 2002).

Replace note 67 with:

67　*See* National Consumer Law Center, Unfair and Deceptive Acts and Practices § 2.3.4 (5th ed. 2001 and Supp.).

Addition to note 68.

68　*Replace NCLC citation with*: National Consumer Law Center, Unfair and Deceptive Acts and Practices § 7.5.3 (5th ed. 2001 and Supp.).

1.4.7 Definition of "Buyer"

Replace note 70 with:

70　Kirby v. NMC/Continue Care, 993 P.2d 951, 40 U.C.C. Rep. Serv. 2d 368 (Wyo. 1999).

Add to text after sentence containing note 70:

A person who buys real property to which the goods have already been affixed may not be a "buyer" of those goods.[70.1]

70.1　Heffernan v. Reinhold, 73 S.W.3d 659, 48 U.C.C. Rep. Serv. 2d 126 (Mo. Ct. App. 2002) (storm sewer pipe installed underground).

Page 11

1.4.8 Requirement that Sale Be for "Personal, Family, or Household Purposes"

Add to text after subsection's second paragraph:

California is one of the few states that has a comprehensive consumer warranty law, the Song-Beverly Consumer Warranty Act.[74.1] It applies only to "consumer goods," defined as new products that are acquired primarily for personal, family, or household purposes.[74.2] An intermediate appellate court decision holds that roofing shingles do not meet this definition because they do not fit into the statutory scheme, which gives the manufacturer three options: repairing the goods on-site, picking them up for repair, or arranging for them to be transported to a repair facility.[74.3] The court noted that shingles could not be removed from the home and taken to a repair facility without damaging the home, but could only be repaired on-site, so the manufacturer would only have the option of on-site repair. From this fact the court concluded that the legislature could not have intended shingles to fall within the definition of consumer goods. The decision ignores the fact that another part of the statute specifically refers to goods that can not be returned to the manufacturer because of "size and weight, or method of attachment, or method of installation," clearly contemplating that such goods are covered.[74.4] A separate chapter of California's warranty law requires a written contract when roofing materials are sold with a warranty, and requires certain disclosures.[74.5]

74.1   Cal. Civ. Code §§ 1790 to 1795.7 (West).
74.2   Cal. Civ. Code § 1791(a) (West).
74.3   Atkinson v. Elk Corp., 109 Cal. App. 4th 739, 135 Cal. Rptr. 2d 433 (2003).
74.4   Cal. Civ. Code § 1793.2(c) (West).
74.5   Cal. Civ. Code §§ 1797.90 to 1797.96 (West).

Replace § 1.4.9 with:

1.4.9 Federal Preemption

1.4.9.1 Overview

Federal preemption of state warranty-type claims is an issue for a few highly-regulated types of products, primarily medical devices, pesticides and herbicides.[77] Manufacturers also sometimes argue, usually without success, that federal regulation of motor vehicle safety issues preempts consumer claims. The effect of the National Manufactured Housing Construction and Safety Standards Act on mobile home warranty claims is discussed in another chapter of this manual.[78]

1.4.9.2 Medical Devices and Drugs

The Medical Device Amendments to the Federal Food, Drug, and Cosmetic Act set up a system for Food and Drug Administration review of medical devices. The statute provides that no state or political subdivision of a state "may establish or continue in effect with respect to a device intended for human use any requirement—(1) which is different from, or in addition to, any requirement applicable under this chapter to the device, and (2) which relates to the safety or effectiveness of the device or to any other matter included in a requirement applicable to the device under this chapter."[79] The United States Supreme Court interpreted this preemption language in 1996.[80] The Court held that negligence

claims (failure to use reasonable care in design, assembly, manufacture and sale) and strict liability claims against a pacemaker manufacturer were not preempted. The pacemaker had not undergone the FDA's most rigorous review, but was grandfathered in because it was substantially equivalent to a pre-amendment device.[81] The Fourth Circuit has applied this same reasoning to a breach of implied warranty claim.[82]

Unfortunately, only a plurality of the Court joined in some critical portions of the opinion, leaving many issues still unclear.[83] In general, it appears that preemption issues for medical devices have to be decided on a case-by-case, fact-intensive basis. The more specific the Food and Drug Administration's requirements for a product and the more detailed its review, the more likely a court will find that state law is preempted.[84] Courts may still find that even the most

---

77   *See also In re* Wireless Tel. Radio Frequency Emissions Products Liab. Litig., 248 F. Supp. 2d 452 (D. Md. 2003) (federal standards for cell phone radio frequency radiation emissions preempt state claims); Churchill Vill. v. Gen. Elec. Co., 169 F. Supp. 2d 1119 (N.D. Cal. 2000) (Consumer Product Safety Act did not preempt suit under state law to force manufacturer to repair damaged products).

78   *See* § 15.3.5, *infra.*

79   21 U.S.C. § 360k(a); *see also* 21 C.F.R. § 808.1(d) (narrowly interpreting preemption provision).

80   Medtronic, Inc. v. Lohr, 518 U.S. 470, 116 S. Ct. 2240, 135 L. Ed. 2d 700 (1996). The FDA also has a regulation on preemp-

tion, 21 C.F.R. § 808, to which the Supreme Court gave some weight.

81   Premarket approval is the most rigorous process. It is required for Class III devices, which are those that present the greatest risk to human safety. Class III devices that were introduced into interstate commerce before May 28, 1976, however, can be grandfathered in without such rigorous review. Products that are substantially equivalent to grandfathered products can also be grandfathered in. Mitchell v. Collagen, 126 F.3d 902, 33 U.C.C. Rep. 2d 750 (5th Cir. 1997).

82   Duvall v. Bristol-Myers-Squibb Co., 103 F.3d 324 (4th Cir. 1996) (no preemption of state law claims re design, manufacture, marketing and sale, failure to warn, or implied warranty where device was grandfathered in under substantial equivalence test even though it had also been tested as an investigational device).

83   *See* Webster v. Pacesetter, Inc., 171 F. Supp. 2d 1 (D.D.C. 2001) (detailed analysis of questions on which the various opinions agreed and disagreed).

84   *See, e.g.,* Brooks v. Homedica, Inc., 273 F.3d 785 (8th Cir. 2001) (failure to warn claims asserted by nurse harmed by exposure to product preempted when FDA dictated exact language of warning label); Martin v. Medtronic, Inc., 254 F.3d 573 (5th Cir. 2001) (state common law tort claims based on design, manufacturing, warnings, and labeling preempted as to device that went through full pre-market review); Goodlin v. Medtronic, 167 F.3d 1367

rigorous review does not result in preemption of a claim that the manufacturer failed to follow the manufacturing process approved by the FDA.[85] State law claims that parallel federal safety requirements are less likely to be preempted.[86]

The Supreme Court interpreted the statute again in 2001 in a case involving a "fraud-on-the-FDA" claim in which the plaintiffs were injured by a device that they claimed the FDA approved only because of false information submitted by the manufacturer.[87] Even though the preemption clause in

the statute did not apply, the court held that such a claim was preempted because it conflicted with the FDA's mission to police the medical device market and to maintain the delicate balance between protecting the public from unsafe devices and giving people access to devices that might help them.

There is no comparable preemption provision in the portion of the Food, Drug, and Cosmetic Act that applies to prescription drugs. Accordingly, courts have held that state claims regarding prescription drugs are not preempted.[88]

Over-the-counter drugs can not be marketed unless the FDA has approved them as safe and effective for their intended use.[89] The statute preempts state requirements that relate to the regulation of non-prescription drugs and that are different from, or in addition to, or otherwise not identical with a requirement under the federal statute.[90] A savings clause states, however, that nothing in the federal statute should be construed to modify or affect any action or the liability of any person under state product liability law.[91] One court has limited the savings clause to traditional product liability actions for non-economic loss, not fraud or breach of warranty claims.[92] As part of the FDA's authority includes approving or specifying requirements for labels, courts may conclude that warranty and fraud claims that are based on a medication's label are preempted.[93]

1.4.9.3 Pesticides, Herbicides, and Veterinary Medicines

A second area in which preemption is an issue involves pesticides and herbicides, which are regulated under the Federal Insecticide, Fungicide, and Rodenticide Act (FIFRA).[94] The statute requires manufacturers to submit information to the Environmental Protection Agency (EPA), which reviews the claims made for the product and approves the label under which the product is to be marketed. While states are allowed to regulate the sale or use of federally-

---

(11th Cir. 1999) (full FDA review of device did not warrant preemption where FDA's requirements were generic rather than device-specific); Mitchell v. Collagen, 126 F.3d 902, 33 U.C.C. Rep. 2d 750 (5th Cir. 1997) (premarket approval process preempts strict liability, negligence, mislabeling, misbranding, adulteration, fraud and implied warranty claims, but not claims that manufacturer failed to follow the standards set by the PMA process); Martin v. Telectronics Pacing Sys., Inc., 105 F.3d 1090 (6th Cir. 1997) (design defect claim preempted where FDA had approved the design; failure to warn claim preempted where FDA had approved the consent form; express warranty claims preempted where FDA had approved all claims made for an investigational device); Enlow v. St. Jude Med., Inc., 210 F. Supp. 2d 853 (W.D. Ky. 2001) (MDA preempts claims for failure to warn, defective design, and breach of express and implied warranty, and claim of manufacturing defect despite adherence to FDA-approved manufacturing process); Webster v. Pacesetter, Inc., 171 F. Supp. 2d 1 (D.D.C. 2001) (even most rigorous review process did not impose specific enough requirements to preempt state claims); Dunlap v. Medtronic, Inc., 47 F. Supp. 2d 888 (N.D. Ohio 1999) (state implied warranty claims were preempted where device had undergone FDA's most rigorous review); Worthy v. Collagen Corp., 967 S.W.2d 360 (Tex. 1998) (negligence, warranty, strict liability and fraud claims preempted where product had undergone FDA's most rigorous review); *see also* Flynn v. Am. Home Products Corp., 627 N.W.2d 342 (Minn. Ct. App. 2001) (fraud-on-FDA claim is preempted). *But see* Armstrong v. Optical Radiation Corp., 50 Cal. App. 4th 580, 57 Cal. Rptr. 2d 763 (1996) (full premarket review does not preempt claims involving negligence in design, manufacture, marketing and distribution; failure to warn; strict liability claim that manufacturer failed to follow manufacturing protocol approved by FDA; or implied warranty of fitness); Weiland v. Telectronics Pacing Sys., Inc., 188 Ill. 2d 415, 242 Ill. Dec. 618, 721 N.E.2d 1149, 40 U.C.C. Rep. 2d 1001 (1999) (premarket approval process does not impose substantive requirements on manufacture or design so does not preempt state warranty and defective design claims).

85 Pipitone v. Biomatrix, Inc., 288 F.3d 239 (5th Cir. 2002); Mitchell v. Collagen, 126 F.3d 902, 33 U.C.C. Rep. 2d 750 (5th Cir. 1997) (premarket approval process preempts strict liability, negligence, mislabeling, misbranding, adulteration, fraud and implied warranty claims, but not claims that manufacturer failed to follow the standards set by the PMA process); Valente v. Sofamor, 48 F. Supp. 2d 862 (E.D. Wis. 1999) (claim based on manufacturer's failure to comply with standards set through MDA process is not preempted); *see also* Enlow v. St. Jude Med., Inc., 210 F. Supp. 2d 853 (W.D. Ky. 2001) (noting distinction between claim of manufacturing defect despite adherence to FDA-approved manufacturing process, which is preempted, and claim of defect caused by failure to follow that process).

86 Buckman Co. v. Plaintiffs' Legal Comm., 531 U.S. 341, 353, 121 S. Ct. 1012, 148 L. Ed. 2d 854 (2001).

87 *Id.*; *cf.* Bryant v. Hoffmann-La Roche, Inc., 262 Ga. App. 401,

585 S.E.2d 723 (2003) (distinguishing *Buckman*; plaintiff's claims not properly characterized as fraud on the agency). *But cf.* Woods v. Gliatech, Inc., 218 F. Supp. 2d 802 (W.D. Va. 2002) (no preemption of negligence, breach of warranty, and fraud claims when FDA's premarketing approval was conditional upon submission of clinical trial results and revision of label, and manufacturer fraudulently submitted false information, for which it was criminally prosecuted).

88 *See, e.g.,* Eve v. Sandoz Pharmaceutical Corp., 2002 WL 181972 (S.D. Ind. Jan. 28, 2002); Caraker v. Sandoz Pharmaceuticals Corp., 172 F. Supp. 2d 1018 (S.D. Ill. 2001).

89 21 U.S.C. § 355.

90 21 U.S.C. § 379r(a).

91 21 U.S.C. § 379r(e).

92 Kanter v. Warner-Lambert Co., 99 Cal. App. 4th 780, 122 Cal. Rptr. 2d 72 (2002).

93 *See id.*; Green v. BDI Pharmaceuticals, 803 So. 2d 68 (La. Ct. App. 2001) (failure to warn claim preempted).

94 7 U.S.C. §§ 136–136y.

registered pesticides or devices, they may not permit any sale or use that is prohibited by the federal statute.[95]

FIFRA provides that states "shall not impose or continue in effect any requirements for labeling or packaging in addition to or different from those required under" FIFRA.[96] While it is clear that FIFRA does not preempt all state law causes of action,[97] a number of courts have seized on this language as a basis for precluding state warranty, negligence and strict liability claims.[98] These courts adopt the theory that any state law claim that could make the manufacturer want to change the label is preempted. Courts taking a more sensible approach point out that if a product does not perform as promised, manufacturers have other choices besides changing the label, such as restricting sales or paying claims.[99] Claims based on false advertising may also avoid preemption,[99.1] but some courts even preempt claims based on statements made by the manufacturer's representatives or in advertisements.[99.2] The Texas Supreme Court

---

95 7 U.S.C. § 136v(a); *see* Wis. Public Intervenor v. Mortier, 501 U.S. 597, 111 S. Ct. 2476, 115 L. Ed. 2d 532 (1991) (FIFRA does not preempt local governmental authority to regulate use of pesticides, so village had authority to deny or restrict permit for pesticide application).

96 7 U.S.C. § 136v(b). The Federal Hazardous Substances Act, 15 U.S.C. § 1261 (historical note), Pub. L. No. 94-284, § 17(a), contains similar language. *See* Cole v. Sunnyside Corp., 234 Wis. 2d 149, 610 N.W.2d 511 (Ct. App. 2000) (declining to rule on preemption question until trial court determines whether label actually complies with federal requirement that it describe the product's hazards, precautionary measures, and instructions for handling and storage).

97 Hart v. Bayer Corp., 199 F.3d 239 (5th Cir. 2000) (FIFRA does not completely preempt state law, so case cannot be removed to federal court on the basis of defendant's FIFRA defense); Sun Valley Packing v. Consep, Inc., 94 Cal. App. 4th 315, 114 Cal. Rptr. 2d 237, 46 U.C.C. Rep. Serv. 2d 982 (2001) (FIFRA does not preempt claims that are not label-based, for example, when manufacturer has voluntarily warranted product's fitness for a particular purpose; FIFRA does not preempt state law restrictions on remedy limitation clauses); Dow Chem. Co. v. Ebling, 723 N.E.2d 881 (Ind. Ct. App. 2000) (FIFRA does not occupy the entire field of pesticide regulation), *aff'd in relevant part, rev'd in part on other grounds*, 753 N.E.2d 633 (Ind. 2001).

98 *See, e.g.*, Dow Agrosciences Ltd. Liab. Co. v. Bates, 332 F.3d 323, 51 U.C.C. Rep. Serv. 2d 384 (5th Cir. 2003) (fraud, warranty, UDAP, defective design, and negligent manufacture claims preempted); Nathan Kimmel, Inc. v. DowElanco, 275 F.3d 1199 (9th Cir. 2002) (claim of fraud on the agency is preempted; aggrieved person may be able to bring administrative action within the agency or sue the agency under the Administrative Procedures Act); Andrus v. Agrevo USA Co., 178 F.3d 395 (5th Cir. 1999) (warranty claims preempted where herbicide did not perform as advertised on the label); Kuiper v. Am. Cyanamid Co., 131 F.3d 656 (7th Cir. 1997) (FIFRA preempts state law claims of negligent manufacture and failure to warn); Grenier v. Vermont Log Bldgs., Inc., 96 F.3d 559 (1st Cir. 1996) (FIFRA preempts failure to warn claim, some design defect or manufacturing defect claims, and claim that language in EPA-approved label created express warranty); Anderson v. Dow Agrosciences Ltd. Liab. Co., 262 F. Supp. 2d 1280, 51 U.C.C. Rep. Serv. 2d 686 (W.D. Okla. 2003) (claims akin to failure to warn and design or manufacturing defect are preempted, but not claims based on post-sale off-label statements); Williams v. Dow Chem. Co., 255 F. Supp. 2d 219 (S.D.N.Y. 2003) (claims of failure to warn are preempted); Dahlman Farms, Inc. v. FMC Corp., 240 F. Supp. 2d 1012 (D. Minn. 2002) (extending preemption even when the specific language on the label is not mandated or regulated by the Environmental Protection Agency); Jeffers v. Wal-Mart Stores, Inc., 171 F. Supp. 2d 617 (S.D. W. Va. 2001) (claims based on labeling and failure to warn preempted, but not design defect claims); Gooch v. E.I. DuPont de Nemours & Co., 40 F. Supp. 2d 863, 38

U.C.C. Rep. 2d 796 (W.D. Ky. 1999) (express warranty claim preempted where herbicide did not do what label said it would do); Dow Chem. Co. v. Ebling, 723 N.E.2d 881 (Ind. Ct. App. 2000) (FIFRA preempts claims that manufacturer should have taken steps to disseminate warnings to ultimate users, that manufacturer should have provided better training to people who applied pesticide, that manufacturer negligently failed to report adverse incidents to EPA, and that applicator violated duty to warn, but not claim of design defect against manufacturer), *aff'd in part, rev'd in part on other grounds*, 753 N.E.2d 633 (Ind. 2001) (claim that pesticide applicator should have warned homeowner is also not preempted); Wright v. Cropmate Co., 599 N.W.2d 668, 39 U.C.C. Rep. Serv. 2d 696 (Iowa 1999) (FIFRA preempts negligence claims where product did not do what label said it would do); Eyl v. Ciba-Geigy Corp., 650 N.W.2d 744 (Neb. 2002) (bystander's failure to warn claim preempted).

99 Brown v. Chas. H. Lilly Co., 161 Or. App. 402, 985 P.2d 846, 38 U.C.C. Rep. 2d 1147 (1999) (FIFRA does not preempt duty to warn and negligence claims where consumer suffered burns and lost foot due to use of herbicide fertilizer product); *see also* Dow Chem. Co. v. Ebling, 723 N.E.2d 881 (Ind. Ct. App. 2000) (design defect claim against pesticide manufacturer in personal injury suit not preempted), *aff'd in relevant part, rev'd in part on other grounds*, 753 N.E.2d 633 (Ind. 2001) (FIFRA does not preempt failure to warn claim against applicator); DePetrillo v. Dow Chem. Co., 729 A.2d 677, 40 U.C.C. Rep. 2d 684 (R.I. 1999) (pre-1972 version of statute, which did not include preemption language, applied to claims based on pre-1972 exposure).

99.1 *See* Wright v. Cropmate Co., 599 N.W.2d 668, 39 U.C.C. Rep. Serv. 2d 696 (Iowa 1999) (declining to rule on question whether false advertising claims would be preempted); *see also* Mitchell v. Collagen, 126 F.3d 902, 33 U.C.C. Rep. 2d 750 (7th Cir. 1997) (Medical Device Amendments would not preempt fraud claims based on advertisements, but only to the extent that they did not conform to FDA's requirements).

99.2 *See, e.g.*, Dow Agrosciences Ltd. Liab. Co. v. Bates, 332 F.3d 323, 51 U.C.C. Rep. Serv. 2d 384 (5th Cir. 2003) (claims based on off-label statements preempted unless statements deviate from label; claims based on post-sale off-label statements not preempted); Andrus v. Agrevo USA Co., 178 F.3d 395 (5th Cir. 1999) (claims based on salesman's statements preempted where they repeated information contained in the label; court does not decide whether claims based on statements going beyond the label would also be preempted); Kuiper v. Am. Cyanamid Co., 131 F.3d 656 (7th Cir. 1997) (FIFRA preempts claims of false representations in advertising and marketing); *see also* Eyl v. Ciba-Geigy Corp., 650 N.W.2d 744 (Neb. 2002) (claim that manufacturer should have supplied flags to warn bystanders and general public is label-based and therefore preempted). *But see* Sun Valley Packing v. Consep, Inc., 94 Cal. App. 4th 315, 114 Cal. Rptr. 2d 237, 46 U.C.C. Rep. Serv. 2d 982 (2001) (statement by manufacturer's representative that went beyond and in

has ruled that claims that relate to aspects of products that the EPA has chosen not to regulate are not preempted.[99.3] A few courts have accepted an estoppel argument that the manufacturer should not be able to hide behind FIFRA if it has failed to comply with FIFRA's requirements.[99.4]

Similar issues arise with respect to veterinary medicines, which are regulated by the federal Viruses, Serums, Toxins, and Analogous Products Act.[99.5] This statute does not itself preempt state laws, but a statement issued by the Animal and Plant Health Inspection Service does.[99.6] Courts have given effect to this agency statement and held that common law claims relying on bases of liability different from or in addition to federal requirements are preempted, but claims are not preempted to the extent they seek relief for violation of the federal substantive standards.[99.7]

1.4.9.4 Boats and Motor Vehicles

The Supreme Court unanimously rejected a seller's claim that the Federal Boat Safety Act preempted common law tort claims by the husband of a woman who fell out of a boat and was killed by the boat's unguarded propeller blades.[99.8] This important decision holds that an express preemption clause that says that a state "may not establish, continue in effect, or enforce a law or regulation" establishing a performance or other safety standard that is not identical to the federal regulations only preempts statutes and regulations, not common law claims. The court relied on a very careful grammatical analysis of the language of the clause. In seeking to avoid preemption, other preemption clauses should be carefully compared to the clause at issue in this case, and the similarities stressed. The Court concluded that the goal of the preemption clause was to limit state authority to regulate boats, and contrasted that to the goal of common law tort claims, which is to provide compensation to victims. The Court also rejected the manufacturer's implicit preemption arguments.

Preemption issues are also likely to arise in claims based on defects that affect the safety of motor vehicles, which are generally governed by the National Highway Traffic and Motor Vehicle Safety Act[99.9] and the regulations promul-

gated thereunder.[99.10] The Act contains an express preemption provision which provides that a state can not maintain a motor vehicle safety standard that is applicable to the same aspect of vehicle performance as a federal standard, unless it is identical to the federal standard.[99.11] The Act also contains a savings clause, however, which provides that compliance with the federal standards does not exempt any person from liability at common law,[99.12] as well as a provision that the Act does not establish or affect any warranty obligation under federal or state law.[99.13]

The Supreme Court recently decided that despite its savings clause, the Act preempted a tort action alleging that a manufacturer's failure to include an airbag was negligent and constituted a defective design.[99.14] The Court, by a vote of five to four, ruled that the premise on which the plaintiff's case was based, that the manufacturer had a duty to install an airbag, conflicted with the federal standard which gradually phased in passive restraints and gave manufacturers various options for compliance.[99.15] The *Geier* decision turned in large part on the Court's assessment of the particular goals of the passive restraint standards, which did not require the use of airbags, but instead "deliberately provided the manufacturer with a range of choices among different passive restraint devices," designed to "bring about a mix of different devices introduced gradually over time" thereby lowering costs, overcoming technical safety problems, encouraging technological development, and winning widespread consumer acceptance—all of which would promote the standard's

---

fact contradicted label's instructions created warranty that FIFRA does not preempt).

99.3 Am. Cyanamid Co. v. Geye, 79 S.W.3d 21 (Tex. 2002).

99.4 *See* Dow Chem. Co. v. Ebling, 723 N.E.2d 881 (Ind. Ct. App. 2000) (citing cases), *aff'd in relevant part, rev'd in part on other grounds*, 753 N.E.2d 633 (Ind. 2001) (FIFRA does not preempt failure to warn claim against applicator).

99.5 21 U.S.C. §§ 151–159.

99.6 57 Fed. Reg. 38,758 (Aug. 27, 1992).

99.7 Symens v. Smithkline Beecham Corp., 152 F.3d 1050 (8th Cir. 1998); Lynbrook Farms v. Smithkline Beecham Corp., 79 F.3d 620 (7th Cir. 1996); Behrens v. United Vaccines, Inc., 198 F. Supp. 2d 945 (D. Minn. 2002).

99.8 Sprietsma v. Mercury Marine, 537 U.S. 51, 123 S. Ct. 518, 154 L. Ed. 2d 466 (2002).

99.9 49 U.S.C. § 30103(b).

99.10 *See, e.g.,* 49 Fed. Reg. 28,962 (July 17, 1984) (Federal Motor Vehicle Safety Standard (FMVSS) 208, relating to air bags and other passive restrain systems).

99.11 49 U.S.C. § 30103(b).

99.12 49 U.S.C. § 30103(e).

99.13 49 U.S.C. § 30103(d); *see also* Martin v. Ford Motor Co., 914 F. Supp. 1449 (S.D. Tex. 1996) (express warranty claims not preempted because not based on state law but imposed by warrantor).

99.14 Geier v. Am. Honda Motor Co., 529 U.S. 861, 120 S. Ct. 1913, 146 L. Ed. 2d 914 (2000); *see* M. Tankersley, *Measuring the Shadow that Federal Regulations Cast Over State Remedies*, The Consumer Advoc., July/August 2000, at 15; *see also* Griffith v. Gen. Motors Corp., 303 F.3d 1276 (11th Cir. 2002) (claim that manufacturer should not have chosen lap belt only restraint system is preempted); Moser v. Ford Motor Co., 2001 WL 1387600 (4th Cir. Nov. 8, 2001) (unpublished) (claim that seat belt system had defect that would be common to all seat belt systems is preempted, as is duty to warn claim, but claim that this particular seat belt system was defectively designed would not be preempted if it caused plaintiff's injuries); Anthony v. Abbott, 289 F. Supp. 2d 667 (D. V.I. 2003) (claim that manufacturer should have included side airbag is preempted); Carrasquilla v. Mazda Motor Corp., 166 F. Supp. 2d 169 (M.D. Pa. 2001) (challenges to manufacturer's choice of restraint system are preempted, but claims of defective design of other safety features are not); Hernandez-Gomez v. Volkswagen of Am., Inc., 32 P.3d 424 (Ariz. Ct. App. 2001) (federal law preempts claim that manufacturer should have added a manual lap belt to restraint system it chose).

99.15 *Geier*, 529 U.S. at 880, 881.

safety objectives.[99.16] Requiring the use of one form of passive restraint—airbags—would frustrate these objectives.[99.17] Significantly, the Court did not find complete preemption (because of the existence of the savings clause and because Congress did not intend to completely occupy the field of vehicle safety) but only *conflict* preemption, when a claim directly conflicts with the federal standard.[99.18]

When the objective of the standard at issue is not to encourage choices, but to set minimum standards (a "floor"), state claims should not be preempted on the basis of a conflict.[99.19] In addition, when a federal standard is not directly implicated, no conflict preemption should be found.[99.20] For example, in a case alleging that certain Jeeps contained a design defect which caused them to self-shift from park to reverse, raising claims of breach of warranty and violation of state consumer protection statutes, the court found that there was no specific federal standard with respect to prevention of an "unintended park-reverse shift," and therefore there was no specific conflict.[99.21] Even a claim based on the failure of a vehicle's restraint system to protect an occupant is not preempted if it challenges the design of the restraint system rather than the manufacturer's choice of that particular type of restraint.[99.22] Claims based on express warranties should not be preempted because such warranties are not imposed by state law, but are created by the warrantor.[99.23]

Some courts have allowed plaintiffs to seek court-ordered recalls of defective vehicles or parts, particularly in cases in which a defect is alleged but the plaintiffs or the members of the plaintiff class have not yet suffered injuries as a result of the defect.[99.24] This result is supported by the Motor Vehicle Safety Act itself, which states that a recall conducted pursuant to 49 U.S.C. § 30120(b) does not displace any other "rights and remedies under other laws of the United States or a State."[99.25] While a recall is in process, courts have allowed suits for damages to proceed, holding that compensating injured plaintiffs does not interfere with the administration of a voluntary recall.[99.26]

When preemption is not found, a defendant may argue that under the doctrine of primary jurisdiction the court should nonetheless defer to the jurisdiction of the National Highway Traffic Safety Administration in cases involving issues of vehicle safety. The doctrine of primary jurisdiction suggests that a court should defer to an agency charged with particular regulatory duties when necessary to ensure uniformity or when the agency is better equipped to address the issues raised by the plaintiffs' claims.[99.27] This notion has been rejected when the plaintiff does not directly challenge a federal standard or regulation, and thus does not put

---

99.16 *Geier*, 529 U.S. at 875.

99.17 *Id.*

99.18 *Accord* McGettigan v. Ford Motor Co., 265 F. Supp. 2d 1291 (S.D. Ala. 2003) (no complete preemption; remanding case to state court); *see also* Farkas v. Bridgestone/Firestone, Inc., 113 F. Supp. 2d 1107 (W.D. Ky. Sept. 22, 2000) (federal motor vehicle laws do not completely preempt state law). *But cf.* Stewart v. Gen. Motors Corp., 222 F. Supp. 2d 845 (W.D. Ky. 2002) (conflict preemption bars claim that manufacturer's airbag warnings were inadequate).

99.19 *Geier*, 529 U.S. at 868; *see also* Littel v. Bridgestone/Firestone, Inc., 259 F. Supp. 2d 1016 (C.D. Cal. 2003) (state law claims not completely preempted). *But see* Majia v. White GMC Trucks, Inc., 336 Ill. App. 3d 702, 784 N.E.2d 345 (2002) (claim of defect in design of vehicle door is preempted; persuasive dissent).

99.20 Kent v. DaimlerChrysler Corp., 200 F. Supp. 2d 1208 (N.D. Cal. 2002); Talalai v. Cooper Tire & Rubber Co., 360 N.J. Super. 547, 823 A.2d 888 (Super. Ct. App. Div. 2001) (UDAP damage suit does not seek to impose regulations or standards so is not preempted); *see also* Freightliner Corp. v. Myrick, 514 U.S. 280, 115 S. Ct. 1483, 131 L. Ed. 2d 385 (1995) (Safety Act did not expressly preempt state common-law design defect claims against manufacturers of trucks that were not equipped with anti-lock braking system because no federal standard was in effect, and no evidence of intent to have no standard).

99.21 Kent v. DaimlerChrysler Corp., 200 F. Supp. 2d 1208, 1215, 1216 (N.D. Cal. 2002); *see also* Talalai v. Cooper Tire & Rubber Co., 2001 WL 1877265 (D.N.J. Jan. 8, 2001) (no preemption when suit seeks damages rather than judicial recall).

99.22 Volkswagen of Am., Inc. v. Gentry, 254 Ga. App. 888, 564 S.E.2d 733 (2002).

99.23 Martin v. Ford Motor Co., 914 F. Supp. 1449, 1454 (S.D. Tex.

1996); Martin v. Ford Motor Co., 2001 WL 253865 (E.D. Pa. Jan. 31, 1996) (express warranty claims not preempted because not based on state law but imposed by warrantor) (citing Cipollone v. Liggett Group, Inc., 505 U.S. 504, 525, 112 S. Ct. 2608, 120 L. Ed. 2d 407 (1992)); *see also* Korthas v. Suzuki Motor Co., 289 A.D.2d 1093, 735 N.Y.S.2d 322 (2001) (claim concerning defective design of motorcycle side stand not preempted because claim did not conflict with federal standards or frustrate their objectives).

99.24 *See* Burgo v. Volkswagen of Am., 183 F. Supp. 2d 683 (D.N.J. 2001) (Motor Vehicle Safety Act does not completely preempt state authority over automobile tire recalls); Kagan v. Carwell Corp., 2001 U.S. Dist. LEXIS 4544 (C.D. Cal. Mar. 30, 2001); Mazerolle v. DaimlerChrysler Corp., 48 U.C.C. Rep. Serv. 2d 1310 (Me. Super. Ct. 2002) (allowing judicial recall suit to proceed when NHTSA had not taken any action); *see also* McGettigan v. Ford Motor Co., 265 F. Supp. 2d 1291 (S.D. Ala. 2003) (Motor Vehicle Safety Act does not completely preempt warranty class action even if case seeks relief similar to recall). *But see In re* Bridgestone/Firestone Inc. Tires Products Liab. Litig., 153 F. Supp. 2d 935, 945 (S.D. Ind. 2001) (ruling that Safety Act preempts any state law recall, noting the comprehensiveness of the Safety Act with regard to recalls demonstrates that any state law providing for a recall would frustrate the purposes of the Act).

99.25 49 U.S.C. § 30103(d).

99.26 *See* Nolan v. Cooper Tire, 2001 WL 253865 (E.D. Pa. Mar. 14, 2001); Dorian v. Bridgestone/Firestone, Inc., 2000 WL 1570627 (E.D. Pa. Oct. 19, 2000); Lennon v. Bridgestone/Firestone, Inc., 2000 WL 1570645 (E.D. Pa. Oct. 19, 2000); Miller v. Bridgestone/Firestone, Inc., 2000 WL 1570732 (E.D. Pa. Oct. 19, 2000); Talalai v. Cooper Tire & Rubber Co., 360 N.J. Super. 547, 823 A.2d 888 (Super. Ct. App. Div. 2001) (UDAP suit for damages not preempted).

99.27 *See* Nader v. Allegheny Airlines, Inc., 426 U.S. 290, 303, 304, 96 S. Ct. 1978, 48 L. Ed. 2d 643 (1976).

uniformity at risk.[99.28] Moreover, claims based on alleged vehicle defects are typically "within the conventional competence of the courts."[99.29]

1.4.9.5 Arguing Against Preemption

Two points should be stressed in arguing against preemption. First, particularly in fields which the states have traditionally occupied, courts should "start with the assumption that the historic police powers of the States were not to be superseded by [a] Federal Act unless that was the clear and manifest purpose of Congress."[99.30]

Second, the intent of Congress is the ultimate touchstone.[99.31] The stated purpose of the Medical Device Amendments is to "provide for the safety and effectiveness of medical devices intended for human use."[99.32] Congress stated its purpose in passing the FIFRA registration requirements as preventing adverse effects on the environment, defined to include not only land, air and water, but also humans and animals.[99.33] Neither statute provides for a federal cause of action to replace state warranty-type claims, and the courts have not cited anything in the legislative history that shows that Congress was considering manufacturers' post-marketing liability when it passed these statutes.[99.34]

Choice of forum may be critical in these cases. As a broad generalization, state courts have tended to be less willing than federal courts to abrogate warranty and tort remedies in favor of a federal regulatory scheme that affords no remedy to injured persons.[99.35]

99.28 Kent v. DaimlerChrysler Corp., 200 F. Supp. 2d 1208, 1218 (N.D. Cal. 2002); *see also* Mazerolle v. DaimlerChrysler Corp., 48 U.C.C. Rep. Serv. 2d 1310 (Me. Super. Ct. 2002) (declining to refer case to NHTSA's primary jurisdiction because plaintiff sought damages as well as recall).

99.29 *Kent*, 200 F. Supp. 2d at 1219.

99.30 Medtronic, Inc. v. Lohr, 518 U.S. 470, 485, 116 S. Ct. 2240, 135 L. Ed. 2d 700 (1996); *cf.* Buckman Co. v. Plaintiffs' Legal Comm., 531 U.S. 341, 121 S. Ct. 1012, 148 L. Ed. 2d 854 (2001) (presumption against preemption only appropriate in fields that states have traditionally occupied).

99.31 *Medtronic, Inc.*, 518 U.S. at 487 (noting "perverse effect of granting complete immunity from design defect liability to an industry that, in the judgment of Congress, needed more stringent regulation . . ."); Weiland v. Telectronics Pacing Sys., Inc., 188 Ill. 2d 415, 242 Ill. Dec. 618, 721 N.E.2d 1149, 40 U.C.C. Rep. 2d 1001 (1999).

99.32 *Medtronic, Inc.*, 518 U.S. at 490.

99.33 7 U.S.C. § 136a(a); Brown v. Chas. H. Lilly Co., 161 Or. App. 402, 985 P.2d 846, 38 U.C.C. Rep. 2d 1147, 1149 (1999).

99.34 *See also* Choate v. Champion Home Builders Co., 222 F.3d 788 (10th Cir. 2000) (construing National Manufactured Housing Construction and Safety Standards Act not to preempt mobile home buyers' strict liability suit is consistent with Act's purposes to reduce personal injuries and deaths resulting from mobile home accidents and to improve quality and durability of mobile homes).

99.35 *Compare* Mitchell v. Collagen, 126 F.3d 902, 33 U.C.C. Rep. 2d 750 (7th Cir. 1997) (premarket approval process preempts most state claims) *with* Weiland v. Telectronics Pacing Sys., Inc., 188 Ill. 2d 415, 242 Ill. Dec. 618, 721 N.E.2d 1149, 40 U.C.C. Rep. 2d 1001 (1999) (premarket approval process does not impose substantive requirements on manufacture or design so does not preempt state warranty and defective design claims).

1.5 Cumulation of Rights and Remedies

Page 14

1.5.2 *Cumulation of Rights Under UCC and State and Federal Consumer Legislation*

Addition to note 103.

103   *See also* Hitachi Constr. Mach. Co. v. Amax Coal Co., 737 N.E.2d 460 (Ind. Ct. App. 2000) (product liability statute does not displace U.C.C. warranty law).

Replace note 108 with:

108   *See* § 11.1.1, *infra; see also* National Consumer Law Center, Unfair and Deceptive Acts and Practices (5th ed. 2001 and Supp.).

1.6 Liberal Construction of Consumer Warranty Laws

Page 15

1.6.1 *Magnuson-Moss Act, Lemon Laws and UDAP Statutes*

Addition to notes 116, 117, 119.

116   *Replace DiCintio citation with*: DiCintio v. DaimlerChrysler Corp., 185 Misc. 2d 667, 713 N.Y.S.2d 808 (Sup. Ct. 2000), *aff'd in part, modified in part on other grounds*, 282 A.D.2d 276, 724 N.Y.S.2d 717 (2001), *rev'd on other grounds*, 97 N.Y.2d 463, 742 N.Y.S.2d 182, 768 N.E.2d 1121 (2002).

117   Singer v. Land Rover N. Am., 955 F. Supp. 359 (D.N.J. 1997); Rothermel v. Safari Motor Coaches, 1994 U.S. Dist. LEXIS 21591 (N.D. Ohio July 29, 1994); Harvill v. Fleetwood Enterprises, Inc., 2003 WL 21702375 (Cal. Ct. App. July 23, 2003) (unpublished); Oregel v. Am. Isuzu Motors, Inc., 90 Cal. App. 4th 1094, 109 Cal. Rptr. 2d 583 (2001) (lemon law should be given construction consistent with its remedial purpose); Kwan v. Mercedes-Benz of N. Am., Inc., 23 Cal. App. 4th 174, 28 Cal. Rptr. 2d 371 (1994)

(Song-Beverly Act); Harmon v. Concord Volkswagon, Inc., 598 A.2d 696 (Del. Super. Ct. 1991) (as remedial statute intended to provide additional remedies and protection to buying public, should be interpreted with reasonable breadth); King v. King Motor Co., 780 So. 2d 937 (Fla. Dist. Ct. App. 2001); Collins v. Mullinax E., Inc., 153 Ohio App. 3d 534, 795 N.E.2d 68 (2003).

119 *Replace DiCintio citation with*: DiCintio v. DaimlerChrysler Corp., 185 Misc. 2d 667, 713 N.Y.S.2d 808 (Sup. Ct. 2000) (applicability of lemon law to leased vehicle), *aff'd in part, modified in part on other grounds*, 282 A.D.2d 276, 724 N.Y.S.2d 717 (2001), *rev'd on other grounds*, 97 N.Y.2d 463, 742 N.Y.S.2d 182, 768 N.E.2d 1121 (2002); *add*: Rothermel v. Safari Motor Coaches, 1994 U.S. Dist. LEXIS 21591 (N.D. Ohio July 29, 1994).

Replace note 123 with: 123 *See* National Consumer Law Center, Unfair and Deceptive Acts and Practices §§ 2.1.3, 3.1.2 (5th ed. 2001 and Supp.).

1.6.2 Uniform Commercial Code

1.6.2.1 Requirement of Liberal Construction

Addition to note 124.   124 *See* Ameristar Jet Charter, Inc. v. Signal Composites, Inc., 271 F.3d 624, 46 U.C.C. Rep. Serv. 2d 425 (5th Cir. 2001) (requirement of notice of breach).

Replace note 125 with: 125 U.C.C. § 1-102 comment 1 is preserved without significant change as U.C.C. § 1-103 comment 1 in revised Article 1, which the National Conference of Commissioners on Uniform State Laws (NCCUSL) approved in 2001 for adoption by the states. *See also* U.C.C. § 1-106(1) ("The remedies provided by this Act shall be liberally construed.") [*redesignated as U.C.C. § 1-305 by revised Article 1 without substantive change*].

Add to text at end of subsection's first paragraph: Section 1-106(1) states that "[t]he remedies provided by this Act shall be liberally administered to the end that the aggrieved party may be put in as good a position as if the other party had fully performed."

Page 16

1.6.2.2 Application of Policy to Consumer Transactions

Replace note 134 with: 134 U.C.C. § 1-201 cmt. 19 [*This particular comment is not retained in the comparable provision of revised Article 1, U.C.C. § 1-304, which the National Conference of Commissioners on Uniform State Laws (NCCUSL) approved in 2001 for adoption by the states. As of early 2004, Texas, Virginia, and the Virgin Islands had adopted revised Article 1 and several other states were considering it.*].

Replace note 135 with: 135 U.C.C. § 1-102 cmt. 1 [*redesignated as U.C.C. § 1-103 by revised Article 1, approved by NCCUSL in 2001 for adoption by the states*].

Addition to notes 136, 138.   136 *Add at end of note*: [*redesignated as U.C.C. § 1-302 cmt. 1 by revised Article 1, which NCCUSL approved in 2001 for adoption by the states*].
138 *Replace "U.C.C. § 1-102 cmt. 1" with*: U.C.C. § 1-102 cmt. 1 [*redesignated as U.C.C. § 1-103 cmt. 1 by revised Article 1, which NCCUSL approved in 2001 for adoption by the states*].

Page 17

1.6.2.3 Flexible Statutory Standards of the UCC

Replace note 141 with: 141 U.C.C. § 1-102 cmt. 1 [*redesignated as U.C.C. § 1-103 cmt. 1 by revised Article 1, which NCCUSL approved in 2001 for adoption by the states*].

Add note 142.1 after "section 1-102" in last sentence of subsection's first paragraph.   142.1 Revised Article 1, which NCCUSL approved in 2001 for adoption by the states, redesignates this provision as U.C.C. § 1-103 cmt. 1 without material change.

1.7 Warranty Law in a Nutshell

1.7.1 Creation of Express and Implied Warranties

1.7.1.1 Introduction

Some courts, however, hold that UCC warranty remedies displace the UCC remedies for breach of contract, so a buyer can not recast a UCC warranty claim as a breach of contract.[159.1]

159.1   Alcan Aluminum Corp. v. BASF Corp., 46 U.C.C. Rep. Serv. 2d 690 (N.D. Tex. 2001), *aff'd.*, 2002 U.S. App. LEXIS 21828 (5th Cir. Sept. 30, 2002) (table); Ellis v. Precision Engine Rebuilders, Inc., 68 S.W.3d 894, 47 U.C.C. Rep. Serv. 2d 992 (Tex. App. 2002); *see also* Lyda Constructors, Inc. v. Butler Mfg. Co., 103 S.W.3d 632, 50 U.C.C. Rep. Serv. 2d 100 (Tex. App. 2003) (contrasting breach of contract with breach of warranty).

Chapter 2 The Magnuson-Moss Warranty Act

2.1 Getting Started

Page 23

2.1.1 Overview

Addition to note 1.

1 *Add at end of note*: The most significant items from the legislative history can be found on the companion CD-Rom to this volume.

2.2 Scope

2.2.2 Covered Consumer Products

Page 25

2.2.2.1 General

Addition to note 23.

23 *See also* Champion Home Builders Co. v. ADT Sec. Services, Inc., 179 F. Supp. 2d 16 (N.D.N.Y. 2001) (industrial alarm system probably not a consumer product); People *ex rel.* Mota v. Cent. Sprinkler Corp., 174 F. Supp. 2d 824 (C.D. Ill. 2001) (commercial water sprinkler system not covered); *In re* Ford Motor Co. Vehicle Paint Litig., 1996 U.S. Dist. LEXIS 11063 (E.D. La. July 30, 1996) (electrocoat paint sold to manufacturer for application to cars as part of manufacturing process not covered); Szubski v. Mercedes-Benz, U.S.A., Ltd. Liab. Co., 124 Ohio Misc. 2d 82, 796 N.E.2d 81 (C.P. 2003) (car is consumer product).

2.2.2.2 Whether Consumer Use Is Normal Use

Addition to notes 28, 33, 35.

28 Champion Home Builders Co. v. ADT Sec. Services, Inc., 179 F. Supp. 2d 16 (N.D.N.Y. 2001) (industrial alarm system probably not covered).

33 Hasek v. DaimlerChrysler Corp., 319 Ill. App. 3d 780, 745 N.E.2d 627, 44 U.C.C. Rep. Serv. 2d 108 (2001) (car is consumer product).

Page 26

35 Frank v. Allstate Auto Sales, 1992 Ohio App. LEXIS 2295 (Ohio Ct. App. Apr. 30, 1992) (tow truck not covered when plaintiff purchased it for business and produced no evidence that tow trucks are normally used for personal, family, or household purposes).

Add to text after subsection's fourth paragraph:

The Federal Trade Commission (FTC) stated at one point that small airplanes are not consumer products,[35.1] and two courts have agreed.[35.2] However, a blanket exclusion of small planes seems inconsistent with the Act. The cost of the product should not be determinative because many consumer products, such as high-end vehicles, are as expensive as small planes. Indeed, the Act's $50,000 amount in controversy requirement for federal court jurisdiction demonstrates that the drafters contemplated that expensive products would fall within the definition of consumer product. Attorneys who are seeking to bring a Magnuson-Moss claim regarding a product such as a small plane should use factual investigation and discovery to determine the extent to which the product is marketed to consumers for personal transportation. Do advertisements promote it for personal use? Does the manufacturer or dealer have figures on the percentage of sales that are for personal use? Do either the manufacturer or dealer have any special programs for non-business buyers?

35.1 Fed. Trade Comm'n, Modification of Implementation and Enforcement Policy, 41 Fed. Reg. 26,757 (June

29, 1976); *see* § 2.1.2, *supra* (current status of the FTC's Implementation and Enforcement Policy).

35.2   Cinquegrani v. Sandel Avionics, 2001 U.S. Dist. LEXIS 7802 (N.D. Ill. June 7, 2001); CAT Aircraft Leasing Inc. v. Cessna Aircraft Co., 1990 U.S. Dist. LEXIS 14720 (D. Kan. Oct. 3, 1990).

Addition to notes 36, 41, 45, 47.

36   Cinquegrani v. Waypoint Aviation Servs., Inc., 2001 U.S. Dist. LEXIS 7802 (N.D. Ill. June 7, 2001) ($500,000 airplane not consumer product as a matter of law).

41   *See also In re* Ford Motor Co. Vehicle Paint Litig., 1996 U.S. Dist. LEXIS 11063 (E.D. La. July 30, 1996) (electrocoat paint, purchased by manufacturer for application to cars as part of manufacturing process, not a consumer product because sold to commercial buyer for commercial purposes).

45   *Cf.* People *ex rel.* Mota v. Cent. Sprinkler Corp., 174 F. Supp. 2d 824 (C.D. Ill. 2001) (refusing to import C.P.S.A. definition into Magnuson-Moss because C.P.S.A. is broader).

Page 27

47   *Replace last sentence of note with*: *But see* Kanter v. Warner-Lambert Co., 99 Cal. App. 4th 780, 122 Cal. Rptr. 2d 72 (2002) (non-prescription drug not a consumer product because exempted from CPSA).

Add to text after sentence containing note 47:

Indeed, following this reasoning would mean that motor vehicles are not consumer products, as the CPSA also explicitly exempts motor vehicles.[47.1] The exclusions to the CPSA's definition of consumer product are merely designed to allocate oversight of the safety of particular products to agencies with specialized expertise, and should not be read into the Magnuson-Moss Act.

47.1   15 U.S.C. § 2052(a)(1)(C).

2.2.2.3 Personalty vs. Realty

Addition to notes 50, 55, 58.

50   *See also* Marshall v. U.S. Home Corp., 2002 WL 274457 (Ohio Ct. App. Feb. 27, 2002) (construction of home not covered).

55   *See also* People *ex rel.* Mota v. Cent. Sprinkler Corp., 174 F. Supp. 2d 824 (C.D. Ill. 2001) (sprinkler system not covered because it was integral component of the structure and because structure was not a consumer dwelling).

58   *Add to Miller citation*: *aff'd on other grounds*, 249 F.3d 629 (7th Cir. 2001) (court states in dictum that it is doubtful that it would disagree with trial court).

Replace § 2.2.2.5 with:

2.2.2.5 Leases

The Act should apply to leases, for example, an automobile consumer lease subject to the manufacturer's new car warranty. Nowhere in the Act did Congress attempt to exempt leases. As one court has pointed out, a narrower construction would be inconsistent with the Act's intent to provide more meaningful protections to consumers entitled to Article 2 warranty protections.[61] But the most compelling argument is a straightforward analysis of the plain language of the Act.

Typically, a new vehicle is selected by the consumer at the showroom and is sold by the dealer to the leasing company, such as a bank or the manufacturer's financing subsidiary, which becomes the registered owner/lessor. The sale to the leasing company is solely predicated on and motivated by the consumer's agreement to lease the vehicle, and the leasing company then entrusts the car to the consumer/lessee for the lease term.[62] Notwithstanding that ownership remains with the lessor, the consumer/lessee is the beneficiary of the manufacturer's warranty.[63] This arrangement meets all of the requirements of the Act.

The fact that the owner/buyer is the financing entity/lessor rather than the ultimate user distinguishes the typical lease from an installment sale, but this difference is of no consequence under the Act. The Act defines a consumer in the disjunctive as any one of the following: (1) the "buyer (other than for purposes of resale)" of the product, (2) a person to whom the product is "transferred" during the duration of the warranty, or (3) "any other person who is entitled . . . to enforce" the warranty by its terms or under state law.[64] In contrast to a retail purchaser, the individual lessee does not qualify as a consumer under the first clause if the court adopts a strict interpretation of the term buyer. However, the third option fully covers the lessee,[64.1] and the second should as well under any ordinary definition of the word transferred. Therefore, the lessee is a "consumer" entitled to enforce the Act.[64.2]

That the buyer is the financing entity/lessor is otherwise unimportant. So long as the product itself "is normally used for personal, family, or household purposes," whether the owner intends or uses it for commercial purposes is irrelevant.[64.3] Similarly, the definition of written warranty requires a "sale by a supplier" but does not state that this initial sale must be made to a consumer.[64.4] Rather, this definition of written warranty requires that the initial sale be to a "buyer for purposes other than resale of such product." The financing entity/lessor that is the buyer does not intend to resell the vehicle but instead intends to lease it. The fact that the lessor intends to sell the car at the end of the lease period should have no bearing on its current intended purposes. After all, almost every new car purchaser intends to resell the vehicle at some point. This qualification in the definition is meaningless unless the "for purposes other than resale" language is limited to the initial use.[64.5]

Therefore, under its plain language, the Act applies to a typical lease. Three recent cases applying the Act to leased vehicles reached their results based on such an analysis of the plain language of the Act.[64.6] The courts conducted thorough statutory analyses paralleling the above outline and bolstered their conclusions with discussions of the Act's legislative history. Other courts have split on the question, but neither those courts that find a lease subject to the Act[64.7] nor those that do not[64.8] have considered this plain language analysis. Additionally, to the extent that any of these cases even address the requirement that a written warranty becomes part of the "basis of the bargain between a supplier and a buyer for purposes other than resale,"[64.9] they fail to consider that this requirement is necessarily fact based.

A New York Court of Appeals decision[64.10] illustrates the flaw in those cases that disregard the Act's plain language. The court initially opines that "the case hinges on whether DiCintio's lease qualifies as a 'sale,'" a formulation that is relevant only to the first clause of the definition of consumer. The second clause merely requires a "transfer," a broader term that should encompasses leases. Ultimately, the court devotes only a few sentences at the end of the opinion to the third clause of the definition of consumer, which covers any person entitled to enforce the warranty against the warrantor. The court rejects the application of this clause of the definition by holding that the manufacturer's warranty in a lease situation does not meet the Magnuson-Moss definition of written warranty. First, the court, without citing any facts or other authority, holds that the warranty does not meet this definition because it does not become part of the basis of the bargain between the manufacturer and the financing entity/buyer.[64.11] To the contrary, the manufacturer's warranty is, as a practical matter, an essential element of the sale to the financing entity/lessor, from the perspective of both the financing entity and the lessee. Indeed, Congress has required as a core disclosure under the Consumer Leasing Act "[a] statement identifying all express warranties and guarantees made by the manufacturer or lessor with respect to the leased property."[64.12] More importantly, the court fails to note that the "basis of the bargain" language is a term of art that as a matter of law unambiguously covers this sale to the financing entity/lessor.[64.13] Second, the court holds that the manufacturer's warranty does not qualify as a written warranty because the financing entity that buys the vehicle does so with the intent of reselling it at the end of the lease term. But the financing entity's probable ultimate resale of the vehicle is, as noted above, no different from all other new car buyers' intentions after a similarly extended period of time. If that ultimate, delayed, and secondary purpose were controlling, no new car buyer would ever be subject to the Act.[64.14] Based on this faulty reasoning, the court concludes that, because the warranty does not qualify as a written warranty, the consumer/lessor can not be a person entitled to enforce a written warranty, and therefore can not satisfy the third clause of the definition of consumer.

A sale disguised as a lease does not raise this issue. In that case, the transaction is treated as a sale and is subject to the Act.[64.15]

61   Henderson v. Benson-Hartman Motors, Inc., 33 Pa. D. & C.3d 6, 41 U.C.C. Rep. Serv. 782, 794 (C.P. Allegheny County 1983).

62   *See* § 19.2.3.1, *infra.*

63   Disclosure of the manufacturer's express warranty is required by Regulation M, 12 C.F.R. § 213.4(p). *See* National Consumer Law Center, Truth in Lending § 10.3.6.17.1 (5th ed. 2003).

64   15 U.S.C. § 2301(3).

64.1   Potente v. Peugeot Motors of Am., Inc., 62 Ohio Misc. 2d 335, 598 N.E.2d 907 (Ct. Com. Pl. 1991) (applying identical state lemon law definition of a consumer to cover an automobile lease).

64.2   *See* 15 U.S.C. § 2310(d)(1); *see also* Cohen v. AM Gen. Corp., 264 F. Supp. 2d 616 (N.D. Ill. 2003);

Dekelaita v. Nissan Motor Corp., 799 N.E.2d 367 (Ill. App. Ct. 2003); Szubski v. Mercedes-Benz, U.S.A., 796 N.E.2d 81 (Ohio C.P. 2003).

64.3   *See* § 2.2.2.2, *supra.*

64.4   15 U.S.C. § 2301(6); *see also* Cohen v. AM Gen. Corp., 264 F. Supp. 2d 616 (N.D. Ill. 2003).

64.5   Cohen v. AM Gen. Corp., 264 F. Supp. 2d 616 (N.D. Ill. 2003); Dekelaita v. Nissan Motor Corp., 799 N.E.2d 367 (Ill. App. Ct. 2003); Szubski v. Mercedes-Benz, U.S.A., 796 N.E.2d 81 (Ohio C.P. 2003).

64.6   Cohen v. AM Gen. Corp., 264 F. Supp. 2d 616 (N.D. Ill. 2003); Dekelaita v. Nissan Motor Corp., 799 N.E.2d 367 (Ill. App. Ct. 2003); Szubski v. Mercedes-Benz, U.S.A., 796 N.E.2d 81 (Ohio C.P. 2003).

64.7   Voelker v. Porsche Cars N. Am., Inc., 353 F.3d 516 (7th Cir. 2003) (sale to leasing company is for the ultimate purpose of resale at expiration of the lease term, but the lease is still subject to the Act because the lessee is a "consumer" who may enforce the warranty under state law); Freeman v. Hubco Leasing, 253 Ga. 698, 324 S.E.2d 462 (1985) (leased vehicle is a consumer product and lessor is a supplier); Stuart Becker & Co. v. Steven Kessler Motor Cars, Inc., 135 Misc. 2d 1069, 517 N.Y.S.2d 692 (Sup. Ct. 1987); Bus. Modeling Techniques, Inc. v. Gen. Motors Corp., 123 Misc. 2d 605, 474 N.Y.S.2d 258 (Sup. Ct. 1984); Henderson v. Benson-Hartman Motors, Inc., 33 Pa. D. & C.3d 6, 41 U.C.C. Rep. Serv. 782, 794 (C.P. Allegheny County 1983).

64.8   Weisberg v. Jaguar Cars, 2003 WL 1337983 (N.D. Ill. Mar. 18, 2003) (lease not covered because the sale is to the leasing company and not to the consumer); Diamond v. Porsche Cars N. Am., Inc., 2002 WL 31155064 (N.D. Ill. Sept. 26, 2002) (lease not covered because the sale is to the leasing company and not to the consumer), *vacated on other grounds*, 2003 WL 21698795 (7th Cir. July 26, 2003) (unpublished); Sellers v. Frank Griffin AMC Jeep, Inc., 526 So. 2d 147 (Fla. Dist. Ct. App. 1988) (pure lease not covered); Corral v. Rollins Protective Services Co., 240 Kan. 678, 732 P.2d 1260 (1987) (true lease of service, not disguised sale, not covered); DiCintio v. DaimlerChrysler Corp., 97 N.Y.2d 463, 742 N.Y.S.2d 182, 768 N.E.2d 1121 (2002); Brandt & Brandt v. Porsche/Audi Manhattan, Inc., 130 A.D.2d 986, 514 N.Y.S.2d 920, 1986-2 Trade Cas. (CCH) ¶ 67,358 (1986); Barco Auto Leasing Corp. v. PSI Cosmetics, 125 Misc. 2d 68, 478 N.Y.S.2d 505 (Civ. Ct. 1984) (true lease not covered); Alpiser v. Eagle Pontiac-GMC-Isuzu, Inc., 97 N.C. App. 610, 389 S.E.2d 293 (1990).

64.9   See the last clause of 15 U.S.C. § 2301(6).

64.10   DiCintio v. DaimlerChrysler Corp., 97 N.Y.2d 463, 742 N.Y.S.2d 182, 768 N.E.2d 1121 (2002).

64.11   *See* 15 U.S.C. § 2301(7) (including "basis of the bargain" in the definition of written warranty).

64.12   15 U.S.C. § 1667a(6); *see also* Reg. M, 12 C.F.R. § 213.4(p).

64.13   *See* § 2.2.5.4, *infra.*

64.14   A more recent case relied on *DiCintio* to exclude leases from Magnuson-Moss coverage based on the same limitation in the definition of a written warranty, the requirement that it be given in a transaction "between a supplier and a buyer for purposes other than resale." Diamond v. Porsche Cars N. Am., Inc., 2002 WL 31155064 (N.D. Ill. Sept. 26, 2002), *vacated on other grounds*, 2003 WL 21698795 (7th Cir. July 16, 2003) (unpublished). As in *DiCintio*, the *Diamond* court ignored the absurd result that its focus on the buyer's ultimate intent after the initial use would also exclude virtually all new car sales from Magnuson-Moss coverage. The *Diamond* holding was later adopted by Weisberg v. Jaguar Cars, 2003 WL 1337983 (N.D. Ill. Mar. 18, 2003).

64.15   Stuart Becker & Co. v. Steven Kessler Motor Cars, Inc., 135 Misc. 2d 1069, 517 N.Y.S.2d 692 (Sup. Ct. 1987).

Page 28

2.2.4 Other Federal Regulation of Warranties

Add to text after sentence containing note 73:

A state court has held that this exemption applies to medication labels that are approved or mandated by federal law.[73.1]

73.1   Kanter v. Warner-Lambert Co., 99 Cal. App. 4th 780, 122 Cal. Rptr. 2d 72 (2002).

2.2.5 Covered Written Warranties

2.2.5.1 General

Addition to notes 77, 79, 80.

Page 29

77   *See also* Poli v. DaimlerChrysler Corp., 349 N.J. Super. 169, 793 A.2d 104, 47 U.C.C. Rep. Serv. 2d 260 (Super. Ct. App. Div. 2002) (repair or replace warranty is "written warranty").

79   *Cf.* Caboni v. Gen. Motors Corp., 278 F.3d 448 (5th Cir. 2002) (statement in owner's manual that air bag should inflate in certain circumstances may create express warranty under similar definition in La. Prod. Liab. Act). *But cf.* Laznovsky v. Hyundai Motor Am., Inc., 190 Misc. 2d 537, 738 N.Y.S.2d 820 (Dist. Ct. 2002) (written warranty required by N.Y. Used Car Lemon Law is not Magnuson-Moss written warranty; court relies solely on silence by an intermediate appellate court in another decision).

80   *See also* Horton Homes, Inc. v. Brooks, 2001 Ala. LEXIS 431 (Ala. Nov. 30, 2001) (certificate of quality assurance stating that mobile home had been carefully inspected to ensure quality was written warranty).

Add to text at end of subsection:

A statement in a sales brochure and the owner's manual that because of a vehicle's anti-theft features it would not start without a specially coded key was a statement that the anti-theft system was defect-free and therefore was a written warranty.[80.1]

80.1 Greines v. Ford Motor Co., 2003 WL 42524 (Cal. Ct. App. Jan. 7, 2003) (unpublished).

2.2.5.2 Statements and Representations Not Meeting Definition of a "Written Warranty"

Add note 81.1 at end of subsection's third bulleted item.

81.1 *See, e.g.,* Lewis v. Conseco Fin. Corp., 845 So. 2d 920 (Ala. 2002) (statement that mobile home was "new" was not written warranty).

Addition to note 83.

83 Lewis v. Conseco Fin. Corp., 845 So. 2d 920 (Ala. 2002) (statement that mobile home was "new" was not written warranty).

Page 31

2.2.5.4 Basis of the Bargain

Addition to note 97.

97 *Add to Miller citation: aff'd on other grounds,* 249 F.3d 629 (7th Cir. 2001).

2.2.6 Buyer Must Be a Consumer

Replace first word of subsection's first sentence with:

The Act includes a three-pronged definition of consumer: 1) a buyer (other than for purposes of resale) of any consumer product; 2) any person to whom such product is transferred during the duration of an implied or written warranty or service contract; or 3) any person who is entitled by the terms of such warranty or service contract or under applicable state law to enforce against the warrantor (or service contractor) the obligations of the warranty (or service contract).[106.1] To be a consumer, a person need only meet one of the three prongs of this definition.[106.2]

The first prong of the definition of consumer

106.1 15 U.S.C. § 2302(3).
106.2 Dekelaita v. Nissan Motor Corp., 2003 WL 22240509 (Ill. App. Ct. Sept. 29, 2003); Szubski v. Mercedes-Benz, U.S.A., Ltd. Liab. Co., 124 Ohio Misc. 2d 82, 796 N.E.2d 81 (C.P. 2003).

Addition to note 108.

108 *But see* Dekelaita v. Nissan Motor Corp., 2003 WL 22240509 (Ill. App. Ct. Sept. 29, 2003) (leasing company that buys vehicle in order to lease it to consumer is not buying it for purposes of resale as that term is used in 15 U.S.C. § 2302(6)).

Page 32

Add to text after subsection's first paragraph:

A consumer who buys the product for purposes other than resale, but then sells it (perhaps because of its defects) is still a consumer.[110.1] The consumer can seek damages only for the period of time that the consumer owned the product, however.[110.2]

110.1 Bartow v. Ford Motor Co., 342 Ill. App. 3d 480, 794 N.E.2d 1027 (2003).
110.2 *Id.*

Addition to note 112.

112 *Add to Coghlan citation: rev'd on other grounds,* 240 F.3d 449 (5th Cir. 2001).

Add to text at end of subsection:

An allegation that the product was not delivered in the bargained-for condition should, however, be sufficient under state law, without the need for any allegation that the product has actually malfunctioned or caused injury.[112.1] The definition of consumer in the context of vehicle leases is discussed in § 2.2.2.5, *supra.*

112.1 Coghlan v. Aquasport Marine Corp., 240 F.3d 449 (5th Cir. 2001) (allegation sufficient to claim benefit-of-bargain damages, which are allowed for many contract and fraud claims).

2.2.7 *Parties Liable Under the Act*

2.2.7.2 Manufacturer Liability

Add note 117.1 at end of subsection's first sentence.

117.1   *See, e.g.,* Szubski v. Mercedes-Benz, U.S.A., Ltd. Liab. Co., 124 Ohio Misc. 2d 82, 796 N.E.2d 81 (C.P. 2003).

2.2.7.3 Dealer Liability Under the Act

Page 33

Add to text at end of subsection's second paragraph:

The dealer would also be liable for any Magnuson-Moss violations that did not involve enforcing rights "thereunder," that is, under the written warranty.

2.2.7.4 Creditors and Lessors

Replace note 135 with:

135   *See* National Consumer Law Center, Unfair and Deceptive Acts and Practices § 6.6 (5th ed. 2001 and Supp.).

Addition to note 137.

137   *See* § 2.2.2.5, *supra.*

Page 34

Replace note 141 with:

141   *See* National Consumer Law Center, Unfair and Deceptive Acts and Practices § 6.6.3.8.1 (5th ed. 2001 and Supp.).

Add new subsection to text after § 2.2.7.4.

2.2.7.5 Individuals

The Act defines supplier as "any person" engaged in the business of making a consumer product directly or indirectly available to consumers, and defines warrantor as any supplier "or other person" who gives or offers to give a written warranty or who is or may be obligated under an implied warranty.[142.1] These definitions are not restricted to corporations or businesses, but include natural persons.

Individuals will often meet the definition of supplier. Many salespersons and corporate owners are engaged in the business of making consumer products available to consumers, at least indirectly. However, the Act imposes fewer substantive duties upon suppliers than upon warrantors.[142.2]

Whether an individual is a warrantor will depend on whether the individual can be found to have given or offered to give a written warranty or to be liable on an implied warranty.[142.3] An individual selling her own property may meet this definition. One unreported decision finds the owner of a used car lot not to meet this standard when he had no personal involvement in the sale.[142.4] The result might be different if the owner of a used car lot also acted as the manager of the lot, dealt personally with the buyer, and personally negotiated and provided the warranty.

142.1   15 U.S.C. § 2301(4), (5).
142.2   *See* § 2.2.7.3, *supra.*
142.3   15 U.S.C. §§ 2301(5), 2310(f); *see* § 2.2.7.3, *supra.*
142.4   Rowan v. Max Auto Mall, Inc., 2002 U.S. Dist. LEXIS 2202 (N.D. Ill. Jan. 29, 2002).

2.3 Act Enforcement of Implied and "Written" Warranties; Regulation of Service Contracts

2.3.1 *Act Prohibits Breach of Implied Warranties Even Where No Written Warranty Provided*

Addition to note 143.

143   *See also* Chase v. Kawasaki Motors Corp., U.S.A., 140 F. Supp. 2d 1280 (M.D. Ala. 2001) (the Act "essentially provides a federal cause of action for breach of an implied warranty which arises under state

law''); Forest River, Inc. v. Posten, 847 So. 2d 957 (Ala. Civ. App. 2002) (fees could be awarded under Magnuson-Moss Act when buyers won implied warranty claim even though they lost a separate Magnuson-Moss count); Dildine v. Town & Country Truck Sales, Inc., 259 Ga. App. 732, 577 S.E.2d 882, 50 U.C.C. Rep. Serv. 2d 761 (2003) (recovery denied because plaintiff failed to prove breach of implied warranty); Alvarez v. Am. Isuzu Motors, 321 Ill. App. 3d 696, 749 N.E.2d 16 (2001) (failure of proof under state implied warranty); Polaris Indus., Inc. v. McDonald, 2003 WL 21940115 (Tex. App. Aug. 13, 2003); Michels v. Monaco Coach Co., 2003 WL 23194248 (E.D. Mich. Dec. 31, 2003); Hawkins v. Ford Motor Co., 211 W. Va. 487, 566 S.E.2d 624 (2002).

Page 35

Add to text at end of subsection:

But, for matters not directly addressed by the Magnuson-Moss Act, courts are likely to borrow state warranty law. Thus, for example, the general rule that expert testimony is unnecessary to prove the existence of a defect as long as the subject can be understood by the average juror applies in Magnuson-Moss cases.[153.1]

153.1   Thorner v. Fleetwood, 2002 WL 844610 (N.D. Ill. May 1, 2001), *vacated in part on other grounds*, 2002 WL 1998285 (N.D. Ill. Aug. 28, 2002).

2.3.2 Prohibitions on Disclaimers and Modifications of Implied Warranties

2.3.2.1 General

Addition to notes 154, 155, 157, 158.

154   *See* Crowe v. Joliet Dodge, 2001 U.S. Dist. LEXIS 10066 (N.D. Ill. July 17, 2001) (dealer entered into service contract); Pitchford v. Oakwood Mobile Homes, Inc., 2001 U.S. Dist. LEXIS 4992 (W.D. Va. Apr. 11, 2001) (seller can not disclaim implied warranties after giving written warranty required by state mobile home warranty law); Horton Homes, Inc. v. Brooks, 2001 Ala. LEXIS 431 (Ala. Nov. 30, 2001); Beyer v. DaimlerChrysler Corp., 287 A.D.2d 427, 730 N.Y.S.2d 541 (2001), *vacated on other grounds*, 293 A.D.2d 434 (2002) (following higher court decision that Magnuson-Moss Act does not apply to leases); Lawhorn v. Joseph Toyota, 141 Ohio App. 3d 153, 750 N.E.2d 610 (2001); Robertson v. Ford Motor Co., 40 Va. Cir. 231 (1996). *But cf.* Frank Griffin Volkswagen, Inc. v. Smith, 610 So. 2d 597 (Fla. Dist. Ct. App. 1992) (vehicle repair order that was executed by selling dealer within ninety days of sale and that warranted the repairs for six months was not a service contract, so "as is" clause was valid).

Page 36

155   *Add at end of note*: These reports are included on the companion CD-Rom to this volume.

157   Miles v. Barrington Motor Sales, Inc., 2003 WL 22889373 (N.D. Ill. Dec. 8, 2003) (dealer does not adopt manufacturer's warranty merely by delivering it); Haight v. Dale's Used Cars, Inc., 51 U.C.C. Rep. Serv. 2d 1017 (Idaho Ct. App. 2003) (dealer's acknowledgment of manufacturer's express warranty insufficient); Filipovic v. Fairchild Chevrolet, 2001 Ohio App. LEXIS 4340 (Ohio Ct. App. Sept. 27, 2001) (absence of proof of a written warranty permits seller to disclaim implied warranties).

158   Watson v. Damon Corp., 2002 WL 32059736 (W.D. Mich. Dec. 17, 2002) (seller who passed along manufacturer's express warranties but did not adopt them could disclaim implied warranties); Lytle v. Roto Lincoln Mercury & Subaru, Inc., 167 Ill. App. 3d 508, 521 N.E.2d 201 (1988) (dealer did not adopt manufacturer's warranty by issuing it to buyer); Beyer v. DaimlerChrysler Corp., 287 A.D.2d 427, 730 N.Y.S.2d 541 (2001), *vacated on other grounds*, 293 A.D.2d 434 (2002) (following higher court decision that Magnuson-Moss Act does not apply to leases).

Add to text after subsection's second paragraph:

Even if the seller gives a highly restricted service contract or written warranty, the implied warranties can not be disclaimed.[159.1] For example, if the seller gives a written warranty on a used car's drive train, it can not disclaim the implied warranty of merchantability either for the drive train or for the car as a whole. Likewise, copayment requirements or restrictive approval procedures that are written into a service contract do not restrict the implied warranty of merchantability.

159.1   *See* Kimpel v. Del. Pub. Auto Auction, 2001 WL 1555932 (Del. Ct. Com. Pl. Mar. 6, 2001) (sale of extremely limited service contract, which did not cover any of the needed repairs, prevented disclaimer of implied warranty).

Add note 160.1 at end of subsection's third paragraph.

160.1   *See* Watson v. Damon Corp., 2002 WL 32059736 (W.D. Mich. Dec. 17, 2002) (no bar against manufacturer's disclaimer of implied warranties because lack of privity prevented implied warranties from arising; *see* § 4.2.2.1, *infra*, for opposing analysis).

Addition to notes 161, 164.

161   *But see* Rokicsak v. Colony Marine Sales & Serv., Inc., 219 F. Supp. 2d 810 (E.D. Mich. 2002) (erroneously stating that invalidation of disclaimer under Magnuson-Moss Act does not revive state law implied warranty claims).

164   *See* Lawhorn v. Joseph Toyota, Inc., 141 Ohio App. 3d 153, 750 N.E.2d 610 (2001) (reversing summary judgment for dealer on Magnuson-Moss and UDAP claims when contract granted express warranty but purported to disclaim implied warranties; general language of Buyers Guide, which stated that "implied warranties may give you even more rights," did not cure this violation); Hachet v. Smedley's Chevrolet Sales, Inc., Clearinghouse No. 54,571 (Ohio C.P. Sept. 5, 2002) (following *Lawhorn*).

2.3.2.2 Service Contract Sale Prevents Disclaimers

Addition to notes 165, 166.

165   *See also* Kimpel v. Del. Pub. Auto Auction, 2001 WL 1555932 (Del. Ct. Com. Pl. Mar. 6, 2001); Shuldman v. DaimlerChrysler Corp., 2003 WL 22502204 (N.Y. App. Div. Nov. 3, 2003).

166   Kimpel v. Del. Pub. Auto Auction, 2001 WL 1555932 (Del. Ct. Com. Pl. Mar. 6, 2001).

Page 37

Add to text after first sentence of subsection's third paragraph:

Discovery is essential.

Add to text at end of subsection's third paragraph:

What are the terms of the agreement between the dealer and the company that offers the service contract?

Addition to note 167.

167   *Change name of Priebe citation to*: Priebe v. Autobarn, Ltd.

Add to text at end of subsection's sixth paragraph:

The dealer's acts may also amount to adoption of the service contract as its own.[167.1]

167.1   *See* § 6.2.6, *infra*.

Add to text after first sentence of subsection's third-to-last paragraph:

A dealership employee may sign the service contract as an "authorized representative" of the service contract company.

Replace "owing" in third sentence of subsection's third-to-last paragraph with:

owning

Add to text after subsection's third-to-last paragraph:

It may also be helpful to point out that the UCC defines the dealer as a party to the contract. Under Section 1-201(29), " '[p]arty', as distinct from 'third party', means a person who has engaged in a transaction or made an agreement within this Act." As most courts find that the UCC applies to incidental services in a predominantly goods transaction,[167.2] this definition should mean that the dealer is a party to the service contract as well as the contract for the product itself.

A Seventh Circuit decision[167.3] holds that a dealer did not "enter into" a service contract when it sold a third-party contract to a consumer. That decision can be distinguished in that there was apparently no evidence—at least the court cited none—that the dealer did anything more than pass on the service contract. Detailed factual investigation and allegations about the dealer's involvement are critical to any claim that the sale of a third-party service contract prevents disclaimer.

167.2   *See* § 17.3.4, *infra*.
167.3   Priebe v. Autobarn Ltd., 240 F.3d 584 (7th Cir. 2001).

Page 38

2.3.2.3 Permitted Restrictions on Duration of Implied Warranties

Addition to note 171.

171   *Add to end of note*: This opinion is included on the CD-Rom accompanying this volume.

Add note 173.1 at end of subsection's third paragraph.

173.1   *See* Montgomery v. Mobile Home Estates, Inc., 1984 Ohio App. LEXIS 9239 (Ohio Ct. App. Apr. 20, 1984) (limitation on duration of implied warranty ineffective when not disclosed in clear and unmistakable language).

Addition to note 174.

174　See also In re Ford Motor Co. Ignition Switch Products Liab. Litig., 1999 WL 33495352 (D.N.J. May 14, 1999) (limitation of duration of implied warranty would be unconscionable if manufacturer knew of defect at time of original retail sale).

Page 39

2.3.3 Act Restrictions on Limitations on Remedies

Addition to note 181.

181　Shuldman v. DaimlerChrysler Corp., 2003 WL 22502204 (N.Y. App. Div. Nov. 3, 2003).

2.3.4 Act Prohibits Breaches of Written Warranties

Addition to notes 185, 186.

185　See also Universal Motors, Inc. v. Waldock, 719 P.2d 254 (Alaska 1986).
186　Hasek v. DaimlerChrysler Corp., 319 Ill. App. 3d 780, 745 N.E.2d 627, 44 U.C.C. Rep. Serv. 2d 108 (2001) (Magnuson-Moss incorporates the elements of U.C.C. express warranty claim).

Add to text at end of subsection:

But, for matters not directly addressed by the Magnuson-Moss Act, courts are likely to borrow state warranty law. Thus, for example, the general rule that expert testimony is unnecessary to prove the existence of a defect as long as the subject can be understood by the average juror applies in Magnuson-Moss cases.[187.1] Courts also follow the general UCC rule that the consumer need only prove the existence of a defect, not its cause.[187.2]

187.1　Thorner v. Fleetwood, 2002 WL 844610 (N.D. Ill. May 1, 2001), *vacated in part on other grounds*, 2002 WL 1998285 (N.D. Ill. Aug. 28, 2002); *see* § 7.5, *infra*.
187.2　Mason v. Porsche Cars of N. Am., 688 So. 2d 361 (Fla. Dist. Ct. App. 1997); *see* § 7.4.2, *infra*.

2.3.6 Restrictions on Vertical Privity Requirement

Page 40

2.3.6.1 No Privity Required for Claim of Breach of Written Warranty

Addition to note 199.

199　Schimmer v. Jaguar Cars, Inc., 2003 WL 21518589 (N.D. Ill. July 2, 2003) (Magnuson-Moss Act allows revocation of acceptance against manufacturer); Shuldman v. DaimlerChrysler Corp., 2003 WL 22502204 (N.Y. App. Div. Nov. 3, 2003).

Add to text at end of subsection:

Not only damages, but also revocation of acceptance may be available against the manufacturer.[199.1]

199.1　Shuldman v. DaimlerChrysler Corp., 2003 WL 22502204 (N.Y. App. Div. Nov. 3, 2003) (case involved limited warranty).

2.3.6.2 Does the Act Eliminate Vertical Privity Requirements for Breach of Implied Warranties?

Replace "the view that" in sentence containing note 203 with:

the view that, when a manufacturer or other indirect party gives a written warranty,

Addition to note 203.

203　Cohen v. AM Gen. Corp., 264 F. Supp. 2d 616 (N.D. Ill. 2003) (following *Szajna*); Dekelaita v. Nissan Motor Corp., 2003 WL 22240509 (Ill. App. Ct. Sept. 29, 2003) (following *Szajna*).

Replace "Second Circuit" in sentence containing note 204 with:

Second and Seventh Circuits

Addition to note 204.

204　Voelker v. Porsche Cars N. Am., Inc., 2003 WL 22930364 (7th Cir. Dec. 12, 2003); Hamdan v. Land Rover N. Am., Inc., 2003 WL 21911244 (N.D. Ill. Aug. 8, 2003); Kutzle v. Thor Indus., Inc., 2003 WL 21654260 (N.D. Ill. July 14, 2003); Schimmer v. Jaguar Cars, Inc., 2003 WL 21518589 (N.D. Ill. July 2, 2003); Pederson v. Monaco Coach Corp., 2002 WL 31834679 (N.D. Ill. Dec. 12, 2002); Diamond v. Porsche Cars N. Am., Inc., 2002 WL 31155064 (N.D. Ill. Sept. 26, 2002), *vacated on other grounds*, 2003 WL 21698795 (7th Cir. July 16, 2003) (unpublished); Shuldman v. DaimlerChrysler Corp., 2003 WL 22502204 (N.Y. App. Div. Nov. 3, 2003) (following *Abraham*).

Add to text at end of subsection's sixth paragraph:

One approach that largely solves the practical problems is to establish that the dealer is the manufacturer's sales agent.[204.1]

> 204.1   DiCintio v. DaimlerChrysler Corp., 282 A.D.2d 276, 724 N.Y.S.2d 717 (2001) (dismissal erroneous without allowing plaintiff to pursue discovery about whether dealer was manufacturer's sales agent), *rev'd on other grounds*, 97 N.Y.2d 463, 742 N.Y.S.2d 182, 768 N.E.2d 1121 (2002).

Page 41

Addition to note 207.

> 207   *But see In re* Ford Motor Co. Ignition Switch Products Liab. Litig., 194 F.R.D. 484 (D.N.J. 2000) (declining to certify class despite elaborately restricted class definition).

Add to text at end of subsection:

Another approach is to argue that the law of the manufacturer's home state, if it allows suits without a privity requirement, applies to the entire class.[207.1]

> 207.1   *See* Ysbrand v. DaimlerChrysler Corp., 49 U.C.C. Rep. Serv. 2d 1062 (Okla. 2003) (certifying nationwide class action). *But see In re* Bridgestone/Firestone, Inc., 288 F.3d 1012 (7th Cir. 2002) (reversing trial court's decision to certify class and apply warranty law of manufacturer's home state).

2.3.8 Act Regulation of Service Contracts

Page 42

2.3.8.2 Act Enforcement of Service Contract Obligations; Other Act Regulation of Service Contracts

Addition to note 224.

> 224   Lysek v. Elmhurst Dodge, Inc., 325 Ill. App. 3d 536, 259 Ill. Dec. 454, 758 N.E.2d 862 (2001) (breach of service contract may be remedied under the Act and not simply under state contract law).

Page 43

2.3.8.3 Does the Act Apply to Service Contracts Regulated as Insurance?

Addition to note 233.

> 233   *See also* Moore v. Liberty Nat'l Ins. Co., 267 F.3d 1209 (11th Cir. 2001) (Civil Rights statutes do not impede state insurance discrimination statute).

2.4 Act Restrictions on Written Warranties (Applicable Both to Limited and Full Warranties)

Page 44

2.4.1 Prohibition of Tie-Ins

Addition to note 248.

> 248   *Replace Federal Register citation with*: 64 Fed. Reg. 19,700, 19,703 (Apr. 22, 1999).

Add to text after sentence containing note 248:

An Ohio trial court has agreed, holding that it is a Magnuson-Moss violation, and therefore a UDAP violation as well, to include a 50-50 warranty in the contract documents.[248.1]

> 248.1   Brown v. P.A. Days, Inc., Clearinghouse No. 54,572 (Ohio C.P. Aug. 27, 2002).

Add to text at end of subsection's eighth paragraph:

However, at the end of 2002 the FTC issued a letter disavowing its previous statement that 50-50 warranties amounted to an illegal tie-in.[248.2] The FTC reasoned that, unlike a warranty that is conditioned on the consumer's purchase of a separate product, a 50-50 warranty can not be severed into two parts, one that the warrantor would perform and another that a different repair shop would perform. The Commission stressed, however, that it would likely be a deceptive practice and a breach of warranty if the dealer inflated the cost of warranted repairs in order to impose all or most of the repair costs on the consumer. Also, 50-50 warranties are often just scrawled on a purchase order and do not include the disclosures that the Magnuson-Moss Act mandates.[248.3]

> 248.2   Letter from the Fed. Trade Comm'n to Keith E. Whann (Dec. 31, 2002), *available at* www.ftc.gov/os/2003/01/niadaresponseletter.htm. The letter is also included on the CD-Rom accompanying this volume.
>
> 248.3   *See* § 2.6, *infra*.

Page 45

2.4.3 Warranty Registration Cards

Add to text at end of subsection:

A California law, effective January 1, 2004, requires paper and on-line warranty registration cards to state that failure to complete and return the card does not diminish the buyer's warranty rights.[256.1]

256.1   Cal. Civ. Code § 1793.1(a)(1) (West).

2.5 Full Warranties

Page 46

2.5.1 Distinguishing Full From Limited Warranties

Addition to note 263.

263   *See* Jones v. Fleetwood Motor Homes, 127 F. Supp. 2d 958 (N.D. Ill. 2000); Lara v. Hyundai Motor Am., 331 Ill. App. 3d 53, 264 Ill. Dec. 416, 770 N.E.2d 721 (2002) (noting that this restriction only applies to full warranties).

2.5.3 Remedy Defects Within a Reasonable Time, Without Charge

Page 47

2.5.3.3 Liens

Addition to note 284.

284   *See* Lara v. Hyundai Motor Am., 331 Ill. App. 3d 53, 264 Ill. Dec. 416, 770 N.E.2d 721 (2002) (requirement of return of vehicle only applies to full warranties and only when consumer elects refund or replacement).

Page 48

Add to text at end of subsection's third paragraph:

The requirement that the product be made available free and clear of liens only applies when the consumer seeks a refund or replacement, not when the consumer seeks damages.[287.1]

287.1   King v. King Motor Co., 780 So. 2d 937 (Fla. Dist. Ct. App. 2001).

2.5.5 Exclusion of Consequential Damages

Addition to notes 291, 294.

291   *Replace United States Code citation with*: 15 U.S.C. § 2304(a)(3); *see* Lara v. Hyundai Motor Am., 331 Ill. App. 3d 53, 264 Ill. Dec. 416, 770 N.E.2d 721 (2002) (noting that this restriction only applies to full warranties).

294   *See* Jones v. Fleetwood Motor Homes, 127 F. Supp. 2d 958 (N.D. Ill. 2000) (conspicuous exclusion of consequential damages under a full warranty not enforced in accordance with state law).

Page 49

2.5.6 Consumer Election of Refund or Replacement

Add to text after sentence containing note 303:

Repair attempts by an authorized dealership count toward this requirement.[303.1]

303.1   Browning v. Am. Isuzu Motors, Inc., 2002 WL 32063978 (Ohio C.P. Mar. 21, 2003).

Addition to note 304.

304   Jones v. Fleetwood Motor Homes, 127 F. Supp. 2d 958 (N.D. Ill. 2000); Browning v. Am. Isuzu Motors, Inc., 2002 WL 32063978 (Ohio C.P. Mar. 21, 2003).

Add to text at end of subsection's second paragraph:

Expert testimony is not necessary to establish whether a certain number of repair attempts is unreasonable, although expert testimony about the difficulty of a particular repair may be helpful.[304.1]

304.1   Jones v. Fleetwood Motor Homes, 127 F. Supp. 2d 958 (N.D. Ill. 2000).

2.6 Disclosure Requirements for Written Warranties

2.6.4 Ten Terms Required to Be Disclosed

Page 52

2.6.4.1 General

Replace note 348 with:

> 348   15 U.S.C. § 1632; 12 C.F.R. § 226.17(a)(1); National Consumer Law Center, Truth in Lending § 4.2.4 (5th ed. 2003).

2.6.4.3 Warranty Coverage

Add to text after sentence containing note 354:

Nor need the warranty list every item that is excluded if it clearly describes the items that are covered.[354.1]

> 354.1   Testan v. Carlsen Motor Cars, Inc., 2002 Cal. App. Unpub. LEXIS 159837 (Cal. Ct. App. Feb. 19, 2002) (unpublished).

2.7 Magnuson-Moss Litigation and Remedies

2.7.1 Violations Leading to Private Remedies

Page 57

Addition to note 411.

> 411   *See also* Pierce v. Catalina Yachts, Inc., 2 P.3d 618 (Alaska 2000) (Magnuson-Moss provides action for breach of written warranty whether warranty is full or limited).

Replace note 415 with:

> 415   This second set of instructions is also available in National Consumer Law Center, Consumer Law Pleadings No. 5, § 6.3 (2003 Cumulative CD-Rom and Index Guide).

2.7.2 Mandatory Arbitration of Magnuson-Moss Claims

Replace first two sentences of subsection with:

Although opinion is far from unanimous, a number of courts have held that warrantors can not precondition written warranties on consumers agreeing to submit warranty disputes or Magnuson-Moss claims to binding arbitration. Such a precondition explicitly violates FTC Rules and the legislative intent.

2.7.3 Federal and State Court Jurisdiction

2.7.3.1 $50,000 Amount in Controversy Requirement for Federal Court Jurisdiction

Addition to notes 418–420.

> 418   *See also* Loff v. Am. Arms, Inc., 2002 WL 29502 (D. Minn. Jan. 4, 2002) (general federal question jurisdiction is not independent basis for jurisdiction over Magnuson-Moss claims, which must meet Magnuson-Moss Act's specific requirements); Buie v. Palm Springs Motors, Inc., 2001 U.S. Dist. LEXIS 13756 (C.D. Cal. May 14, 2001) (declining jurisdiction over Magnuson-Moss claim under $50,000), *aff'd on other grounds*, 36 Fed. Appx. 328, 2002 U.S. App. LEXIS 11046 (9th Cir. June 7, 2002).
>
> 419   Vyshnevsky v. Park Ridge Oldsmobile, 2003 WL 21518568 (N.D. Ill. July 2, 2003) (awarding attorney fees to consumer when defendant removed Magnuson-Moss Act suit even though amount in controversy was clearly less than $50,000; Loff v. Am. Arms, Inc., 2002 WL 29502 (D. Minn. Jan. 4, 2002).
>
> 420   Diamond v. Porsche Cars N. Am., Inc., 2003 WL 21698795 (7th Cir. July 16, 2003) (unpublished).

Add to text after sentence containing note 420:

Merely referring to the Magnuson-Moss Act as setting a standard of care or conduct for a state law claim does not create federal jurisdiction regardless of whether the jurisdictional amount is met.[420.1]

> 420.1   Greene v. Gen. Motors Corp., 261 F. Supp. 2d 414 (W.D.N.C. 2003).

Addition to note 422.

> 422   *But see* Messana v. Mercedes-Benz of N. Am., Inc., 248 F.3d 1158 (7th Cir. 2001) (unpublished) (text

available at 2001 U.S. App. LEXIS 3924) (the plaintiff must support its allegation of the amount in controversy if challenged by "competent proof").

Add to text at end of subsection's third paragraph:

The Seventh Circuit has reduced the calculation to a formula in a typical new car lemon law case: the cost of the new vehicle less the value of the car with defects less the benefit or use value to the consumer plus any remaining damages available under state law.[422.1]

422.1   Voelker v. Porsche Cars N. Am., Inc., 2003 WL 22930364 (7th Cir. Dec. 12, 2003); Messana v. Mercedes-Benz of N. Am., Inc., 248 F.3d 1158 (7th Cir. 2001) (unpublished) (text available at 2001 U.S. App. LEXIS 3924) (remanding case for application of formula), *on remand*, 2001 U.S. Dist. LEXIS 17785 (N.D. Ill. Oct. 26, 2001) (applying formula and finding no jurisdiction); *see also* Pederson v. Monaco Coach Corp., 2002 WL 31834679 (N.D. Ill. Dec. 12, 2002) (amount in controversy is amount paid plus unpaid balance would be canceled, minus the actual value of the vehicle).

Page 58

Addition to notes 423–426, 428.

423   *Cf.* Golden v. Gorno Bros., Inc., 274 F. Supp. 2d 913 (E.D. Mich. 2003) (confused opinion holding that only diminution in value, not revocation of acceptance, is available in Magnuson-Moss suit).

424   Salter v. Al-Hallaq, 50 U.C.C. Rep. Serv. 2d 348 (D. Kan. 2003) (not available under Kansas law); Poindexter v. Morse Chevrolet, Inc., 270 F. Supp. 2d 1286 (D. Kan. 2003) (punitive damages available on a pendent fraud claim do not count toward jurisdictional amount); *see* § 2.7.5.3, *infra. But cf.* Neilon v. Chrysler Corp., 1997 U.S. Dist. LEXIS 20327 (E.D. Pa. Dec. 11, 1997) (no punitive damages for Magnuson-Moss claim in Pennsylvania because not allowed for state law warranty claims).

425   Oliver v. Homes of Legend, Inc., 2000 U.S. Dist. LEXIS 10960 (M.D. Ala. Apr. 17, 2000) (personal injury damages not available for Magnuson-Moss breach of warranty claim so can not be used to reach jurisdictional amount).

426   *See* § 2.7.5.3, *infra.*

428   Golden v. Gorno Bros., Inc., 274 F. Supp. 2d 913 (E.D. Mich. 2003); Ferrer Santiago v. Daimler Chrysler Corp., 265 F. Supp. 2d 171 (D. P.R. 2003); Donahue v. Bill Page Toyota, Inc., 164 F. Supp. 2d 778 (E.D. Va. 2001).

Add to text after sentence containing note 428:

But a federal court has held that the finance charges under the contract that the consumer seeks to revoke are not excluded from the amount in controversy by this language.[428.1]

428.1   Roberts v. Chandaleur Homes Inc., 237 F. Supp. 2d 696 (S.D. Miss. 2002).

Replace first four words of sentence containing note 429 with:

Incidental and consequential damages generally may be used to calculate the amount in controversy if allowed by state law[428.2] but

428.2   Messana v. Mercedes-Benz of N. Am., Inc., 248 F.3d 1158 (7th Cir. 2001) (unpublished) (text available at 2001 U.S. App. LEXIS 3924).

Replace note 430 with:

430   Rodriguez v. Colon, 248 F.3d 1127 (1st Cir. 2000); Ferrer Santiago v. Daimler Chrysler Corp., 265 F. Supp. 2d 171 (D. P.R. 2003).

Addition to note 431.

431   Vyshnevsky v. Park Ridge Oldsmobile, 2003 WL 21518568 (N.D. Ill. July 2, 2003); Critney v. Nat'l City Ford, Inc., 255 F. Supp. 2d 1146 (S.D. Cal. 2003); Grant v. Cavalier Mfg., Inc., 229 F. Supp. 2d 1332 (M.D. Ala. 2002) (damages for emotional distress); Donahue v. Bill Page Toyota, Inc., 164 F. Supp. 2d 778 (E.D. Va. 2001).

Add to text at end of subsection's fourth paragraph:

The value of any equitable relief sought may be used to meet the jurisdictional amount.[431.1] However, the legal basis for calculating the value of equitable relief is complicated, and the ultimate result is unlikely to increase the case's value if the damages themselves are not already sufficient.[431.2]

431.1   Samuel-Bassett v. Kia Motors Am., Inc., 143 F. Supp. 2d 503 (E.D. Pa. 2001); McIntire v. Ford Motor Co., 142 F. Supp. 2d 911 (S.D. Ohio 2001).

431.2   Samuel-Bassett v. Kia Motors Am., Inc., 143 F. Supp. 2d 503 (E.D. Pa. 2001); McIntire v. Ford Motor Co., 142 F. Supp. 2d 911 (S.D. Ohio 2001).

Page 59

2.7.3.2 Appending Magnuson-Moss Claims to Other Federal Action

Addition to notes 437, 440, 441.

437   *But cf.* O'Keefe v. Mercedes-Benz USA, 2002 U.S. Dist. LEXIS 6973 (E.D. Pa. Jan. 31, 2002) (refusing to allow plaintiff to add Magnuson-Moss class claim with less than one-hundred plaintiffs to complaint that defendants had removed to federal court on diversity grounds; court would have accepted jurisdiction if class claim had been in original state court complaint).

440   McGettigan v. Ford Motor Co., 265 F. Supp. 2d 1291 (S.D. Ala. 2003) (declining diversity jurisdiction over warranty class action; refusing to aggregate class claims to reach jurisdictional amount).

441   Lastih v. Elk Corp. of Ala., 140 F. Supp. 2d 166 (D. Conn. 2001) ("strains credulity" to believe that individual's attorney fees would approach jurisdictional amount).

Add to text at end of subsection's second paragraph:

In addition, the plaintiff may reach the jurisdictional threshold by asserting fraud claims or personal injury claims that involve damages that can not be recovered on the Magnuson-Moss claim, in which case the court would have supplemental jurisdiction over the Magnuson-Moss claim.[441.1]

441.1   Barnes v. West, Inc., 249 F. Supp. 2d 737 (E.D. Va. 2003).

Addition to notes 442, 443.

442   Samuel-Bassett v. Kia Motors Am., Inc., 143 F. Supp. 2d 503 (E.D. Pa. 2001) (trebled damages, attorney fees, costs, and costs of repairs and alternate transportation exceed $75,000 to support removal to federal court).

443   Lastih v. Elk Corp. of Ala., 140 F. Supp. 2d 166 (D. Conn. 2001) (allegations insufficient).

Add to text at end of subsection's third paragraph:

Punitive damages are possible on tort counts and in some jurisdictions for particularly egregious contract violations.[443.1]

443.1   *See* § 10.8, *infra.*

Add to text at end of subsection's fourth paragraph:

But the Seventh Circuit has held that a district court does have discretion to exercise supplemental jurisdiction over a Magnuson-Moss claim when the complaint raises claims under other statutes, such as the Truth in Lending Act or the Fair Credit Reporting Act, over which the court has original jurisdiction.[448.1]

448.1   Voelker v. Porsche Cars N. Am., Inc., 2003 WL 22930364 (7th Cir. Dec. 12, 2003).

Page 60

2.7.3.3 Class Actions in Federal Court

Addition to notes 454, 455.

454   *See also* McGettigan v. Ford Motor Co., 265 F. Supp. 2d 1291 (S.D. Ala. 2003) (no federal jurisdiction over Magnuson-Moss class action with only three named plaintiffs); Loff v. Am. Arms, Inc., 2002 WL 29502 (D. Minn. Jan. 4, 2002) (remanding class action to state court when it did not include one-hundred named plaintiffs); Miller v. Bridgestone/Firestone, Inc., 2000 U.S. Dist. LEXIS 15292 (E.D. Pa. Oct. 19, 2000) (Magnuson-Moss can not support removal because fewer than one-hundred named plaintiffs); Dorian v. Bridgestone/Firestone, Inc., 2000 WL 1570627 (E.D. Pa. Oct. 19, 2000) (same). *But cf.* O'Keefe v. Mercedes-Benz USA, 2002 U.S. Dist. LEXIS 6973 (E.D. Pa. Jan. 31, 2002) (refusing to allow plaintiff to add Magnuson-Moss class claim with less than one-hundred plaintiffs to complaint that defendants had removed to federal court on diversity grounds; court would have accepted jurisdiction if class claim had been in original state court complaint).

455   *Add at end of note*: (this report is also reproduced on the CD-Rom accompanying this volume).

Replace last sentence of subsection's first paragraph with:

State court class actions do not have to meet these requirements,[456.1] and a state court class action that does not meet them can not be removed to federal court.[456.2]

456.1   15 U.S.C. § 2310(d)(3) (referring only to suits brought under § 2310(d)(1)(B)).

456.2   O'Keefe v. Mercedes-Benz USA, Ltd. Liab. Co., 214 F.R.D. 266 (E.D. Pa. 2003).

Page 61

Add note 466.1 at end of second sentence of subsection's last paragraph.

466.1   Ysbrand v. DaimlerChrysler Corp., 49 U.C.C. Rep. Serv. 2d 1062 (Okla. 2003) (certifying class action against manufacturer; law of manufacturer's home state will apply to class).

Add to text at end of subsection:

Prosecuting the class action only for related state law claims under federal supplemental jurisdiction appended to the individual Magnuson-Moss claim may not be an option.[467.1] The only court apparently to consider the issue refused to exercise supplemental jurisdiction so as not to "effectuate an end run around Magnuson-Moss" and its requirement of one hundred plaintiffs.[467.2]

467.1   *See generally* § 2.7.3.2, *supra.*

467.2   Hatfield v. Oak Hill Banks, 115 F. Supp. 2d 893 (S.D. Ohio 2000); *cf.* Almenares v. Wyman, 453 F.2d 1075 (2d Cir. 1971) (permitting generally a pendent class for corresponding injunctive relief).

2.7.4 Preconditions to Suit

Addition to note 470.

470   Teerling v. Fleetwood Motor Homes of Ind., Inc., 2001 U.S. Dist. LEXIS 7481 (N.D. Ill. May 31, 2001) (the refund or replacement remedy in § 2304(a)(4) "after a reasonable number of [repair] attempts" is stated in the plural and therefore requires giving the defendant more than one opportunity to repair); Sharkus v. Daimler Chrysler Corp., 2002 WL 31319119 (Ohio Ct. App. Oct. 17, 2002) (unpublished) (no Magnuson-Moss claim when dealer made repairs whenever consumer complained, although sporadic screeching noise may have remained).

Page 62

Add to text after subsection's third paragraph:

The buyer satisfies this requirement by affording the manufacturer's authorized representative, that is, the dealer, the opportunity to cure.[471.1]

471.1   Ventura v. Ford Motor Co., 180 N.J. Super. 45, 433 A.2d 801 (Super. Ct. App. Div. 1981).

Addition to note 472.

472   *See also* Greines v. Ford Motor Co., 2003 WL 42524 (Cal. Ct. App. Jan. 7, 2003) (unpublished) (Magnuson-Moss Act does not require reasonable number of repair attempts).

2.7.5 Available Relief Under the Act

2.7.5.1 Actual Damages

Addition to notes 481–483, 485.

481   *Add to H.R. Rep. No. 1107 citation*: (this report is also reproduced on the CD-Rom accompanying this volume).

482   *Replace Price citation with*: 765 A.2d 800, 43 U.C.C. Rep. Serv. 2d 593 (Pa. Super. Ct. 2000); *add*: Grant v. Cavalier Mfg., Inc., 229 F. Supp. 2d 1332 (M.D. Ala. 2002) (court should look to state law for measure of damages, but Magnuson-Moss Act controls as to what types of damages are available); Jones v. Fleetwood Motor Homes, 127 F. Supp. 2d 958 (N.D. Ill. 2000) (conspicuous exclusion of consequential damages under a full warranty not enforced in accordance with state law); Ventura v. Ford Motor Co., 180 N.J. Super. 45, 433 A.2d 801 (Super. Ct. App. Div. 1981) (nominal damages available under N.J. law even without proof of actual damages); Shuldman v. DaimlerChrysler Corp., 2003 WL 22502204 (N.Y. App. Div. Nov. 3, 2003).

Page 63

483   Schimmer v. Jaguar Cars, Inc., 2003 WL 21518589 (N.D. Ill. July 2, 2003) (Magnuson-Moss Act allows revocation of acceptance); Lara v. Hyundai Motor Am., 331 Ill. App. 3d 53, 264 Ill. Dec. 416, 770 N.E.2d 721 (2002) (buyer need not return vehicle to obtain damages remedy); Boyle v. Daimler Chrysler Corp., 2002 WL 1881157 (Ohio Ct. App. Aug. 16, 2002) (evidence of diminished value, although imprecise, was sufficient to go to the jury). *But see* Golden v. Gorno Bros., Inc., 274 F. Supp. 2d 913 (E.D. Mich. 2003) (confused opinion holding that only diminution in value, not revocation of acceptance, is available in Magnuson-Moss suit).

485   Shuldman v. DaimlerChrysler Corp., 2003 WL 22502204 (N.Y. App. Div. Nov. 3, 2003).

Add to text after sentence containing note 485:

If the consumer is seeking damages rather than a refund or replacement, the consumer need not make the product available to the seller free and clear of liens.[485.1]

485.1   King v. King Motor Co., 780 So. 2d 937 (Fla. Dist. Ct. App. 2001); Bartow v. Ford Motor Co., 342 Ill. App. 3d 480, 794 N.E.2d 1027 (2003).

Add to text at end of subsection:

To maintain a Magnuson-Moss claim, there is no requirement that a consumer have suffered any injury beyond receiving the defective product.[490.1] It is sufficient that the consumer is saddled with a non-conforming product.

490.1   *In re* Bridgestone/Firestone Inc. ATX, ATX II & Wilderness Tires Prods. Liab. Litig., 155 F. Supp. 2d 1069 (S.D. Ind. 2001), *rev'd in part on other grounds*, 288 F.3d 1012 (7th Cir. 2002).

2.7.5.2 Personal Injury Damages

Addition to note 491.

491   *See also* Voelker v. Porsche Cars N. Am., Inc., 2003 WL 22930364 (7th Cir. Dec. 12, 2003); Grant v. Cavalier Mfg., Inc., 229 F. Supp. 2d 1332 (M.D. Ala. 2002); Sanks v. Parke-Davis, 2000 U.S. Dist. LEXIS 20739 (M.D. Ala. Oct. 30, 2000); Oliver v. Homes of Legend, Inc., 2000 U.S. Dist. LEXIS 10960 (M.D. Ala. Apr. 17, 2000).

2.7.5.3 Statutory, Punitive Damages

Page 64

Addition to note 497.

497   Salter v. Al-Hallaq, 50 U.C.C. Rep. Serv. 2d 348 (D. Kan. 2003) (not available under Kansas law).

2.7.5.4 Revocation and Equitable Relief

Page 65

Replace note 501 with:

501   Jones v. Fleetwood Motor Homes, 127 F. Supp. 2d 958 (N.D. Ill. 2000) (erroneously concluding that refund and rescission is an equitable remedy, so plaintiff must show absence of adequate remedy at law; only Magnuson-Moss case cited for this proposition is one seeking an injunction, not revocation); *see also* § 8.1, *infra.*

Add to text after sentence containing note 501:

Unlike rescission, which is an equitable remedy, revocation of acceptance is a remedy at law.[501.1]

501.1   *See* § 8.1, *infra.*

Addition to note 502.

502   *But see* Golden v. Gorno Bros., Inc., 274 F. Supp. 2d 913 (E.D. Mich. 2003) (confused opinion holding that only diminution in value, not revocation of acceptance, is available in Magnuson-Moss suit).

Add to text after sentence containing note 502:

Even if a suit for revocation of acceptance were not a suit for damages, it would be encompassed by the Act's authorization of "other legal . . . relief."[502.1]

502.1   15 U.S.C. § 2310(d)(1).

2.7.6 Attorney Fees and Costs

2.7.6.1 General Standards for Attorney Fees

Add to text after sentence containing note 504:

This provision makes fees part of "expenses" and not costs, an important distinction when considering the cost-shifting effects of Rule 68 offers of judgment.[504.1] Until the consumer prevails, the fee claim is not in issue and discovery of the retainer agreement and time records is unwarranted.[504.2]

504.1   Jones v. Fleetwood Motor Homes, 127 F. Supp. 2d 958 (N.D. Ill. 2000).

504.2   Hussain v. Gen. Motors Corp., 276 A.D.2d 452, 715 N.Y.S.2d 394 (2000).

Addition to note 507.

507   *Add to Messana citation: remanded on other grounds,* 248 F.3d 1158 (7th Cir. 2001) (unpublished) (text available at 2001 U.S. App. LEXIS 3924) (questioning jurisdiction); *replace Alvine citation with:* 620 N.W.2d 608 (S.D. 2001); *add: See, e.g.,* Horton Homes, Inc. v. Brooks, 2001 Ala. LEXIS 431 (Ala. Nov. 30, 2001) ($34,612.50 in fees); *see also* Basselen v. Gen. Motors Corp., 341 Ill. App. 3d 278, 792 N.E.2d 498 (2003) (trial court's complete denial of fees erroneous; even if many entries were not clear or specific enough, court should have awarded fees for hours that were adequately documented).

Add to text at end of subsection's first paragraph:

The West Virginia Supreme Court has held that a plaintiff may obtain attorney fees under the Magnuson-Moss Act after winning an implied warranty claim even without specifically pleading a Magnuson-Moss cause of action, as long as the defendant is on notice that the plaintiff is seeking fees.[507.1] Similarly, an Alabama decision holds that fees may be awarded under the authority of the Magnuson-Moss Act when the plaintiff wins an implied warranty claim, even when the consumer loses on a separate Magnuson-Moss claim.[507.2]

507.1   Hawkins v. Ford Motor Co., 211 W. Va. 487, 566 S.E.2d 624 (2002); *see also* Maconi v. Price Motorcars, 1993 WL 542571 (Del. Super. Ct. Dec. 1, 1993) (unpublished) (awarding fees under Magnuson-Moss Act when consumers pleaded the claim but did not submit it to the jury).

507.2   Forest River, Inc. v. Posten, 847 So. 2d 957 (Ala. Civ. App. 2002).

Page 66

Addition to note 511.

511   *See also* Ventura v. Ford Motor Co., 180 N.J. Super. 45, 433 A.2d 801 (Super. Ct. App. Div. 1981) (fees of $5165 awarded against manufacturer even though consumer was only entitled to nominal damages against manufacturer).

2.7.6.2 Attorney Fees Available for Breach of Written and Implied Warranties and for Cancellation Under the UCC

Addition to notes 514, 515.

514 *See also* Love v. Kenneth Hammersley Motors, Inc., 556 S.E.2d 764 (Va. 2002) (awarding Magnuson-Moss attorney fees for state law breach of warranty claim; defendant conceded entitlement).

515 *See also* Kimpel v. Del. Pub. Auto Auction, 2001 WL 1555932 (Del. Ct. Com. Pl. Mar. 6, 2001) (fees awarded for breach of implied warranty; seller also sold service contract but contract did not cover any of the needed repairs).

2.7.6.3 Determining the Size of Attorney Fees

Replace note 520 with:

520 *See* National Consumer Law Center, Truth in Lending § 8.9 (5th ed. 2003); National Consumer Law Center, Unfair and Deceptive Acts and Practices § 8.8 (5th ed. 2001 and Supp.); National Consumer Law Center, Consumer Class Actions: A Practical Litigation Guide Ch. 15 (5th ed. 2002 and Supp.).

Add to text after sentence containing note 520:

Courts in Magnuson-Moss cases are likely to follow the general standards developed under other fee-shifting statutes.[520.1]

520.1 *See* Hawkins v. Ford Motor Co., 211 W. Va. 487, 566 S.E.2d 624 (2002) (listing factors).

Replace note 521 with:

521 Universal Motors, Inc. v. Waldock, 719 P.2d 254 (Alaska 1986) (affirming fees of $36,576.00 and costs of $8659.80 when award to consumer was $17,785.80); Specialized Med. Sys., Inc. v. Lemmerling, 252 N.J. Super. 180, 599 A.2d 578 (Super. Ct. App. Div. 1991).

Addition to notes 522, 525. Page 67

522 Love v. Kenneth Hammersley Motors, Inc., 556 S.E.2d 764 (Va. 2002).

525 Jones v. Fleetwood Motor Homes, 127 F. Supp. 2d 958 (N.D. Ill. 2000); Cannon v. William Chevrolet/Geo, Inc., 341 Ill. App. 3d 674, 794 N.E.2d 843 (2003); S. Rep. No. 93-151, at 23, 24 (1975) (reproduced on the CD-Rom accompanying this volume).

Replace sentence containing note 526 with:

The legislative history indicates: "It should be noted that an attorney's fee is to be based upon actual time expended rather than being tied to any percentage of the recovery. This requirement is designed to make the pursuit of consumer rights involving inexpensive consumer products economically feasible."[526]

526 S. Rep. No. 93-151, at 23, 24 (1975) (reproduced on the CD-Rom accompanying this volume); *see also* Droun v. Fleetwood Enterprises, 163 Cal. App. 3d 486, 209 Cal. Rptr. 623 (1985) (quoting language of Senate report); Cannon v. William Chevrolet/Geo, Inc., 341 Ill. App. 3d 674, 794 N.E.2d 843 (2003) (same).

Addition to note 529.

529 *Add to Messana citation*: *remanded on other grounds*, 248 F.3d 1158 (7th Cir. 2001) (unpublished) (text available at 2001 U.S. App. LEXIS 3924) (questioning jurisdiction); *replace Alvine citation with*: 620 N.W.2d 608 (S.D. 2001); *add*: *see also* Cannon v. William Chevrolet/Geo, Inc., 341 Ill. App. 3d 674, 794 N.E.2d 843 (2003).

2.7.6.4 Are Magnuson-Moss Fees Available for Work on Closely Related State Claims?

Addition to notes 532–534.

532 *Replace Alvine citation with*: 620 N.W.2d 608 (S.D. 2001).

533 Jones v. Fleetwood Motor Homes, 127 F. Supp. 2d 958 (N.D. Ill. 2000).

534 Cannon v. William Chevrolet/Geo, Inc., 794 N.E.2d 843 (Ill. App. Ct. 2003); Basselen v. Gen. Motors Corp., 341 Ill. App. 3d 278, 792 N.E.2d 498 (2003).

Replace § 2.7.6.5 with:

2.7.6.5 Fees If Case Is Settled

The entitlement to fees following a settlement has been thrown into confusion by the Supreme Court's decision in *Buckhannon Board & Care Home, Inc. v. West Virginia Department of Health and Human Resources.*[540] In *Buckhannon*, the Court rejected decades of federal decisions that awarded fees to plaintiffs as prevailing parties under the "catalyst" rule. The catalyst rule had held that a plaintiff prevails, and is therefore entitled to recover under a federal statutory fee provision, when the lawsuit causes a change in the defendant's conduct, even if a favorable order on the merits is never entered.

The plaintiff in *Buckhannon* had sought an injunction against enforcement of certain rules governing assisted living homes. During the course of the litigation, the state legislature repealed the contested rules, and the court dismissed the case as moot. The Supreme Court affirmed the denial of fees, holding that a "material alteration of the legal relationship of the parties" was necessary in order for a plaintiff to be the prevailing party.[541] While this standard can be met by "enforceable judgments on the merits and court-ordered consent decrees,"[542] the plaintiff's case lacked "the necessary judicial imprimatur."[543]

Although *Buckhannon* dealt with the fee-shifting provisions of the fair housing laws and the Americans with Disabilities Act, the Supreme Court made clear that it was announcing a general rule that applied to most if not all federal fee-shifting statutes.[544] Courts have applied the ruling to the civil rights fee-shifting statute,[545] the Equal

Access to Justice Act,[546] and the Individuals with Disabilities Education Act,[547] all of which, like the statute construed in *Buckhannon*, use the term "prevailing party." One court has held that *Buckhannon* applies even to consumer protection statutes that use the term "successful action" rather than "prevailing party."[547.1]

The language of the Magnuson-Moss Act, which allows fees if the consumer "finally prevails,"[547.2] is similar to that construed in *Buckhannon*, so it is likely that courts will find *Buckhannon* to apply.[547.3] One possible distinction, however, is the Magnuson-Moss Act's language authorizing a plaintiff who finally prevails to recover fees "reasonably incurred by the plaintiff for or in connection with the commencement and prosecution" of the action.[547.4] The focus on the preliminary and interim stages of the case—commencement and prosecution—suggests that fees should be available even if the case is resolved short of an enforceable judgment or court order.[547.5]

The most troubling aspect of *Buckhannon* is its apparent support for the argument that a settlement agreement may be insufficient to trigger the consumer's right to attorney fees because the consumer is not a prevailing party. The decision states that a "court-ordered consent decree" is sufficient, contrasted in a footnote to "private settlements," which "do not entail the judicial approval and oversight involved in consent decrees."[547.6] Although the Court stopped short of an explicit holding that a "private settlement" does not make a plaintiff a

---

540   532 U.S. 598, 121 S. Ct. 1835, 149 L. Ed. 2d 855 (2001). *See generally* Gill Deford, *The Prevailing Winds After Buckhannon*, 36 Clearinghouse Rev. 313 (Sept.-Oct. 2002).

541   *Buckhannon*, 121 S. Ct. at 1840.

542   *Id.*

543   *Id.*

544   *Id.*, 121 S. Ct. at 1838 ("Numerous federal statutes allow courts to award attorney's fees and costs to the 'prevailing party.' The question presented here is whether this term includes a party that has failed to secure a judgment on the merits or a court-ordered consent decree."), 1839 n.4 (citing various fee-shifting statutes, referring to the list of additional statutes in Marek v. Chesny, 473 U.S. 1, 105 S. Ct. 3012, 87 L. Ed. 2d 1 (1985), and saying that all are interpreted consistently). *But cf.* Loggerhead Turtle v. County Council, 307 F.3d 1318 (11th Cir. 2002) (*Buckhannon* does not apply to Endangered Species Act's unique attorney fee provision).

545   42 U.S.C. § 1988; *see* Walker v. City of Mesquite, 313 F.3d 246 (5th Cir. 2002); Chambers v. Ohio Dep't of Human Services, 273 F.3d 690 (6th Cir. 2001); Nat'l Coalition for Students with Disabilities v. Bush, 173 F. Supp. 2d 1272 (N.D. Fla. 2001); *see also* Johnny's Icehouse, Inc. v. Amateur Hockey Ass'n, 2001 U.S. Dist. LEXIS 11671 (N.D. Ill. Aug. 2, 2001) (Title IX).

546   28 U.S.C. § 2412(d)(1); *see* Perez-Arellano v. Smith, 279 F.3d 791 (9th Cir. 2002); Former Employees of Motorola Ceramic Products v. United States, 336 F.3d 1360 (Fed. Cir. 2003); Brickwood Contractors, Inc. v. United States, 288 F.3d 1371 (Fed. Cir. 2002); Sileikis v. Perryman, 2001 U.S. Dist. LEXIS 12737 (N.D. Ill. Aug. 20, 2001); Vaughn v. Principi, 15 Vet. App. 277 (2001); Thayer v. Principi, 15 Vet. App. 204 (2001).

547   20 U.S.C. § 1415(I)(3); *see* J.C. v. Reg'l Sch. Dist. 10, 278 F.3d 119 (2d Cir. 2002); Brandon K. v. New Lenox Sch. Dist., 2001 U.S. Dist. LEXIS 20006 (N.D. Ill. Nov. 30, 2001); John T. v. Del. County Intermediate Unit, 318 F.3d 545 (3d Cir. 2003); Jose Luis R. v. Joliet Township High Sch. Dist. 204, 2001 U.S. Dist. LEXIS 13951 (N.D. Ill. Aug. 27, 2001).

547.1   *See* Crabill v. Trans Union, 259 F.3d 662 (7th Cir. 2001) (applying *Buckhannon* to the Fair Credit Reporting Act and concluding that attorney fees are not available unless the plaintiff wins "formal judicial relief").

547.2   15 U.S.C. § 2310(d)(2).

547.3   *See* Pitchford v. Oakwood Mobile Homes, Inc., 212 F. Supp. 2d 613 (W.D. Va. 2002) (*Buckhannon* applies to Magnuson-Moss Act); Bruemmer v. Compaq Computer Corp., 329 Ill. App. 3d 755, 263 Ill. Dec. 516, 768 N.E.2d 276 (2002) (applying *Buckhannon* to Magnuson-Moss claims).

547.4   15 U.S.C. § 2310(d)(2).

547.5   *But see* Pitchford v. Oakwood Mobile Homes, Inc., 212 F. Supp. 2d 613 (W.D. Va. 2002).

547.6   *Buckhannon*, 121 S. Ct. at 1840 n.7.

prevailing party, and the Ninth Circuit has characterized this language as *dictum*,[547.7] most courts have concluded that a "private settlement" can not be a basis for a fee award.[547.8]

What is a "court-ordered consent decree" and what is a "private settlement"? The key distinction is likely to be that a consumer has prevailed and is entitled to fees when a final order is entered in the case which permits the court, under the standards set forth in *Kokkonen v. Guardian Life Insurance Co.*,[547.9] to retain jurisdiction for enforcement purposes.[547.10] An order need not include an admission of liability by the defendant to qualify as a consent decree.[547.11] If an order meets these standards, it need not be titled "Consent Decree," and it is immaterial whether it repeats the terms of the parties' agreement or incorporates them by referring to a separate document.[547.12] Thus, an order that recites or incorporates a stipulation that sets forth steps that the defendant agrees to take, thereby subjecting the parties' agreement to judicial oversight and enforcement, qualifies as a court-ordered consent decree.[547.13] Even an order of dismissal can meet these standards if the court retains jurisdiction to enforce compliance with the parties' agree-

ment.[547.14] In some circumstances a remand to an administrative agency may meet *Buckhannon*'s requirements.[547.15] But a stipulation of dismissal that does not retain jurisdiction to enforce the agreement,[547.16] or a favorable preliminary or procedural ruling[547.17] will probably not suffice to qualify the plaintiff as a prevailing party. On the other hand, a preliminary injunction that, in effect, provides irreversible relief may be sufficient as a basis for fees.[547.18] And the Ninth Circuit has held that a preliminary injunction may suffice even if it merely preserves the status quo.[547.19]

The typical warranty case seeks money damages, not declaratory and injunctive relief as in *Buckhannon*. It is harder for a defendant to take unilateral steps to moot a claim for money than a claim for injunctive relief, as few defendants will pay money unilaterally without getting a release.[547.20] Nonetheless, the issues raised by *Buckhannon*

547.7 Barrios v. Cal. Interscholastic Fed'n, 277 F.3d 1128, 1134 n.5 (9th Cir. 2002).

547.8 *See, e.g.,* Smyth v. Rivero, 282 F.3d 268 (4th Cir. 2002); Nat'l Coalition for Students with Disabilities v. Bush, 173 F. Supp. 2d 1272 (N.D. Fla. 2001) (construing *Buckhannon* to disallow fees for "private settlements").

547.9 511 U.S. 375, 114 S. Ct. 1673, 128 L. Ed. 2d 391 (1994).

547.10 Richard S. v. Dep't of Developmental Services, 317 F.3d 1080 (9th Cir. 2003); Truesdell v. Philadelphia Hous. Auth., 290 F.3d 159 (3d Cir. 2002) (district court's order incorporating plaintiff's settlement in mandatory terms is sufficient); Am. Disability Ass'n v. Chmielarz, 289 F.3d 1315 (11th Cir. 2002); Smyth v. Rivero, 282 F.3d 268 (4th Cir. 2002) (consent decree on which fees can be based is one that is enforceable as a judicial decree by the court that entered it); Vasquez v. County of Lake, 2002 WL 31256166 (N.D. Ill. Oct. 7, 2002).

547.11 *Buckhannon*, 121 S. Ct. at 1840.

547.12 Am. Disability Ass'n v. Chmielarz, 289 F.3d 1315 (11th Cir. 2002); Smyth v. Rivero, 282 F.3d 268 (4th Cir. 2002); Nat'l Coalition for Students with Disabilities v. Bush, 173 F. Supp. 2d 1272, 1278, 1279 (N.D. Fla. 2001) ("the appropriateness of an award of fees surely ought not turn on whether the court does or does not retype the provisions of a settlement agreement as part of an order compelling compliance").

547.13 Labotest, Inc. v. Bonta, 297 F.3d 892 (9th Cir. 2002) (order incorporating stipulation about steps defendant would take to resolve two claims made plaintiff a prevailing party even though the stipulation stated that it was not a determination of "the issue of plaintiff's entitlement to attorney fees"); Johnny's Icehouse, Inc. v. Amateur Hockey Ass'n, 2001 U.S. Dist. LEXIS 11671 (N.D. Ill. Aug. 7, 2001); *see* Am. Disability Ass'n v. Chmielarz, 289 F.3d 1315 (11th Cir. 2002) (order of dismissal that approved, adopted, and ratified settlement, and retained jurisdiction to enforce it, was consent decree and plaintiff was prevailing party). *But cf.* Smyth v. Rivero, 282 F.3d 268 (4th Cir. 2002) (entry dismissing case as moot because of defendant's change of policy was not a consent decree even though it referred to the parties' agreement on one of the issues).

547.14 Am. Disability Ass'n v. Chmielarz, 289 F.3d 1315 (11th Cir. 2002).

547.15 *Compare* Former Employees of Motorola Ceramic Products v. United States, 336 F.3d 1360 (Fed. Cir. 2003) (plaintiffs who obtained remand to agency were prevailing parties) *with* Vaughn v. Principi, 336 F.3d 1351 (Fed. Cir. 2003) (claimant who obtained remand was not prevailing party).

547.16 Oil, Chem. & Atomic Workers Int'l Union v. Dep't of Energy, 288 F.3d 452 (D.C. Cir. 2002) (stipulation of dismissal insufficient even though signed by judge); Perez-Arellano v. Smith, 279 F.3d 791 (9th Cir. 2002); Dorfsman v. Law Sch. Admission Council, 2001 U.S. Dist. LEXIS 24044 (E.D. Pa. Nov. 28, 2001) (stipulation followed by dismissal); John T. v. Del. County Intermediate Unit, 318 F.3d 545 (3d Cir. 2003); Sileikis v. Perryman, 2001 U.S. Dist. LEXIS 12737 (N.D. Ill. Aug. 20, 2001) (suit which sought order requiring Immigration and Naturalization Service to adjudicate two applications was dismissed when I.N.S. did so); Thayer v. Principi, 15 Vet. App. 204 (2001); *see also* J.C. v. Reg'l Sch. Dist. 10, 278 F.3d 119 (2d Cir. 2002) (order dismissing hearing as moot after school board adopted individualized educational plan granting all relief sought was insufficient for fee award).

547.17 Oil, Chem. & Atomic Workers Int'l Union v. Dep't of Energy, 288 F.3d 452 (D.C. Cir. 2002) (order that government complete its review of records within sixty days did not make plaintiffs the prevailing parties in Freedom of Information Act case because it did not order relief on the merits); Smyth v. Rivero, 282 F.3d 268 (4th Cir. 2002) (preliminary injunction, followed by change of policy, does not make plaintiff the prevailing party); Pitchford v. Oakwood Mobile Homes, Inc., 212 F. Supp. 2d 613 (W.D. Va. 2002) (defeat of motion to compel arbitration and winning of magistrate's recommendation to deny motion to dismiss are insufficient); *see also* New Eng. Reg'l Council of Carpenters v. Kinton, 284 F.3d 9 (1st Cir. 2002) (judge's statements to defendants during preliminary proceedings about advisability of adopting new regulations, after which defendants did so, did not make plaintiff the prevailing party).

547.18 Watson v. County of Riverside, 300 F.3d 1092 (9th Cir. 2002).

547.19 Richard S. v. Dep't of Developmental Services, 317 F.3d 1080 (9th Cir. 2003).

547.20 *See Buckhannon*, 121 S. Ct. at 1842, 1843 (contrasting claims for money with claims for injunctive or declaratory relief). *But cf.* Bruemmer v. Compaq Computer Corp., 329 Ill. App. 3d 755, 263 Ill. Dec. 516, 768 N.E.2d 276 (2002) (class plaintiff's

can arise in Magnuson-Moss suits for money damages unless careful attention is paid to the format of the documents that resolve the case.

After *Buckhannon*, the following ways of settling a case are likely to preserve entitlement to fees:

- Negotiation of payment of fees in an acceptable amount as part of the settlement on the merits.

- An agreed judgment for money, as long as it is clear that fees have not been waived. A money judgment is a "material alteration of the legal relationship of the parties,"[547.21] as it creates an obligation of one party to the other that is enforceable by judicial process. The ability to enforce a money judgment by judicial process should be considered the functional equivalent of the judicial oversight that was the hallmark of a court-ordered consent decree for the *Buckhannon* court.[547.22]

- An agreed order that specifies steps, sought by the plaintiff in the case, that the defendant will take (for example, repair of a vehicle, accepting return of a vehicle, or canceling a security interest), as long as the court retains jurisdiction to enforce it.[547.23] It is clearer that the plaintiff is the prevailing party if the order the court signs actually recites the steps the defendant will take, rather than referring to a separate document, although courts have held that the latter format is also sufficient.[547.24]

- An agreed order of any sort that includes a finding or stipulation that the plaintiff is the prevailing party or is entitled to fees in an amount to be determined by the court.[547.25] Even a stipulation between the parties, not

signed by the court, that the plaintiff is the prevailing party is probably sufficient. While *Buckhannon* does not explicitly endorse this method of preserving the right to attorney fees, the Supreme Court never indicated that winning an enforceable judgment or a court-ordered consent decree is a jurisdictional requirement that can not be satisfied by a stipulation. Merely reserving the issue of attorney fees for the court, without stipulating that the plaintiff is the prevailing party, may be insufficient, however.[547.26]

Settlement methods that are less likely to preserve the right to fees are:

- A stipulation resolving the merits of the case, even if filed with the court, that is signed only by the parties and does not state that the plaintiff is the prevailing party.

- An entry of dismissal, even if the case is dismissed pursuant to an agreement signed by the parties under which the defendant agrees to the relief the plaintiff sought, unless the order embodies the settlement agreement or retains jurisdiction to enforce it.[547.27]

Warranty cases that primarily seek declaratory or injunctive relief rather than damages are more vulnerable to being rendered moot by unilateral action on the part of the defendant. In this situation, however, the *Buckhannon* court stressed that rendering the declaratory and injunctive claims moot will not prevent consumers from proceeding with damage claims and recovering attorney fees.[547.28] Even as to the declaratory and injunctive relief, the *Buckhannon* court reiterated the doctrine that voluntary cessation of a practice does not render a case moot "unless it is absolutely clear that the allegedly wrongful behavior could not reasonably be

---

acceptance of Rule 68 tender, followed by judge's dismissal of all claims, precludes fees).

547.21 *Buckhannon*, 121 S. Ct. at 1840.

547.22 *Buckhannon*, 532 U.S. at 603 (defining "prevailing party" as one in whose favor a judgment is rendered); Utility Automation 2000, Inc. v. Choctawhatchee Elec. Coop., Inc., 298 F.3d 1238 (11th Cir. 2002) (entry of Rule 68 judgment is basis for attorney fees if Marek v. Chesny, 473 U.S. 1, 105 S. Ct. 3012, 87 L. Ed. 2d 1 (1985), does not bar them); Dennis v. Columbia Collection Med. Ctr., Inc., 290 F.3d 639 (4th Cir. 2002) (party who obtains a judgment prevails); Pitchford v. Oakwood Mobile Homes, Inc., 212 F. Supp. 2d 613 (W.D. Va. 2002) (implying that settlement would have been basis for fees if it had been incorporated into court order); *see also* Walker v. City of Mesquite, 313 F.3d 246 (5th Cir. 2002) (adopting functional equivalence as standard).

547.23 *See* Am. Disability Ass'n v. Chmielarz, 289 F.3d 1315 (11th Cir. 2002) (dismissal order that approved, adopted, and ratified settlement, and retained jurisdiction to enforce it, was consent decree and plaintiff was prevailing party).

547.24 Labotest, Inc. v. Bonta, 297 F.3d 892 (9th Cir. 2002).

547.25 *See* Pitchford v. Oakwood Mobile Homes, Inc., 212 F. Supp. 2d 613 (W.D. Va. 2002) (settlement that merely reserved fee issue for court insufficient; court says that it would have sufficed if parties had stipulated that plaintiff was entitled to fees and that court would decide amount); *see also* Chase v. DaimlerChrysler Corp., 587 S.E.2d 521 (Va. 2003) (consent order stating that plaintiff was prevailing party would have been sufficient).

547.26 Dorfsman v. Law Sch. Admission Council, 2001 U.S. Dist. LEXIS 24044 (E.D. Pa. Nov. 28, 2001); *see also* Oil, Chem. & Atomic Workers Int'l Union v. Dep't of Energy, 288 F.3d 452 (D.C. Cir. 2002) (no fees despite stipulation that dismissal is "without prejudice to the right of plaintiff to obtain . . . an award of attorney's fees"; court does not discuss whether this provision amounted to a stipulation that plaintiff was the prevailing party); Pitchford v. Oakwood Mobile Homes, Inc., 212 F. Supp. 2d 613 (W.D. Va. 2002) (settlement that reserved fee issue for court insufficient; court says that it would have sufficed if settlement had said plaintiff was entitled to fees and that court would decide amount). *But cf.* Richard S. v. Dep't of Developmental Services, 317 F.3d 1080 (9th Cir. 2003) (stipulation that court retained jurisdiction to resolve attorney fee issues was sufficient when settlement agreement was binding and enforceable by court order).

547.27 *See* Smyth v. Rivero, 282 F.3d 268 (4th Cir. 2002) (dismissal order that merely acknowledges, refers to, or approves settlement agreement is insufficient); *see also* Pitchford v. Oakwood Mobile Homes, Inc., 212 F. Supp. 2d 613 (W.D. Va. 2002) (order that meets *Kokkonen* standards would be sufficient to preserve fee claim).

547.28 *Buckhannon*, 121 S. Ct. at 1842.

expected to recur."[547.29] While a government agency's agreement to change its regulations or a legislature's revision of a statute may make it unlikely that the challenged conduct will recur, a company's unilateral cessation of a practice provides little or no such assurance. If a claim for declaratory or injunctive relief is settled, the consumer's attorney should take care that the settlement includes an order granting substantive relief that is signed by the judge and that allows continuing jurisdiction, or that the agreement at least includes a stipulation that the consumer is the prevailing party.

If the case is resolved by the court rather than by settlement, the Fourth Circuit has held that the party in whose favor judgment is entered is the prevailing party regardless of the amount of damages awarded.[547.30] Even extremely limited success on a claim under a fee-shifting statute is enough, although a limited success will be a factor in determining the amount of fees.[547.31]

Of course, *Buckhannon* only controls as to federal law. Courts interpreting state fee-shifting statutes may find *Buckhannon* persuasive[547.32] but are free to adopt their own views about the catalyst theory and the formal requirements of settlements. Nonetheless, it is prudent to assume that state courts will impose the same requirements and to draft settlement documents accordingly.

547.29 *Id.* at 1842, 1843.

547.30 Dennis v. Columbia Collection Med. Ctr., Inc., 290 F.3d 639 (4th Cir. 2002).

547.31 *Id.*; Truesdell v. Philadelphia Hous. Auth., 290 F.3d 159 (3d Cir. 2002).

547.32 *Compare* Graham v. Daimlerchrysler Corp., 2002 WL 31732556 (Cal. Ct. App. Dec. 16, 2002) (unpublished) (rejecting *Buckhannon* and adhering to catalyst theory for state law warranty claim), *review granted* (Feb. 19, 2003) *and* Moedt v. Gen. Motors Corp., 60 P.3d 240 (Ariz. Ct. App. 2002) (awarding fees for settlement of state lemon law claim even though *Buckhannon* might have precluded fees for federal claim) *with* Pitchford v. Oakwood Mobile Homes, Inc., 212 F. Supp. 2d 613 (W.D. Va. 2002) (adopting interpretation of Virginia UDAP fee award standard similar to *Buckhannon*) *and* Wallerstein v. Stew Leonard's Dairy, 258 Conn. 299, 780 A.2d 916 (2001) (citing *Buckhannon* as authority that judgment entered under Connecticut equivalent of Rule 68 made plaintiff the prevailing party) *and* Chase v. DaimlerChrysler Corp., 587 S.E.2d 521 (Va. 2003) (adopting interpretation of "successful" party similar to *Buckhannon*'s under Virginia lemon law).

2.7.6.6 Defendant's Fees Not Recoverable

Addition to note 548.

548   Jones v. Fleetwood Motor Homes, 127 F. Supp. 2d 958 (N.D. Ill. 2000).

Page 69

2.7.6.7 Costs

Addition to notes 555–557.

555   *Add to Messana citation*: *remanded on other grounds*, 248 F.3d 1158 (7th Cir. 2001) (unpublished) (text available at 2001 U.S. App. LEXIS 3924) (questioning jurisdiction).

556   *Add to Messana citation*: *remanded on other grounds*, 248 F.3d 1158 (7th Cir. 2001) (unpublished) (text available at 2001 U.S. App. LEXIS 3924) (questioning jurisdiction).

557   *See generally* Teerling v. Fleetwood Motor Homes of Ind., Inc., 2001 U.S. Dist. LEXIS 11704 (N.D. Ill. Aug. 8, 2001) (applying Rule 54(d)(i) for the prevailing defendant).

2.7.7 Class Actions

Addition to note 564.

564   *Replace Cheminova citation with*: 779 So. 2d 1175 (Ala. 2000); *add*: *See, e.g.*, *In re* Bridgestone/Firestone, Inc., 288 F.3d 1012 (7th Cir. 2002).

Add to text after sentence containing note 564:

Applying the law of the jurisdiction where the manufacturer is located would simplify the issues considerably, but at least one appellate decision has rejected this approach.[564.1]

564.1   *See In re* Bridgestone/Firestone, Inc., 288 F.3d 1012 (7th Cir. 2002) (reversing trial court's decision to certify class and apply warranty law of manufacturer's home state).

Addition to notes 565, 566.

565   *See also* Miller v. Gen. Motors Corp., 2003 WL 168626 (N.D. Ill. Jan. 26, 2003) (declining to certify nationwide UDAP class action regarding vehicle defect, but not foreclosing certification of subsets of states in which UDAP statutes are similar).

Page 70

566   *See also In re* Bridgestone/Firestone, Inc., 288 F.3d 1012 (7th Cir. 2002) (differences in facts and law preclude certification of class of buyers of tires).

2.7.8 Statute of Limitations

Addition to notes 568–573.

568　　Murungi v. Mercedes Benz Credit Corp., 192 F. Supp. 2d 71 (W.D.N.Y. 2001); Dalton v. Ford Motor Co., 2002 WL 338081 (Del. Super. Ct. Feb. 28, 2002); Nowalski v. Ford Motor Co., 781 N.E.2d 578 (Ill. App. Ct. 2002); Poli v. DaimlerChrysler Corp., 349 N.J. Super. 169, 793 A.2d 104, 47 U.C.C. Rep. Serv. 2d 260 (Super. Ct. App. Div. 2002).

569　　*Add to end of note*: Note that a few states, such as Wisconsin, have non-uniform statutes of limitations for U.C.C. claims.

570　　*Replace Perez citation with*: 1999 U.S. Dist. LEXIS 9462 (N.D. Ill. June 10, 1999), *rev'd on other grounds*, 223 F.3d 617 (7th Cir. 2000), *cert. denied*, 531 U.S. 1153 (2001); *replace Adams citation with*: 39 U.C.C. Rep. Serv. 2d 769 (Ohio Ct. App. 1999).

571　　*Replace Perez citation with*: 1999 U.S. Dist. LEXIS 9462 (N.D. Ill. June 10, 1999), *rev'd on other grounds*, 223 F.3d 617 (7th Cir. 2000), *cert. denied*, 531 U.S. 1153 (2001); *replace Adams citation with*: 39 U.C.C. Rep. Serv. 2d 769 (Ohio Ct. App. 1999).

572　　*Replace Adams citation with*: 39 U.C.C. Rep. Serv. 2d 769 (Ohio Ct. App. 1999).

573　　*Replace Adams citation with*: 39 U.C.C. Rep. Serv. 2d 769 (Ohio Ct. App. 1999).

Add to text at end of subsection's second paragraph:

It is also arguable that, when the Magnuson-Moss Act gives the seller the right to a reasonable opportunity to cure,[574.1] the cause of action does not accrue until the seller's cure attempts are complete, and therefore the statute of limitations runs from that time.[574.2]

574.1　　*See* § 2.7.4, *supra*.

574.2　　Lowe v. Volkswagen of Am., 879 F. Supp. 28, 30 (E.D. Pa. 1995).

2.8 Informal Dispute Resolution Mechanisms

2.8.1 Precondition to Suit

Page 71

Add to text after sentence containing note 589:

In 2001, however, based on industry reports, it concluded that all domestic manufacturers and most importers now include a prior resort requirement in their warranties.[589.1]

589.1　　Fed. Trade Comm'n, Comment Request, 66 Fed. Reg. 42,538, 42,540 (Aug. 13, 2001).

Add to text at end of subsection's fourth paragraph:

Discovery about the structure and features of the mechanism may be necessary in order to demonstrate that it does not meet the Magnuson-Moss requirements.[590.1]

590.1　　*See* § 2.8.5, *infra* (discussion of requirements for mechanisms and records they must keep).

2.8.4 Disclosure of Mechanism Availability

Page 72

The warrantor must also take reasonable steps to make consumers aware of the existence of the mechanism at the time the consumer experiences a warranty dispute.[608.1]

608.1　　16 C.F.R. § 703.2(d).

2.9 Effect on State Laws

2.9.1 No General Preemption

Page 74

Addition to note 646.

646　　McIntire v. Ford Motor Co., 142 F. Supp. 2d 911 (S.D. Ohio 2001) (the Act "does not completely preempt the field of informed settlement mechanisms for warranty disputes").

Chapter 3   Express Warranties

Page 77

3.1 Introduction

Addition to notes 5, 7.

5   *See also* James River Equip. Co. v. Beadle County Equip., Inc., 646 N.W.2d 265, 48 U.C.C. Rep. Serv. 2d 105 (S.D. 2002).

7   *See* Prishwalko v. Bob Thomas Ford, Inc., 33 Conn. App. 575, 636 A.2d 1383 (1994) (mistaken statement of car's mileage was warranty).

Add to text at end of subsection:

The revised version of Article 2, approved by the National Conference of Commissioners on Uniform State Laws in 2003 for consideration by state legislatures, creates several new categories of obligations that were formerly encompassed by the definition of express warranty. First, it defines "remedial promise" as "a promise by the seller to repair or replace goods or to refund all or part of the price of goods upon the happening of a specified event."[8.1] The standard "repair or replace" warranty falls within this definition. In contrast to the current version of Article 2, such a promise is not a warranty,[8.2] although most of the rules for it are the same as for warranties. One significant difference, however, is that the statute of limitations for breach of a remedial promise begins to run only when the seller fails to perform the promise.[8.3]

Second, the revised version of Article 2 adds section 2-313A, which covers obligations to remote purchasers created by documents or other records that are packaged with or accompany the goods. The obligation may be created by an affirmation of fact or promise that relates to the goods, a description of the goods, or a remedial promise.[8.4] Examples are a product label, a card or booklet inside the container, or a booklet handed to the buyer at the time of sale. These obligations bind the remote seller without the need to show that they formed part of the basis of the bargain.[8.5]

Similarly, new section 2-313B covers obligations to remote purchasers created by advertisements or similar communications to the public that contain an affirmation of fact or promise that relates to the goods, a description of the goods, or a remedial promise.[8.6] The remote seller has an obligation created by such advertisements if the remote purchaser enters into the transaction with knowledge of the advertisement and with the expectation that the goods will conform to it or that the remote seller will fulfill the remedial promise.[8.7]

Both sections 2-313A and 2-313B create obligations on the part of the remote manufacturer only to persons who buy or lease the goods in the normal chain of distribution.[8.8] Both apply only to new goods or to goods sold or leased as new goods.[8.9] They both also have an effect on privity questions in that they create obligations that run directly from the manufacturer to remote buyers. Section 2-318, the general section on privity, deals with the extent to which the right to sue extends *beyond* remote buyers whose rights are recognized by sections 2-313A and 2-313B.[8.10]

Having created these new categories of obligations on the part of the manufacturer to remote buyers, Article 2 then provides that section 2-313 warranties are made only to the immediate buyer.[8.11] In other words, revised Article 2 confines traditional express warranties to immediate buyers, and creates two new categories of warranty-like obligations that run directly from the manufacturer to the remote buyer. If the buyer buys directly from the manufacturer, the traditional express warranty provisions of section 2-313 apply.[8.12]

Under revised Article 2's scheme, the major differences among these three categories of warranties and warranty-like obligations are:

EXPRESS WARRANTIES	LABELS, WARRANTY BOOKLETS	ADVERTISEMENTS
§ 2-313	§ 2-313A	§ 2-313B
Only made to immediate buyer	Made to remote purchaser	Made to remote purchaser
Can arise for new or used goods	Only arise for new goods	Only arise for new goods
Must be part of basis of bargain	Need not be part of basis of bargain; must be packaged with or accompany the goods	Obligation arises only if remote buyer enters into transaction with knowledge of the advertisement and with an expectation that the goods will conform to it
Section specifically contemplates warranties by model or sample	No mention of warranties by model or sample	No mention of warranties by model or sample, but if communication to public included a model or sample it would presumably create an obligation
No restrictions on incidental or consequential damages	No lost profit damages	No lost profit damages
Cause of action accrues upon delivery to immediate buyer and completion of any agreed installation or assembly	Cause of action accrues when remote buyer receives the goods	Cause of action accrues when remote buyer receives the goods

Section 2-313 is broader than sections 2-313A and 2-313B in that it creates warranties based on model or sample. By contrast, sections 2-313A and 2-313B do not specifically mention any obligation created by model or sample. An advertisement or other communication to the public could include a model or sample, however, in which case section 2-313B would create an obligation to the remote buyer. Sections 2-313A and 2-313B are also narrower than section 2-313 in that they preclude recovery of lost profits from the remote seller.[8.13]

Both sections 2-313A and 2-313B have their own remedy subsections that make it clear that the buyer has the right to recover damages from the remote seller for breach of these warranty-like obligations.[8.14] It is not completely clear whether those remedy sections supplement or supplant Article 2's general rules about breach and remedies. Both sections 2-313A and 2-313B include general provisions that would not be necessary if Article 2's general rules about breach and remedies applied.[8.15]

Section 2-711, which lists the buyer's remedies in general under Article 2 for the seller's breach of contract, provides little clarification. It does not confine these remedies to the "immediate buyer," even though both sections 2-313A and 2-313B use this term. It defines breach of contract to include several enumerated events. One is the seller's "wrongful failure to . . . perform a contractual obligation."[8.16] There is no indication whether the obligations created by sections 2-313A and 2-313B are "contractual obligations," but the UCC's broad definition of "contract"[8.17] suggests that it would include these obligations. Section 2-711's remedies are also available if the seller makes a "nonconforming tender,"[8.18] and noncompliance with the obligations created by sections 2-313A and 2-313B may make a tender nonconforming. Moreover, as section 2-711 merely states that a breach of contract "includes" the enumerated events, it can be argued that it applies to other breaches that are not enumerated. This latter view is consistent with the requirement that UCC remedies be liberally administered.[8.19]

An examination of revised section 2-608, which authorizes revocation, also supports the view that revocation is available for breach of the warranty-like obligations created by revised sections 2-313A and 2-313B. Revised section 2-608 is virtually unchanged from the pre-revision version. It applies to any ''nonconformity'' that substantially impairs the value of the goods, without reference to whether that nonconformity is based on a contract or on one of the new warranty-like obligations. It is not limited to the ''immediate buyer'' even though other sections of revised Article 2 are. In addition, the use of ''seller'' in revised sections 2-313A and 2-313B to refer to a remote manufacturer makes it clear that the same meaning can be attached to the use of the term in revised section 2-608.

The seller may limit the remedies that are available to the remote purchaser for breach of these warranty-like obligations.[8.20] The remedy limitation must be furnished to the remote purchaser no later than the time of purchase or along with the document containing the affirmation of fact, promise, or description, or included as part of the advertisement.[8.21] The general rules about remedy limitations—for example, that if a limited remedy fails of its essential purpose the buyer may recover without regard to the limitation—apply to limitations of remedies for breach of these warranty-like obligations.[8.22]

8.1   Revised U.C.C. § 2-103(1)(n).
8.2   Official Comment 7 to Revised U.C.C. § 2-103.
8.3   Revised U.C.C. § 2-725(2)(c); *see* § 10.3.3aS, *infra*.
8.4   Revised U.C.C. § 2-313A(3).
8.5   Official Comment 1 to Revised U.C.C. § 2-313A.
8.6   Revised U.C.C. § 2-313B(3).
8.7   Revised U.C.C. § 2-313B(3).
8.8   Revised U.C.C. §§ 2-313A(1)(b), 2-313B(1)(b).
8.9   Revised U.C.C. §§ 2-313A(2), 2-313B(2).
8.10   *See* § 6.1, *infra*.
8.11   Revised U.C.C. § 2-313(2).
8.12   Official Comment 1 to Revised U.C.C. § 2-313A.
8.13   Revised U.C.C. §§ 2-313A(5)(b), 2-313B(5)(b).
8.14   Revised U.C.C. §§ 2-313A(5), 2-313B(5).
8.15   *See* Revised U.C.C. §§ 2-313A(5)(c), 2-313B(5)(c) (authorizing damages).
8.16   Revised U.C.C. § 2-711(1).
8.17   U.C.C. § 1-201(11).
8.18   U.C.C. § 1-201(11).
8.19   *See* Official Comment 3 to Revised U.C.C. § 2-711.
8.20   Revised U.C.C. §§ 2-313A(5)(a), 2-313B(5)(a).
8.21   Revised U.C.C. §§ 2-313A(5)(a), 2-313B(5)(a).
8.22   Official Comment 7 to Revised U.C.C. § 2-313A; Official Comment 2 to Revised U.C.C. § 2-313B; *see* Ch. 9, *infra* (discussion of U.C.C. rules on remedy limitations).

3.2 Express Warranty by Affirmation of Fact or Promise

3.2.2 *"Any Affirmation of Fact or Promise"*

Page 78

3.2.2.2 Statements of Quality, Characteristics, or Condition

Addition to notes 21, 24, 27, 31.

Page 79

21   *But cf.* Rokicsak v. Colony Marine Sales & Serv., Inc., 219 F. Supp. 2d 810 (E.D. Mich. 2002) (no express warranty created by seller's statement that, to the extent any warranties existed despite disclaimer, repair and replacement was exclusive remedy).

24   *Replace NCLC citation with*: National Consumer Law Center, Unfair and Deceptive Acts and Practices § 4.9.4 (5th ed. 2001 and Supp.) (discussing UDAP cases on sale of used items as new); *add: See also* Morehouse v. Behlmann Pontiac-GMC Truck Serv., Inc., 31 S.W.3d 55 (Mo. Ct. App. 2000) (evidence that vehicle had multiple prior owners, contrary to salesman's statement, was admissible as tending to show its poor condition).

27   Terrell v. R & A Mfg. Partners, Ltd., 835 So. 2d 216, 50 U.C.C. Rep. Serv. 2d 151, 162, 163 (Ala. Civ. App. 2002).

31   Morehouse v. Behlmann Pontiac-GMC Truck Serv., Inc., 31 S.W.3d 55 (Mo. Ct. App. 2000) (van was in "good condition," "excellent condition," "tip-top shape").

Page 80

3.2.2.3 Representations of Gas Mileage and Prior Repairs or Maintenance

Addition to note 34.

34   *See* Moore v. Mack Trucks, Inc., 40 S.W.3d 888, 44 U.C.C. Rep. Serv. 2d 416 (Ky. Ct. App. 2001) (salesman's oral statement that transmission had been redone created warranty).

Page 81

3.2.2.4 Promises of Seller's Future Actions or Product's Future Performance

Addition to notes 40, 41.

40   *See also* Watson & Son Landscaping v. Power Equip. Co., 2003 WL 22326967 (Tenn. Ct. App. Apr. 29, 2003) (promise to repair machine's defective hydraulic system is a warranty).

41   *See* Fassi v. Auto Wholesalers, 145 N.H. 404, 762 A.2d 1034 (2000) (promise to repair any problems with car found within first thirty days was express warranty). *But see* Voelker v. Porsche Cars N. Am., Inc., 2003 WL 22930364 (7th Cir. Dec. 12, 2003) (repair or replace warranty is not U.C.C. warranty); Schimmer v. Jaguar Cars, Inc., 2003 WL 21518589 (N.D. Ill. July 2, 2003) (repair or replace warranty is not a warranty under U.C.C. definition); Cosman v. Ford Motor Co., 285 Ill. App. 3d 250, 674 N.E.2d 61 (1996) (in applying U.C.C. statute of limitations, finds that repair or replace warranty is not a warranty under U.C.C. definition).

Page 82

Add to text after sentence containing note 46:

Statements in the owner's manual about how the vehicle can be expected to function can be express warranties.[46.1]

46.1   Caboni v. Gen. Motors Corp., 278 F.3d 448 (5th Cir. 2002) (definition of warranty under La. Prod. Liab. Act).

3.2.2.5 Affirmation or Promise Created Orally, By Advertisements, Brochures or Labels

Addition to notes 49, 50.

49   *See, e.g.,* Daley v. McNeil Consumer Products Co., 164 F. Supp. 2d 367, 45 U.C.C. Rep. Serv. 2d 770 (S.D.N.Y. 2001) (statement by customer service representative in toll-free telephone call that product could not cause rash could be warranty if buyer relied on it and it became part of basis of bargain); Moore v. Mack Trucks, Inc., 40 S.W.3d 888, 44 U.C.C. Rep. Serv. 2d 416 (Ky. Ct. App. 2001) (salesman's oral statement that transmission had been redone created warranty); *see also* Hercules Mach. Corp. v. McElwee Bros., Inc., 49 U.C.C. Rep. Serv. 2d 72 (E.D. La. 2002) (construing statements in facsimiles as part of contract); Keller v. Inland Metals All Weather Conditioning, Inc., 76 P.3d 977 (Idaho 2003) (seller's letter created express warranty).

50   *See, e.g.,* Select Pork, Inc. v. Babcock Swine, Inc., 640 F.2d 147 (8th Cir. 1981) (warranty by description incorporated details contained in advertisement); Berg Chilling Sys., Inc. v. Hull Corp., 49 U.C.C. Rep. Serv. 2d 189 (E.D. Pa. 2002) (product literature); Hobbs v. Gen. Motors Corp., 134 F. Supp. 2d 1277, 44 U.C.C. Rep. Serv. 2d 148 (M.D. Ala. 2001) (statements on window sticker and in owner's manual could create warranties); Carrau v. Marvin Lumber & Cedar Co., 93 Cal. App. 4th 281, 112 Cal. Rptr. 2d 869, 46 U.C.C. Rep. Serv. 2d 1036 (2001) (assertion in advertisement, if read and relied on by buyer, may act as warranty); Triple E, Inc. v. Hendrix & Dail, Inc., 543 S.E.2d 245, 43 U.C.C. Rep. Serv. 2d 533 (S.C. Ct. App. 2001) (advertisements); Bobholz v. Banaszak, 655 N.W.2d 547, 49 U.C.C. Rep. Serv. 2d 25 (Wis. Ct. App. 2002) (advertisements); Selzer v. Brunsell Bros., Ltd., 652 N.W.2d 806, 48 U.C.C. Rep. Serv. 2d 629 (Wis. Ct. App. 2002) (advertisements created warranty); *see also In re* Bridgestone/Firestone, Inc. Tires Products Liab. Litig., 47 U.C.C. Rep. Serv. 2d 140 (S.D. Ind. 2001) (Mich. and Tenn. law) (advertisement is part of basis of bargain only if consumer saw it), *rev'd on other grounds*, 288 F.3d 1012 (7th Cir. 2002). *But cf.* Anthony v. Country Life Mfg., Ltd. Liab. Co., 2003 WL 21540975 (7th Cir. July 2, 2003) (unpublished) (action of placing product on shelf for sale is not an affirmation); Malul v. Capital Cabinets, Inc., 740 N.Y.S.2d 828, 47 U.C.C. Rep. Serv. 2d 502 (Civ. Ct. 2002) (statements in advertisements not part of basis of bargain when buyer did not see them before contracting).

Page 83

Add to text at end of subsection:

Even an advertisement that the buyer did not see may be admissible because it tends to prove that other statements that the buyer did see or hear were consistent with it.[53.1]

53.1   Bobholz v. Banaszak, 655 N.W.2d 547 (Wis. Ct. App. 2002) (table) (text available at 2002 WL 31521364).

3.2.2.6 Pictures, Conduct, and the Product Itself as Affirmations of Fact

Addition to note 54.

54   *But cf.* Boud v. SDNCO, Inc., 54 P.3d 1131 (Utah 2002) (picture of yacht moving across a body of water was not a representation about mechanical or electrical systems, quality, or reliability).

3.2.2.7 Opinion or Puffing

Page 84

3.2.2.7.1 *General*

Addition to notes 61, 64, 65, 67, 68, 70, 71, 74.

61   Baughn v. Honda Motor Co., 727 P.2d 655, 669 (Wash. 1986) ("You meet the nicest people on a Honda" not a warranty).

64   *But see* Bumgarner v. Lowe's Companies, 51 U.C.C. Rep. Serv. 2d 112 (N.C. Ct. App. 2003) (unpublished) ("runs and drives good" is puffing).

65   *Accord* Morehouse v. Behlmann Pontiac-GMC Truck Serv., Inc., 31 S.W.3d 55 (Mo. Ct. App. 2000) (van was in "excellent condition," "tip-top shape").

67   *See also* Bobb Forest Products, Inc. v. Morbark Indus., Inc., 151 Ohio App. 3d 63, 783 N.E.2d 560, 50 U.C.C. Rep. Serv. 2d 106 (2002) (statement that sawmill would accurately cut various types of lumber was warranty); Packard Norfolk, Inc. v. Miller, 198 Va. 557, 95 S.E.2d 207 (1956) ("perfect condition" not puffing); Bobholz v. Banaszak, 655 N.W.2d 547, 49 U.C.C. Rep. Serv. 2d 25 (Wis. Ct. App. 2002) ("in perfect condition" is warranty; rule is same for casual sellers as for merchants).

Page 85

68   *See also* Daley v. McNeil Consumer Products Co., 164 F. Supp. 2d 367, 45 U.C.C. Rep. Serv. 2d 770 (S.D.N.Y. 2001) (statement by customer service representative that product could not cause rash goes directly to character and quality and therefore presents jury question).

70   *See also* Malul v. Capital Cabinets, Inc., 740 N.Y.S.2d 828, 47 U.C.C. Rep. Serv. 2d 502 (Civ. Ct. 2002) (statement that cabinets were built to last a lifetime was puffing).

71   *See also* Sheffield v. Darby, 244 Ga. App. 437, 535 S.E.2d 776 (2000) (statements that horse had no problems and would make a good show horse were either true or merely puffing).

74   *See, e.g.*, Bagley v. Mazda Motor Corp., 2003 WL 21040506 (Ala. May 9, 2003) (statements that car was "good car" and "about the best one" on the lot were not express warranties); Greines v. Ford Motor Co., 2003 WL 42524 (Cal. Ct. App. Jan. 7, 2003) (unpublished) (representation that "vehicle won't start" without specially coded key is not puffing); Bumgarner v. Lowe's Companies, 51 U.C.C. Rep. Serv. 2d 112 (N.C. Ct. App. 2003) (unpublished) ("runs and drives good" is puffing); Boud v. SDNCO, Inc., 54 P.3d 1131 (Utah 2002) ("best performance . . . in its class" not a warranty).

Page 86

3.2.2.7.2 *Buyer and seller's sophistication as a factor*

Addition to note 76.

76   Hercules Mach. Corp. v. McElwee Bros., Inc., 49 U.C.C. Rep. Serv. 2d 72 (E.D. La. 2002) (representation is express warranty when seller asserts fact of which buyer is ignorant); Morehouse v. Behlmann Pontiac-GMC Truck Serv., Inc., 31 S.W.3d 55 (Mo. Ct. App. 2000); Norcold, Inc. v. Gateway Supply Co., 51 U.C.C. Rep. Serv. 2d 88 (Ohio Ct. App. 2003) (unpublished) (express written warranty is enforceable regardless of reliance).

3.2.5 *Basis of the Bargain*

Page 89

3.2.5.1 General

Addition to notes 99, 100, 106, 107.

99   PPG Indus., Inc. v. JMB/Houston Centers Partners, 41 S.W.3d 270 (Tex. App. 2001) (warranty is part of the basis of bargain even though not incorporated into written contract).

100   *Add to Yates citation*: 514 S.E.2d 605.

106   Murrin v. Ford Motor Co., 303 A.D.2d 475, 756 N.Y.S.2d 596 (2003) (no express warranty created when buyer was unaware of advertisements); *see also In re* Bridgestone/Firestone, Inc. Tires Products Liab. Litig., 47 U.C.C. Rep. Serv. 2d 140 (S.D. Ind. 2001) (Mich. and Tenn. law) (advertisement is part of basis of bargain only if consumer saw it), *rev'd on other grounds*, 288 F.3d 1012 (7th Cir. 2002); Boyd v. Johnson & Johnson, 47 U.C.C. Rep. Serv. 2d 164 (Pa. C.P. 2002) (no express warranty claim without an allegation that plaintiff saw the documents).

107   *See, e.g.*, Rudder v. K Mart Corp., 44 U.C.C. Rep. Serv. 2d 101 (S.D. Ala. 1997); *see also* Arkwright-Boston Manufacturers Mut. Ins. Co. v. Westinghouse, 844 F.2d 1174 (5th Cir. 1988) (statements in proposal that were not included in final contract, which two large commercial entities signed after months of negotiation and which expressly overrode prior documents, were not basis of bargain).

Add to text at end of subsection:

One court has characterized the basis of the bargain test as encompassing "what the seller sold to the buyer."[107.1]

    107.1   *In re* Bridgestone/Firestone, Inc. Tires Products Liab. Litig., 47 U.C.C. Rep. Serv. 2d 140 (S.D. Ind. 2001) (Mich. and Tenn. law), *rev'd on other grounds*, 288 F.3d 1012 (7th Cir. 2002).

3.2.5.2 Reliance Not Required

Addition to note 108.

    108   *Add to Yates citation*: 514 S.E.2d 605; *add: See, e.g., In re* Bridgestone/Firestone, Inc. Tires Products Liab. Litig., 47 U.C.C. Rep. Serv. 2d 140 (S.D. Ind. 2001) (Mich. and Tenn. law), *rev'd on other grounds*, 288 F.3d 1012 (7th Cir. 2002); Greines v. Ford Motor Co., 2003 WL 42524 (Cal. Ct. App. Jan. 7, 2003) (unpublished); Keller v. Inland Metals All Weather Conditioning, Inc., 76 P.3d 977 (Idaho 2003); Norcold, Inc. v. Gateway Supply Co., 51 U.C.C. Rep. Serv. 2d 88 (Ohio Ct. App. 2003) (unpublished) (express written warranty is enforceable regardless of reliance); PPG Indus., Inc. v. JMB/Houston Centers Partners, 41 S.W.3d 270 (Tex. App. 2001); Baughn v. Honda Motor Co., 727 P.2d 655, 669 (Wash. 1986) (reliance unnecessary but buyer must be aware of seller's statement). *But see* Pressalite Corp. v. Matsushita Elec. Corp., 50 U.C.C. Rep. Serv. 2d 410 (N.D. Ill. 2003) (equating basis of bargain and reliance); Austin v. Will-Burt Co., 232 F. Supp. 2d 682, 50 U.C.C. Rep. Serv. 2d 121 (N.D. Miss. 2002) (no express warranty without reliance); Monte v. Toyota Motor Corp., 46 U.C.C. Rep. Serv. 2d 967 (Mich. Ct. App. 2001) (unpublished) (affirmation in owner's manual received after consummation of lease can not be express warranty because plaintiff can not have relied on it); Selzer v. Brunsell Bros., Ltd., 652 N.W.2d 806, 48 U.C.C. Rep. Serv. 2d 629 (Wis. Ct. App. 2002) (listing reliance as an element, but citing as authority only a case under a pre-U.C.C. statute that explicitly required reliance); *cf.* McManus v. Fleetwood Enterprises, Inc., 320 F.3d 545, 49 U.C.C. Rep. Serv. 2d 1124 (5th Cir. 2003) (Tex. law) (basis of bargain requirement is close enough to reliance that it precludes class certification).

Replace § 3.2.5.3 heading with:

3.2.5.3 Presumption That Statements Are Part of Basis of Bargain

Addition to notes 109, 111.

    109   *Add to Yates citation*: 514 S.E.2d 605; *add*: Greines v. Ford Motor Co., 2003 WL 42524 (Cal. Ct. App. Jan. 7, 2003) (unpublished).

    111   Williams v. Dow Chem. Co., 255 F. Supp. 2d 219 (S.D.N.Y. 2003) (no express warranties when plaintiffs did not hear, see, or rely on any statements by manufacturer before allowing product to be used in their homes); Murrin v. Ford Motor Co., 303 A.D.2d 475, 756 N.Y.S.2d 596, 50 U.C.C. Rep. Serv. 2d 745 (2003) (no express warranty claim when plaintiff did not allege that he was aware of the advertisements before his purchase); Baughn v. Honda Motor Co., 727 P.2d 655, 669 (Wash. 1986) (buyer must at least have been aware of statement).

3.2.5.4 Nullification of Express Warranties Due to Buyer's Pre-Sale Inspection

Add to text at end of subsection's third paragraph:

Furthermore, as section 2-316(3)(b) refers only to the effect of inspection on implied warranties, it is reasonable to argue that express warranties are unaffected by inspection.[119.1]

    119.1   James River Equip. Co. v. Beadle County Equip., Inc., 646 N.W.2d 265, 48 U.C.C. Rep. Serv. 2d 105 (S.D. 2002).

3.3 Express Warranty by Description of Goods

Addition to notes 123, 128.

    123   *Add to Streeks citation*: 605 N.W.2d 110; *add: Accord* Select Pork, Inc. v. Babcock Swine, Inc., 640 F.2d 147 (8th Cir. 1981) (description of breed of pig in contract was non-disclaimable warranty by description, and it incorporated details contained in advertising brochure); Smart Online, Inc. v. Opensite Technologies, Inc., 51 U.C.C. Rep. Serv. 2d 47 (N.C. Super. Ct. 2003) (when contract referred to documentation that came with software, its description of the software's capacity may be part of the basis of the bargain, notwithstanding a merger clause); James River Equip. Co. v. Beadle County Equip., Inc., 646 N.W.2d 265, 48 U.C.C. Rep. Serv. 2d 105 (S.D. 2002) (description of features of equipment attached to purchase order).

    128   *E.g.*, Cheminova Am. Corp. v. Corker, 779 So. 2d 1175 (Ala. 2000) (label).

3.4 Express Warranty by Sample or Model

Page 94

3.4.1 Sample and Model Distinguished

Addition to note 136.

136 Materials Mktg. Corp. v. Spencer, 40 S.W.3d 172, 43 U.C.C. Rep. Serv. 2d 1131 (Tex. App. 2001). *But cf.* Pioneer Peat, Inc. v. Quality Grassing & Services, Inc., 653 N.W.2d 469, 49 U.C.C. Rep. Serv. 2d 440 (Minn. Ct. App. 2002) (commercial case) (no express warranty by sample when there was no evidence that parties considered first shipment to be a sample).

3.5 Can Postsale Statements Be Part of the Basis of the Bargain?

Page 96

3.5.1 Statements Made or Read at Delivery

Addition to notes 147, 148.

147 *See* Mich. Dessert Corp. v. A.E. Staley Mfg. Corp., 46 U.C.C. Rep. Serv. 2d 642 (6th Cir. 2001) (Mich. law) (post-sale statements can be part of basis of bargain if bargaining process is still going on, but a statement made much later was not).

148 *See also* Hercules Mach. Corp. v. McElwee Bros., Inc., 49 U.C.C. Rep. Serv. 2d 72 (E.D. La. 2002) (documents executed around same time as contract, including facsimiles sent during contract formation, should be construed together as a whole).

Page 97

3.5.2 Written Statements Provided at or Before Delivery That Are Not Read Until After Delivery

Addition to notes 156, 160, 164.

156 *But cf.* Sun-Lite Glazing Contractors, Inc. v. J.E. Berkowitz, Ltd. P'ship, 49 U.C.C. Rep. Serv. 2d 483 (4th Cir. 2002) (unpublished) (Md. law) (because of limited warranty, buyer had no warranty claim for erroneous installation instructions included with product; court only analyzes implied warranty theories, not express warranty).

160 *See, e.g.,* Monte v. Toyota Motor Corp., 46 U.C.C. Rep. Serv. 2d 967 (Mich. Ct. App. 2001) (unpublished) (affirmation in owner's manual received after consummation of lease can not be express warranty because plaintiff can not have relied on it).

Page 98

164 *Replace entire U.C.C. citation with: See* U.C.C. § 1-103 (principles of law and equity, including the law of estoppel, supplement the U.C.C. unless displaced by a particular provision of the U.C.C.) [*redesignated as U.C.C. § 1-103(b) by revised Article 1, which the National Conference of Commissioners on Uniform State Laws (NCCUSL) approved in 2001 for adoption by the states*].

Add to text at end of subsection:

A final approach is the concept of "layered contracting," in which the buyer and seller reach agreement initially on some basic terms, with additional terms added at later points.[166.1] While this concept has mostly been used to validate disclaimers found in shrink-wrap licenses, it can also be a basis for recognizing warranties created by post-sale assurances.

166.1 *See, e.g.,* M.A. Mortensen Co. v. Timberline Software Corp., 140 Wash. 2d 568, 998 P.2d 305 (2000).

Replace § 3.5.3 heading with:

3.5.3 Statements Made After Delivery

3.5.3.1 General

Addition to note 169.

169 *But see* Williams v. Dow Chem. Co., 255 F. Supp. 2d 219 (S.D.N.Y. 2003) (statements made after buyers had already allowed product to be used in their homes are not part of basis of bargain).

Page 99

3.5.3.2 Postsale Statements as Modifications of the Original Bargain

Addition to notes 175, 178.

175 *See* Sara Lee Corp. v. Quality Mfg., Inc., 201 F. Supp. 2d 608, 47 U.C.C. Rep. Serv. 2d 1314 (M.D.N.C. 2002) (modification of term can operate as waiver even if it does not meet statute of frauds), *aff'd*, 2003 WL 1564377 (4th Cir. Mar. 27, 2003) (*per curiam*) (unpublished); *see also* ePresence, Inc. v. Evolve Software, Inc., 47 U.C.C. Rep. Serv. 2d 132 (D. Mass. 2002) (oral modification allowed, despite clause requiring signed writing, if there is clear factual evidence (such as a course of conduct) showing the modification; not shown in this case).

178 *Add to Miller citation*: aff'd on other grounds, 249 F.3d 629 (7th Cir. 2001); *add*: *Cf.* i.LAN Sys., Inc. v. Netscout Serv. Level Corp., 183 F. Supp. 2d 328 (D. Mass. 2002) (adopting idea of "payment first, terms later" to uphold disclaimer and remedy limitation in clickwrap license that was delivered only with the product).

Page 100

3.5.3.3 Must The Modification Be in Writing?

Addition to note 179.

179 *Add at beginning of note*: Revised U.C.C. § 2-201, part of a general overhaul of Article 2 that the National Conference of Commissioners on Uniform State Laws approved in 2003 for consideration by state legislatures, would raise the statute of frauds threshold to $5000.

3.5.3.4 Enforcing an Oral Modification Even if Statute of Frauds Requires It to Be in Writing

Addition to notes 182, 183.

182 *Add at end of note*: *See also* Marley Cooling Tower Co. v. Caldwell Energy & Envtl., Inc., 280 F. Supp. 2d 651, 51 U.C.C. Rep. Serv. 2d 376 (W.D. Ky. 2003) (words and conduct can waive contractual requirement despite contract clause barring oral modification, but not shown here).

183 Thorn's Diesel Serv., Inc. v. Houston Ship Repair, Inc., 253 F. Supp. 2d 1332, 49 U.C.C. Rep. Serv. 2d 380 (N.D. Ala. 2002); Securities Indus. Automation Corp. v. United Computer Capital Corp., 723 N.Y.S.2d 668, 45 U.C.C. Rep. Serv. 2d 745 (App. Div. 2001); *see also* Wireless Distributors, Inc. v. Sprintcom, Inc., 51 U.C.C. Rep. Serv. 2d 676 (N.D. Ill. 2003) (buyer sufficiently alleged that seller's actions were waiver).

3.6 Effect of Seller's Disclaimer of Responsibility for Oral Statements

Page 103

3.6.2 Primacy of the Parties' Actual Intent and Understanding

Addition to notes 198, 199.

198 *Add after second sentence of note*: [*Note that revised Article 1, approved by the National Conference of Commissioners on Uniform State Laws (NCCUSL) in 2001 for adoption by state legislatures, transfers the definition of course of performance to U.C.C. § 1-303(d). It eliminates this specific comment, while preserving the general point in revised U.C.C. § 1-303 cmt. 1. Revised U.C.C. § 1-303 and the comments thereto are reprinted in Appx. E.6, infra.*]

199 *See, e.g.,* Oakwood Mobile Homes, Inc. v. Cabler, 73 S.W.3d 363 (Tex. App. 2002) (clause buried in boilerplate language that disavowed oral statements was unenforceable when signed by unsophisticated buyer).

3.6.3 Has the Consumer Agreed to the Merger Clause?

Addition to notes 205, 206, 211, 217.

Page 104

205 *See, e.g.,* Tibco Software, Inc. v. Gordon Food Serv., Inc., 51 U.C.C. Rep. Serv. 2d 102 (W.D. Mich. 2003) (commercial case).

206 *See also* Oakwood Mobile Homes, Inc. v. Cabler, 73 S.W.3d 363 (Tex. App. 2002) (clause buried in boilerplate language that disavowed oral statements was unenforceable when signed by unsophisticated buyer); *cf.* Telecom Int'l Am., Ltd. v. AT & T Corp., 280 F.3d 175 (2d Cir. 2001) (New Jersey would allow admission of evidence of parties' intent despite integration clause but, in this case, parties intended the bargain set forth in the writing).

211 *But see* Hessler v. Crystal Lake Chrysler-Plymouth, Inc., 338 Ill. App. 3d 1010, 788 N.E.2d 405, 50 U.C.C. Rep. Serv. 2d 330 (2003) (fact that integration clause was preprinted and not specifically negotiated, without more, does not render it inoperative).

Page 105

217 *See also* Brewer v. Poole Constr. Co., 13 Mass. L. Rep. 97, 2001 Mass. Super. LEXIS 151 (Mass. Super. Ct. May 3, 2001) (non-U.C.C. case).

3.6.4 Merger Clause Cannot Prevent Oral Statements From Interpreting Ambiguous Contract Terms

Addition to note 219.

219 Golden Peanut Co. v. Bass, 275 Ga. 145, 563 S.E.2d 116, 48 U.C.C. Rep. Serv. 2d 514 (2002); Hessler v. Crystal Lake Chrysler-Plymouth, Inc., 338 Ill. App. 3d 1010, 788 N.E.2d 405, 50 U.C.C. Rep. Serv. 2d 330 (2003).

Page 106

3.6.5 Merger Clause Ineffective if Inconspicuous, Unconscionable, in Bad Faith, or Unfair or Deceptive

Addition to note 228.

228 *See also* Oakwood Mobile Homes, Inc. v. Cabler, 73 S.W.3d 363 (Tex. App. 2002) (clause buried in boilerplate language that disavowed oral statements was unenforceable when unsophisticated buyer was induced to sign contract by seller's fraudulent representations).

3.6.7 Merger Clause Does Not Protect Persons Not Parties to the Contract

Addition to note 232.

232 *Add after KLPR TV, Inc. citation: See also* Holden Farms, Inc. v. Hog Slat, Inc., 347 F.3d 1055 (8th Cir. 2003) (parol evidence rule does not protect entity that is not a party to the contract).

3.6.8 Oral Claims Are Actionable Under Other Legal Theories Despite Merger Clause

Replace note 238 with:

238 *See In re* Ivernux, Inc., 298 B.R. 442, 51 U.C.C. Rep. Serv. 2d 563 (Bankr. D. Colo. 2003) (parol evidence rule has no application to claim of mutual mistake); § 11.4.1, *infra; see also* Restatement (Second) of Contracts § 152 cmt. a (parol evidence rule does not preclude use of prior or contemporaneous agreements or negotiations to establish mistake).

3.7 Parol Evidence: Can Oral Statements Expand on a Written Warranty?

Page 107

3.7.1 General

Replace note 242 with:

242 U.C.C. §§ 1-205(1), 2-208 (course of dealing and course of performance are contract terms arising from parties' conduct) [*Note that revised Article 1, approved by the National Conference of Commissioners on Uniform State Laws (NCCUSL) in 2001 for adoption by state legislatures, consolidates U.C.C. §§ 1-205 and 2-208 as revised U.C.C. § 1-303*]; *see* § 3.2.2.6, *supra* (discussion of express warranties by conduct).

Addition to notes 245, 249.

245 *See, e.g.,* Sagent Tech., Inc. v. Micros Sys., Inc., 276 F. Supp. 2d 464, 51 U.C.C. Rep. Serv. 2d 59 (D. Md. 2003).

Page 108

249 *See also* Golden Peanut Co. v. Bass, 275 Ga. 145, 563 S.E.2d 116, 48 U.C.C. Rep. Serv. 2d 514 (2002) (U.C.C. was intended to liberalize the common law parol evidence rule).

3.7.2 Procedure for Evaluating Parol Evidence

3.7.2.1 Question for Judge or Jury?

Addition to note 254.

254 *See also* Fox v. Montell Corp., 44 U.C.C. Rep. Serv. 2d 370 (N.D. Ill. 2001) (whether contract is ambiguous is question of law).

Page 109

3.7.2.2 Parol Evidence Must Be Examined Before It Can Be Excluded

Addition to note 257.

257 *See* Sagent Tech., Inc. v. Micros Sys., Inc., 276 F. Supp. 2d 464, 51 U.C.C. Rep. Serv. 2d 59 (D. Md. 2003).

Page 111

3.7.2.5 Postsale Conduct

Addition to note 269.

269 *Cf.* Pioneer/Eclipse Corp. v. Kohler Co., 113 F. Supp. 2d 811 (W.D.N.C. 2000) (parties' course of dealing demonstrated acceptance of remedy limitation despite absence of formal assent).

3.7.3 Rejection of the Four Corners Test

Addition to note 270.

270   Dakota Pork Indus. v. City of Huron, 638 N.W.3d 884 (S.D. 2002) (commercial contract); Boud v. SDNCO, Inc., 54 P.3d 1131 (Utah 2002).

Page 112

3.7.4 Form Contracts

Addition to note 275.

275   *But see* Shook v. Counterman, 43 U.C.C. Rep. Serv. 2d 1144 (Ohio Ct. App. 2000) (giving effect to integration clause in consumer sale and excluding evidence that boat was "a good boat").

3.7.6 Writing May Be Final Expression on Some Terms, But Not on Others

Addition to note 282.

282   De La Morena v. Ingeniera E Maquinaria De Guadalupe, S.A., 56 S.W.3d 652, 45 U.C.C. Rep. Serv. 2d 391 (Tex. App. 2001) (parol evidence admissible to show consistent additional terms).

Page 113

3.7.7 The Contract Was Intended to Be Final, but the Parol Evidence and the Contract Terms Can Be Construed Harmoniously

Addition to note 283.

283   Paul v. Timco, Inc., 356 N.J. Super. 180, 811 A.2d 948 (Super. Ct. App. Div. 2002).

Page 114

3.7.8 Parol Evidence Admissible to Interpret a Contract Term

Addition to notes 302, 304, 306.

302   Busch v. Dyno Nobel, Inc., 48 U.C.C. Rep. Serv. 2d 874 (6th Cir. 2002) (unpublished) (Mich. law); Fox v. Montell Corp., 44 U.C.C. Rep. Serv. 2d 370 (N.D. Ill. 2001) (parol evidence admissible to explain ambiguities notwithstanding integration clause); Golden Peanut Co. v. Bass, 275 Ga. 145, 563 S.E.2d 116, 48 U.C.C. Rep. Serv. 2d 514 (2002); Hessler v. Crystal Lake Chrysler-Plymouth, Inc., 338 Ill. App. 3d 1010, 788 N.E.2d 405, 50 U.C.C. Rep. Serv. 2d 330 (2003).

Page 115

304   *Cf.* Mohave Valley Irrigation & Drainage Dist. v. Norton, 244 F.3d 1164, 44 U.C.C. Rep. Serv. 2d 40 (9th Cir. 2001) (to determine whether a contract term, clear on its face, is ambiguous, the only extrinsic evidence a court can consider is course of dealing, trade usage, or course of performance).

306   *Add to end of note:* [*This comment is redesignated U.C.C. § 1-103 cmt. 1 by revised Article 1, which the National Conference of Commissioners on Uniform State Laws (NCCUSL) approved in 2001 for adoption by the states.*]

3.7.9 Parol Evidence Goes to Course of Dealing, Usage of Trade, or Course of Performance to Explain or Supplement the Writing

Addition to notes 313–316.

313   *Add to end of note:* [*Note that revised Article 1, approved by the National Conference of Commissioners on Uniform State Laws (NCCUSL) in 2001 for adoption by state legislatures, consolidates U.C.C. §§ 1-205 and 2-208 as revised U.C.C. § 1-303. Revised Article 1 includes a companion revision to U.C.C. § 2-202(a) that revises these cross-references.*]

314   Telecom Int'l Am., Ltd. v. AT & T Corp., 280 F.3d 175 (2d Cir. 2001) (N.J. law); Bank of Am. v. C.D. Smith Motor Co., 106 S.W.3d 425, 50 U.C.C. Rep. Serv. 2d 670 (Ark. 2003); *see also* Herman Bros. Sales Corp. v. Hill's Pet Prods. Div., 875 F.2d 864, 44 U.C.C. Rep. Serv. 2d 695 (6th Cir. 1989) (noting that Kansas comments to § 2-202 go beyond Official Comments in allowing admission of this evidence). *But see* Mies Equip., Inc. v. NCI Bldg. Sys., 167 F. Supp. 2d 1077, 44 U.C.C. Rep. Serv. 2d 1017 (D. Minn. 2001) (commercial case) (evidence of course of dealing or consistent additional terms admissible only if clear and convincing).

315   Watkins & Son Pet Supplies v. The Iams Co., 254 F.3d 607, 44 U.C.C. Rep. Serv. 2d 708 (6th Cir. 2001) (not admissible if it would contradict the contract terms); *see also* Pioneer/Eclipse Corp. v. Kohler Co., 113 F. Supp. 2d 811, 44 U.C.C. Rep. Serv. 2d 59 (W.D.N.C. 2000) (commercial parties' course of dealing demonstrated their assent to limitations on seller's warranty).

316   Allapattah Services, Inc. v. Exxon Corp., 333 F.3d 1248, 50 U.C.C. Rep. Serv. 2d 1047 (11th Cir. 2003); Bank of Am. v. C.D. Smith Motor Co., 106 S.W.3d 425, 50 U.C.C. Rep. Serv. 2d 670 (Ark. 2003).

Add to text at end of subsection's first paragraph:

Implied warranties can also be created by a course of dealing or trade usage.[316.1]

316.1 U.C.C. § 2-316(3); *see* Conductores Monterrey v. Remee Prods. Corp., 45 U.C.C. Rep. Serv. 2d 111 (S.D.N.Y. 2000).

Page 116

Replace note 318 with:

318 U.C.C. § 1-205(1) [*The definition of course of dealing is carried over without change in revised U.C.C. § 1-303(b), which was approved by NCCUSL in 2001 for adoption by state legislatures. Revised U.C.C. § 1-303 is reprinted in Appx. E.6, infra.*]; *see* Duffin v. Idaho Crop Improvement Co., 126 Idaho 1002, 895 P.2d 1195 (Idaho 1995) (evidence of course of dealing admissible to show meaning of contract term).

Replace note 322 with:

322 U.C.C. § 1-205(2) [*This definition is carried over without change in revised U.C.C. § 1-303(b), which was approved by NCCUSL in 2001 for adoption by state legislatures. Revised U.C.C. § 1-303 is reprinted in Appx. E.6, infra.*]

Replace sentence containing note 323 with:

Unlike course of dealing and usage of trade, the current version of the UCC deals with course of performance in Article 2 rather than in Article 1. Section 2-208(1) provides: "Where a contract for sale involves repeated occasions for performance by either party with knowledge of the nature of the performance and opportunity for objection to it by the other, any course of performance accepted or acquiesced in without objection shall be relevant to determine the meaning of the agreement." Revised Article 1, approved by the National Conference of Commissioners on Uniform State Laws in 2001 for adoption by state legislatures, moves the treatment of course of performance to UCC § 1-303.[323] The definition of the term and the substantive rules are slightly reformulated but essentially the same. The major effect of the change is to apply course of performance rules to transactions governed by any Article of the UCC, not just those transactions covered by Articles 2 and 2A.

323 Revised U.C.C. § 1-303 is reprinted in Appx. E.6, *infra.*

Add new subsection to text after § 3.7.9.

3.7.9a The Parol Evidence Rule Does Not Protect Non-Parties to the Contract

The parol evidence rule is also inapplicable if it is being asserted by someone who is not a party to the contract that contains the integration clause. For example, the Eighth Circuit dealt with a case in which the buyers' contract with the dealer was integrated and set forth the final expression of the parties' agreement.[327.1] While the parol evidence rule barred the buyers from introducing evidence of any prior or contemporaneous agreements with the dealer, the parol evidence rule offered no protection to the manufacturer.

327.1 Holden Farms, Inc. v. Hog Slat, Inc., 347 F.3d 1055 (8th Cir. 2003).

Page 118

Add new subsection to text after § 3.7.11.

3.7.12 Parol Evidence Rule Does Not Affect Fraud and UDAP Claims

Regardless of whether parol evidence is admissible to supplement, explain, or contradict a contract, it is admissible in support of other claims such as fraud[342.1] and deceptive practices.[342.2] Even the traditional version of the parol evidence rule, as expressed by the Restatement (Second) of Contracts § 214, recognizes that agreements and negotiations prior to or contemporaneous with the adoption of a writing are admissible to establish "illegality, fraud, duress, mistake, lack of consideration, or other invalidating cause," and as grounds for "rescission, reformation, specific performance, or other remedy."

342.1 *See* § 11.1.1.2, *infra.*
342.2 *See* § 11.4.1, *infra.*

3.8 Does Express Warranty Conflict With Implied Warranties or Other Express Warranties?

3.8.1 Warranties Are To Be Construed To Cumulate Whenever Possible

Addition to note 344.

344   *See, e.g.*, Lara v. Hyundai Motor Am., 331 Ill. App. 3d 53, 264 Ill. Dec. 416, 770 N.E.2d 721 (2002) (existence of express warranty does not preclude claim for breach of implied warranty of merchantability).

Chapter 4   Implied Warranties

Page 123

4.1 Introduction

Addition to note 3.

3   *Add after "U.C.C. § 2-314(3)" citation*: Conductores Monterrey v. Remee Prods. Corp., 45 U.C.C. Rep. Serv. 2d 111 (S.D.N.Y. 2000); *cf.* Ramos v. Ford Motor Co., 655 N.W.2d 447 (S.D. 2002) (no implied warranty of merchantability arose from buyer's series of vehicle purchases, absent some conduct by seller that would establish a warranty).

Add to text at end of subsection's first paragraph:

Louisiana and Puerto Rico have non-UCC statutes that give buyers similar protections.[5.1]

5.1   La. Civ. Code Ann. art. 2520 (West) (creating a warranty against defects that render the item useless, or that make its use so inconvenient that the buyer would presumably not have bought it with knowledge of the defects); 31 P.R. Laws Ann. §§ 3841 (vendor is bound to give warranty against hidden defects), 3843 (buyer has right to either a partial price reduction or rescission of the contract).

4.2 Implied Warranty of Merchantability

4.2.1 Nature of the Warranty

Add to text after second sentence of subsection's first paragraph:

Louisiana, although it has not adopted UCC Article 2, recognizes a similar doctrine that there is an implied warranty that the item sold is free of hidden defects and reasonably fit for the buyer's intended use.[9.1]

9.1   Morrison v. Allstar Dodge, Inc., 792 So. 2d 9 (La. Ct. App. 2001).

Addition to note 11.

11   *But cf.* Evans v. Chrysler Fin. Corp., 13 Mass. L. Rptr. 156, 44 U.C.C. Rep. Serv. 2d 1003 (Mass. Super. Ct. 2001) (warranty does not arise unless possessory interest in goods is transferred; no warranty arose when potential buyer test-started car).

Page 124

Add to text at end of subsection's second paragraph:

A buyer who specifies a particular brandname does not thereby exclude or modify the implied warranty of merchantability.[12.1]

12.1   Commonwealth v. Johnson Insulation, 425 Mass. 650, 682 N.E.2d 1323 (1997); *see also* U.C.C. § 2-316 cmt. 9 (if buyer gives precise and complete specifications, implied warranty of merchantability may be displaced by express warranties); § 3.8, *supra*.

Add to text at end of subsection's third paragraph:

A specific designation of goods by the buyer does not exclude the implied warranty that they be fit for the general purposes appropriate for such goods.[15.1]

15.1   U.C.C. § 2-314 cmt. 3; Malul v. Capital Cabinets, Inc., 740 N.Y.S.2d 828, 47 U.C.C. Rep. Serv. 2d 502 (Civ. Ct. 2002); *cf.* U.C.C. § 2-316 cmt. 9 (if implied warranty of merchantability is inconsistent with express warranty that goods will comply with the designation, the express warranty displaces the implied warranty). *See generally* § 3.8.3, *supra*.

Add to text at end of subsection:

The defect must relate to the goods sold, not to other components of the product into which they are installed.[19.1]

19.1   Easley v. Day Motors, Inc., 796 So. 2d 236, 44 U.C.C. Rep. Serv. 2d 407 (Miss. Ct. App. 2001).

4.2.2 Parties Who Create Implied Warranty of Merchantability

4.2.2.1 Manufacturers and Other Non-Retailers

Addition to notes 21, 22.

21   *Replace Tucker citation with*: Tucker v. Gen. Motors Corp. (*Ex parte* Gen. Motors Corp.), 769 So. 2d 903, 40 U.C.C. Rep. Serv. 2d 123; *add*: Michels v. Monaco Coach Co., 2003 WL 23194248 (E.D. Mich. Dec. 31, 2003).

22   *Add at end of note: But cf.* Horton Homes, Inc. v. Brooks, 2001 Ala. LEXIS 431 (Ala. Nov. 30, 2001) (implied warranties do not normally arise against manufacturer but do when product has been specially manufactured for particular customer).

Page 125

4.2.2.2 "Merchant"

Addition to notes 28, 34.

28   *Replace Tucker citation with*: Tucker v. Gen. Motors Corp. (*Ex parte* Gen. Motors Corp.), 769 So. 2d 903, 40 U.C.C. Rep. Serv. 2d 123.

34   Ladner v. Jordan, 848 So. 2d 870, 49 U.C.C. Rep. Serv. 2d 138 (Miss. Ct. App. 2002).

Page 127

4.2.2.3 Merchant Must Be a Merchant With Respect to Goods of that Kind

Addition to note 44.

44   Malul v. Capital Cabinets, Inc., 740 N.Y.S.2d 828, 47 U.C.C. Rep. Serv. 2d 502 (Civ. Ct. 2002).

4.2.3 Standards for Determining if Good Is Merchantable

4.2.3.2 Fitness for the Ordinary Purposes

Page 128

4.2.3.2.1 Ordinary purposes

Addition to notes 48, 50, 54.

48   *Cf.* Pleasurecraft Marine Engine Co. v. Thermo Power Corp., 272 F.3d 654 (4th Cir. 2001) (Ohio law) (fact that goods are obsolete may make them unsellable, but not unmerchantable).

50   Kimpel v. Del. Pub. Auto Auction, 2001 WL 1555932 (Del. Ct. Com. Pl. Mar. 6, 2001) (car that could not pass state inspection was not merchantable because it was not fit for use on public highways).

54   *See also* Battersby v. Boyer (Am. Honda Motor Co. v. Boyer), 241 Ga. App. 115, 526 S.E.2d 159 (1999) (ATV was merchantable when it was fit for single rider use and seller did not know a passenger would ride it).

4.2.3.2.2 General meaning of fitness

Addition to note 57.

57   *But cf.* Hertzog v. WebTV Networks, Inc., 112 Wash. App. 1043, 48 U.C.C. Rep. Serv. 2d 558 (2002) ("universal" remote control device was merchantable even though it was not compatible with all television sets).

Page 129

4.2.3.2.3 Able to do ordinary job

Addition to notes 59, 60, 64.

59   Phoenix Color Corp. v. Krause Am., Inc., 46 U.C.C. Rep. Serv. 2d 442 (4th Cir. 2001) (unpublished) (Conn. law) (machine was not merchantable when design defects caused lengthy periods of down time for repairs); Eggl v. Letvin Equip. Co., 632 N.W.2d 435, 45 U.C.C. Rep. Serv. 2d 538 (N.D. 2001) (tractor that continually stalled was not merchantable); Mitchell v. BBB Services Co., 261 Ga. App. 240, 582 S.E.2d 470, 51 U.C.C. Rep. Serv. 2d 393 (2003) (bone chip made hamburger unmerchantable; rejecting foreign/natural test). *But cf.* Bako v. Crystal Cabinet Works, Inc., 44 U.C.C. Rep. Serv. 2d 1048 (Ohio Ct. App. 2001) (wood stain was merchantable when it properly colored the wood, even though it was incompatible with the sealer buyer used).

60   *Replace Tucker citation with*: Tucker v. Gen. Motors Corp. (*Ex parte* Gen. Motors Corp.), 769 So. 2d 903, 40 U.C.C. Rep. Serv. 2d 123.

64   Malul v. Capital Cabinets, Inc., 740 N.Y.S.2d 828, 47 U.C.C. Rep. Serv. 2d 502 (Civ. Ct. 2002) (kitchen cabinets).

4.2.3.2.4 Reasonable safety, efficiency, and comfort

Page 130

Add note 65.1 at end of subsection's first sentence.

65.1 *See, e.g.,* Spain v. Brown & Williamson Tobacco Corp., 50 U.C.C. Rep. Serv. 2d 1091 (Ala. 2003) (recognizing viability of claim that cigarettes' health hazards made them unmerchantable).

Addition to notes 66–70.

66 Holtzman v. Gen. Motors Corp., 48 U.C.C. Rep. Serv. 2d 1020 (Mass. Super. Ct. 2002) (dangerous vehicle jack is unmerchantable even if it has not yet caused injury); Solarz v. DaimlerChrysler Corp., 47 U.C.C. Rep. Serv. 2d 969 (Pa. C.P. 2002).

67 *See also* Erpelding v. Skipperliner Indus., Inc., 45 U.C.C. Rep. Serv. 2d 722 (D. Minn. 2001) (product that suddenly and without provocation bursts into flame is not merchantable); Cheminova Am. Corp. v. Corker, 779 So. 2d 1175 (Ala. 2000) (medicine had undisclosed ingredient that made it unsafe to use); Mitchell v. BBB Services Co., 261 Ga. App. 240, 582 S.E.2d 470, 51 U.C.C. Rep. Serv. 2d 393 (2003) (bone chip made hamburger unmerchantable; rejecting foreign/natural test); Wright v. Brooke Group Ltd., 652 N.W.2d 159 (Iowa 2002) (implied warranty of merchantability is breached by cigarettes' health dangers if the breach is based on defective design or inadequate warnings, even though they are in the condition intended by the manufacturer); Commonwealth v. Johnson Insulation, 425 Mass. 650, 682 N.E.2d 1323 (1997) (failure to warn of dangers made product unmerchantable); Otis Spunkmeyer, Inc. v. Blakely, 30 S.W.3d 678, 43 U.C.C. Rep. Serv. 2d 856 (Tex. App. 2000) (hard object in cookie dough).

68 *See* Austin v. Will-Burt Co., 232 F. Supp. 2d 682, 50 U.C.C. Rep. Serv. 2d 121 (N.D. Miss. 2002) (telescoping mast not unmerchantable when it functioned properly for many years, even though someone was ultimately electrocuted after it came into contact with power line).

69 Erpelding v. Skipperliner Indus., Inc., 45 U.C.C. Rep. Serv. 2d 722 (D. Minn. 2001) (product that suddenly and without provocation bursts into flame is not merchantable).

70 *See, e.g.,* Daley v. McNeil Consumer Products Co., 164 F. Supp. 2d 367, 45 U.C.C. Rep. Serv. 2d 770 (S.D.N.Y. 2001) (product still merchantable if a small percentage of people have allergic reaction); Mitchell v. BBB Services Co., 261 Ga. App. 240, 582 S.E.2d 470, 51 U.C.C. Rep. Serv. 2d 393 (2003) (bone chip made hamburger unmerchantable; rejecting foreign/natural test); Wright v. Brooke Group Ltd., 652 N.W.2d 159, 48 U.C.C. Rep. Serv. 2d 934 (Iowa 2002) (consumer has no implied warranty claim under manufacturing defect theory when cigarettes were in condition intended by manufacturer, but may recover if implied warranty claim arises from defective design or inadequate instructions or warnings).

4.2.3.2.5 Standards for used goods

Page 131

Addition to note 79.

79 Lipinski v. Martin J. Kelly Oldsmobile, Inc., 325 Ill. App. 3d 1139, 259 Ill. Dec. 586, 759 N.E.2d 66 (2001) (used car must be fit for ordinary purpose of driving, *i.e.*, must be safe and substantially free of defects; excessive oil consumption would be breach); Berney v. Rountree Olds-Cadillac Co., 763 So. 2d 799 (La. Ct. App. 2000) (implied warranty arises under Louisiana Civil Code that used goods will operate reasonably well for a reasonable period of time).

Replace note 80 with:

80 Cartillar v. Turbine Conversions, Ltd., 187 F.3d 858, 39 U.C.C. Rep. Serv. 2d 708 (8th Cir. 1999) (Ark. law).

4.2.3.2.6 Quality of similar goods

Addition to note 84.

84 *But cf.* Norcold, Inc. v. Gateway Supply Co., 51 U.C.C. Rep. Serv. 2d 88 (Ohio Ct. App. 2003) (unpublished) (newly-designed product could not be compared to other goods so did not breach implied warranty).

Page 132

Replace note 87 with:

87 For further discussion of odometer rollbacks as breaches of warranty, see § 14.5.2, *infra*, and National Consumer Law Center, Automobile Fraud § 8.2 (2d ed. 2003).

4.2.3.2.8 Government or industry standards

Addition to note 92.

92 *See also* § 14.10, *infra*.

Add to text after first sentence of subsection's third paragraph:

A car that, because of its inability to pass state inspection, can not be legally operated on the public highways is not fit for its ordinary purposes.[92.1]

92.1 Kimpel v. Del. Pub. Auto Auction, 2001 WL 1555932 (Del. Ct. Com. Pl. Mar. 6, 2001).

Addition to note 97.

> 97   CEF Enterprises v. Betts, 838 So. 2d 999 (Miss. Ct. App. 2003) (food can be unmerchantable even if it does not violate adulterated food laws).

Page 134

4.2.3.3 Adequately Contained, Packaged, and Labeled and in Conformity with the Container or Label

Addition to note 103.

> 103   Commonwealth v. Johnson Insulation, 425 Mass. 650, 682 N.E.2d 1323 (1997). *But see* Bako v. Crystal Cabinet Works, Inc., 44 U.C.C. Rep. Serv. 2d 1048 (Ohio Ct. App. 2001) (seller did not breach implied warranty of merchantability by delivering cans of wood stain without labels when parties' agreement did not require labeling).

4.2.3.4 Passing Without Objection in the Trade

Add note 104.1 at end of subsection's first paragraph.

> 104.1   *See* Contreras v. Ford Motor Co., 2002 WL 31727261 (Cal. Ct. App. Dec. 5, 2002) (unpublished) (error for trial court to give instruction that defined merchantability solely as fitness for ordinary purposes, because passing without objection in the trade has clearer focus on trade usage, similar goods, and the seller's conduct).

Add to text after sentence containing note 106:

A discrepancy in the model year alone may breach the implied warranty of merchantability, as a 2001 vehicle will not pass as a 2002 vehicle without exception.[106.1]

> 106.1   Terrell v. R & A Mfg. Partners, Ltd., 835 So. 2d 216, 50 U.C.C. Rep. Serv. 2d 151 (Ala. Civ. App. 2002).

Addition to note 107.

> 107   *But cf.* Norcold, Inc. v. Gateway Supply Co., 51 U.C.C. Rep. Serv. 2d 88 (Ohio Ct. App. 2003) (newly-designed product was not unmerchantable as there was no trade in goods of its kind).

4.3 Implied Warranty of Fitness for a Particular Purpose

4.3.2 Elements of the Warranty

Page 135

4.3.2.2 "The Seller"

Addition to note 114.

> 114   *Add after Renze Hybrids citation*: Ford Motor Co. v. Gen. Accident Ins. Co., 365 Md. 321, 779 A.2d 362, 45 U.C.C. Rep. Serv. 2d 319 (2001) (privity unnecessary if remote seller knows of particular purpose); *add after Duall Building Restoration, Inc. citation*: *See also* Morris Concrete v. Warrick, 2003 WL 21205836 (Ala. Civ. App. May 23, 2003) (ultimate user was third party beneficiary of warranty of fitness). *But cf.* Austin v. Will-Burt Co., 232 F. Supp. 2d 682, 50 U.C.C. Rep. Serv. 2d 121 (N.D. Miss. 2002) (warranty did not arise when buyer had no contact with remote seller).

Add to text after sentence containing note 114:

A dealer's actions can also create the warranty as to the manufacturer if the dealer is the manufacturer's agent.[114.1]

When a corporate buyer relies on the judgment of its own employee, but that employee is secretly in the pay of the seller, one court held that it was a question of fact whether an implied warranty of fitness for a particular purpose arose.[114.2]

> 114.1   Chase v. Kawasaki Motors Corp., 140 F. Supp. 2d 1280 (M.D. Ala. 2001) (dealer could create implied particular purpose warranty if manufacturer's agent, but not shown in this case).
> 114.2   Longwall-Associates, Inc. v. Wolfgang Preintalk GmbH, 46 U.C.C. Rep. Serv. 2d 651 (W.D. Va. 2002).

Add to text at end of subsection:

And the warranty only extends to the item of goods the seller sells, not the other components of the product into which it is installed.[115.1]

> 115.1   Easley v. Day Motors, Inc., 796 So. 2d 236, 44 U.C.C. Rep. Serv. 2d 407 (Miss. Ct. App. 2001).

4.3.2.3 "At the Time of Contracting Has Reason to Know"

Add to text after second sentence of subsection's first paragraph:

Simply communicating the buyer's purpose or requirements to the seller also suffices, without an explicit request that the seller select suitable goods.[115.2]

115.2   *In re* Simitar Entm't, Inc., 275 B.R. 331, 47 U.C.C. Rep. Serv. 2d 1343 (Bankr. D. Minn. 2002).

Page 136

Addition to note 120.

120   *See also* Ford Motor Co. v. Gen. Accident Ins. Co., 365 Md. 321, 779 A.2d 362, 45 U.C.C. Rep. Serv. 2d 319 (2001) (manufacturer's knowledge that chassis cab could be modified for use as tow truck did not, without more, create implied fitness warranty).

4.3.2.4 "Any Particular Purpose"

Page 137

4.3.2.4.1 General

Addition to note 125.

125   *See also* Bako v. Crystal Cabinet Works, Inc., 44 U.C.C. Rep. Serv. 2d 1048 (Ohio Ct. App. 2001) (implied warranty of fitness would be breached if seller sold stain that was incompatible with sealant buyer stated she was using; however, buyer failed to give timely notice of breach).

Replace § 4.3.2.4.2 heading with:

4.3.2.4.2 Case law finding ordinary purpose as particular purpose

Addition to note 129.

129   *Add to Thomas citation: questioned by* Ford Motor Co. v. Gen. Accident Ins. Co., 365 Md. 321, 779 A.2d 362, 45 U.C.C. Rep. Serv. 2d 319 (2001); *add*: Earls v. Condor Capital Corp., 2001 Conn. Super. LEXIS 2595 (Conn. Super. Ct. Aug. 30, 2001) (request for "safe and reliable" transportation is particular purpose).

Add to text after sentence containing note 136:

Likewise, the Alabama Supreme Court held that roadway transportation could be a particular purpose for a car.[136.1] A federal court interpreting Nebraska law held that the warranty can arise even though the buyer did not put the goods to an abnormal use.[136.2]

136.1   Bagley v. Mazda Motor Corp., 2003 WL 21040506 (Ala. May 9, 2003).
136.2   Outlook Windows P'ship v. York Int'l Corp., 112 F. Supp. 2d 877 (D. Neb. 2000).

Page 138

4.3.2.4.3 Case law finding ordinary purpose cannot be particular purpose

Addition to notes 140, 141, 145.

140   State *ex rel.* Stovall v. DVM Enterprises, Inc., 275 Kan. 243, 62 P.3d 653 (2003); Gall v. Allegheny County Health Dept., 521 Pa. 68, 555 A.2d 786, 790 (1989); *see also* Ford Motor Co. v. Gen. Accident Ins. Co., 365 Md. 321, 779 A.2d 362, 45 U.C.C. Rep. Serv. 2d 319 (2001) (quoting treatises which state that ordinary purpose can not be particular purpose, but stating in lengthy footnote that it is not deciding the issue); Malul v. Capital Cabinets, Inc., 740 N.Y.S.2d 828, 47 U.C.C. Rep. Serv. 2d 502 (Civ. Ct. 2002) (relying on seller's selection of "something good" is not a particular purpose).
141   *See also* Solarz v. DaimlerChrysler Corp., 47 U.C.C. Rep. Serv. 2d 969 (Pa. C.P. 2002) (safe and reliable family transportation is not a particular purpose).
145   *See also* Lithuanian Commerce Corp. v. Sara Lee Hosiery, 219 F. Supp. 2d 600, 48 U.C.C. Rep. Serv. 2d 922 (D.N.J. 2002) (use of pantyhose by Lithuanian women not a particular purpose); Oppenheimer v. York Int'l, 2002 WL 31409949 (Pa. C.P. Oct. 25, 2002) (efficiency, reliability, and economy of furnace are not particular purposes).

Page 140

4.3.2.5 "And That the Buyer Is Relying"

Addition to note 158.

158   *Replace Tucker citation with*: Tucker v. Gen. Motors Corp. (*Ex parte* Gen. Motors Corp.), 769 So. 2d 903, 40 U.C.C. Rep. Serv. 2d 123.

Add to text at end of subsection's first paragraph:

The person injured by the breach of the implied particular purpose warranty need not be the buyer and need not have relied on the seller.[160.1] Once the warranty arises, the question of who may recover for its breach is determined by the state's approach to horizontal privity.[160.2]

160.1   Chase v. Kawasaki Motors Corp., 140 F. Supp. 2d 1280 (M.D. Ala. 2001).
160.2   *See* § 6.3, *infra.*

Addition to notes 161, 162, 165.

Page 141

161   *But cf.* Norcold, Inc. v. Gateway Supply Co., 51 U.C.C. Rep. Serv. 2d 88 (Ohio Ct. App. 2003) (buyer who provided design sketches may still have relied on seller's skill and judgment).

162   Commonwealth v. Johnson Insulation, 425 Mass. 650, 682 N.E.2d 1323, 1327 (1997).

165   Jenkins v. Gen. Motors Corp., 240 Ga. App. 636, 524 S.E.2d 324 (1999) (no reliance on seller when commercial buyer owned many trucks).

Page 142

4.3.2.7 "To Select or Furnish Suitable Goods"

Addition to note 175.

175   *Add to end of note's second paragraph*: U.C.C. § 2-316 cmt. 9; Malul v. Capital Cabinets, Inc., 740 N.Y.S.2d 828, 47 U.C.C. Rep. Serv. 2d 502 (Civ. Ct. 2002).

4.3.4 Existence of Warranty Is Factual Issue

Page 143

4.3.4.1 General

Addition to note 189.

189   *See, e.g.,* Longwall-Associates, Inc. v. Wolfgang Preintalk GmbH, 46 U.C.C. Rep. Serv. 2d 651 (W.D. Va. 2002) (question of fact whether use of seller's mining equipment for a particular type of mining was a particular purpose).

Page 144

Add to text after "buyer's purpose" in subsection's last sentence:

, what the ordinary purpose is for certain goods,[189.1]

189.1   Longwall-Associates, Inc. v. Wolfgang Preintalk GmbH, 46 U.C.C. Rep. Serv. 2d 651 (W.D. Va. 2002) (question of fact whether use of seller's mining equipment for a particular type of mining was a particular purpose).

4.4 Effect of Presale Inspection

4.4.1 General

Addition to note 194.

194   *See* Hays v. Gen. Elec. Co., 151 F. Supp. 2d 1001, 45 U.C.C. Rep. Serv. 2d 449 (N.D. Ill. 2001) (no implied warranties for motors purchased after commercial buyer's testing showed that they were overheating).

Page 145

Add to text after subsection's third paragraph:

Section 2-316(3)(b) applies only to implied warranties, not express warranties.[200.1] Express warranties are vitiated, however, if the buyer has actual knowledge of the nonconformity before buying because, in that case, the express warranties can not be part of the basis of the bargain.[200.2]

200.1   *See* Johann, Inc. v. City Motors, Inc., 2002 WL 31684970 (Cal. Ct. App. Dec. 2, 2002) (unpublished); Goldwater v. Ollie's Garage, 1998 Conn. Super. LEXIS 456 (Conn. Super. Ct. Feb. 17, 1998).

200.2   *See* § 3.2.5.4, *supra*.

4.4.2 Ways to Avoid Presale Inspection Problems

4.4.2.1 Defects That Could Not Reasonably Have Been Discovered

Addition to note 203.

203   Rawson v. Conover, 20 P.3d 876, 44 U.C.C. Rep. Serv. 2d 420 (Utah 2001). *But see* Bumgarner v. Lowe's Companies, 51 U.C.C. Rep. Serv. 2d 112 (N.C. Ct. App. 2003) (unpublished) (no implied warranty of merchantability when invoice said "as is" and buyer examined truck when he submitted bid, even though defect arose after inspection).

Page 146

4.4.2.4 Necessity of Demand by Seller Where Consumer Fails to Inspect Goods

Addition to note 211.

211   *Cf.* Ladner v. Jordan, 848 So. 2d 870, 49 U.C.C. Rep. Serv. 2d 138 (Miss. Ct. App. 2002) (no implied warranty of fitness when buyer twice refused to examine goods; court does not say whether seller made demand).

Add to text at end of subsection:

The revised version of Article 2, which the National Conference of Commissioners on Uniform State Laws approved in 2003 for consideration by state legislatures, moves this requirement into the text of the statute.[211.1]

211.1   Revised U.C.C. § 2-316(3)(b). Selected portions of revised Article 2 are reproduced in Appx. E.7S, *infra*, and on the CD-Rom accompanying this volume.

Page 147

4.4.3 Dealing With Contract Clauses Stating That the Buyer Has Examined the Goods

Replace note 217 with:

217   National Consumer Law Center, Unfair and Deceptive Acts and Practices (5th ed. 2001 and Supp.).

Add to text at end of subsection:

Such a clause may also be unconscionable.[217.1]

217.1   Tri-Continental Leasing Corp. v. Law Office of Richard W. Burns, 710 S.W.2d 604 (Tex. App. 1985).

Replace § 4.5 with:

4.5 Warranty of Title

4.5.1 Nature and Creation of Warranty of Title

Every contract for sale implies a warranty by the seller that the title conveyed is good and its transfer rightful, and that the goods will be delivered free from any security interest or other lien or encumbrance of which the buyer at the time of contracting has no knowledge.[221] Under the revised version of UCC Article 9, effective July 1, 2001 in most states, the implied warranty of title is also made by a secured party upon resale of repossessed goods.[222] To defeat the warranty, the buyer must have actual knowledge of the title defect, not merely constructive knowledge.[223]

Warranty of title can be excluded or modified only by specific language or by circumstances which give the buyer reason to know of the title defect.[224] A disclaimer must describe what the seller is or is not conveying, rather than merely describing how the seller's liability will be limited.[225]

A warranty of title claim should be considered if a seller transfers goods that are stolen or subject to an undisclosed lien to the consumer. Many cases hold that the warranty is breached when another claimant merely asserts a colorable challenge to the buyer's title, forcing the buyer into a contest over ownership.[226] There is no need to show that the seller knew of the problem with the title, as the warranty arises by operation of law regardless of the seller's knowledge.[227] There must be more than a mere temporary interference with the buyer's possession, however. For example, if the police seize the property because of a false report that it is stolen, but then promptly return it to the buyer, the buyer does not have a claim for breach of the warranty of title.[228]

The warranty of title may also be breached when there is a discrepancy between what the title describes and what the consumer receives. For example, giving the consumer title to a 1985 Corvette with a certain vehicle identification number (VIN), but delivering a car that is partly a 1985 Corvette and partly made up of components of other vehicles with an assortment of VINs is a breach of the warranty of title.[229]

The warranty of title is also breached if the seller fails to transfer title after selling the goods to the consumer.[230] In such a case, the goods subject to the contract for sale are not delivered free of encumbrances. Failure to deliver title documents may be sufficient to constitute a breach of the implied warranty of title.[231] But when a seller had and conveyed legal title and made it clear to the buyer, another car dealer, that the vehicle was flood-damaged and had an out-of-state salvage title, there was no implied representation about the type of in-state title for which the vehicle would qualify, that is, whether the state would issue a rebuilt salvage title.[232]

Another situation in which warranty of title issues arise is the sale of "gray market" vehicles—vehicles manufactured for sale outside the United States—which may not meet U.S. safety and emissions standards.[233] If the state refuses to issue a certificate of title because of these defects, it is a breach of the implied warranty of title.[234] Particularly when the seller is not acting in good faith, the requirement of a timely notice of breach should be very liberally construed in favor of the buyer.[235]

4.5.2 Defending the Buyer's Title

Sometimes the seller who breached the warranty of title has disappeared or it would be impossible to collect a judgment against them. In such a case the buyer may want to defend her right to the goods. While a thief cannot transfer good title to a vehicle, a person who acquires a vehicle by fraud may obtain title that is merely voidable rather than void.[236] Then that person may be able to transfer good title to a good faith purchaser.[237]

In addition, in contrast to the common law, UCC § 2-403 provides that, when an owner entrusts goods to a merchant who deals in goods of that kind, the merchant has the power to transfer all rights of the entruster to a buyer in the ordinary course of business.[238] This is so notwithstanding any conditions agreed to between the entruster and the merchant, and even if the merchant procured the entrustment of the goods by criminal fraud.[239] Thus, when individuals placed their vehicles with a car dealer on consignment, the dealer had the power to transfer good title to buyers, even though the dealer misappropriated the buyers' payments.[240] In another case, the title owner sold a car to a dealer, but then the dealer's check bounced and the owner refused to sign the title over to the dealer. The dealer still had authority to pass good title to a good faith retail buyer.[241]

The issue is more complicated, however, in strict title states where by statute or case law the sale is absolutely void unless the certificate of title has been delivered to the buyer.[242] The Ohio Supreme Court resolved a case in which the title owner sold vehicles to a dealer but held back the titles.[243] The dealer sold the vehicles to a commercial buyer but never paid the title owner, and the title owner refused to turn over the titles. The court held that the state's motor vehicle title law controlled over UCC § 2-403 and that, therefore, the commercial buyer did not acquire title to the vehicles.[244] However, a decision from Missouri, a strict title state, holds that a consumer who buys a car from a dealer can force the dealer's floor plan financer to turn over the title to the consumer even though the dealer's pay-off check to the floor plan financer bounced.[245]

4.5.3 Available Causes of Action

In addition to claims under the UCC, the consumer will probably have a cause of action under the state unfair and deceptive acts and practices (UDAP) statute if the seller breaches the implied warranty of title.[246] The buyer will often have a fraud claim against a seller who sells goods without title. An advantage of a warranty claim is that many insurance policies exclude fraud. Breach of the warranty of title may also amount to a breach of the implied warranty of merchantability, especially if the car can not be driven or transferred because of the title problems. Other possible claims include breach of contract and negligent misrepresentation.

If the dealer made a practice of selling cars without title because it was not paying the prior owners of the cars, the liability of other parties involved in the transactions should be investigated. The dealer's floor plan financer, for example, probably knew that the dealer was becoming slower and slower in paying the prior owners of the vehicles. The financing entity to which the dealer referred buyers may have known that the dealer was failing to obtain titles promptly for the vehicles it was selling. By continuing to finance deals, these players may have assisted the fraud.

221   U.C.C. § 2-312(1).

222   U.C.C. § 9-610(d) ("a contract for sale, lease, license, or other disposition [by secured party] includes the warranties relating to title, possession, quiet enjoyment, and the like which by operation of law accompany a voluntary disposition of property of the kind subject to the contract"); *see also* U.C.C. § 2-312 cmt. 5 (revised "Section 9-610 provides that a disposition of collateral includes warranties such as those provided by" section 2-312).

223   U.C.C. § 2-312 cmt. 1; *see, e.g.,* Christopher v. McGehee, 124 Ga. App. 310, 183 S.E.2d 624, *aff'd*, 228 Ga. 466 (1971).

224   U.C.C. § 2-312(2); *see also* U.C.C. § 2-312 cmt. 6. See also revised U.C.C. § 9-610(d) and (e), which provides that, unless disclaimed, a secured creditor gives implied warranties of title upon resale of repossessed collateral. Revised U.C.C. § 9-610(f) provides the following sample disclaimer language: "There is no warranty relating to title, possession, quiet enjoyment, or the like in this disposition."

225   Moore v. Pro-Team Corvette Sales, Inc., 786 N.E.2d 903, 48 U.C.C. Rep. Serv. 2d 528 (Ohio Ct. App. 2002).

226   *See, e.g.,* Frank Arnold Contractors, Inc. v. Vilsmeier Auction Co., 806 F.2d 462 (3d Cir. 1986) (cloud on title is sufficient; plaintiff need not establish existence of paramount or superior title in third party); Crook Motor Co. v. Goolsby, 703 F. Supp. 511 (N.D. Miss. 1988); Sumner v. Fel-Air, Inc., 680 P.2d 1109 (Alaska 1984) ("substantial shadow" on title is a breach); Smith v. Russ, 13 S.W.3d 920, 44 U.C.C. Rep. Serv. 2d 1036 (Ark. Ct. App. 2000) (buyer did not have burden of proving that car was stolen); Maroone Chevrolet, Inc. v. Nordstrom, 587 So. 2d 514 (Fla. Dist. Ct. App. 1991); Jefferson v. Jones, 408 A.2d 1036 (Md. 1979); Saber v. Dan Angelone Chevrolet, Inc., 811 A.2d 644 (R.I. 2002) (police impoundment breaches warranty of title even if car is ultimately determined not to be stolen); Colton v. Decker, 540 N.W.2d 172, 30 U.C.C. Rep. 2d 206 (S.D. 1995) (when police questioned buyer's ownership of truck because of conflicting vehicle identification numbers and improper title, buyer has claim for breach of warranty of title; citing cases); Trial v. McCoy, 553 S.W.2d 199 (Tex. Civ. App. 1977) (buyer had claim for breach of warranty of title when police took the goods on information that they were stolen; buyer did not have to prove that they actually were stolen). Revised U.C.C. § 2-312(1)(a), approved by the National Conference of Commissioners on Uniform State Laws in 2003 for consideration by state legislatures, explicitly adopts this view.

227   Robinson v. Durham, 537 So. 2d 966 (Ala. Civ. App. 1988) (innocent sale of stolen car is breach); Brokke v. Williams, 766 P.2d 1311 (Mont. 1989); Shelton v. Tidwell, 2001 Tenn. App. LEXIS 628 (Tenn. Ct. App. Aug. 21, 2001); *see also* Smith v. Russ, 13 S.W.3d 920, 44 U.C.C. Rep. Serv. 2d 1036 (Ark. Ct. App. 2000) (buyer did not have to prove that car was stolen).

228   Ammons v. Baker-Jackson Nissan, 2001 Tex. App. LEXIS 6174 (Tex. App. Sept. 6, 2001). *But cf.* Saber v. Dan Angelone Chevrolet, Inc., 811 A.2d 644 (R.I. 2002) (long-term police impoundment is breach even if car is ultimately determined not to be stolen).

229   Saber v. Dan Angelone Chevrolet, Inc., 811 A.2d 644 (R.I. 2002).

230   *See, e.g.,* Bunch v. Signal Oil & Gas Co., 505 P.2d 41 (Colo. Ct. App. 1972) (construing certificate of title statute with U.C.C.); *see also* Smith v. Russ, 13 S.W.3d 920, 44 U.C.C. Rep. Serv. 2d 1036 (Ark. Ct. App. 2000).

231   *See* Bunch v. Signal Oil & Gas Co., 505 P.2d 41 (Colo. Ct. App. 1972) (construing certificate of title statute with U.C.C.); Robinson v. Densman, 470 S.W.2d 451 (Tex. Civ. App. 1971) (construing certificate of title statute alone); 67A Am. Jur. 2d *Sales* § 808 (1985); *see also* Ammons v. Baker-Jackson Nissan, 2001 Tex. App. LEXIS 6174 at n.6 (Tex. App. Sept. 6, 2001); H.E.D. Sales, Inc. v. Szelc, 596 S.W.2d 299 (Tex. Civ. App. 1980), *rev'd on other grounds*, 603 S.W.2d 803 (Tex. 1980); *cf.* Trial v. McCoy, 553 S.W.2d 199 (Tex. Civ. App. 1977).

232   Roberts v. D & W Auto Sales, 2002 WL 770652 (Tex. App. Apr. 30, 2002) (unpublished).

233   *See* § 13.7, *infra.*

234   *See* Elmore v. Doenges Bros. Ford, Inc., 21 P.3d 65 (Okla. Civ. App. 2000).

235   U.C.C. § 2-312 cmt. 2.

236   Midway Auto Sales, Inc. v. Clarkson, 71 Ark. App. 316, 29 S.W.3d 788, 45 U.C.C. Rep. Serv. 2d 1062 (2000); Marlow v. Conley, 787 N.E.2d 490, 50 U.C.C. Rep. Serv. 2d 712 (Ind. Ct. App. 2003); Kubota Credit Corp. v. Tillman, 49 U.C.C. Rep. Serv. 2d 926 (Tenn. Ct. App. 2002); Saenz v. Big H Auto Auction, Inc., 653 S.W.2d 521 (Tex. App. 1983), *aff'd on other grounds,* 665 S.W.2d 756 (Tex. 1984).

237   Midway Auto Sales, Inc. v. Clarkson, 71 Ark. App. 316, 29 S.W.3d 788, 45 U.C.C. Rep. Serv. 2d 1062 (2000); Marlow v. Conley, 787 N.E.2d 490, 50 U.C.C. Rep. Serv. 2d 712 (Ind. Ct. App. 2003) (buyers were good faith purchasers even though they knew title was not in seller's name, when seller offered an explanation).

238   U.C.C. § 2-403; *see, e.g.,* Duke Wholesale, Inc. v. Pitchford, 56 S.W.3d 399 (Ark. Ct. App. 2001) (good faith buyer obtained good title to car bought from dealer even though wholesaler kept title certificate); Keybank Nat'l Ass'n v. Mascarenas, 17 P.3d 209, 43 U.C.C. Rep. Serv. 2d 580 (Colo. Ct. App. 2000); Right Touch of Class, Inc. v. Super. Bank, 244 Ga. App. 473, 536 S.E.2d 181, 44 U.C.C. Rep. Serv. 2d 1055 (2000); Christopher v. McGehee, 124 Ga. App. 310, 183 S.E.2d 624 (1971); Marlow v. Conley, 787 N.E.2d 490, 50 U.C.C. Rep. Serv. 2d 712 (Ind. Ct. App. 2003); Madrid v. Bloomington Auto Co., 782 N.E.2d 386, 49 U.C.C. Rep. Serv. 2d 795 (Ind. Ct. App. 2003); Byrne Fund Mgmt., Inc. v. Jim Lynch Cadillac, Inc., 922 S.W.2d 434 (Mo. Ct. App. 1996) (by entrusting vehicle to dealer, floor plan financer gave dealer power to transfer it to buyer in ordinary course of business); KDG Auto Sales, Inc. v. Asta Funding, Inc., 781 A.2d 202, 45 U.C.C. Rep. Serv. 2d 800 (Pa. Super. Ct. 2001).

239   U.C.C. § 2-403.

240   Keybank Nat'l Ass'n v. Mascarenas, 17 P.3d 209, 43 U.C.C. Rep. Serv. 2d 580 (Colo. Ct. App. 2000); Madrid v. Bloomington Auto Co., 782 N.E.2d 386, 49 U.C.C. Rep. Serv. 2d 795 (Ind. Ct. App. 2003).

241   Right Touch of Class, Inc. v. Super. Bank, 244 Ga. App. 473, 536 S.E.2d 181, 44 U.C.C. Rep. Serv. 2d 1055 (2000); *accord* Mitchell Motors, Inc. v. Barnett, 549 S.E.2d 445, 46 U.C.C. Rep. Serv. 2d 655 (Ga. Ct. App. 2001).

242   *See* National Consumer Law Center, Repossessions and Foreclosures § 3.5.7 (5th ed. 2002 and Supp.).

243   Saturn of Kings Automall, Inc. v. Mike Albert Leasing, Inc., 92 Ohio St. 3d 513, 751 N.E.2d 1019, 45 U.C.C. Rep. Serv. 2d 478 (2001).

244   *But cf.* Marlow v. Conley, 787 N.E.2d 490, 50 U.C.C. Rep. Serv. 2d 712 (Ind. Ct. App. 2003) (buyer obtained title even though manner of transferring title violated state law).

245   Bradley v. K & E Investments, Inc., 847 S.W.2d 915 (Mo. Ct. App. 1993); *see also* Strebler v. Hampton Metro Bank, 686 S.W.2d 28 (Mo. Ct. App. 1985) (reversing dismissal of buyer's petition for order requiring lienholder to transfer title to buyer even though seller's pay-off check bounced).

246   Antle v. Reynolds, 15 S.W.3d 762 (Mo. Ct. App. 2000); Cardwell v. Tom Harrigan Oldsmobile, Inc., 1984 Ohio App. LEXIS 10104 (Ohio Ct. App. June 27, 1984); Saenz v. Big H Auto Auction, Inc., 665 S.W.2d 756 (Tex. 1984); Trial v. McCoy, 553 S.W.2d 199 (Tex. Civ. App. 1977). *See generally* § 11.1, *infra*.

Chapter 5

Fourteen Ways to Defeat Warranty Disclaimers

Page 150

5.2 No Disclaimer of Express Warranties

Addition to notes 6, 9, 12.

6 *See* Select Pork, Inc. v. Babcock Swine, Inc., 640 F.2d 147 (8th Cir. 1981); Hercules Mach. Corp. v. McElwee Bros., Inc., 49 U.C.C. Rep. Serv. 2d 72 (E.D. La. 2002); Fassi v. Auto Wholesalers, 145 N.H. 404, 762 A.2d 1034 (2000) (holding that N.H. Rev. Stat. Ann. § 382-A:2-316(3)(a) only applies to implied warranties); Fletcher v. Don Foss of Cleveland, Inc., 90 Ohio App. 3d 82, 628 N.E.2d 60 (1993) (language that car had warranty overrode contrary language); Materials Mktg. Corp. v. Spencer, 40 S.W.3d 172, 43 U.C.C. Rep. Serv. 2d 1131 (Tex. App. 2001); *see also* Smart Online, Inc. v. Opensite Technologies, Inc., 51 U.C.C. Rep. Serv. 2d 47 (N.C. Super. Ct. 2003) (warranty by description is very hard to waive). *But see* Boud v. SDNCO, Inc., 54 P.3d 1131 (Utah 2002) (disclaimer of any express warranties created during negotiation was effective); *cf.* Sun-Lite Glazing Contractors, Inc. v. J.E. Berkowitz, Ltd. P'ship, 49 U.C.C. Rep. Serv. 2d 483 (4th Cir. 2002) (unpublished) (Md. law) (because of limited warranty, buyer had no warranty claim for erroneous installation instructions included with product; court only analyzes implied warranty theories, not express warranty).

Page 151

9 James River Equip. Co. v. Beadle County Equip., Inc., 646 N.W.2d 265, 48 U.C.C. Rep. Serv. 2d 105 (S.D. 2002). *But see* T.T. Exclusive Cars, Inc. v. Christie's Inc., 1996 WL 737204 (S.D.N.Y. Dec. 24, 1996) (auction house's disclaimer overrode description of goods printed in catalog).

Page 152

12 Blankenship v. Northtown Ford, Inc., 95 Ill. App. 3d 303, 420 N.E.2d 167 (1981) (new car).

Page 153

5.3 Magnuson-Moss Warranty Act Bar on Implied Warranty Disclaimers

Add to text after bulleted item containing note 27:

• Implied warranties can not be limited in duration at all if the seller enters into a service contract with the buyer.[27.1]

27.1 Advisory Opinion, 92 F.T.C. 1050, 1978 FTC LEXIS 73 (Fed. Trade Comm'n Nov. 30, 1978). This opinion is included on the CD-Rom accompanying this volume.

Addition to note 31.

31 *See* Montgomery v. Mobile Home Estates, Inc., 1984 Ohio App. LEXIS 9239 (Ohio Ct. App. Apr. 20, 1984).

5.4 State Statutory Restrictions on Implied Warranty Disclaimers

Add to text after subsection's first paragraph:

Alabama precludes disclaimers as to personal injury claims in the case of consumer goods.[35.1]

35.1 Ala. Code § 7-2-316(5); *see* Bagley v. Mazda Motor Corp., 2003 WL 21040506 (Ala. May 9, 2003).

Addition to notes 39, 40, 46.

39 *See also* State *ex rel.* Stovall v. DVM Enterprises, Inc., 275 Kan. 243, 62 P.3d 653 (2003) (any attempt to disclaim implied warranties is void; seeking waiver is not a UDAP violation in and of itself but is one factor to be considered in determining unconscionability); *cf.* Tufts v. Newmar Corp., 53 F. Supp. 2d 1171 (D. Kan. 1999) (not a UDAP violation to include disclaimer in Kansas contract when it clearly stated that it did not apply in states that prohibited it).

Page 154

40 *See also* Berney v. Rountree Olds-Cadillac Co., 763 So. 2d 799 (La. Ct. App. 2000) (waiver of warranty was ineffective because not clear and unambiguous); Chaudoir v. Porsche Cars of N. Am., 667 So. 2d 569 (La. Ct. App. 1996) (waiver ineffective when not brought to buyer's attention).

46 *See* Cooper Indus., Inc. v. Tarmac Roofing Sys., Inc., 276 F.3d 704 (5th Cir. 2002) (prohibition only applies to consumer transactions); Mercury Marine v. Clear River Constr. Co., 839 So. 2d 508, 49 U.C.C. Rep. Serv. 2d 989 (Miss. 2003) (noting prohibition of disclaimers).

Add to text after sentence containing note 53:

This prohibition overrides the UCC disclaimer provisions.[53.1] It preserves implied warranties even when the seller gives a short-term, limited express warranty.[53.2]

> 53.1   Wolfe v. Welton, 210 W. Va. 563, 558 S.E.2d 363 (2001).
>
> 53.2   *Id.*

5.5 UCC Requires Use of the Word "Merchantability" or Language Such As "As Is"

Addition to note 56.

> 56   U.C.C. § 2-316(3)(a).

Add to text at end of subsection:

The revised version of Article 2, which the National Conference of Commissioners on Uniform State Laws adopted in 2003 for consideration by state legislatures, changes the language that must be used to disclaim implied warranties in consumer contracts. Instead of mentioning merchantability, a disclaimer of the implied warranty of merchantability must state: "The seller undertakes no responsibility for the quality of goods except as otherwise provided in this contract."[57.1] To disclaim the implied warranty of fitness for a particular purpose the seller must state: "The seller assumes no responsibility that the goods will be fit for any particular purpose for which you may be buying these goods, except as otherwise provided in the contract."[57.2] In the alternative, the seller can use a term such as "as is" to disclaim both implied warranties.[57.3]

> 57.1   Revised U.C.C. § 2-316(2).
>
> 57.2   Revised U.C.C. § 2-316(2), (3).
>
> 57.3   Revised U.C.C. § 2-316(3).

5.6 Only Party Drafting the Disclaimer Usually Protected

Addition to note 65.

> 65   *See also* Hou-Tex, Inc. v. Landmark Graphics, 26 S.W.3d 103, 43 U.C.C. Rep. Serv. 2d 306 (Tex. App. 2000) (disclaimer applied to customer of retail buyer).

5.7 Where Disclaimer Not Available Before Contract Is Signed

Addition to note 66.

> 66   Terrell v. R & A Mfg. Partners, Ltd., 835 So. 2d 216, 50 U.C.C. Rep. Serv. 2d 151 (Ala. Civ. App. 2002); Womco, Inc. v. Navistar Int'l Corp., 84 S.W.3d 272, 48 U.C.C. Rep. Serv. 2d 130 (Tex. App. 2002) (disclaimer must be communicated to buyer before contract is finalized). *But see* i.LAN Sys., Inc. v. Netscout Serv. Level Corp., 183 F. Supp. 2d 328 (D. Mass. 2002) (adopting idea of "payment first, terms later" to uphold disclaimer and remedy limitation in clickwrap license that was delivered only with the product).

Add to text after phrase containing note 70:

printed on a post-sale repair order,[70.1]

> 70.1   Contreras v. Ford Motor Co., 2002 WL 31727261 (Cal. Ct. App. Dec. 5, 2002) (unpublished) (repair order's disclaimer, which was illegible on consumer's copy, ineffective when it was inconsistent with warranty given at sale).

Add to text at end of subsection:

Another problem with a post-sale disclaimer from the seller's point of view is that it may be difficult to prove that the buyer received the disclaimer if it is not part of the signed contract. If the buyer never received the disclaimer, it is not effective.[76.1]

> 76.1   McLaughlin v. Denharco, Inc., 129 F. Supp. 2d 32, 43 U.C.C. Rep. Serv. 2d 1122 (D. Me. 2001); S.H. Nevers Corp. v. Husky Hydraulics, Inc., 408 A.2d 676 (Me. 1979); Materials Mktg. Corp. v. Spencer, 40 S.W.3d 172, 43 U.C.C. Rep. Serv. 2d 1131 (Tex. App. 2001).

Replace § 5.8 heading with: **5.8 Disclaimer Must Be Conspicuous**

5.8.1 General Requirement

Replace subsection's first sentence with:

The buyer's expectations from the transaction are further protected by the requirement of section 2-316(2) that any disclaimer of the implied warranty of fitness for a particular purpose must be in writing and conspicuous, and that any written disclaimer of the implied warranty of merchantability must be conspicuous.[77]

> 77   [*Retain as in main edition.*]

Add to text after subsection's first paragraph:

The language of section 2-316(2) appears to contemplate that the implied warranty of merchantability, although not the implied warranty of fitness for a particular purpose, can be excluded orally. Courts may invalidate oral disclaimers that are not drawn to the buyer's attention. One court held that an oral disclaimer at the start of an auction was ineffective when it was not stressed or amplified in any way, it was stated only once even though the auction lasted several hours, and the buyer had not in fact heard it.[80.1] The revised version of Article 2, which the National Conference of Commissioners on Uniform State Laws (NCCUSL) approved in 2003 for consideration by state legislatures, requires that, in a consumer contract, a disclaimer of the implied warranty of merchantability or the implied warranty of fitness be in a written or electronic document (termed a "record").[80.2] There is an exception, however, when the seller uses a term such as "as is" or "with all faults" to disclaim the warranty. In that case, the disclaimer need be in a written or electronic document only if the contract is evidenced by a record.[80.3] This exception appears to allow, for example, "as is" disclaimers to be in signs located above the goods. For non-consumer contracts, revised Article 2 does not require that a disclaimer of the implied warranty of merchantability be in a document. A disclaimer of the implied warranty of fitness, however, must be in a document unless a term such as "as is" is used.[80.4]

> 80.1   Regan Purchase & Sales Corp. v. Primavera, 328 N.Y.S.2d 490, 10 U.C.C. Rep. Serv. 858 (Civ. Ct. 1972).
> 80.2   *See* Revised U.C.C. § 2-103(m); Revised U.C.C. § 1-201(a)(31) (definition of record). Selected portions of revised Article 2 are reproduced in Appx. E.7S, *infra*, and on the CD-Rom accompanying this volume.
> 80.3   Revised U.C.C. § 2-316(2), (3).
> 80.4   Revised U.C.C. § 2-316(2), (3); *see* Official Comment 3 to Revised U.C.C. § 2-316.

Page 159

Addition to note 81.

> 81   Mich. Dessert Corp. v. A.E. Staley Mfg. Corp., 46 U.C.C. Rep. Serv. 2d 642 (6th Cir. 2001) (Mich. law) (disclaimer placed at bottom of each page of data sheet was conspicuous in commercial case).

Add to text at end of subsection:

In 2001, NCCUSL approved a revised version of UCC Article 1 that includes a revised definition of "conspicuous":[81.1]

> "Conspicuous," with reference to a term, means so written, displayed, or presented that a reasonable person against which it is to operate ought to have noticed it. Whether a term is "conspicuous" is a decision for the court. Conspicuous terms include the following:
>   (A) a heading in capitals equal to or greater in size than the surrounding text, or in contrasting type, font, or color to the surrounding text of the same or lesser size; and
>   (B) language in the body of a record or display in larger type than the surrounding text, or in contrasting type, font, or color to the surrounding text of the same size, or set off from surrounding text of the same size by symbols or other marks that call attention to the language.

This definition deletes the outmoded reference to telegrams, and adds the concept that language can be conspicuous if it is set off from other text by symbols or marks. The comments add an important point: that text that has the listed characteristics of conspicuousness—font size, contrasting color, and so forth—can still fail to meet the standard if it is not written, displayed, or presented in a way so that a reasonable person ought to have noticed it. Thus, text that has the bells and whistles of conspicuousness but is cleverly designed to be overlooked by the consumer is not conspicuous.[81.2]

The revised version of Article 2 takes this definition verbatim from the revised version of Article 1, but then adds a special example of conspicuousness for electronic transactions: "a term that is so placed in a record or display that the person or electronic agent may not proceed without taking action with respect to the particular term."[81.3] The Official Comments to revised Article 2 reiterate that, regardless of type size, color, font, or other features, a term is not conspicuous unless a reasonable person ought to have noticed it.[81.4]

81.1   Revised U.C.C. § 1-201(b)(10).
81.2   Official Comment 10 to Revised U.C.C. § 1-201.
81.3   Revised U.C.C. § 2-103(1)(b). Selected portions of revised Article 2 are reproduced in Appx. E.7S, *infra*, and on the CD-Rom accompanying this volume.
81.4   Official Comment 2 to Revised U.C.C. § 2-103.

5.8.2 Type Size and Appearance

Addition to notes 82, 85.

82   *See, e.g.*, Erpelding v. Skipperliner Indus., Inc., 45 U.C.C. Rep. Serv. 2d 722 (D. Minn. 2001) (fact that agreement as a whole was conspicuous not sufficient when disclaimer was in same font and was capitalized the same as rest of contract); *see also* UPS Truck Leasing, Inc. v. Leaseway Transfer Pool, Inc., 27 S.W.3d 174, 45 U.C.C. Rep. Serv. 2d 380 (Tex. App. 2000) (bold headings did not make indemnity agreement conspicuous as headings merely said "Customer Agrees").

Page 160

85   *Replace Vision Graphics citation with*: 41 F. Supp. 2d 93, 38 U.C.C. Rep. Serv. 2d 78; *replace Gooch citation with*: 40 F. Supp. 2d 863, 38 U.C.C. Rep. Serv. 2d 796; *add: See, e.g.*, Voelker v. Porsche Cars N. Am., Inc., 2003 WL 22930364 (7th Cir. Dec. 12, 2003) (bold type on face of lease); McLaughlin v. Denharco, Inc., 129 F. Supp. 2d 32, 43 U.C.C. Rep. Serv. 2d 1122 (D. Me. 2001) (disclaimer in larger type, all capitals, set apart from other text, was conspicuous); Haight v. Dale's Used Cars, Inc., 51 U.C.C. Rep. Serv. 2d 1017 (Idaho Ct. App. 2003) (bold capital lettering above buyer's signature and on Buyers Guide); Basselen v. Gen. Motors Corp., 341 Ill. App. 3d 278, 792 N.E.2d 498 (2003) ("as is" in all caps and large font, halfway down buyer's order, is conspicuous); Smith v. Radam, Inc., 51 S.W.3d 413, 45 U.C.C. Rep. Serv. 2d 796 (Tex. App. 2001) ("as is" in large capital letters and in bold face on buyer's guide was effective).

Page 161

5.8.3 Disclaimers on the Back of Contract

Addition to notes 87, 88.

87   Rawson v. Conover, 20 P.3d 876, 44 U.C.C. Rep. Serv. 2d 420 (Utah 2001) (disclaimer in capital letters on back of contract upheld; buyer also signed Buyers Guide stating "no warranty" and knew there was no warranty).

88   *See* Watson v. Damon Corp., 2002 WL 32059736 (W.D. Mich. Dec. 17, 2002) (conspicuous disclaimer on back, referred to by conspicuous language on front, is effective); Christopher v. Larson Ford Sales, Inc., 557 P.2d 1009 (Utah 1976) (disclaimer in fine print on back of contract is ineffective unless called to buyer's attention); *cf.* Moorer v. Hartz Seed Co., 120 F. Supp. 2d 1283 (M.D. Ala. 2000) (disclaimer in all caps on back, referenced by bold caps on front, was effective in commercial transaction).

Page 163

5.8.4 Disclaimers Buried in Other Text

Addition to note 93.

93   *Accord* Hercules Mach. Corp. v. McElwee Bros., Inc., 49 U.C.C. Rep. Serv. 2d 72 (E.D. La. 2002) (commercial case) (disclaimer that was tucked into last sentence of confusing paragraph and was inconsistent with express warranty is not conspicuous); Erpelding v. Skipperliner Indus., Inc., 45 U.C.C. Rep. Serv. 2d 722 (D. Minn. 2001) (fact that agreement as a whole was conspicuous not sufficient when disclaimer was in same font and was capitalized the same as rest of contract); *see also In re* Bassett, 285 F.3d 882, 47 U.C.C. Rep. Serv. 2d 17 (9th Cir. 2002) (applying U.C.C. by analogy and finding statement in a two-page agreement conspicuous even though it was lower case and other text paragraph was all upper case). *But cf.* McLaughlin v. Denharco, Inc., 129 F. Supp. 2d 32, 43 U.C.C. Rep. Serv. 2d 1122 (D. Me. 2001) (disclaimer was conspicuous when it was set apart in text).

Page 164

5.8.5 Disclaimers Found Outside the Contract

Add to text after sentence containing note 100:

A disclaimer in a purchase order may also be ineffective if the order states that it is not binding unless signed by the seller, and the seller has not signed it.[100.1]

100.1 *But see* Rokicsak v. Colony Marine Sales & Serv., Inc., 219 F. Supp. 2d 810 (E.D. Mich. 2002) (disclaimer in purchase order that seller had not signed upheld when buyer had taken delivery).

Addition to note 101.

101 *See, e.g.*, Miles v. Barrington Motor Sales, Inc., 2003 WL 22889373 (N.D. Ill. Dec. 8, 2003) (disclaimer in earlier document not part of contract which provided that it superseded all prior agreements); McLaughlin v. Denharco, Inc., 129 F. Supp. 2d 32, 43 U.C.C. Rep. Serv. 2d 1122 (D. Me. 2001) (disclaimer ineffective without proof that buyer received it); Materials Mktg. Corp. v. Spencer, 40 S.W.3d 172, 43 U.C.C. Rep. Serv. 2d 1131 (Tex. App. 2001) (disclaimer on invoice ineffective without proof that seller gave it to buyer).

Page 165

5.8.7 Special Conspicuousness Requirements of FTC Used Car Rule

Replace note 111 with:

111 *See* National Consumer Law Center, Unfair and Deceptive Acts and Practices (5th ed. 2001 and Supp.); *see also* § 14.7.8, *infra*.

5.8.8 Reasonable Person Standard

Addition to notes 112, 113.

112 *In re* Bassett, 285 F.3d 882, 47 U.C.C. Rep. Serv. 2d 17 (9th Cir. 2002) (applying U.C.C. by analogy); Gelles & Sons Gen. Contracting, Inc. v. Jeffrey Stack, Inc., 264 Va. 285, 569 S.E.2d 406, 48 U.C.C. Rep. Serv. 2d 1429 (2002).

Page 166

113 *In re* Bassett, 285 F.3d 882, 47 U.C.C. Rep. Serv. 2d 17 (9th Cir. 2002) (applying U.C.C. by analogy and phrasing test as whether reasonable person in buyer's position would have been surprised to find the term in the contract).

5.8.9 Effect of State Plain Language Laws

Replace note 119 with:

119 *See* National Consumer Law Center, Unfair and Deceptive Acts and Practices § 5.2.2 (5th ed. 2001 and Supp.) (citations to state plain language statutes and plain language requirements in other statutes).

Page 167

5.8.10 Electronic Documents as Disclaimers

Replace note 120 with:

120 15 U.S.C. §§ 7001–7031.

Add to text after subsection's first sentence:

These statutes are described in more detail in NCLC's *Consumer Banking and Payments Law*.[121.1]

121.1 National Consumer Law Center, Consumer Banking and Payments Law Ch. 9 (2d ed. 2002 and Supp.).

Add to text at end of subsection's first paragraph:

Neither requires any party to use electronic means of contracting.[122.1]

122.1 15 U.S.C. § 7001(b)(2); UETA § 5.

Addition to note 123.

123 *Replace last sentence of note with*: These requirements are discussed in more detail in National Consumer Law Center, Truth in Lending § 4.2.9 (5th ed. 2003) and National Consumer Law Center, Consumer Banking and Payments Law § 9.4 (2d ed. 2002 and Supp.).

Add to text immediately before sentence containing note 124:

Most importantly, the consumer must give or confirm consent electronically, "in a manner that reasonably demonstrates that the consumer can access information in the electronic form" that the seller will use.[123.1] Therefore, merely signing a contract that contains a clause saying that the warranty terms will be e-mailed to the consumer or posted on-line is insufficient. The consumer must demonstrate the ability to go on-line and or receive e-mailed documents in the specific format that the seller will use.

123.1 15 U.S.C. § 7001(c)(1)(C)(ii).

Replace "law" in sentence containing note 125 with:

laws

Replace "suggessts" in sentence following sentence containing note 128 with:

suggests

Replace subsection's fourth paragraph with:

When enacting UETA many state legislatures chose to preserve E-Sign's consumer consent requirements instead of allowing UETA to supersede them. The National Conference of Commissioners on Uniform State Laws has bowed to this trend by proposing language for states to adopt along with UETA that preserves E-Sign's consumer consent requirements.[128.1]

> 128.1   Nat'l Conference of Commissioners on Unif. State Laws, Memorandum to Standby Committee for UETA, Clearinghouse 53,549 (Aug. 2, 2001).

Page 168

Add to text after sentence containing note 129:

A term that has never appeared on the consumer's computer screen, or to which the consumer has never explicitly been asked to agree, is unlikely to be found to be part of the contract.[129.1] Under the revised version of Article 2, which the National Conference of Commissioners on Uniform State Laws approved in 2003 for consideration by state legislatures, a term in an electronic transaction is conspicuous if the term is so placed that the party can not proceed without taking action with respect to the term.[129.2] This principle is just an example of conspicuousness, however, and revised Article 2 does not rule out other ways to meet the standard in electronic transactions, as long as the term is so displayed or presented that a reasonable person against whom the disclaimer is to operate ought to have noticed it.[129.3]

> 129.1   Specht v. Netscape Communications Corp., 306 F.3d 17 (2d Cir. 2002); *see also* Softman Products Co. v. Adobe Sys., Inc., 171 F. Supp. 2d 1075, 45 U.C.C. Rep. Serv. 2d 945 (C.D. Cal. 2001) (shrink-wrap contract that was displayed only when user loaded software onto computer did not bind middleman who merely bought and then resold the software without ever installing it).
>
> 129.2   Revised U.C.C. § 2-103(1)(b)(ii). Selected portions of revised Article 2 are reproduced in Appx. E.7S, *infra*, and on the CD-Rom accompanying this volume.
>
> 129.3   Revised U.C.C. § 2-103(1)(b).

5.9 Consumer Must Have Actual Knowledge of Disclaimer

Addition to note 135.

> 135   Chaudoir v. Porsche Cars of N. Am., 667 So. 2d 569 (La. Ct. App. 1996) (non-U.C.C. case); *see also* Softman Products Co. v. Adobe Sys., Inc., 171 F. Supp. 2d 1075, 45 U.C.C. Rep. Serv. 2d 945 (C.D. Cal. 2001) (shrink-wrap contract that was displayed only when user loaded software onto computer did not bind middleman who merely bought and then resold the software without ever installing it); Oakwood Mobile Homes, Inc. v. Cabler, 73 S.W.3d 363 (Tex. App. 2002) (clause disavowing oral statements unenforceable when buried in boilerplate language of contract signed by unsophisticated buyer); Materials Mktg. Corp. v. Spencer, 40 S.W.3d 172, 43 U.C.C. Rep. Serv. 2d 1131 (Tex. App. 2001) (limitation of liability clause on back of contract ineffective without evidence that buyer was aware of it or that it was given to buyer).

Add note 136.1 after "Section 1-201(10)" in third sentence of subsection's second paragraph.

> 136.1   Revised Article 1, which the National Conference of Commissioners on Uniform State Laws (NCCUSL) approved in 2001 for adoption by the states, preserves this basic test without change as part of revised U.C.C. § 1-201(b)(10).

Page 169

Addition to note 143.

> 143   *Replace NCLC citation with*: National Consumer Law Center, Unfair and Deceptive Acts and Practices § 5.2.1 (5th ed. 2001 and Supp.).

Page 170

5.10 Construction of Disclaimer Language to Protect Buyer

Addition to notes 145, 147.

> 145   *See, e.g.*, Hercules Mach. Corp. v. McElwee Bros., Inc., 49 U.C.C. Rep. Serv. 2d 72 (E.D. La. 2002); Fletcher v. Don Foss of Cleveland, Inc., 90 Ohio App. 3d 82, 628 N.E.2d 60 (1993) (language that car had warranty overrode contrary language); James River Equip. Co. v. Beadle County Equip., Inc., 646 N.W.2d 265, 48 U.C.C. Rep. Serv. 2d 105 (S.D. 2002).
>
> 147   *See also* Mills v. Burkey, 2002 WL 31521423 (Ohio Ct. App. Nov. 4, 2002) (unpublished) (trial court did not err in refusing to rely on ambiguous buyer's order which dealer had not signed).

Page 171

Add to text after subsection's fourth paragraph:

The seller will have even more difficulty disclaiming implied warranties if it has sold a service contract. In that case, the FTC Used Car Rule requires the dealer to check the box marked "WARRANTY" on the Buyers Guide and also a box stating that state law implied warranties may give the buyer additional rights.[150.1] Regardless of whether the Magnuson-Moss Act invalidates a disclaimer of implied warranties when a service contract is sold, by checking the "WARRANTY" box the dealer is probably making it impossible to disclaim implied warranties successfully under the UCC.

150.1 16 C.F.R. § 455.2(b)(3); *see* Appx. D, *infra*.

Addition to note 153.

153 *Cf.* Pioneer/Eclipse Corp. v. Kohler Co., 113 F. Supp. 2d 811 (W.D.N.C. 2000) (parties' course of dealing demonstrated acceptance of remedy limitation despite absence of formal assent).

5.11 "As Is" Disclaimer Invalid If "Circumstances Indicate Otherwise"

5.11.1 General Rule

Addition to note 155.

155 Knipp v. Weinbaum, 351 So. 2d 1081 (Fla. Dist. Ct. App. 1977).

Page 173

5.11.3 Seller's Conduct May Invalidate "As Is" Disclaimer

Add note 165.1 after "section 1-203" in subsection's final sentence.

165.1 Revised Article 1, approved by the National Conference of Commissioners on Uniform State Laws (NCCUSL) in 2001 for adoption by the states, redesignates the good faith requirement as U.C.C. § 1-304 without substantive change. It expands the definition of good faith, however, to include not only honesty in fact but also the observance of reasonable commercial standards of fair dealing, regardless of whether the actor is a merchant. Revised U.C.C. § 1-201(b)(20).

Add to text at end of subsection:

An "as is" clause may also be unenforceable if the buyer was induced to sign the contract by the seller's fraudulent representations or omissions.[166.1]

166.1 Oakwood Mobile Homes, Inc. v. Cabler, 73 S.W.3d 363 (Tex. App. 2002).

5.12 Unconscionability of Disclaimer

Addition to notes 169, 173.

169 *In re* Ford Motor Co. Ignition Switch Prods. Liab. Litig., 1999 U.S. Dist. LEXIS 22892 (D.N.J. May 14, 1999) (denial of motion for judgment on the pleadings), *vacated in part on other grounds*, 1999 U.S. Dist. LEXIS 22891 (D.N.J. July 27, 1999); *see also In re* Ford Motor Co. Ignition Switch Products Liab. Litig., 1999 WL 33495352 (D.N.J. May 14, 1999) (limitation of duration of implied warranty would be unconscionable if manufacturer knew of defect at time of original retail sale).

173 *But cf.* Basselen v. Gen. Motors Corp., 341 Ill. App. 3d 278, 792 N.E.2d 498 (2003) (consumer must show both procedural and substantive unconscionability; seller's failure to show disclaimer to consumer before contract signed is insufficient).

5.13 Disclaimer Invalid for Lack of Good Faith

Page 174

Add note 174.1 at end of subsection's first sentence.

174.1 Revised Article 1, approved by the National Conference of Commissioners on Uniform State Laws (NCCUSL) in 2001 for adoption by the states, redesignates the good faith requirement as U.C.C. § 1-304 without substantive change. It expands the definition of good faith, however, to include not only honesty in fact but also the observance of reasonable commercial standards of fair dealing, regardless of whether the actor is a merchant. Revised U.C.C. § 1-201(b)(20).

Addition to note 176.

176 *Accord* Richie v. Bank of Am. Auto Fin. Corp., 2002 Cal. App. Unpub. LEXIS 6077 (Cal. Ct. App. June 28, 2002) (unpublished).

Replace note 177 with:

177 *See* National Consumer Law Center, Unfair and Deceptive Acts and Practices (5th ed. 2001 and Supp.).

Page 175

5.14 Disclaimer May Not Affect Consumer's Ability to Revoke Acceptance

Addition to note 180.

180   *See also* Van Bibber Homes Sales v. Marlow, 778 N.E.2d 852 (Ind. Ct. App. 2002) (allowing rescission of contract despite dealer's disclaimer of warranties). *But see* Watson v. Damon Corp., 2002 WL 32059736 (W.D. Mich. Dec. 17, 2002).

5.15 No Disclaimer of Tort, Deceptive Practices Statute, or Other Non-Warranty Liability

Page 176

5.15.1 Tort Claims

Addition to note 191.

191   *Add*: *See also* D & M Jupiter, Inc. v. Friedopfer, 853 So. 2d 485 (Fla. Dist. Ct. App. 2003) (non-U.C.C. case; fraud in inducement vitiates every part of contract, including "as is" clause); Viene v. Concours Auto Sales, Inc., 787 S.W.2d 814 (Mo. Ct. App. 1990) (case involved UDAP claims; court also says that "as is" clause is no defense to fraud); MacFarlane v. Manly, 274 S.C. 392, 264 S.E.2d 838 (S.C. 1980); Self v. Miller, 2001 Tex. App. LEXIS 6026 (Tex. App. Aug. 30, 2001) (unpublished); Merriman v. Auto Excellence, Inc., 55 Va. Cir. 330 (2001); *add at end of note*: See § 11.4.1, *infra*.

Add to text at end of subsection's second paragraph:

Even if the buyer asserts a warranty claim rather than a fraud claim, an "as is" clause may be unenforceable if the buyer was induced to sign the contract by the seller's fraudulent representations or omissions.[194.1]

194.1   Oakwood Mobile Homes, Inc. v. Cabler, 73 S.W.3d 363 (Tex. App. 2002).

Page 177

5.15.2 Statutory Claims

Addition to note 199.

199   Campbell v. Beak, 568 S.E.2d 801 (Ga. Ct. App. 2002); Oakwood Mobile Homes, Inc. v. Cabler, 73 S.W.3d 363 (Tex. App. 2002) (declining to extend *Prudential Ins. Co. v. Jefferson Associates*, 896 S.W.2d 156 (Tex. 1995), to clause disavowing oral statements, when unsophisticated buyer was induced to sign it by dealer's fraudulent representations).

Chapter 6

Avoiding Vertical and Horizontal Privity Requirements

Page 179

6.1 Introduction

Add to text at end of subsection:

The revised version of Article 2, which the National Conference of Commissioners on Uniform State Laws approved in 2003 for consideration by state legislatures, would make some significant changes with respect to vertical privity. The primary change is that revised Article 2 defines a new set of obligations that run directly from the remote seller to the ultimate purchaser. First, a "remedial promise" (defined to include the standard repair or replace warranty) that is packaged with the goods or accompanies the goods creates an obligation on the part of the remote seller to perform.[2.1] In addition, any description of the goods and any affirmation of fact or promise relating to the goods that is packaged with or accompanies the goods, creates an obligation to the remote buyer that the goods will conform to it.[2.2] Finally, an advertisement or similar communication to the public that contains a remedial promise, a description of the goods, or an affirmation of fact or promise relating to the goods also creates an obligation from the remote seller to the remote buyer.[2.3] The remote seller is directly liable to the ultimate purchaser for breach of these warranty-like obligations.[2.4] All of these obligations only apply to new goods, however.[2.5] Revised Article 2's general privity rules deal with the extent to which the right to sue extends *beyond* the remote purchasers covered by these new sections.[2.6]

2.1   Revised U.C.C. § 2-313A.
2.2   Revised U.C.C. § 2-313A.
2.3   Revised U.C.C. § 2-313B.
2.4   Revised U.C.C. § 2-313A(5)(b), (c); Revised U.C.C. § 2-313B(5)(b), (c). Note that these sections provide that the remote seller is not liable for the ultimate buyer's lost profits, however.
2.5   Revised U.C.C. §§ 2-313A(2), 2-313B(2).
2.6   Revised U.C.C. § 2-318(2); *see* Official Comment 4 to Revised U.C.C. § 2-318 ("Obligations and remedial promises under Sections 2-313A and 2-313B arise initially in a non-privity context but are extended under this section to the same extent as warranties and remedial promises running to a buyer in privity.").

6.2 Vertical Privity and the Liability of Indirect Sellers

Page 181

6.2.3 Manufacturer's Liability for Express Warranties That Are Not "Written Warranties"

Replace "applied warranties" in sentence containing note 14 with:

implied warranties

Addition to notes 14, 15, 19, 22, 24, 27, 30.

14   *Add to Texas entry:* U.S. Tire-Tech, Inc. v. Boeran, B.V., 110 S.W.3d 194, 50 U.C.C. Rep. Serv. 2d 780 (Tex. App. 2003) (privity not required for deceptive trade practices claim against manufacturer for violation of express warranty).

15   *Cf.* Hobbs v. Gen. Motors Corp., 134 F. Supp. 2d 1277, 44 U.C.C. Rep. Serv. 2d 148 (M.D. Ala. 2001) (discussing but not resolving question under Alabama law).

Page 182

19   *Replace subsequent history in Rheem citation with*: rev'd and remanded on other grounds, 746 N.E.2d 941 (Ind. 2001).

22 Murrin v. Ford Motor Co., 303 A.D.2d 475, 756 N.Y.S.2d 596 (2003); DiCintio v. DaimlerChrysler Corp., 282 A.D.2d 276, 724 N.Y.S.2d 717 (2000), *rev'd on other grounds*, 97 N.Y.2d 463, 742 N.Y.S.2d 182, 768 N.E.2d 1121 (2002).

24 Bobb Forest Products, Inc. v. Morbark Indus., Inc., 151 Ohio App. 3d 63, 783 N.E.2d 560, 50 U.C.C. Rep. Serv. 2d 106 (2002); *accord* Johnson v. Monsanto Co., 48 U.C.C. Rep. Serv. 2d 586 (Ohio Ct. App. 2002).

27 *Replace Baxter citation with*: 168 Wash. 456, 15 P.2d 1118; *add*: Tex Enterprises, Inc. v. Brockway Standard, Inc., 66 P.3d 625, 50 U.C.C. Rep. Serv. 2d 317 (Wash. 2003); Baughn v. Honda Motor Co., 727 P.2d 655, 669 (Wash. 1986); Urban Dev., Inc. v. Evergreen Bldg. Products, 59 P.3d 112, 49 U.C.C. Rep. Serv. 2d 372 (Wash. Ct. App. 2002) (commercial case), *review granted*, 149 Wash. 2d 1027 (2003).

30 *Replace Mgmt. Catalysts citation with*: 119 Idaho 626, 809 P.2d 487.

6.2.4 Manufacturer Liability to Consumer for Implied Warranties

6.2.4.2 Liability Under State Law

Page 183

6.2.4.2.1 Analyzing state law

Addition to note 38.

38 *See also* Tex Enterprises, Inc. v. Brockway Standard, Inc., 66 P.3d 625, 50 U.C.C. Rep. Serv. 2d 317 (Wash. 2003) (noting that Alternative A leaves vertical privity issues to the courts).

Page 185

6.2.4.2.2 State law surveyed

Addition to notes 49–51.

49 *Add at end of California entry*: A retail seller includes a building contractor who buys items from a manufacturer for installation in the consumer's home. Atkinson v. Elk Corp., 109 Cal. App. 4th 739, 135 Cal. Rptr. 2d 433 (2003) (decision also holds that shingles are not consumer goods); *add after first sentence of Delaware entry*: St. Paul Fire & Marine Ins. Co. v. Elkay Mfg. Co., 2003 WL 139775 (Del. Super. Ct. Jan. 17, 2003) (Delaware's version of Alternate C, which is limited to natural persons, means that corporations must establish privity); *add to Kansas entry*: *See also* Limestone Farms, Inc. v. Deere & Co., 29 P.3d 457 (Kan. Ct. App. 2001) (abolition of privity only applies to consumers and sole proprietors); *cf.* Full Faith Church of Love W., Inc. v. Hoover Treated Wood Products, Inc., 224 F. Supp. 2d 1285, 48 U.C.C. Rep. Serv. 2d 1331 (D. Kan. 2002) (commercial case) (public policy exception to privity requirement for dangerous products applies only if the product has caused personal injury); *add to Massachusetts entry*: *See also* W.R. Constr. & Consulting, Inc. v. Jeld-Wen, Inc., 2002 WL 31194870 (D. Mass. Sept. 10, 2002) (vertical privity still required in non-consumer cases, but builder's purchase of windows for home owners was for consumer purposes; *cf.* Super. Kitchen Designs, Inc. v. Valspar Indus. (U.S.A.), Inc., 263 F. Supp. 2d 140, 50 U.C.C. Rep. Serv. 2d 748 (D. Mass. 2003) (vertical privity still required when commercial buyer seeks economic loss); *add to end of first paragraph of New Jersey entry*: *See also* Paramount Aviation Corp. v. Gruppo Agusta, 288 F.3d 67, 47 U.C.C. Rep. Serv. 2d 431 (3d Cir. 2002); *add to Pennsylvania entry*: Teledyne Tech. v. Freedom Forge Corp., 47 U.C.C. Rep. Serv. 2d 520 (Pa. C.P. 2002); *add to Texas entry after citation to Nobility Homes*: Hou-Tex, Inc. v. Landmark Graphics, 26 S.W.3d 103, 43 U.C.C. Rep. Serv. 2d 306 (Tex. App. 2000).

Page 187

50 *Add explanatory parenthetical to Connecticut entry after Koellmer citation*: (implying that result would be different if plaintiff had shown that dealer was agent of manufacturer); *replace sentence following "Alternative A" in Illinois entry with*: Courts hold that the Magnuson-Moss Act allows suit on implied warranties for economic loss against a remote manufacturer who gives a written warranty, but there is no independent abolition of privity requirements under state law; *add to Illinois entry after Connick citation*: *Accord* Cohen v. AM Gen. Corp., 264 F. Supp. 2d 616 (N.D. Ill. 2003) (following *Szajna*); Dekelaita v. Nissan Motor Corp., 2003 WL 22240509 (Ill. App. Ct. Sept. 29, 2003) (following *Szajna*); *add to Illinois entry after Connick citation*: However, the Seventh Circuit has held that the Magnuson-Moss Act does not affect state law privity requirements: Voelker v. Porsche Cars N. Am., Inc., 2003 WL 22930364 (7th Cir. Dec. 12, 2003); *add at end of Illinois entry*: *But see* Hamdan v. Land Rover N. Am., Inc., 2003 WL 21911244 (N.D. Ill. Aug. 8, 2003) (Magnuson-Moss Act does not abrogate vertical privity requirement for implied warranties); Kutzle v. Thor Indus., Inc., 2003 WL 21654260 (N.D. Ill. July 14, 2003) (same); Schimmer v. Jaguar Cars, Inc., 2003 WL 21518589 (N.D. Ill. July 2, 2003) (same); *add to Michigan entry before Landings Ass'n citation*: Michels v. Monaco Coach Co., 2003 WL 23194248 (E.D. Mich. Dec. 31, 2003) (buyer can seek economic loss damages for breach of implied warranty against manufacturer regardless of privity); *In re* Bridgestone/Firestone, Inc. Tires Products Liab. Litig., 47 U.C.C. Rep. Serv. 2d 140 (S.D. Ind. 2001) (Mich. law), *rev'd on other grounds*, 288 F.3d 1012 (7th Cir. 2002); *add at end of Michigan entry*: Cova v. Harley Davidson Motor Co., 182 N.W.2d 800 (Mich. Ct. App. 1970); *see also* Watson v. Damon Corp., 2002 WL 32059736 (W.D. Mich. Dec. 17, 2002) (privity is necessary for implied warranty claims seeking economic loss); Mt. Holly Ski Area v. U.S. Elec. Motors, 666 F. Supp. 115 (E.D. Mich. 1987) (privity required in suit by business for economic loss); Auto Owners Ins. Co. v. Chrysler

Corp., 341 N.W.2d 223 (Mich. Ct. App. 1983) (privity necessary in suit for economic loss by insurance company (buyer's subrogor) against manufacturer); *add to Ohio entry before Midwest Ford citation*: Norcold, Inc. v. Gateway Supply Co., 51 U.C.C. Rep. Serv. 2d 88 (Ohio Ct. App. 2003); Johnson v. Monsanto Co., 48 U.C.C. Rep. Serv. 2d 586 (Ohio Ct. App. 2002); *add to Ohio entry after Chemtrol citation*: *See also* Teledyne Tech. v. Freedom Forge Corp., 47 U.C.C. Rep. Serv. 2d 520 (Pa. C.P. 2002) (commercial case) (contrasting Ohio law with Pa. and Ky. law); *add to Ohio entry before Iocono citation*: Bobb Forest Products, Inc. v. Morbark Indus., Inc., 151 Ohio App. 3d 63, 783 N.E.2d 560, 50 U.C.C. Rep. Serv. 2d 106 (2002) (privity is required for contract-based implied warranty claim, but if manufacturer is so involved in the sale that distributor is its agent, privity exists); *add to Virginia entry after Genito Glenn citation*: *Accord* Stoney v. Franklin, 44 U.C.C. Rep. Serv. 2d 1211 (Va. Cir. Ct. June 18, 2001); *add to Virginia entry before Darden citation*: *But see* Glass v. Trafalgar House Prop., Inc., 58 Va. Cir. 437 (2002) (no economic loss recovery without privity); *add at end of Virginia entry*: In Pulte Home Corp. v. Parex, Inc., 265 Va. 518, 579 S.E.2d 188, 50 U.C.C. Rep. Serv. 2d 766 (2003), the court again held that consequential damages are unavailable in the absence of privity. It held that a home builder's claim against its subcontractor's supplier for damages the builder was required to pay to the home buyer amounted to consequential damages; *add to Washington entry before Anderson citation:* In Baughn v. Honda Motor Co., 727 P.2d 655, 669 (Wash. 1986), the court held that lack of privity bars implied warranty claims for personal injuries. A later decision, Tex Enterprises, Inc. v. Brockway Standard, Inc., 66 P.3d 625, 50 U.C.C. Rep. Serv. 2d 317 (Wash. 2003), a commercial case, holds that a remote buyer can not be a third party beneficiary of the manufacturer's implied warranties when the manufacturer's contract with the middleman disclaims implied warranties, even when the manufacturer has made direct oral representations to the remote buyer. The court stated that vertical non-privity plaintiffs must show either an express warranty or that they are third party beneficiaries.; *add at end of Washington entry*: see also Urban Dev., Inc. v. Evergreen Bldg. Products, 59 P.3d 112, 49 U.C.C. Rep. Serv. 2d 372 (Wash. Ct. App. 2002) (commercial case) (general contractor can not make warranty claim against subcontractor's suppliers because of lack of privity), *review granted*, 149 Wash. 2d 1027 (2003).

Page 189

51   *Add to Alabama entry*: Rampey v. Novartis Consumer Health, Inc., 2003 WL 21246560 (Ala. May 30, 2003); Copenhagen Reinsurance Co. v. Champion Home Builders Co., 2003 WL 21850441 (Ala. Civ. App. Aug. 8, 2003); Certainteed Corp. v. Russell, 51 U.C.C. Rep. Serv. 2d 418 (Ala. Civ. App. 2003); *in Indiana entry, replace subsequent history in Rheem citation with*: *rev'd and remanded on other grounds*, 746 N.E.2d 941 (Ind. 2001); *add to Kentucky entry*: *See also* Teledyne Tech. v. Freedom Forge Corp., 47 U.C.C. Rep. Serv. 2d 520 (Pa. C.P. 2002) (commercial case) (contrasting Ky. law with Pa. and Ohio law); *add to Tennessee entry before Walter Truck citation*: *See also* In re Bridgestone/Firestone, Inc. Tires Products Liab. Litig., 47 U.C.C. Rep. Serv. 2d 140 (S.D. Ind. 2001) (Tenn. law), *rev'd on other grounds*, 288 F.3d 1012 (7th Cir. 2002).

6.2.5 *Manufacturer Liability Even Where Privity Required*

Page 191

6.2.5.1 Consumer as Third Party Beneficiary of Manufacturer Warranty

Addition to note 54.

54   Bobb Forest Products, Inc. v. Morbark Indus., Inc., 151 Ohio App. 3d 63, 783 N.E.2d 560, 50 U.C.C. Rep. Serv. 2d 106 (2002) (when product was specially manufactured for buyer, buyer was third party beneficiary); *see also* Morris Concrete v. Warrick, 2003 WL 21205836 (Ala. Civ. App. May 23, 2003) (employee bought product from employer at employee discount rate and supplied it, with employer's knowledge, to third party as partial payment for car; third party was third party beneficiary of this contract).

Add to text after sentence containing note 56:

However, the theory applies to implied warranties as well as express warranties.[56.1]

56.1 Tex Enterprises, Inc. v. Brockway Standard, Inc., 66 P.3d 625, 50 U.C.C. Rep. Serv. 2d 317 (Wash. 2003) (third party beneficiaries can enforce implied warranties but not in this case because manufacturer's contract with middleman disclaimed them).

6.2.5.2 Dealer as Manufacturer's Agent

Addition to note 59.

59   *Add at beginning of note*: See also W.R. Constr. & Consulting, Inc. v. Jeld-Wen, Inc., 2002 WL 31194870 (D. Mass. Sept. 10, 2002) (question of fact whether dealer was manufacturer's agent). *But cf.* Kutzle v. Thor Indus., Inc., 2003 WL 21654260 (N.D. Ill. July 14, 2003) (finding allegation of agency insufficient); *add before Gaha citation*: DiCintio v. DaimlerChrysler Corp., 282 A.D.2d 276, 724 N.Y.S.2d 717 (2000), *rev'd on other grounds*, 97 N.Y.2d 463, 742 N.Y.S.2d 182, 768 N.E.2d 1121 (2002); Bobb Forest Products, Inc. v. Morbark Indus., Inc., 151 Ohio App. 3d 63, 783 N.E.2d 560, 50 U.C.C. Rep. Serv. 2d 106 (2002) (privity is required for contract-based implied warranty claim, but if manufacturer is so involved in the sale that distributor is its agent, privity exists); *add after Gaha citation*: Oakwood Mobile Homes, Inc. v. Cabler, 73 S.W.3d 363 (Tex. App. 2002); *add at end of note*: Cooper Indus., Inc. v. Tarmac Roofing Sys.,

Inc., 276 F.3d 704 (5th Cir. 2002) (contractor was not manufacturer's agent when contractor was certified for installation of many other manufacturers' products; buyer shopped for a contractor rather than for a particular manufacturer's product, and the contractor chose to use this manufacturer's product; insufficient evidence that manufacturer held contractor out as its agent or had control over contractor).

Replace sentence following sentence containing note 59 with:

Although the law is not entirely clear, agency may be found in three situations.

Addition to note 60.

60   *See also* Wolfe v. Chrysler Corp., 734 F.2d 701 (11th Cir. 1984) (dealer was manufacturer's agent for purpose of delivering new car warranty that led buyer to believe that car was new).

Page 192

Add to text at end of subsection:

Finally, the dealer can be held to be the manufacturer's agent when the manufacturer exercises substantial control over the dealer's operations, such as controlling the dealer's location, operations, pricing, and so forth.[61.1] For example, discovery may show that the manufacturer requires dealers to report sales and service data, maintain an Internet connection with the manufacturer, participate in manufacturer-sponsored training for sales and technical personnel, submit to testing and certification of sales and technical staff, participate in customer satisfaction surveys, follow a host of rules and policies, use the manufacturer's parts in repairs, submit to audits and site visits by the manufacturer, and use the manufacturer's software. The manufacturer probably provides technical service bulletins, service messages, vehicle history data, and trouble-shooting services to the dealer, and authorizes the dealer to bind it to service contracts. Documents that tend to show the manufacturer's control are discussed in § 10.1.4.2, *infra.*

61.1   Bruce v. ICI Americas, Inc., 933 F. Supp. 781 (D. Iowa 1996) (dealers may be manufacturer's agents when manufacturer has the right to control their operations).

6.2.5.3 Manufacturer as Direct Seller

Addition to note 63.

63   *But see* Kutzle v. Thor Indus., Inc., 2003 WL 21654260 (N.D. Ill. July 14, 2003) (manufacturer's advertising does not create privity).

Add to text after sentence containing note 63:

Many motor vehicle manufacturers issue rebates directly to consumers, which may also be enough to create privity.

Add to text at end of subsection:

It is also possible that a manufacturer is a seller if it has a direct relationship with the buyer through a rebate program or some other sales incentive. The manufacturer may also have a direct enough relationship with the buyer to obviate privity concerns when the dealer has a warranty from the manufacturer and assigns that warranty to the buyer.

Page 193

6.2.5.4 Manufacturer Liability Based on Equitable Estoppel

Add to text at end of subsection:

Estoppel may also preclude a manufacturer from avoiding liability when the manufacturer induces the buyer to proceed with a sale by conveying promises through the dealer to correct defects.[66.1]

66.1   *Ex parte* Grand Manor, Inc., 778 So. 2d 173 (Ala. 2000).

6.2.5.5 Non-Warranty Claims

Addition to note 67.

67   *Add to Southwest Pet Products citation*: *aff'd in part, rev'd in part on other grounds*, 2002 WL 460280 (9th Cir. Feb. 8, 2002); *add*: *See, e.g., Ex parte* Grand Manor, Inc., 778 So. 2d 173 (Ala. 2000) (privity not a bar to negligence claim, but damage to product itself not recoverable).

6.2.6 *Direct Seller's Liability on Indirect Seller's Warranty*

Addition to notes 70, 71.

70 Miles v. Barrington Motor Sales, Inc., 2003 WL 22889373 (N.D. Ill. Dec. 8, 2003); Lytle v. Roto Lincoln Mercury & Subaru, Inc., 167 Ill. App. 3d 508, 521 N.E.2d 201 (1988); *see also* Waterloo Coal Co. v. Komatsu Mining Sys., Inc., 2003 WL 124137 (S.D. Ohio Jan. 9, 2003) (merely performing warranty service was not adoption of manufacturer's warranty).

71 Felde v. Chrysler Credit Corp., 219 Ill. App. 3d 530, 580 N.E.2d 191 (1991) (dealer's invoice, which stated that manufacturer's warranty "is incorporated herein and made a part hereof," was adoption of manufacturer's warranty); *see also* Rokicsak v. Colony Marine Sales & Serv., Inc., 219 F. Supp. 2d 810 (E.D. Mich. 2002) (revocation claim based on manufacturer's warranties can proceed against dealer even though dealer effectively disclaimed its warranties).

6.3 Horizontal Privity and the Claims of Nonbuyers

6.3.3 *State Law May Also Abandon Horizontal Privity*

Page 197

6.3.3.2 Analysis of State Law Variations

Addition to notes 95, 99, 102, 106.

95 St. Paul Fire & Marine Ins. Co. v. Elkay Mfg. Co., 2003 WL 139775 (Del. Super. Ct. Jan. 17, 2003) (Delaware's version of Alternate C, which is limited to natural persons, means that corporations must establish privity).

99 *But see* Whitaker v. Lian Feng Mach. Co., 156 Ill. App. 3d 316, 108 Ill. Dec. 895, 509 N.E.2d 591 (1987) (employee of buyer can sue even though state has adopted Alternative A, as courts are allowed to develop horizontal privity law beyond § 2-318); *cf.* Frank v. Edward Hines Lumber Co., 327 Ill. App. 3d 113, 761 N.E.2d 1257, 46 U.C.C. Rep. Serv. 2d 419 (2001) (employee of buyer may be able to recover, but not employee of contractor doing work on buyer's premises).

102 *See, e.g.,* Mugavero v. A-1 Auto Sales, Inc., 944 P.2d 151 (Idaho Ct. App. 1997) (seller of car with defects that caused collision has no warranty liability to driver of other car); *see also* Paramount Aviation Corp. v. Gruppo Agusta, 288 F.3d 67, 47 U.C.C. Rep. Serv. 2d 431 (3d Cir. 2002) (person hired to perform services for owner of goods who suffers solely economic injury because of goods' malfunction can not sue manufacturer for breach of warranty).

Page 198

106 *See, e.g.,* Whitaker v. Lian Feng Mach. Co., 156 Ill. App. 3d 316, 108 Ill. Dec. 895, 509 N.E.2d 591 (1987) (employee of buyer can sue even though state has adopted Alternative A). *But see* United Technologies Corp. v. Saren Eng'g, Inc., 48 U.C.C. Rep. Serv. 2d 1349 (Conn. Super. Ct. 2002) (declining to expand horizontal liability in commercial case).

6.3.3.3 Survey of State Law

Addition to notes 107, 108.

107 *Replace Kansas entry with*: *Kansas*: Abolishes horizontal privity by separate statute for consumer transactions, defined to include transactions with individuals, sole proprietors, and, by virtue of a 2001 amendment, family partnerships. Kan. Stat. Ann. §§ 50-639, 50-624. Otherwise, horizontal privity is required unless a natural person suffers personal injury. *See* Limestone Farms, Inc. v. Deere & Co., 29 P.3d 457 (Kan. Ct. App. 2001).

Page 199

108 *Add to Illinois entry after Thomas citation*: *But see* Reed v. City of Chicago, 263 F. Supp. 2d 1123, 50 U.C.C. Rep. Serv. 2d 146 (N.D. Ill. 2003) (warranties given by manufacturer that supplied product to prison for prisoners' use run to prisoner; courts may expand privity beyond U.C.C. § 2-318); Whitaker v. Lian Feng Mach. Co., 156 Ill. App. 3d 316, 108 Ill. Dec. 895, 509 N.E.2d 591 (1987) (employee of buyer can sue even though state has adopted Alternative A, as courts are allowed to develop horizontal privity law beyond § 2-318); *add to New Jersey entry*: *See* Paramount Aviation Corp. v. Gruppo Agusta, 288 F.3d 67, 47 U.C.C. Rep. Serv. 2d 431 (3d Cir. 2002) (person hired to perform services for owner of goods who suffers solely economic injury because of goods' malfunction can not sue manufacturer for breach of warranty); *replace Hou-Tex citation in Texas entry with*: 26 S.W.3d 103 (Tex. App. 2000).

Page 201

6.3.5 *Asserting Warranty Rights as a Third Party Beneficiary*

Addition to note 111.

111 Reed v. City of Chicago, 263 F. Supp. 2d 1123, 50 U.C.C. Rep. Serv. 2d 146 (N.D. Ill. 2003) (prisoner is third party beneficiary of warranties given by seller of product that prison supplied to prisoner); River Rouge Sch. Dist. v. Mestek, Inc., 48 U.C.C. Rep. Serv. 2d 1036 (Mich. Ct. App. 2002) (unpublished).

6.3.6 *Horizontal Privity Not Required for Non-Warranty Claims*

*Add to text after sentence
containing note 116:*

Common law warranty claims, applicable to transactions not covered by Article 2, may have different privity rules.[116.1]

116.1   *See* Szabo v. Rosenberg, 1998 Ohio App. LEXIS 2790 (Ohio Ct. App. June 24, 1998) (horizontal privity required for suit against independent contractor who performed services on home but not for suit against home builder-vendor); *see also* § 16.3.2, *infra.*

Chapter 7

Establishing Breach of Warranty: Notice, Standards, Proof and Defenses

7.2 Notice of Breach

7.2.1 *General Requirement*

Page 203

Addition to notes 1, 3.

1   *See, e.g.,* Adams v. Wacaster Oil Co., 98 S.W.3d 832, 50 U.C.C. Rep. Serv. 2d 774 (Ark. Ct. App. 2003) (buyer can not avoid notice requirement by pleading breach of contract instead of breach of warranty). *But cf.* Old Kent Bank v. Kal Kustom, Inc., 255 Mich. App. 524, 660 N.W.2d 384 (2003) (under separate provision of U.C.C. § 2-607(5)(a), middleman is permitted but not required to notify manufacturer of buyer's breach of warranty suit; failure to give notice means only that factual findings in buyer's suit are not binding on manufacturer, and manufacturer need not defend that suit).

3   *See* Am. Bumper & Mfg. Co. v. Transtechnology Corp., 252 Mich. App. 340, 652 N.W.2d 252 (2002) (adopting *Aqualon* statement of purposes).

Page 204

Add to text at end of subsection:

The revised version of Article 2, which the National Conference of Commissioners on Uniform State Laws approved in 2003 for consideration by state legislatures, requires notice of breach but takes a different approach as to the effect of failure to give timely notice. It would bar the buyer from a remedy only to the extent that the seller is prejudiced by the buyer's failure to give timely notice.[4.1]

4.1   Revised U.C.C. § 2-607(3)(a). Selected portions of revised Article 2 are reproduced in Appx. E.7S, *infra*, and on the CD-Rom accompanying this volume.

7.2.2 *When Notice of Breach Is Not Required*

Addition to notes 10, 11.

10   *But see* Christian v. Sony Corp., 152 F. Supp. 2d 1184, 45 U.C.C. Rep. Serv. 2d 510 (D. Minn. 2001) (actual knowledge can not excuse failure to give notice).

Page 205

11   *See also* Anthony v. Country Life Mfg., Ltd. Liab. Co., 2003 WL 21540975 (7th Cir. July 2, 2003) (unpublished) (seller must have knowledge not just of facts constituting breach but also of buyer's claim).

7.2.3 *Reasonable Time Within Which to Give Notice of Breach*

7.2.3.1 General

Addition to notes 13, 15.

13   Hays v. Gen. Elec. Co., 151 F. Supp. 2d 1001, 45 U.C.C. Rep. Serv. 2d 449 (N.D. Ill. 2001) (jury could find that eight to nine month delay was not unreasonable); Wal-Mart Stores, Inc. v. Wheeler, 586 S.E.2d 83, 51 U.C.C. Rep. Serv. 2d 133 (Ga. Ct. App. 2003) (in light of policies behind notice requirement, two-year delay may be reasonable if it does not prejudice seller, when defects caused personal injury); Johnson v. Monsanto Co., 48 U.C.C. Rep. Serv. 2d 586 (Ohio Ct. App. 2002) (question of fact whether notice given in July that herbicide was not working was timely when problems developed in June); Bako v. Crystal Cabinet Works, Inc., 44 U.C.C. Rep. Serv. 2d 1048 (Ohio Ct. App. 2001) (seven-month delay too long).

Page 206

15   Ameristar Jet Charter, Inc. v. Signal Composites, Inc., 271 F.3d 624, 46 U.C.C. Rep. Serv. 2d 425 (5th Cir. 2001); Calbert v. Volkswagen of Am., Inc., 1991 WL 215669 (Del. Super. Ct. Oct. 1, 1991) (reasonableness of notice is question of fact); Wal-Mart Stores, Inc. v. Wheeler, 586 S.E.2d 83, 51 U.C.C. Rep. Serv. 2d 133 (Ga. Ct. App. 2003).

Page 207   **7.2.3.2 Consumer Cases**

Addition to note 22.

22   Solarz v. DaimlerChrysler Corp., 47 U.C.C. Rep. Serv. 2d 969 (Pa. C.P. 2002) (complaint can serve as notice of breach, even in cases not involving personal injury). *But see* Anthony v. Country Life Mfg., Ltd. Liab. Co., 2003 WL 21540975 (7th Cir. July 2, 2003) (unpublished) (complaint can serve as notice only in personal injury cases); Hobbs v. Gen. Motors Corp., 134 F. Supp. 2d 1277, 44 U.C.C. Rep. Serv. 2d 148 (M.D. Ala. 2001) (filing of lawsuit not sufficient notice); Brookings Mun. Utilities, Inc. v. Amoco Chem. Co., 103 F. Supp. 2d 1169, 42 U.C.C. Rep. Serv. 2d 470 (D.S.D. 2000).

Page 209   **7.2.4 Contractual Specification of Time to Give Notice**

Addition to note 30.

30   *Replace "U.C.C. § 1-102(3)" with:* U.C.C. § 1-103(3) [*redesignated as U.C.C. § 1-302 by revised Article 1, which the National Conference of Commissioners on Uniform State Laws (NCCUSL) approved in 2001 for adoption by the states*].

Add note 31.1 at end of first sentence of subsection's second paragraph.

31.1 Revised Article 1, which NCCUSL approved in 2001 for adoption by the states, redesignates this provision as U.C.C. § 1-205 without substantive change.

Addition to note 34.

34   *But cf.* Hangzhou Silk Imp. & Exp. Corp. v. P.C.B. Int'l Indus., Inc., 48 U.C.C. Rep. Serv. 2d 1367 (S.D.N.Y. 2002) (thirty days not manifestly unreasonable when defects were not difficult to detect); Xuchang Rihetai Human Hair Goods Co. v. Hanyu Int'l, 45 U.C.C. Rep. Serv. 2d 1077 (S.D.N.Y. 2001) (thirty-day period for experienced commercial buyers to inspect is not manifestly unreasonable even for latent defects).

7.2.5 Form and Content of Notice

Page 210   **7.2.5.1 Minimal Requirements**

Addition to notes 37–39, 43, 44, 47, 48, 55.

37   *See, e.g.,* Hangzhou Silk Imp. & Exp. Corp. v. P.C.B. Int'l Indus., Inc., 48 U.C.C. Rep. Serv. 2d 1367 (S.D.N.Y. 2002) (notice need not demand damages); Quality Bus. Forms v. Secured Choice, Inc., 51 U.C.C. Rep. Serv. 2d 447 (Minn. Ct. App. 2003) (unpublished); Johnson v. Monsanto Co., 48 U.C.C. Rep. Serv. 2d 586 (Ohio Ct. App. 2002). *But cf.* Am. Bumper & Mfg. Co. v. Transtechnology Corp., 252 Mich. App. 340, 652 N.W.2d 252 (2002) (manufacturer's initial notification of problems to supplier insufficient when manufacturer subsequently investigated the problems and concluded that supplier was not at fault, and then sued three and a half years later without further notice).

38   *See* Am. Bumper & Mfg. Co. v. Transtechnology Corp., 252 Mich. App. 340, 652 N.W.2d 252 (2002) (remarking on inconsistency).

39   *But see* Quality Bus. Forms v. Secured Choice, Inc., 51 U.C.C. Rep. Serv. 2d 447 (Minn. Ct. App. 2003) (unpublished) (notice need not state that errors constitute a breach or that buyer intends to seek damages).

Page 211

43   *See, e.g.,* Dunleavy v. Paris Ceramics USA, Inc., 819 A.2d 945, 49 U.C.C. Rep. Serv. 2d 515 (Conn. Super. Ct. 2002).

44   *See* Hays v. Gen. Elec. Co., 151 F. Supp. 2d 1001, 45 U.C.C. Rep. Serv. 2d 449 (N.D. Ill. 2001) (sending motors with melted parts back to manufacturer could be sufficient notice).

47   *See In re* Bridgestone/Firestone Inc. ATX, ATX II & Wilderness Tires Prods. Liab. Litig., 155 F. Supp. 2d 1069 (S.D. Ind. 2001) (Tenn. and Mich. law), *rev'd on other grounds*, 288 F.3d 1012 (7th Cir. 2002). *But see* Adams v. Wacaster Oil Co., 98 S.W.3d 832, 50 U.C.C. Rep. Serv. 2d 774 (Ark. Ct. App. 2003).

Page 212

48   *See* Quality Bus. Forms v. Secured Choice, Inc., 51 U.C.C. Rep. Serv. 2d 447 (Minn. Ct. App. 2003).

55   *Replace U.C.C. citation and parenthetical with:* U.C.C. § 1-201(26) ("A person 'notifies' or 'gives' a notice or notification to another by taking such steps as may be reasonably required to inform the other in ordinary course whether or not such other actually comes to know of it.") [*redesignated as U.C.C. § 1-202 by revised Article 1, which the National Conference of Commissioners on Uniform State Laws (NCCUSL) approved in 2001 for adoption by the states*].

Add to text at end of subsection's sixth paragraph:

Courts have split, however, on whether a pleading can serve as notice of breach.[57.1]

57.1 *See* § 7.2.3.2, *supra.*

Replace note 59 with:

59   S. Energy Homes, Inc. v. Washington, 774 So. 2d 505, 40 U.C.C. Rep. Serv. 2d 986 (Ala. 2000); *see also* Copenhagen Reinsurance Co. v. Champion Home Builders Co., 2003 WL 21850441 (Ala. Civ. App. Aug. 8, 2003) (warranty mandated written notice).

Addition to note 64.   64   Smart Online, Inc. v. Opensite Technologies, Inc., 51 U.C.C. Rep. Serv. 2d 47 (N.C. Super. Ct. 2003).

7.2.6 Notice of Breach to Indirect Sellers and by Nonbuyers

Page 213

7.2.6.2 Indirect Sellers

Addition to note 69.   69   Johnson v. Monsanto Co., 48 U.C.C. Rep. Serv. 2d 586 (Ohio Ct. App. 2002). *But see* U.S. Tire-Tech, Inc.
v. Boeran, B.V., 110 S.W.3d 194, 50 U.C.C. Rep. Serv. 2d 780 (Tex. App. 2003) (buyer must give notice
to remote manufacturer but has longer time to do so); *cf.* Hobbs v. Gen. Motors Corp., 134 F. Supp. 2d
1277, 44 U.C.C. Rep. Serv. 2d 148 (M.D. Ala. 2001) (buyer must give notice to manufacturer either
directly or through notice provided by direct seller).

7.3 Warranty Standards and Nonconformity

Page 214

7.3.1 Standards for Nonconformity Vary With the Type of Warranty

*Delete sentences containing
notes 74 and 75.*

*Add to text at end of
subsection:*

The buyer's dissatisfaction with a product does not alone establish a breach of warranty.[80.1] Courts have consistently held, for example, that automobile "engine noise" without proof of a specific defect is not enough to establish a breach of express warranty.[80.2] Unless the buyer can show that as a result of the noise the vehicle has failed in its essential purpose or poses an unreasonable danger,[80.3] or that the noise diminished the value of the vehicle,[80.4] courts are unlikely to find a breach. A buyer's concern about a product or inconvenience to the buyer is normally not compensable in a breach of warranty case.[80.5]

7.3.1a Defects That Have Not Yet Caused a Malfunction

If a specific defect can be established some courts have allowed a claim of breach of warranty to go forward even though the defect has not yet caused the product to malfunction.[80.6] For example, in *In Re Bridgestone/Firestone, Inc. ATX, ATX II & Wilderness Tires Products Liability Litigation*,[80.7] the federal court in Indiana denied a motion to dismiss the complaint in a class action claiming that tires on Ford Explorers had an unreasonably dangerous propensity to suffer tread separation, creating a substantial risk that the vehicles would roll over, despite the fact that the class did not allege that the tires had actually malfunctioned as to any individual class member. The plaintiffs claimed that the tire manufacturer breached the warranty of merchantability and the express warranty that the tires would be free of defects, because the tires subjected the plaintiffs to an undue risk of physical injury and death.[80.8] The court held that the plaintiffs were not required to prove that the tires actually malfunctioned in order to prove a breach of warranty.[80.9] They need only prove that the tires were not merchantable at the time of purchase because of the defect.[80.10] The court also cited UCC § 2-725(2), which provides in part: "A cause of action accrues when the breach occurs, regardless of the aggrieved party's lack of knowledge of the breach." Therefore, the court noted, "by the plain language of the statute, each Plaintiff's cause of action for breach of implied warranty accrued at the time he or she purchased [an Explorer or the tires] and there is no requirement that Plaintiffs demonstrate any injury to their person or property as a result of the breach, but only that they purchased an unmerchantable product."[80.11]

Likewise, in *Microsoft Corp. v. Manning*,[80.12] a Texas court of appeals upheld the certification of a class in an action for breach of express and implied warranties in connection with the sale of computer operating system software, in which the plaintiffs did not allege that the operating system had in fact malfunctioned but only that it contained a defect which *could* cause users to lose data. The class plaintiffs claimed that the data compression feature of the software was faulty.[80.13] The court took note that, shortly after the release of the software at issue (MS-DOS 6.0), Microsoft released an update which corrected the disk compression problem, which it sold for $9.95.[80.14] The court held that the plaintiffs could prevail if they proved that an individual defect existed in all original MS-DOS 6.0 software, whether or not the purchasers had actually suffered a loss of data as a result of that defect.[80.15] The purchasers suffered damage because they received less than they bargained for when they purchased the product—specifically, they received a product which they believed contained a functioning compression program but which did not—and the measure of their loss was the $9.95 Microsoft charged to correct the defect in their software.[80.16] The court rejected Microsoft's argument that, because the software had not malfunctioned as to most class members, they had received the benefit of their bargain.[80.17] The software *could* malfunction in the future, the court noted, if the purchaser risked using the data compression feature, and therefore it was less than was warranted at the time of purchase.[80.18]

In home construction cases, some courts have held that the cost of repairing latent construction defects can be recovered under a breach of warranty theory without proof that the defects have resulted in property damage.[80.19] In an action for repair or replacement of defective foundations containing "Fibermesh" rather than customary wire mesh, a court again took note of the almost indefinite useful life of a home's foundation and also took note of evidence which showed that foundations containing Fibermesh would someday "most likely crack badly," causing problems such as insect and vermin infestation.[80.20] The court held that breach of warranty does not require proof that the product has malfunctioned but only that the product contains an inherent defect which is substantially certain to malfunction during the useful life of the product.[80.21]

Other courts have held, however, that proof of some damage is an element of a breach of warranty claim and the possibility of future harm is insufficient to meet this burden.[80.22] For example, in *In Re Air Bag Products Liability Litigation*,[80.23] a Louisiana district court dismissed breach of warranty claims that air bags are dangerously defective because they are designed to deploy with sufficient speed and force to seriously injure or kill front seat passengers, especially women, children, the elderly, and short adults. The court dismissed the class action's breach of warranty claims because the plaintiffs had not alleged that a single air bag "functioned improperly under normal use" which, it held, is a prerequisite for recovery under a breach of warranty theory.[80.24] In addition, the court found that the plaintiffs were on constructive notice of the risks posed by air bags by virtue of a warning on the visor as well as numerous articles in the media, thus making any defects apparent.[80.25] The court rejected the plaintiffs' argument that they should not be required to allege manifest injury because the claimed defect was a "life-threatening condition," noting that other courts had dismissed claims for failure to allege injury even when the plaintiffs claimed that the defect increased the risk of deadly injury.[80.26]

Another court held that claims of negligence, strict liability, breach of the implied warranty of merchantability, fraud, and deceptive practices could not be based on the tendency of a vehicle seat to collapse in an accident.[80.27] The court held that the consumers' recourse was to petition the National Highway Traffic Safety Administration to conduct an investigation and order a product recall.

Another case involved a drug that the manufacturer later withdrew from the market because it caused side effects under certain conditions. The Fifth Circuit held that purchasers for whom the product had worked and who had not suffered side effects did not have standing to assert an implied warranty of merchantability claim.[80.28] It appears from the court's recitation of the facts that the purchasers were seeking compensation for medication they had already used, as the manufacturer had already established a program to refund users for any unused portion of their prescription.[80.29]

In another case, a court held that the absence of an interlock feature that prevented a vehicle from being inadvertently shifted from "park" to "drive" did not suffice to support a warranty claim except for buyers who had actually experienced an inadvertent shift.[80.30] The decision failed to recognize that the development of this defect was not contingent on deterioration or some particular use, but it was already entirely apparent and objectively demonstrable.

One decision questions the view that recovery for defects that have not yet caused injury will result in over-compensation.[80.31] This view is correct only if the court ignores some of the losses that buyers suffer. For example, imagine that a manufacturer sells 50,000 defective widgets and 1000 catch fire because of the defect. If each fire causes $100,000 damage, the manufacturer should pay $10,000,000 in damages for the fires. That is full compensation for the fires. But if the owners of the remaining widgets discard them or sell them at a loss because of the defect, that is an additional loss that should not go uncompensated.[80.32] The decisions allowing recovery for defects that have not yet caused an injury or malfunction properly recognize this loss. If the buyers use the product for its entire economic life without injury, rather than selling it at a loss or discarding it, then the sellers' argument makes more sense.

Though the cases are not entirely consistent, the more speculative the harm, the less likely the court will be to find a breach. Many of the decisions, while couched in terms of failure to plead manifest injury, in fact found that the product had substantially performed as warranted during its useful life.[80.33]

A deceptive practices (UDAP) claim may offer advantages when the defective product has not yet malfunctioned. Some state UDAP statutes are interpreted broadly to allow suit whenever the consumer has received something less than she bargained for.[80.34]

80.1   *See* Iskander v. Ford Motor Co., 59 Ohio App. 2d 325, 394 N.E.2d 1017, 27 U.C.C. Rep. Serv. 387 (1978) (affirming dismissal of car purchaser's claim that pronounced wind noise heard inside vehicle breached express and implied warranties, causing him emotional distress and anxiety).

80.2   *Id.*; Hasek v. DaimlerChrysler Corp., 319 Ill. App. 3d 780, 745 N.E.2d 627, 44 U.C.C. Rep. Serv. 2d 108 (2001) ("engine noise" is subjective complaint, not sufficient to establish breach of warranty); Tokar v. Crestwood Imports, Inc., 177 Ill. App. 422, 532 N.E.2d 382 (1988) (plaintiff failed to establish that "grinding noise" in transmission was a defect that constituted a breach of express warranty); Collum v. Fred Tuch Buick, 6 Ill. App. 3d 317, 322, 285 N.E.2d 532, 536 (1972) (fact that car engine made "squeaky noise" is not proof of defects in material or workmanship, finding no breach of express warranty).

80.3   Hasek v. DaimlerChrysler Corp., 319 Ill. App. 3d 780, 745 N.E.2d 627, 638, 44 U.C.C. Rep. Serv. 2d 108 (2001) (citing McGrady v. Chrysler Motors Corp., 46 Ill. App. 3d 136, 4 Ill. Dec. 705, 360 N.E.2d 818, 821 (1977)).

80.4   *Id.* at 634.

80.5   *Id.* at 638; *see also* Khan v. Shiley Inc., 217 Cal. App. 3d 848, 266 Cal. Rptr. 106 (1990); Grant v. Bridgestone/Firestone, Inc., 55 Pa. D. & C.4th 438, 46 U.C.C. Rep. Serv. 2d 990 (Pa. C.P. 2001) (no warranty recovery for worry about dangers of defective product unless there is physical injury or impact). *But see* Phillips v. Restaurant Mgmt., 552 S.E.2d 686, 45 U.C.C. Rep. 2d 790 (N.C. Ct. App. 2001) (sale of food on which an employee had spat breached implied warranty of merchantability even though buyer suffered no physical injury and no physical manifestation of emotional distress).

80.6   *In re* St. Jude Med., Inc. Silzone Heart Valves Products Liab. Litig., 2003 WL 1589527 (D. Minn. Mar. 27, 2003) (plaintiffs have standing to assert claim for medical monitoring of defective heart valves even though valves have not yet malfunctioned); Miller v. William Chevrolet/Geo, Inc., 326 Ill. App. 3d 642, 762 N.E.2d 1, 11, 260 Ill. Dec. 735 (2001).

80.7   155 F. Supp. 2d 1069 (S.D. Ind. 2001) (but dismissing claims for negligence and RICO violations because of lack of injury), *rev'd on other grounds*, 288 F.3d 1012 (7th Cir. 2002) (reversing class certification because each state's law must be applied); *see also* Talalai v. Cooper Tire & Rubber Co., 360 N.J. Super. 547, 823 A.2d 888 (Super. Ct. App. Div. 2001) (UDAP claim may proceed when buyers got worse product than they bargained for, even if it has not yet caused injury or required repairs); Tietsworth v. Harley-Davidson, Inc., 661 N.W.2d 450 (Wis. Ct. App. 2003), *review granted by* 665 N.W.2d 375 (Wis. 2003). *But cf.* Grant v. Bridgestone/Firestone, Inc., 55 Pa. D. & C.4th 438, 46 U.C.C. Rep. Serv. 2d 990 (Pa. C.P. 2001) (warranty claim can not be based on diminution in value due to defect unless plaintiff has tried to resell the product), *later opinion at* 46 U.C.C. Rep. Serv. 2d 995 (Pa. C.P. 2002) (no claim for breach of implied warranty of merchantability unless defect has manifested itself).

80.8   155 F. Supp. 2d 1069 (S.D. Ind. 2001), *rev'd on other grounds*, 288 F.3d 1012 (7th Cir. 2002).

80.9   *Id.* at 1100.

80.10   *Id.*

80.11   *Id.* at 1099.

80.12   914 S.W.2d 602 (Tex. App. 1995).

80.13   *Id.* at 605.

80.14   *Id.*

80.15   *Id.* at 609.

80.16   *Id.* at 609; *accord* McManus v. Fleetwood Enterprises, Inc., 320 F.3d 545, 49 U.C.C. Rep. Serv. 2d 1124 (5th Cir. 2003) (Tex. law) (plaintiffs can press claim that motor home could not safely tow amount of weight it was represented as being able to tow, even though plaintiffs had not suffered physical injury; not receiving the benefit of their bargain is sufficient for damages).

80.17   Microsoft Corp. v. Manning, 914 S.W.2d 602, 609 (Tex. App. 1995).

80.18   *Id. But cf.* Polaris Indus., Inc. v. McDonald, 2003 WL 21940115 (Tex. App. Aug. 13, 2003) (no implied warranty claim when plaintiff did not contend that he got less than he paid for; distinguishing *Manning*).

80.19   *See* Coghlan v. Wellcraft Marine Corp., 240 F.3d 449 (5th Cir. 2001) (buyer may seek benefit of the bargain damages if product has defect, even if product has not malfunctioned); Hicks v. Kaufman & Broad Home Corp., 89 Cal. App. 4th 908, 107 Cal. Rptr. 2d 761 (2001) (if plaintiffs prove their foundations contain an inherent defect which is substantially certain to malfunction during its useful life, they have established a breach of express and implied warranties, and do not have to prove that their foundations had already cracked or caused property damage); Aas v. Superior Court, 24 Cal. 4th 627, 635, 101 Cal. Rptr. 2d 718, 12 P.3d 1125, 1130 (2000) (in discussing breach of warranty claims for construction defects, stating that "tort law provides a remedy for construction defects that cause property damage or personal injury . . . but the difference between price paid and value received and deviations from standards of quality that have not resulted in property damage or personal injury, are primarily the domain of contract and warranty law . . . rather than of negligence").

80.20   Hicks v. Kaufman & Broad Home Corp., 89 Cal. App. 4th 908, 918, 107 Cal. Rptr. 2d 761 (2001).

80.21   *Id.*

80.22   *See* Briehl v. Gen. Motors Corp., 172 F.3d 623, 627 (8th Cir. 1998) (affirming dismissal of warranty claims seeking lost resale value of vehicles with anti-lock brake system that tended to fail if driver stepped hard on brakes, when plaintiffs' vehicles never exhibited the alleged defect); Carlson v. Gen. Motors Corp., 883 F.2d 287 (4th Cir. 1989) (loss of resale value due to defects that have not yet manifested themselves is not breach of implied warranty of merchantability); Jarman v. United Indus. Corp., 98 F. Supp. 2d 757 (S.D. Miss. 2000) (dismissing breach of warranty and other claims when buyer claimed that termite control product was not as effective as advertised but it had not failed to perform); Yost v. Gen. Motors Corp., 651 F. Supp. 656, 657, 658 (D.N.J. 1986) (likelihood of coolant leak due to design defect insufficient for warranty claim when no leak had actually occurred); Am. Suzuki Motor Corp. v. Super. Ct., 44 Cal. Rptr. 2d 526 (Ct. App. 1995) (design defect that created rollover risk not a breach of implied warranty of merchantability when vehicle has not yet malfunctioned); Zwiercan v. Gen. Motors Corp., 2002 WL 1472335 (Pa. C.P. May 22, 2002) (no warranty claim when seat belt that provides inadequate protection in rear-end collisions has not yet malfunctioned, but buyer may assert UDAP claim if repairs are required); Polaris Indus., Inc. v. McDonald, 2003 WL 21940115 (Tex. App. Aug. 13, 2003) (dangers in jet ski design did not breach warranty when no injury had occurred, plaintiff continued to use it, alleged defect was a design feature that was clearly disclosed before sale, and plaintiff did not contend he got less than he paid for); *see also* Delahunt v. Cytodyne Technologies, 241 F. Supp. 2d 827 (S.D. Ohio 2003) (no fraud claim for plaintiffs whose defective medications had not caused injuries, but UDAP claim is viable without injury other than payment of purchase price); Ford Motor Co. v. Rice, 726 So. 2d 626 (Ala. 1998) (no fraud claim when vehicles' alleged design defect had not caused injury to person or property).

80.23   7 F. Supp. 2d 792 (E.D. La. 1998).

80.24   *Id.* at 803.

80.25   *Id.*

80.26   *Id.* at 804 ("[P]laintiffs disregard the common thread of the cases: that the absence of manifest injury is so fundamental a deficiency in tort or implied warranty claims that such claims are more appropriately dismissed than preserved."), *citing* Martin v. Ford Motor Co., 914 F. Supp. 1449 (S.D. Tex. 1996) (granting summary judgment against vehicle owners who had not sustained any injuries but who claimed that an inadequate visor warning rendered their restraint system unsafe); *see In re* Gen. Motors Corp. Anti-Lock Brake Prods. Liab. Litig., 966 F. Supp. 1525, 1530 (E.D. Mo. 1997) (dismissing implied warranty of merchantability claims because "plaintiffs do not allege that the defect manifested itself in their vehicles, i.e. they do not explain when, where or how their vehicles exhibited the defects"), *aff'd*, 172 F.3d 623 (8th Cir. 1999). *But see* Holtzman v. Gen. Motors Corp., 48 U.C.C. Rep. Serv. 2d 1020 (Mass. Super. Ct. 2002) (denying motion to dismiss implied warranty claim when product was dangerous but had not yet caused injury).

80.27   Frank v. DaimlerChrysler Corp., 292 A.D.2d 118, 741 N.Y.S.2d 9, 48 U.C.C. Rep. Serv. 2d 563 (2002); *accord* Green v. Gen. Motors Corp., 2003 WL 21730592 (N.J. Super. Ct. App. Div. July 10, 2003) (unpublished).

80.28   Rivera v. Wyeth-Ayerst Laboratories, 283 F.3d 315 (5th Cir. 2002).

80.29   *Id.* at 317.

80.30   Solarz v. DaimlerChrysler Corp., 47 U.C.C. Rep. Serv. 2d 969 (Pa. C.P. 2002).

80.31   *In re* Bridgestone/Firestone, Inc., 288 F.3d 1012, 1017 n.1 (7th Cir. 2002); *see also* Delahunt v. Cytodyne Technologies, 241 F. Supp. 2d 827 (S.D. Ohio 2003) (no fraud claim for plaintiffs whose defective medications had not caused injuries, but UDAP claim is viable without injury other than payment of purchase price).

80.32   *See* Holtzman v. Gen. Motors Corp., 48 U.C.C. Rep. Serv. 2d 1020 (Mass. Super. Ct. 2002) (consumer who replaces dangerous product with a safer one should be able to recover cost of cover; consumer who keeps the dangerous product may recover diminution in value).

80.33   *See* Hicks v. Kaufman & Broad Home Corp., 89 Cal. App. 4th 908, 107 Cal. Rptr. 2d 761 (2001) ("Those implied warranty cases [in which claim was dismissed for failure to allege manifest injury] were not decided on the ground a defect must have resulted in the product malfunctioning in order to give rise to a suit for breach of warranty. Rather, they were decided on the ground that since there was no history of the products failing they were not, as a matter of law, defective.").

80.34 *See, e.g.*, Coley v. Champion Home Builders Co., 590 S.E.2d 20 (N.C. Ct. App. 2004) (manufacturer's provision of inadequate mobile home tie-down system is sufficient injury for UDAP claim).

7.3.4 Nonconformity With Express Warranties

7.3.4.1 Present Characteristics Express Warranties

Page 216

Addition to notes 94, 96.

Page 217

Page 222

Add new subsection to text after § 7.3.4.2.4.

7.3.4.1.1 Specific warranties created by affirmation of fact

94 *See* Hasek v. DaimlerChrysler Corp., 319 Ill. App. 3d 780, 745 N.E.2d 627, 44 U.C.C. Rep. Serv. 2d 108 (2001) (interpreting "defect" not to include engine noise that caused inconvenience and concern but did not interfere with operation, pose danger, or reduce value).

96 *Replace NCLC citation with*: National Consumer Law Center, Unfair and Deceptive Acts and Practices § 4.9.4 (5th ed. 2001 and Supp.).

7.3.4.3 Interpretation of Express Warranties

As discussed in Chapter 3, express warranties can be created by written guarantees, by oral statements, by advertising, or by pictures, models or labels. Generally, the question of whether certain language creates an express warranty is a question of fact.[128.1] The scope or meaning of the language creating the express warranty will be a question of fact whenever the language is "reasonably susceptible to different interpretations."[128.2]

In general, warranties are treated like other types of contracts, interpreted according to general contract principles.[128.3] They should be construed so as to give effect to the warranty.[128.4]

If the language of the warranty is ambiguous, and the language appears in a form prepared by the seller (which will almost always be the case in a consumer transaction), then the ambiguity must be resolved against the drafter.[128.5] This rule applies to contracts in which the warranty and a limitation or disclaimer of warranty appear to conflict.[128.6] For example, in *Southern Energy Homes, Inc. v. Washington*, a case against a mobile home manufacturer for defects including a roof leak, the court resolved an inconsistency between the warranty and the limitation of warranty to find that the leak was not excluded from the warranty.[128.7] The contract's express warranty provided that the mobile home would be free from defects for one year, "assuming reasonable maintenance and servicing of the home by the owner as described in the Owner's Manual," and excluded defects arising from the homeowner's "failure to perform reasonable maintenance and servicing as described in the Owner's Manual." The warranty also stated that the manufacturer would "have no obligation to repair roof leaks unless the roof of the home has been coated or painted as provided for on page 4 of the homeowner's manual." However, the owner's manual provided only that the roof should be coated after the first twelve months and each year thereafter, and that the roof should be inspected twice a year and "recoated" as necessary. Because the maintenance directions did not indicate that the homeowner must coat or paint the roof during the warranty period, the roof leaks were not excluded from the warranty for "failure to perform reasonable maintenance and servicing as described in the homeowner's manual."[128.8] The court noted that, although the warranty could have been read to exclude coverage until the roof was coated, such an interpretation would have been inconsistent with Southern's warranty that the mobile home, "assuming reasonable maintenance and servicing," will be free of substantial defects for one year from the date of the initial delivery of the home to the owner.[128.9]

Express warranties must be reasonably construed taking into consideration the nature of the product, the situation of the parties, and surrounding circumstances.[128.10] The terms of the warranty must be interpreted as an ordinary person would understand their meaning.[128.11] Thus, in a case against Rolls-Royce Motors for paint defects on a $185,000 Corniche convertible, the court held that the express warranty that the vehicle will be "free from defects in material and workmanship" must be read to include the description of quality of workmanship contained in the Rolls-Royce advertising brochure.[128.12] The warranty could not fairly be construed, as the manufacturer argued, to assure no more than a safe and operable vehicle acceptable in the trade. Although the contract purported to limit the express warranty to the terms of the written contract and to disclaim any other representations, the court found that a literal interpretation of the warranty limitation would be unreasonable under the circumstances. The quality of a Rolls-Royce, as described by the advertising brochure, is "intimately intertwined" with Rolls-Royce's promise that the vehicle will be "free from defects in material and workmanship." A standard paint job, acceptable on a Chevrolet or Buick, did not meet the standard of the Rolls-Royce guarantee.

Similarly, in a case against Ford Motor Co. involving paint defects caused by environmental damage, the court construed the terms of an ambiguous contract provision in accordance with their "ordinary meaning" to find an express warranty.[128.13] The contract contained a general express warranty against defects for three years or 36,000 miles, and the following provision regarding paint damage: "With respect to damage caused by airborne material (environmental fallout), where there is no defect involved and therefore no warranty, our policy is to cover paint damage due to airborne material (environmental fallout) for 12 months or 12,000 miles, whichever occurs first." The court found, over Ford's objection, that this was a warranty even though Ford chose to label it a policy rather than a warranty.

Other general principles of contract interpretation have been applied to the terms of express warranties. For example, if two provisions are in conflict, the first will generally prevail over a later-appearing provision; general provisions will yield to specific; handwriting will prevail over printed language; and the interpretation which gives effect to the main purpose of the contract will prevail.[128.14]

Section 2-316(1) of the UCC provides that limitations on express warranties are inoperative to the extent that they can not reasonably be read consistently with the warranty.[128.15] Thus, in a case against Midas Muffler seeking to enforce an express warranty to replace worn out or defective brakes for free for as "long as you own your car," the court nullified a limitation on the warranty which rendered the warranty meaningless.[128.16] Although the warranty promised free replacement of the warranted brakes, it also contained a provision that excluded coverage for "the cost of additional components and labor required to restore the brake system to its proper operation" and required the Midas shop to "restore the entire brake system to its proper operation" at the customer's expense before replacing the worn or defective brakes.[128.17] The court found that the "warranty" was in fact a marketing device, designed to get customers back to Midas where they would be sold other parts and labor. The court ruled that the clause excluding coverage was inconsistent with the express warranty and was therefore inoperable pursuant to UCC § 2-316(1), in addition to being ambiguous and therefore to be construed strictly against the drafter.

Other courts have noted that limitations on warranties will be construed strictly, in accordance with public policy which does not favor modifications of warranties and limitation of remedies.[128.18]

Efforts to modify or limit express warranties may give rise to other statutory claims. If a clause purporting to limit or modify an express warranty is misleading or deceptive, it may violate the state unfair and deceptive acts and practices (UDAP) statute.[128.19] Misrepresenting or failing to disclose material facts about a warranty may also be a UDAP violation.[128.20] The Magnuson-Moss Warranty Act prohibits a supplier from disclaiming or modifying an implied warranty when it has given a written warranty on the product.[128.21] Magnuson-Moss also requires certain limits on the duration of an implied warranty to be disclosed in clear and unmistakable language on the face of the warranty,[128.22] and requires that key terms of the warranty be clearly and conspicuously disclosed.[128.23]

128.1   McLaughlin v. Denharco, Inc., 129 F. Supp. 2d 32, 43 U.C.C. Rep. Serv. 2d 1122, 1128 (D. Me. 2001); Crothers v. Cohen, 384 N.W.2d 562 (Minn. Ct. App. 1986).

128.2   McLaughlin v. Denharco, Inc., 129 F. Supp. 2d 32, 43 U.C.C. Rep. Serv. 2d 1122, 1127 (D. Me. 2001); *see* Fassi v. Auto Wholesalers, 145 N.H. 404, 762 A.2d 1034 (2000) (court would not disturb finding of express warranty when plaintiffs were told by salesperson that they could have their own mechanic examine the vehicle within thirty days, and if problem were discovered, the defendant would take care of it, even though bill of sale stated: "Type of Warranty—30 DAY 1000 Mile Safety Items"). *But see* Canal Elec. Co. v. Westinghouse Elec. Co., 973 F.2d 988 (1st Cir. 1992) (interpretation is a question of fact to be determined by the trier of fact if it depends on the credibility of extrinsic evidence or on a choice among reasonable inferences to be drawn from extrinsic evidence, but a question of interpretation of an integrated agreement is to be determined as a matter of law); Ford Motor Co. v. McMillian, 1995 Conn. Super. LEXIS 247 (Conn. Super. Ct. Jan. 25, 1995) (whether an express warranty for paint defects exists is a question of law to be determined from a review of the language contained in the warranty at issue).

128.3   S. Energy Homes, Inc. v. Washington, 774 So. 2d 505 (Ala. 2000) (express warranties are treated like any other type of contract and are interpreted according to general contract principles); Contreras v. Ford Motor Co., 2002 WL 31727261 (Cal. Ct. App. Dec. 5, 2002) (unpublished) (interpreting dealer's warranty according to general contract principles and finding warranty covered entire car, not just custom features that dealer installed).

128.4   *See id.*; Crothers v. Cohen, 384 N.W.2d 562 (Minn. Ct. App. 1986).

128.5   Wilbur v. Toyota Motor Sales, U.S.A., Inc., 86 F.3d 23 (2d Cir. 1996); Berk v. Gordon Johnson Co., 232 F. Supp. 682 (E.D. Mich. 1964) (ambiguity resolved against drafter); S. Energy Homes, Inc. v. Washington, 774 So. 2d 505 (Ala. 2000) (ambiguity caused by apparent conflict between warranty and limitation of warranty resolved in favor of buyer of mobile home); Gen. Motors Corp. v. Blanchard, 1998 WL 285838 (Conn. Super. Ct. May 19, 1998); Crothers v. Cohen, 384 N.W.2d 562, 564 (Minn. Ct. App. 1986); Giarratano v. Midas Muffler, 166 Misc. 2d 390, 630 N.Y.S.2d 656, 660 (Civ. Ct. 1995); Stream v. Sportscar Salon, Ltd., 91 Misc. 2d 99, 397 N.Y.S.2d 677 (Civ. Ct. 1977) (ambiguity resolved against the drafter, particularly when contract is one of adhesion).

128.6   Berk v. Gordon Johnson Co., 232 F. Supp. 682 (E.D. Mich. 1964); S. Energy Homes, Inc. v. Washington, 774 So. 2d 505 (Ala. 2000).

128.7   774 So. 2d 505, 516 (Ala. 2000).

128.8   *Id.* at 513.

128.9   *Id.* at 517.

128.10   Huebert v. Fed. Pac. Elec. Co., Inc., 208 Kan. 720, 725, 494 P.2d 1210 (1972).

128.11   Crothers v. Cohen, 384 N.W.2d 562, 564 (Minn. Ct. App. 1986).

128.12   Zeff v. Rolls-Royce Motors, Inc., 1988 U.S. Dist. LEXIS 17755, at *20 (E.D. Mich. Aug. 31, 1988).

128.13   Ford Motor Co. v. McMillian, 1995 Conn. Super. LEXIS 247 (Conn. Super. Ct. Jan. 25, 1995).

128.14   Berk v. Gordon Johnson Co., 232 F. Supp. 682, 687 (E.D. Mich. 1964).

128.15   *See* § 5.2, *supra*; *see also* Ford Motor Co. v. Reid, 250 Ark. 176, 465 S.W.2d 80 (Ark. 1971) (applying § 2-316 to find that language stating that all express warranties "shall be fulfilled by selling dealer" was an instruction to the dealer and not a limitation on the warranty); Giarratano v. Midas Muffler, 630 N.Y.S.2d 656, 660 (Civ. Ct. 1995) (clause negating express warranty inoperative because it violates § 2-316).

128.16   Giarratano v. Midas Muffler, 630 N.Y.S.2d 656, 658 (Civ. Ct. 1995).

128.17   *Id.* at 658.

128.18   *See* Hahn v. Ford Motor Co., 434 N.E.2d 943 (Ind. 1982) (Ind. law); Auto-Teria, Inc. v. Ahern, 170 Ind. App. 84, 352 N.E.2d 774 (1976).

128.19   *See* § 11.1.6, *infra*; Giarratano v. Midas Muffler, 630 N.Y.S.2d 656, 662 (Civ. Ct. 1995) ("Midas Warranty Certificate was misleading and deceptive in that it promised the replacement of worn brake pads free of charge and then emasculated that promise by requiring plaintiff to pay for additional brake system repairs which Midas would deem necessary and proper.").

128.20   *See* § 11.6.1, *infra*.

128.21   *See* § 2.3.2, *supra*.

128.22   *See* § 2.3.2.3, *supra*.

128.23   *See* Wilbur v. Toyota Motor Sales, U.S.A., Inc., 86 F.3d 23 (2d Cir. 1996) (manufacturer's interpretation of warranty, which would exclude coverage, would render warranty so cryptic and unclear as to violate Magnuson-Moss Act); § 2.6.4, *supra*.

7.3.5 *Nonconformity With Implied Warranty of Merchantability*

Page 223

7.3.5.1 Standards for Nonconformity

Add to text after bulleted item containing note 142:

- Concrete that could not withstand 3000 lbs. of pressure per square inch, possibly because of substandard components;[142.1]

142.1   Morris Concrete v. Warrick, 2003 WL 21205836 (Ala. Civ. App. May 23, 2003).

Add to text after bulleted item containing note 145:

• Medicine that could cause dangerous side effects, even if it did not cause side effects for the particular consumer;[145.1]

145.1   Rivera v. Wyeth-Ayerst Laboratories, 121 F. Supp. 2d 614 (S.D. Tex. 2000).

Page 224

Addition to note 147.

147   *See also* Erpelding v. Skipperliner Indus., Inc., 45 U.C.C. Rep. Serv. 2d 722 (D. Minn. 2001) (boat component that suddenly burst into flames).

7.3.5.2 Nonconformity Must Exist at Delivery

Addition to notes 154, 155.

154   Dildine v. Town & Country Truck Sales, Inc., 259 Ga. App. 732, 577 S.E.2d 882, 50 U.C.C. Rep. Serv. 2d 761 (2003); Jenkins v. Gen. Motors Corp., 240 Ga. App. 636, 524 S.E.2d 324 (1999).

155   Dildine v. Town & Country Truck Sales, Inc., 259 Ga. App. 732, 577 S.E.2d 882, 50 U.C.C. Rep. Serv. 2d 761 (2003); Sheffield v. Darby, 244 Ga. App. 437, 535 S.E.2d 776 (2000); Ford Motor Co. v. Gen. Accident Ins. Co., 365 Md. 321, 779 A.2d 362, 45 U.C.C. Rep. Serv. 2d 319 (2001).

Replace last sentence of subsection with:

See § 7.5, *infra*, for more detail on proving nonconformity at delivery.

7.4 The Buyer's Burden of Proof and Use of Circumstantial Evidence

Page 226

7.4.1 *The Buyer's Burden of Proof*

Addition to note 168.

168   *See, e.g.*, Hasek v. DaimlerChrysler Corp., 319 Ill. App. 3d 780, 745 N.E.2d 627, 44 U.C.C. Rep. Serv. 2d 108 (2001).

Add to text at end of subsection's first paragraph:

The buyer need not prove any fault on the part of the seller but only that the goods were defective.[169.1]

169.1   Eggl v. Letvin Equip. Co., 632 N.W.2d 435, 45 U.C.C. Rep. Serv. 2d 538 (N.D. 2001).

Add note 169.2 at end of first sentence of subsection's second paragraph.

169.2   Revised Article 1, which the National Conference of Commissioners on Uniform State Laws (NCCUSL) approved in 2001 for adoption by the states, preserves this provision without substantive change as U.C.C. § 1-201(b)(8).

Addition to notes 171, 172, 176, 177, 180.

171   Ford Motor Co. v. Gen. Accident Ins. Co., 365 Md. 321, 779 A.2d 362, 45 U.C.C. Rep. Serv. 2d 319 (2001).

172   Ford Motor Co. v. Gen. Accident Ins. Co., 365 Md. 321, 779 A.2d 362, 45 U.C.C. Rep. Serv. 2d 319 (2001) (engine fire in two-year-old vehicle not sufficient in and of itself to establish breach).

176   Oregel v. Am. Isuzu Motors, Inc., 90 Cal. App. 4th 1094, 109 Cal. Rptr. 2d 583 (2001) (lemon law case); Vanderbrook v. Coachmen Indus., 818 So. 2d 906 (La. Ct. App. 2002) (lay witness could testify that motor home's electrical system was not properly recharging the battery); Dalme v. Blockers Manufactured Homes, Inc., 779 So. 2d 1014 (La. Ct. App. 2001) (decided under La. Civil Code).

Page 227

177   Universal Motors, Inc. v. Waldock, 719 P.2d 254 (Alaska 1986) (once consumer offers credible evidence that defect relates to materials or workmanship, the burden shifts to the warrantor to prove consumer abuse).

180   *See also* CEF Enterprises v. Betts, 838 So. 2d 999 (Miss. Ct. App. 2003) (elements are: 1) defendant is merchant who sold goods of this kind; 2) defect was present when product left defendant's control; and 3) defect proximately caused plaintiff's injuries).

Replace note 181 with:

181   Tucker v. Gen. Motors Corp. (*Ex parte* Gen. Motors Corp.), 769 So. 2d 903, 40 U.C.C. Rep. Serv. 2d 123 (Ala. 1999); *accord* Chase v. Kawasaki Motors Corp., 140 F. Supp. 2d 1280, 45 U.C.C. Rep. Serv. 2d 782 (M.D. Ala. 2001); *see also* Nev. Contract Services, Inc. v. Squirrel Companies, 68 P.3d 896, 50 U.C.C. Rep. Serv. 2d 1066 (Nev. 2003) (elements of warranty claim are that a warranty existed, the defendant breached that warranty, and the defendant's breach was the proximate cause of the loss sustained).

Addition to note 182.

182   *Accord* DeWitt v. Eveready Battery Co., 565 S.E.2d 140, 49 U.C.C. Rep. Serv. 2d 116 (N.C. 2002).

Replace § 7.4.2 heading with:

7.4.2 Circumstantial Evidence of Defective Condition: Proof of Cause Unnecessary

Addition to notes 183–185, 187, 188, 195.

183   *See, e.g.,* Genetti v. Caterpillar, Inc., 261 Neb. 98, 621 N.W.2d 529, 43 U.C.C. Rep. Serv. 2d 829 (2001); DeWitt v. Eveready Battery Co., 565 S.E.2d 140, 49 U.C.C. Rep. Serv. 2d 116 (N.C. 2002) (evidence may include such factors as the malfunction, expert testimony concerning possible causes, timing of appearance of defect, history of the product, similar incidents, elimination of other possible causes, and proof that the accident would not occur without a defect); Earl v. Leiffer Constr., Inc., 2001 Ohio App. LEXIS 3857 (Ohio Ct. App. Aug. 31, 2001) (common law warranty case); Osburn v. Bendix Home Sys., Inc., 613 P.2d 445 (Okla. 1980); *see also* Evans v. Evans, 569 S.E.2d 303, 48 U.C.C. Rep. Serv. 2d 1342 (N.C. Ct. App. 2002) (circumstantial evidence can be sufficient, but insufficient in this case). *But see* Miller v. Daimler-Chrysler Motors Corp., 2001 Ohio App. LEXIS 2450 (Ohio Ct. App. May 31, 2001) (intermittent noise and vibration in steering column were symptoms, not defects in and of themselves, and were not sufficient circumstantial evidence of defect).

184   *Replace Tucker citation with:* Tucker v. Gen. Motors Corp. (*Ex parte* Gen. Motors Corp.), 769 So. 2d 903, 40 U.C.C. Rep. Serv. 2d 123; *add: In re* Simitar Entm't, Inc., 275 B.R. 331, 47 U.C.C. Rep. Serv. 2d 1343 (Bankr. D. Minn. 2002); Oregel v. Am. Isuzu Motors, Inc., 90 Cal. App. 4th 1094, 109 Cal. Rptr. 2d 583 (2001) (lemon law case); Morrison v. Allstar Dodge, Inc., 792 So. 2d 9 (La. Ct. App. 2001) (redhibition claim); Genetti v. Caterpillar, Inc., 261 Neb. 98, 621 N.W.2d 529, 43 U.C.C. Rep. Serv. 2d 829 (2001); Nev. Contract Services, Inc. v. Squirrel Companies, 68 P.3d 896, 50 U.C.C. Rep. Serv. 2d 1066 (Nev. 2003); Taft v. Sports Page Shop, Inc., 226 A.D.2d 974, 640 N.Y.S.2d 698 (1996); Reddin v. Toyota Motor Distributors, Inc., 1991 WL 21522 (Ohio Ct. App. Feb. 22, 1991) (unpublished) (lemon law case); Osburn v. Bendix Home Sys., Inc., 613 P.2d 445 (Okla. 1980); *see also* Jarvis v. Ford Motor Co., 283 F.3d 33 (2d Cir. 2002) (negligence and products liability case); Universal Motors, Inc. v. Waldock, 719 P.2d 254 (Alaska 1986) (once consumer offers credible evidence that defect relates to materials or workmanship, the burden shifts to the warrantor to prove consumer abuse). *But see* Teerling v. Fleetwood Motor Homes of Ind., Inc., 2001 U.S. Dist. LEXIS 7481 (N.D. Ill. May 31, 2001) (aberrant decision denying warranty claim because of, *inter alia*, failure to prove precise cause of excessive windshield fogging); *cf.* Wilder v. Toyota Motor Sales, U.S.A., Inc., 2001 WL 1602043 (4th Cir. Dec. 17, 2001) (proof of malfunction insufficient in product liability case when buyer failed to negate alternative causes suggested by manufacturer); Thorner v. Fleetwood, 2002 WL 1998285 (N.D. Ill. Aug. 28, 2002) (proof of malfunction insufficient when buyer failed to negate other causes advanced by manufacturer).

Page 228

185   Dalme v. Blockers Manufactured Homes, Inc., 779 So. 2d 1014 (La. Ct. App. 2001) (decided under La. Civil Code).

187   *Replace Tucker citation with:* Tucker v. Gen. Motors Corp. (*Ex parte* Gen. Motors Corp.), 769 So. 2d 903, 40 U.C.C. Rep. Serv. 2d 123; *add:* Thorner v. Fleetwood, 2002 WL 844610 (N.D. Ill. May 1, 2001) (defects in motor home not so difficult for layperson to understand that expert testimony necessary), *vacated in part on other grounds,* 2002 WL 1998285 (N.D. Ill. Aug. 28, 2002); Green v. Ford Motor Co., 1996 WL 153214 (E.D. Pa. Apr. 1, 1996); Baker v. Chrysler Corp., 1993 WL 18099 (E.D. Pa. Jan. 25, 1993), *aff'd,* 9 F.3d 1539 (3d Cir. 1993) (table); *see also* Dalme v. Blockers Manufactured Homes, Inc., 779 So. 2d 1014 (La. Ct. App. 2001) (decided under La. Civil Code); Taft v. Sports Page Shop, Inc., 226 A.D.2d 974, 640 N.Y.S.2d 698 (1996) (buyer who relies on circumstantial evidence also bears burden of excluding other causes); Earl v. Leiffer Constr., Inc., 2001 Ohio App. LEXIS 3857 (Ohio Ct. App. Aug. 31, 2001) (expert testimony unnecessary in common law warranty case to show that roofer deviated from common standards of workmanship or failed to exercise ordinary care in allowing water to enter interior of home). *But cf.* Fatovic v. Chrysler Corp., 2003 WL 21481012 (Del. Super. Ct. Feb. 28, 2003) (lay testimony insufficient without negation of other causes).

Page 229

188   *See, e.g.,* Teerling v. Fleetwood Motor Homes of Ind., Inc., 2001 U.S. Dist. LEXIS 7481 (N.D. Ill. May 31, 2001) (expert testimony is necessary to prove that motor home's air suspension system is defective, because it is not a subject of common knowledge or understanding).

Page 230

195   Easley v. Day Motors, Inc., 796 So. 2d 236, 44 U.C.C. Rep. Serv. 2d 407 (Miss. Ct. App. 2001).

7.5 Proving Condition at Delivery

7.5.1 Eyewitness Testimony of Performance

7.5.1.1 Eyewitness and Expert Testimony Compared

Addition to note 198.

198   *See* Gen. Motors Corp. v. Martin, 1997 WL 805137 (Conn. Super. Ct. Dec. 16, 1997) (lemon law case); Adventure Travel World, Ltd. v. Gen. Motors Corp., 107 N.C. App. 573, 421 S.E.2d 173 (1992).

7.5.1.2 Early Detection Adds Credibility to Eyewitness Testimony

Page 231

Addition to note 199.

199   McGough v. Oakwood Mobile Homes, Inc., 779 So. 2d 793 (La. Ct. App. 2000) (appearance of defects in mobile home soon after delivery is evidence that they existed at delivery); *see also* DeWitt v. Eveready Battery Co., 565 S.E.2d 140, 49 U.C.C. Rep. Serv. 2d 116 (N.C. 2002) (batteries leaked twenty-four hours after purchase).

Page 232

7.5.1.3 Problems of Using Eyewitness Testimony Against Indirect Sellers

Addition to note 206.

206   Phillips v. Restaurant Mgmt., 552 S.E.2d 686, 45 U.C.C. Rep. 2d 790 (N.C. Ct. App. 2001).

7.5.2 *Evidence of Proper Use and Maintenance; Negating Other Causes*

Addition to notes 208, 210, 213.

208   *See also* Alvarez v. Am. Isuzu Motors, 321 Ill. App. 3d 696, 255 Ill. Dec. 236, 749 N.E.2d 16 (2001) (recovery denied because plaintiff failed to testify about how she cared for and handled the car, under what conditions she drove it, or how she maintained it).

210   *See also* Wilder v. Toyota Motor Sales, U.S.A., Inc., 2001 WL 1602043 (4th Cir. Dec. 17, 2001) (proof of malfunction insufficient in product liability case when buyer failed to negate alternative causes suggested by manufacturer); Teerling v. Fleetwood Motor Homes of Ind., Inc., 2001 U.S. Dist. LEXIS 7481 (N.D. Ill. May 31, 2001) (insufficient proof of defect when plaintiff failed to show proper use and maintenance and failed to negate other causes); Oregel v. Am. Isuzu Motors, Inc., 90 Cal. App. 4th 1094, 109 Cal. Rptr. 2d 583 (2001) (in lemon law case jury may infer from circumstantial evidence that defect was not caused by fault of the buyer); Alvarez v. Am. Isuzu Motors, 321 Ill. App. 3d 696, 255 Ill. Dec. 236, 749 N.E.2d 16 (2001) (plaintiff's proof failed because did not exclude other causes or abnormal use); Fidele v. Crescent Ford Truck Sales, Inc., 786 So. 2d 147 (La. Ct. App. 2001) (buyer who failed to maintain vehicle did not prove existence of defect); Morehouse v. Behlmann Pontiac-GMC Truck Serv., Inc., 31 S.W.3d 55 (Mo. Ct. App. 2000) (expert identified two possible causes of oil sludge and owner negated one possibility); DeWitt v. Eveready Battery Co., 565 S.E.2d 140, 49 U.C.C. Rep. Serv. 2d 116 (N.C. 2002); Taft v. Sports Page Shop, Inc., 226 A.D.2d 974, 640 N.Y.S.2d 698 (1996) (buyer who relies on circumstantial evidence also bears burden of excluding other causes); Price v. Chevrolet Motor Div., 765 A.2d 800, 43 U.C.C. Rep. Serv. 2d 593 (Pa. Super. Ct. 2000) (failure to negate accident as cause of vehicle's malfunction).

Page 233

213   *See also* DeWitt v. Eveready Battery Co., 565 S.E.2d 140, 49 U.C.C. Rep. Serv. 2d 116 (N.C. 2002) (buyer's expert testified that alleged misuse, even if it had occurred, would not have caused the accident).

Add to text at end of subsection:

The buyer need not, however, negate every theoretically conceivable cause.[214.1]

214.1   DeWitt v. Eveready Battery Co., 565 S.E.2d 140, 49 U.C.C. Rep. Serv. 2d 116 (N.C. 2002).

Page 234

7.5.4 *Evidence of Repairs by the Seller*

Addition to note 219.

219   Linscott v. Smith, 3 Kan. App. 2d 1, 587 P.2d 1271 (1978); Fletcher v. Don Foss of Cleveland, Inc., 90 Ohio App. 3d 82, 628 N.E.2d 60 (1993). *But see* Teerling v. Fleetwood Motor Homes of Ind., Inc., 2001 U.S. Dist. LEXIS 7481 (N.D. Ill. May 31, 2001) (defendant's repairs of the product as if warranty covered these defects was not proof of defect, as sometimes defendant made adjustments or replaced parts even though it could not substantiate plaintiff's complaints); Alvarez v. Am. Isuzu Motors, 321 Ill. App. 3d 696, 255 Ill. Dec. 236, 749 N.E.2d 16 (2001) (seller's history of making repairs does not prove breach of warranty, especially as some repairs were routine maintenance that was not covered by warranty).

7.5.5 *Evidence That Replacement Parts Work Well*

Addition to note 221.

221   Cannan v. Bob Chambers Ford, 432 A.2d 387 (Me. 1981) (citing evidence replacement part worked well as support for conclusion that original work was defective).

Page 235

7.5.6 *Evidence of Similar Claims by Others*

Addition to note 222.

222   Smith v. Ingersoll-Rand Co., 214 F.3d 1235 (10th Cir. 2000) (N.M. law) (evidence of other incidents admissible to prove causation only if they have high degree of similarity to problem with plaintiff's product); DeWitt v. Eveready Battery Co., 565 S.E.2d 140, 49 U.C.C. Rep. Serv. 2d 116 (N.C. 2002);

Cummings v. Glidden Co., 565 S.E.2d 279 (N.C. Ct. App. 2002) (unpublished) (text available at 2002 WL 1419618) (evidence that other paint sprayers had same problem tends to show that defect existed when product left manufacturer's control); *see also* Woodson v. McGeorge Camping Ctr., Inc., 1992 U.S. App. LEXIS 22747 (4th Cir. Sept. 15, 1992) (allowing discovery of complaints by other owners and information that would lead to evidence of similar malfunctions by same model). *But cf. In re* Ford Motor Co. Ignition Switch Prods. Liab. Lit., 194 F.R.D. 484 (D.N.J. 2000) (statistical analysis creates at most a rebuttable presumption that defect was cause of problem).

Add to text at end of subsection's first paragraph:

Similar incidents are relevant for this purpose whether occurring before or after the problem with the plaintiff's product.[222.1] Evidence that subsequent or prior owners experienced the same problems with the product is also admissible, as it tends to show that the problems arose from defects in the product rather than from misuse.[222.2]

222.1 Smith v. Ingersoll-Rand Co., 214 F.3d 1235 (10th Cir. 2000) (N.M. law).

222.2 Chicago Cutlery Co. v. Dist. Ct., 568 P.2d 464 (Colo. 1977) (customer lists discoverable to locate other buyers to show that injuries were caused by design of the product rather than plaintiff's peculiar susceptibilities); Genetti v. Caterpillar, Inc., 261 Neb. 98, 621 N.W.2d 529, 43 U.C.C. Rep. Serv. 2d 829 (2001); *see also* Alvine v. Mercedes-Benz of N. Am., 620 N.W.2d 608 (S.D. 2001) (evidence that prior owners experienced same problems with vehicle admissible to show damages).

Addition to notes 223, 224.

223 *See* White v. Ford Motor Co., 312 F.3d 998 (9th Cir. 2002).

224 White v. Ford Motor Co., 312 F.3d 998 (9th Cir. 2002) (evidence of prior similar accidents admissible to show that manufacturer had notice); *see also* Allen v. Roberts Constr. Co., 138 N.C. App. 557, 532 S.E.2d 534 (2000) (citing photos of similar defects in other houses constructed by same builder as evidence of knowledge). *But cf.* Pierce v. Catalina Yachts, Inc., 2 P.3d 618 (Alaska 2000) (other consumers' letters of complaint were not admissible to support UDAP claim that manufacturer had notice of defects yet continued to sell product without disclosure, unless consumer also introduced evidence that defect actually existed).

Page 236

7.5.8 Expert Testimony

Addition to notes 228, 232.

228 Starks v. Solomon, 2001 Mich. App. LEXIS 1000 (Mich. Ct. App. Mar. 30, 2001) (unpublished) (expert can make reasonable inferences from established facts to form opinion about how long defect existed and whether sellers would have known about it). *But cf.* Thorner v. Fleetwood, 2002 WL 844610 (N.D. Ill. May 1, 2001) (expert in auto mechanics but who had no personal or professional experience with motor homes could not testify concerning defects in coach portion of motor home), *vacated in part on other grounds*, 2002 WL 1998285 (N.D. Ill. Aug. 28, 2002).

232 King v. Taylor Chrysler Plymouth, 184 Mich. App. 204, 457 N.W.2d 42 (1990) (licensed automobile mechanic qualified as expert). *But cf.* Teerling v. Fleetwood Motor Homes of Ind., Inc., 2001 U.S. Dist. LEXIS 7481 (N.D. Ill. May 31, 2001) (barring expert's opinion because he had experience only with cars, not motor homes).

Add to text at end of subsection's next-to-last paragraph:

The American Trial Lawyers Association and some private companies may also be able to help locate experts. Another source of information is reports of jury verdicts in publications and on the Internet, which often identify the experts involved in the case.

7.6 Defenses to Breach of Warranty

7.6.2 Buyer's Conduct as the Cause of Damage

Page 237

7.6.2.1 General

Addition to note 244.

244 *See also* Universal Motors, Inc. v. Waldock, 719 P.2d 254 (Alaska 1986).

Add to text at end of subsection's third paragraph:

The jury may infer from circumstantial evidence that the defect was caused by a breach of the warranty rather than by the fault of the buyer.[244.1]

244.1 Oregel v. Am. Isuzu Motors, Inc., 90 Cal. App. 4th 1094, 109 Cal. Rptr. 2d 583 (2001).

7.6.2.2 Buyer's Negligence

Page 239

Addition to notes 251, 253.

251   *See also* Oddi v. Ford Motor Co., 234 F.3d 136 (3d 2000) (Pa. law).
253   E.D. Smith & Sons v. Ark. Glass Container Corp., 236 F.3d 920 (8th Cir. 2001).

7.6.2.3 Assumption of Risk

Addition to note 254.

254   *See, e.g.,* Spain v. Brown & Williamson Tobacco Corp., 50 U.C.C. Rep. Serv. 2d 1091 (Ala. 2003) (if buyer continued to smoke cigarettes after learning of their dangers, injury would not proximately result from breach of warranty).

7.6.2.4 Misuse of the Product

Page 241

Addition to note 270.

270   Malul v. Capital Cabinets, Inc., 740 N.Y.S.2d 828, 47 U.C.C. Rep. Serv. 2d 502 (Civ. Ct. 2002).

Page 242

Add to text at end of subsection's fifth paragraph:

The nature of the ordinary uses of the product may be defined by any warnings the manufacturer communicates.[273.1]

273.1   Malul v. Capital Cabinets, Inc., 740 N.Y.S.2d 828, 47 U.C.C. Rep. Serv. 2d 502 (Civ. Ct. 2002).

Addition to note 274.

274   Johnson v. Monsanto Co., 48 U.C.C. Rep. Serv. 2d 586 (Ohio Ct. App. 2002) (misuse does not bar claim if it did not contribute to the malfunction).

Replace note 275 with:

275   *See* S. Energy Homes, Inc. v. Washington, 774 So. 2d 505, 40 U.C.C. Rep. Serv. 2d 986 (Ala. 2000) (because maintenance instructions did not clearly state that buyer had to coat or paint the roof during the warranty period, failure to do so was no basis for denying warranty claim); *see also* Malul v. Capital Cabinets, Inc., 740 N.Y.S.2d 828, 47 U.C.C. Rep. Serv. 2d 502 (Civ. Ct. 2002) (if buyer uses product in an abnormal but reasonably foreseeable way, seller may be liable if it failed to warn).

7.6.2.5 Failure to Abide by Directions for Use

Addition to notes 276, 283.

276   *Replace S. Energy Homes citation with*: 774 So. 2d 505, 40 U.C.C. Rep. Serv. 2d 986 (Ala. 2000); *add*: *But cf.* Chapman v. Maytag Corp., 297 F.3d 682 (7th Cir. 2002) (adequate warnings will not render product with a manufacturing defect non-defective in strict liability case).

Page 243

283   Vanderbrook v. Coachmen Indus., 818 So. 2d 906 (La. Ct. App. 2002).

7.6.3 *Noncompliance with Conditions to Warranty Coverage*

Page 244

Add to text at end of subsection's fourth paragraph:

A California law, effective January 1, 2004, requires paper and on-line warranty registration cards to state that failure to complete and return the card does not diminish the buyer's warranty rights.[290.1]

290.1   Cal. Civ. Code § 1793.1(a)(1) (West).

Replace note 293 with:

293   *See* National Consumer Law Center, Unfair and Deceptive Acts and Practices § 9.5 (5th ed. 2001 and Supp.).

7.6.4 *Expiration of Express Warranty Period*

7.6.4.1 Determining When Warranty Expires

Replace § 7.6.4.1 heading with:

Add to text at end of subsection's second paragraph:

There may also be an argument that the running of the warranty period was tolled while the seller had possession of the vehicle for earlier repairs.[297.1] Michigan has a non-uniform UCC amendment that extends the warranty for the duration of any period of time that exceeds either ten days or ten percent of the warranty period, if the product was out of service for warranty repairs during that time.[297.2]

297.1   Fletcher v. Don Foss of Cleveland, Inc., 90 Ohio App. 3d 82, 628 N.E.2d 60 (1993).
297.2   Mich. Comp. Laws § 440.2313b.

Add new subsection heading after subsection's second paragraph.

7.6.4.1a Defects Reported, But Not Repaired Before Period Expires

Addition to note 298.

298   *See also* Nulite Indus. Co. v. Horne, 252 Ga. App. 378, 556 S.E.2d 255 (2001) (question whether defect arose during warranty period does not affect statute of limitations; non-U.C.C. case).

Page 245

Add note 299.1 at end of second sentence of subsection's final paragraph.

299.1   Alvine v. Mercedes-Benz of N. Am., 620 N.W.2d 608 (S.D. 2001) (it was jury question whether problems experienced after warranty expired were the same as earlier problem).

Add to text at end of subsection:

Maryland provides by statute that warranties are automatically extended if the guarantor fails to successfully repair a malfunctioning or defective product within the warranty period.[300.1]

300.1   Md. Code Ann., Com. Law § 14-404(a)(2).

7.6.4.2 Defects Not Discovered Until After Period Expires

Addition to notes 302, 306.

302   *Accord* Tibco Software, Inc. v. Gordon Food Serv., Inc., 51 U.C.C. Rep. Serv. 2d 102 (W.D. Mich. 2003) (rejecting claim that warranty failed of its essential purpose when buyer did not make claim within warranty period).
306   Mazerolle v. Daimlerchrysler Corp., 48 U.C.C. Rep. Serv. 2d 1310 (Me. Super. Ct. 2002).

Add to text at end of subsection's third paragraph:

The manufacturer's failure to disclose a known defect may also be a UDAP violation.[308.1]

308.1   *See* § 11.1.5, *infra.*

Addition to note 309.

309   *See also* § 7.3.4.3, *supra.*

Page 246

Add note 313.1 at end of subsection's seventh paragraph.

313.1   Revised Article 1, which the National Conference of Commissioners on Uniform State Laws (NCCUSL) approved in 2001 for adoption by the states, redesignates this provision as U.C.C. § 1-302(b) without substantive change.

Add note 313.2 at end of first sentence of subsection's last paragraph.

313.2   This comment is preserved as U.C.C. § 1-302 cmt. 1 in revised Article 1, which NCCUSL approved in 2001 for adoption by the states.

Addition to note 315.

315   *Replace Taterka citation parenthetical with*: (for new car 12,000 mile/12-month period is reasonable when subsequently discovered defect was minor and appeared after two and one-half years); *add: But see* Mazerolle v. Daimlerchrysler Corp., 48 U.C.C. Rep. Serv. 2d 1310 (Me. Super. Ct. 2002) (U.C.C. § 1-204 does not permit courts to invalidate limits on express warranties, nor can limit be treated as a remedy limitation and invalidated under U.C.C. § 2-719).

7.6.4.3 Defects Discovered During But Reported After Warranty Period

Addition to notes 317, 318.

317   Nulite Indus. Co. v. Horne, 252 Ga. App. 378, 556 S.E.2d 255 (2001) (non-U.C.C. case) (no duty to give notice during warranty period when warranty did not require notice).
318   *Add to Werwinski citation: aff'd on other grounds,* 286 F.3d 661 (3d Cir. 2002).

Page 247

Replace note 320 with:

320   Revised Article 1, approved by the National Conference of Commissioners on Uniform State Laws (NCCUSL) in 2001 for adoption by the states, redesignates this provision as U.C.C. § 1-302(b) without substantive change. *See* § 7.6.4.2, *supra.*

Chapter 8	# UCC Self-Help Remedies: Cancellation of the Sale; Deducting Damages from the Outstanding Balance

8.1 Overview

Page 249

Addition to note 4.

4   *See* Taylor Inv. Corp. v. Weil, 169 F. Supp. 2d 1046, 44 U.C.C. Rep. Serv. 2d 382 (D. Minn. 2001) (revocation of acceptance under U.C.C. replaces rescission).

Add to text after sentence containing note 4:

Revocation of acceptance is an action at law, so a jury trial is available and the consumer need not meet traditional equitable requirements.[4.1] There may, however, be advantages for some plaintiffs in seeking an equitable remedy. For one thing, the state court system may assign equity cases to a faster or more favorable forum. In such a case the plaintiff may be able to frame the claim as one seeking equitable relief, such as rescission.[4.2]

4.1   Motor Vehicle Manufacturers Ass'n v. O'Neill, 212 Conn. 83, 561 A.2d 917 (1989) (revocation of acceptance is a legal action, but state lemon law claims are equitable because of flexibility of remedies and availability of repair and replacement orders); Henderson v. Chrysler Corp., 191 Mich. App. 337, 477 N.W.2d 505, 16 U.C.C. Rep. Serv. 2d 671 (1991) (complaint sought remedy at law even though it used term "rescission"); Koperski v. Husker Dodge, Inc., 208 Neb. 29, 36, 37, 302 N.W.2d 655 (1981); Gen. Motors Acceptance Corp. v. Jankowitz, 216 N.J. Super. 313, 523 A.2d 695 (Super. Ct. App. Div. 1987); Sudol v. Rudy Papa Motors, 175 N.J. Super. 238, 417 A.2d 1133 (Dist. Ct. 1980); Motor Vehicle Manufacturers Ass'n v. State, 75 N.Y.2d 175, 551 N.Y.S.2d 470, 550 N.E.2d 919 (1990) (revocation of acceptance is an action at law, but state's lemon law remedies are equitable); Merola v. Atlas Lincoln Mercury, Inc., 70 A.D.2d 950, 417 N.Y.S.2d 775 (1979); *see also* Gen. Motors Corp. v. Schmitz, 362 Md. 229, 764 A.2d 838 (2001) (lemon law suit seeking refund need not be filed in court with equity jurisdiction); Genetti v. Caterpillar, Inc., 261 Neb. 98, 621 N.W.2d 529, 43 U.C.C. Rep. Serv. 2d 829 (2001) (lemon law suit for replacement or refund is action at law); Love v. Kenneth Hammersley Motors, Inc., 556 S.E.2d 764 (Va. 2002) (revocation of acceptance claim is a claim for money and can be filed on law side rather than equity). *But see* Thorner v. Fleetwood, 2002 WL 1998285 (N.D. Ill. Aug. 28, 2002) (characterizing revocation as an equitable issue for the court; no rationale or authority cited); Jones v. Fleetwood Motor Homes, 127 F. Supp. 2d 958 (N.D. Ill. 2000) (erroneously characterizing revocation as equitable remedy; decision cites only non-U.C.C. rescission cases that do not involve revocation of acceptance); *cf.* Peppler v. Kasual Kreations, Inc., 416 So. 2d 864 (Fla. Dist. Ct. App. 1982) (revocation is equitable remedy, but plaintiff need only plead the enumerated statutory grounds).

4.2   *See, e.g.*, Van Bibber Homes Sales v. Marlow, 778 N.E.2d 852 (Ind. Ct. App. 2002) (allowing rescission of contract despite dealer's disclaimer of warranties); Hyler v. Garner, 548 N.W.2d 864 (Iowa 1996) (allowing rescission based on dealer's misrepresentations, including misrepresentations about the warranty).

Replace sentence containing note 6 with:

The buyer may either reject the goods[5] or revoke acceptance,[6] and in either case may cancel the contract.[6.1]

5   U.C.C. § 2-601.

6   U.C.C. § 2-608.

6.1   U.C.C. § 2-711(1).

Add to text at end of subsection's seventh paragraph:

The buyer can, however, keep the goods instead of rejecting them, and then deduct or recover damages.[11.1]

Another distinction between rejection and revocation of acceptance is the effect upon ownership of the goods. Under UCC section 2-401, rejection by the buyer, whether or not justified, revests title to the goods in the seller, while revocation does so only if justified. This language may make it easier for the buyer to argue that rejection automatically unwinds the deal, without the need for any judicial determination.[11.2]

11.1 U.C.C. § 2-714; *see* Dunleavy v. Paris Ceramics USA, Inc., 819 A.2d 945, 49 U.C.C. Rep. Serv. 2d 515 (Conn. Super. Ct. 2002); Beaver Valley Alloy Foundry Co. v. Therma-Fab, Inc., 814 A.2d 217, 49 U.C.C. Rep. Serv. 2d 507 (Pa. Super. Ct. 2002).

11.2 Even though rejection returns ownership of the goods to the seller, the buyer has the option of selling the goods if the seller does not provide instructions about what to do with them. A buyer who has made payments or incurred certain other expenses also can sell the goods pursuant to the security interest granted by U.C.C. § 2-711. *See* §§ 8.4.2, 8.4.4, *infra*.

8.2 Buyer's Rejection of Goods

8.2.2 Acceptance by Failure to Reject After Reasonable Opportunity to Inspect

Page 251

8.2.2.1 Timeliness of Inspection and of Notice of Rejection

Addition to note 25.

25 Weil v. Murray, 161 F. Supp. 2d 250, 44 U.C.C. Rep. Serv. 2d 482 (S.D.N.Y. 2001) (buyer who had possession of painting for four-and-one-half months and inspected it at least twice had accepted it as a matter of law).

Page 252

8.2.2.2 Length of Reasonable Opportunity to Inspect

Addition to note 28.

28 *E.g.*, Wang Laboratories, Inc. v. Lee, 44 U.C.C. Rep. Serv. 2d 470 (Del. Super. Ct. 1989) (one year too long).

Add note 29.1 at end of sentence containing note 29.

29.1 Keller v. Inland Metals All Weather Conditioning, Inc., 76 P.3d 977 (Idaho 2003).

Addition to note 30.

30 *Add to Smith citation*: 587 N.W.2d 660, *aff'd on other grounds*, 618 N.W.2d 452 (Neb. 2000); *add: See, e.g*, Jacob Hartz Seed Co. v. Coleman, 271 Ark. 756, 612 S.W.2d 91 (Ark. 1981) (June 1 rejection of seeds delivered on April 8 and May 5 was timely when testing was necessary); *cf.* Weil v. Murray, 161 F. Supp. 2d 250, 44 U.C.C. Rep. Serv. 2d 482 (S.D.N.Y. 2001) (buyer who had possession of painting for four-and-one-half months and inspected it at least twice had accepted it as a matter of law). *But see* China Nat'l Metal Prods. Imp./Exp. Co. v. Apex Digital, Inc., 141 F. Supp. 2d 1013 (C.D. Cal. 2001) (magistrate's decision) (four months too long), *vacated on other grounds*, 155 F. Supp. 2d 1174 (C.D. Cal. 2001).

Page 254

8.2.2.3 Contractual Specification of Time to Inspect

Addition to note 42.

42 China Nat'l Metal Prods. Imp./Exp. Co. v. Apex Digital, Inc., 141 F. Supp. 2d 1013 (C.D. Cal. 2001) (magistrate's decision) (precluding commercial buyer from rejecting beyond date specified in contract), *vacated on other grounds*, 155 F. Supp. 2d 1174 (C.D. Cal. 2001); Wang Laboratories, Inc. v. Lee, 44 U.C.C. Rep. Serv. 2d 470 (Del. Super. Ct. 1989) (failure to notify seller of rejection within sixty days as specified by contract is acceptance; commercial transaction).

Add note 42.1 after "section 1-204(1)" in sentence containing note 43.

42.1 Revised Article 1, which the National Conference of Commissioners on Uniform State Laws (NCCUSL) approved in 2001 for adoption by the states, redesignates this provision as U.C.C. § 1-302(b) without substantive change.

Addition to note 43.

43 *See* Bus. Communications, Inc. v. KI Networks, Inc., 580 S.E.2d 77, 50 U.C.C. Rep. Serv. 2d 799 (N.C. Ct. App. 2003) (enforcing contractual rejection period).

Replace subsection's last sentence with:

Such a clause is unconscionable and does not result in acceptance if the buyer has not in fact had a reasonable opportunity to inspect the goods, as is the case when such a clause is contained in a receipt the buyer signs upon delivery.[44.1] The unenforceability of such clauses in the context of implied warranties is discussed at § 4.4.3, *supra*.

44.1 Tri-Continental Leasing Corp. v. Law Office of Richard W. Burns, 710 S.W.2d 604 (Tex. App. 1985).

Page 257

8.2.4 Buyer's Acceptance by Acts Inconsistent With Seller's Ownership

Addition to notes 60, 61, 64–67, 70.

60 China Nat'l Metal Prods. Imp./Exp. Co. v. Apex Digital, Inc., 141 F. Supp. 2d 1013 (C.D. Cal. 2001) (magistrate's decision) (selling the goods to retailers, and ordering more despite discovery of defect, was acceptance), *vacated on other grounds*, 155 F. Supp. 2d 1174 (C.D. Cal. 2001); *see* Jacob Hartz Seed Co. v. Coleman, 271 Ark. 756, 612 S.W.2d 91 (Ark. 1981) (entering into contract to resell goods while unaware of defects was not acceptance).

61 *See, e.g.*, Berg Chilling Sys., Inc. v. Hull Corp., 49 U.C.C. Rep. Serv. 2d 189 (E.D. Pa. 2002) (incorporating goods into equipment and then shipping the equipment to a buyer is acceptance); Weil v. Murray, 161 F. Supp. 2d 250, 44 U.C.C. Rep. Serv. 2d 482 (S.D.N.Y. 2001) (cleaning and restoration of Degas painting were acts inconsistent with seller's ownership); Imex Int'l, Inc. v. Wires Eng'g, 583 S.E.2d 117, 50 U.C.C. Rep. Serv. 2d 448 (Ga. Ct. App. 2003) (using the goods as raw materials in manufacturing is acceptance); Bacchus Indus., Inc. v. Frontier Mech. Contractors, 36 S.W.3d 579, 42 U.C.C. Rep. Serv. 2d 1011 (Tex. App. 2000) (unpublished) (repairing the goods is inconsistent with seller's ownership).

64 *See also* Trinity Indus., Inc. v. McKinnon Bridge Co., 77 S.W.3d 159, 46 U.C.C. Rep. Serv. 2d 119 (Tenn. Ct. App. 2001).

65 MacSteel Int'l USA Corp. v. Superior Products Co., 47 U.C.C. Rep. Serv. 2d 468 (N.D. Ill. 2002).

66 *But cf.* Credit Inst. v. Veterinary Nutrition Corp., 62 P.3d 339, 49 U.C.C. Rep. Serv. 2d 1160 (N.M. Ct. App. 2002) (not acceptance when buyer promptly rejected but seller instructed buyer to use the defective goods until it could remedy the problem).

67 *See* Hangzhou Silk Imp. & Exp. Corp. v. P.C.B. Int'l Indus., Inc., 48 U.C.C. Rep. Serv. 2d 1367 (S.D.N.Y. 2002); Fabrica de Tejidos Imperial v. Brandon Apparel Group, Inc., 218 F. Supp. 2d 974, 48 U.C.C. Rep. Serv. 2d 960 (N.D. Ill. 2002); MacSteel Int'l USA Corp. v. Superior Products Co., 47 U.C.C. Rep. Serv. 2d 468 (N.D. Ill. 2002); China Nat'l Metal Prods. Imp./Exp. Co. v. Apex Digital, Inc., 141 F. Supp. 2d 1013 (C.D. Cal. 2001) (magistrate's decision) (selling the goods to retailers, and ordering more despite discovery of defect, was acceptance), *vacated on other grounds*, 155 F. Supp. 2d 1174 (C.D. Cal. 2001); Dunleavy v. Paris Ceramics USA, Inc., 819 A.2d 945, 49 U.C.C. Rep. Serv. 2d 515 (Conn. Super. Ct. 2002) (resale of goods is acceptance); Crady v. Ned Hiatt Country Sales, Inc., 815 P.2d 1133 (Kan. Ct. App. 1991) (consumer's resale of goods precluded revocation). *But cf.* Cumberland County Improvement Auth. v. GSP Recycling Co., 358 N.J. Super. 484, 818 A.2d 431, 49 U.C.C. Rep. Serv. 2d 1186 (Super. Ct. App. Div. 2003) (retention and sale of goods was not acceptance when parties' contract allowed buyer to retain non-conforming goods and deduct additional expenses from purchase price).

Page 258

70 Jacob Hartz Seed Co. v. Coleman, 271 Ark. 756, 612 S.W.2d 91 (Ark. 1981).

8.2.5 Notice of Rejection

8.2.5.1 Notice Must Be Timely

Addition to notes 77, 78.

77 *Add at beginning of note*: Northwest Airlines, Inc. v. Aeroservice, Inc., 168 F. Supp. 2d 1052, 46 U.C.C. Rep. Serv. 2d 962 (D. Minn. 2001) (contractual period for inspection of goods is also the period within which rejection must be communicated to seller).

78 *Add before McClure citation*: Imex Int'l, Inc. v. Wires Eng'g, 583 S.E.2d 117, 50 U.C.C. Rep. Serv. 2d 448 (Ga. Ct. App. 2003) (commercial case) (notice not seasonable when buyer used machine for over a month without giving notice of rejection); *add before DeJesus citation*: Pioneer Peat, Inc. v. Quality Grassing & Services, Inc., 653 N.W.2d 469, 49 U.C.C. Rep. Serv. 2d 440 (Minn. Ct. App. 2002) (commercial case) (rejection ineffective due to delay between discovery of unsuitability and notification to seller).

Page 259

8.2.5.2 Form of Notice of Rejection

Add to text after subsection's first paragraph:

One unreported decision holds that notice that the buyer had not accepted the product was insufficient when it was sent by the seller's service agent rather than by the buyer.[85.1] The case might have been decided differently if there had been some evidence that the buyer had communicated non-acceptance to the seller's service agent with the intent that the message be conveyed to the seller.

85.1 River Rouge Sch. Dist. v. Mestek, Inc., 48 U.C.C. Rep. Serv. 2d 1036 (Mich. Ct. App. 2002) (unpublished).

Add new subsection to text after § 8.2.5.2.

8.2.5.2a Practical Tips for Giving Notice

When rejecting a product, remember that there is often a delay between the time of sale and the time when the entity financing the sale pays the dealer. Faxing a copy of the rejection notice to the putative financer and asking it not to fund the transaction until the dispute is resolved may make it easier to unwind the sale. For products that carry certificates of title, the consumer might also consider contacting the state titling agency and asking that it hold up the transfer of the title.

Page 260

8.2.5.3 Content of Notice of Rejection

Addition to notes 93, 95, 96.

93   Fabrica de Tejidos Imperial v. Brandon Apparel Group, Inc., 218 F. Supp. 2d 974, 48 U.C.C. Rep. Serv. 2d 960 (N.D. Ill. 2002).

95   *Add at beginning of note*: *See* A.P.S., Inc. v. Standard Motor Products, Inc., 295 B.R. 442, 51 U.C.C. Rep. Serv. 2d 398, 412 (D. Del. 2003) (denying rejection when buyer did not specify defect).

96   *See* Imex Int'l, Inc. v. Wires Eng'g, 583 S.E.2d 117, 50 U.C.C. Rep. Serv. 2d 448 (Ga. Ct. App. 2003) (commercial case) (rejection notice ineffective because it did not particularize machine's defects but just stated machine did not perform in a superior manner).

Page 261

8.2.6 Any Nonconformity Is Sufficient to Reject

Addition to note 102.

102   Jakowski v. Carole Chevrolet, Inc., 180 N.J. Super. 122, 433 A.2d 841 (Super. Ct. Law Div. 1981).

8.2.7 Seller's Right to Cure After Buyer's Rejection

8.2.7.1 Introduction

Add to text after sentence containing note 104:

The seller must take the initiative to cure and can not shift any part of the burden to the buyer.[104.1]

104.1   Sinco, Inc. v. Metro-N. Commuter R.R. Co., 133 F. Supp. 2d 308, 44 U.C.C. Rep. Serv. 2d 137 (S.D.N.Y. 2001).

Add note 107.1 at end of sentence following sentence containing note 107.

107.1   Linscott v. Smith, 3 Kan. App. 2d 1, 587 P.2d 1271 (1978).

Add note 107.2 at end of subsection's second paragraph.

107.2   Dunleavy v. Paris Ceramics USA, Inc., 819 A.2d 945, 49 U.C.C. Rep. Serv. 2d 515 (Conn. Super. Ct. 2002); *cf.* Mercury Marine v. Clear River Constr. Co., 839 So. 2d 508, 49 U.C.C. Rep. Serv. 2d 989 (Miss. 2003) (finding a U.C.C. right to cure as condition of damages suit; this was a repair or replace warranty which required an opportunity to cure in any event).

8.2.7.2 Distinguishing Cure Before and After Time for Performance Has Expired

Page 262

8.2.7.2.2 *Determining whether time for performance has expired*

Addition to note 117.

117   *Add at end of note*: [*redesignated as U.C.C. § 1-205 with immaterial changes by revised Article 1, which the National Conference of Commissioners on Uniform State Laws (NCCUSL) approved in 2001 for adoption by the states*].

8.2.7.3 Seller Must Give Seasonable Notice of Intention To Cure

Replace note 120 with:

120   U.C.C. § 1-204(3) [*redesignated as U.C.C. § 1-205(b) by revised Article 1, which NCCUSL approved in 2001 for adoption by the states*].

Addition to notes 122, 124.

122   *Replace "U.C.C. § 1-204(2)" with*: U.C.C. § 1-204(2) [*redesignated as U.C.C. § 1-205(a) by revised Article 1, which NCCUSL approved in 2001 for adoption by the states*].

Page 263

124   United Wholesale Supply, Inc. v. Wear, 106 Wash. App. 1042, 45 U.C.C. Rep. Serv. 2d 1067 (2001) (unpublished) (notice of intent to cure was condition precedent even though buyer failed to return four phone calls from seller and stated that he refused to accept the nonconforming goods under any circumstances).

8.2.7.4 Cure Before Time of Performance Has Expired and the Shaken Faith Doctrine

Add to text after subsection's first sentence:

The cure must conform to the contract in all respects.[124.1]

124.1   Sinco, Inc. v. Metro-N. Commuter R.R. Co., 133 F. Supp. 2d 308, 44 U.C.C. Rep. Serv. 2d 137 (S.D.N.Y. 2001) (replacement parts had not gone through quality control process required by contract so did not constitute cure).

Addition to note 128.

128   *But cf.* Sinco, Inc. v. Metro-N. Commuter R.R. Co., 133 F. Supp. 2d 308, 44 U.C.C. Rep. Serv. 2d 137 (S.D.N.Y. 2001) (declining to adopt shaken faith doctrine, but cure must conform to contract in all respects).

8.2.7.8 Cost of Returning Goods to Seller to Allow a Cure

Page 267

8.2.7.8.1 *Seller bears the expense*

Add note 152.1 at end of second sentence of subsection's last paragraph.

152.1   Revised Article 1, approved by the National Conference of Commissioners on Uniform State Laws (NCCUSL) in 2001 for adoption by the states, preserves the duty of good faith as U.C.C. § 1-304. It also expands the definition of "good faith" in revised U.C.C. § 1-201(b)(20) to include not only honesty in fact but also the observance of reasonable commercial standards of fair dealing, regardless of whether the actor is a merchant.

8.3 Revocation of Acceptance

Page 268

8.3.1 *Introduction*

Add note 160.1 at end of subsection's first sentence.

160.1   *See also* 31 P.R. Laws Ann. §§ 3841, 3843 (providing comparable right of redhibition in case of hidden defects); Correa v. Cruisers, 298 F.3d 13 (1st Cir. 2002) (applying Puerto Rico's comparable redhibition statutes); Johnson v. CHL Enterprises, 115 F. Supp. 2d 723 (W.D. La. 2000) (describing elements of Louisiana's comparable right of redhibition).

Add note 160.2 after "Section 2-608," in subsection's second sentence.

160.2   In Louisiana, which has not adopted article 2 of the U.C.C., the right of redhibition under La. Civ. Code art. 2520 is somewhat comparable to revocation of acceptance. *See, e.g.*, Dalme v. Blockers Manufactured Homes, Inc., 779 So. 2d 1014 (La. Ct. App. 2001); McGough v. Oakwood Mobile Homes, Inc., 779 So. 2d 793 (La. Ct. App. 2000) (allowing redhibition of defective mobile home); Carpenter v. Lafayette Woodworks, 653 So. 2d 1187 (La. Ct. App. 1995) (reversing trial court's denial of redhibition of motor home).

Addition to note 161.

161   Calbert v. Volkswagen of Am., Inc., 1991 WL 215669 (Del. Super. Ct. Oct. 1, 1991); Bus. Communications, Inc. v. KI Networks, Inc., 580 S.E.2d 77, 50 U.C.C. Rep. Serv. 2d 799 (N.C. Ct. App. 2003) (whether revocation occurred within reasonable time is question of fact, but here facts are undisputed and only one reasonable inference can be drawn); Eggl v. Letvin Equip. Co., 632 N.W.2d 435, 45 U.C.C. Rep. Serv. 2d 538 (N.D. 2001); Ramos v. Ford Motor Co., 655 N.W.2d 447 (S.D. 2002) (what constitutes substantial impairment is question of fact); *see also* Barker v. Fleetwood Enterprises, Inc., 2002 WL 453931 (Cal. Ct. App. Mar. 26, 2002) (unpublished) (substantial impairment under state lemon law is question of fact for jury).

Page 269

Add to text at end of subsection:

A buyer may base revocation of acceptance on breach of express or implied warranties[163.1] or on breach of other contractual obligations.[163.2]

163.1   Mercedes-Benz Credit Corp. v. Lotito, 328 N.J. Super. 491, 746 A.2d 480 (Super. Ct. App. Div. 2000).

163.2   *See* § 8.3.2.6, *infra*.

8.3.2 Substantial Impairment of Value of Goods to Buyer

8.3.2.1 General

Addition to notes 166, 167.

166   *Add after Sessa citation*: Cissell Mfg. Co. v. Park, 36 P.3d 85, 43 U.C.C. Rep. Serv. 2d 889 (Colo. Ct. App. 2001).

167   *Replace O'Bryant citation with*: 1999 Tenn. App. LEXIS 245 (Tenn. Ct. App. Apr. 15, 1999); *add*: Ramos v. Ford Motor Co., 655 N.W.2d 447 (S.D. 2002) (revocation not allowed when defect did not exist at time of revocation).

Page 270

8.3.2.2 Is the Test Objective or Subjective?

Addition to notes 171, 174.

171   *Replace O'Bryant citation with*: 1999 Tenn. App. LEXIS 245 (Tenn. Ct. App. Apr. 15, 1999); *add*: Phoenix Color Corp. v. Krause Am., Inc., 46 U.C.C. Rep. Serv. 2d 442 (4th Cir. 2001) (unpublished) (Conn. law) (design defects that caused lengthy periods of down time for repairs were substantial impairment); Jaramillo v. Gonzales, 50 P.3d 554 (N.M. Ct. App. 2002); Herring v. Home Depot, Inc., 565 S.E.2d 773 (S.C. Ct. App. 2002).

174   Pifer v. DaimlerChrysler Corp., 2003 WL 22850124 (Mich. Ct. App. Dec. 2, 2003) (unpublished) (test has both objective and subjective components).

Page 272

8.3.2.3 Rationale for Subjective View of Substantial Impairment

Replace note 182 with:

182   1999 Tenn. App. LEXIS 245 (Tenn. Ct. App. Apr. 15, 1999).

8.3.2.4 Application of the Subjective View

Addition to notes 183, 186.
Page 273

183   Pifer v. DaimlerChrysler Corp., 2003 WL 22850124 (Mich. Ct. App. Dec. 2, 2003) (unpublished).

186   *But cf.* Ramos v. Ford Motor Co., 655 N.W.2d 447 (S.D. 2002) (rejecting loss of confidence argument when vehicle was not defective at time of revocation).

Add to text after subsection's second paragraph:

A major failure soon after purchase may be sufficient to justify revocation of acceptance even if the manufacturer stands ready to replace all defective or damaged parts. Such a failure can shake the buyer's faith. Furthermore, the replacement parts may be rebuilt rather than new, and the buyer may legitimately lack confidence that the replacement parts will work any better than the original ones.

8.3.2.5 Failure to Repair as a Substantial Nonconformity

Addition to notes 192, 194, 195.

192   Phoenix Color Corp. v. Krause Am., Inc., 46 U.C.C. Rep. Serv. 2d 442 (4th Cir. 2001) (unpublished) (Conn. law) (design defects that caused lengthy periods of down time for repairs were substantial impairment); Bland v. Freightliner Ltd. Liab. Co., 206 F. Supp. 2d 1202, 49 U.C.C. Rep. Serv. 2d 524 (M.D. Fla. 2002); Earls v. Condor Capital Corp., 2001 Conn. Super. LEXIS 2595 (Conn. Super. Ct. Aug. 30, 2001) (buyer could revoke when he knew of defects but seller breached promise to repair them).

Page 274

194   Ramos v. Ford Motor Co., 655 N.W.2d 447 (S.D. 2002).

195   *But see* Haight v. Dale's Used Cars, Inc., 51 U.C.C. Rep. Serv. 2d 1017 (Idaho Ct. App. 2003) (need for repairs costing ten percent of purchase price not a substantial impairment).

8.3.3 Buyer's Justification for Having Accepted the Nonconforming Goods

8.3.3.2 Acceptance Based on Reasonable Assumption of Repair

Page 275

Addition to note 206.

206   *See, e.g.*, Earls v. Condor Capital Corp., 2001 Conn. Super. LEXIS 2595 (Conn. Super. Ct. Aug. 30, 2001).

8.3.3.3 Buyer Unaware of Nonconformity at Time of Acceptance

Page 276

Add note 212.1 at end of subsection's first sentence.

212.1   *See also* 31 P.R. Laws Ann. §§ 3841, 3843 (providing comparable right of redhibition in case of hidden defects); Johnson v. CHL Enterprises, 115 F. Supp. 2d 723 (W.D. La. 2000) (describing elements of Louisiana's similar redhibition action; defect must be non-apparent).

Addition to note 213.

213   *See also* McGough v. Oakwood Mobile Homes, Inc., 779 So. 2d 793 (La. Ct. App. 2000) (under La. Civil Code, buyer can cancel sale only if reasonable inspection would not have revealed the defects).

8.3.4 Reasonable Time for Revocation

Add note 217.1 after "Section 1-204(2)" in sentence containing note 218.

217.1   Revised Article 1, approved by the National Conference of Commissioners on Uniform State Laws (NCCUSL) in 2001 for adoption by the states, preserves this provision without substantive change as U.C.C. § 1-205(a).

Page 277

Addition to notes 219, 220.

219   Sumner v. Fel-Air, Inc., 680 P.2d 1109 (Alaska 1984); Jaramillo v. Gonzales, 50 P.3d 554 (N.M. Ct. App. 2002).

220   *See, e.g.*, Bus. Communications, Inc. v. KI Networks, Inc., 580 S.E.2d 77, 50 U.C.C. Rep. Serv. 2d 799 (N.C. Ct. App. 2003).

Add to text at end of subsection's first paragraph:

The buyer has the burden of proving that revocation occurred within a reasonable time.[220.1]

220.1   Rose v. Colo. Factory Homes, 10 P.3d 680, 43 U.C.C. Rep. Serv. 2d 1160 (Colo. Ct. App. 2000).

Addition to notes 221–223.

221   Magnum Press Automation, Inc. v. Thomas & Betts Corp., 758 N.E.2d 507 (Ill. App. Ct. 2001); *see* Sumner v. Fel-Air, Inc., 680 P.2d 1109 (Alaska 1984) (assurances that title problems would be cured extended time for revocation); Montgomery v. Mobile Home Estates, Inc., 1984 Ohio App. LEXIS 9239 (Ohio Ct. App. Apr. 20, 1984).

222   *Replace Micro Prods., Inc. citation with*: 47 Va. Cir. 24, 39 U.C.C. Rep. Serv. 2d 428 (1999); *add: See also* Sorce v. Naperville Jeep Eagle, Inc., 309 Ill. App. 3d 313, 242 Ill. Dec. 738, 722 N.E.2d 227 (1999) (jury question whether revocation thirty-one months after purchase of truck, and after thirty repair attempts, was timely); Jaramillo v. Gonzales, 50 P.3d 554 (N.M. Ct. App. 2002) (five years reasonable when mobile home had latent plumbing defects); Montgomery v. Mobile Home Estates, Inc., 1984 Ohio App. LEXIS 9239 (Ohio Ct. App. Apr. 20, 1984) (notice of revocation of acceptance of mobile home nine-and-one-half months after delivery was timely). *But see* MacSteel Int'l USA Corp. v. Superior Products Co., 47 U.C.C. Rep. Serv. 2d 468 (N.D. Ill. 2002) (notice of revocation sent in July untimely in commercial transaction when goods were delivered in February); Imex Int'l, Inc. v. Wires Eng'g, 583 S.E.2d 117, 50 U.C.C. Rep. Serv. 2d 448 (Ga. Ct. App. 2003) (commercial case) (revocation six months after delivery too late).

Page 278

223   Eggl v. Letvin Equip. Co., 632 N.W.2d 435, 45 U.C.C. Rep. Serv. 2d 538 (N.D. 2001) (tractor).

Page 279

8.3.5 Condition of Goods at Revocation

Add to text at end of subsection's first paragraph:

The seller has the burden of proving and quantifying a change in the condition of the goods.[230.1]

230.1   Jaramillo v. Gonzales, 50 P.3d 554 (N.M. Ct. App. 2002).

Page 280

Add to text at end of subsection:

Normal depreciation alone is not a substantial change in the condition of the goods.[239.1]

239.1   Deere & Co. v. Johnson, 271 F.3d 613 (5th Cir. 2001) (Miss. law).

8.3.6 Notice of Revocation

8.3.6.1 Timeliness of Notice

Addition to note 240.

240   Eggl v. Letvin Equip. Co., 632 N.W.2d 435, 45 U.C.C. Rep. Serv. 2d 538 (N.D. 2001).

8.3.6.2 Form of Notice

Add note 241.1 at end of subsection's first sentence.

241.1   Cissell Mfg. Co. v. Park, 36 P.3d 85, 43 U.C.C. Rep. Serv. 2d 889 (Colo. Ct. App. 2001).

Addition to notes 242, 247.

242   Calkins v. Valley Mobile Homes, Inc., 306 N.W.2d 304 (Wis. Ct. App. 1981) (unpublished) (text available at 1981 Wisc. App. LEXIS 4025).

Page 281

247   *Accord* King v. Taylor Chrysler Plymouth, 184 Mich. App. 204, 457 N.W.2d 42 (1990) (complaint was sufficient notice of revocation); Calkins v. Valley Mobile Homes, Inc., 306 N.W.2d 304 (Wis. Ct. App. 1981) (unpublished) (text available at 1981 Wisc. App. LEXIS 4025).

8.3.6.3 Content of Notice

Addition to notes 254, 257, 258, 261.

254   Sumner v. Fel-Air, Inc., 680 P.2d 1109 (Alaska 1984).

257   *Accord* Phoenix Color Corp. v. Krause Am., Inc., 46 U.C.C. Rep. Serv. 2d 442 (4th Cir. 2001) (unpublished) (Conn. law) (notice saying buyer wanted seller to remove the goods sufficed); Cissell Mfg. Co. v. Park, 36 P.3d 85, 43 U.C.C. Rep. Serv. 2d 889 (Colo. Ct. App. 2001) (notice need only tell seller that buyer wants to return the goods and receive a refund or replacement).

258   China Nat'l Metal Prods. Imp./Exp. Co. v. Apex Digital, Inc., 141 F. Supp. 2d 1013 (C.D. Cal. 2001) (magistrate's decision), *vacated on other grounds*, 155 F. Supp. 2d 1174 (C.D. Cal. 2001).

Page 282

261   Phoenix Color Corp. v. Krause Am., Inc., 46 U.C.C. Rep. Serv. 2d 442 (4th Cir. 2001) (unpublished) (Conn. law) (not necessary to specify defects when parties had previously communicated about defects).

Add to text after subsection's third paragraph:

However, for non-consumer contracts, the revised version of Article 2, which the National Conference of Commissioners on Uniform State Laws approved in 2003 for consideration by state legislatures, would give the seller the right to cure after revocation of acceptance[262.1] and would require the buyer to specify the defects.[262.2]

262.1   Revised U.C.C. § 2-508. Selected portions of revised Article 2 are reproduced in Appx. E.7S, *infra*, and on the CD-Rom accompanying this volume.

262.2   Revised U.C.C. § 2-605; *see* Official Comment 1 to Revised U.C.C. § 2-605 (notice requirement does not apply when consumer seeks to revoke acceptance).

8.3.6.4 Sending the Notice to Third Parties

Addition to note 264.

264   *But cf.* Calkins v. Valley Mobile Homes, Inc., 306 N.W.2d 304 (Wis. Ct. App. 1981) (unpublished) (text available at 1981 Wisc. App. LEXIS 4025) (notice of revocation given through third party may be effective).

8.3.7 Seller's Cure After Revocation

Page 283

8.3.7.1 No Right to Cure Under the UCC

Addition to notes 267, 268.

267   *Replace O'Bryant citation with*: 1999 Tenn. App. LEXIS 245 (Tenn. Ct. App. Apr. 15, 1999); *add*: *See, e.g.*, Dunleavy v. Paris Ceramics USA, Inc., 819 A.2d 945, 49 U.C.C. Rep. Serv. 2d 515 (Conn. Super. Ct. 2002).

268   *See* Magnum Press Automation, Inc. v. Thomas & Betts Corp., 758 N.E.2d 507, 46 U.C.C. Rep. Serv. 2d 97 (Ill. App. Ct. 2001) (finding that buyer gave seller sufficient opportunity to cure before revoking acceptance; no discussion of whether seller had right to attempt cure); Shook v. Counterman, 43 U.C.C. Rep. Serv. 2d 1144 (Ohio Ct. App. 2000) (applying right to cure to revocation of acceptance case without discussing rationale); *cf.* Johnson v. CHL Enterprises, 115 F. Supp. 2d 723 (W.D. La. 2000) (listing opportunity for seller to cure as one element of Louisiana right of redhibition).

Add to text at end of subsection:

The revised version of Article 2, which the National Conference of Commissioners on Uniform State Laws approved in 2003 for consideration by state legislatures, gives the seller the right to cure if the buyer, in a non-consumer transaction,[272.1] justifiably revokes acceptance.[272.2] This new right to cure is available only to a seller who has performed in good faith, and the seller must compensate the buyer for all the buyer's reasonable expenses caused by the breach and the cure.

272.1   *See* Revised U.C.C. § 2-103(1)(c), (d) (definitions of "consumer" and "consumer contract"). Selected portions of revised Article 2 are reproduced in Appx. E.7S, *infra*, and on the CD-Rom accompanying this volume.

272.2   Revised U.C.C. § 2-508.

Page 284

8.3.7.3 Cure Based on Contractual Limitation on Remedies

Add to text after subsection's first sentence:

Then the buyer's failure to allow repair of the product may preclude further remedies.[277.1]

277.1   *See, e.g.,* Terrell v. R & A Mfg. Partners, Ltd., 835 So. 2d 216, 50 U.C.C. Rep. Serv. 2d 151, 159–161 (Ala. Civ. App. 2002); Olson v. Ford Motor Co., 258 Ga. App. 848, 575 S.E.2d 743, 50 U.C.C. Rep. Serv. 2d 166 (2002) (buyer who refused to allow repair attempts can not make claim under repair or replace warranty).

8.3.8 Cancelling the Sale Against the Indirect Seller

8.3.8.1 Introduction

Add to text after sentence following sentence containing note 279:

For manufacturing defects it serves both justice and judicial efficiency to allow the consumer to sue the responsible party directly, rather than confining the consumer to suing the retailer and then requiring the retailer to assert a separate claim against the manufacturer.

Page 285

Add to text at end of subsection:

The force of the arguments in favor of the right to revoke acceptance against the manufacturer is heightened by the National Conference of Commissioners on Uniform State Laws' 2003 revisions to Article 2, which add special definitions of "immediate buyer" and "remote purchaser" to several sections of Article 2.[288.1] If the drafters of Article 2 had wanted to confine revocation of acceptance to immediate purchasers, presumably they would have inserted similar language in section 2-608. Furthermore, sections 2-313A and 2-313B recognize new categories of warranty-like obligations that run from "sellers" to remote purchasers. This usage makes it clear that the term "seller," a term that is also used in section 2-608, encompasses not just immediate sellers but also manufacturers. In addition, nothing in the language of section 2-608 suggests that a failure to conform to these warranty-like obligations can not be a nonconformity that justifies revocation of acceptance. The fact that the remedy provisions of the new sections on manufacturers' warranty-like obligations[288.2] do not mention revocation of acceptance does not undercut this conclusion. Revised section 2-608 stands on its own as authorizing revocation of acceptance for breach of these obligations. Neither the general comments by the drafters of revised Article 2[288.3] nor the specific comments to these new sections indicate any intent to confine revocation of acceptance to the immediate seller.

288.1   Revised U.C.C. §§ 2-313(1), 2-313A(1), 2-313B(1), 2-318. Selected portions of revised Article 2 are reproduced in Appx. E.7S, *infra*, and on the CD-Rom accompanying this volume.

288.2   Revised U.C.C. §§ 2-313A(5), 2-313B(5); *see* § 3.1, *supra*.

288.3   *See* Prefatory Note to Revised Article 2.

8.3.8.2 Precedent Allowing Revocation Against the Indirect Seller

Add note 293.1 at end of subsection's third paragraph.

293.1   *See also* Shuldman v. DaimlerChrysler Corp., 2003 WL 22502204 (N.Y. App. Div. Nov. 3, 2003) (buyer may revoke acceptance against remote manufacturer under Magnuson-Moss Act).

Addition to note 297.

297   *Accord* Schimmer v. Jaguar Cars, Inc., 2003 WL 21518589 (N.D. Ill. July 2, 2003).

Add to text at end of subsection:

A New York appellate court has held that a buyer can revoke acceptance against the manufacturer under the Magnuson-Moss Warranty Act because it allows suit directly against a remote manufacturer.[299.1]

299.1   Shuldman v. DaimlerChrysler Corp., 2003 WL 22502204 (N.Y. App. Div. Nov. 3, 2003) (case involved limited written warranty).

8.3.8.3 Precedent Not Allowing Revocation Against the Indirect Seller

Addition to notes 300, 302.

300   *See, e.g.*, Kutzle v. Thor Indus., Inc., 2003 WL 21654260 (N.D. Ill. July 14, 2003); Neal v. SMC Corp., 99 S.W.3d 813, 49 U.C.C. Rep. Serv. 2d 1179 (Tex. App. 2003); *see also* Rokicsak v. Colony Marine Sales & Serv., Inc., 219 F. Supp. 2d 810 (E.D. Mich. 2002) (revocation claim based on manufacturer's warranties can proceed against dealer even though dealer effectively disclaimed its warranties).

Page 286

302   *See* Neal v. SMC Corp., 99 S.W.3d 813, 49 U.C.C. Rep. Serv. 2d 1179 (Tex. App. 2003).

Page 287

8.3.8.4 Tactics to Optimize Chances of Revoking Against the Indirect Seller

Replace note 310 with:

310   Revised Article 1, which the National Conference of Commissioners on Uniform State Laws (NCCUSL) approved in 2001 for adoption by the states, preserves this provision as U.C.C. § 1-305(a) without substantive change. *See* § 1.6, *supra.*

8.4 What the Buyer May Do With the Goods After Cancellation

8.4.1 Introduction

Add to text after subsection's second paragraph:

In cases involving cars the buyer often needs to use the goods but may want to minimize the risk that continued use will bar cancellation. One strategy is to have the buyer stop making payments for several months after revoking acceptance. Once the buyer has saved up enough payments to make a down payment on a replacement vehicle, the buyer returns the original car to the dealer (or the buyer can return the vehicle earlier if other arrangements for temporary transportation are possible). In pursuing this strategy, it is often helpful to file suit soon after sending the notice of revocation, and to file a petition for injunctive relief asking for an order preserving the status quo, including a prohibition against making any negative credit report. A negative credit report can make it impossible for the buyer to obtain financing for a replacement vehicle.

8.4.2 Holding the Goods for Seller

Addition to note 323.

323   *See, e.g.*, Queen v. Lynch Jewelers, Ltd. Liab. Co., 55 P.3d 914 (Kan. Ct. App. 2002).

Page 289

8.4.3 Returning the Goods to the Seller

Add to text after subsection's second paragraph:

Taking the following steps may reduce the loss of leverage caused by returning the goods. First, the buyer's attorney should obtain a stipulation that the buyer's security interest in the goods continues. Otherwise, as the security interest is possessory, it will be lost if the buyer surrenders the goods.[334.1] The attorney may also want to ask the seller to obtain a bond in the amount of the buyer's security interest, or to deposit that amount into the attorney's trust account, before the goods are surrendered. The attorney should consider requiring that the bond or deposit be maintained until all appeals are exhausted; otherwise, if the buyer loses at trial and has to appeal, the bond or deposit will no longer provide any protection. At the very least, there should be an agreement that the proceeds of the resale of the goods will be held in the buyer's attorney's trust account or in escrow until the dispute is resolved. The attorney should also obtain a stipulation that return of the goods is without prejudice to either party's position, and should consider whether the stipulation should also include an agreement to a motion in limine precluding mention at trial of the return and sale of the vehicle. It is also wise to work out the specifics of insurance coverage and to stipulate that the dealer will indemnify the buyer for all damages, accidents, personal injury, and property damage that may occur after the dealer takes possession, regardless of whether the damage would be covered by the buyer's insurance.[334.2]

334.1   *See* § 8.4.4.1, *infra.*

334.2   *See also* § 10.1.2.2, *infra* (strategic issues to consider in deciding whether to keep or return the goods).

Add note 336.1 at end of first sentence of subsection's fifth paragraph.

336.1   *See* Miranda v. All Car Sales Inc., 2003 WL 22056729 (N.Y. Civ. Ct. June 25, 2003) (dealer was constructive bailee and was sufficiently negligent to be liable for disappearance of car after buyer returned it).

Page 290

Add note 336.2 at end of subsection's next-to-last sentence.

336.2   *See* McLain v. Cuccia, 259 So. 2d 337 (La. Ct. App. 1972) (court appears willing, depending on specific facts, to credit consumer with return of vehicle to unwilling dealer, even though vehicle disappeared).

Add to text at end of subsection:

A defiant dealer may try to redeliver a vehicle after the consumer has returned it, for example by parking it in front of the consumer's house and leaving the keys on the seat or in the consumer's mailbox. The consumer should avoid taking this bait, which is intended to create a new acceptance of the goods. The consumer should write the dealer a series of letters, reiterating the revocation of acceptance, declining to accept the vehicle, insisting that the vehicle be removed, and explaining why the vehicle is at risk and why it is embarrassing or inconvenient to have it sitting in the street. Even if the dealer claims that the consumer's revocation of acceptance is ineffective and it still has only a security interest in the vehicle, UCC § 9-207 requires the dealer to use reasonable care in the custody and preservation of the collateral.

8.4.4 Selling the Goods Where Buyer Has Made Payments or Incurred Expenses

8.4.4.1 Right to Sell the Goods

Addition to note 338.

338   Queen v. Lynch Jewelers, Ltd. Liab. Co., 55 P.3d 914 (Kan. Ct. App. 2002).

Replace note 341 with:

341   *See* Crady v. Ned Hiatt Country Sales, Inc., 815 P.2d 1133 (Kan. Ct. App. 1991); *see also* § 8.2.4, *supra.*

Page 292

8.4.4.5 Sale Procedures

Add to text at end of subsection's second paragraph:

In addition, sale of the goods without enough advance notice to enable opposing parties to inspect them can constitute spoliation of evidence.[352.1]

352.1   *See* § 10.1.2.5, *infra.*

Addition to note 353.

353   *Replace NCLC citation with*: National Consumer Law Center, Repossessions and Foreclosures (5th ed. 2002 and Supp.).

8.4.5 Buyer's Rights Where Seller or Creditor Also Retains Security Interest in the Goods

8.4.5.1 Introduction

Add to text at end of subsection:

While the UCC envisions resale of the goods as a self-help remedy, the difficulties of reselling goods that are subject to a security interest may make it necessary for the buyer to seek a court order allowing the goods to be sold free of the security interest. The order can provide either that the proceeds are to go to the secured party or, if the buyer's claims run against the secured party as well as the seller, that they are to be held in escrow pending the outcome of the case.

8.4.5.2 Buyer's Security Interest as Superior to That of Seller

Addition to note 357.

357   *Replace "U.C.C. § 9-404" with*: U.C.C. § 9-513; *add at end of note: See* § 8.5.2, *infra.*

Page 293

8.4.5.3 Reselling the Goods Where the Seller Holds the Security Interest and Has Not Filed a Financing Statement

Addition to note 359.

359   *Replace second sentence of note with*: By mid-2001, all state legislatures had adopted revised Article 9, although a few postponed the effective date and many included non-uniform amendments. *See* National Consumer Law Center, Repossessions and Foreclosures Appx. B (5th ed. 2002 and Supp.).

Page 294

8.4.5.5 Reselling the Goods When an Assignee Has a Security Interest

Addition to notes 373, 374.

373   *Replace NCLC citation with*: National Consumer Law Center, Unfair and Deceptive Acts and Practices § 6.6 (discussion of rule), Appx. B.2.1 (text of rule) (5th ed. 2001 and Supp.).

374   *Replace Valentino citation with:* 317 Ill. App. 3d 524, 251 Ill. Dec. 457, 740 N.E.2d 538 (2000); *add*: Jaramillo v. Gonzales, 50 P.3d 554 (N.M. Ct. App. 2002); *see also* Detroit & N. Sav. & Loan Ass'n v. Woodworth, 54 Mich. App. 517, 221 N.W.2d 190 (1974) (buyer's withholding of payments due to warranty defects is defense to replevin action brought by assignee).

Add note 374.1 at end of subsection's first paragraph.

374.1   Ford Motor Credit Co. v. Britton, 1996 Conn. Super. LEXIS 504 (Conn. Super. Ct. Feb. 23, 1996); Jaramillo v. Gonzales, 50 P.3d 554 (N.M. Ct. App. 2002); Green Tree Acceptance, Inc. v. Pierce, 768 S.W.2d 416 (Tex. App. 1989); *see also* Music Acceptance Corp. v. Lofing, 32 Cal. App. 4th 610, 39 Cal. Rptr. 2d 159 (1995) (assignee is liable for warranty claims against seller under both FTC Rule and state law).

Add to text at end of subsection's first paragraph:

The assignee's rights and duties should be exactly the same as if it were the original seller: because the buyer has revoked, the buyer no longer has a duty to pay, so nonpayment is not a default that triggers the right to repossess. Article 2 makes this result clear by providing that the buyer's cancellation discharges all executory obligations,[374.2] which would include the buyer's obligation to pay. Furthermore, once there is no longer an obligation that the collateral can secure, the security interest terminates.[374.3] Indeed, if there is no longer an obligation secured by the collateral, UCC Article 9 requires that the secured party formally document the release of the security interest.[374.4]

The FTC agrees with this analysis. Soon after adopting the Holder Rule the Federal Trade Commission issued an advisory opinion that, if the consumer, under applicable law, is entitled to withhold payment from the seller, the Holder Notice allows the consumer to withhold payment from the assignee.[374.5] An Illinois Supreme Court decision, while erroneously construing the Holder Rule in other respects, agrees that it means that the buyer can withhold payment from the assignee when a car is a "lemon."[374.6] Other Illinois courts, however, have confused the issue with an analysis of UCC Article 9's rules regarding the priority among competing security interests.[374.7] This approach is wrong, because after revocation both the obligation and the creditor's security interest cease to exist, so the only security interest is the consumer's. It also ignores the fact that the consumer who revokes acceptance is not in default. The factor that may have troubled these courts was that the consumer's revocation of acceptance was unilateral, neither accepted by the seller or creditor nor approved by a court. While the UCC recognizes revocation as a self-help remedy, courts are more likely to accept the effect of the Holder Rule on the creditor's security interest if the consumer is seeking or has obtained a court ruling that the revocation is valid.

374.2   U.C.C. § 2-106(3), (4).
374.3   U.C.C. § 1-201(b)(35).
374.4   U.C.C. § 9-513(a), (c).
374.5   Advisory Opinion, 89 F.T.C. 675 (Fed. Trade Comm'n 1977).

374.6   Jackson v. S. Holland Dodge, 197 Ill. 2d 39, 258 Ill. Dec. 79, 755 N.E.2d 462 (2001); *accord* Ellis v. Gen. Motors Acceptance Corp., 160 F.3d 703, 709 (11th Cir. 1998); Ransom v. Rohr-Gurnee Volkswagen, Inc., 2001 U.S. Dist. LEXIS 17363 (N.D. Ill. Oct. 22, 2001).

374.7   Ambre v. Joe Madden Ford, 881 F. Supp. 1182 (N.D. Ill. 1995); Valentino v. Glendale Nissan, Inc., 317 Ill. App. 3d 524, 740 N.E.2d 538 (2000).

Page 295

8.4.5.6 Reselling the Goods When a Third-Party Direct Lender Has Security Interest

Replace note 377 with:

377   16 C.F.R. § 422; *see* National Consumer Law Center, Unfair and Deceptive Acts and Practices § 6.6 (5th ed. 2001 and Supp.).

Add to text at end of subsection's second paragraph:

If the consumer has the right, under the UCC, to withhold payments from the seller due to the revocation, then the consumer may withhold payments from the lender.[377.1]

377.1   *See* Advisory Opinion, 89 F.T.C. 675 (Fed. Trade Comm'n 1977).

Addition to note 378.

378   *Replace NCLC citation with*: National Consumer Law Center, Unfair and Deceptive Acts and Practices § 6.6 (5th ed. 2001 and Supp.).

Add to text after third sentence of subsection's tenth paragraph:

If the proceeds are insufficient to pay the full balance, the consumer will remain liable, but the lender may prefer to take the debt off its books by having the consumer roll the deficiency into a personal loan. The additional interest might be damages that could be claimed against the seller.

Page 296

Add to text at end of subsection:

Even if sale of the vehicle can not be worked out with the lender, the lender may be willing to cooperate with the buyer in reducing or suspending the buyer's payments during the litigation against the seller if the buyer agrees to pay the lender out of the proceeds of the suit. This may be better from the lender's point of view than a repossession sale of a defective vehicle. The buyer should obtain enforceable guarantees that the lender will not report the non-payment to any credit reporting agency as a default.

8.4.6 Using the Goods—Does It Negate Cancellation?

8.4.6.1 General

Addition to note 383.

383   MacSteel Int'l USA Corp. v. Super. Products Co., 47 U.C.C. Rep. Serv. 2d 468 (N.D. Ill. 2002) (commercial case); Imex Int'l, Inc. v. Wires Eng'g, 583 S.E.2d 117, 50 U.C.C. Rep. Serv. 2d 448 (Ga. Ct. App. 2003) (commercial case); Olson v. Ford Motor Co., 258 Ga. App. 848, 575 S.E.2d 743, 50 U.C.C. Rep. Serv. 2d 166 (2002) (refusal to allow seller to arrange repairs, continued payment of note, insurance, and taxes, and other acts amounted to reacceptance); Jenkins v. Gen. Motors Corp., 240 Ga. App. 636, 524 S.E.2d 324 (1999) (commercial buyer's continued use of truck was inconsistent with revocation of acceptance).

Add to text at end of subsection:

Courts may be more willing to allow revocation despite continued use if the cost of replacement is high, if continuing to use the goods mitigates the buyer's damages, and if the seller has refused to accept return of the goods.[386.1] Continued use will mitigate damages when the buyer needs to use the goods in order to avoid significant losses or expenses. For example, the buyer may lose income without a car, or may have to incur rental costs.[386.2]

The revised version of Article 2, which the National Conference of Commissioners on Uniform State Laws approved in 2003 for consideration by state legislatures, takes a different approach. Any use by the buyer that is "reasonable under the circumstances" is not wrongful as against the seller and is not an acceptance.[386.3] However, in an appropriate case the buyer is obligated to the seller for the value to the buyer of the use of the goods.[386.4] Any use by the buyer that is unreasonable under the circumstances is wrongful as against the seller but is still not an acceptance unless the seller ratifies the use.[386.5] As an example of reasonable use, the Official Comments cite a consumer buyer who has incurred an unavoidable obligation to a third-party financier and has no reasonable alternative but to use the goods while waiting for the seller to refund the price.[386.6]

386.1   Deere & Co. v. Johnson, 271 F.3d 613 (5th Cir. 2001) (Miss. law); Keller v. Inland Metals All Weather Conditioning, Inc., 76 P.3d 977 (Idaho 2003).

386.2   *See, e.g.*, Fargo Tool & Mach. Co. v. Kearney & Trecker Corp., 428 F. Supp. 364, 378 (E.D. Mich. 1977).

386.3   Revised U.C.C. § 2-608(4)(b). Selected portions of revised Article 2 are reproduced in Appx. E.7S, *infra*, and on the CD-Rom accompanying this volume.

386.4   Revised U.C.C. § 2-608(4)(b).

386.5   Revised U.C.C. § 2-608(4)(a).

386.6   Official Comment 8 to Revised U.C.C. § 2-608.

Page 297

Addition to note 390.

8.4.6.2 Continued Use of a Mobile Home

390   *Cf.* Fargo Mach. & Tool Co. v. Kearney & Trecker Corp., 428 F. Supp. 364, 378 (E.D. Mich. 1977) (continued use can mitigate damages, but not proven here).

Page 298

Add to text at end of subsection:

The revised version of Article 2, which the National Conference of Commissioners on Uniform State Laws approved in 2003 for consideration by state legislatures, allows post-revocation use that is "reasonable under the circumstances," but provides that in an appropriate case the buyer is obligated to the seller for the value to the buyer of the use of the goods.[392.1] As an example of reasonable use, the Official Comments cite a buyer's continued use of a mobile home that provides needed shelter.[392.2]

392.1   Revised U.C.C. § 2-608(4)(b). Selected portions of revised Article 2 are reproduced in Appx. E.7S, *infra*, and on the CD-Rom accompanying this volume.

392.2   Official Comment 8 to Revised U.C.C. § 2-608.

8.4.6.3 Continued Use of a Motor Vehicle

Addition to notes 393, 396, 400.

393   *Accord* Cuesta v. Classic Wheels, Inc., 358 N.J. Super. 512, 818 A.2d 448, 50 U.C.C. Rep. Serv. 2d 791 (Super. Ct. App. Div. 2003). *Contra* Basselen v. Gen. Motors Corp., 341 Ill. App. 3d 278, 792 N.E.2d 498 (2003) (buyers who drove van 23,000 miles before and 19,000 miles after revocation, and who showed no special circumstances, could not revoke acceptance).

396   *But cf.* Basselen v. Gen. Motors Corp., 341 Ill. App. 3d 278, 792 N.E.2d 498 (2003) (revocation barred when buyers were apparently able to finance another purchase).

Page 299

400   *But cf.* Basselen v. Gen. Motors Corp., 341 Ill. App. 3d 278, 792 N.E.2d 498 (2003) (continued use of van unreasonable when plaintiffs had other vehicle).

8.5 Deducting Buyer's Damages from the Outstanding Balance

Page 301

Replace § 8.5.2 heading with:

8.5.2 Avoiding Repossession When Buyer Deducts Damages

Move paragraph containing note 422 to end of § 8.5.1.

Add to text at beginning of subsection:

In the typical consumer transaction, the entity that financed the sale will have a security interest in the items purchased and possibly in other property as well. If the consumer's claims or defenses offset the entire remaining debt, then there is no longer any obligation for the collateral to secure. In this event, the secured party has a duty under Article 9 of the Uniform Commercial Code to document that the security interest has terminated.[422.1] Likewise, if the consumer's claims reduce the amount of the debt, the collateral secures only the reduced obligation, and the creditor must file a termination statement once the consumer pays the reduced amount. In either event, the creditor no longer has the right to repossess the goods.

In addition, if the consumer is rightfully withholding payments under UCC § 2-717, the consumer is not in default. The Official Comments make this point clear.[422.2] As a default is a precondition to the right to repossess,[422.3] the creditor has no right to repossess the goods when the consumer is deducting damages from the payments.

422.1 U.C.C. § 9-513.

422.2 Official Comment 2 to U.C.C. § 2-717 ("The buyer . . . must give notice of his intention to withhold all or part of the price if he wishes to avoid a default within the meaning of the section on insecurity and right to assurances."); *see* Purofied Down Products Corp. v. Royal Down Products, Inc., 87 F.R.D. 685 (W.D. Mich. 1980) (buyer who withholds payments under § 2-717 is not in breach of contract).

422.3 U.C.C. § 9-609.

Replace note 423 with:

423 Detroit & N. Sav. & Loan Ass'n v. Woodworth, 54 Mich. App. 517, 221 N.W.2d 190 (1974); *see also* Chrysler Fin. Co. v. Flynn, 88 S.W.3d 142 (Mo. Ct. App. 2002) (breach of warranty is defense to replevin based on non-payment); Created Gemstones, Inc. v. Union Carbide Corp., 47 N.Y.2d 250, 417 N.Y.S.2d 905, 391 N.E.2d 987 (1979).

Replace note 424 with:

424 *See* National Consumer Law Center, Repossessions and Foreclosures §§ 5.5.5, 5.8.1 (5th ed. 2002 and Supp.).

Replace note 426 with:

426 *See* National Consumer Law Center, Consumer Law Pleadings No. 2, § 12.2.2 (2003 Cumulative CD-Rom and Index Guide).

Addition to notes 428, 429.

428 *See* Advisory Opinion, 89 F.T.C. 67 n.5 (Fed. Trade Comm'n 1977) (if applicable law allows buyer to withhold payment from seller, Holder Notice allows buyer to withhold payment from assignee).

429 *Replace NCLC citation with*: National Consumer Law Center, Fair Credit Reporting (5th ed. 2002 and Supp.).

Add to text at end of subsection:

Some courts have had difficulty with this analysis when the consumer revokes acceptance of the goods. Under Article 2 of the UCC, after revoking acceptance, the consumer no longer owes any part of the purchase price to the seller.[429.1] Furthermore, Article 2 gives the consumer a security interest in the goods until the seller refunds the purchase price and reimburses the consumer for these expenses.[429.2]

Properly analyzed, the Holder Rule places the assignee or related lender in exactly the same shoes as the seller: the revocation of acceptance cancels the consumer's obligation to pay for the goods, so there is no obligation for the collateral to secure. As the assignee or related lender is subject to the same revocation claims as the dealer, the consumer owes no money and can not be in default. As the Federal Trade Commission stated in a formal opinion letter soon after the Holder Rule was adopted: "if the consumer, under applicable law, is entitled to withhold payments from the seller, he may, pursuant to the notice, withhold payment from the holder."[429.3]

429.1 U.C.C. § 2-711.

429.2 U.C.C. § 2-711.

429.3 Advisory Opinion, 89 F.T.C. 675 (Fed. Trade Comm'n 1977); *accord* Ellis v. Gen. Motors Acceptance Corp., 160 F.3d 703, 709 (11th Cir. 1998) (Holder Notice "affirms the right of buyers to withhold payment from sellers or assignees, if the cars they purchase turn out to be lemons"); Ransom v. Rohr-Gurnee Volkswagen, Inc., 2001 U.S. Dist. LEXIS 17363 (N.D. Ill. Oct. 22, 2001); Jackson v. S. Holland Dodge, 197 Ill. 2d 39, 258 Ill. Dec. 79, 755 N.E.2d 462 (2001) (erroneously confining affirmative actions against assignees to those in which seller's breach is so substantial that rescission is warranted, but confirming the right to withhold payment from the assignee if a car is a lemon).

Page 302

8.5.3 *Deductions from Installment Payments*

Replace note 430 with:

430 U.C.C. § 1-106 [*redesignated as U.C.C. § 1-305(a) by revised Article 1, approved by the National Conference of Commissioners on Uniform State Laws (NCCUSL) in 2001 for adoption by the states*].

Add note 435.1 at end of sentence containing note 435.

435.1 *See* Advisory Opinion, 89 F.T.C. 675 (Fed. Trade Comm'n 1977) (if consumer, under applicable law, is entitled to withhold payment from the seller, Holder Notice allows withholding of payment from assignee); Jackson v. S. Holland Dodge, 197 Ill. 2d 39, 258 Ill. Dec. 79, 755 N.E.2d 467 (2001) (Holder Rule allows buyer to withhold payment from assignee when car is a lemon).

Withholding payments from the assignee or lender is a particularly helpful remedy if the goods are defective and the original seller is defunct or in bankruptcy. In such a case, the buyer is unlikely to be able to force the seller to make repairs, replace the product, or pay damages. Deducting damages from the payments is a way to make the buyer whole while bypassing the seller.

8.5.4 *Practical Problems with Withholding Installment Payments*

Add to text after sentence containing note 436:

Even though deduction of damages from payments under UCC § 2-717 is not a default,[436.1] the secured party may threaten repossession.

436.1   *See* § 8.5.2, *supra.*

Replace note 437 with:

437   *See* National Consumer Law Center, Repossessions and Foreclosures § 4.9 (5th ed. 2002 and Supp.); *see also* Appx. J.2, *infra* (sample letter).

Page 304

8.5.6 *Deducting Damages for Breach of Manufacturer's Warranty When Direct Seller Has Disclaimed Warranties*

Add note 450.1 at end of first sentence of subsection's third paragraph.

450.1   *See, e.g.,* Mich. Comp. Laws § 492.114a (making any holder of a motor vehicle installment sales contract subject to all claims and defenses of the buyer arising out of the installment transaction, up to the amount paid by the buyer).

Add to text after subsection's fourth paragraph:

Even if the claim is only against the manufacturer, not the dealer, in many cases the creditor is an assignee that is a wholly-owned subsidiary of the manufacturer. In this situation, deducting damages from the amount owed to the assignee is the equivalent of deducting them from the manufacturer.

Add to text at end of subsection:

A Missouri appellate decision, on the other hand, held that buyers could assert breach of the manufacturer's express warranty against the dealer's assignee as a defense to an action seeking replevin if the transaction was deemed to be for consumer purposes and therefore governed by a state law making assignees liable for all claims of the debtor "arising from or out of such sale."[456]

456   Chrysler Fin. Co. v. Flynn, 88 S.W.3d 142 (Mo. Ct. App. 2002).

Chapter 9

Ten Ways to Avoid Contractual Limitations on Remedies

Page 305

9.1 Introduction

Addition to note 4.

4   *See, e.g.,* Webco Indus., Inc. v. Thermatool Corp., 278 F.3d 1120, 46 U.C.C. Rep. Serv. 2d 698 (10th Cir. 2002) (Mich. law) (warranty limiting remedies to repair or refund is analyzed the same as repair-or-replace warranty).

9.2 Contract Language Must Unambiguously Limit the Consumer's Remedies

Addition to notes 5, 6.

5   *See also* Triple E, Inc. v. Hendrix & Dail, Inc., 543 S.E.2d 245, 43 U.C.C. Rep. Serv. 2d 533 (S.C. Ct. App. 2001) (construing direct damages to include lost profits because otherwise buyer would have no meaningful remedy).

Page 306

6   *See also* Traina v. Nationsbank, 2001 U.S. Dist. LEXIS 14612 (E.D. La. Sept. 7, 2001) (remedy limitation in lease must be unambiguous and brought to the attention of the lessee).

Add to text at end of subsection:

    In another case, a clause disclaimed warranties and limited damages unless the seller provided a separate written warranty. The court held that the certificate of title to the vehicle was an express written warranty of title, so the remedy limitation was not effective as to damages flowing from a breach of the warranty of title.[15.1]

15.1   Elmore v. Doenges Bros. Ford, Inc., 21 P.3d 65 (Okla. Civ. App. 2000).

9.3 Has the Consumer Agreed to the Remedy Limitation?

Addition to notes 16, 20.

16   *See also* Materials Mktg. Corp. v. Spencer, 40 S.W.3d 172, 43 U.C.C. Rep. Serv. 2d 1131 (Tex. App. 2001) (limitation of liability clause on back of contract ineffective without evidence that buyer was aware of it and agreed to it).

Page 307

20   Terrell v. R & A Mfg. Partners, Ltd., 835 So. 2d 216, 50 U.C.C. Rep. Serv. 2d 151 (Ala. Civ. App. 2002); *see also* Beaver Valley Alloy Foundry Co. v. Therma-Fab, Inc., 814 A.2d 217, 49 U.C.C. Rep. Serv. 2d 507 (Pa. Super. Ct. 2002) (remedy limitation effective when court found that seller's facsimile included the reverse side of the quote, which recited the limitation). *But cf.* Pioneer/Eclipse Corp. v. Kohler Co., 113 F. Supp. 2d 811 (W.D.N.C. 2000) (remedy limitation on packing slip enforced when commercial parties' course of dealing incorporated it).

9.4 Claims Unaffected By Contractual Remedy Limitations

9.4.4 Tort and Consumer Protection Claims

Page 308

Addition to note 32.

32   Dow Agrosciences Ltd. Liab. Co. v. Bates, 332 F.3d 323, 51 U.C.C. Rep. Serv. 2d 384 (5th Cir. 2003) (remedy limitation does not apply to fraud claim but may apply to estoppel and waiver claims).

Replace note 33 with:

33   *See* National Consumer Law Center, Unfair and Deceptive Acts and Practices § 4.2.15 (5th ed. 2001 and Supp.).

9.5 When Limited Remedy "Fails of Its Essential Purpose"

Page 309

9.5.1 General

Addition to notes 38, 39, 41.

38   Moorer v. Hartz Seed Co., 120 F. Supp. 2d 1283 (M.D. Ala. 2000) (limited remedy might fail of its essential purpose if seeds' defects became apparent only when it was too late to plant replacement crop).

39   *Add to Star-Shadow Prods. citation:* 730 A.2d 1081; *add:* Bernath v. Potato Services, 2004 WL 73280 (D. Me. Jan. 15, 2004); Rheem Mfg. Co. v. Phelps Heating & Air Conditioning, Inc., 746 N.E.2d 941 (Ind. 2001) (limited remedy maintained reasonable division of responsibilities between manufacturer and dealer); BOC Group v. Chevron Chem. Co., 359 N.J. Super. 135, 819 A.2d 431, 50 U.C.C. Rep. Serv. 2d 489 (Super. Ct. App. Div. 2003) (commercial case).

Page 310

41   *But see* Taylor Inv. Corp. v. Weil, 169 F. Supp. 2d 1046, 44 U.C.C. Rep. Serv. 2d 382 (D. Minn. 2001) (remedy limitation in commercial case upheld when it allowed repair, replacement, or refund).

9.5.2 Application to Repair or Replace Remedies

Addition to notes 46, 48, 49, 51–53, 57.

46   Webco Indus., Inc. v. Thermatool Corp., 278 F.3d 1120, 46 U.C.C. Rep. Serv. 2d 698 (10th Cir. 2002) (Mich. law) (if seller does not perform obligation to repair or refund within reasonable time, limited remedy fails of its essential purpose and consequential damages are recoverable); Hercules Mach. Corp. v. McElwee Bros., Inc., 49 U.C.C. Rep. Serv. 2d 72 (E.D. La. 2002) (commercial case); Rose v. Colo. Factory Homes, 10 P.3d 680, 43 U.C.C. Rep. Serv. 2d 1160 (Colo. Ct. App. 2000); Forster v. Navistar Int'l Transp. Corp., 48 U.C.C. Rep. Serv. 2d 1384 (Mich. Ct. App. 2002) (unpublished) (twenty-nine repairs to truck in three and a half years raises factual question whether limited remedy failed of its essential purpose); King v. Taylor Chrysler Plymouth, 184 Mich. App. 204, 457 N.W.2d 42 (1990); Trinity Indus., Inc. v. McKinnon Bridge Co., 77 S.W.3d 159, 46 U.C.C. Rep. Serv. 2d 119 (Tenn. Ct. App. 2001) (inability or unwillingness to repair or replace within realistic time would avoid limitation, but not shown here when buyer never requested repair or replacement). *But cf.* Christian v. Sony Corp., 152 F. Supp. 2d 1184, 45 U.C.C. Rep. Serv. 2d 510 (D. Minn. 2001) (remedy limitation precluded claim when buyers had not asked manufacturer to repair or replace); Delmarva Power & Light Co. v. ABB Power T & D Co., 47 U.C.C. Rep. Serv. 2d 1033 (Del. Super. Ct. 2002) (upholding remedy limitation clause when seller made diligent attempts to repair complex equipment, even though repairs took two months).

Page 311

48   *See, e.g.,* Jones v. Fleetwood Motor Homes, 127 F. Supp. 2d 958 (N.D. Ill. 2000). *But cf.* Moore v. Mack Trucks, Inc., 40 S.W.3d 888, 44 U.C.C. Rep. Serv. 2d 416 (Ky. Ct. App. 2001) (clause upheld when buyer only sought repair twice, four months apart); River Rouge Sch. Dist. v. Mestek, Inc., 48 U.C.C. Rep. Serv. 2d 1036 (Mich. Ct. App. 2002) (unpublished) (upholding remedy limitation when seller successfully repaired product within days each time it broke); Mercury Marine v. Clear River Constr. Co., 839 So. 2d 508, 49 U.C.C. Rep. Serv. 2d 989 (Miss. 2003) (no failure of essential purpose when boat required repairs three times in ten months).

49   Johnson v. Monsanto Co., 48 U.C.C. Rep. Serv. 2d 586 (Ohio Ct. App. 2002); Osburn v. Bendix Home Sys., Inc., 613 P.2d 445 (Okla. 1980) (mobile home water leakage not repaired until after interior was damaged).

51   Forest River, Inc. v. Posten, 2002 WL 1264011 (Ala. Civ. App. June 7, 2002) (repairs were unsuccessful, and seller's expert testified that problem was uncorrectable); Rose v. Colo. Factory Homes, 10 P.3d 680, 43 U.C.C. Rep. Serv. 2d 1160 (Colo. Ct. App. 2000); Lara v. Hyundai Motor Am., 331 Ill. App. 3d 53, 264 Ill. Dec. 416, 770 N.E.2d 721 (2002); Forster v. Navistar Int'l Transp. Corp., 48 U.C.C. Rep. Serv. 2d 1384 (Mich. Ct. App. 2002) (unpublished) (repeated need for repairs); King v. Taylor Chrysler Plymouth, 184 Mich. App. 204, 457 N.W.2d 42 (1990).

52   Arabian Agric. Services Co. v. Chief Indus., Inc., 309 F.3d 479, 48 U.C.C. Rep. Serv. 2d 1394 (8th Cir. 2002) (Neb. law); Amsan, Ltd. Liab. Co. v. Prophet 21, Inc., 45 U.C.C. Rep. Serv. 2d 1089 (E.D. Pa. 2001) (denying motion to dismiss when buyer alleged that seller refused to repair or replace software); Cocchiola Paving, Inc. v. Peterbilt, 50 U.C.C. Rep. Serv. 2d 136 (Conn. Super. Ct. 2003).

Page 312

53   *See* Forster v. Navistar Int'l Transp. Corp., 48 U.C.C. Rep. Serv. 2d 1384 (Mich. Ct. App. 2002) (unpublished) (twenty-nine repairs to truck over three and one-half years for multiple problems).

57   Forest River, Inc. v. Posten, 2002 WL 1264011 (Ala. Civ. App. June 7, 2002) (repairs were unsuccessful, and seller's expert testified that problem was uncorrectable).

Page 313

9.5.3 Effect of Failure of Repair or Replace Remedy on Seller's Limitation of Incidental or Consequential Damages

Addition to notes 63, 64, 67, 68.

63   *Replace Rheem Mfg. Co. citation with:* 746 N.E.2d 941 (Ind. 2001) (court stresses that this is a commercial case; also rejects use of commercial reasonableness test to determine validity of clause); *add: See* Patapsco

Designs, Inc. v. Dominion Wireless, Inc., 276 F. Supp. 2d 472, 51 U.C.C. Rep. Serv. 2d 159 (D. Md. 2003) (commercial case); Hercules Mach. Corp. v. McElwee Bros., Inc., 49 U.C.C. Rep. Serv. 2d 72 (E.D. La. 2002); Taylor Inv. Corp. v. Weil, 169 F. Supp. 2d 1046, 44 U.C.C. Rep. Serv. 2d 382 (D. Minn. 2001) (clauses held independent in commercial setting between two merchants of equal bargaining power); Pierce v. Catalina Yachts, Inc., 2 P.3d 618 (Alaska 2000) (holding clauses independent in consumer case, but finding limitation unconscionable for other reasons); Parker-Smith v. STO Corp., 52 Va. Cir. 577, 43 U.C.C. Rep. Serv. 2d 606 (1999) (consumer case), *aff'd on other grounds*, 262 Va. 432, 551 S.E.2d 615 (2001).

64   *See* Arabian Agric. Services Co. v. Chief Indus., Inc., 309 F.3d 479, 48 U.C.C. Rep. Serv. 2d 1394 (8th Cir. 2002) (commercial case) (Neb. law); Webco Indus., Inc. v. Thermatool Corp., 278 F.3d 1120, 46 U.C.C. Rep. Serv. 2d 698 (10th Cir. 2002) (Mich. law) (commercial case); Amsan, Ltd. Liab. Co. v. Prophet 21, Inc., 45 U.C.C. Rep. Serv. 2d 1089 (E.D. Pa. 2001) (commercial case); Curragh Queensland Mining Ltd. v. Dresser Indus., Inc., 55 P.3d 235, 47 U.C.C. Rep. Serv. 2d 1064 (Colo. Ct. App. 2002) (commercial case); Lara v. Hyundai Motor Am., 331 Ill. App. 3d 53, 264 Ill. Dec. 416, 770 N.E.2d 721 (2002).

Page 314   67   Jones v. Fleetwood Motor Homes, 127 F. Supp. 2d 958 (N.D. Ill. 2000).

68   Jones v. Fleetwood Motor Homes, 127 F. Supp. 2d 958 (N.D. Ill. 2000).

9.6 Unconscionability of Limitation of Remedies

Page 316

9.6.3 *Factors Used to Determine Unconscionability of a Limitation of Remedies Clause*

Addition to notes 85, 92.   85   *See* Dow Agrosciences Ltd. Liab. Co. v. Bates, 332 F.3d 323, 51 U.C.C. Rep. Serv. 2d 384 (5th Cir. 2003) (lack of opportunity to read clause before sale may make it unconscionable). *But cf.* Roossinck v. Orkin Exterminating Co., 1998 U.S. Dist. LEXIS 7161 (W.D. Mich. Apr. 24, 1998) (remedy limitation clause not unconscionable in non-U.C.C. service contract when it was clearly spelled out).

Page 317   92   *See* Taylor Inv. Corp. v. Weil, 169 F. Supp. 2d 1046, 44 U.C.C. Rep. Serv. 2d 382 (D. Minn. 2001) (clause not unconscionable when sophisticated commercial entities had relatively equal bargaining power and agreement was not overly one-sided); Moorer v. Hartz Seed Co., 120 F. Supp. 2d 1283 (M.D. Ala. 2000) (upholding limitation of remedies for defective seeds); Parker-Smith v. STO Corp., 52 Va. Cir. 577, 43 U.C.C. Rep. Serv. 2d 606 (1999) (remedy limitation clause not unconscionable when warranty ran to large group of users and for a long period of time), *aff'd on other grounds*, 262 Va. 432, 551 S.E.2d 615 (2001); *see also* Triple E, Inc. v. Hendrix & Dail, Inc., 543 S.E.2d 245, 43 U.C.C. Rep. Serv. 2d 533 (S.C. Ct. App. 2001) (treating profits lost due to defective crop treatment as direct rather than consequential damages that would be excluded by remedy limitation clause).

Add to text at end of subsection's third paragraph: Another important factor is the seller's bad faith: if the seller acts in bad faith in failing to honor the warranty, it is unconscionable to enforce the parties' allocation of risks.[94.1]

94.1   Pierce v. Catalina Yachts, Inc., 2 P.3d 618 (Alaska 2000).

Page 318

Addition to notes 95, 96, 99.   95   *See also* Adcock v. Ramtreat Metal Tech., Inc., 105 Wash. App. 1058, 44 U.C.C. Rep. Serv. 2d 1026 (2001) (unpublished) (distinguishing between consumer and commercial transactions).

96   Patapsco Designs, Inc. v. Dominion Wireless, Inc., 276 F. Supp. 2d 472, 51 U.C.C. Rep. Serv. 2d 159 (D. Md. 2003) (not unconscionable to exclude consequential damages for breach of commercial contract for production of complex electronic components); Pierce v. Catalina Yachts, Inc., 2 P.3d 618 (Alaska 2000); *see also* Trinity Indus., Inc. v. McKinnon Bridge Co., 77 S.W.3d 159, 46 U.C.C. Rep. Serv. 2d 119 (Tenn. Ct. App. 2001) (not unconscionable when commercial parties had equal bargaining power).

99   *But see* Lara v. Hyundai Motor Am., 331 Ill. App. 3d 53, 264 Ill. Dec. 416, 770 N.E.2d 721 (2002) (erroneously stating that nothing in Magnuson-Moss Act governs limitation of remedies in limited warranties; court does not mention § 2302(a) or 16 C.F.R. § 701.3(a)(8)).

9.7 Inconspicuousness of Limitations Provision Will Defeat Its Effect

9.7.2 *UCC Requirements Concerning Conspicuous Disclosure*

Page 319

Addition to note 106.

106 *See also* Materials Mktg. Corp. v. Spencer, 40 S.W.3d 172, 43 U.C.C. Rep. Serv. 2d 1131 (Tex. App. 2001) (limitation of liability clause on back of contract ineffective without evidence that buyer was aware of it and agreed to it). *But see* Lara v. Hyundai Motor Am., 331 Ill. App. 3d 53, 264 Ill. Dec. 416, 770 N.E.2d 721 (2002).

9.7.3 *Effect of State Plain Language Statute*

Replace note 110 with:

110 *See* National Consumer Law Center, Unfair and Deceptive Acts and Practices § 5.2.2 (5th ed. 2001 and Supp.) (citations to state plain language statutes and plain language requirements in other statutes).

Page 320

9.10 Seller's Bad Faith

Replace note 118 with:

118 U.C.C. § 1-102 [*redesignated as U.C.C. § 1-302(b) by revised Article 1, approved by the National Conference of Commissioners on Uniform State Laws (NCCUSL) in 2001 for adoption by the states*].

Replace note 119 with:

119 U.C.C. § 1-203 [*redesignated as U.C.C. § 1-304 by revised Article 1, approved by NCCUSL in 2001 for adoption by the states; note also the expanded definition of "good faith" in revised § 1-201(b)(2)*]; *see also* § 11.3, *infra.*

Replace note 120 with:

120 Long Island Lighting Co. v. Transamerica Delaval, Inc., 646 F. Supp. 1442 (S.D.N.Y. 1986); *see* Select Pork v. Babcock Swine, 640 F.2d 147 (8th Cir. 1981); Werner Kammann Maschinenfabrik v. Max Levy Autograph, Inc., 47 U.C.C. Rep. Serv. 2d 1023 (E.D. Pa. 2002) (misrepresentation of features of product); Jannus Group, Inc. v. Indep. Container, Inc., 1999 WL 294846 (S.D.N.Y. May 10, 1999) (Ky. law); Christiana Marine Serv. Corp. v. Seaboard Shipping Corp., 1997 WL 587292 (E.D. Pa. Sept. 10, 1997); *see also* Int'l Connectors Indus., Ltd. v. Litton Sys., Inc., 1995 WL 253089 (D. Conn. Apr. 25, 1995) (non-warranty case).

9.11 Remedy Limitations that Make Warranty Unfair or Deceptive

Addition to note 124.

124 *Replace NCLC citation with*: National Consumer Law Center, Unfair and Deceptive Acts and Practices § 5.2.7.3 (5th ed. 2001 and Supp.); *add: See also* Roelle v. Orkin Exterminating Co., 2000 Ohio App. LEXIS 5141 (Ohio Ct. App. Nov. 7, 2000) (termite retreatment guarantee).

Page 321

Replace note 125 with:

125 *See* National Consumer Law Center, Unfair and Deceptive Acts and Practices § 4.2.14 (5th ed. 2001 and Supp.).

Replace note 128 with:

128 *See* National Consumer Law Center, Unfair and Deceptive Acts and Practices § 4.3 (5th ed. 2001 and Supp.).

Chapter 10

Warranty Litigation Under the UCC

10.1 Strategy and Practice

10.1.1 Evaluating and Framing the Case

10.1.1.1 Initial Contacts With the Client

Page 323

Add note 1.1 at end of first bulleted item.

1.1   If the client does not have a copy of the warranty for their vehicle, information may appear in "The Official Warranty Guide," published by J & L Warranty Pros (copies may be ordered from J & L Warranty Pros at (800) 852-6298).

Add note 1.2 at end of second bulleted item.

1.2   If the consumer does not have the owner's manual, it may be possible to obtain one through a commercial service such as TMC Publications Automobile Literature, 5817 Park Heights Ave., Baltimore, MD 21215; telephone: (410) 367-4490; website: www.tmcpubl.com.

Add to text at end of subsection:

Consumers who have defective vehicles and no other means of daily transportation can find warranty litigation frustrating. It is important to advise the client from the outset about how the case is likely to progress and about the delays inherent in the process, for example, periods spent waiting for discovery responses. The attorney's office procedures for accepting client telephone calls should also be explained. The attorney may want to encourage the client to relay day-to-day questions through a paralegal or office assistant. The attorney may want to explain to the client that the client has two problems: a legal problem, which the attorney will handle, and a transportation problem, which the client needs to develop a plan to handle.

Attorney fees should be thoroughly explained to the consumer at the outset of the relationship. If the monetary value of the case is small and it involves a claim under a fee-shifting statute, the consumer should know that, unless the defendants resolve the matter promptly, the attorney's fee may end up being larger than the consumer's recovery. Many attorneys include provisions in their retainers that if the consumer abandons the case or settles it, the attorney is entitled to be paid at his or her prevailing hourly rate. Such a provision, and the likelihood that the defendant will pressure the client to settle without provision for fees, should be carefully explained to the client.

Page 324

10.1.1.2 Obtain and Analyze All Relevant Documents

Replace note 10 with:

10   See National Consumer Law Center, Automobile Fraud Ch. 2 (2d ed. 2003) for suggestions on researching a vehicle's title history.

Addition to note 12.

12   *Replace "http://www.free2incorporate.com/Secretary of State.htm" with:* www.nass.org.

10.1.1.3 Go Behind the Written Documents

Replace note 17 with:

17   *See* National Consumer Law Center, Unfair and Deceptive Acts and Practices § 4.2.14 (5th ed. 2001 and Supp.); *see also* § 11.4, *infra.*

Replace note 19 with:

19   U.C.C. §§ 2-202(a), 1-205, 1-208(1) [*The latter two provisions are consolidated as U.C.C. § 1-303 by revised Article 1, which the National Conference of Commissioners on Uniform State Laws (NCCUSL) approved in 2001 for adoption by state legislatures.*]

10.1.2 Strategic Decisions

Page 326

10.1.2.2 Should the Buyer Cancel the Sale or Keep the Goods?

Add to text at end of subsection:

If the buyer wants to cancel the sale under a lemon law, it is important to work out in advance whether the client wants a refund or a replacement. The process of selecting a replacement vehicle potentially raises complications about whether it is truly comparable, and is likely to consume additional attorney time. The implementation of a refund is much simpler.

10.1.2.3 How to Deal With Secured Creditors

Add to text at end of subsection:

Even though revocation of acceptance is intended to be a self-help remedy, the buyer may find it necessary to file suit in order to enforce the revocation and prevent repossession.

Page 327

10.1.2.5 Avoiding Spoliation of Evidence Problems

Addition to notes 49, 52.

49   *Replace Oliver citation with*: 297 Mont. 336, 993 P.2d 11; *add after Meyn citation*: Fletcher v. Dorchester Mut. Ins. Co., 437 Mass. 544, 773 N.E.2d 420 (2002).

52   Fletcher v. Dorchester Mut. Ins. Co., 437 Mass. 544, 773 N.E.2d 420 (2002); Manorcare Health Servs., Inc. v. Osmose Wood Preserving, Inc., 336 N.J. Super. 218, 764 A.2d 475 (Super. Ct. App. Div. 2001) (excluding all evidence obtained during or after repairs that destroyed evidence); *see also* Copenhagen Reinsurance Co. v. Champion Home Builders Co., 2003 WL 21850441 (Ala. Civ. App. Aug. 8, 2003) (barring plaintiff from attempting to prove that fire was caused by any parts of mobile home other than those that plaintiff preserved).

Add to text at end of sentence containing note 52:

, or dismissal of the action.[52.1]

52.1   Silvestri v. Gen. Motors Corp., 271 F.3d 583 (4th Cir. 2001).

Addition to note 54.

54   *See also* Simons v. Mercedes-Benz of No. Am., 1996 WL 103796 (E.D. Pa. Mar. 7, 1996) (weighing factors and denying manufacturer's motion for summary judgment when its expert and service technicians had opportunity to examine car before consumer traded it in).

Page 328

Addition to note 55.

55   *But see* Silvestri v. Gen. Motors Corp., 271 F.3d 583 (4th Cir. 2001) (case dismissed as sanction for spoliation even though plaintiff did not own car, when he had access to it and could have taken steps to preserve it or to give defendant opportunity to inspect it).

Add to text after subsection's fourth paragraph:

If the consumer sells the goods or agrees that the seller or secured party can sell them, negotiating a stipulation about the conduct of the sale is a good precaution. The stipulation could include such terms as: 1) authorization for the sale; 2) an agreement that the secured party will execute whatever documents are necessary for the sale to go forward; 3) a requirement that the goods be retained for a specified period of time and be made available to the parties so that they can inspect them; 4) directions for the disposition of the proceeds; 5) an agreement that the seller will hold the consumer harmless for any claims by any subsequent buyer, user, or lessor of the vehicle arising out of any defect in the vehicle or any defect in the title; and 6) a provision that the sale of the vehicle is without prejudice to any parties' rights, duties, claims, or defenses.

Sometimes the buyer consults an attorney after having returned the product to the dealer in an attempt to undo the transaction. In this situation, it may be best for the buyer to retrieve the product, keep it insured, preserve it, and have it examined. The danger that these steps will be construed as reacceptance can be reduced, although not completely avoided, by carefully documenting and communicating the purpose of retrieving the goods. An alternate course of action is to file a motion to preserve the evidence, seeking an injunction to prevent the seller from disposing of, destroying, or altering the product.

Add to text at end of subsection:

The buyer should also continue insurance on the goods while awaiting resolution of the claim.

10.1.2.6 Provide Complete and Timely Notice to the Seller

Replace note 64 with:

64   *See* National Consumer Law Center, Unfair and Deceptive Acts and Practices § 7.5.4 (5th ed. 2001 and Supp.).

Add to text at end of subsection's first paragraph:

In addition, early demands for relief can help persuade the judge that a later attorney fee claim is reasonable, by showing that the defendant refused the opportunity to resolve the case on a reasonable basis when substantial fees had not yet been incurred.

Add to text at end of subsection:

In addition to the notices required by the UCC, the attorney may want to send a demand letter. A demand letter can be viewed as a pre-suit discovery device, as it is likely to flush out major defenses or hidden weaknesses in the consumer's case. It also makes the suit seem more justified in the eyes of an overworked trial judge if the defendant spurned the consumer's requests before suit. Having made a pre-suit demand is especially helpful when seeking fees under a fee-shifting statute, and demand letters should be drafted keeping the possibility in mind that the letter will be evidence in support of a fee petition.[67.1] On the other hand, the imminent expiration of the statute of limitations, or the fear that the defendant will destroy evidence if alerted before suit is filed, may make a demand letter impossible. If a demand letter is sent, the attorney should caution the consumer to refer any calls from the potential defendant to the attorney.

67.1   *See* Moedt v. Gen. Motors Corp., 60 P.3d 240 (Ariz. Ct. App. 2002).

10.1.2.7 Consumer Publicity Efforts

Add to text at end of subsection's first paragraph:

The consumer should be careful not to overstate the facts, as the defendants may use such statements against the consumer at trial. The consumer should also avoid an over-energetic publicity campaign that might enable the defendants to portray her as unbalanced. The First Amendment protects publicity campaigns and peaceful informational picketing to some extent.[67.2]

67.2   Boemler Chevrolet Co. v. Combs, 808 S.W.2d 875 (Mo. Ct. App. 1991); Sid Dillon Chevrolet-Oldsmobile-Pontiac, Inc. v. Sullivan, 251 Neb. 722, 559 N.W.2d 740 (1997); Brammer v. KB Home Lone Star, Ltd. P'ship, 114 S.W.3d 101 (Tex. App. 2003).

10.1.3 Pleading Warranty Claims

10.1.3.1 Plead Both UCC and Non-UCC Claims

Page 329

Replace note 72 with:

72   *See* § 11.1, *infra. See generally* National Consumer Law Center, Unfair and Deceptive Acts and Practices (5th ed. 2001 and Supp.).

Page 330

Replace note 83 with:

83   *See* § 11.1, *infra*; National Consumer Law Center, Unfair and Deceptive Acts and Practices (5th ed. 2001 and Supp.).

Replace note 84 with:

84   *See* § 11.1.1, *infra*; National Consumer Law Center, Unfair and Deceptive Acts and Practices § 4.2.15 (5th ed. 2001 and Supp.).

10.1.3.3 Pleading Revocation or Rejection

Add to text at end of subsection:

It is probably proper to characterize these claims as causes of action rather than remedies, at least when the seller has not complied with the buyer's attempt to reject or revoke acceptance.[94.1]

94.1   Crowe v. Joliet Dodge, 2001 U.S. Dist. LEXIS 10066 (N.D. Ill. July 17, 2001).

Page 331

10.1.3.4 Pleading Breach of Warranty

Addition to notes 95, 98.

95   *E.g.,* Smart Online, Inc. v. Opensite Technologies, Inc., 51 U.C.C. Rep. Serv. 2d 47 (N.C. Super. Ct. 2003); U.S. Tire-Tech, Inc. v. Boeran, B.V., 110 S.W.3d 197, 50 U.C.C. Rep. Serv. 2d 780 (Tex. App. 2003).

98   *But cf.* Pressalite Corp. v. Matsushita Elec. Corp., 50 U.C.C. Rep. Serv. 2d 410 (N.D. Ill. 2003) (finding warranty complaint sufficiently specific); Kutzle v. Thor Indus., Inc., 2003 WL 21654260 (N.D. Ill. July 14, 2003) (finding complaint sufficiently specific).

Page 332

10.1.3.6 Determining What Parties to Name as Defendants

Addition to note 106.

106   *Replace NCLC citation with*: National Consumer Law Center, Unfair and Deceptive Acts and Practices § 6.6 (5th ed. 2001 and Supp.) (full discussion of the Holder Rule); *add: See, e.g.,* Ford Motor Credit Co. v. Britton, 1996 Conn. Super. LEXIS 504 (Conn. Super. Ct. Feb. 23, 1996); Jaramillo v. Gonzales, 50 P.3d 554 (N.M. Ct. App. 2002) (assignee stands in shoes of seller); Green Tree Acceptance, Inc. v. Pierce, 768 S.W.2d 416 (Tex. App. 1989).

Add to text after subsection's next-to-last sentence:

Another technique is to serve a request to admit and an interrogatory on this question along with the complaint or promptly thereafter.

Replace website citation in subsection's last sentence with:

www.nass.org, www.residentagentinfo.com, and www.statelocalgov.net.

Add new subsection to text after § 10.1.3.6.

10.1.3.6a Warranty Class Actions

Warranty class actions offer great promise, yet face a number of hurdles. A class action may be filed in federal court under the Magnuson-Moss Act only if there are one hundred or more named plaintiffs, each individual claim equals $25 or more, and the total amount in controversy is at least $50,000.[109.1] State court class actions can raise Magnuson-Moss claims without meeting these requirements, however.[109.2]

The differences in warranty law from state to state complicate multi-state warranty class actions.[109.3] One approach is to define the class to include only buyers in states that have similar laws.[109.4] Another approach is to seek to apply the law of the manufacturer's home state to all class members,[109.5] which is constitutionally permissible in some circumstances.[109.6] Dividing states with similar laws into subclasses is another possibility.[109.7] Sometimes there is a large enough number of buyers in a single state to allow a class action to proceed without having to deal with choice of law questions.[109.8]

A number of courts have certified warranty class actions.[109.9] Claims based on the implied warranty of merchantability have some advantages because there is no need to show that the warranty was part of the basis of the bargain, as is required for express warranties.[109.10] Individual issues can still arise in implied warranty cases, however. For example, one court refused to certify an implied warranty class action because examination would have revealed the existence of the defect and the court concluded that individual inquiry was necessary as to whether the buyer had examined the product before the sale.[109.11] In many express warranty cases, it will be clear that the warranty was part of the basis of the bargain except in such highly unusual factual circumstances that this requirement should not preclude certification. Even if there are individual questions, the court can still certify the class and conduct separate proceedings to resolve the individual issues.[109.12] Consumer class actions are discussed in detail in another NCLC manual.[109.13]

109.1   15 U.S.C. § 2310(d)(3); *see* § 2.7.3.3, *supra.*

109.2   *See* 15 U.S.C. § 2310(d)(3) (referring only to suits brought under § 2310(d)(1)(B)).

109.3   *See, e.g.,* Chin v. Chrysler Corp., 182 F.R.D. 448 (D.N.J. 1998); *see also* §§ 2.3.6.2 (effect of privity requirements on multi-state warranty class actions), 2.7.7, *supra.*

109.4   *But see In re* Ford Motor Co. Ignition Switch Products Liab. Litig., 194 F.R.D. 484 (D.N.J. 2000) (declining to certify class despite elaborately restricted class definition).

109.5   *See* Ysbrand v. DaimlerChrysler Corp., 49 U.C.C. Rep. Serv. 2d 1062 (Okla. 2003) (certifying nationwide class action). *But see In re* Bridgestone/Firestone, Inc., 288 F.3d 1012 (7th Cir. 2002) (reversing trial court's decision to certify class and apply warranty law of manufacturer's home state).

109.6   Phillips Petroleum Co. v. Shutts, 472 U.S. 797, 105 S. Ct. 2965, 86 L. Ed. 2d 628 (1985); *see* National Consumer Law Center, Unfair and Deceptive Acts and Practices § 8.5.5 (5th ed. 2001 and Supp.).

109.7   *See, e.g., In re* St. Jude Med., Inc. Silzone Heart Valves Products Liab. Litig., 2003 WL 1589527 (D. Minn. Mar. 27, 2003).

109.8   *See, e.g.,* McManus v. Fleetwood Enterprises, Inc., 330 F.3d 545, 49 U.C.C. Rep. Serv. 2d 1124 (5th Cir. 2003).

109.9   *See* O'Keefe v. Mercedes-Benz USA, 214 F.R.D. 266 (E.D. Pa. 2003) (certifying settlement class); Joseph v. Gen. Motors Corp., 109 F.R.D. 635 (D. Colo. 1986) (certifying class of Colorado purchasers of vehicle; individual causation, reliance, and damages issues can be resolved in separate proceedings); Gordon v. Boden, 224 Ill. App. 3d 195, 586 N.E.2d 461 (1991) (affirming certification of nationwide class of purchasers of mislabeled orange juice); Martin v. Amana Refrigeration, Inc., 435 N.W.2d 364 (Iowa 1989) (affirming certification of class of Des Moines area furnace buyers); *In re* Cadillac V8-6-4 Class Action, 93 N.J. 412, 461 A.2d 736 (1983) (certifying class of New Jersey buyers of vehicle); Delgozzo v. Kenny, 266 N.J. Super. 169, 628 A.2d 1080 (Super. Ct. App. Div. 1993) (reversing denial of class certification; remanding with instructions to certify at least a single-state class of furnace buyers); National Consumer Law Center, Consumer Class Actions: A Practical Litigation Guide § 9.3.4.4 (5th ed. 2002 and Supp.). *But see* Jacobs v. Osmose, Inc., 213 F.R.D. 607 (S.D. Fla. 2003) (too many individual factual issues prevent certification of class on claims of contamination and health hazards caused by leaching of preservative from wood).

109.10   *See* McManus v. Fleetwood Enterprises, Inc., 330 F.3d 545, 49 U.C.C. Rep. Serv. 2d 1124 (5th Cir. 2003) (upholding class certification of implied warranty of merchantability claims but reversing certification of express warranty claims); Murrin v. Ford Motor Co., 756 N.Y.S.2d 596, 50 U.C.C. Rep. Serv. 2d 745 (App. Div. 2003).

109.11   *See* Polaris Indus., Inc. v. McDonald, 2003 WL 21940115 (Tex. App. Aug. 13, 2003) (denying class certification).

109.12   *See, e.g., In re* St. Jude Med., Inc. Silzone Heart Valves Products Liab. Litig., 2003 WL 1589527 (D. Minn. Mar. 27, 2003) (conditionally certifying class on common law claims involving defective heart valves); Joseph v. Gen. Motors Corp., 109 F.R.D. 635 (D. Colo. 1986) (certifying class of Colorado purchasers of vehicle; individual causation, reliance, and damages issues can be resolved in separate proceedings).

109.13   National Consumer Law Center, Consumer Class Actions: A Practical Litigation Guide § 9.3.4.4 (5th ed. 2002 and Supp.).

10.1.3.7 The Seller's Answer

Add to text after sentence containing note 110:

Although it is not specifically listed in Federal Rule of Civil Procedure 8(c), at least one court has concluded that failure to mitigate damages is also an affirmative defense that must be pleaded.[110.1]

110.1   Hays v. Gen. Elec. Co., 151 F. Supp. 2d 1001, 45 U.C.C. Rep. Serv. 2d 449 (N.D. Ill. 2001).

Addition to note 111.

111   Hays v. Gen. Elec. Co., 151 F. Supp. 2d 1001, 45 U.C.C. Rep. Serv. 2d 449 (N.D. Ill. 2001) (analogizing claim of disclaimer to waiver, which must be affirmatively pleaded as defense). *But see* Basselen v. Gen. Motors Corp., 341 Ill. App. 3d 278, 792 N.E.2d 498 (2003).

Add to text at end of subsection:

By contrast, a claim that the buyer failed to give notice of breach merely controverts an element of the plaintiff's proof and so may not need to be affirmatively pleaded.[111.1]

111.1   Hays v. Gen. Elec. Co., 151 F. Supp. 2d 1001, 45 U.C.C. Rep. Serv. 2d 449 (N.D. Ill. 2001).

10.1.4 Discovery

10.1.4.1 Interrogatories

Addition to notes 113, 115.

113   *Replace first sentence of note with:* A set of interrogatories about the defense's expert witnesses can be found in National Consumer Law Center, Consumer Law Pleadings No. 4, § 15.6 (2003 Cumulative CD-Rom and Index Guide) and on the CD-Rom accompanying this volume.

Page 333

115   *See* Ericson v. Ford Motor Co., 107 F.R.D. 92 (E.D. Ark. 1985) (evidence of prior accidents is relevant to show that manufacturer knew of vehicle's defects before manufacturing the one sold to plaintiff); *Ex parte* Horton, 711 So. 2d 979 (Ala. 1998); Chicago Cutlery Co. v. Dist. Ct., 568 P.2d 464 (Colo. 1977) (customer lists discoverable to locate other buyers to show that injuries were caused by design of the product rather than plaintiff's peculiar susceptibilities).

10.1.4.2 Document Requests

Replace note 116 with:

116   National Consumer Law Center, Consumer Law Pleadings No. 1, §§ 3.2 (odometer rollback and breach of warranty), 4.5, 4.6 (bank's liability for dealer's sale of defective vehicles), 9.2 (auto lease) (2003 Cumulative CD-Rom and Index Guide); National Consumer Law Center, Consumer Law Pleadings No. 2, Ch. 5 (2003 Cumulative CD-Rom and Index Guide) (new car defects); National Consumer Law Center, Consumer Law Pleadings No. 4, §§ 15.2–15.6 (2003 Cumulative CD-Rom and Index Guide) (discovery and requests for admissions to dealer and manufacturer); National Consumer Law Center, Consumer Law Pleadings No. 5, Chs. 4, 7 (2003 Cumulative CD-Rom and Index Guide) (mobile home and pre-fabricated housing cases); National Consumer Law Center, Consumer Law Pleadings No. 6, Ch. 11 (2003 Cumulative CD-Rom and Index Guide) (gray market vehicle case). All of these discovery requests are also included on the CD-Rom accompanying this volume.

Add to text at end of subsection:

A recurring issue in many car cases is whether the selling dealer is the manufacturer's agent. Various theories establishing the dealer's agency are discussed in § 6.2.5.2, *supra*. When, in order to establish agency, it is necessary to demonstrate the manufacturer's control over the dealer, a request for the following documents may be helpful:

• Franchise agreement, sales and service agreement, or similar document (note that there may be a generic franchise agreement, plus a separate set of paragraphs that are specific to the particular dealer);
• Warranty and Policy Manual, or similar document;
• All documents establishing the manufacturer's requirements for dealer facilities, equipment, capitalization, and net working capital;
• Vehicle Terms of Sale Bulletin or similar document;
• Customer Service Bulletin or similar document;
• All pre-delivery and conditioning schedules or similar documents;
• All documents regarding the manufacturer's approval of dealership facilities;
• All documents regarding manufacturer's requirements for dealership identification and sign design; and
• All documents regarding manufacturer's requirements for dealership accounting procedures.

A careful reading of the documents received pursuant to such a request should lead the advocate to additional manufacturer-specific documents.

Page 334

10.1.4.4 Deposition of the Consumer

Add to text at end of subsection:

Sometimes defense attorneys will ask a "contention question" at the plaintiff's deposition, asking the plaintiff to describe all facts that establish a contention in the complaint. At least one court has held that these questions are improper at deposition.[117.1] A lay plaintiff presumably knows at least some of the facts, but can hardly be expected to know their legal consequences, or sort through the facts and apply them on the spot to the legal theories. This same rationale may be a basis for objecting to questions asking the plaintiff what her damages are or what she wants out of the case, a question that plaintiffs often answer at deposition without adequate care. Another strategy to prepare for questions about damages is to help the plaintiff make a written itemization of damages in advance of the deposition. The plaintiff can then pull out the list and refer to it in response to questions about damages. Before allowing the plaintiff to answer the question, the plaintiff's attorney may want to put an objection on the record that the plaintiff is not an attorney and does not necessarily know the law of damages.

117.1   Rifkind v. Super. Ct., 22 Cal. App. 4th 1255, 27 Cal. Rptr. 2d 822 (1994).

10.1.5 Inspections

10.1.5.1 Inspection by the Buyer's Expert

Add to text at end of subsection's first paragraph:

If the goods have found their way into the hands of an uncooperative third party, it may be necessary to use the state's procedure for subpoenaing documents and objects from a non-party.

Page 335

Addition to note 121.

121   *See, e.g.*, Woodson v. McGeorge Camping Ctr., Inc., 1992 U.S. App. LEXIS 22747 (4th Cir. Sept. 15, 1992) (mechanical engineer with B.S. degree and experience with trailer design, hitches, and sway control could give opinion about whether hitch was defective); Forest River, Inc. v. Posten, 847 So. 2d 957 (Ala. Civ. App. 2002) (recreational vehicle (RV) salesperson testified as to actual value of RV); Schreidel v. Am. Honda Motor Co., 34 Cal. App. 4th 1242, 40 Cal. Rptr. 2d 576 (1995) (nineteen years of experience in auto repairs and mechanics qualified expert to testify); Sibley v. Bauers, 1999 Mich. App. LEXIS 1267 (Mich. Ct. App. July 16, 1999) (witness who had owned used car business for seventeen years, had worked for agency that performed financing-related appraisals, and had experience in auto repair and refinishing was qualified to testify on value of used vehicle); King v. Taylor Chrysler Plymouth, 184 Mich. App. 204, 457 N.W.2d 42 (1990) (licensed automobile mechanic qualified as expert).

Add to text at end of subsection's fifth paragraph:

It is a good idea to consult with the expert before starting discovery, in order to be sure to ask in discovery for the items the expert will need.

Add to text at end of subsection's seventh paragraph:

If the vehicle is still under warranty, the expert should make sure not to do anything that would invalidate the warranty.

Add to text after subsection's eighth paragraph:

If outside testing of oil or other fluids is necessary the consumer's attorney may want to invite the opposing parties to attend when the sample is drawn. It is best to have an expert take the sample rather than having the consumer or an interested party do so. The consumer's attorney should ask the testing company beforehand about its protocol for marking and identifying samples. Placing signed seals on the containers and photographing them before mailing may be helpful.

Add to text after bulleted item containing note 126:

The expert who evaluates the defect should always evaluate whether the defect creates a safety hazard, which will have ramifications for revocation of acceptance, punitive damages, and UDAP violations.

Add to text at end of subsection:

The attorney should not press the expert to take a position with which the expert is uncomfortable, as this approach has the potential to backfire during cross-examination.

Page 336

10.1.5.2 Inspection by the Seller

Add to text after subsection's fifth paragraph:

If a seller requests a pre-litigation inspection of a vehicle to verify the existence of the defects, the same guidelines as for an inspection during litigation should be used. Some consumer attorneys also require the seller to pay the fees for the buyer's expert to attend the inspection. In the alternative, some attorneys allow the inspection only if the seller stipulates that it will be the only inspection allowed during the course of any future litigation. In determining how to respond to a request for a pre-litigation inspection, the consumer's attorney should take into account whether the court is likely to admit evidence of any lack of cooperation if the case goes to trial.

Replace § 10.1.6 with:

10.1.6 Settlement[129]

10.1.6.1 Negotiating Settlement

Preparation for settlement should start with the initial client contact and continue throughout the case. The client's expectations should be probed at the initial contact. Both overly high and overly low expectations create problems. The client's non-pecuniary goals should be explored and clearly understood. If the case will be litigated, the client must be prepared to spend time, attend depositions and hearings, and live with uncertainty. The client should understand the negotiation and settlement process, the likely duration of the process, and the implications of such issues as confidentiality clauses, *cy pres* awards, and defendants' use of low attorney fee offers to drive a wedge between attorney and client.

The attorney should have potential settlement in mind when framing the complaint. Not only parties but also claims should be chosen that will make settlement possible. For example, the primary defendant may have insurance coverage for negligent but not intentional acts. If so, the attorney should make sure to assert any claims of negligence that are available.

Investigating, documenting, and analyzing the facts before suit enables the consumer's attorney to start the case in a strong position. Obtaining an expert opinion before filing suit may be helpful. Assessing the likability of the client is also important. The defendant will have a number of occasions to observe the consumer over the course of the litigation, and in formulating a settlement position will be evaluating how a jury will respond to the consumer.

The first settlement approach to the defendants is crucial for setting the tone of the negotiations. The consumer's demand should be high but realistic, and—most critically— the attorney and client should be prepared to follow through. An initial demand that is low or equivocal signals to the defendant that the case is not serious. By the same token, an inflated, unsupported demand from which the consumer's attorney quickly retreats signals not only that the case is weak but also that the consumer is not prepared to litigate it. Pressing forward unabated with trial preparation unless and until a settlement is final tells the defendants that the case is serious and the consumer is prepared to try it.

The consumer's attorney should strive for constructive engagement with defendants' counsel. Easing the defendants' and opposing attorneys' ego issues can be important in settling a case. The way a settlement is packaged may make it easier for a defendant to accept. For example, paying actual damages, other reimbursements, and attorney fees is much more palatable to defendants than paying punitive damages or emotional distress damages. It may take time and considerable litigation pressure before the defendants and opposing attorneys are prepared to recognize the strength of the plaintiff's case and reach the conclusion that settlement is better than trial. Granting a concession near the end of a negotiation, after a strong and determined course of pretrial preparation and negotiation, may enable the opponent to save face and accept a settlement.

Making and documenting settlement proposals is important. Even if the case is not settled but goes to trial, the court may look on an attorney fee petition more favorably if it is clear that the defendants passed up many opportunities to settle the case for a reasonable amount at an earlier point when the plaintiff's fees were lower.

An attorney with a high-volume warranty or lemon law practice may find it useful to tabulate the respective percentages of cases against various manufacturers that settle before suit. Clients find this information helpful in evaluating their options.

Many manufacturers, especially vehicle manufacturers, have in-house dispute settlement offices that seek to resolve warranty problems without litigation. Or the manufacturer may contract out this function to an independent entity. Attorneys report varying degrees of success with these offices. Sometimes these offices are bound by manufacturer policies that prevent them from offering reasonable settlements.

Publications that report settlements can be useful in determining the settlement value of a case. *Lawyers Weekly USA* and similar state publications report settlements, and some maintain websites that can be visited without charge. Westlaw carries jury verdicts on-line, and the American Trial Lawyers Association reports trials and settlements in its newsletter. These and other materials may also be available in a local law library.

10.1.6.2 Settlement Terms

When settling a lemon law case, remember that the client will not want to be left without transportation while waiting for the settlement check to arrive. If the client will be required to return the vehicle before receiving the settlement check, the settlement amount should include the costs of renting a replacement vehicle for a week or two.

If the settlement figure includes the amount necessary to pay off a debt to a bank or other financier, remember that it should cover the amount that will be due when the check arrives, not the amount due at the time the settlement agreement is reached. The figure should cover not only

---

129 Many of the suggestions in this subsection were provided by Ronald L. Burdge, an Ohio attorney, and Bernard Brown, a Kansas City attorney, both of whom specialize in consumer law. Their contributions are gratefully acknowledged.

interest that accrues up to the time the check arrives but also the loan payment that the client will have to make while waiting for the check.

Another helpful provision is that any court costs owed to the clerk of court beyond the deposit paid by the plaintiff at the beginning of the case will be paid by the defendant. Then the defendant, not the consumer or the consumer's attorney, is responsible for any late-arriving court cost bills.

It is important to incorporate into the settlement agreement a deadline for the settlement proceeds to be paid. If the defendant misses the deadline, the agreement can provide that the consumer has the option of 1) enforcing the settlement agreement[130] or 2) declaring the settlement agreement null and void, with the result that the case returns to the trial calendar.

Two particular provisions may be helpful if there is concern about delay in payment. First, it is helpful if the settlement agreement obligates the defendant to pay any costs and attorney fees incurred to enforce the agreement. Second, the agreement could require a lower settlement amount if prompt payment is made. For example, the agreement could state that the defendant agrees to pay $40,000 but that the plaintiff will release all claims if the defendant pays $30,000 by a certain date. Another approach is to specify, when proposing a settlement, that the settlement offer can be accepted only by actual payment.

Another important provision of any settlement agreement is protection of the consumer's credit record. If the manufacturer is going to pay the balance on the debt as part of the settlement, the attorney should get proof of payment before the buyer signs a release. If the manufacturer pays late, the creditor may report a delinquency to the credit bureau. If the buyer withheld payments because of defects, the attorney should ask the creditor, in return for the manufacturer's payment of the balance, to submit a revised report to the credit reporting agency.[131] If the creditor already reported a default to any credit reporting agencies because the consumer was withholding payments, the settlement agreement should require the creditor to submit a Universal Data Form to the agencies, instructing them to delete the report. The settlement agreement should also require the creditor to correct its internal records so that the information is not re-reported, a very common problem. Sample language may be found in another NCLC manual.[132]

If the product has been damaged while in the consumer's possession, responsibility for the damage should be resolved during the settlement negotiations. If insurance will cover the damage, the manufacturer may prefer to have the insurance money paid to it rather than having the damage repaired. Undisclosed damage can torpedo a settlement when the buyer returns the product.

The tax implications of settlements are discussed in another manual.[133] As tax law is complex, changeable, and generally outside the expertise of consumer attorneys, the consumer's attorney may prefer simply to advise the consumer to seek advice from an accountant or tax expert about the tax implications.

The manufacturer or dealer may ask for a confidentiality agreement as part of the settlement. While agreeing that the exact amount of the settlement will be confidential is fairly common, a clause that requires the fact of settlement or the details of the case to be kept confidential is very troubling. A confidentiality clause may prevent the disclosure and correction of safety problems that could affect other people. The seller may want a confidentiality clause in order to avoid branding the vehicle as a lemon, contrary to state law. Such a clause may also amount to a restriction on the attorney's right to practice, contrary to the Rules of Professional Conduct.[133.1] It also places a great and usually lifelong burden on the consumers, forcing them to live under the threat of suit if they ever disclose the settlement or if the defendant ever believes they disclosed it. Some local court rules or state statutes restrict such clauses, especially if they involve sealing court records.[133.2] It is a good idea to discuss these issues with the client before suit is filed, so that a last-minute demand by the defendant for a confidentiality agreement does not catch the consumer unprepared.

Buyers should reject any clause in a proposed release that states that the product was not defective or that the vehicle was not a lemon. The seller or manufacturer is likely seeking this language in order to protect itself if it foists the product off on another buyer without disclosing the product's history. By signing such a release the consumer would be assisting in this effort and contradicting the position taken in the lawsuit. The consumer could be in a very awkward position if a future buyer brought litigation about the product. Such a settlement might also amount to paying a lay witness for testimony, which may be a crime.

Often a settlement is reached on the key issues, but then the defendant's attorney seeks to add other, unbargained-for terms when the settlement documents are drafted. When a settlement is reached in court or at a deposition, one way to

---

130 *See* Latson v. Chrysler Corp., 2000 WL 762793 (Ohio Ct. App. June 14, 2000) (affirming award of $5000 in attorney fees and sanctions for contempt when manufacturer failed to implement settlement by delivering replacement vehicle and check).

131 *See* National Consumer Law Center, Fair Credit Reporting (5th ed. 2002 and Supp.).

132 National Consumer Law Center, Fair Credit Reporting §§ 13.5.4.3–13.5.4.5 (5th ed. 2002 and Supp.).

133 National Consumer Law Center, Repossessions and Foreclosures § 21.7.3 (5th ed. 2002 and Supp.).

133.1 Model Rules of Prof'l Conduct R. 5.6(b); ABA Comm. on Ethics and Prof'l Responsibility, Formal Op. 00-417 (2000); *see Settlement Agreements Create Ethical Dilemma*, N.Y.L.J., Oct. 12, 2000 (discussing New York State Bar Ass'n ethics opinion); *see also* National Consumer Law Center, Automobile Fraud § 9.11.2.4 (2d ed. 2003).

133.2 *See, e.g.*, Gleba v. Daimler Chrysler Corp., 13 Mass. L. Rptr. 576, 2001 Mass. Super. LEXIS 364 (Super. Ct. Aug. 6, 2001) (refusing to seal documents in product liability case).

guard against this problem is to take careful notes about the agreement, read it into the record, and then ask defense counsel on the record whether that is correct and whether it represents all the terms of the settlement. Another good idea is to ask the judge to retain jurisdiction to enforce the settlement if necessary.

10.1.6.3 Protecting Against the Defendant's Bankruptcy

If the defendant is in such bad financial shape that bankruptcy is a possibility, the consumer's attorney should take special care in handling the settlement. A bankruptcy trustee can recapture property that a debtor transferred to or for the benefit of a creditor on account of an antecedent debt while the debtor was insolvent, if the transfer took place within ninety days prior to the debtor's bankruptcy filing and enables the creditor to receive more than the creditor would receive if the transfer had not taken place.[133.3] If the consumer's attorney receives the settlement amount and forwards it to the consumer, and the defendant then files for bankruptcy within ninety days, the consumer—or the consumer's attorney—may be required to return the settlement money to the bankruptcy trustee. It may be best for the consumer's attorney to hold the money, with the client's consent, until the ninety-day period passes.

Conditioning the consumer's release upon receipt of the settlement money, as suggested in § 10.1.6.2, *supra*, may also be helpful if the defendant files bankruptcy. While a settlement agreement does not prevent the bankruptcy court from finding that the debt is for money obtained by fraud and is therefore nondischargeable, it is still possible that issues of collateral estoppel might preclude a finding of nondischargeability.[133.4]

10.1.6.4 Mediation

Courts often suggest or mandate mediation to resolve cases. Careful preparation for mediation is essential.

Mediation is likely to be fruitful only if the defendant is seriously engaged in trying to settle the case. For this reason, many attorneys insist on a serious settlement offer from the defendant before they will agree to mediation. If the parties are taking incompatible postures about the value of the case, it may be best to postpone mediation until the case has been developed further. It is also important to make sure that the defendant sends someone to the mediation who has the authority to offer the settlement that the consumer wants.

If it appears that mediation may be fruitful, selection of the mediator is critical. It is important that the mediator be someone that the opposing party trusts. Mediation may be a

pleasant experience with a mediator who favors the consumer, but the chances of reaching an agreement are much greater if the defendant perceives the mediator as neutral and trustworthy.

The mediator is likely to ask the consumer directly what would be a satisfactory resolution of the case. The consumer should be carefully prepared for this question. Sometimes consumers are so eager to appear compliant and cooperative with the mediator that they understate their case. If the consumer intends to go to trial if the defendant does not come to terms, the consumer has to be prepared to say so in a convincing manner and stick with it. The consumer should also be warned not to respond to settlement suggestions conveyed by the mediator without first speaking privately to the attorney. The consumer should also be warned about fatigue, and not to abandon his or her position because of exhaustion.

As with any settlement negotiation, it is best to start high. It is easy to drop to a lower figure but almost impossible to move higher. The consumer's initial proposal should, however, be serious and realistic. Ridiculous settlement proposals undermine the consumer's credibility. When making a high early demand, the consumer should be cautioned that the case is unlikely to settle for the high initial demand.

Mediation is often the first time the decision-maker for the defendant actually has contact with the plaintiff and gets the real story of what happened. The mediator's impression of the strength of the consumer's case is also important. For these reasons, the consumer should be prepared to present a convincing, well-organized case. Charts and tables may be helpful.

The consumer's position at mediation should be reasonable and well-supported. Even if mediation does not resolve the case, it is important that the consumer be perceived by the trial judge as having participated fully and reasonably in settlement efforts.

10.1.6.5 Effect of Settlement upon Other Parties

If the consumer settles with the entity that financed the purchase, remember that it may have a recourse agreement with the seller. If the seller repurchases the paper, the seller may demand the payments that the consumer thought were forgiven by the agreement with the financier. This issue should be analyzed before the terms of settlement with the financier are finalized. Conversely, if the consumer settles with the dealer only, state law should be carefully researched if the consumer wants to preserve claims against the financer. Including a covenant not to sue the seller in the agreement may be less likely to extinguish claims against the financer than a release of the seller. Settlement with a dealer when the manufacturer is also a defendant, or vice-versa, raises the same issues.

133.3 11 U.S.C. § 547.

133.4 Archer v. Warner, 2003 WL 1611437 (U.S. Mar. 31, 2003).

Even if the settlement does not extinguish the claim against the remaining party, the amount of the settlement may operate as a credit against any judgment ultimately won.[133.5] It may be possible to minimize this effect by designating the settlement as compensation for injuries for which the settling party alone is liable. One factor in determining whether the settlement will operate as a set-off is whether the trier of fact was informed of the settlement.[133.6]

133.5　*See, e.g.*, Dynasty Hous., Inc. v. McCollum, 832 So. 2d 73 (Ala. Civ. App. 2001); Buccaneer Homes v. Pelis, 43 S.W.3d 586 (Tex. App. 2001). *See generally* National Consumer Law Center, Automobile Fraud § 9.11.1.4 (2d ed. 2003).

133.6　Dynasty Hous., Inc. v. McCollum, 832 So. 2d 73 (Ala. Civ. App. 2001) (when defense exercised its option to inform trier of fact of settlement with other party, judge's refusal to set off settlement was not error); Barker v. Fleetwood Enterprises, Inc., 2002

10.1.6.6　Preserving Attorney Fees Under Fee-Shifting Statutes

If the buyer has sued under a statute allowing attorney fees, care should be taken to preserve this claim when settling the case. A recent Supreme Court decision has rejected the "catalyst" theory as a basis for awarding fees under federal fee-shifting statutes.[133.7] Defendants can be expected to argue that this rule should be applied to state fee-shifting statutes as well. This issue is discussed in detail in § 2.7.6.5, *supra*.

　　WL 453931 (Cal. Ct. App. Mar. 26, 2002) (unpublished).

133.7　Buckhannon Bd. & Care Home v. W. Va. Dep't of Health & Human Res., 532 U.S. 598, 121 S. Ct. 1835, 149 L. Ed. 2d 855 (2001).

10.1.7　Trial

Page 337

10.1.7.1　Most Elements of Warranty Cases Are Questions for the Trier of Fact

Addition to note 136.

136　*See, e.g.*, Pressalite Corp. v. Matsushita Elec. Corp., 50 U.C.C. Rep. Serv. 2d 410 (N.D. Ill. 2003) (whether express warranty exists is question of fact); McLaughlin v. Denharco, Inc., 129 F. Supp. 2d 32, 43 U.C.C. Rep. Serv. 2d 1122 (D. Me. 2001) (interpretation of ambiguous express warranty is jury question); Oppenheimer v. York Int'l, 2002 WL 31409949 (Pa. C.P. Oct. 25, 2002); Bobholz v. Banaszak, 655 N.W.2d 547, 49 U.C.C. Rep. Serv. 2d 25 (Wis. Ct. App. 2002) (whether a statement constitutes a warranty is a question of fact); *see also* James River Equip. Co. v. Beadle County Equip., Inc., 646 N.W.2d 265, 48 U.C.C. Rep. Serv. 2d 105 (S.D. 2002) (whether certain words were spoken or written is question of fact but their meaning is question of law); *cf.* Carrau v. Marvin Lumber & Cedar Co., 93 Cal. App. 4th 281, 112 Cal. Rptr. 2d 869, 46 U.C.C. Rep. Serv. 2d 1036 (2001) (existence of warranty can be proven by inference, but in this case evidence was insufficient). *But see* Hercules Mach. Corp. v. McElwee Bros., Inc., 49 U.C.C. Rep. Serv. 2d 72 (E.D. La. 2002) (if agreement is entirely in writing, whether an express warranty was created is for the court).

Page 338

Add note 136.1 after "puffing" in sentence following first bulleted list.

136.1　Triple E, Inc. v. Hendrix & Dail, Inc., 543 S.E.2d 245, 43 U.C.C. Rep. Serv. 2d 533 (S.C. Ct. App. 2001).

Add to text after sentence containing note 137:

There may also be factual questions as to who is liable under the warranty, for example, whether the dealer or distributor is liable along with the manufacturer.[137.1]

137.1　Miller v. Crabtree Mazda, Inc., 146 Misc. 2d 658, 552 N.Y.S.2d 526 (Civ. Ct. 1990).

Add to text after bulleted item containing note 141:

There may also be factual issues regarding whether an implied warranty arose, such as whether the seller was a merchant, or whether a purpose was a particular purpose or an ordinary one.[141.1]

141.1　*See* Longwall-Associates, Inc. v. Wolfgang Preintalk GmbH, 46 U.C.C. Rep. Serv. 2d 651 (W.D. Va. 2002) (question of fact whether use of seller's mining equipment for a particular type of mining was a particular purpose).

Add to text after bulleted item containing note 144:

• Whether the buyer's revocation is effective despite continued use of the goods;[144.1]

144.1　Deere & Co. v. Johnson, 271 F.3d 613 (5th Cir. 2001) (Miss. law).

Page 339

Replace note 147 with:

147　Johnson v. Monsanto Co., 48 U.C.C. Rep. Serv. 2d 586 (Ohio Ct. App. 2002); *see* § 7.2.3.1, *supra*.

Add to text after bulleted item containing note 149:

    • Whether goods or services predominate in a contract that involves both goods and services;[149.1]

149.1   Busch v. Dyno Nobel, Inc., 48 U.C.C. Rep. Serv. 2d 874 (6th Cir. 2002) (unpublished) (Mich. law).

Addition to note 150.

150   Johnson v. Monsanto Co., 48 U.C.C. Rep. Serv. 2d 586 (Ohio Ct. App. 2002).

Replace note 152 with:

152   Schawk, Inc. v. Donruss Trading Cards, Inc., 319 Ill. App. 3d 640, 746 N.E.2d 18, 43 U.C.C. Rep. Serv. 2d 1109 (2001); *see* § 11.3, *infra*.

10.1.7.2 Jury Selection

A *voir dire* question that may be helpful in weeding out jurors who are prejudiced against consumer protection lawsuits is "How many of you think there are too many lawsuits against car dealers (or whatever type of seller or lender is involved in the case) for cheating people?"

Add to text at end of subsection's fourth paragraph:

Page 340

Add to text after second sentence of subsection's last paragraph:

Voir dire is also a good occasion to bring up potentially damaging evidence or themes that the defense is likely to raise. The consumer's attorney can characterize these issues in a way sympathetic to the plaintiff, and ask whether any of the jurors agree with the defense position.

10.1.7.3 Proving that the Goods Were Defective and Caused Damages

Add note 165.1 after "section 1-106" in subsection's final paragraph.

165.1   Revised Article 1, which the National Conference of Commissioners on Uniform State Laws (NCCUSL) approved in 2001 for adoption by the states, redesignates this provision as U.C.C. § 1-305 cmt. 1 without material change.

10.1.7.4 Evidence Issues

10.1.7.4.1 Introduction

Add to text at end of subsection:

Evidentiary issues in proving the value of the goods, including problems with admitting repair estimates, are discussed in § 10.5, *infra*.

10.1.7.4.3 Recall notices

Addition to note 171.

171   Baker v. Chrysler Corp., 1993 WL 18099 (E.D. Pa. Jan. 25, 1993), *aff'd*, 9 F.3d 1539 (3d Cir. 1993) (table); Bowers v. Wal-Mart Stores, Inc., 827 So. 2d 63 (Ala. 2001) (recall notices and technical service bulletins issued by other defendant were relevant to defendant's claim that defects were fault of other defendant).

Page 341

10.1.7.4.6 Evidence of other bad acts

Addition to note 181.

181   *See* Smith v. Ingersoll-Rand Co., 214 F.3d 1235 (10th Cir. 2000) (N.M. law) (evidence of other incidents admissible to support punitive damages on negligence and strict liability claims).

Replace note 182 with:

182   *See* National Consumer Law Center, Unfair and Deceptive Acts and Practices § 8.4.2.3.1 (5th ed. 2001 and Supp.).

Replace note 183 with:

183   *See* National Consumer Law Center, Unfair and Deceptive Acts and Practices § 7.5.3 (5th ed. 2001 and Supp.).

Addition to notes 184, 186, 187.

184   *See* White v. Ford Motor Co., 312 F.3d 998 (9th Cir. 2002) (evidence of prior similar accidents admissible to show that manufacturer had notice); Smith v. Ingersoll-Rand Co., 214 F.3d 1235 (10th Cir. 2000) (N.M. law) (evidence of other similar accidents admissible to show that manufacturer had notice of defect).

186   Ericson v. Ford Motor Co., 107 F.R.D. 92 (E.D. Ark. 1985) (evidence of prior accidents is relevant to show that manufacturer knew of vehicle's defects before manufacturing the vehicle sold to plaintiff).

Page 342

187   *See* S. Energy Homes, Inc. v. Washington, 774 So. 2d 505 (Ala. 2000) (evidence that other buyers alleged that manufacturer did not respond to their complaints allowed in impeachment of witness who asserted that manufacturer always responded promptly).

Add to text at end of subsection's fourth paragraph:

Even raw complaints from other consumers may be admissible to show that the manufacturer had notice of the existence of a problem. The National Highway Traffic Safety Administration (NHTSA) sends consumer complaint information to the manufacturer whenever it opens an investigation of a specific defect. Even if it does not open an investigation, it makes the complaint information available on its website, and the consumer may be able to establish that the manufacturer checks the NHTSA website on a regular basis.

Replace note 190 with:

190   National Consumer Law Center, Automobile Fraud § 9.8.1 (2d ed. 2003).

10.1.7.4.7 Subsequent remedial measures

Add to text at end of subsection:

A manufacturer's offer to repair a vehicle was admissible to rebut the consumer's testimony about undue delay, even though the offer was made after the litigation began.[194.1]

194.1   Boyle v. Daimler Chrysler Corp., 2002 WL 1881157 (Ohio Ct. App. Aug. 16, 2002).

10.1.7.4.8 Demonstrative evidence

Add to text at end of subsection:

Videotapes with high-quality audio are particularly useful to prove that a defect such as a loud noise in a vehicle is a substantial impairment.

If the product is too big to be brought into the courtroom, or must be observed in operation to detect the defect, the court may be willing to allow a jury view. Such a request makes sense only if the defect occurs constantly rather than intermittently and if it is easily perceived by laypersons.

Add new subsection to text after § 10.1.7.4.8.

10.1.7.4.9 History of vehicle

Evidence of a vehicle's collision history, odometer history, and buyback history is relevant and admissible in suits based on nondisclosure or misrepresentation of these facts. The title history, showing the number of times the vehicle has been transferred, may even be relevant on the question of the vehicle's condition. A Missouri appellate court has held that the trial court erred in excluding evidence that a van had multiple owners.[195.1] The court held that this evidence would tend to prove that it was not in good condition, which had motivated the prior owners to sell it.

195.1   Morehouse v. Behlmann Pontiac-GMC Truck Serv., Inc., 31 S.W.3d 55 (Mo. Ct. App. 2000).

10.1.7.5 Admissibility of Expert Testimony Under *Daubert*

Replace §§ 10.1.7.5.1 and 10.1.7.5.2 with:

10.1.7.5.1 The gatekeeping function established by Daubert

In *Daubert v. Merrell Dow Pharmaceuticals, Inc.*, the U.S. Supreme Court interpreted the Federal Rules of Evidence to require federal courts, before admitting expert testimony, to make "a preliminary assessment of whether the reasoning or methodology underlying the testimony is scientifically valid and of whether that reasoning or methodology properly can be applied to the facts in issue."[197] Six years later, in *Kumho Tire v. Carmichael*,[198] the Court held that this gatekeeping obligation applies to *all* expert testimony. Effective December 1, 2000, this obligation is codi-

fied by the Federal Rules of Evidence.[199] These changes

197   509 U.S. 579, 113 S. Ct. 2786, 2796, 125 L. Ed. 2d 469 (1993).
198   526 U.S. 137, 119 S. Ct. 1167, 143 L. Ed. 2d 238 (1999).

199   Fed. R. Evid. 702. The revised rules, along with the Supreme Court's message to Congress, can be found at www.uscourts.gov/rules/approved.htm. Also effective on December 1, 2000 are changes to Rules 701 and 703 of the Federal Rules of Evidence. Rule 701 has been revised to prevent experts from testifying as lay witnesses as a means of avoiding the *Daubert* test. Instead, all expert testimony must be assessed under Rule 702. Rule 703 provides that an expert can testify to an opinion that is based on facts or data that are reasonably relied upon by experts in the field, even if those facts or data are not admissible in evidence. This aspect of the rule is unchanged, but the rule now also states that facts or data that are otherwise inadmissible are not to be disclosed to the jury by the proponent of the expert's testimony unless the court determines that their probative value in helping the jury evaluate the expert's opinion outweighs their prejudicial effect.

have spawned an enormous number of decisions, as a *Daubert* motion to exclude the opponent's expert witnesses' testimony has quickly become a routine part of pretrial practice. This subsection can only sketch out several important issues in this rapidly developing area.

Prior to *Daubert*, expert testimony was admissible if the scientific theories were generally accepted in the field.[200] In one sense, *Daubert* liberalizes admission of expert testimony because it allows testimony based on new theories that have not yet been widely accepted. On the other hand, the *Daubert* test has placed federal courts in the role of gatekeepers, often requiring an exacting defense of the expert's methodology before the testimony can go to the jury. This defense can be required even when the expert is relying on widely accepted techniques. The new test also goes beyond the former rule in that it requires scrutiny not only of testimony based on hard science, but also of testimony from experts such as accountants,[201] economists,[202] appraisers,[203] social scientists and experts in survey technique,[204] psychologists, human factor experts,[205] and statisticians.[206] Even such routinely accepted expert witnesses as auto mechanics, mobile home repair technicians, carpenters and plumbers will have to be prepared to meet the *Daubert* test in warranty cases. While the concerns that prompted the *Daubert* rule are of less significance in a bench trial, the *Daubert* standards must nevertheless be met.[207]

Many state courts have also adopted *Daubert*.[208] On the other hand, a substantial number continue to follow the prior rule.[209] Because state courts are free to fashion their own

---

200 Frye v. United States, 293 F. 1013 (D.C. Cir. 1923).

201 *See, e.g.*, Maiz v. Virani, 253 F.3d 641 (11th Cir. 2001) (affirming admission of forensic accountant's testimony, including testimony about his assumptions about the meaning of the contracts whose financial implications he evaluated).

202 *See, e.g.*, Maiz v. Virani, 253 F.3d 641 (11th Cir. 2001) (allowing Ph.D. economist with background in estimating damages to testify as to amount of economic loss); Total Containment, Inc. v. Dayco Products, Inc., 2001 U.S. Dist. LEXIS 15838 (E.D. Pa. Sept. 6, 2001) (excluding testimony of economic expert because it was based on unjustified assumptions); Coleman v. Dydula, 139 F. Supp. 2d 388 (W.D.N.Y. 2001) (allowing economic expert to testify).

203 *See, e.g.*, Cayuga Indian Nation v. Pataki, 83 F. Supp. 2d 318 (N.D.N.Y. 2000) (precluding testimony of one real estate appraiser but allowing testimony of two others).

204 *See* Metro. St. Louis Equal Hous. Opportunity Council v. Gordon A. Gundaker Real Estate Co., 130 F. Supp. 2d 1074 (E.D. Mo. 2001) (excluding testimony of individuals who conducted and analyzed fair housing survey).

205 *See, e.g.*, Alfred v. Caterpillar, Inc., 262 F.3d 1083 (10th Cir. 2001).

206 *See, e.g.*, Munoz v. Orr, 200 F.3d 291 (5th Cir. 2000) (excluding statistician's testimony).

207 Seaboard Lumber Co. v. United States, 308 F.3d 1283 (Fed. Cir. 2003).

208 *See, e.g.*, State v. Coon, 974 P.2d 386 (Alaska 1999); Farm Bureau Mut. Ins. Co. v. Foote, 341 Ark. 105, 14 S.W.3d 512 (Ark. 2000); State v. Porter, 241 Conn. 57, 698 A.2d 739 (1997); M.G. Bancorporation v. Le Beau, 737 A.2d 513 (Del. 1999); Goodyear Tire & Rubber Co. v. Thompson, 11 S.W.3d 575 (Ky. 2000) (adopting *Kumho Tire*); Mitchell v. Commonwealth, 908

S.W.2d 100 (Ky. 1995) (adopting *Daubert*); Indep. Fire Ins. Co. v. Sunbeam Corp., 755 So. 2d 226 (La. 2000) (reiterating adoption of *Daubert* and applying it at summary judgment stage); Canavan's Case, 432 Mass. 304, 733 N.E.2d 1042 (2000) (adopting *Daubert* and *Kumho Tire*); Schafersman v. Agland Coop, 262 Neb. 215, 631 N.W.2d 862 (2001) (adopting *Daubert* and citing *Kumho Tire* favorably); State v. Torres, 127 N.M. 20, 976 P.2d 20 (N.M. 1999) (*Daubert* test applies in New Mexico courts and is not limited to novel theories); State v. Machmuller, 630 N.W.2d 495 (S.D. 2001) (noting adoption of *Daubert*); E. I. du Pont de Nemours & Co. v. Robinson, 923 S.W.2d 549 (Tex. 1995) (adopting *Daubert*); Purina Mills v. Odell, 948 S.W.2d 927 (Tex. App. 1997) (Texas courts must ensure that expert's underlying scientific technique or principle is reliable before testimony can be admitted); State v. Kinney, 171 Vt. 239, 762 A.2d 833 (2000) (noting adoption of *Daubert* standard, but courts can take judicial notice of reliability when other courts have admitted the evidence); Bunting v. Jamieson, 984 P.2d 467 (Wyo. 1999) (adopting *Daubert*); *see also* State v. Vliet, 95 Haw. 94, 19 P.3d 42 (Haw. 2001) (requiring reliability determination similar to *Daubert* and *Kumho Tire*); McGrew v. State, 682 N.E.2d 1289 (Ind. 1997) (*Daubert* concerns are consistent with Indiana rules; *Daubert* is helpful but not controlling); State v. Hungerford, 142 N.H. 110, 697 A.2d 916 (1997) (terming *Daubert* helpful and applying its tests); State v. Harvey, 151 N.J. 117, 699 A.2d 596 (1997) (adopting a more flexible standard than *Frye*, but requiring general acceptance by scientific community in criminal cases); State v. Nemeth, 82 Ohio St. 3d 202, 694 N.E.2d 1332 (1999) (Ohio evidentiary rule requires showing of reliability of scientific, technical, or other specialized information, and court uses *Daubert* factors to interpret it); State v. Lyons, 324 Or. 256, 924 P.2d 802 (1996) (*Daubert* has not been adopted but is instructive); State v. O'Key, 321 Or. 285, 899 P.2d 663 (1995) (making extensive use of *Daubert* factors); DiPetrillo v. Dow Chem. Co., 729 A.2d 677 (R.I. 1999) (endorsing *Daubert* principles for both scientific and technical evidence, but noting that court can take judicial notice of reliability if theories are not novel); State v. Crosby, 927 P.2d 638 (Utah 1996) (adhering to prior Utah formulation of test, but noting its similarity to *Daubert*). *But cf.* Fugate v. State, 993 S.W.2d 931 (Ky. 1999) (*Daubert* hearing will no longer be required in each case involving admission of DNA evidence).

209 *See, e.g.*, Bagley v. Mazda Motor Corp., 2003 WL 21040506 (Ala. May 9, 2003) (declining to decide whether to adopt *Daubert*); S. Energy Homes v. Washington, 774 So. 2d 505, 40 U.C.C. Rep. 2d 986 (Ala. 2000) (declining to decide whether to adopt *Daubert* test); Logerquist v. McVey, 196 Ariz. 470, 1 P.3d 113 (Ariz. 2000) (declining to adopt *Daubert*); People v. Leahy, 8 Cal. 4th 587, 34 Cal. Rptr. 2d 663, 882 P.2d 321 (1994) (declining to adopt *Daubert*); Bryant v. Hoffmann-La Roche, Inc., 262 Ga. App. 401, 585 S.E.2d 723 (2003); Leaf v. Goodyear Tire & Rubber Co., 590 N.W.2d 525 (Iowa 1999) (declining to adopt *Daubert*, although trial courts may find it helpful in assessing reliability); Goeb v. Tharaldson, 615 N.W.2d 800 (Minn. 2000) (rejecting *Daubert*); Kan. City S. Ry. Co. v. Johnson, 798 So. 2d 374 (Miss. 2001) (reiterating refusal to adopt *Daubert* and adherence to *Frye*); Dow Chem. Co. v. Mahlum, 114 Nev. 1468, 970 P.2d 98 (1998) (declining to adopt *Daubert*, at least until the doctrine is developed further); State v. Jones, 130 Wash. 2d 302, 922 P.2d 806 (1996) (rejecting *Daubert* and continuing its adherence to *Frye*); *see also* People v. Shreck, 22 P.3d 68 (Colo. 2001) (rejecting *Frye* as too inflexible but declining to endorse *Daubert* analysis, although

criteria for admission of expert testimony, the practitioner should research the forum state's recent rulings before presenting expert testimony.

States may impose requirements in addition to the *Daubert* tests. For example, in Ohio expert testimony must relate to matters beyond the knowledge or experience of laypersons, or dispel a misperception common among laypersons.[210]

10.1.7.5.2 Factors in the court's evaluation of expert testimony

Daubert establishes a two-step approach to determine the admissibility of expert testimony or evidence. First, the court must decide whether the expert testimony is based on a reliable and valid methodology. Second, the court must determine if there is a legal fit between the expert testimony and the disputed issues of the case.

Revised Rule 702 of the Federal Rules of Evidence adopts these two criteria and adds a third. Under the revised rule, a witness qualified as an expert by knowledge, skill, experience, training or education may present expert testimony if: "(1) the testimony is based upon sufficient facts or data; (2) the testimony is the product of reliable principles and methods, and (3) the witness has applied the principles and methods reliably to the facts of the case."

The objective of *Daubert* gatekeeping is "to ensure the reliability and relevancy of expert testimony."[211] The court must ensure that an expert, whether basing testimony upon professional studies or personal experience, employs the

same level of intellectual rigor in the courtroom that characterizes the practice of an expert in the relevant field.[212] The expert's self-proclaimed accuracy is insufficient: "nothing in either *Daubert* or the Federal Rules of Evidence requires a district court to admit opinion evidence that is connected to existing data only by the *ipse dixit* of the expert."[213]

The *Daubert* opinion lists five non-exclusive[214] factors to guide a district court in its preliminary assessment of the admissibility of expert testimony:

- Whether the theory or technique has been tested;[215]
- Whether the technique has been subjected to peer review and publication;
- The known or potential error rate of the technique employed;
- The maintenance of standards controlling the technique's operation; and
- Whether the theory or technique is "generally accepted" in the scientific (or relevant) community.[216]

---

courts may consider *Daubert* factors when appropriate); Brooks v. People, 975 P.2d 1105 (Colo. 1999) (declining to apply *Daubert* to experience-based specialized knowledge); Gilkey v. Schweitzer, 295 Mont. 345, 983 P.2d 869 (1999) (*Daubert* test will be applied only to novel scientific testimony); Harris v. State, 13 P.3d 489 (Okla. Crim. App. 2000) (noting adoption of *Daubert* and referring favorably to *Kumho Tire* but applying both only to novel theories); State v. Council, 335 S.C. 1, 515 S.E.2d 508 (S.C. 1999) (rejecting *Frye*; declining to adopt *Daubert* but requiring determination of reliability); Coe v. State, 17 S.W.3d 193, 226 n.17 (Tenn. 2000) (acknowledging general principles of *Daubert* but declining to adopt it, as Tennessee rules are narrower than federal rules); Tamez v. Mack Trucks, Inc., 100 S.W.3d 549 (Tex. App. 2003) (applying factors similar to those identified by *Daubert*); Watson v. Inco Alloys Int'l, Inc., 209 W. Va. 234, 545 S.E.2d 294 (2001) (reiterating previous adoption of *Daubert* test for scientific evidence but declining to apply it to testimony of engineer, which court considers technical rather than scientific).

210 Ohio R. Evid. 702(A); *see* Pearn v. DaimlerChrysler Corp., 148 Ohio App. 3d 228, 772 N.E.2d 712 (2002) (expert's testimony concerning diminished value of vehicle was admissible, but testimony about dealer practices may not have been beyond knowledge or experience of laypersons); *see also* Pa. R. Evid. 702 (expert may testify concerning scientific, technical, or other specialized knowledge beyond that possessed by a layperson).

211 Kumho Tire v. Carmichael, 526 U.S. 137, 152, 119 S. Ct. 1167, 143 L. Ed. 2d 238 (1999).

212 *Id.*

213 *Id.* at 157 (quoting Gen. Elec. v. Joiner, 522 U.S. 136, 146, 118 S. Ct. 512, 139 L. Ed. 2d 508 (1997)).

214 That these are non-exclusive factors is reiterated in *Kumho Tire*, 526 U.S. at 150–151.

215 Chapman v. Maytag Corp., 297 F.3d 682 (7th Cir. 2002) (scientific testimony inadmissible when unsupported by tests, studies, or experiments); *see, e.g.*, Dhillon v. Crown Controls Corp., 269 F.3d 865 (7th Cir. 2001) (precluding testimony by design defect experts because of their failure to test alternate designs).

216 The industry may be the relevant community for some purposes. *See* Dhillon v. Crown Controls Corp., 269 F.3d 865 (7th Cir. 2001) (fact that no manufacturer or professional body had adopted design defect expert's views supports exclusion of testimony); Alfred v. Caterpillar, Inc., 262 F.3d 1083 (10th Cir. 2001) (engineer's application of professional body's standards to specific product was admissible); Hynes v. Energy W., Inc., 211 F.3d 1193 (10th Cir. 2000) (evidence that industry adheres to a certain practice implies a degree of reliability and supports expert's conclusion); *see also* Correa v. Cruisers, 298 F.3d 13 (1st Cir. 2002) (visual inspection sufficient when opposing expert's testimony corroborated that it was an accepted method); Chapman v. Maytag Corp., 297 F.3d 682 (7th Cir. 2002) (novel theory inadmissible when unsupported by anything produced by others in field); Rider v. Sandoz Pharmaceuticals Corp., 295 F.3d 1194 (11th Cir. 2002) (epidemiological studies are best but not only acceptable proof that medication caused injury; case reports can support finding of causation but can not be sole proof); Meister v. Med. Eng'g Corp., 267 F.3d 1123 (D.C. Cir. 2001) (evidence on which plaintiff's experts based their opinions was insufficient in light of overwhelming contrary evidence from epidemiological studies); Coleman v. Dydula, 139 F. Supp. 2d 388 (W.D.N.Y. 2001) (general acceptance of techniques sufficient to allow admission); Metro. St. Louis Equal Hous. Opportunity Council v. Gordon A. Gundaker Real Estate Co., 130 F. Supp. 2d 1074 (E.D. Mo. 2001) (general acceptance of theories insufficient when expert could point to no authority beyond his own belief).

The Advisory Committee Note to the revised Rule lists the following additional factors as relevant:

- Whether the expert developed his or her opinion expressly for the purpose of testifying or whether it grew naturally and directly out of independent research;[217]
- Whether the expert has unjustifiably extrapolated from an accepted premise to an unfounded conclusion;[218]
- Whether the expert has adequately accounted for obvious alternative explanations;[219]
- Whether the expert is being as careful as he or she would be in regular professional work outside paid litigation consulting;[220]
- Whether the field of expertise claimed by the expert is known to reach reliable results for the type of opinion the expert would give.[221]

Many courts rely on the Federal Judicial Center's *Reference Manual on Scientific Evidence*[222] in evaluating scientific evidence.[222.1] The expert's opinion must also be sufficiently related to the facts of the case to aid the jury in resolving the factual dispute.[222.2] The expert need not accept the plaintiff's version of events exactly, however, if other eyewitness testimony supports the expert's analysis.[222.3]

These lists of factors should not obscure the fact that the district court's gatekeeper role is a flexible one. The factors are simply useful measures, not mandatory hurdles that a party must overcome in order to have expert testimony admitted. For example, *Daubert* recognizes that some propositions are too particular, too new, or of too limited interest to have been published in a peer-reviewed journal.[222.4] A party seeking to admit (or exclude) expert testimony must do more than enumerate the factors listed in *Daubert* and tally the number that are or are not met by a particular expert's testimony.

Courts have applied these factors to exclude expert testimony when the expert's opinion was based on insufficient or unreliable data,[222.5] was based on a methodology that was untested, unsupported or misapplied,[222.6] did not spell out

---

217 *See* Lauzon v. Senco Products, Inc., 270 F.3d 681 (8th Cir. 2001) (slight negative impact of expert's introduction to the field through litigation was outweighed by independent testing and other factors); Metabolife Int'l v. Wornick, 264 F.3d 832 (9th Cir. 2001) (if evidence is not based on independent research, then peer review or at least reference to some objective source such as a treatise is essential).

218 *See* Phelan v. Synthes, 2002 WL 1058900 (4th Cir. May 28, 2002) (unpublished) (expert applied basic engineering principles to product without quantitative or other systematic examination of the product); Rider v. Sandoz Pharmaceuticals Corp., 295 F.3d 1194 (11th Cir. 2002) (excluding testimony when experts could not justify application to humans of results of animal studies, or of conclusions drawn regarding one drug from properties of related drugs).

219 *See* Pipitone v. Biomatrix, Inc., 288 F.3d 239 (5th Cir. 2002) (citing expert's meticulous elimination of alternate explanations as a factor in allowing testimony); Phelan v. Synthes, 2002 WL 1058900 (4th Cir. May 28, 2002) (unpublished); Lauzon v. Senco Products, Inc., 270 F.3d 681 (8th Cir. 2001) (expert need not rule out every possible cause); In re Propulsid Products Liab. Litig., 261 F. Supp. 2d 603, 618 (E.D. La. 2003) (testimony inadmissible because of failure to rule out alternate explanations); Soldo v. Sandoz Pharmaceuticals Corp., 244 F. Supp. 2d 434, 518–524 (W.D. Pa. 2003); McGuire v. Davidson Mfg. Corp., 238 F. Supp. 2d 1096 (N.D. Iowa 2003) (investigating all known causes and eliminating all except one is an acceptable methodology).

220 *See, e.g.*, Cooper v. Smith & Nephew, Inc., 259 F.3d 194 (4th Cir. 2001) (doctor's development of opinion without physical examination of patient, contrary to his usual practice, is a factor in excluding testimony).

221 Advisory Committee on Evidence Rules Note to amended Fed. R. Evid. 702 at 43, 44.

222 (2d ed. 2000).

222.1 *See, e.g.*, Soldo v. Sandoz Pharmaceuticals Corp., 244 F. Supp. 2d 434 (W.D. Pa. 2003); Smith v. Wyeth-Ayerst Laboratories Co., 278 F. Supp. 2d 684 (W.D.N.C. 2003).

222.2 Rider v. Sandoz Pharmaceuticals Corp., 295 F.3d 1194 (11th Cir. 2002) (excluding testimony when experts could not justify application to humans of results of animal studies, or of conclusions drawn regarding one drug from properties of related drugs); Lauzon v. Senco Products, Inc., 270 F.3d 681 (8th Cir. 2001).

222.3 Lauzon v. Senco Products, Inc., 270 F.3d 681 (8th Cir. 2001).

222.4 Daubert v. Merrell Dow Pharmaceuticals, Inc., 509 U.S. 579, 593, 113 S. Ct. 2786, 125 L. Ed. 2d 469 (1993); *accord* Lauzon v. Senco Products, Inc., 270 F.3d 681 (8th Cir. 2001); *see also* Miller v. Burlington N. Santa Fe Ry. Co., 2001 U.S. Dist. LEXIS 16650 (N.D. Tex. Oct. 16, 2001) (magistrate's ruling) (math is not a proper subject of peer review); Coleman v. Dydula, 139 F. Supp. 2d 388 (W.D.N.Y. 2001) (admitting evidence based on generally accepted methods for calculating future lost wages even though expert did not cite scholarly treatises in support). *But cf.* Nelson v. Tenn. Gas Pipeline Co., 243 F.3d 244 (6th Cir. 2001) (citing lack of peer review as reason for excluding testimony despite plaintiff's claim that expert's novel opinions were at forefront of his field).

222.5 Munoz v. Orr, 200 F.3d 291 (5th Cir. 2000) (calculation errors one of reasons for excluding testimony), *cert. denied*, 121 S. Ct. 45 (2000); Irvine v. Murad Skin Research Laboratories, 194 F.3d 313 (1st Cir. 1999); Dunn v. Sandoz Pharmaceuticals Corp., 275 F. Supp. 2d 672 (M.D.N.C. 2003) (small study size); *In re* Propulsid Products Liab. Litig., 261 F. Supp. 2d 603 (E.D. La. 2003); Soldo v. Sandoz Pharmaceuticals Corp., 244 F. Supp. 2d 434, 539–541 (W.D. Pa. 2003) (anecdotal case reports and adverse event reports are insufficient basis for conclusions about causation); Cayuga Indian Nation v. Pataki, 83 F. Supp. 2d 318 (N.D.N.Y 2000) (data errors one of reasons for excluding testimony); Telecomm Technical Services v. Siemens Rolm Communications, Inc., 1999 U.S. Dist. LEXIS 21415 (N.D. Ga. Aug. 24, 1999) (use of too many estimates made underlying data unreliable); *see also* Metro. St. Louis Equal Hous. Opportunity Council v. Gordon A. Gundaker Real Estate Co., 130 F. Supp. 2d 1074 (E.D. Mo. 2001) (expert's failure to review accuracy of underlying survey data one factor in excluding his testimony); *In re* Ford Motor Co. Ignition Switch Products Liab. Litig., 194 F.R.D. 484 (D.N.J. 2000) (unreliability of data on which statistical analysis was based renders it unpersuasive).

222.6 Meister v. Med. Eng'g Corp., 267 F.3d 1123 (D.C. Cir. 2001) (affirming exclusion of medical opinion that was based on case

the analysis in a step-by-step way so that others could review it for error,[222.7] was overly subjective,[222.8] strayed into areas beyond the witness's expertise,[222.9] or made selective use of evidence.[222.10] Nonetheless, courts are not to apply *Daubert* in a way that usurps the jury's role.[222.11] Nor are they to evaluate the expert's conclusions, as long as the expert's methodology is reliable and relevant to the case.[222.12] The fact that experts in other fields might also be able to form opinions about a question and would base those opinions on other factors does not disqualify an expert from testifying based on the factors that are relevant to his or her expertise.[222.13]

The requirement that expert testimony meet the *Daubert* standards does not mean that expert witnesses must have academic credentials. The Supreme Court[222.14] and many lower courts[222.15] have recognized that experts can base their

testimony on skill or experience-based observation.[222.16] In such cases, many of the factors recited in *Daubert* will be irrelevant,[222.17] although some may be relevant, such as error rate or acceptance in the field.[222.18] The Notes of the Advisory Committee accompanying the amended rules state that an expert witness who relies solely or primarily on experience "must explain how that experience leads to the conclusion reached, why that experience is a sufficient basis for the opinion, and how that experience is reliably applied to the facts."[222.19] The expert's testimony need not be based on first-hand knowledge.[222.20]

A court's decision whether to admit or exclude expert testimony as part of its gatekeeping function is only subject to review pursuant to an abuse of discretion standard.[222.21] Practitioners should be cognizant, however, of the possible consequences of reversal of a trial court ruling that an expert's testimony was admissible. In *Weisgram v. Marley Co.*,[222.22] the trial court had admitted the plaintiff's expert testimony over the defendant's *Daubert* objections. The Court of Appeals, upon holding that the testimony did not meet the *Daubert* standards and should have been excluded, determined that the admissible evidence was insufficient to support a verdict for the plaintiff and ordered judgment entered for the defendant. The Supreme Court affirmed, rejecting the argument that the plaintiff should have been granted a new trial.

---

reports rather than epidemiological studies); Dunn v. Sandoz Pharmaceuticals Corp., 275 F. Supp. 2d 672 (M.D.N.C. 2003); Metro. St. Louis Equal Hous. Opportunity Council v. Gordon A. Gundaker Real Estate Co., 130 F. Supp. 2d 1074 (E.D. Mo. 2001) (survey's reliability was undercut by variations in forms and protocols); Rockwell Int'l Corp. v. Wilhite, 83 S.W.3d 516 (Ky. 2002). *But cf.* Smith v. Wyeth-Ayerst Laboratories Co., 278 F. Supp. 2d 684 (W.D.N.C. 2003) (case reports and an epidemiological study were sufficient basis for opinion).

222.7 Ebenhoech v. Koppers Indus., Inc., 239 F. Supp. 2d 455 (D.N.J. 2002) (report cited sources but failed to apply them to the analysis; also did not suggest modifications, alternate designs, or alternate warnings); Rogers v. Horseshoe Entm't, 766 So. 2d 595 (La. Ct. App. 2000).

222.8 Cayuga Indian Nation v. Pataki, 83 F. Supp. 2d 318 (N.D.N.Y. 2000).

222.9 McGuire v. Davidson Mfg. Corp., 238 F. Supp. 2d 1096 (N.D. Iowa 2003) (excluding a portion of testimony); Gray v. Briggs, 45 F. Supp. 2d 316 (S.D.N.Y. 1999).

222.10 Concord Boat Corp. v. Brunswick Corp., 207 F.3d 1039 (8th Cir. 2000).

222.11 Maiz v. Virani, 253 F.3d 641 (11th Cir. 2001).

222.12 Union Bank v. Deutsche Fin. Services Co., 2000 U.S. Dist. LEXIS 1481 (S.D.N.Y. Feb. 14, 2000); Cayuga Indian Nation v. Pataki, 83 F. Supp. 2d 318 (N.D.N.Y 2000).

222.13 Smith v. BMW N. Am., Inc., 308 F.3d 913 (8th Cir. 2002).

222.14 Kumho Tire v. Carmichael, 526 U.S. 137, 151, 119 S. Ct. 1167, 143 L. Ed. 2d 238 (1999).

222.15 Tuf Racing Products v. Am. Suzuki Motor Corp., 223 F.3d 585 (7th Cir. 2000) (accountant could testify about damages despite lack of degree in academic field); U.S. v. Majors, 196 F.3d 1206 (11th Cir. 1999) (witness could testify as financial expert based on training and experience, despite having only associate's degree in accounting), *cert. denied*, 120 S. Ct. 2022 (2000); Lauria v. Nat'l R.R. Passenger Corp., 145 F.3d 593 (3d Cir. 1998); *In re* Bonham, 251 B.R. 113 (Bankr. D. Alaska 2000) (qualifying witness as expert in reconstructive accounting based on her training and experience, despite lack of a CPA degree or certification).

222.16 *Accord* Advisory Committee on Evidence Rules Note to amended Fed. R. Evid. 702 at 49 ("[i]n certain fields, experience is the predominant, if not sole, basis for a great deal of reliable expert testimony").

222.17 First Tenn. Bank v. Barreto, 268 F.3d 319 (6th Cir. 2001) (expertise based on experience within an industry does not easily lend itself to scholarly review or scientific evaluation).

222.18 *See Kumho Tire*, 526 U.S. at 151.

222.19 Advisory Committee on Evidence Rules Note to amended Fed. R. Evid. 702 at 49; *see* Metro. St. Louis Equal Hous. Opportunity Council v. Gordon A. Gundaker Real Estate Co., 130 F. Supp. 2d 1074 (E.D. Mo. 2001) (excluding testimony by witnesses who lacked academic credentials and who could not establish a basis for their expertise).

222.20 Daubert v. Merrell Dow Pharmaceuticals, Inc., 509 U.S. 579, 592, 113 S. Ct. 2786, 125 L. Ed. 2d 469 (1993); Smith v. Ingersoll-Rand Co., 214 F.3d 1235 (10th Cir. 2000) (N.M. law).

222.21 Gen. Elec. v. Joiner, 522 U.S. 136, 138, 139, 118 S. Ct. 512, 139 L. Ed. 2d 508 (1997). This holding was reiterated in Kumho Tire v. Carmichael, 526 U.S. 137, 152, 119 S. Ct. 1167, 143 L. Ed. 2d 238 (1999).

222.22 528 U.S. 440, 120 S. Ct. 1011, 145 L. Ed. 2d 958 (2000); *see also* Nelson v. Tenn. Gas Pipeline Co., 243 F.3d 244 (6th Cir. 2001) (there is no right to an opportunity to cure the exclusion of expert testimony). *But cf.* Wilhite v. Rockwell Int'l Corp., 83 S.W.3d 516 (Ky. 2002) (when other evidence was sufficient to go to jury, court remands for new trial).

Page 345

Addition to note 226.

10.1.7.5.4 Burden of proof and conduct of the Daubert *hearing*

226   *But see* Nelson v. Tenn. Gas Pipeline Co., 243 F.3d 244 (6th Cir. 2001) (whether to hold hearing is within trial court's discretion).

Page 346

Addition to note 232.

10.1.7.5.5 *Timing of the inquiry into admissibility*

232   *See* U.S. v. Alatorre, 222 F.3d 1098 (9th Cir. 2000) (trial court may resolve *Daubert* objections after *voir dire* of expert at trial); *see also* Macsenti v. Becker, 237 F.3d 1223 (10th Cir. 2001) (*Daubert* objection at trial must be made contemporaneously with the testimony).

Add to text after sentence containing note 232:

Except in rare circumstances, the trial court should reject as untimely a motion to strike the expert's testimony that is made after the proponent has rested.[232.1]

232.1   Alfred v. Caterpillar, Inc., 262 F.3d 1083 (10th Cir. 2001).

Add note 233.1 at end of subsection.

233.1   *See, e.g.,* Nelson v. Tenn. Gas Pipeline Co., 243 F.3d 244 (6th Cir. 2001) (fairness does not require that plaintiff whose expert testimony has been excluded by pretrial motion be given second chance to marshal expert opinions).

10.1.7.6 Presenting the Testimony of the Plaintiff's Expert

Add to text at beginning of subsection:

It is important that the consumer's expert witness be prepared to explain and justify each step in the inspection and analysis of the defects. For many experts a set of diagnostic or investigatory procedures will have become so thoroughly ingrained that they will not be able to explain why they take those steps without some research. The expert should be prepared to refer to industry standards, such as a repair manual or a repair database, whenever possible.

10.1.7.8 Trial Themes

Page 348

10.1.7.8.1 *Tie the facts to the policies behind applicable law*

Add to text at end of subsection:

The consumer's presentation will be more effective if all the evidence relates to the main theory of the case. For example, evidence of violations of consumer protection regulations that do not have any bearing on the breach of warranty may detract from the overall impact of a breach of warranty case. But if those violations can be tied to the main theme—for example, by showing that the violations helped the dealer delay the consumer's discovery of the warranty problems—they can enhance the consumer's case.

10.1.7.9 Jury Forms

Addition to note 243.

243   *See also* Brzezinski v. Feuerwerker, 2000 Ohio App. LEXIS 4145 (Ohio Ct. App. Sept. 14, 2000) (refusing to treble damages because court could not tell from jury's general verdict whether its damage award related to a UDAP violation).

Add to text at end of subsection:

A case may go to the jury on claims for both revocation of acceptance and damages for breach of warranty, but the two claims are inconsistent and the jury must choose one or the other.[243.1]

243.1   Herring v. Home Depot, Inc., 565 S.E.2d 773 (S.C. Ct. App. 2002).

Replace § 10.2 with:

10.2 The Enforceability of Binding Arbitration Agreements

10.2.1 Introduction

The enforceability of binding arbitration agreements is now analyzed in a separate NCLC volume. That volume contains not only detailed analysis, but reprints the rules from major arbitration service providers and includes a number of sample briefs and discovery on this topic.

This section briefly lists ways to challenge a binding arbitration clause, as set out in more detail in that other NCLC volume. This section does develop in more detail several of these challenges that have special applicability to warranty transactions, including the effect of the Magnuson-Moss Warranty Act on an arbitration clause, whether revocation of acceptance is subject to arbitration, and whether service contracts regulated as insurance are subject to state or federal arbitration law.

10.2.2 The Enforceability of Arbitration Clauses in a Nutshell

NCLC's *Consumer Arbitration Agreements*[244] examines a number of important exceptions to the general rule that the Federal Arbitration Act (FAA) requires enforcement of arbitration agreements. All of these exceptions potentially have applicability to warranty litigation.

A number of state arbitration laws restrict the enforceability of consumer arbitration agreements. While, in general, the FAA preempts these state limitations, there are two exceptions.

State arbitration law applies instead of the FAA in insurance transactions, because of the operation of the McCarran-Ferguson Act.[245] This rule has special applicability when a state regulates service contracts as insurance.

In addition, the FAA applies only to transactions within the reach of the Constitution's Commerce Clause, that is, to transactions affecting interstate commerce.[246] For example, if a home sale were viewed as not being in interstate commerce, then state arbitration law and not the FAA would apply.

Importantly, the FAA itself states that whether an agreement to arbitrate is binding is to be determined by state contract law principles.[247] Only if there is a binding agree-

ment under state law does the FAA come into play. An arbitration clause thus is not enforceable if:

- A binding agreement has never been formed, such as when the document is not signed, it was not entered into voluntarily and knowingly, or the arbitration agreement was sent after the contract was consummated;[248]
- The arbitration clause is unconscionable, because it is not mutual, it restricts statutory remedies or rights, it creates excessive fees and costs, it involves arbitrator bias or an inconvenient venue, or the agreement is procedurally unconscionable;[249]
- The contract is void because of fraud in the factum, illegality, or because the contract has been canceled;[250]
- The arbitration clause, not the whole contract, is induced by misrepresentation;[251]
- The corporation has waived its rights under the arbitration clause by instituting litigation or by waiting too long to demand that a case be sent to arbitration;[252] or
- Other standard contract defenses apply or a state statute limits the arbitration clause in the same way that it limits any contract clause.[253]

In addition, when an arbitration agreement limits federal statutory rights or remedies, a conflict is created between the federal statute and the FAA. A court may determine that the congressional intent is that the other federal statute prevail over the FAA, and that the arbitration agreement should not be enforced. The most important example of this conflict is the interplay of the Magnuson-Moss Warranty Act with the FAA.[254] This section examines this issue in some detail in § 10.2.4, *infra*.

Other examples of possible conflict between federal law and the FAA include:

- The Bankruptcy Code's requirement that claims be presented to the bankruptcy court;[255]
- Arbitration clauses that limit a federal law's statutory remedies, such as the awarding of attorney fees, statutory damages, the right to bring a class action, injunctive relief, and the statute of limitations;[256] and
- High arbitration fees that effectively prevent vindication of federal statutory rights.[257]

---

244 (3d ed. 2003).
245 *See* National Consumer Law Center, Consumer Arbitration Agreements § 2.3.3 (3d ed. 2003).
246 *Id.* § 2.3.1.
247 *Id.* § 2.4.

248 *Id.* Ch. 3.
249 *Id.* §§ 4.2, 4.3.
250 *Id.* § 4.5.
251 *Id.* § 4.6.
252 *Id.* Ch. 7.
253 *Id.* §§ 4.7–4.9.
254 *Id.* § 5.2.2.
255 *Id.* § 5.2.3.
256 *Id.* § 5.3.
257 *Id.* § 5.4.

An arbitration agreement is just an agreement between two parties to send certain disputes to arbitration. If the parties have not agreed that certain disputes between them should be arbitrated, then those disputes need not be arbitrated even though an arbitration clause covers other disputes. An arbitration clause may have no effect concerning disputes outside the scope of the clause.[258] Similarly, an arbitration clause does not apply to consumer self-help remedies, such as rejection, revocation of acceptance, or withholding of payments, as the consumer is not disputing anything but merely exercising a statutory right. *See* § 10.2.3.1, *infra*.

A more difficult issue is whether an arbitration clause still applies to litigation initiated after the consumer cancels the transaction. If the transaction was properly cancelled, then the arbitration clause should no longer be enforceable. These issues are examined at § 10.2.3.2, *infra*.

Of particular relevance to warranty litigation, the arbitration clause may not apply when the consumer is suing someone not a party to the arbitration agreement.[259] For example, can a manufacturer or a service contract company avail itself of an arbitration agreement signed by a dealer and a consumer? Similarly, issues are raised as to the enforceability of an arbitration agreement when the consumer bringing the suit has not signed the arbitration agreement.[260]

NCLC's *Consumer Arbitration Agreements* also covers such key topics as:

- The consumer's right to discovery relating to the enforceability of the arbitration clause;[261]
- The right for a jury to decide whether the clause is enforceable;[262]
- Whether the determination as to enforceability can be removed to federal court;[263]
- Whether arbitration claims can proceed on a class-wide basis;[264]
- Appeals from judicial orders relating to arbitration;[265] and
- The consumer's judicial review of the arbitrator's decision.[266]

10.2.3 Effect of Arbitration Clause When Consumer Cancels the Transaction or Withholds Payments

10.2.3.1 Arbitration Clause Does Not Apply to Self-Help Remedies Such As Rejection, Revocation or Withholding Payments

Arbitration agreements require consumers to submit "claims" or "disputes" or "controversies" to arbitration. When a consumer rightfully rejects or revokes acceptance of a good, or withholds payments because of a breach of contract, the consumer is not making a claim, is not disputing anything, and is not engaged in a controversy. The consumer has a right to take these actions, and is exercising that right.

These are self-help remedies, and they do not require court action, only notice to the seller. A court action may follow if the seller refuses to acknowledge the self-help remedy, and there may be issues as to whether that subsequent court action must be submitted to arbitration. But the self-help remedy itself need not be. Article 2 allows a revoking consumer to sell the collateral to pay off any amount due from the seller. Again, such an action is a self-help remedy and need to be subjected to arbitration.

In addition, a number of arbitration clauses exclude "self-help remedies" from the arbitration requirement, often listing repossessions and foreclosures as examples. Rejection and revocation of acceptance are also such self-help remedies and should thus be excluded from the arbitration requirement by the very language of the arbitration clause.[267]

10.2.3.2 Does Consumer's Cancellation of the Contract Invalidate the Arbitration Requirement?

When a consumer revokes acceptance or rejects a good, the UCC allows the consumer to cancel.[268] If the contract is cancelled, then the rights and obligations of the parties as spelled out by the contract are cancelled. Instead, the parties' rights and obligations are determined only by Article 2. The arbitration clause is cancelled with the rest of the contract, and is no longer binding on the consumer.

Nevertheless, courts may not accept this view when the seller disputes whether the cancellation was proper. In other words, some courts may refer to arbitration any dispute as to whether the contract has in fact been cancelled.[269] But when

---

258 *Id.* § 6.1.
259 *Id.* § 6.3.
260 *Id.* § 6.4.
261 *Id.* § 9.1.
262 *Id.* § 9.2.
263 *Id.* § 9.3.
264 *Id.* § 9.4.
265 *Id.* § 9.5.
266 *Id.* Ch. 10.

267 *See* Franklin v. Harland Mortgage Centers, Inc., 2001 WL 726986 (N.D. Ill. June 28, 2001) (Truth in Lending Act rescission is a self-help remedy, not covered by arbitration clause).
268 U.C.C. § 2-711(1).
269 *Cf.* Thompson v. Irwin Home Equity Corp., 300 F.3d 88 (1st Cir. 2002) (Truth in Lending Act rescission case); Large v. Conseco Fin. Servicing Corp., 292 F.3d 49 (1st Cir. 2002) (same).

the seller accepts that the revocation, and thus the cancellation, are valid, then there should be no basis for the seller to argue that subsequent litigation must be referred to arbitration.[270] The arbitration clause is no longer binding on the parties.

Finally, there is a question whether an arbitration clause can force an injunctive action into arbitration, or whether only a court has the authority to issue such relief.[271] Consequently, when a consumer has revoked acceptance and seeks injunctive relief preventing repossession or ordering the seller to fulfill its duties under the revocation, it may be that such an action can not be referred to arbitration.

10.2.4 Does the Magnuson-Moss Act Prohibit Binding Arbitration When Warranty Offered?

10.2.4.1 Introduction

The federal Magnuson-Moss Warranty Act[272] permits warrantors to require that consumers resort to informal dispute resolution mechanisms to resolve their claims arising under the Act, but specifies that these mechanisms must be non-binding, and that consumers retain the right to go to court to assert their claims. The text of the Act appears to explicitly prohibit binding informal dispute resolution procedures and guarantees consumers access to the courts to resolve their claims. Statements in the legislative history likewise demonstrate that the Act's sponsors understood that claimants would retain access to the courts. In light of this evidence, a number of courts have rejected warrantors' motions to compel binding arbitration and have held that the Magnuson-Moss Warranty Act only permits non-binding arbitration of consumer claims. But a number of courts, including two federal circuit courts, have come to the opposite conclusion.

Although the party seeking access to court must demonstrate Congress's intent to prohibit a waiver of access to court, this burden is not meant to be prohibitive. The Supreme Court has explained that arbitration of federal statutory claims is a matter of congressional intent which the Federal Arbitration Act alone does not resolve.[273] "Like any other statutory directive, the Arbitration Act's mandate may be overridden by a contrary congressional command."[274] Congress's intent to carve out an exception to the policies of

the Arbitration Act need not be explicit.[275] Congress's intent to preserve claimants' access to court thus may simply be inferred from the text, history, and underlying purposes of the Magnuson-Moss Act. The inference that Congress intended to preserve claimants' access to court is properly drawn because Magnuson-Moss places extensive restrictions on the use of informal dispute resolution procedures.

10.2.4.2 The Text and Structure of the Act

The Magnuson-Moss Warranty Act sets out specific requirements for disclosures, duties, remedies, and procedures relating to warranties on consumer products, creating an unqualified right of access to the courts for consumers claiming breach of warranty. "[A] consumer who is damaged by the failure of a supplier, warrantor, or service contractor to comply with an obligation under this title or under a written warranty, implied warranty, or service contract, may bring suit for damages and other legal and equitable relief."[276] While Magnuson-Moss also permits warrantors to use informal dispute resolution procedures, the Act makes such procedures a non-binding pre-litigation exhaustion requirement rather than a substitute for litigation:

> One or more warrantors may establish an informal dispute settlement procedure which meets the requirements of the Commission's rules under paragraph (2). If—
>   (A) a warrantor establishes such a procedure,
>   (B) such procedure, and its implementation, meets the requirements of such rules; and
>   (C) he incorporates in a written warranty a requirement that the consumer resort to such procedure *before pursuing any legal remedy under this section respecting such warranty*, then (i) the consumer may not commence a civil action (other than a class action) under subsection (d) of this section unless he *initially resorts to such procedure*. . . . In any civil action arising out of a warranty obligation and relating to a matter considered in such a procedure, any decision in such procedure shall be admissible in evidence.[277]

In placing restrictions on the use of alternative dispute resolution, Magnuson-Moss both embraces adjudication after exhaustion of informal proceedings and establishes that the decision reached in the proceedings only constitutes relevant evidence for courts to consider. The Act's plain language thus strongly supports the conclusion that binding arbitration of written warranty claims is prohibited.[278]

---

270 *Cf.* Large v. Conseco Fin. Servicing Corp., 292 F.3d 49 (1st Cir. 2002) (seeming to accept this argument).

271 *See* National Consumer Law Center, Consumer Arbitration Agreements § 4.3.6.3 (3d ed. 2003).

272 15 U.S.C. §§ 2301–2312.

273 Mitsubishi Motors Corp. v. Soler Chrysler-Plymouth, Inc., 473 U.S. 614, 627, 105 S. Ct. 3346, 87 L. Ed. 2d 444 (1985).

274 Shearson/American Express, Inc. v. McMahon, 482 U.S. 220, 226, 107 S. Ct. 2332, 96 L. Ed. 2d 185 (1987).

---

275 *Id.* (citation omitted).

276 15 U.S.C. § 2310(d)(1).

277 15 U.S.C. § 2310(a)(3) (emphasis added).

278 The discussion of the Magnuson-Moss Act and binding arbitration herein does not apply to state law claims for breach of *oral* warranties, which fall outside the scope of the federal Act's

10.2.4.3 The Act's Legislative History

The legislative history of the Magnuson-Moss Warranty Act provides further support for the argument that Congress intended to ban the use of binding arbitration clauses in written warranties. Congressman Moss, the named sponsor of the Act, explained in floor remarks that these provisions allow an opportunity for private dispute resolution, without limiting a warranty claimant's ultimate right to a judicial resolution:

> First, the bill provides the consumer with an economically feasible private right of action so that when a warrantor breaches his warranty or service contract obligations, the consumer can have effective redress. Reasonable attorney's fees and expenses are provided for the successful consumer litigant, and the bill is further refined so as to place a minimum extra burden on the courts by requiring as *a prerequisite to suit* that the purchaser give the [warrantor] reasonable opportunity to settle the dispute out of court, including the use of a fair and formal dispute settlement mechanism. . . .[279]

The House report accompanying this legislation further states that "[a]n adverse decision in any informal dispute settlement proceeding would not be a bar to a civil action on the warranty involved in the proceeding."[280]

10.2.4.4 The Act's Implementing Regulations

The Magnuson-Moss Warranty Act contains an express delegation of authority to the Federal Trade Commission (FTC) to make rules governing informal proceedings[281] and the FTC has promulgated such regulations.[282] The FTC rules are entitled to considerable judicial deference.[283]

FTC Rule 703 establishing minimum standards that warrantors must follow in any informal dispute settlement procedure specifically provides that such a procedure *can not* be binding on the consumer.[284] Rule 703 applies to *any*

informal dispute settlement procedure which is incorporated into the terms of a written warranty,[285] and the FTC in promulgating Rule 703 was very explicit that the Rule prohibits binding arbitration as a warranty condition: "reference within the written warranty to any binding, nonjudicial remedy is prohibited by the Rule and the Act."[286]

The FTC reiterated this ban in 1999 after a three-year review of its Magnuson-Moss rules:[287]

> The Commission examined the legality and the merits of mandatory binding arbitration clauses in written consumer product warranties when it promulgated Rule 703 in 1975. Although several industry representatives at that time had recommended that the Rule allow warrantors to require consumers to submit to binding arbitration, the Commission rejected that view as being contrary to the Congressional intent.
>
> The Commission based this decision on its analysis of the plain language of the Warranty Act. Section 110(a)(3) of the Warranty Act provides that if a warrantor establishes an IDSM that complies with Rule 703 and incorporates that IDSM in its written consumer product warranty, then "(t)he consumer may not commence a civil action (other than a class action) * * * *unless he initially resorts to such procedure.*" (Emphasis added.) This language clearly implies that a mechanism's decision can not be legally binding, because if it were, it would bar later court action. The House Report supports this interpretation by stating that "(a)n adverse decision in any informal dispute settlement proceeding would not be a bar to a civil action on the warranty involved in the proceeding."[fn69] In summarizing its position at the time Rule 703 was adopted, the Commission stated:
>
> > The Rule does not allow (binding arbitration) for two reasons. First * * * Congressional intent was that decisions of section 110 Mechanisms not be legally binding. Second, even if binding Mechanisms were contemplated by section 110 of the Act, the Commission is not prepared, at this point in time, to develop guidelines for a system in which consumers would commit themselves, at the time of product purchase, to resolve any difficulties in a binding, but nonjudicial proceeding. *The Commission is not now convinced that any guidelines which it set out could ensure sufficient protection for consumers.* (Emphasis added.)[fn70]
>
> Based on its analysis, the Commission deter-

---

279 119 Cong. Rec. 972 (1973) (statement of Rep. Moss).

relevant provisions. *See, e.g.,* Richardson v. Palm Harbor Homes, Inc., 254 F.3d 1321, 1325 (11th Cir. 2001) ("the Act's preference for nonbinding dispute resolution, arguably to the exclusion of binding arbitration, expressly applies only to dispute-resolution mechanisms for which *written* warranties provide as a prerequisite to suit").

279 119 Cong. Rec. 972 (1973) (statement of Rep. Moss).

280 H.R. Rep. No. 93-1107, at 41 (1974), *reprinted in* 1974 U.S.C.C.A.N. 7702, 7723.

281 15 U.S.C. § 2310(a)(2) ("The Commission shall prescribe rules setting forth minimum requirements for any informal dispute settlement procedure which is incorporated into the terms of a written warranty to which any provision of this title applies.").

282 16 C.F.R. § 703.

283 *See generally* Chevron U.S.A., Inc. v. Natural Res. Def. Council, Inc., 467 U.S. 837, 104 S. Ct. 2778, 81 L. Ed. 2d 694 (1984).

284 *See* 16 C.F.R. § 703.5(j); *see also* 16 C.F.R. § 703.5(g)(1) (consumers must be informed that they can pursue legal rem-

edies if they are dissatisfied with the resolution of the informal dispute settlement procedure).

285 *See* 16 C.F.R. § 703.1(e).

286 *See* 40 Fed. Reg. 60,168, 60,211 (Dec. 31, 1975).

287 Final Action Concerning Review of Interpretations of Magnuson-Moss Warranty Act § C(2), 64 Fed. Reg. 19,700, 19,708 (Apr. 22, 1999).

mined that "reference within the written warranty to any binding, non-judicial remedy is prohibited by the Rule and the Act."[fn71] The Commission believes that this interpretation continues to be correct.[fn72] Therefore, the Commission has determined not to amend section 703.5(j) to allow for binding arbitration. Rule 703 will continue to prohibit warrantors from including binding arbitration clauses in their contracts with consumers that would require consumers to submit warranty disputes to binding arbitration.

fn69 House Report (to accompany H.R. 7917), H. Report, No. 93-1107, 93d Cong., 2d Sess. 41 (1974). [*Ed. note*: reprinted in 1974 U.S.C.C.A.N. 7702, 7723.]

fn70 40 Fed. Reg. 60168, 60210 (1975). The Commission noted, however, that warrantors are not precluded from offering a binding arbitration option to consumers *after* a warranty dispute has arisen. 40 Fed. Reg. 60168, 60211 (1975).

fn71 40 Fed. Reg. 60168, 60211 (1975).

fn72 At least one federal district court has upheld the Commission's position that the Warranty Act does not intend for warrantors to include binding arbitration clauses in written warranties on consumer products. Wilson v. Waverlee Homes, Inc., 954 F. Supp. 1530 (M.D. Ala. 1997). The court ruled that a mobile home warrantor could not require consumers to submit their warranty dispute to binding arbitration based on the arbitration clauses in the installment sales and financing contracts between the consumers and the dealer who sold them the mobile home. The court noted that a contrary result would enable warrantors and the retailers selling their products to avoid the requirements of the Warranty Act simply by inserting binding arbitration clauses in sales contracts. *Id.* at 1539–1540.[288]

10.2.4.5 Magnuson-Moss Case Law Prohibiting Binding Arbitration

For a number of years, reported federal court decisions were unanimous in holding that the Magnuson-Moss Warranty Act (MMWA) prohibits binding arbitration requirements imposed by warrantors on consumers.[289] Although

several of these decisions have been overturned by recent federal appellate court rulings,[290] a number of federal and state courts alike continue to hold that Magnuson-Moss claims can not be subject to pre-dispute binding arbitration clauses.

In *Rickard v. Teynor's Homes, Inc.*,[291] a federal district court found that the FTC rules prohibit binding arbitration of written warranty disputes. *Rickard* explicitly rejected two federal court decisions that refused to defer to the FTC, and instead bowed to the FTC's expertise, particularly as the FTC rules are based on a reasonable construction of the statute. *Rickard* finds further support for its ruling because:

> The federal policy favoring arbitration should give way to the pro-consumer policy embodied in the MMWA. The creators of the FAA understood that arbitration agreements historically were entered into in the commercial or contractual context where the parties were sophisticated and deliberately desired to avoid the expense and delay attendant on the civil trial system. That policy does not acknowledge the practical circumstances of cases such as this, where the principal consequence of the "agreement" to arbitrate is to deprive the plaintiff of her right to judicial resolution of the dispute, and thus, of meaningful opportunity for redress. Therefore, notwithstanding the Supreme Court's recent expansion of the FAA, the statute's "liberal policy" should not encroach on or undermine the manifest pro-consumer policy of the MMWA.[292]

In *Browne v. Kline Tysons Imports, Inc.*,[293] a federal district court held that Magnuson-Moss "prohibits binding arbitration of a claim arising under a written warranty because any informal dispute procedure proffered by a warrantor cannot be final."[294] *Browne* held that 15 U.S.C. § 2310(a)(1) establishes the Act's policies with regard to out-of-court dispute resolution procedures and that 15 U.S.C. § 2310(d)(1) requires that such procedures be non-binding by allowing consumers to bring actions in federal court after exhausting the warrantor's informal dispute settlement procedures.[295] The court further found that this interpretation of the Act was supported by the FTC's regulations which echo the statutory language and mandate that consumers retain access to the courts.[296]

---

288 At least two federal district courts continue to uphold the validity of the FTC's ban on binding arbitration under Magnuson-Moss. *See* Pitchford v. Oakwood Mobile Homes, Inc., 124 F. Supp. 2d 958, 963, 964 (W.D. Va. 2000); Browne v. Kline Tyson's Imports, Inc., 190 F. Supp. 827, 831 (E.D. Va. 2002).

289 *See, e.g.*, Raesley v. Grand Hous., Inc., 105 F. Supp. 2d 562 (S.D. Miss. 2000), *overruled by* Walton v. Rose Mobile Homes, Ltd. Liab. Co., 298 F.3d 470 (5th Cir. 2002); Wilson v. Waverlee

Homes, Inc., 954 F. Supp. 1530 (M.D. Ala.), *aff'd*, 127 F.3d 40 (11th Cir. 1997), *overruled by* Davis v. S. Energy Homes, Inc., 305 F.3d 1268 (11th Cir. 2002).

290 *See* § 10.2.4.6, *infra*.

291 279 F. Supp. 2d 910 (N.D. Ohio 2003).

292 *Id.* at 921 (footnote omitted).

293 190 F. Supp. 2d 827 (E.D. Va. 2002).

294 *Id.* at 831.

295 *Id.* at 830, 831.

296 *Id.* at 831.

Similarly, in *Pitchford v. Oakwood Mobile Homes, Inc.*,[297] the court denied a mobile home seller's motion to compel arbitration and held that "there can be no agreement at the time of sale to enter into binding arbitration on a written warranty."[298] The *Pitchford* court found both that the clear intent of Magnuson-Moss was to encourage alternative dispute resolution without depriving parties of their right of access to the courts, and that the FTC's regulations prohibiting binding dispute resolution procedures are entitled to judicial deference.[299]

In *Parkerson v. Smith*,[300] a majority of the Mississippi Supreme Court embraced the reasoning of these federal decisions and likewise held that Magnuson-Moss prohibits all binding arbitration of disputes arising under the Act. The court in *Parkerson* found that "Congress intended to preserve for consumers the right to bring suit for breach of written or implied warranties" and therefore that "the Magnuson-Moss Warranty Act has superceded the FAA in regard to breach of consumer warranties, and binding arbitration cannot be compelled . . . without contravening the purposes of the Act."[301]

In *Borowiec v. Gateway 2000, Inc.*,[302] an Illinois appellate court joined these other courts in holding that Magnuson-Moss prohibits warrantors from imposing pre-dispute binding arbitration requirements on consumers. The court in *Borowiec* found that the plain text of Magnuson-Moss compelled the conclusion that Congress only meant to permit non-binding dispute resolution procedures for claims under the Act, that the Act's legislative history further demonstrates the congressional intent to preserve access to the courts for consumers, and that the FTC's regulations and commentary solidifies the conclusion that the Act precludes binding arbitration requirements.[303]

10.2.4.6 Case Law Finding Binding Arbitration Permissible Under Magnuson-Moss

Two federal circuit courts have recently held that Magnuson-Moss does not prohibit warrantors from imposing binding arbitration requirements on consumers. In *Walton v. Rose Mobile Homes, Inc.*,[304] a divided panel of the Fifth Circuit held that Magnuson-Moss does not preclude binding arbitration. *Walton* reached this conclusion after finding that

the text of Magnuson-Moss does not explicitly address arbitration, that the statutory reference to "informal dispute settlement procedure[s]" does not extend to arbitration, that the legislative history of Magnuson-Moss was inconclusive on this point, that binding arbitration was consistent with the underlying purposes of the Act, and that the FTC's regulations were not entitled to deference because the Act does not empower the FTC to ban arbitration.[305] In an extensive dissenting opinion, Chief Judge King of the Fifth Circuit argued that the textual ambiguity of Magnuson-Moss with regard to binding arbitration compelled courts to defer to the FTC's interpretation that the Act prohibited binding arbitration.[306]

In *Davis v. Southern Energy Homes, Inc.*,[307] the Eleventh Circuit joined the Fifth Circuit in holding that Magnuson-Moss does not preclude enforcement of binding arbitration clauses in written warranties.[308] *Davis* held that the Magnuson-Moss Act's explicit regulation of informal dispute settlement procedures does not demonstrate Congress's intent to preclude binding arbitration, that the Act's legislative history was inconclusive on this point, that binding arbitration would not conflict with the Act's underlying purposes, and that the FTC's prohibition of binding arbitration was not a reasonable construction of the Act because it relied on an interpretation of statutory provisions that the Supreme Court had rejected under other statutes.[309] Therefore, the Eleventh Circuit held that claims for breach of a written warranty arising under Magnuson-Moss may be subject to binding arbitration.[310] Several state courts before and after these decisions have adopted similar interpretations that Magnuson-Moss permits binding arbitration of claims arising under the Act.[311]

---

297 124 F. Supp. 2d 958 (W.D. Va. 2000).

298 *Id.* at 965; *see also* Philyaw v. Platinum Enterprises, Inc., 54 Va. Cir. 364 (Va. Cir. Ct. 2001) (denying used car dealer's motion to compel arbitration of buyers' breach of express warranty claims, finding *Pitchford*'s interpretation of Magnuson-Moss Act persuasive).

299 124 F. Supp. 2d at 963, 964.

300 817 So. 2d 529 (Miss. 2002).

301 *Id.* at 534.

302 331 Ill. App. 3d 842, 772 N.E.2d 256 (2002).

303 *Id.*, 331 Ill. App. 3d at 848–851.

304 298 F.3d 470 (5th Cir. 2002).

305 *Id.* at 475–478.

306 *Id.* at 480–492 (King, C.J., dissenting); *see also* Rickard v. Teynor's Homes, Inc., 2003 WL 22060320 (N.D. Ohio Aug. 25, 2003).

307 305 F.3d 1268 (11th Cir. 2002).

308 *But see also* Cunningham v. Fleetwood Homes of Ga., 253 F.3d 611 (11th Cir. 2001) (holding that Magnuson-Moss prohibits warrantor from enforcing arbitration clause not included in warranty based on Act's "one document rule"); National Consumer Law Center, Consumer Arbitration Agreements § 5.2.2.8.2 (3d ed. 2003) (addressing one document rule).

309 305 F.3d at 1274–1280. *Contra* Rickard v. Teynor's Homes, Inc., 279 F. Supp. 2d 910 (N.D. Ohio 2003).

310 305 F.3d at 1280.

311 *See, e.g.*, S. Energy Homes, Inc. v. Ard, 772 So. 2d 1131 (Ala. 2000); S. Energy Homes, Inc. v. Lee, 732 So. 2d 994 (Ala. 1999) (See, J., dissenting) (opinion adopted by majority of the court in *Ard*); Stacy David, Inc. v. Consuegra, 845 So. 2d 303 (Fla. Dist. Ct. App. 2003) (noting authority holding that Magnuson-Moss permits binding arbitration); Howell v. Cappaert Manufactured Hous., Inc., 819 So. 2d 461 (La. Ct. App. 2002) (split panel decision holding by 2–1 vote that Magnuson-Moss permits binding arbitration); Abela v. Gen. Motors Corp., 2003 WL 21664686 (Mich. Ct. App. July 15, 2003); *In re* Am. Homestar of Lancaster, Inc., 50 S.W.3d 480 (Tex. 2001); *cf. Ex parte* Homes of Legend, Inc., 831 So. 2d 13 (Ala. 2002) (denying writ

The primary state court decision holding that binding arbitration is permissible under Magnuson-Moss serves to highlight the vulnerabilities of the opinions adopting this position. In *Southern Energy Homes, Inc. v. Lee*,[312] a divided Alabama Supreme Court originally denied a mobile home manufacturer's motion to compel arbitration of the buyers' written warranty claims and adopted then prevailing federal court interpretations of Magnuson-Moss with respect to such claims.[313] Soon thereafter, however, the court in *Southern Energy Homes, Inc. v. Ard*[314] used a change of one member in the court's composition to reverse *Lee*'s interpretation of Magnuson-Moss. Instead, without further explanation, the court adopted the *Lee* dissent as the opinion of the court and held that the manufacturer of a mobile home could compel binding arbitration of buyers' claims for breach of written warranty.[315] To reach this conclusion the *Ard* majority/*Lee* dissent relies on numerous debatable interpretations of federal law.

First, by averring that "the text of the Magnuson-Moss Act does not expressly preclude arbitration[,]"[316] the *Lee* dissent transforms the United States Supreme Court's holdings that a statute's intent to preclude mandatory arbitration need only be "discernible" or "deducible" into a plain statement requirement that has no basis in federal law.

More fundamentally, the *Lee* dissent misapplies the holding of *Gilmer v. Interstate/Johnson Lane Corp.*[317] regarding the effect of informal *public* administrative proceedings on arbitration requirements to the very different context of Magnuson-Moss's regulation of *private* dispute resolution.[318] The issue before the Supreme Court in *Gilmer* was whether the requirement under the Age Discrimination in Employment Act (ADEA)[319] that parties use informal public procedures established by the Equal Employment Opportunity Commission (EEOC) served to prohibit all private arbitration of ADEA claims. The Supreme Court held that it did not because informal conciliation by the EEOC "sug-gests that out-of-court dispute resolution, such as arbitration, is consistent with the statutory scheme established by Congress."[320] By contrast, the question under Magnuson-Moss is whether the Act's explicit limitations on privately administered informal dispute resolution procedures apply to regulate the use of arbitration. Under the reasoning of *Gilmer*, Magnuson-Moss should be found to prohibit binding arbitration. While the ADEA's requirement of informal dispute resolution is entirely consistent with binding arbitration, Magnuson-Moss, by its express terms, makes *all* informal dispute resolution procedures non-binding. The *Lee* dissent and its progeny thus ignore crucial differences between Magnuson-Moss and the statutory scheme at issue in *Gilmer*.

Furthermore, the *Lee* dissent's discussion of Magnuson-Moss's legislative history is not persuasive. The *Lee* dissent dismisses as irrelevant the House Report's statement that claimants retain the right to bring a civil action after any informal proceeding, contending that the report "does not expressly deal with arbitration."[321] Once again, this plain statement requirement ignores the Supreme Court's holdings that the intent of Congress to restrict private use of arbitration may be *deducible* from a statute's legislative history and the requirement relies on an erroneous differentiation between arbitration and other informal dispute resolution procedures.

The *Lee* dissent and several of its progeny also draw a mistaken analogy between the legislative history of the Magnuson-Moss Act and that of the Securities Act, which the Supreme Court addressed in *Shearson/American Express, Inc. v. McMahon*.[322] In *McMahon*, the Supreme Court noted that Congress had favorably discussed anti-arbitration precedent regarding Securities Act claims but had done so "without enacting into law any provision remotely addressing that subject."[323] Therefore, the Supreme Court found that this legislative history did not support the interpretation that the Securities Act prohibits arbitration. Under Magnuson-Moss, in contrast, the committee report and sponsor's floor statements noting that consumers would retain access to court corresponded with the enactment of section 2310(a)(3). This legislative history therefore does support the conclusion that Magnuson-Moss prohibits binding arbitration. In any case, discussions of the legislative history of *other* statutes do not answer the question of whether Congress intended to prohibit binding arbitration under Magnuson-Moss.

Finally, the Alabama Supreme Court's rejection of the Federal Trade Commission's interpretation of Magnuson-

---

of *mandamus*, discussing without deciding whether trial court's order requiring use of informal dispute settlement mechanism under Magnuson-Moss constitutes an arbitration order).

312 732 So. 2d 994 (Ala. 1999).

313 *Id.* at 999, 1000.

314 772 So. 2d 1131 (Ala. 2000).

315 *Id.* at 1135; *see also* S. Energy Homes, Inc. v. McCray, 2000 Ala. LEXIS 524 (Ala. Dec. 1, 2000) (affirming *Ard*); *In re* Am. Homestar of Lancaster, Inc., 50 S.W.3d 480 (Tex. 2001) (holding that Magnuson-Moss permits binding arbitration, relying heavily on reasoning of Alabama Supreme Court in *Ard*).

316 *Lee*, 732 So. 2d at 1008 (See, J., dissenting); *see also* Walton v. Rose Mobile Homes, Inc., 298 F.3d 470, 475 (5th Cir. 2002); *In re* Am. Homestar of Lancaster, Inc., 50 S.W.3d 480, 487 (Tex. 2001) ("neither the Magnuson-Moss Act nor the FTC regulations mention arbitration or the FAA").

317 500 U.S. 20, 111 S. Ct. 1647, 114 L. Ed. 2d 26 (1991).

318 *See* S. Energy Homes, Inc. v. Lee, 732 So. 2d 994, 1008 (Ala. 1999) (See, J., dissenting); *see also In re* Am. Homestar of Lancaster, Inc., 50 S.W.3d 480, 487 (Tex. 2001).

319 29 U.S.C. §§ 621–634.

320 *Gilmer*, 500 U.S. at 29.

321 *Lee*, 732 So. 2d at 1009 (See, J., dissenting); *see also* Davis v. S. Energy Homes, Inc., 305 F.3d 1268, 1275, 1276 (11th Cir. 2002); *In re* Am. Homestar of Lancaster, Inc., 50 S.W.3d 480, 488 (Tex. 2001).

322 482 U.S. 220, 107 S. Ct. 2332, 96 L. Ed. 2d 185 (1987).

323 *McMahon*, 482 U.S. at 237.

Moss to prohibit binding arbitration, despite the deference that is generally accorded an agency's interpretation of the statute that it is charged with administering, also involves a misapplication of United States Supreme Court precedent.[324] In addition, the *Lee* dissent cites a string of decisions rejecting anti-arbitration arguments that are based *solely* on a statute's provision of a judicial forum,[325] while ignoring the additional Magnuson-Moss provisions requiring that all informal dispute resolution proceedings be non-binding.

10.2.4.7 The Act Prevents Use of Arbitration Agreements in Only Certain Consumer Transactions

In those jurisdictions in which courts agree with the conclusion that binding arbitration agreements are not allowed for claims under the Magnuson-Moss Warranty Act for breach of explicit written warranties,[326] merchants are prevented from using arbitration agreements in many types of consumer transactions. Manufacturers typically provide written warranties on virtually all new consumer products, from cars and mobile homes to appliances and electronic equipment. Retailers who sell these new goods to consumers may add their own written warranties as well, although frequently these merchants attempt to disclaim that they are making warranties, and instead tell the consumer to rely solely on the manufacturer's written warranties.

When a consumer purchases used goods, the remainder of the manufacturer's written warranty or an implied warranty may still apply, and the consumer can not be required to arbitrate warranty disputes with the manufacturer. More typically in the purchase of used cars and other used goods, the consumer's dispute is with the dealer selling the goods to the consumer. In some such circumstances, the dealer will offer a written warranty. In that case, an attendant arbitration agreement will violate Magnuson-Moss.

More commonly, the dealer offers no written warranty, but state law provides that the dealer offers implied warranties in the transaction or the dealer may sell an extended warranty (also called a service contract). The Magnuson-Moss Warranty Act provides a private right of action for breach of such implied warranties or extended warranties,[327] and the issue is then whether a merchant who only provides implied warranties or sells an extended warranty can include a binding arbitration requirement in the sales agreement.

The Act's rules as to informal dispute settlement procedures only apply if a written warranty is provided, so the analysis must be different than when a written warranty is provided. Courts may find the inclusion of an arbitration agreement not automatically inconsistent with the Magnuson-Moss Act.[328] This conclusion still begs the question whether the congressional intent behind the Magnuson-Moss Act in encouraging a practical remedial scheme for small consumer warranty disputes is inconsistent with an arbitration mechanism that prevents class actions, refuses to award attorney fees to a prevailing consumer, or that assesses high arbitration costs to the consumer.[329] This type of conflict is examined in NCLC's *Consumer Arbitration Agreements*.[330]

10.2.5 Arbitration, When Permitted, Must Still Comply with the Act's Provisions Concerning Disclosures and Tie-Ins

10.2.5.1 Introduction

In jurisdictions where courts permit binding arbitration of written warranty disputes, the arbitration agreement still must comply with Magnuson-Moss Warranty Act disclosure requirements[331] and prohibitions concerning tie-ins.[332] In addition, Magnuson-Moss tie-in prohibitions relate not only to written, but also to *implied* warranties,[333] while its disclosure requirements apply both to written warranties and to *service contracts*.[334] Magnuson-Moss, being a federal statute, is not preempted by the Federal Arbitration Act (FAA), and compliance with these requirements is not inconsistent with FAA requirements.

The precise application of these requirements to arbitration clauses is unclear because case law is sparse and Federal Trade Commission (FTC) regulations do not directly address this issue, which is not surprising considering that the FTC maintains that Magnuson-Moss prohibits bind-

---

324 *See* § 10.2.4.4, *supra*.

325 *See* S. Energy Homes, Inc. v. Lee, 732 So. 2d 994, 1010, 1011 (Ala. 1999); *see also* Walton v. Rose Mobile Homes, Inc., 298 F.3d 470, 474–476 (5th Cir. 2002); Davis v. S. Energy Homes, Inc., 305 F.3d 1268, 1277–1279 (11th Cir. 2002). *But see also* Walton, 298 F.3d at 480–492 (King, C.J., dissenting) (arguing that FTC's interpretation is entitled to judicial deference).

326 The term "written warranty" is defined at 15 U.S.C. § 2301(6). *See* § 2.2.5, *supra*.

327 15 U.S.C. § 2310(d)(1).

328 *See* Rhode v. E & T Investments, Inc., 6 F. Supp. 2d 1322 (M.D. Ala. 1998); Boyd v. Homes of Legend, Inc., 981 F. Supp. 1423 (M.D. Ala. 1997), *remanded on jurisdictional grounds*, 188 F.3d 1294 (11th Cir. 1999).

329 *But see* Boyd v. Homes of Legend, Inc., 981 F. Supp. 1423 (M.D. Ala. 1997) (legislative intent to encourage Magnuson-Moss litigation concerning implied warranty claims can not override the FAA), *remanded on jurisdictional grounds*, 188 F.3d 1294 (11th Cir. 1999).

330 National Consumer Law Center, Consumer Arbitration Agreements § 5.3 (3d ed. 2003).

331 15 U.S.C. § 2302(a).

332 15 U.S.C. § 2302(c).

333 15 U.S.C. § 2302(c).

334 15 U.S.C. § 2306(b).

ing arbitration.[335] Why specify how to disclose a requirement that the FTC has already prohibited?

This section examines three issues: whether an arbitration requirement must be disclosed in a written warranty, whether such a requirement must be disclosed in an extended warranty or service contract, and whether a company offering a written or implied warranty may designate the name of the arbitration service provider, or whether such a designation is a prohibited tie-in. If a court determines that written warranty disputes are not subject to binding arbitration, then the first issue described above is largely moot. But even if written warranty disputes are not subject to arbitration, the Magnuson-Moss provisions still apply to regulate whether an arbitration requirement must be disclosed in a *service contract* and whether a merchant can designate the name of an arbitration service provider to resolve a dispute relating to *implied* warranties.

10.2.5.2 Arbitration Requirement Must Be Disclosed in Written Warranties

In *Cunningham v. Fleetwood Homes of Georgia, Inc.*,[336] the Eleventh Circuit held that a mobile home manufacturer could not compel arbitration of a home buyer's written warranty claims when the arbitration requirement was not disclosed in the warranty itself. Even though the Eleventh Circuit in a later case would hold that Magnuson-Moss does not generally prohibit warrantors from imposing binding arbitration upon consumers,[337] the court in *Cunningham* found that a binding arbitration requirement is a material contract term that must be disclosed in accordance with the Act's explicit disclosure requirements, and therefore could not be presented to consumers in a document separate from the warranty.[338]

Likewise the Alabama Supreme Court, despite its earlier holdings generally permitting binding arbitration under Magnuson-Moss, held in *Ex parte Thicklin* that a warrantor's "failure to disclose in the warranty the requirement that [a consumer] arbitrate her claims against it violates the disclosure requirements of the Magnuson-Moss Act" and therefore prohibits the warrantor from forcing the consumer into arbitration.[339] The court in *Thicklin* concluded that the Eleventh Circuit's reasoning in *Cunningham* was persuasive

and therefore overturned its own prior decision enforcing an arbitration clause found in a separate document from the warranty.[340]

The Magnuson-Moss Act's disclosure requirement applies to written warranties. It does not require disclosure of an arbitration clause when a written warranty is not offered,[341] and at least one court finds that the failure to disclose the arbitration clause in the written warranty only prevents the arbitration of written warranty disputes, and not other legal claims.[342]

The holdings in *Cunningham* and *Thicklin* are grounded in the text, legislative history, and underlying policy goals of Magnuson-Moss. The core purposes of the Act are to "improve the adequacy of information available to consumers, prevent deception, and improve competition in the marketing of consumer products."[343]

Towards these ends, the Act requires warrantors to "fully and conspicuously disclose in simple and readily understood language the terms and conditions of such warranty" and empowers the Federal Trade Commission (FTC) to:

require inclusion in the written warranty of any of the following items among others:

. . .

(4) A statement of what the warrantor will do in the event of a defect, malfunction, or failure to conform with such written warranty—at whose expense—and for what period of time.

(5) A statement of what the consumer must do and expenses he must bear.

(6) Exceptions and exclusions from the terms of the warranty.

(7) The step-by-step procedure which the consumer should take in order to obtain performance of any obligation under the warranty, including the identification of any person or class of persons authorized to perform the obligations set forth in the warranty.

(8) Information respecting the availability of any informal dispute settlement procedure offered by the warrantor and a recital, where the warranty so provides, that the purchaser may be required to resort to such procedure before pursuing any legal remedies in the courts.

. . .

(13) The elements of the warranty in words or phrases which would not mislead a reason-

---

335 *See* § 10.2.4.4, *supra.*

336 253 F.3d 611, 622 (11th Cir. 2001).

337 *See* Davis v. S. Energy Homes, Inc., 305 F.3d 1268 (11th Cir. 2002).

338 *Cunningham*, 253 F.3d at 622, 623. It is worth emphasizing that, because Magnuson-Moss is a federal statute, there is no question regarding preemption when the Act's disclosure requirements are applied to arbitration clauses that are also governed by the FAA. *Cf.* Doctor's Associates, Inc. v. Casarotto, 517 U.S. 681, 686, 687, 116 S. Ct. 1652, 134 L. Ed. 2d 902 (1996) (holding that FAA preempts *state* laws imposing special disclosure rules for arbitration clauses).

339 *Ex parte* Thicklin, 824 So. 2d 723, 730 (Ala. 2002).

340 *Id.* at 730 (overruling Cavalier Mfg., Inc. v. Jackson, 823 So. 2d 1237 (Ala. 2001)).

341 Lewis v. Conseco Fin. Corp., 848 So. 2d 920 (Ala. 2002) (when party's representation did not constitute a written warranty, Magnuson-Moss rules regarding binding arbitration clauses do not apply); Huegel v. Mifflin Constr. Co., 2002 Pa. Super. 94, 796 A.2d 350 (Pa. Super. Ct. 2002) (same).

342 Stevens v. Phillips, 852 So. 2d 123 (Ala. 2002) (Magnuson-Moss one-document rule is not applicable when party's claims are not for breach of written warranty).

343 15 U.S.C. § 2302(a).

able, average consumer as to the nature or scope of the warranty.[344]

Magnuson-Moss thus expressly contemplates the one-document rule for disclosure of material terms that both the Eleventh Circuit and Alabama Supreme Court found applies to warrantors' mandatory arbitration clauses.

Pursuant to Magnuson-Moss's disclosure requirements and the Act's express delegation of authority, the FTC promulgated regulations requiring that any warrantor "shall clearly and conspicuously disclose *in a single document* in simple and readily understood language" the information identified in the statutory provisions quoted above.[345]

The Eleventh Circuit found that the FTC's "comprehensive disclosure requirements . . . are an integral, if not the central feature of the Act."[346] Accordingly, *Cunningham* held that a warrantor's attempt to force a consumer into arbitration when the arbitration requirement is not disclosed in the warranty itself "contravenes the text, legislative history, and purpose of the Magnuson-Moss Warranty Act."[347]

10.2.5.3 Disclosure Requirement Has Significant, Widespread Application

The cases recognizing that Magnuson-Moss requires that arbitration clauses comply with the Act's one-document rule provide support for the argument that a manufacturer can not obtain the benefit of a *dealer's* arbitration clause with consumers if the manufacturer did not disclose the clause *in its own written warranty*. A manufacturer's failure to disclose the details of an arbitration clause in its warranty would run afoul of the Act's requirement that material terms relating to the warranty be disclosed in a single document.

It may not even be sufficient for the manufacturer to disclose in its warranty the bare fact that the consumer is bound by an arbitration clause that is fully disclosed elsewhere.[348] Instead, the manufacturer should coordinate with the dealer so that the manufacturer's description of the dealer's arbitration clause is full and accurate.

Similarly, an arbitration clause in a sales contract between consumer and seller should not be effective for written warranty claims if the clause is not also disclosed in the seller's written warranty. As the written warranty-related disclosures must all be contained within the single warranty document, the seller can not rely exclusively on a separate document to impose binding arbitration.

A seller's attempt to achieve the converse also may not work, for example by placing the arbitration clause *only* in the warranty or other warranty-related documents. For starters, if the arbitration clause in the warranty only requires arbitration of claims under the written warranty, then it does not prevent the consumer from litigating claims under an implied warranty or other consumer law claims.[349]

The seller is also vulnerable if it puts the arbitration clause not in the written warranty itself but in the owner's manual. The consumer typically does not see the owner's manual until after consummation of the transaction, reading the owner's manual does not indicate assent to its terms, and the seller may even have difficulty proving the consumer saw the owner's manual. Courts may find an arbitration clause in an owner's manual to have no effect on the consumer's claims, even claims relating to the written warranty.[350]

Sellers may find themselves in a similar quandry if the arbitration clause is only in the written warranty. Proof questions may arise as to whether the consumer ever saw the warranty or agreed to its terms.[351] Even if the seller can prove the consumer received the written warranty, the question remains whether the consumer is bound by terms in a warranty the consumer sees only after the transaction is consummated, particularly when the consumer takes no steps to ratify or attempt to benefit from that warranty.[352] On the other hand, courts have found that a consumer's written warranty claims must be arbitrated if there is an arbitration clause in the warranty, because bringing a claim under the written warranty indicates a ratification of the warranty provisions.[353]

---

344 15 U.S.C. § 2302(a).

345 *See* 16 C.F.R. § 701.3(a) (emphasis added); *see also* 16 C.F.R. § 701.3(a)(3), (5), (6). Also potentially relevant is the requirement of 16 C.F.R. § 701.3(a)(8) that the warranty disclose "any exclusions of or limitations on relief," which would require the warranty to disclose any arbitration clause terms which either explicitly limit a consumer's remedies or do so indirectly by adopting an arbitration service provider's rules that limit remedies.

346 Cunningham v. Fleetwood Homes of Ga., Inc., 253 F.3d 611, 621 (11th Cir. 2001); *see also Ex parte* Thicklin, 824 So. 2d 723, 729 (Ala. 2002) (quoting *Cunningham*).

347 *Cunningham*, 253 F.3d at 622; *see also id.* at 623 ("consumers confronted with warranties that do not contain arbitration clauses that are nonetheless subject to arbitration will have no basis for judging the suitability of a warranty").

348 *But see* Adkins v. Palm Harbor Homes, 157 F. Supp. 2d 1256 (M.D. Ala. 2001) (speculating, but not holding, that mere reference may be sufficient), *aff'd*, 2002 U.S. App. LEXIS

12972 (11th Cir. Apr. 29, 2002).

349 *See, e.g.,* Lyles v. Pioneer Hous. Sys., Inc., 858 So. 2d 226 (Ala. 2003).

350 *See, e.g., Ex parte* Cain., 838 So. 2d 1020 (Ala. 2002); S. Energy Homes, Inc. v. Hennis, 776 So. 2d 105 (Ala. 2000).

351 *See, e.g.,* S. Energy Homes, Inc. v. Kennedy, 774 So. 2d 540 (Ala. 2000).

352 *See* Lyles v. Pioneer Hous. Sys., Inc., 858 So. 2d 226 (Ala. 2003) (finding that the consumer did in fact avail himself of the warranty and is thus bound by the arbitration clause, but indicating consumer would not be bound if he had not availed himself of the warranty); *see also* Licitra v. Gateway, Inc., 189 Misc. 2d 721, 734 N.Y.S.2d 389 (Civ. Ct. 2001).

353 *See* Lyles v. Pioneer Hous. Sys., Inc., 858 So. 2d 226 (Ala. 2003); *see also* S. Energy Homes, Inc. v. Kennedy, 774 So. 2d 540 (Ala. 2000).

10.2.5.4 Does Disclosure Requirement Extend to Service Contracts and Extended Warranties?

Consumers are often sold service contracts, extended warranties, or mechanical breakdown insurance when they purchase products. Service contracts and extended warranties are distinguished from written warranties because they must be separately purchased and do not come free with the product. They may be offered by the warrantor or by a separate party. Magnuson-Moss disclosure provisions relating to written warranties do not apply to such contracts, and service contract providers often insert requirements that service contract disputes are subject to binding arbitration.

Nevertheless, Magnuson-Moss has its own disclosure requirements for service contracts. Companies can enter "into a service contract with consumer in addition to or in lieu of a written warranty if such contract fully, clearly, and conspicuously discloses its terms and conditions in simple and readily understood language."[354] One of the terms and conditions that should be disclosed is the requirement for resort to binding arbitration instead of a court proceeding, just as such a condition must be disclosed in a written warranty.

Magnuson-Moss authorizes the Federal Trade Commission (FTC) to prescribe by rule the manner and form in which the terms and conditions of service contracts are to be fully, clearly, and conspicuously disclosed,[355] but the FTC has not issued such regulations. Nevertheless, the statute makes it clear that service contracts must fully disclose their terms whether or not specific standards have been set by the FTC.[356]

Service contracts present similar practical issues as written warranties. If the service contract company tries to rely on an arbitration agreement between the consumer and the seller, the agreement should fail if it is not disclosed in the service contract. At the same time, putting the arbitration agreement only in the service contract is not enough because the consumer typically does not even see the service contract until weeks after its purchase, if even then. Nor does the typical policy provide an option for the consumer to cancel for a full refund if the consumer is dissatisfied with its terms. The terms are presented unilaterally. At least one court has found such a unilateral imposition of an arbitration requirement in a service contract not to be enforceable.[357]

If a service contract is regulated by a state as insurance, this classification will pose additional issues. On the one hand, the Magnuson-Moss Warranty Act may not apply, and then neither would the Act's disclosure requirements.[358] On the other hand, because of the operation of the federal McCarran-Ferguson Act, states have the authority to limit binding arbitration in insurance transactions, and a number of states have done so, at least for certain lines of insurance.[359]

10.2.5.5 Can Agreement Designate Named Arbitration Service Provider to Settle Written or Implied Warranty Disputes?

An important consumer safeguard under the Magnuson-Moss Act is that the warrantor can not "condition his written or implied warranty of such product on the consumer's using, in connection with such product, any article or service (other than article or service provided without charge under the terms of the warranty) which is identified by brand, trade, or corporate name. . . ."[360] Congress was concerned that warrantors would diminish the "free" aspect of a warranty by conditioning its coverage on the consumer's use of a designated product or service, whose price would be in excess of the price available elsewhere in the marketplace.

The restriction on tie-ins should apply to an arbitration requirement, as it is a condition on obtaining relief under a written or implied warranty. If the warrantor designates the service provider by name (for example, the American Arbitration Association (AAA) or National Arbitration Forum (NAF)), then the consumer can be forced to pay a higher price for arbitration than would be available elsewhere. Of course, if there is no charge for the arbitration, this provision does not apply. Unlike the disclosure requirements that apply only to written warranties, this tie-in provision applies to written or *implied* warranties. Consequently, it applies even when a written warranty is not offered, and when the seller only provides implied warranties.

---

354 15 U.S.C. § 2306(b).
355 15 U.S.C. § 2306(a).
356 15 U.S.C. § 2306(b).

357 *See* Paul v. Timco, Inc., 811 A.2d 948 (N.J. Super. Ct. App. Div. 2002).
358 *See* § 2.3.8.3, *supra*.
359 *See* National Consumer Law Center, Consumer Arbitration Agreements § 2.3.3 (3d ed. 2003).
360 15 U.S.C. § 2302(c).

10.3 Statute of Limitations

10.3.1 The UCC Limitations Period: Four Years After Tender of Delivery

Add note 446.1 at end of subsection's first sentence.

446.1 A few states, such as Wisconsin, have non-uniform versions of U.C.C. § 2-725(1) that set a limitation period other than four years. Colorado has a three-year limitations period: Colo. Rev. Stat. §§ 4-2-725,

13-80-101; *see* Loughridge v. Goodyear Tire & Rubber Co., 192 F. Supp. 2d 1175 (D. Colo. 2002). Mass. Gen. Laws ch. 106, § 2-318 provides a three-year statute of limitations for actions brought pursuant to it, while Mass. Gen. Laws ch. 106, § 2-725 includes the standard four-year limitations period. *See* Fine v. Huygens, DiMella, Shaffer & Associates, 49 U.C.C. Rep. Serv. 2d 1218 (Mass. App. Ct. 2003) (applying three-year statute of limitations; plaintiffs did not raise question whether four-year statute might apply).

Page 373

Addition to note 448.

448 *But see* Spain v. Brown & Williamson Tobacco Corp., 50 U.C.C. Rep. Serv. 2d 1091 (Ala. 2003) (applying non-uniform Alabama provision that action for personal injury from consumer goods accrues when injury occurs).

Add to text at end of subsection:

The revised version of Article 2, which the National Conference of Commissioners on Uniform State Laws approved in 2003 for consideration by state legislatures, would also generally adopt a discovery rule.[451.1]

451.1 Revised U.C.C. § 2-275(1); *see* § 10.3.3aS, *infra*.

10.3.2 Defining When Delivery Occurs

Add to text at beginning of subsection's first paragraph:

The date of delivery may be a disputed question of fact.[451.2]

451.2 Carll v. McClain Indus., Inc., 45 U.C.C. Rep. Serv. 2d 158 (D.N.H. 2001).

Addition to note 452.

452 *But cf.* Webco Indus., Inc. v. Thermatool Corp., 278 F.3d 1120, 46 U.C.C. Rep. Serv. 2d 698 (10th Cir. 2002) (Mich. law) (contractual duty to inspect and test does not, unlike duty to install, extend statute of limitations); Kittitas Reclamation Dist. v. Spider Staging Corp., 107 Wash. App. 468, 27 P.3d 645, 46 U.C.C. Rep. Serv. 2d 144 (2001) (seller's post-delivery field testing obligation does not extend statute of limitations).

Page 374

Add to text at end of subsection:

But when the warranty claim is against the retailer, the statute of limitations runs from the date the product was delivered to the retail buyer.[457.1]

457.1 Lipinski v. Martin J. Kelly Oldsmobile, Inc., 325 Ill. App. 3d 1139, 259 Ill. Dec. 586, 759 N.E.2d 66 (2001).

10.3.3 UCC Limitations Period for Future Performance Warranties

10.3.3.1 General

Addition to notes 459–462, 464, 465, 468, 469.

459 *See, e.g.*, Controlled Environments Constr., Inc. v. Key Indus. Refrigeration Co., 670 N.W.2d 771 (Neb. 2003).

460 *Accord* Full Faith Church of Love W., Inc. v. Hoover Treated Wood Products, Inc., 224 F. Supp. 2d 1285, 48 U.C.C. Rep. Serv. 2d 1331 (D. Kan. 2002) (commercial case) (warranty that treated wood would last as long as untreated wood is future performance warranty); Loughridge v. Goodyear Tire & Rubber Co., 192 F. Supp. 2d 1175 (D. Colo. 2002) (specific oral promises of longevity were future performance warranties); Berg Chilling Sys., Inc. v. Hull Corp., 49 U.C.C. Rep. Serv. 2d 189 (E.D. Pa. 2002) (question of fact whether assurances that product would be maintenance-free for ten years, and brochure promising long product life, created future performance warranty); Mills v. Forestex Co., 108 Cal. App. 4th 625, 134 Cal. Rptr. 2d 273 (2003) (warranties that siding would be free of buckling for twenty-five years and that paint would not blister or peel for five years extended to future performance).

461 *See also* Sherman v. Sea Ray Boats, Inc., 649 N.W.2d 783, 47 U.C.C. Rep. Serv. 2d 1011 (Mich. Ct. App. 2002) (assurance of "years of trouble free boating" and "family fun for years to come" did not create future performance warranty).

Page 375

462 *See also* Loughridge v. Goodyear Tire & Rubber Co., 192 F. Supp. 2d 1175, 48 U.C.C. Rep. Serv. 2d 53 (D. Colo. 2002) (denying summary judgment on statute of limitations issue in light of evidence of specific oral warranties extending to future performance).

464 *Replace "review granted" portion of Gladhart citation with*: *rev'd on other grounds*, 332 Or. 226, 26 P.3d 817 (2001); *add*: City of Cleveland v. N. Pac. Group, 48 U.C.C. Rep. Serv. 2d 191 (Ohio Ct. App. 2002) (chart showing expected life, shipped with the product, did not create future performance warranty); *see also* Carrau v. Marvin Lumber & Cedar Co., 93 Cal. App. 4th 281, 112 Cal. Rptr. 2d 869, 46 U.C.C. Rep.

Serv. 2d 1036 (2001) (general assertion as to performance or duration of warranty insufficient); Kittitas Reclamation Dist. v. Spider Staging Corp., 107 Wash. App. 468, 27 P.3d 645, 46 U.C.C. Rep. Serv. 2d 144 (2001) (warranty's reference to testing and training did not make it a future performance warranty).

Page 376

465 *See, e.g.*, Donatelle Plastics Inc. v. Stonhard, Inc., 48 U.C.C. Rep. Serv. 2d 1399 (D. Minn. 2002); *cf.* Holbrook, Inc. v. Link-Belt Constr. Equip. Co., 103 Wash. App. 279, 12 P.3d 638 (2000) (suggesting that warranty would be a future performance warranty if it promised to repair or replace any defects that arose during warranty period, not just those present at delivery).

468 *But see* Ouellette Mach. Sys. v. Clinton Lindberg Cadillac Co., 60 S.W.3d 618, 45 U.C.C. Rep. Serv. 2d 163 (Mo. Ct. App. 2001) (warranty that car is free from defects for a period of time is future performance warranty).

469 *See also* Coady v. Marvin Lumber & Cedar Co., 167 F. Supp. 2d 166, 46 U.C.C. Rep. Serv. 2d 1047 (D. Mass. 2001) (even with future performance warranty, statute of limitations on defect begins to run when defect is capable of discovery).

Replace note 470 with:

470 U.C.C. § 2-725(2); *see* Mills v. Forestex Co., 108 Cal. App. 4th 625, 134 Cal. Rptr. 2d 273 (2003) (claim barred); Controlled Environments Constr., Inc. v. Key Indus. Refrigeration Co., 670 N.W.2d 771 (Neb. 2003) (all facts and circumstances must be considered to determine when buyer discovered or should have discovered defect).

10.3.3.2 Use of a Specific Time Period Can Create a Future Performance Warranty

Addition to notes 473–475.

473 *See* Berg Chilling Sys., Inc. v. Hull Corp., 49 U.C.C. Rep. Serv. 2d 189 (E.D. Pa. 2002) (question of fact whether assurances that product would be maintenance-free for ten years, and brochure promising long product life, created future performance warranty); Full Faith Church of Love W., Inc. v. Hoover Treated Wood Products, Inc., 224 F. Supp. 2d 1285, 48 U.C.C. Rep. Serv. 2d 1331 (D. Kan. 2002) (commercial case) (warranty that treated wood would last as long as untreated wood specifies time period sufficiently so extends to future performance); Ouellette Mach. Sys. v. Clinton Lindberg Cadillac Co., 60 S.W.3d 618, 45 U.C.C. Rep. Serv. 2d 163 (Mo. Ct. App. 2001) (four-year/50,000 mile car warranty); Controlled Environments Constr., Inc. v. Key Indus. Refrigeration Co., 670 N.W.2d 771 (Neb. 2003) (warranty that goods would be free from defects for one year extends to future performance).

474 *See, e.g.*, Selzer v. Brunsell Bros., Ltd., 652 N.W.2d 806, 48 U.C.C. Rep. Serv. 2d 629 (Wis. Ct. App. 2002) (promise that product would "permanently protect" did not extend to future performance).

Page 377

475 F.F. Hitchcock Co. v. Herrmidifier Co., 46 U.C.C. Rep. Serv. 2d 151 (Conn. Super. Ct. 2001) (not a future performance warranty when no specific time limit and no express reference to future performance).

10.3.3.3 Does Limitation of Remedy to Repair or Replace Create a Future Performance Warranty?

Addition to notes 476, 477, 480.

476 *See also* Brainard v. Freightliner Corp., 2002 WL 31207467 (W.D.N.Y. Oct. 1, 2002) (claim for breach of service contract not barred even though implied warranty claims are barred); Lowe v. Volkswagen of Am., 879 F. Supp. 28, 30 (E.D. Pa. 1995) (limitations period for Magnuson-Moss and lemon law claims runs from date seller performs reasonable number of repair attempts); Cocchiola Paving, Inc. v. Peterbilt, 50 U.C.C. Rep. Serv. 2d 136 (Conn. Super. Ct. 2003) (statute of limitations ran from seller's failure or refusal to make repairs); Ouellette Mach. Sys. v. Clinton Lindberg Cadillac Co., 60 S.W.3d 618, 45 U.C.C. Rep. Serv. 2d 163 (Mo. Ct. App. 2001) (statute of limitations for breach of repair or replace warranty runs from date of discovery of defect); Poli v. DaimlerChrysler Corp., 349 N.J. Super. 169, 793 A.2d 104, 47 U.C.C. Rep. Serv. 2d 260 (Super. Ct. App. Div. 2002); Parker-Smith v. STO Corp., 52 Va. Cir. 577, 43 U.C.C. Rep. Serv. 2d 606 (1999) (implying that statute of limitations would begin to run from date of refusal to repair or replace), *aff'd on other grounds*, 262 Va. 432, 551 S.E.2d 615 (2001); *cf.* Holbrook, Inc. v. Link-Belt Constr. Equip. Co., 103 Wash. App. 279, 12 P.3d 638 (2000) (suggesting that warranty would be a future performance warranty if it promised to repair or replace any defects that arose during warranty period, not just those present at delivery).

477 Brainard v. Freightliner Corp., 2002 WL 31207467 (W.D.N.Y. Oct. 1, 2002); Controlled Environments Constr., Inc. v. Key Indus. Refrigeration Co., 670 N.W.2d 771 (Neb. 2003) (while repair and replace language does not make warranty extend to future performance, neither does it preclude such a conclusion); Gianakakos v. Commodore Home Sys. Inc., 285 A.D.2d 907, 727 N.Y.S.2d 806, 45 U.C.C. Rep. Serv. 2d 816 (2001).

Page 378

480 *See also* Brainard v. Freightliner Corp., 2002 WL 31207467 (W.D.N.Y. Oct. 1, 2002) (claim for breach of service contract not barred even though implied warranty claims are barred); Parker-Smith v. STO Corp., 52 Va. Cir. 577, 43 U.C.C. Rep. Serv. 2d 606 (1999) (suggesting that warranty would be a future performance warranty if it promised to repair or replace any defects that arose during warranty period, not just those present at delivery, but only if plaintiff made demand for that remedy), *aff'd on other grounds*,

262 Va. 432, 551 S.E.2d 615 (2001); Poli v. DaimlerChrysler Corp., 349 N.J. Super. 169, 793 A.2d 104, 47 U.C.C. Rep. Serv. 2d 260 (Super. Ct. App. Div. 2002) (finding it unnecessary to decide between theories); Richard A. Rosenblatt & Co. v. Davidge Data Sys. Corp., 295 A.D.2d 168, 743 N.Y.S.2d 471, 47 U.C.C. Rep. Serv. 2d 1390 (2002) (U.C.C. statute of limitations for claim for breach of service agreement that was part of mixed goods/services transaction runs from date of breach, not from date of delivery of goods). *But see* Nowalski v. Ford Motor Co., 781 N.E.2d 578 (Ill. App. Ct. 2002) (criticizing reasoning of *Cosman* and refusing to apply it to a repair or replace warranty that did not extend beyond four years).

Add to text at end of subsection:

One Illinois appellate court has done just that,[480.1] but another disagrees,[480.2] finding it impossible to characterize the commitment to repair or replace as a promise rather than a warranty, at least when the effective period does not exceed the four year UCC statute of limitations.

480.1   Cosman v. Ford Motor Co., 285 Ill. App. 3d 250, 220 Ill. Dec. 790, 674 N.E.2d 61 (1996).
480.2   Nowalski v. Ford Motor Co., 781 N.E.2d 578 (Ill. App. Ct. 2002).

10.3.3.4 Does Future Performance Exception Apply to Implied Warranties?

Addition to note 481.

481   Brainard v. Freightliner Corp., 2002 WL 31207467 (W.D.N.Y. Oct. 1, 2002); *In re* Bridgestone/Firestone Inc. ATX, ATX II & Wilderness Tires Prods. Liab. Litig., 155 F. Supp. 2d 1069 (S.D. Ind. 2001) (Tenn. & Mich. law), *rev'd on other grounds*, 288 F.3d 1012 (7th Cir. 2002) (reversing class certification because each state's law must be applied); Controlled Environments Constr., Inc. v. Key Indus. Refrigeration Co., 670 N.W.2d 771 (Neb. 2003); Selzer v. Brunsell Bros., Ltd., 652 N.W.2d 806, 48 U.C.C. Rep. Serv. 2d 629 (Wis. Ct. App. 2002).

Add new subsection to text after § 10.3.3.4.

10.3.3a Revised Article 2's Statute of Limitations

The revised version of Article 2, which the National Conference of Commissioners on Uniform State Laws approved in 2003 for consideration by state legislatures, takes a fresh approach to the statute of limitations. If adopted by the states, revised Article 2 would adopt the discovery rule generally for breach of contract.[483.1] An action would have to be commenced within four years after the right of action accrued or one year after the breach was or should have been discovered, whichever comes later, but in no case longer than five years after the right of action accrued.[483.2]

Revised Article 2's rules as to when a cause of action accrues vary depending on the type of claim. If an express warranty extends to future performance and discovery of the breach must await the time of performance, the right of action accrues only when the buyer discovers or should have discovered the breach.[483.3] Reading this provision in conjunction with the general rule means that for a future performance warranty the statute of limitations is four years from discovery—the same as under the current version of Article 2.

Similarly, for breach of the implied warranty of title the cause of action accrues when the aggrieved party discovers or should have discovered the breach.[483.4] Thus, the statute of limitations is four years from that date.[483.5]

For breach of the implied warranties of merchantability or fitness, the cause of action accrues when the seller tenders delivery to the immediate buyer and completes performance of any agreed installation or assembly of the goods.[483.6] This rule means that the ultimate buyer has four years from that date to sue, or one year from the date the defect was or should have been discovered, whichever is later, but suit must be brought no later than five years after the seller tendered delivery and completed any required installation or assembly. The same rules apply to express warranties created by affirmation of fact or promise, by description of the goods, or by sample or model.[483.7] The result is that, for all these types of warranties, a buyer who does not discover the defect within the old four-year statute of limitations has up to one more year to discover the defect and file suit.

The revised version of Article 2 creates two new categories of warranty-like obligations: those created by a written or electronic document packaged with or accompanying the goods[483.8] and those created by advertisements.[483.9] A cause of action for breach of these obligations accrues when the remote purchaser receives the goods.[483.10] This rule means that the statute of limitations for these claims is the later of four years from receipt of the goods or one year from discovery of the defect, but suit must be brought within five years after receiving the goods. This result improves the statute of limitations for buyers in two respects: first, by adding a discovery rule, and second, by starting the statute of limitations from the date the ultimate buyer, rather than the retailer, received the goods.[483.11]

For breach of a "remedial promise," a new category created for repair-or-replace warranties by revised Article 2,[483.12] the cause of action accrues when the remedial promise is not performed when performance is due.[483.13] The statute of limitations would therefore be the later of four years after the seller's failure to perform, or one year after the buyer discovered the seller's failure to perform, but in no event more than five years after the seller's failure to perform.

The revised version of Article 2 also prohibits contractual shortening of the statute of limitations in consumer contracts.[483.14]

483.1 Revised U.C.C. § 2-725(1). Selected portions of revised Article 2 are reproduced in Appx. E.7S, *infra*, and on the CD-Rom accompanying this volume.

483.2 Revised U.C.C. § 2-725(1). The limitation to five years appears to mean that, if the buyer discovers the defect four years and six months after the cause of action accrued, the buyer has only six more months to file suit.

483.3 Revised U.C.C. § 2-725(3)(c).

483.4 Revised U.C.C. § 2-725(3)(d).

483.5 Note, however, that when the breach of the warranty of title is based on a claim of infringement asserted against the buyer, the buyer has only six years after tender of delivery to bring an action against the seller. Revised U.C.C. § 2-725(3)(d).

483.6 Revised U.C.C. § 2-725(3)(a).

483.7 Revised U.C.C. § 2-725(3)(a); *see* Revised U.C.C. § 2-313.

483.8 Revised U.C.C. § 2-313A; *see* § 3.1, *supra*.

483.9 Revised U.C.C. § 2-313B; *see* § 3.1, *supra*.

483.10 Revised U.C.C. § 2-725(3)(b).

483.11 *See* § 10.3.2, *supra*.

483.12 *See* Revised U.C.C. § 2-103(1)(n) (definition of "remedial promise"). Under Article 2, a remedial promise is not a warranty and is not governed by the rules for warranties.

483.13 Revised U.C.C. § 2-725(c).

483.14 Revised U.C.C. § 2-725(1).

10.3.4 Seller's Repair Attempts May Toll the Limitations Period

Page 379

Addition to notes 484, 486.

484 *But see* Kittitas Reclamation Dist. v. Spider Staging Corp., 107 Wash. App. 468, 27 P.3d 645, 46 U.C.C. Rep. Serv. 2d 144 (2001) (repair attempts do not extend statute of limitations); Holbrook, Inc. v. Link-Belt Constr. Equip. Co., 103 Wash. App. 279, 12 P.3d 638 (2000) (rejecting repair doctrine; commercial case).

486 Curragh Queensland Mining Ltd. v. Dresser Indus., Inc., 55 P.3d 235, 47 U.C.C. Rep. Serv. 2d 1064 (Colo. Ct. App. 2002); *see also* Miner Group v. Stamson & Blair, Inc., 2000 Minn. App. LEXIS 770 (Minn. Ct. App. July 25, 2000) (unpublished) (non-U.C.C. case). *But cf.* Coady v. Marvin Lumber & Cedar Co., 167 F. Supp. 2d 166, 46 U.C.C. Rep. Serv. 2d 1047 (D. Mass. 2001) (no equitable estoppel when manufacturer denied responsibility).

Add to text after sentence containing note 486:

This view is consistent with policy considerations. Penalizing buyers for waiting until the outcome of repairs was known would foster unnecessary litigation, compromise business relationships, burden courts with unripe claims, and discourage the voluntary resolution of disputes.[486.1]

486.1 Curragh Queensland Mining Ltd. v. Dresser Indus., Inc., 55 P.3d 235, 47 U.C.C. Rep. Serv. 2d 1064 (Colo. Ct. App. 2002).

Addition to notes 488, 489.

488 Berg Chilling Sys., Inc. v. Hull Corp., 49 U.C.C. Rep. Serv. 2d 189 (E.D. Pa. 2002) (no tolling when seller made no assurances and buyer, not seller, made the repairs); Gus' Catering, Inc. v. Menusoft Sys., 762 A.2d 804, 43 U.C.C. Rep. Serv. 2d 1163 (Vt. 2000) (promise to assist in installing product and fixing it did not toll limitation period).

Page 380

489 F.F. Hitchcock Co. v. Herrmidifier Co., 46 U.C.C. Rep. Serv. 2d 151 (Conn. Super. Ct. 2001) (installation of part as remedial measure did not extend statute of limitations).

10.3.5 *Fraudulent Concealment Tolls the Limitation Period*

Addition to notes 491, 492.

491   Full Faith Church of Love W., Inc. v. Hoover Treated Wood Products, Inc., 224 F. Supp. 2d 1285, 48 U.C.C. Rep. Serv. 2d 1331 (D. Kan. 2002); Northwestern Pub. Serv. v. Union Carbide Corp., 236 F. Supp. 2d 966 (D.S.D. 2002) (fraudulent concealment will toll warranty statute of limitations, but not shown here); *In re* Bridgestone/Firestone Inc. ATX, ATX II & Wilderness Tires Prods. Liab. Litig., 155 F. Supp. 2d 1069 (S.D. Ind. 2001) (Tenn. & Mich. law), *rev'd on other grounds*, 288 F.3d 1012, 1017 n.1 (7th Cir. 2002); *In re* Ford Motor Co. Ignition Switch Prods. Liab. Litig., 1999 U.S. Dist. LEXIS 22892 (D.N.J. May 14, 1999) (denial of motion for judgment on the pleadings), *vacated in part on other grounds*, 1999 U.S. Dist. LEXIS 22891 (D.N.J. July 27, 1999).

492   Olcott Int'l & Co. v. Micro Data Base Sys., Inc., 793 N.E.2d 1063, 51 U.C.C. Rep. Serv. 2d 352 (Ind. Ct. App. 2003).

10.3.6 *A Timely Action That Is Dismissed May Be Refiled Within Six Months*

Replace subsection's final sentence with:

In Illinois,[494] Ohio,[494.1] and Utah[494.2] the supreme courts have held that in UCC cases this savings provision prevails over other more general savings provisions in state law.

494   Portwood v. Ford Motor Co., 183 Ill. 2d 459, 233 Ill. Dec. 828, 701 N.E.2d 1102 (1998).

494.1   Int'l Periodical Distributors v. Bizmart, Inc., 95 Ohio St. 3d 452, 768 N.E.2d 1167, 47 U.C.C. Rep. Serv. 2d 1227 (2002).

494.2   Grynberg v. Questar Pipeline Co., 70 P.3d 1 (Utah 2003) (also holds that U.C.C. § 2-725(3) applies when U.C.C. claim but not entire suit is dismissed, and that the six-month period begins to run upon the dismissal of the U.C.C. claim).

Page 381

10.3.7 *Warranty Defenses to Seller's Collection Action Can Be Raised After the Limitations Period Has Expired*

Replace note 495 with:

495   *See, e.g.*, Bethlehem Steel Corp. v. Chicago E. Corp., 863 F.2d 508 (7th Cir. 1988) (Ill. law). *See generally* National Consumer Law Center, Truth in Lending § 7.2.5 (5th ed. 2003).

Replace note 496 with:

496   *See* National Consumer Law Center, Repossessions and Foreclosures § 12.7 (5th ed. 2002 and Supp.).

10.3.8 *Effect of Contract Provision Shortening the Limitation Period*

Add note 497.1 at end of subsection's first sentence.

497.1   Colorado's non-uniform version of § 2-725(1), Colo. Rev. Stat. § 4-2-275(1), prohibits contract clauses that vary the UCC statute of limitations. It also, by cross-reference to Colo. Rev. Stat. § 13-80-101, adopts a three-year rather than a four-year statute of limitations for breach of contracts for sale.

Addition to note 499.

499   *But see* Rokicsak v. Colony Marine Sales & Serv., Inc., 219 F. Supp. 2d 810 (E.D. Mich. 2002) (upholding reduction of statute of limitations in sale of $418,800 boat to individual); Hensley v. Ray's Motor Co., 580 S.E.2d 721, 50 U.C.C. Rep. Serv. 2d 695 (N.C. Ct. App. 2003) (enforcing one-year contractual limitation period in consumer case; court does not mention any challenge by the consumer to the enforceability of the limitation).

Add to text at end of subsection's first paragraph:

The statutes of limitation for non-UCC claims may be unaffected by such a contract term.[499.1]

499.1   *See* Cocchiola Paving, Inc. v. Peterbilt, 50 U.C.C. Rep. Serv. 2d 136 (Conn. Super. Ct. 2003) (misrepresentation and UDAP claims unaffected).

Add note 499.2 at end of second sentence of subsection's last paragraph.

499.2   *See* 16 C.F.R. § 701.3(a)(4), (5), (8) (requiring disclosure of: the time period or other measurement of warranty duration, the step-by-step procedure that the consumer should follow to obtain performance, and any limitations on the duration of implied warranties).

Add to text at end of subsection:

The UCC specifically prohibits the parties from extending the UCC statute of limitations in their "original agreement."[499.3] The reference to the original agreement implies that the parties may extend the statute of limitations by a post-sale agreement, and this interpretation is consistent with the recognition that other post-sale actions, such as repair attempts or fraudulent concealment,[499.4] can extend the statute of limitations.

499.3   U.C.C. § 2-725(1); *see* Olcott Int'l & Co. v. Micro Data Base Sys., Inc., 793 N.E.2d 1063, 51 U.C.C. Rep. Serv. 2d 352 (Ind. Ct. App. 2003) (refusing to interpret contract as extending time to bring suit).

499.4   *See* §§ 10.3.4, 10.3.5, *supra.*

Page 382

Addition to notes 501, 503.

10.3.9 Limitations Periods for Non-UCC Claims

501   *Replace NCLC citation with*: National Consumer Law Center, Unfair and Deceptive Acts and Practices § 7.3.2 (5th ed. 2001 and Supp.); *add*: *But see* Coady v. Marvin Lumber & Cedar Co., 167 F. Supp. 2d 166, 46 U.C.C. Rep. Serv. 2d 1047 (D. Mass. 2001) (applying warranty statute of limitations rules to UDAP claim).

503   *See* Kambury v. DaimlerChrysler Corp., 185 Or. App. 635, 60 P.3d 1103 (2003) (two-year product liability statute of limitations applies to warranty claim involving wrongful death).

10.4 Buyer's Direct Damages Upon Cancellation

10.4.1 General

Add to text at end of subsection's first paragraph:

The goal of the UCC's remedy provision is to place the aggrieved party "in as good a position as if the other party had fully performed," and its remedies are to be liberally administered to achieve that end.[503.1]

503.1   U.C.C. § 1-106(1); *see* IMI Norgren Inc. v. D & D Tooling & Mfg., Inc., 247 F. Supp. 2d 966, 50 U.C.C. Rep. Serv. 2d 1072 (N.D. Ill. 2002); Bobb Forest Products, Inc. v. Morbark Indus., Inc., 151 Ohio App. 3d 63, 783 N.E.2d 560, 50 U.C.C. Rep. Serv. 2d 106 (2002).

Add to text after sentence containing note 505:

A buyer who cancels is no longer obligated to pay the purchase price.[505.1]

505.1   Cissell Mfg. Co. v. Park, 36 P.3d 85, 43 U.C.C. Rep. Serv. 2d 889 (Colo. Ct. App. 2001); Keller v. Inland Metals All Weather Conditioning, Inc., 76 P.3d 977 (Idaho 2003); Brenner Marine, Inc. v. George J. Goudreau, Jr. Trust, 1995 Ohio App. LEXIS 62 (Ohio Ct. App. Jan. 13, 1995).

Page 383

Addition to note 510.

10.4.2 Recovery of Purchase Price

510   *See also* Conductores Monterrey v. Remee Prods. Corp., 45 U.C.C. Rep. Serv. 2d 111 (S.D.N.Y. 2000); Mercedes-Benz Credit Corp. v. Lotito, 328 N.J. Super. 491, 746 A.2d 480 (Super. Ct. App. Div. 2000).

10.4.3 Cover: Cost of Substitute Goods

Page 384

Addition to notes 522, 525.

10.4.3.2 Goods Qualifying as Substitutes

522   *Add at end of note*: *But see* Keller v. Inland Metals All Weather Conditioning, Inc., 76 P.3d 977 (Idaho 2003) (buyer could not recover higher cost of more suitable equipment).

525   *Replace "U.C.C. § 1-201(32)" with*: U.C.C. § 1-201(32) [*redesignated as U.C.C. § 1-201(b)(29) without relevant change by revised Article 1, which the National Conference of Commissioners on Uniform State Laws (NCCUSL) approved in 2001 for adoption by the states*].

Page 385

Add to text at end of subsection's third paragraph:

Revised Article 1, approved by the National Conference of Commissioners on Uniform State Laws (NCCUSL) in 2001 for adoption by the states, makes this conclusion even clearer by adding leases to the list of examples of types of purchases.[527.1]

527.1   Revised U.C.C. § 1-201(b)(29). As of early 2004, revised Article 1 had been adopted by Texas, Virginia, and the Virgin Islands, and was under consideration by several other states.

10.4.3.3 Requirements of Good Faith and Reasonableness

Addition to note 529.

529   *See also* Hessler v. Crystal Lake Chrysler-Plymouth, Inc., 338 Ill. App. 3d 1010, 788 N.E.2d 405, 50 U.C.C. Rep. Serv. 2d 330 (2003) (finding buyer's cover reasonable).

Page 386

10.4.3.5 Offset for Expenses Saved in Consequence of Breach

Replace note 535 with:

535   U.C.C. § 1-106(1) [*redesignated as U.C.C. § 1-305 by revised Article 1, approved by the National Conference of Commissioners on Uniform State Laws (NCCUSL) in 2001 for adoption by the states*].

Page 387

10.4.6 Offset for Buyer's Use

Add to text after subsection's second paragraph:

The revised version of Article 2, which the National Conference of Commissioners on Uniform State Laws approved in 2003 for consideration by state legislatures, would add explicit authority for requiring the buyer, "in an appropriate case," to compensate the seller for use of the goods after revocation or rejection.[546.1]

546.1   Revised U.C.C. § 2-608(4)(b). Selected portions of revised Article 2 are reproduced in Appx. E.7S, *infra*, and on the CD-Rom accompanying this volume.

Replace "section 718(3)" in subsection's third paragraph with:

section 2-718(3)

Addition to note 548.

548   *See also* Price v. Chevrolet Motor Div., 765 A.2d 800, 43 U.C.C. Rep. Serv. 2d 593 (Pa. Super. Ct. 2000) (dictum).

Page 388

Add note 556.1 at end of sentence following sentence containing note 556.

556.1   *But see* Messana v. Mercedes-Benz of N. Am., Inc., 2001 U.S. App. LEXIS 3924, at *4 n.2 (7th Cir. Mar. 7, 2001) (unpublished) (using IRS business deduction for usage allowance to establish damages for purposes of determining amount in controversy; court does not discuss why this rate is appropriate, and opinion suggests that parties stipulated to it).

Add note 556.2 at end of second sentence following sentence containing note 556.

556.2   Johnson v. Gen. Motors Corp., 233 Kan. 1044, 668 P.2d 139 (1983) (rejecting use of depreciation to calculate offset; proper measure is value received by buyer).

Add to text after subsection's fifth paragraph:

The revised version of Article 2, approved by NCCUSL in 2003 for consideration by state legislatures, clarifies the issue somewhat by stating that, when it is appropriate to charge the buyer for post-revocation use of the goods, the standard should be the value "to the buyer" of the use of the goods.[556.3] Under this standard, a car should have no value to the buyer if it is in a repair shop because of its defects. Similarly, a car that is so defective that the buyer is afraid to drive it or drives it only occasionally has little or no value to the buyer.

Another way to estimate a value for buyer's use is to divide the purchase price by the expected useful life of the product and then to discount that figure to take account of the defects. For example, if a vehicle costs $15,000 and has an expected useful life of 150,000 miles, its use could be valued at ten cents per mile if it did not have significant defects. Some lemon laws adopt this approach.[556.4] Another approach to determining the offset is to subtract the blue book value of the vehicle with its current mileage from its blue book value at the time of purchase. Yet another possibility is to base a per-mile offset on the locally prevailing rate for excess mileage in long-term auto leases.

556.3   Revised U.C.C. § 2-608(4)(b). Selected portions of revised Article 2 are reproduced in Appx. E.7S, *infra*, and on the CD-Rom accompanying this volume.

556.4   *See* § 13.2.8.7, *infra*.

Addition to note 557.

557   *See* Dalme v. Blockers Manufactured Homes, Inc., 779 So. 2d 1014 (La. Ct. App. 2001) (seller entitled to no offset for use in redhibition action because of severity of defects in mobile home); *see also* Fruge v. Toyota Motor Sales, 692 So. 2d 467 (La. Ct. App. 1997) (offset for use not required in redhibition action

when buyer endured great inconvenience and interruption in service); Bingham v. Ryan Chevrolet-Subaru, Inc., 691 So. 2d 817 (La. Ct. App. 1997) (no offset for use of defective, unreliable vehicle in fraud case). *But cf.* Deere & Co. v. Johnson, 271 F.3d 613 (5th Cir. 2001) (Miss. law) (evidence of rental value of non-defective product was sufficient to support jury's finding of rental value of defective product).

Add to text after sentence containing note 557:

If the defect makes the vehicle unreliable or dangerous, what market is there for such a vehicle? What experience does the witness have with that market?

Add to text after sentence containing note 559:

Mileage that was on the vehicle before the sale must also be subtracted.

Addition to notes 560, 561.

560   Gawlick v. Am. Builders Supply, 519 P.2d 313 (N.M. Ct. App. 1974); Clark v. Ourisman Fairfax, Inc., 59 Va. Cir. 129 (2002).

561   *See also* Deere & Co. v. Johnson, 271 F.3d 613 (5th Cir. 2001) (Miss. law) (when offset for use exceeded buyer's damages, buyer is entitled to zero recovery, but seller who had not pleaded *quantum meruit* could not recover for use under that theory).

Add to text at end of subsection:

It is arguable that a product that is unreliable or dangerous has no value or virtually no value. A consumer with a car that runs sometimes, but sometimes does not start, must always worry about being left stranded, and probably has had to invest considerable time in obtaining repairs and finding alternate transportation. Just like an alarm clock that works some of the time, such a vehicle causes at least as much harm as good, and therefore has little or no value. There is also authority that no offset for use is appropriate when the consumer prevails on a fraud claim.[561.1]

561.1   *See, e.g.,* Cowart v. Claude Nolan, Inc., 281 So. 2d 907 (Fla. Dist. Ct. App. 1973); Osterberger v. Hites Constr., 599 S.W.2d 221, 229, 230 (Mo. Ct. App. 1980).

10.5 Buyer's Direct Damages Where No Cancellation

10.5.1 General

Add to text at end of subsection's first paragraph:

Direct damages "result from an act without the intervention of any intermediate controlling or self-efficient cause."[561.2] By contrast, consequential damages "are not produced without the concurrence of some other event attributable to the same origin or cause."[561.3]

561.2   IMI Norgren Inc. v. D & D Tooling & Mfg., Inc., 247 F. Supp. 2d 966, 970, 50 U.C.C. Rep. Serv. 2d 1072 (N.D. Ill. 2002) (repair costs are direct damages and are not capped at value of the transaction).

561.3   *Id.; see also* Pulte Home Corp. v. Parex, Inc., 265 Va. 518, 579 S.E.2d 188, 50 U.C.C. Rep. Serv. 2d 766 (2003) ("such damage, loss, or injury as does not flow directly and immediately from the act of the party, but only from some of the consequences or results of such act").

Add to text at beginning of subsection's second paragraph:

In contrast to rejection or revocation of acceptance, an action for breach of warranty is an action affirming the contract: the buyer retains the goods and sues for damages.[561.4]

561.4   Herring v. Home Depot, Inc., 565 S.E.2d 773 (S.C. 2002).

Add to text at end of subsection's second paragraph:

The rule adopted by many jurisdictions that precludes recovery of this type of "economic loss" in negligence actions has no application to warranty claims.[561.5]

561.5   Ohio Cas. Ins. Co. v. Vermeer Mfg. Co., 2004 WL 60487 (W.D. Ky. Jan. 12, 2004); *see* § 12.2, *infra.*

Addition to notes 562–566.

562   *Replace "U.C.C. § 1-106(1)" with:* U.C.C. § 1-106(1) [*redesignated as U.C.C. § 1-305 by revised Article 1, which the National Conference of Commissioners on Uniform State Laws (NCCUSL) approved in 2001 for adoption by the states*].

563   Beaver Valley Alloy Foundry Co. v. Therma-Fab, Inc., 814 A.2d 217, 49 U.C.C. Rep. Serv. 2d 507 (Pa. Super. Ct. 2002).

564   *See, e.g.,* Triple E, Inc. v. Hendrix & Dail, Inc., 543 S.E.2d 245, 43 U.C.C. Rep. Serv. 2d 533 (S.C. Ct. App. 2001) (allowing lost profits as direct damages for defective crop treatment).

Page 389

565   Price v. Chevrolet Motor Div., 765 A.2d 800, 43 U.C.C. Rep. Serv. 2d 593 (Pa. Super. Ct. 2000).

566   *See* Ford Motor Co. v. Cooper, 2004 WL 34859 (Tex. App. Jan. 8, 2004) (UDAP claim); JHC Ventures, Ltd. P'ship v. Fast Trucking, Inc., 94 S.W.3d 762, 49 U.C.C. Rep. Serv. 2d 167 (Tex. App. 2002).

10.5.2 Difficulties in Proving Value of Goods

Add to text at end of subsection:

If the particular defect is one that does not change over time, the consumer may also be able to persuade the court that evidence of value at a later point is probative of the value at the time of delivery.[582.1]

582.1   Elmore v. Doenges Bros. Ford, Inc., 21 P.3d 65 (Okla. Ct. App. 2001) (title defect).

10.5.3 Cost of Repair as a Measure of Damages

Addition to note 583.

583   IMI Norgren Inc. v. D & D Tooling & Mfg., Inc., 247 F. Supp. 2d 966, 50 U.C.C. Rep. Serv. 2d 1072 (N.D. Ill. 2002) (repair costs are direct damages and are not capped at value of the transaction); Cambridge Technologies, Inc. v. Argyle Indus., Inc., 807 A.2d 125, 48 U.C.C. Rep. Serv. 2d 966 (Md. Ct. Spec. App. 2002); Fassi v. Auto Wholesalers, 145 N.H. 404, 762 A.2d 1034 (2000) (upholding award based on cost of repair); Malul v. Capital Cabinets, Inc., 740 N.Y.S.2d 828, 47 U.C.C. Rep. Serv. 2d 502 (Civ. Ct. 2002) (awarding purchase price as replacement cost for defective cabinets that had at most a nominal salvage value); Watson & Son Landscaping v. Power Equip. Co., 2003 WL 22326967 (Tenn. Ct. App. Apr. 29, 2003) (trade-in value two years later insufficient); Bobholz v. Banaszak, 655 N.W.2d 547, 49 U.C.C. Rep. Serv. 2d 25 (Wis. Ct. App. 2002). *But see* Shoemaker v. KraftMaid Cabinetry, Inc., 639 N.W.2d 224 (Wis. Ct. App. 2001) (cost of replacement of kitchen fixture insufficient as measure of damages without proof of value of item as delivered); *cf.* Rheem Mfg. Co. v. Phelps Heating & Air Conditioning, Inc., 746 N.E.2d 941 (Ind. 2001) (manufacturer not liable to dealer for dealer's costs of repairing defective goods sold to consumers, but dealer may have indemnification claim).

Add to text at end of subsection's first paragraph:

The cost of repair is an appropriate estimate of the diminution in value even if the buyer does not intend to make the repairs.[585.1]

585.1   Fassi v. Auto Wholesalers, 145 N.H. 404, 762 A.2d 1034 (2000).

Addition to notes 587, 593, 597.
Page 392

587   IMI Norgren Inc. v. D & D Tooling & Mfg., Inc., 247 F. Supp. 2d 966, 50 U.C.C. Rep. Serv. 2d 1072 (N.D. Ill. 2002).

593   Forest River, Inc. v. Posten, 847 So. 2d 957 (Ala. Civ. App. 2002) (cost of repair not an appropriate measure of damages when repairs would not restore motor home to warranted condition).

597   *See* Shoemaker v. KraftMaid Cabinetry, Inc., 639 N.W.2d 224 (Wis. Ct. App. 2001).

Add note 598.1 at end of sentence following sentence containing note 598.

598.1   *See* Taylor v. Elkins Home Show, Inc., 210 W. Va. 612, 558 S.E.2d 611 (2001) (cost of replacement can not be awarded as damages unless there is evidence that replacement is necessary to put product into warranted condition).

Add to text after sentence following sentence containing note 598:

The repair estimate itself may be hearsay.[598.2]

598.2   Shoemaker v. KraftMaid Cabinetry, Inc., 639 N.W.2d 224 (Wis. Ct. App. 2001).

Add to text after subsection's seventh paragraph:

One court has held that repair estimates are hearsay if they are presented by the consumer rather than by the person who prepared the estimate.[599.1] But a repair estimate is an offer, which may be introduced in evidence not to prove the truth of some matter stated by the offeror, but simply to prove that the offer was made.[599.2] Thus it should be possible for the consumer to introduce a repair estimate either to establish the amount of damages or to show that the cost of repairs already performed is reasonable because it is within the range of other offers. The typical repair estimate will probably not, however, fit under the business record rule, because it is not a memo or report of acts, events or conditions.[599.3] The estimates would show that the consumer had conducted a thorough and fair analysis of the reduction in value.[599.4] Estimates may also be admissible to show some other fact, such as the consumer's attempt to mitigate damages by seeking to repair the product, or they might be admissible if the jurisdiction has adopted a residual exception to the hearsay rule.[599.5] The best approach, however, is to seek admissions, or stipulations allowing admission of the repair estimates.

599.1   Urich v. Fish, 261 Conn. 575, 804 A.2d 795 (2002) (price quotes from third parties for replacement items were hearsay; not admissible as non-hearsay verbal acts).

599.2   Ways v. City of Lincoln, 206 F. Supp. 2d 978 (D. Neb. 2002); Puma v. Sullivan, 746 A.2d 871, 874–876 (D.C. 2000); Colonial Sch. Dist. v. Unemployment Compensation Bd. of Review, 416 A.2d 1152, 1154 n.4 (Pa. Commw. Ct. 1980); *see also* Pa. R. Evid. 801 cmt. c (listing offers as an example of out-of-court statement that is not hearsay because it has direct legal significance).

599.3   *See* Fed. R. Evid. 803(6).

599.4   *See* Vreeman v. Davis, 348 N.W.2d 756, 38 U.C.C. Rep. Serv. 850 (Minn. 1984) (citing consumer's comparison shopping as evidence supporting his testimony regarding reduced value); *see also* § 10.5.5, *infra*.

599.5   *See* Fed. R. Evid. 804.

Add to text at end of subsection:

If some of the defects can be repaired but others can not, the buyer may recover the repair costs for the repairable defects plus the diminution in value caused by the unrepairable ones.[601.1]

601.1   Prather v. Crane, 2004 WL 51115 (Wis. Ct. App. Jan. 13, 2004).

10.5.4 Resale Price as a Measure of Damages

Add to text after sentence containing note 602:

Of course, the buyer will have to disclose the defect when reselling the goods; to foist defective goods off on an unsuspecting person would make the buyer just as culpable as the original seller, or would demonstrate that the defects are not actually serious.[602.1]

602.1   *See* Fidele v. Crescent Ford Truck Sales, Inc., 786 So. 2d 147 (La. Ct. App. 2001) (buyer's failure to disclose defects upon resale shows they are not significant).

Page 393

Add to text at end of subsection's first paragraph:

If the defective goods are resold for the same price that goods without the defect would bring, however, it is some evidence that the defect does not affect market value.[603.1]

603.1   Valenti v. Mitsubishi Motor Sales, 332 Ill. App. 3d 969, 773 N.E.2d 1199 (2002); *cf.* Cohen v. AM Gen. Corp., 264 F. Supp. 2d 616 (N.D. Ill. 2003) (resale price is circumstantial evidence of quality of vehicle).

Add note 603.2 at end of first sentence of subsection's second paragraph.

603.2   *See* § 10.5.3, *supra.*

Addition to note 604.

604   Watson & Son Landscaping v. Power Equip. Co., 2003 WL 22326967 (Tenn. Ct. App. Apr. 29, 2003); *see also* Ford v. Chrysler Corp., 1996 WL 363914 (E.D. Pa. June 28, 1996) (plaintiff's testimony about trade-in value insufficient proof of damages; court suggests that any repair costs that plaintiff had to pay would have been recoverable); *cf.* Cohen v. AM Gen. Corp., 264 F. Supp. 2d 616 (N.D. Ill. 2003) (credit received at trade-in three years after purchase is some evidence of quality of vehicle). *But see* Valenti v. Mitsubishi Motor Sales, 332 Ill. App. 3d 969, 773 N.E.2d 1199 (2002) (accepting trade-in allowance for car, over two years after original sale, as evidence that buyer had suffered no damages; decision appears to be based primarily on buyer's failure to prove some basis for damage claim).

Add to text at end of subsection:

When the consumer has traded the vehicle in before trial for a trade-in allowance consistent with the average for that vehicle, one court has held that the consumer suffered no damages.[604.1] A more carefully reasoned decision finds the trade-in allowance to be some evidence of the vehicle's fair market value at the time of resale, but recognizes that the consumer could still show damages by presenting testimony that the appraiser offered a reduced trade-in amount because of the defects, or that the difference between the purchase price and the trade-in allowance was due to factors other than usage and passage of time.[604.2] The buyer may also have claims for incidental and consequential damages regardless of the amount received for the trade-in.[604.3]

604.1   Valenti v. Mitsubishi Motor Sales, 332 Ill. App. 3d 969, 773 N.E.2d 1199 (2002).

604.2   Kruse v. Chevrolet Motor Div., 1997 WL 408039 (E.D. Pa. July 17, 1997).

604.3   *Id.*; Bartow v. Ford Motor Co., 342 Ill. App. 3d 480, 794 N.E.2d 1027 (2003).

10.5.5 Buyer's Testimony as a Measure of Damages

Addition to note 606.

606   *See also* Acheson v. Shafter, 107 Ariz. 576, 490 P.2d 832 (Ariz. 1971); King v. O'Rielly Motor Co., 16 Ariz. App. 518, 494 P.2d 718 (1972); Town & Country Chrysler Plymouth v. Porter, 11 Ariz. App. 369, 464 P.2d 815 (1970) (owner of rolled-back vehicle is competent to give opinion as to difference in value); Cash v. Styers, 2003 WL 129046 (Ark. Ct. App. Jan. 15, 2003); Alvine v. Mercedes-Benz of N. Am., 620 N.W.2d 608 (S.D. 2001) (jury was justified in accepting owner's testimony that defective car had zero

value and rejecting manufacturer's evidence of blue book value of generic vehicle of same model); JHC Ventures, Ltd. P'ship v. Fast Trucking, Inc., 94 S.W.3d 762, 49 U.C.C. Rep. Serv. 2d 167 (Tex. App. 2002) (buyer's testimony, based on commercial quotes for comparable product, sufficient evidence of value as warranted); Prather v. Crane, 2004 WL 51115 (Wis. Ct. App. Jan. 13, 2004).

Add to text at end of subsection's first paragraph:

The buyer should take care to focus on market value rather than the personal value to the buyer.[608.1]

608.1   Ford Motor Co. v. Cooper, 2004 WL 34859 (Tex. App. Jan. 8, 2004) (UDAP claim).

Page 394

10.5.6 Expert Testimony of Extent of Buyer's Damages

Addition to note 613.

613   *See* King v. O'Rielly Motor Co., 16 Ariz. App. 518, 494 P.2d 718 (1972) (experienced repair shop worker can testify that poor repair job would greatly reduce new car's value).

10.5.7 Blue Books and Other Market Compilations

Addition to note 618.

618   *Add to State v. Erickstad citation*: 620 N.W.2d 136.

Add to text at end of subsection's first paragraph:

If there is significant variation in the values shown by the different blue books, or if the vehicle has unusual characteristics that make it hard to place on the chart, it may be necessary to have an expert analyze these questions. The buyer must also present evidence of the car's condition, features, mileage, and any other factors that are necessary to determine which blue book value applies to it.[618.1]

618.1   Transmission Shop v. Chacon Autos, Ltd., 2002 WL 1402368 (Tex. App. July 1, 2002) (unpublished).

Add to text after sentence containing note 619:

If the purpose of the evidence is to show a vehicle's value in a particular local market, it usually makes sense to use the guide that dealers use in that market.

Page 395

Add to text at end of subsection:

As the standard measure of damages is the difference between the value as warranted and the value as delivered, the blue book value as of the date of delivery rather than the current value should be obtained. Many public libraries keep back copies of blue books. For a fee, the publisher may also be willing to look up the value as of the date of delivery.

Blue books generally do not give values for vehicles with serious defects, such as odometer rollbacks.[619.1] In these circumstances, the blue book may help establish what the vehicle's value would have been if it had been as warranted but will not accurately reflect its value in its actual condition.

619.1   *See* National Consumer Law Center, Automobile Fraud § 9.10.1.4 (2d ed. 2003).

10.5.9 Subjective Value

Replace note 622 with:

622   Revised Article 1, which the National Conference of Commissioners on Uniform State Laws (NCCUSL) approved in 2001 for adoption by the states, redesignates this provision as U.C.C. § 1-305 without substantive change. *See* § 10.6.1, *supra*.

10.5.10 Where Seller Did Not Have Title to Goods Sold

Add to text at end of subsection:

If the buyer still has possession of the goods but their market value is reduced because of the title defect, damages can be calculated as the difference between their value if title had been as warranted and their value with the title defect.[627.1]

627.1   Elmore v. Doenges Bros. Ford, Inc., 21 P.3d 65 (Okla. Ct. App. 2001).

10.6 Buyer's Incidental and Consequential Damages (Whether or Not Buyer Cancels)

10.6.1 General

Page 396

Add to text at end of subsection's first paragraph:

The goal is to place the buyer in as good a position as if the breach had not occurred.[628.1]

628.1   U.C.C. § 1-106(1); *see* Leanin' Tree v. Thiele Technologies, Inc., 48 U.C.C. Rep. Serv. 2d 991 (10th Cir. 2002) (unpublished) (Colo. law); IMI Norgren Inc. v. D & D Tooling & Mfg., Inc., 247 F. Supp. 2d 966, 50 U.C.C. Rep. Serv. 2d 1072 (N.D. Ill. 2002).

10.6.2 Incidental Damages

Page 397

Add to text after sentence containing note 636:

The cost of maintaining insurance on the goods while storing them should also be incidental damages.

Add note 636.1 at end of sentence following sentence containing note 636.

636.1   Keller v. Inland Metals All Weather Conditioning, Inc., 76 P.3d 977 (Idaho 2003) (affirming award of compensation for time employees spent testing defective equipment); Mitsui O.S.K. Lines v. Consol. Rail Corp., 327 N.J. Super. 343, 743 A.2d 362, 43 U.C.C. Rep. Serv. 2d 897 (Super. Ct. App. Div. 2000) (Pa. law) (applying U.C.C. by analogy).

Addition to note 639.

639   *See, e.g.,* Williams v. Planet Motor Car, Inc., 190 Misc. 2d 22, 738 N.Y.S.2d 170, 47 U.C.C. Rep. Serv. 2d 1000 (Civ. Ct. 2001) (cost of unsuccessful repairs are incidental damages because they are part of diagnosis; cost of successful repairs also recoverable when buyer revokes because they confer benefit on seller). *But cf.* Magnum Press Automation, Inc. v. Thomas & Betts Corp., 325 Ill. App. 3d 613, 259 Ill. Dec. 384, 758 N.E.2d 507 (2001) (cost of unsuccessful repairs may be recoverable by revoking buyer, depending on whether seller had advance notice of planned repairs or should have anticipated them).

Page 398

Add to text at end of subsection:

Incidental damages are recoverable if they were "reasonably incurred" by the buyer.[641.1] The buyer should take care to introduce evidence that any expenses claimed as incidental damages are reasonable.[641.2]

641.1   U.C.C. § 2-715.
641.2   *See* JHC Ventures v. Fast Trucking, Inc., 94 S.W.3d 762, 49 U.C.C. Rep. Serv. 2d 167 (Tex. App. 2002).

10.6.3 Consequential Damages

10.6.3.1 Economic Loss Consequential Damages

10.6.3.1.1 General standards

Addition to notes 643, 653.

643   *See also* Parker Tractor & Implement Co. v. Johnson, 819 So. 2d 1234, 48 U.C.C. Rep. Serv. 2d 1025 (Miss. 2002) (seller is liable for consequential damages when its representative knew of buyer's intended use, even though buyer's application stated different use).

Page 399

653   *See, e.g.,* State v. Polley, 2 S.W.3d 887, 892 (Mo. Ct. App. 1999) (UDAP case involving shoddy home repairs).

Add to text at end of subsection:

The buyer should take care to document consequential damages. For example, if the buyer needs transportation and borrows a car from a family member, any expectation of reimbursement by the family member should be specified and documented rather than left vague. If the buyer pays others for transportation to work or errands, the buyer should document these costs. The buyer should keep track of lost wages and telephone costs, and save all pay records and telephone bills.

Page 400

10.6.3.1.2 Substitute transportation and housing, lost wages

Addition to note 663.

663 Elmore v. Doenges Bros. Ford, Inc., 21 P.3d 65 (Okla. Ct. App. 2001); *see also* Bland v. Freightliner Ltd. Liab. Co., 206 F. Supp. 2d 1202, 49 U.C.C. Rep. Serv. 2d 524 (M.D. Fla. 2002) (denying motion to dismiss claim for damages, including missed work opportunities, due to defects in Freightliner truck).

10.6.3.1.3 Financing costs

Addition to notes 664, 665, 672.

664 Webco Indus., Inc. v. Thermatool Corp., 278 F.3d 1120, 46 U.C.C. Rep. Serv. 2d 698 (10th Cir. 2002) (Mich. law); Bland v. Freightliner Ltd. Liab. Co., 206 F. Supp. 2d 1202, 49 U.C.C. Rep. Serv. 2d 524 (M.D. Fla. 2002) (denying motion to dismiss claim for damages, including loan finance charges, due to defects in Freightliner truck).

665 *Add before Bair citation*: *Compare* Webco Indus., Inc. v. Thermatool Corp., 278 F.3d 1120, 46 U.C.C. Rep. Serv. 2d 698 (10th Cir. 2002) (Mich. law) (financing costs are recoverable when seller had reason to know of financing or it was reasonably foreseeable at time of contract that additional interest would result from a breach); *add after Fortin citation*: *Compare* Bobb Forest Products, Inc. v. Morbark Indus., Inc., 151 Ohio App. 3d 63, 783 N.E.2d 560, 50 U.C.C. Rep. Serv. 2d 106 (2002) (finance costs recoverable when seller could tell from other circumstances that buyer would have to finance the purchase).

Page 401

672 *See* Webco Indus., Inc. v. Thermatool Corp., 278 F.3d 1120, 46 U.C.C. Rep. Serv. 2d 698 (10th Cir. 2002) (Mich. law) (plaintiff can get financing costs as consequential damages plus prejudgment interest); M.S. Distrib. Co. v. Web Records, Inc., 51 U.C.C. Rep. Serv. 2d 716 (N.D. Ill. 2003) (finding no basis under U.C.C. or other law to award pre-judgment interest).

10.6.3.1.4 Damage to the consumer's credit rating

Addition to note 673.

673 *See also* Maberry v. Said, 927 F. Supp. 1456 (D. Kan. 1996).

Replace note 675 with:

675 *See* National Consumer Law Center, Fair Credit Reporting § 10.2.3.3 (5th ed. 2002 and Supp.).

Add note 676.1 at end of sentence following sentence containing note 676.

676.1 *See, e.g.*, Jaramillo v. Gonzales, 50 P.3d 554 (N.M. Ct. App. 2002) (affirming commercial defamation award against bank that reported buyers as delinquent after they revoked acceptance).

Replace note 677 with:

677 15 U.S.C. § 1681h(e); *see* National Consumer Law Center, Fair Credit Reporting § 10.3.5 (5th ed. 2002 and Supp.).

Replace note 678 with:

678 *See* National Consumer Law Center, Fair Credit Reporting § 10.4.2 (5th ed. 2002 and Supp.); *see also* Gaddy v. Galarza Motor Sport L.T.D., 2000 WL 1364451 (N.D. Ill. Sept. 18, 2000) (declining to dismiss claim that creditor committed UDAP violation by reporting deficiency claim to credit reporting agency without reporting that it was disputed).

Add to text at end of subsection:

If litigation is underway before the creditor makes an adverse credit report, the consumer may want to consider seeking injunctive relief forbidding the creditor from making an adverse report while the case is pending. Such an order may be attractive to the court because it merely preserves the status quo.

Page 402

10.6.3.1.5 Damage due to repossession of the goods

Addition to note 679.

679 Fruge v. Toyota Motor Sales, 692 So. 2d 467 (La. Ct. App. 1997) (redhibition action).

10.6.3.2 Consequential Damages Based on Injury to Person or Property

Addition to note 681.

681 *See* Chase v. Kawasaki Motors Corp., 140 F. Supp. 2d 1280 (M.D. Ala. 2001) (no recovery when injuries were caused by factors other than the alleged breach of warranty).

10.6.3.3 Mental Anguish Damages

Addition to notes 689, 691.

689 *See* Horton Homes, Inc. v. Brooks, 2001 Ala. LEXIS 431 (Ala. Nov. 30, 2001) (affirming award that included $138,000 in mental anguish damages for defective mobile home); Cook v. Skyline Corp., 135

Idaho 26, 13 P.3d 857 (Idaho 2000) (recovery allowed if buyers prove physical manifestations of the emotional distress); *cf.* Morris Concrete v. Warrick, 2003 WL 21205836 (Ala. Civ. App. May 23, 2003) (mental anguish damages allowed for breach of contract only in exceptional cases, not shown here). *But see* McGough v. Oakwood Mobile Homes, Inc., 779 So. 2d 793 (La. Ct. App. 2000) (mental anguish damages not allowed for defective mobile home because contract was not intended to satisfy significant nonpecuniary interest); *cf.* Bowers v. Wal-Mart Stores, Inc., 827 So. 2d 63 (Ala. 2001) (emotional distress damages not available for breach of car repair warranty; only available for cases in which it is highly foreseeable that egregious breach will result in significant emotional distress); Grant v. Bridgestone/ Firestone, Inc., 55 Pa. D. & C.4th 438, 46 U.C.C. Rep. Serv. 2d 990 (Pa. C.P. 2001) (no warranty recovery for worry about dangers of defective product unless there is physical injury or impact).

Page 403

691　*Accord* Forest River, Inc. v. Posten, 847 So. 2d 957 (Ala. Civ. App. 2002) (affirming $2000 mental anguish damages for defects in motor home, which was a second home to buyers).

Page 404

10.6.3.4 Damages for Inconvenience, Aggravation, Loss of Time

Addition to note 699.

699　*See* Calbert v. Volkswagen of Am., Inc., 1991 WL 215669 (Del. Super. Ct. Oct. 1, 1991).

Page 405

10.6.4 Proving Incidental and Consequential Damages

Add to text after subsection's first sentence:

Circumstantial evidence is acceptable.[706.1]

706.1　Quality Bus. Forms v. Secured Choice, Inc., 51 U.C.C. Rep. Serv. 2d 447 (Minn. Ct. App. 2003).

Addition to note 708.

708　Watson & Son Landscaping v. Power Equip. Co., 2003 WL 22326967 (Tenn. Ct. App. Apr. 29, 2003) (proof of lost profits too imprecise).

10.7 Punitive Damages

Replace note 711 with:

711　U.C.C. § 1-106(1) [*redesignated as U.C.C. § 1-305 by revised Article 1, approved by the National Conference of Commissioners on Uniform State Laws (NCCUSL) in 2001 for adoption by the states*].

Addition to notes 712, 713.

712　Salter v. Al-Hallaq, 50 U.C.C. Rep. Serv. 2d 348 (D. Kan. 2003) (Kansas allows punitive damages for an accompanying tort, not for the breach of contract itself); Poindexter v. Morse Chevrolet, Inc., 270 F. Supp. 2d 1286 (D. Kan. 2003) (punitive damages available only for independent tort); Robinson Helicopter Co. v. Dana Corp., 2003 WL 164734 (Cal. Ct. App. Jan. 24, 2003) (punitive damages not available in actions based on breach of contract in non-insurance cases), *review granted, opinion superseded by* 68 P.3d 344 (Cal. 2003).

713　Rhodes v. McDonald, 345 S.C. 500, 548 S.E.2d 220, 46 U.C.C. Rep. Serv. 2d 114 (Ct. App. 2001) (no punitive damages in breach of contract case unless breach accompanied by fraudulent act); Highland Constr. Co. v. Union Pacific R.R. Co., 683 P.2d 1042, 1049 (Utah 1984); Jorgensen v. John Clay & Co., 660 P.2d 229 (Utah 1983) (punitive damages allowed if breach of contract amounts to independent tort but willful and malicious breach is insufficient); *see also* N.Y. Univ. v. Cont'l Ins. Co., 87 N.Y.2d 308, 639 N.Y.S.2d 283, 662 N.E.2d 763 (1995) (when tort claim arises from contract, punitive damages available if defendant's conduct is 1) actionable as independent tort, 2) egregious, 3) directed toward plaintiff, and 4) part of a pattern directed at the public generally). *But see* Neilon v. Chrysler Corp., 1997 U.S. Dist. LEXIS 20327 (E.D. Pa. Dec. 11, 1997); Rose v. A & L Motor Sales, 699 F. Supp. 75 (W.D. Pa. 1988) (stating that punitive damages are unavailable but citing only non-warranty cases as authority).

Page 406

Add to text at end of subsection's second paragraph:

Claiming punitive damages on the contract count rather than on a separate tort count may avoid problems such as election of remedies issues that arise when contract and tort claims are pleaded separately.

Addition to notes 716, 717.

716　*Cf.* Horton Homes, Inc. v. Brooks, 2001 Ala. LEXIS 431 (Ala. Nov. 30, 2001) (affirming award of punitive damages; buyer raised both warranty and negligence claims but opinion does not state which formed basis for award).

717　*But see* Salter v. Al-Hallaq, 50 U.C.C. Rep. Serv. 2d 348 (D. Kan. 2003) (Kansas allows punitive damages for an accompanying tort, not for the breach of contract itself).

Replace note 721 with:

721　*See, e.g.,* Aguilera v. Palm Harbor Homes, Inc., 54 P.3d 993 (N.M. 2002) (affirming trial court's entry of arbitrator's award of $100,000 punitive damages under state UDAP statute for violation of mobile home warranty law); *see also* § 11.1.1, *infra*.

10.8 Attorney Fees

Addition to note 725.

725   *See* Idaho Code § 12-120(3) (Michie) (party who prevails on breach of contract claim relating to sale of goods entitled to fees); La. Civ. Code Ann. art. 2545 (West) (seller who fails to disclose known defect or knowingly misrepresents quality is liable for attorney fees); *see also* Nulite Indus. Co. v. Horne, 252 Ga. App. 378, 556 S.E.2d 255 (2001) (Georgia's Rule 11-type statute, Ga. Code Ann. § 13-6-11, applies to performance of contracts and can be basis for fees in contract claims such as breach of warranty); Haight v. Dale's Used Cars, Inc., 51 U.C.C. Rep. Serv. 2d 1017 (Idaho Ct. App. 2003) (awarding fees to prevailing seller); Morrison v. Allstar Dodge, Inc., 792 So. 2d 9 (La. Ct. App. 2001) (awarding fees against seller who failed to disclose known wreck damage); Dalme v. Blockers Manufactured Homes, Inc., 779 So. 2d 1014 (La. Ct. App. 2001) (attorney fees may be awarded against manufacturer, who is deemed by statute to know of defects); McGough v. Oakwood Mobile Homes, Inc., 779 So. 2d 793 (La. Ct. App. 2000) (awarding fees in mobile home redhibition action); Chaudoir v. Porsche Cars of N. Am., 667 So. 2d 569 (La. Ct. App. 1996) (affirming award of fees when dealer knew of acid rain damage); Osburn v. Bendix Home Sys., Inc., 613 P.2d 445 (Okla. 1980) (awarding fees for defending damage award on appeal); Elmore v. Doenges Bros. Ford, Inc., 21 P.3d 65 (Okla. Ct. App. 2001) (affirming award of fees); Hawkins v. Ford Motor Co., 211 W. Va. 487, 566 S.E.2d 624, 632 n.4 (2002) (fees are recoverable for breach of implied warranty under W. Va. Code §§ 46A-6-108 and 46A-5-104); Wolfe v. Welton, 210 W. Va. 563, 558 S.E.2d 363 (2001) (when seller unsuccessfully defended warranty claim based on disclaimer prohibited by West Virginia Consumer Credit & Protection Act, consumer could recover fees under that Act). *But see* JHC Ventures, Ltd. P'ship v. Fast Trucking, Inc., 94 S.W.3d 762, 49 U.C.C. Rep. Serv. 2d 167 (Tex. App. 2002) (commercial case) (warranty is not a contract claim, so provision of Tex. Civ. Prac. & Rem. Code Ann. § 38.001(8) (Vernon) allowing fees for contract claims inapplicable).

Page 407

Add note 725.1 at end of sentence containing note 725.

725.1 *See, e.g.*, United Wholesale Supply, Inc. v. Wear, 106 Wash. App. 1042, 45 U.C.C. Rep. Serv. 2d 1067 (2001) (unpublished).

Replace note 727 with:

727   *See, e.g.*, Wolfe v. Welton, 210 W. Va. 563, 558 S.E.2d 363 (2001) (when seller unsuccessfully defended warranty claim based on disclaimer prohibited by West Virginia Consumer Credit & Protection Act, consumer could recover fees under that Act). *See generally* § 11.1, *infra*; National Consumer Law Center, Unfair and Deceptive Acts and Practices § 8.8 (5th ed. 2001 and Supp.).

Chapter 11

Deception, Unfairness, Unconscionability, Lack of Good Faith and Fraud

11.1 State UDAP Statutes

11.1.1 Application of UDAP Statutes to Warranty Problems

11.1.1.1 Introduction

Page 409

Replace NCLC citation in subsection's second paragraph with:

Unfair and Deceptive Acts and Practices (5th ed. 2001 and Supp.)

11.1.1.2 Advantages of a UDAP Claim

Add to text at end of subsection's first paragraph:

A violation of another consumer protection law, such as the Magnuson-Moss Act or a state warranty law, may be a per se UDAP violation,[1.1] thus allowing the buyer to recover UDAP remedies, which often include treble damages and attorney fees.[1.2]

    1.1   *See* § 11.1.8, *infra.*

    1.2   *See generally* National Consumer Law Center, Unfair and Deceptive Acts and Practices § 8.8 (5th ed. 2001 and Supp.).

Replace note 2 with:

    2   *See* National Consumer Law Center, Unfair and Deceptive Acts and Practices § 7.2.2 (5th ed. 2001 and Supp.) (discussion of alternatives to private UDAP actions in Iowa).

Addition to notes 4, 5, 7.

    4   Mike Castrucci Ford Sales, Inc. v. Krull, Clearinghouse No. 53,534 (Ohio C.P. Clermont County, June 1, 2000); Oakwood Mobile Homes, Inc. v. Cabler, 73 S.W.3d 363 (Tex. App. 2002).

Page 410

    5   Campbell v. Beak, 568 S.E.2d 801 (Ga. Ct. App. 2002).

    7   Shannon v. Boise Cascade, 336 Ill. App. 3d 533, 783 N.E.2d 1105 (2003) (UDAP claim regarding defective siding), *leave to appeal granted*, 792 N.E.2d 314 (Ill. 2003) (table); *see* National Consumer Law Center, Unfair and Deceptive Acts and Practices § 4.2.15.4 (5th ed. 2001 and Supp.).

Replace note 8 with:

    8   *See* National Consumer Law Center, Unfair and Deceptive Acts and Practices § 7.5.4 (5th ed. 2001 and Supp.).

Page 411

11.1.1.3 Advantages of a UCC Claim

Replace note 14 with:

    14   *See* National Consumer Law Center, Unfair and Deceptive Acts and Practices § 7.3 (5th ed. 2001 and Supp.).

11.1.2 Standards of Deception and Unfairness

Replace note 17 with:

    17   National Consumer Law Center, Unfair and Deceptive Acts and Practices § 4.2 (5th ed. 2001 and Supp.).

Add to text after sentence containing note 18:

Breach of the duty of good faith can be a UDAP violation.[18.1]

    18.1   Marx v. Globe Newspaper Co., 13 Mass. L. Rptr. 190, 43 U.C.C. Rep. Serv. 2d 812 (Super. Ct. 2001).

Page 412

11.1.3 Breach of Warranty or Service Contract as a UDAP Violation

Addition to notes 20–22, 24.

20   W.R. Constr. & Consulting, Inc. v. Jeld-Wen, Inc., 2002 WL 31194870 (D. Mass. Sept. 10, 2002) (denial of manufacturer's motion for summary judgment); *In re* Ford Motor Co. Ignition Switch Products Liab. Litig., 1999 U.S. Dist. LEXIS 22892 (D.N.J. May 14, 1999) (breach of implied warranty of merchantability, if one arises and is enforceable against this defendant under state law, may be UDAP violation), *vacated in part on other grounds*, 1999 U.S. Dist. LEXIS 22891 (D.N.J. July 27, 1999); Earls v. Condor Capital Corp., 2001 Conn. Super. LEXIS 2595 (Conn. Super. Ct. Aug. 30, 2001) (used car); Sparks v. Re/Max Allstar Realty, Inc., 55 S.W.3d 343 (Ky. Ct. App. 2000) (grossly negligent performance of services may be UDAP violation); Gadula v. Gen. Motors Co., 2001 Mich. App. LEXIS 692 (Mich. Ct. App. Jan. 5, 2001); Boyle v. Daimler Chrysler Corp., 2002 WL 1881157 (Ohio Ct. App. Aug. 16, 2002); Estate of Cattano v. High Touch Homes, Inc., 2002 WL 1290411 (Ohio Ct. App. May 24, 2002) (unpublished) (sale of modular home that did not conform to model, and failure to make adequate repairs); Lump v. Best Door & Window, Inc., 2002 Ohio App. LEXIS 1381 (Ohio Ct. App. Mar. 27, 2002); Jones v. Star Houston, Inc., 45 S.W.3d 350 (Tex. App. 2001) (failure to perform repairs in workmanlike manner is UDAP violation); Materials Mktg. Corp. v. Spencer, 40 S.W.3d 172, 43 U.C.C. Rep. Serv. 2d 1131 (Tex. App. 2001); *see also* Brace v. Titcomb, 2002 WL 1335871 (Me. Super. Ct. May 17, 2002) (defective home improvement work is UDAP violation).

21   *See* Vt. Code R. 06-031-009, § 102.02.

22   McLaughlin v. Denharco, Inc., 129 F. Supp. 2d 32, 43 U.C.C. Rep. Serv. 2d 1122 (D. Me. 2001); Kleczek v. Jorgensen, 328 Ill. App. 3d 1012, 263 Ill. Dec. 187, 767 N.E.2d 913 (2002); Sampson v. Winnie, 2001 Tenn. App. LEXIS 894 (Tenn. Ct. App. Dec. 11, 2001); Brooks v. Ibsen, 2001 Tenn. App. LEXIS 630 (Tenn. Ct. App. Aug. 24, 2001); *see also* Wolfe v. Welton, 210 W. Va. 563, 558 S.E.2d 363 (2001) (enforcing West Virginia Consumer Credit & Protection Act prohibition of warranty disclaimers; remanding for entry of judgment plus attorney fees).

Page 413

24   *But cf.* Bonaccoloto v. Coca-Cola Enterprises, Inc., 1999 U.S. Dist. LEXIS 22732 (D. Mass. Feb. 11, 1999) (magistrate's recommended decision) (negligence in repairing leaky soft drink cooler, which caused plaintiff to slip and fall, not a UDAP violation).

Add to text after sentence containing note 24:

Alleging specific facts that meet the jurisdiction's standard for unfairness or deception will help withstand a motion to dismiss.

Addition to note 25.

25   Earls v. Condor Capital Corp., 2001 Conn. Super. LEXIS 2595 (Conn. Super. Ct. Aug. 30, 2001) (misrepresentation that vehicle had been repaired pursuant to warranty); Perkins v. Stapleton Buick-GMC Truck, Inc., 2001 Ohio App. LEXIS 2651 (Ohio Ct. App. June 15, 2001) (misrepresentation that repairs had been made when they had not been successful).

Replace NCLC citation in subsection's last sentence with:

National Consumer Law Center, *Unfair and Deceptive Acts and Practices* §§ 5.2.5, 5.3 (5th ed. 2001 and Supp.)

11.1.4 Unfair and Deceptive Conduct After Warranty Breach

Addition to note 29.

29   *Add to Jones citation*: *aff'd on other grounds*, 1986 Ohio App. LEXIS 6904 (Ohio Ct. App. May 22, 1986).

Add to text after sentence containing note 31:

It is a UDAP violation for a bank to refuse to acknowledge its liability under the FTC Holder Rule after the buyer revokes acceptance.[31.1]

31.1   Ford Motor Co. v. Mayes, 575 S.W.2d 480 (Ky. Ct. App. 1978) (manufacturer's policy of refusing to acknowledge revocation of acceptance even when vehicle could not be repaired was unfair practice under state UDAP statute); Jaramillo v. Gonzales, 50 P.3d 554 (N.M. Ct. App. 2002); *see also* Mich. Comp. Laws § 445.903(1)(u) (defining UDAP violations to include failing to make prompt refund after consumer has rescinded, canceled, or terminated a contract in accord with an agreement, advertisement, representation, or provision of law).

Replace note 32 with:

32   *See* National Consumer Law Center, Unfair and Deceptive Acts and Practices § 4.9.3 (5th ed. 2001 and Supp.). *But see* Churchill Vill., L.L.C. v. Gen. Elec. Co., 169 F. Supp. 2d 1119 (N.D. Cal. 2000) (denying preliminary injunction to force manufacturer to repair defects in dishwashers rather than offering rebate coupon for replacement).

Replace NCLC citation in subsection's last sentence with:

Unfair and Deceptive Acts and Practices § 5.3 (5th ed. 2001 and Supp.)

Page 414

11.1.5 Defective Product as a UDAP Violation

Replace note 34 with:

34 *See* § 5.15.2, *supra*; National Consumer Law Center, Unfair and Deceptive Acts and Practices § 4.9.3 (5th ed. 2001 and Supp.).

Add to text at end of subsection's first paragraph:

Egregiously poor construction work may be a UDAP violation.[34.1]

34.1 Budner v. Lake Erie Homes, 2001 Ohio App. LEXIS 4446 (Ohio Ct. App. Sept. 28, 2001).

Addition to notes 35, 37.

35 Delahunt v. Cytodyne Technologies, 241 F. Supp. 2d 827 (S.D. Ohio 2003) (failure to warn buyers of danger is UDAP violation, even as to buyers who suffered no damages other than paying purchase price); Check v. Clifford Chrysler-Plymouth, 342 Ill. App. 3d 150, 794 N.E.2d 829 (2003) (making substandard repairs and then selling vehicle as new without inspecting the repairs); Lipinski v. Martin J. Kelly Oldsmobile, Inc., 325 Ill. App. 3d 1139, 259 Ill. Dec. 586, 759 N.E.2d 66 (2001).

37 *But cf.* Lambert v. Downtown Garage, Inc., 262 Va. 707, 553 S.E.2d 714 (2001) (seller did not commit UDAP violation by failing to disclose defects when seller was unaware of specific defects and buyer knew of wreck damage).

11.1.6 Misrepresentations re Warranties

Replace note 40 with:

40 National Consumer Law Center, Unfair and Deceptive Acts and Practices § 5.2.8 (5th ed. 2001 and Supp.).

Addition to notes 41, 44, 47.

41 *See also* Rose v. Kemp Ford, 2003 WL 21495081 (Cal. Ct. App. June 30, 2003) (unpublished) (misrepresentation that vehicle was still under manufacturer's warranty); Garcia v. Overland Bond & Inv. Co., 282 Ill. App. 3d 486, 668 N.E.2d 199 (1996) (deceptive to misrepresent availability of warranties); Forton v. Laszar, 239 Mich. App. 711, 609 N.W.2d 850 (2000) (builder violated UDAP statute by representing that he would build home according to blueprints and then failing to do so).

44 *But see* Tufts v. Newmar Corp., 53 F. Supp. 2d 1171 (D. Kan. 1999) (not a UDAP violation to include disclaimer in Kansas contract when it clearly stated that it did not apply in states that prohibited it).

Page 415

47 Roelle v. Orkin Exterminating Co., 2000 Ohio App. LEXIS 5141 (Ohio Ct. App. Nov. 7, 2000) (termite retreatment guarantee); *see also* Vincent v. Safeco Ins. Co., 136 Idaho 107, 29 P.3d 943 (Idaho 2001) (insurance policy that provides no coverage or extremely minimal coverage is illusory and void).

Add to text at end of subsection's third paragraph:

Another deceptive tactic is to start the warranty period running prior to the actual sale to the buyer. An earlier sale may have been reported to the manufacturer but then the buyer backed out of the deal, or the dealership may be attempting to inflate its sales figures by prematurely reporting cars as sold.

Replace note 49 with:

49 Lawhorn v. Joseph Toyota, Inc., 141 Ohio App. 3d 153, 750 N.E.2d 610 (2001); *see also* National Consumer Law Center, Unfair and Deceptive Acts and Practices §§ 4.2.12, 5.2.9 (5th ed. 2001 and Supp.).

Addition to note 52.

52 *See also* Lawhorn v. Joseph Toyota, Inc., 141 Ohio App. 3d 153, 750 N.E.2d 610 (2001) (parties conceded that Magnuson-Moss violation would be UDAP violation).

Replace note 53 with:

53 National Consumer Law Center, Unfair and Deceptive Acts and Practices § 5.2.8 (5th ed. 2001 and Supp.).

Replace note 56 with:

56 Brooks v. Midas-Int'l Corp., 47 Ill. App. 3d 266, 361 N.E.2d 815, 5 Ill. Dec. 492 (1977); Conn. Agencies Regs. §§ 42-110b-1 to 42-110b-8 (Representations of Guarantees); Mass. Regs. Code tit. 940, § 3.3 (Deceptive Advertising of Guarantees); *see also* Oakwood Mobile Homes, Inc. v. Cabler, 73 S.W.3d 363 (Tex. App. 2002) (promising repairs but failing to disclose that warranty only covered certain types of problems is deceptive). *But cf.* Testan v. Carlsen Motor Cars, Inc., 2002 Cal. App. Unpub. LEXIS 1837 (Cal. Ct. App. Feb. 19, 2002) (unpublished) (failure to disclose parts not covered by warranty not a UDAP violation when warranty clearly listed the parts that were covered).

The FTC Guides for Advertising of Warranties and Guarantees, 16 C.F.R. § 239.2, require advertisers that mention a warranty to disclose that buyers can view the warranty at the store. This rule only applies to written warranties as defined by the Magnuson-Moss Act, however. *See* § 16 C.F.R. § 239.1. *See generally* § 2.2.5, *supra*.

Replace note 60 with:

60 16 C.F.R. § 239.5 (FTC Guides for the Advertising of Warranties and Guarantees); Conn. Agencies Regs. §§ 42-110b-1 to 42-110b-8 (Representations of Guarantees); Mass. Regs. Code tit. 940, § 3.3 (Deceptive Advertising of Guarantees); *accord* Earls v. Condor Capital Corp., 2001 Conn. Super. LEXIS 2595 (Conn. Super. Ct. Aug. 30, 2001) (misrepresentation that vehicle had been repaired pursuant to warranty); Oakwood Mobile Homes, Inc. v. Cabler, 73 S.W.3d 363 (Tex. App. 2002); Tiger Direct, Inc., 1999 FTC

LEXIS 175 (Fed. Trade Comm'n Nov. 4, 1999) (consent order) (advertising on-site warranty service but not providing it promptly or in all circumstances); Gateway 2000, Inc., 1998 FTC LEXIS 135 (Fed. Trade Comm'n Dec. 22, 1998) (consent order) (advertising on-site warranty service but not providing it in all circumstances); *cf.* Commodore Corp., 85 F.T.C. 472 (Fed. Trade Comm'n 1975) (consent order); Fleetwood Enterprises, 85 F.T.C. 414 (Fed. Trade Comm'n 1975) (consent order); Redman Indus. Inc., 85 F.T.C. 309 (Fed. Trade Comm'n 1975) (consent order); Skyline Corp., 85 F.T.C. 444 (Fed. Trade Comm'n 1975) (consent order). These last four cases involved mobile home manufacturers' failure to perform their warranty obligations. The consent orders in these four cases were vacated by the Federal Trade Commission, 110 F.T.C. 636 (Fed. Trade Comm'n 1988), after the National Manufactured Housing Construction and Safety Standards Act was adopted.

Page 416

Addition to notes 61, 62.

61   *Add after Woods citation*: *But cf. In re* Ford Motor Co. Ignition Switch Prods. Liab. Litig., 1999 U.S. Dist. LEXIS 22892 (D.N.J. May 14, 1999) (manufacturer's express warranty was not a representation that vehicle was defect-free but only a promise to repair or replace if defects arose), *vacated in part on other grounds*, 1999 U.S. Dist. LEXIS 22891 (D.N.J. July 27, 1999).

62   Garcia v. Overland Bond & Inv. Co., 282 Ill. App. 3d 486, 668 N.E.2d 199 (1996).

Add to text at end of subsection:

Regardless of whether it amounts to a UDAP violation, if the parties are under a misapprehension about the existence or scope of a warranty, the buyer may be able to rescind the contract on grounds of mistake.[64.1]

64.1   *See, e.g.*, Bernal v. Long, 836 So. 2d 516 (La. Ct. App. 2002). *See generally* National Consumer Law Center, Automobile Fraud § 8.3 (2d ed. 2003).

Add new subsections to text after § 11.1.6.

11.1.7 Misrepresentation of Condition of Product

If the seller's assurances regarding the condition of a product are false they are UDAP violations.[64.2] They are violations even if the seller's statements do not amount to express warranties because of the parol evidence rule,[64.3] or if the contract contains an "as is" or similar clause.[64.4]

11.1.8 Violation of Other Warranty Statute

Substantial authority holds that a violation of another consumer protection statute is a UDAP violation.[64.5] Using this theory consumers have successfully argued that a violation of the Magnuson-Moss Act[64.6] or the FTC Used Car Rule[64.7] entitles the consumer to UDAP remedies. Similarly, a violation of a state vehicle title law,[64.8] an inspection law, a state warranty law,[64.9] or a dealer licensing statute should be a UDAP violation.

64.2   Delahunt v. Cytodyne Technologies, 241 F. Supp. 2d 827 (S.D. Ohio 2003); Loughridge v. Goodyear Tire & Rubber Co., 192 F. Supp. 2d 1175, 1185, 1186 (D. Colo. 2002); Rose v. Kemp Ford, 2003 WL 21495081 (Cal. Ct. App. June 30, 2003) (unpublished) (false statement that truck was in good working order was UDAP violation); Shannon v. Boise Cascade, 336 Ill. App. 3d 533, 783 N.E.2d 1105 (2003), *leave to appeal granted*, 792 N.E.2d 314 (Ill. 2003) (table); Howard v. Norman's Auto Sales, 2003 WL 21267261 (Ohio Ct. App. June 3, 2003); Oppenheimer v. York Int'l, 2002 WL 31409949 (Pa. C.P. Oct. 25, 2002); Oakwood Mobile Homes, Inc. v. Cabler, 73 S.W.3d 363 (Tex. App. 2002); *see also* People *ex rel.* Spitzer v. Gen. Elec. Co., 302 A.D.2d 314, 756 N.Y.S.2d 520 (2003) (misrepresentation that appliances were not repairable). *See generally* National Consumer Law Center, Unfair and Deceptive Acts and Practices § 5.4.6.8 (5th ed. 2001 and Supp.).

64.3   *See* National Consumer Law Center, Unfair and Deceptive Acts and Practices § 4.2.15.2 (5th ed. 2001 and Supp.).

64.4   *See. e.g.*, Attaway v. Tom's Auto Sales, Inc., 144 Ga. App. 813, 242 S.E.2d 740 (1978); Gaidon v. Guardian Life Ins. Co., 94 N.Y.2d 330, 704 N.Y.S.2d 177, 725 N.E.2d 598 (1999); Oakwood Mobile Homes, Inc. v. Cabler, 73 S.W.3d 363 (Tex. App. 2002). *See generally* §§ 5.15.2, 11.1.1.2, *supra*; National Consumer Law Center, Unfair and Deceptive Acts and Practices §§ 4.2.15.3, 4.2.15.5 (5th ed. 2001 and Supp.).

64.5   *See* National Consumer Law Center, Unfair and Deceptive Acts and Practices § 3.2.7 (5th ed. 2001 and Supp.).

64.6   Fed. Trade Comm'n v. Va. Homes Mfg. Corp., 509 F. Supp. 51 (D. Md. 1981); Buskirk v. Harrell, 2000 Ohio App. LEXIS 3100 (Ohio Ct. App. June 28, 2000) (failure to post window sticker required by used car rule); Brown v. P.A. Days, Inc., Clearinghouse No. 54,572 (Ohio C.P. Aug. 27, 2002); Brown v. Spears, 1979 WL 52451 (Ohio Mun. Ct. Aug. 20, 1979) (failure to designate warranty as full or limited in violation of Magnuson-Moss Act is UDAP violation); *see also* Haun v. Don Mealy Imports, Inc., 285 F. Supp. 2d 1297 (M.D. Fla. 2003) (noting that Florida Deceptive and Unfair Trade Practices Act defines a Magnuson-Moss violation as an unfair or deceptive act, but dismissing claim on other grounds). *But see* Sharpe v. Gen. Motors Corp., 198 Ga. App. 313, 401 S.E.2d 328 (1991).

64.7   *See* § 14.7.8, *infra.*

64.8   *See* National Consumer Law Center, Automobile Fraud § 6.2.3 (2d ed. 2003).

64.9   *See* §§ 14.8 (used car lemon laws), 14.9 (other minimum statutory standards for used cars), 15.4.2 (state mobile home warranty laws), *infra. But cf.* State *ex rel.* Stovall v. DVM Enterprises, Inc., 275 Kan. 243, 62 P.3d 653 (2003) (seeking waiver of implied warranties, which is ineffective under state law, is not a UDAP violation in and of itself but is one factor to be considered in determining unconscionability).

11.2 UCC Unconscionability

11.2.1 Introduction and Scope

Replace note 66 with:

66   Discussed in National Consumer Law Center, Unfair and Deceptive Acts and Practices § 4.4 (5th ed. 2001 and Supp.).

Page 417

Add note 68.1 after "section 1-201(11)" in subsection's second paragraph.

68.1   Revised Article 1, approved by the National Conference of Commissioners on Uniform State Laws (NCCUSL) in 2001 for adoption by the states, redesignates this provision as U.C.C. § 1-201(b)(12).

Add to text at end of subsection:

There is also a common law doctrine of unconscionability that the court may be willing to apply to contracts for services.[74.1]

74.1   *See, e.g.,* Children's Surgical Found., Inc. v. Nat'l Data Corp., 121 F. Supp. 2d 1221 (N.D. Ill. 2000) (Tex. law); Roossinck v. Orkin Exterminating Co., 1998 U.S. Dist. LEXIS 7161 (W.D. Mich. Apr. 24, 1998) (remedy limitation clause not unconscionable); *see also* National Consumer Law Center, The Cost of Credit: Regulation and Legal Challenges § 11.7 (2d ed. 2000 and Supp.).

11.2.2 Unconscionability Is a Question of Law for the Court; Hearing Requirement

Replace note 76 with:

76   National Consumer Law Center, Unfair and Deceptive Acts and Practices § 7.10.2 (5th ed. 2001 and Supp.).

11.2.4 Standards for Determining Unconscionability

11.2.4.4 Substantive Unconscionability

Page 423

11.2.4.4.2 Creditor's remedies

Replace note 119 with:

119   These cases are quite similar to unfair practices decisions. *See* National Consumer Law Center, Unfair and Deceptive Acts and Practices § 5.1.3 (5th ed. 2001 and Supp.).

Page 424

11.2.4.4.3 Penalty clauses

Addition to notes 128, 133.

128   *Add to Honey Dew citation*: *vacated on other grounds*, 241 F.3d 23 (1st Cir. 2001) (remanding because trial court should have allocated burden of proof to party challenging the clause).

133   *Replace NCLC citation with*: National Consumer Law Center, Repossessions and Foreclosures § 14.2 (5th ed. 2002 and Supp.) (detailed analysis of challenges to early lease termination charges).

11.2.4.4.4 Excessive price

Addition to notes 134, 135.

134   *Replace NCLC citation with*: National Consumer Law Center, Unfair and Deceptive Acts and Practices § 4.4.5 (5th ed. 2001 and Supp.).

Page 425

135   *Replace NCLC UDAP citation with*: National Consumer Law Center, Unfair and Deceptive Acts and Practices § 4.4.4 (5th ed. 2001 and Supp.).

Page 426

11.2.5 Unconscionability of Warranty Disclaimers

Replace note 147 with:

147   Revised Article 1, approved by the National Conference of Commissioners on Uniform State Laws (NCCUSL) in 2001 for adoption by the states, redesignates the good faith requirement as U.C.C. § 1-304 without substantive change. It expands the definition of good faith, however, to include not only honesty in fact but also the observance of reasonable commercial standards of fair dealing, regardless of whether the actor is a merchant. Revised U.C.C. § 1-201(b)(20); *see* §§ 5.12, 5.13, *supra*.

Page 427

11.2.6 Unconscionability of Limitations of Remedies Clauses

Replace subsection's last sentence with:

The application of the unconscionability doctrine to remedy limitation clauses is discussed more fully in § 9.6, *supra*.

11.2.8 Remedies for Unconscionable Clauses

Page 430

11.2.8.4 Availability of Monetary Damages

Add note 177.1 after "Section 1-106(1)" in subsection's final paragraph.

177.1   Revised Article 1, which the National Conference of Commissioners on Uniform State Laws (NCCUSL) approved in 2001 for adoption by the states, redesignates this provision as U.C.C. § 1-305 without substantive change.

11.3 Good Faith Obligation

11.3.1 General

Add note 180.1 at end of first sentence of subsection's second paragraph.

180.1   Revised Article 1, approved by NCCUSL in 2001 for adoption by the states, redesignates this provision as U.C.C. § 1-304 and clarifies that it applies to "performance *and* enforcement."

Add to text at end of subsection's second paragraph:

Louisiana, although it has not adopted UCC Article 2, has a doctrine that a seller who knows of defects in the items sold but fails to disclose them is a bad faith seller, and is liable for the return of the price, with interest, plus damages akin to incidental and consequential damages, as well as attorney fees.[181.1] Good faith is a question of fact for the jury.[181.2]

Revised Article 1, approved by the National Conference of Commissioners on Uniform State Laws (NCCUSL) in 2001 for adoption by the states, expands the definition of good faith to include not only honesty in fact but also the observance of reasonable commercial standards of fair dealing.[181.3] In its current form, Article 2 defines the duty of good faith to include reasonable commercial standards of fair dealing only if the party is a merchant.[181.4]

181.1   *See* Morrison v. Allstar Dodge, Inc., 792 So. 2d 9 (La. Ct. App. 2001).

181.2   Schawk, Inc. v. Donruss Trading Cards, Inc., 319 Ill. App. 3d 640, 746 N.E.2d 18, 43 U.C.C. Rep. Serv. 2d 1109 (2001).

181.3   Revised U.C.C. § 1-201(b)(20). A conforming amendment to U.C.C. § 2-103 deletes the existing more limited definition of "good faith."

181.4   U.C.C. § 2-103(1)(b); *see* § 11.3.2, *infra*. Revised Article 2, which the National Conference of Commissioners on Uniform State Laws and the American Law Institute approved in 2003 for consideration by state legislatures, incorporates the expanded definition of good faith into revised U.C.C. § 2-103(1)(j).

Add note 181.5 at end of subsection.

181.5   This comment has been deleted in revised U.C.C. § 1-304, which is the good faith provision in revised Article 1, approved by NCCUSL in 2001 for adoption by the states.

Page 431

11.3.2 Merchants Must Meet Higher Standard of Conduct

Addition to notes 184, 188.

184 *See also* Emerson Radio Corp. v. Orion Sales, Inc., 253 F.3d 159, 44 U.C.C. Rep. Serv. 2d 681 (3d Cir. 2001) (mere compliance with terms of contract is insufficient; common law case). *But see* W. A. Butler Co. v. Colgate-Palmolive Co., 44 U.C.C. Rep. Serv. 2d 704 (E.D. Pa. 1992) (duty of good faith does not require departure from express terms of contract).

188 *But cf.* Rawson v. Conover, 20 P.3d 876, 44 U.C.C. Rep. Serv. 2d 420 (Utah 2001) (no violation of duty of good faith when seller disclosed that van was salvage and was being sold as is).

Add to text at end of subsection:

Revised Article 1, approved by the National Conference of Commissioners on Uniform State Laws (NCCUSL) in 2001 for adoption by the states, eliminates the distinction between merchants and other parties. It defines "good faith," for purposes of all of the Uniform Commercial Code except Article 5, as "honesty in fact and the observance of reasonable commercial standards of fair dealing."[188.1] A companion amendment deletes the inconsistent definition of "good faith" from Article 2. NCCUSL has also now finalized a revised version of Article 2 that reinstates a definition of "good faith"—a definition identical to the expanded Article 1 definition.[188.2]

188.1 Revised U.C.C. § 1-201(b)(2). As of early 2004, revised Article 1 had been adopted by Texas, Virginia, and the Virgin Islands, and was under consideration by several states.

188.2 Revised U.C.C. § 2-103(1)(j), approved by NCCUSL in 2003 for consideration by state legislatures.

11.3.3 Good Faith Applies to Conduct Initiating the Sale and to Contract Terms

Addition to note 189.

189 *See, e.g.,* Race v. Fleetwood Retail Corp., 50 U.C.C. Rep. Serv. 2d 363 (Wash. Ct. App. 2003) (unpublished) (mobile home seller breached duty of good faith by failing to disclose likelihood of problems in obtaining permits for site it arranged for consumer to buy).

Page 432

11.3.4 Common Law Duty of Good Faith

Addition to note 194.

194 *See* Emerson Radio Corp. v. Orion Sales, Inc., 253 F.3d 159, 44 U.C.C. Rep. Serv. 2d 681 (3d Cir. 2001) (adopting U.C.C. definition in common law case).

11.3.5 Remedies for Seller's Lack of Good Faith

Addition to notes 196, 197.

196 Wortley v. Camplin, 333 F.3d 284, 50 U.C.C. Rep. Serv. 2d 1178 (1st Cir. 2003) (Me. law) (does not create independent cause of action or obligation conceptually separate from underlying agreement); Marland v. Safeway, Inc., 49 U.C.C. Rep. Serv. 2d 817 (4th Cir. 2003) (unpublished) (Md. law) (no independent cause of action for violation of duty of good faith); Watson v. Damon Corp., 2002 WL 32059736 (W.D. Mich. Dec. 17, 2002); John Wood Group USA, Inc. v. ICO, Inc., 26 S.W.3d 12 (Tex. App. 2000) (breach of duty of good faith gives rise to cause of action only if tied to a specific contractual duty); *see also* New Pac. Overseas Group v. Excal Int'l Dev. Corp., 43 U.C.C. Rep. Serv. 2d 1149 (S.D.N.Y. 2001) (party is limited to contract damages for breach of duty of good faith unless defendant's conduct violates fundamental public policy); *cf.* Xuchang Rihetai Human Hair Goods Co. v. Hanyu Int'l, 45 U.C.C. Rep. Serv. 2d 1077 (S.D.N.Y. 2001) (no claim for breach of duty of good faith when such a claim would just duplicate a contract claim).

197 *See also* Race v. Fleetwood Retail Corp., 50 U.C.C. Rep. Serv. 2d 363 (Wash. Ct. App. 2003) (affirming judgment against seller for violating U.C.C. duty of good faith); *cf.* Xuchang Rihetai Human Hair Goods Co. v. Hanyu Int'l, 45 U.C.C. Rep. Serv. 2d 1077 (S.D.N.Y. 2001) (no claim for breach of duty of good faith when such a claim would just duplicate a contract claim; implies that cause of action might be available in absence of duplication).

Page 433

Replace note 198 with:

198 U.C.C. § 1-106 [*redesignated as U.C.C. § 1-305(b) by revised Article 1, which the National Conference of Commissioners on Uniform State Laws (NCCUSL) approved in 2001 for adoption by the states*].

Add note 198.1 at end of sentence following sentence containing note 198.	198.1 Revised Article 1, which NCCUSL approved in 2001 for adoption by the states, redesignates U.C.C. § 1-106(2) as U.C.C. § 1-305(b) without substantive change.
Add note 200.1 at end of first sentence of subsection's third paragraph.	200.1 The amended comment has been carried over into revised U.C.C. § 1-304 cmt. 1, part of revised Article 1, which NCCUSL approved in 2001 for adoption by the states.
Addition to notes 201, 202.	201 *Delete "review granted" portion of Best Dist. Co. citation.*
	202 *Replace Northview Motors citation with*: 227 F.3d 78 (3d Cir. 2000); *add to Sauer citation*: *aff'd*, 2001 U.S. App. LEXIS 3833 (2d Cir. 2001); *add*: Caudill Seed & Warehouse Co. v. Prophet 21, Inc., 126 F. Supp. 2d 937, 43 U.C.C. Rep. Serv. 2d 848 (E.D. Pa. 2001) (following *Northview Motors*).

Add to text at end of subsection:

Breach of the duty of good faith can also be actionable as a UDAP violation.[204.1]

204.1   Anthony's Pier Four v. HBC Assocs., 411 Mass. 451, 583 N.E.2d 806 (1991); Marx v. Globe Newspaper Co., 13 Mass. L. Rptr. 190, 43 U.C.C. Rep. Serv. 2d 812 (Super. Ct. 2001).

11.4 Common Law Deceit, Misrepresentation, and Fraud

11.4.1 Relevance to Warranty Cases

Page 434

Addition to notes 211–214.

211   *See* Bickerstaff Auto., Inc. v. Tsepas, 574 S.E.2d 322 (Ga. Ct. App. 2002) (affirming punitive damage award against dealer that did not disclose new car's pre-sale collision damage); Christopher v. Larson Ford Sales, Inc., 557 P.2d 1009 (Utah 1976).

212   *See* Underwood v. Monte Asti Buick Co., 73 Pa. D. & C.2d 773, 20 U.C.C. Rep. Serv. 657 (C.P. Allegheny County 1976).

213   *Add to Ramada Franchise Sys. citation*: *judgment entered*, 2000 U.S. Dist. LEXIS 3511 (D. Kan. Mar. 10, 2000); *replace LEXIS citation to the Alabama Supreme Court decision in Platt with*: 774 So. 2d 592 (Ala. 2000); *add to Wanetick citation*: *rev'd in part, aff'd in part on other grounds*, 163 N.J. 484, 750 A.2d 79 (2000); *add*: Sagent Tech., Inc. v. Micros Sys., Inc., 276 F. Supp. 2d 464, 51 U.C.C. Rep. Serv. 2d 59 (D. Md. 2003) (would have been admissible if fraudulent intent had been shown) CBS Personnel Services, Ltd. Liab. Co. v. Canadian Am. Transp., Inc., 2003 WL 22669236, at *5 (S.D. Ohio Oct. 11, 2003) (fraud in the inducement claim); J.C. Whitney & Co. v. Renaissance Software Corp., 2000 U.S. Dist. LEXIS 6180 (N.D. Ill. Apr. 19, 2000) (commercial case; party can be found to have relied on precontractual oral misrepresentations despite integration clause), *aff'd in relevant part, rev'd in part on other grounds*, 98 F. Supp. 2d 981 (N.D. Ill. 2000); Pac. State Bank v. Greene, 110 Cal. App. 4th 375, 396, 1 Cal. Rptr. 3d 739, 755, 756 (2003) (evidence of promise directly at variance with promise in the contract is not admissible under fraud exception to parol evidence rule, but evidence of misrepresentation of fact about the content of the document is admissible); Harold Cohn & Co. v. Harco Int'l, Ltd. Liab. Co., 72 Conn. App. 43, 804 A.2d 218 (2002); Lindberg v. Roseth, 46 P.3d 518 (Idaho 2002) (plaintiffs could use parol evidence to show that vendor's fraud induced real estate contract); Culinary Connection Holdings, Inc. v. Culinary Connection of Great Neck, Inc., 2003 WL 22799781, at *1 (N.Y. App. Div. Nov. 24, 2003); Gizzi v. Hall, 300 A.D.2d 879, 754 N.Y.S.2d 373 (2002) (general merger clause did not preclude use of parol evidence in fraud claim); Redwend Ltd. P'ship v. Edwards, 354 S.C. 459, 472, 581 S.E.2d 496, 503 (S.C. Ct. App. 2003) (neither parol evidence rule nor merger and integration clause barred evidence of negligent misrepresentation); Packard Norfolk, Inc. v. Miller, 198 Va. 557, 95 S.E.2d 207 (1956); *cf.* Outdoor Recreation Group v. Crymson Co., 2000 U.S. App. LEXIS 28092, at *3 (9th Cir. Nov. 9, 2000) (unpublished) (fraud exception to parol evidence rule allows evidence of those misrepresentations that do not contradict the terms of the agreement); Wang v. Massey Chevrolet, 118 Cal. Rptr. 2d 770, 781, 782 (Cal. Ct. App. 2002) (fraud exception to parol evidence rule permits evidence only of those statements that are independent of, or consistent with, the integrated agreement, and not those that contradict the agreement; thus salesman's false answers to car lessees' specific questions regarding the terms of the lease would be allowed into evidence only for lease which did not have terms that contradicted the salesman's representations); Francis v. Stinson, 2000 ME 173, 760 A.2d 209, 218 (2000) (parol evidence of fraud may not clearly contradict the terms of the contract). *But see* Winters v. Inv. Sav. Plan, 174 F. Supp. 2d 259 (E.D. Pa. 2001) (parol evidence rule bars claims of fraud in the inducement, allows only claims of fraud in the execution).

Page 435

214   *Add to Peerless Wall & Window citation*: *aff'd*, 234 F.3d 1265 (3d Cir. 2000); *add*: Cummins v. Bickel & Brewer, 2001 U.S. Dist. LEXIS 12738, at *3 (N.D. Ill. Aug. 16, 2001); Gershberg v. Kean, 2002 WL 1489532 (Conn. Super. Ct. June 10, 2002) (clause providing that buyer had inspected the premises and was satisfied with their condition did not preclude buyer's claim of innocent misrepresentation based on defects that were unknown to buyer at purchase); Syvrud v. Today Real Estate, Inc., 2003 WL 22459124, at *4, *5 (Fla. Dist. Ct. App. Oct. 31, 2003) (clause in purchase contract that seller and broker made no

representations about the property functioned as equivalent of an "as is" clause and did not alleviate their duty to disclose latent defects to the buyer); Greenfield v. Heckenbach, 797 A.2d 63, 79, 80 (Md. Ct. Spec. App. 2002); Billingham v. Dornemann, 771 N.E.2d 166, 173 (Mass. App. Ct. 2002); Stephan v. Kahler, 2001 WL 1699435 (Mich. Ct. App. Dec. 28, 2001) ("as is" clause did not defeat plaintiff's innocent misrepresentation claim); Artilla Cove Resort, Inc. v. Hartley, 72 S.W.3d 291, 299 (Mo. Ct. App. 2002) (disclaimer clause did not bar misrepresentation action against sellers who failed to disclose foundation damage of which they knew); Culinary Connection Holdings, Inc. v. Culinary Connection of Great Neck, Inc., 2003 WL 22799781, at *1 (N.Y. App. Div. Nov. 24, 2003); Harrel v. Solt, 2000 Ohio App. LEXIS 6312, at *28 (Ohio Ct. App. Dec. 23, 2000); Redwend Ltd. P'ship v. Edwards, 354 S.C. 459, 472, 581 S.E.2d 496, 503 (S.C. Ct. App. 2003) (neither parol evidence rule nor merger and integration clause barred evidence of negligent misrepresentation); Oakwood Mobile Homes, Inc. v. Cabler, 73 S.W.3d 363, 371 (Tex. App. 2002) (seller who induces contract by fraud can not rely on "as is" clause); *see also* Catrett v. Landmark Dodge, Inc. 560 S.E.2d 101, 104 (Ga. Ct. App. 2002) (when buyer elects to rescind rather than affirm purchase contract, merger clause will not defeat fraud claim); *see also* Werremeyer v. K.C. Auto Salvage, Co., 2003 WL 21487311, at *4 (Mo. Ct. App. June 30, 2003) ("as is" clause not a defense when contract induced by fraud), *transferred to Missouri Supreme Court* (Oct. 28, 2003); Logue v. Flanagan, 584 S.E.2d 186, 188–191 (W. Va. 2003) (*per curiam*) ("as is" clause in contract for sale of land did not bar plaintiff's fraud action based on seller's failure to disclose septic system problems); *cf.* Yahner v. Kerlin, 2003 WL 21714917, at *4 (Ohio Ct. App. July 24, 2003) ("as is" clause protects property seller from liability for non-disclosure but not for affirmative misrepresentation). *But see* Solieri v. Polletta, 2002 WL 450073, at *6 (Conn. Super. Ct. Mar. 8, 2002) (disclaimer clause precluded innocent misrepresentation action); Fann v. Mills, 248 Ga. App. 460, 546 S.E.2d 853, 857 (2001) (buyer who chooses to affirm the contract and sue for fraud rather than rescind is bound by terms of contract, including any merger clause, but buyer may nonetheless assert fraud claim because seller suppressed unfavorable termite report despite contract clause requiring seller to provide termite report); Sound Techniques, Inc. v. Hoffman, 50 Mass. App. Ct. 425, 737 N.E.2d 920, 926 (2000) (parol evidence of fraud not allowed to show negligent misrepresentation when agreement contained a merger clause); Ringstreet Northcrest, Inc. v. Bisanz, 890 S.W.2d 713, 722, 723 (Mo. Ct. App. 1995) ("as is" clause barred plaintiff's claim against sellers of apartment complex who failed to fully disclose pipe freezing problems); Malach v. Chuang, 194 Misc. 2d 651, 661, 754 N.Y.S.2d 835, 843 (Civ. Ct. 2002) (representations made in statutorily-required disclosure form merged into the contract pursuant to the merger and integration clause and accordingly home buyers could not base their misrepresentation action on them); Tovar v. Trust, 2002 WL 253838, at *5 (Tex. App. Feb. 21, 2002) ("as is" clause barred purchaser's claim based on substantial fire damage that home had incurred prior to purchase); *cf.* Chleborowicz v. Johnson, 584 S.E.2d 108 (N.C. Ct. App. 2003) (table) (text available at 2003 WL 21961386) (enforcing merger and integration clause in contract for sale of boat when buyer could not show that seller made any affirmative representation or concealed any fact about the boat); Bynum v. Prudential Residential Services, Ltd. P'ship, 2003 WL 22456111, at *4, *5 (Tex. App. Oct. 30, 2003) (holding that "as is" clause barred buyers from recovering for fraudulent misrepresentation when buyers could not show the defendants knew that their representation that remodeling work was done with proper permits was false).

Add to text after sentence containing note 214:

The degree of specificity of the clause, and the extent to which it specifically refers to certain types of claims, may affect its potential to bar fraud claims. Broad, boilerplate clauses that use expansive language are less likely to be given effect than clauses that are more straightforward. Merger and integration clauses also relate to the element of the buyer's justifiable reliance, which is discussed in § 11.4.4a, *infra*.[214.1]

214.1   *See also* National Consumer Law Center, Automobile Fraud § 7.6 (2d ed. 2003).

Replace "These" in sentence containing note 215 with:

Fraud

Add to text following sentence containing note 215:

In many jurisdictions, a fraud claim may not be defeated by an as is clause or other disclaimer in the language of the contract.[215.1] These courts reason that, although parties can agree to allocate the risk of unknown defects, a seller who actually knows of a defect should not be able to shield himself from his failure to disclose the defect.[215.2] Other jurisdictions enforce disclaimers, even in the face of a fraud claim.[215.3] The degree of specificity of the exculpatory language may determine whether the fraud claim may withstand the clause,[215.4] as may the relative bargaining position of the parties.[215.5]

215.1   Xiangyuan Zhu v. Countrywide Realty, Co., 165 F. Supp. 2d 1181, 1204 (D. Kan. 2001) (plaintiff who purchased home "as is" still had a fraud claim if listing agent made misrepresentations in order to induce her to sign the contract); S Dev. Co. v. Pima Capital Mgmt. Co., 31 P.3d 123, 126, 128 (Ariz. Ct. App. 2001) (vendor must disclose known latent defects to the purchaser notwithstanding as is clause, which precludes breach of warranty claims, not tort claims; vendor who precludes buyer from discovering defects may be liable for negligent nondisclosure); White v. J.D. Reece Co., 29 Kan. App. 2d 226, 26 P.3d 701, 706 (2001) (selling broker who took over course of repairs to be made to property had "inserted" himself into the buyer's investigation of the property and could not rely on disclaimer in seller's disclosure statement to preclude negligent misrepresentation action); Billingham v. Dornemann, 771 N.E.2d 166, 173 (Mass. App. Ct. 2002); Stephan v. Kahler, 2001 WL 1699435 (Mich. Ct. App. Dec. 28, 2001) ("as is" clause did not defeat plaintiff's innocent misrepresentation claim); Artilla Cove Resort, Inc. v. Hartley, 72 S.W.3d 291, 299 (Mo. Ct. App. 2002) (disclaimer clause did not bar misrepresentation action against sellers who failed to disclose foundation damage of which they knew); Oakwood Mobile Homes, Inc. v. Cabler, 73 S.W.3d 363, 371 (Tex. App. 2002) (seller who induces contract by fraud can not rely on "as is" clause).

215.2   S Dev. Co. v. Pima Capital Mgmt. Co., 31 P.3d 123, 129 n.4 (Ariz. Ct. App. 2001) (seller owed duty to buyer of building to disclose defective plumbing that could not have reasonably been discovered through inspection).

215.3   Stanley v. Bray Terminals, Inc., 197 F.R.D. 224, 228 (N.D.N.Y. 2000) (when agreement has specific language disclaiming any reliance on oral representations, parol evidence rule will bar showing of either fraud in the inducement or fraud in the execution); Keiser v. Wecker, 2001 Conn. Super. LEXIS 1027, at *7–*9 (Conn. Super. Ct. Apr. 12, 2001) (plaintiffs who not only signed contract that disclaimed representations, but had also conducted their own inspection of septic system in purchased house and put provisions concerning that system in the contract, could not maintain negligent misrepresentation claim against seller); Rader v. Danny Darby Real Estate, Inc., 2001 Tex. App. LEXIS 6198, at *9 (Tex. App. Sept. 10, 2001) (as is clause precluded home buyer's fraud claim when buyer could not substantiate fraudulent inducement because buyer failed to have home inspected despite obvious flaws); Olmsted v. Mulder, 72 Wash. App. 169, 863 P.2d 1355, 1359 (1993) (to be effective, as is clause or disclaimer must be explicitly negotiated or bargained for and must set forth with particularity the qualities and characteristics being disclaimed; handwritten as is clause in real estate contract addendum that did not specify what was being disclaimed did not bar buyer's negligent misrepresentation claim).

215.4   *See, e.g.,* Chicago Printing Co. v. Heidelberg USA, Inc., 2001 U.S. Dist. LEXIS 15331, at *15 (N.D. Ill. Sept. 25, 2001) (when neither as is clause nor disclaimer was sufficiently specific to alert plaintiff to misrepresentations, they did not bar action for deceit).

215.5   *See* Rader v. Danny Darby Real Estate, Inc., 2001 Tex. App. LEXIS 6198, at *14 (Tex. App. Sept. 10, 2001) (though in general the bargaining position of the parties should be considered in determining whether as is clause bars fraud claim, when buyers had clear notice of flaws in house prior to signing the contract, clause would be enforced).

Page 436

11.4.2 Elements of Deceit

Replace note 217 with:

217   *Id.* at 728. The same source contains a detailed analysis of each element of the claim. For a detailed discussion of fraud damages, including analysis of the availability of punitive damages, see National Consumer Law Center, Automobile Fraud §§ 7.9–7.10 (2d ed. 2003).

Add to text at end of subsection:

When pleading deceit, misrepresentation, or fraud, be alert to any special pleading requirements, such as those of Rule 9(b) of the Federal Rules of Civil Procedure which demands that "in all averments of fraud or mistake, the circumstances constituting fraud or mistake shall be stated with particularity."[218.1]

218.1   Fed. R. Civ. P. 9(b). Many state rules duplicate this requirement. *See* National Consumer Law Center, Automobile Fraud § 7.1 (2d ed. 2003). The rule requires the plaintiff to describe the circumstances of the fraud by specifying the time, place, and content of the false representation, the identity of the person making the representation, and the harm caused by the plaintiff's reliance on the representation. *See, e.g.,* Xiangyuan Zhu v. Countrywide Realty, Co., 165 F. Supp. 2d 1181 (D. Kan. 2001) (granting defendants' motion for summary judgment based on plaintiff's failure to comply with Rule 9(b)). However, Rule 9(b) may not apply to allegations of negligent misrepresentation, as opposed to allegations of fraud. Fid. Nat'l Title Ins. Co. v. Intercounty Nat'l Title Ins. Co., 161 F. Supp. 2d 876, 882 (N.D. Ill. 2001).

11.4.3 Where Intent Not Required

11.4.3.1 Negligent Misrepresentation

Add note 220.1 at end of third sentence of subsection's second paragraph.

220.1   Champion Home Builders Co. v. ADT Sec. Services, Inc., 179 F. Supp. 2d 16, 25 (N.D.N.Y. 2001) (elements of negligent misrepresentation claim); Xiangyuan Zhu v. Countrywide Realty, Co., 165 F. Supp. 2d 1181, 1205 (D. Kan. 2001) (tort of negligent misrepresentation only requires proof that defendants failed to exercise reasonable care or competence to obtain or communicate true information); Adams v.

NVR Homes, Inc., 135 F. Supp. 2d 675, 703 (D. Md. 2001) (plaintiff must show that the defendant carelessly made a false statement), *modified in part on other grounds*, 142 F. Supp. 2d 649 (D. Md. 2001); Zanaskis-Pico v. Cutter Dodge, Inc., 47 P.3d 1222, 1234 (Haw. 2002) (elements of negligent misrepresentation claim); *see also* Capiccioni v. Brennan Naperville, Inc., 339 Ill. App. 3d 927, 939, 940, 791 N.E.2d 553, 563, 564 (2003) (property buyers stated negligent misrepresentation claim against broker who misrepresented that home was in "acclaimed" school district).

Addition to notes 221, 222.

221   *See also* Adams v. NVR Homes, Inc., 135 F. Supp. 2d 675, 704 (D. Md. 2001) (claim for negligent misrepresentation could be predicated upon "intimate nexus" that arose between home seller and buyers, denying builder's motion for summary judgment), *modified in part on other grounds*, 142 F. Supp. 2d 649 (D. Md. 2001); Griesi v. Atl. Gen. Hosp. Corp., 360 Md. 1, 756 A.2d 548, 554 (2000) (to demonstrate duty of care in negligent misrepresentation claim, plaintiff must show an "intimate nexus" between plaintiff and defendant; relevant factors include whether the defendant knew that plaintiff intended to rely on the information, and whether the parties' relationship would have led the plaintiff to believe he or she had the right to rely on the information).

222   *Add*: *See, e.g.*, Kingsford Fastener, Inc. v. Koki, 2002 WL 992610, at *3 (N.D. Ill. May 15, 2002) (granting summary judgment to defendants on grounds that they were not in the business of providing information to others in their business transactions); Wilson v. Dryvit Sys., Inc., 206 F. Supp. 2d 749, 754 (E.D.N.C. 2002), *aff'd*, 2003 WL 21805618 (4th Cir. Aug. 7, 2003) (*per curiam*) (unpublished); Fid. Nat'l Title Ins. Co. v. Intercounty Nat'l Title Ins. Co., 161 F. Supp. 2d 876, 882 (N.D. Ill. 2001); Gershberg v. Kean, 2002 WL 1489532, at *4, *5 (Conn. Super. Ct. June 10, 2002) (negligent misrepresentation action may be based on a defendant's failure to fulfill duty to speak); Prime Leasing, Inc. v. Kendig, 773 N.E.2d 84, 95 (Ill. App. Ct. 2002) (holding that if intended end result of relationship is for the defendant to create a product, then the defendant is not in the "business of supplying information"); Mahler v. Keenan Real Estate, Inc., 255 Kan. 593, 876 P.2d 609, 616 (1994) (adopting Restatement (Second) of Torts § 552); Kitner v. CTW Transp., Inc., 762 N.E.2d 867, 874 (Mass. App. Ct. 2002) (upholding jury's verdict for plaintiffs against defendant who had represented that it could obtain insurance coverage for them); Forbes v. Par Ten Group, Inc., 99 N.C. App. 587, 394 S.E.2d 643, 648 (1990) (citing Restatement (Second) of Torts § 552); Harrel v. Solt, 2000 Ohio App. LEXIS 6312, at *18 (Ohio Ct. App. Dec. 27, 2000); Tartera v. Palumbo, 224 Tenn. 262, 453 S.W.2d 780 (1970); Strange v. Peterson, 2001 Tenn. App. LEXIS 23, at *6 (Tenn. Ct. App. Jan. 11, 2001) (following Restatement (Second) of Torts § 552); Trans-Gulf Corp. v. Performance Aircraft Services, Inc., 82 S.W.3d 691, 696 (Tex. App. 2002) (interpreting Restatement (Second) of Torts § 552 to require the speaker to have had actual knowledge of the recipient's identity and a specific intent that the claimant would rely on the misrepresentation; therefore plaintiff could not recover for defendants' misleading entries in aircraft's maintenance records that were made before plaintiff purchased the plane); Rawson v. Conover, 20 P.3d 876, 883 (Utah 2001) (persons who supply information for the guidance of others in their business transactions must use reasonable care in obtaining the information); Denaxas v. Sandstone Court of Bellevue, Ltd. Liab. Co., 2001 Wash. App. LEXIS 1982 (Wash. Ct. App. Aug. 20, 2001) (following Restatement (Second) of Torts § 552), *review granted*, 45 P.2d 552 (Wash. 2002); *add at end of note*: At least one court has held that the defendant need not be exclusively in the business of supplying information to be held liable for negligent misrepresentation; if a business provides both information and goods, that business may still be liable for negligent misrepresentation if the information provided was not central to the sale of goods. Fid. Nat'l Title Ins. Co. v. Intercounty Nat'l Title Ins. Co., 161 F. Supp. 2d 876, 882 (N.D. Ill. 2001). In Texas, the requirement that the defendant provided the information in the course of his business can be met merely by showing that he or she had a pecuniary interest in the transaction. Larsen v. Carlene Langford & Assocs., 41 S.W.3d 245, 249, 250 (Tex. App. 2001).

Add to text after sentence containing note 222:

This liability is justified because the professional knows that the hearer expects to rely on the professional's judgment and expertise. In some jurisdictions, this theory may be used to sue a real estate broker who negligently gives false information to a buyer.[222.1]

222.1   *See, e.g.*, Vahanian v. Kaylor, 2001 Wash. App. LEXIS 1519, at *20 (Wash. Ct. App. July 13, 2001) (seller's broker owed duty to buyer to disclose potential water supply problem).

Page 437

Addition to notes 223, 225, 226.

223   Air Products & Chemicals, Inc. v. Eaton Metal Products Co., 272 F. Supp. 2d 482, 492 (E.D. Pa. 2003) (Idaho law) (granting summary judgment on negligent misrepresentation claim).

225   *Replace Marvin Lumber citation with*: 223 F.3d 873 (8th Cir. 2000); *add*: Florida State Bd. of Admin. v. Eng'g & Envtl. Services, Inc., 262 F. Supp. 2d 1004, 1020 (D. Minn. 2003) (Fla. law) (economic loss doctrine did not bar negligent misrepresentation claim even though it was "closely related" to the plaintiff's breach of contract claim); Kingsford Fastener, Inc. v. Koki, 2002 WL 992610, at *3 (N.D. Ill. May 15, 2002); Gavett v. Roto-Rooter Services, Co., 2001 WL 1688896, at *2 (D. Mass. Nov. 27, 2001); Adams v. NVR Homes, Inc., 135 F. Supp. 2d 675, 703 (D. Md. 2001), *modified in part on other grounds*, 142 F. Supp. 2d 649 (D. Md. 2001); Young v. Oberhelman, 607 So. 2d 719, 721 (La. Ct. App. 1992); May

v. ERA Landmark Real Estate, 302 Mont. 326, 15 P.3d 1179, 1187 (2000); Tankersley v. Hewlett, 2003 WL 22173047, at *3 (Wash. Ct. App. Sept. 22, 2003) (doctrine did not bar negligent misrepresentation claim brought by mobile home park purchasers based on defective septic system).

226 N.Y. Pumping, Inc. v. O'Connor Truck Sales S., Inc., 2003 WL 21499014, at *3, *4 (E.D. Pa. June 20, 2003) (dismissing plaintiff's negligent misrepresentation claim); Full Faith Church of Love W., Inc. v. Hoover Treated Wood Products, Inc., 224 F. Supp. 2d 1285 (D. Kan. 2002) (economic loss rule bars negligent misrepresentation claim); Am. Specialty Sys. v. Chicago Metallic Corp., 47 U.C.C. Rep. Serv. 2d 949 (N.D. Ill. 2002) (Pa. law); Fox Associates, Inc. v. Robert Half Int'l, Inc., 777 N.E.2d 603, 607 (Ill. App. Ct. Sept. 14, 2002) (if information supplied was "merely ancillary" to the sale of a product or service, plaintiff can not recover economic loss); Green v. Gen. Motors Corp., 2002 WL 1575589, at *2 (N.J. Super. Ct. Law Div. Jan. 4, 2002), *aff'd*, 2003 WL 21730592 (N.J. Super. Ct. App. Div. July 10, 2003) (unpublished); SME Indus., Inc. v. Thompson, Ventulett, Stainback & Assocs., Inc., 2001 Utah 54, 28 P.3d 669, 683 (2001) (economic loss rule prevents commercial parties in construction transaction from claiming negligent misrepresentation); Stoney v. Franklin, 54 Va. Cir. 591, 44 U.C.C. Rep. Serv. 2d 1211, 2001 Va. Cir. LEXIS 84, at *11, *12 (June 18, 2001) (economic loss rule bars constructive fraud claims as well as negligence claims when only economic damages alleged); Ivankovic v. Wis. O'Connor Corp., 264 Wis. 2d 893, 664 N.W.2d 126 (Wis. Ct. App. 2003) (table) (text available at 2003 WL 1983485) (economic loss doctrine barred negligent misrepresentation and strict liability claims); Prent Corp. v. Martek Holdings, Inc., 618 N.W.2d 201, 207 (Wis. Ct. App. 2000); *see also* Sun-Lite Glazing Contractors, Inc. v. J.E. Berkowitz, Ltd. P'ship, 37 Fed. Appx. 677, 679, 680 (4th Cir. 2002) (negligent misrepresentation exception to economic loss doctrine did not arise when duty of care rose solely from contract and not from an independent source).

Page 438

11.4.3.2 Innocent Misrepresentation

Addition to note 232.

232 *See also* Orsini Imps. v. Marciano, 2001 Conn. Super. LEXIS 1722, at *8, *9 (Conn. Super. Ct. June 21, 2001) (car buyer who had given incorrect information about balance due on lease of old car liable to dealer for innocent misrepresentation); Catamaran Acquisition Corp. v. Spherion Corp., 2001 Del. Super. LEXIS 227, at *16, *17 (Del. Super. Ct. May 31, 2001) (chancery court may hear action for rescission and rescissionary damages).

Add to text after sentence containing note 234:

It may also be referred to as constructive fraud.[234.1]

234.1 *See, e.g.*, Ford v. Dye, 2000 Ark. App. LEXIS 718, at *13 (Ark. Ct. App. Nov. 15, 2000) ("Constructive fraud, on the other hand, while requiring proof of all the necessary elements of actual fraud, misrepresentation, and deceit, may be proven even when there is a complete absence of any moral wrong or evil intention.").

11.4.4 Deceit by Concealment or Nondisclosure

Page 439

11.4.4.1 General

Addition to note 236.

236 *See also* Brewer v. Poole Constr. Co., 13 Mass. L. Rptr. 97, 2001 Mass. Super. LEXIS 151, at *21, *22 (Super. Ct. May 3, 2001) (buyers of home had no claim that nondisclosure of septic system irregularities amounted to fraud by silence).

Add to text at end of subsection's first paragraph:

In addition to common law claims, some states have enacted laws that specifically impose liability on those who suppress information notwithstanding their duty to disclose it.[236.1]

236.1 *See, e.g.*, Ala. Code § 6-5-102; Cal. Civ. Code §§ 1709, 1710 (West); *see also* Restatement (Second) of Torts § 550 (a party "who by concealment or other action intentionally prevents the other from acquiring material information is subject to the same liability to the other, for pecuniary loss as though he had stated the nonexistence of the matter that the other was thus prevented from discovering"); Lovejoy v. AT & T Corp., 92 Cal. App. 4th 85, 111 Cal. Rptr. 2d 711 (2001) (phone company that "slammed" a customer by appropriating customer's toll-free number for itself through false representations, then suppressed the switch from the customer by hiding the charges in customer's long distance bill, could be liable for fraudulent suppression).

Add to text at end of subsection:

Different jurisdictions put slightly different parameters on the duty to disclose. In Alabama, for example, whether a duty to disclose arises depends upon several factors: the relationship of the parties, the relative knowledge of the parties, the value of the particular fact, the plaintiff's opportunity to ascertain the fact, and the customs of the particular trade.[238.1]

238.1 *Ex parte* Walden, 785 So. 2d 335, 339 (Ala. 2001).

11.4.4.2 Half Truths

Addition to note 239.

239   *See also* Adams v. NVR Homes, Inc., 135 F. Supp. 2d 675, 703 (D. Md. 2001) (a party who has an obligation to speak and fails to do so may be making an implied representation that can be the basis of a claim for negligent misrepresentation), *modified in part on other grounds*, 142 F. Supp. 2d 649 (D. Md. 2001); Globetti v. Sandoz Pharm., Corp., 2001 U.S. Dist. LEXIS 2093, at *27, *28 (N.D. Ala. Feb. 2, 2001) (once pharmaceutical company made some disclosures about drug's safety, it became obligated to tell whole truth); Robichaud v. Hewlett Packard Co., 2001 Conn. Super. LEXIS 1830, at *10 (Conn. Super. Ct. June 29, 2001) (representation by seller of printer that cartridges were included could be viewed as an implicit promise that those cartridges were standard, fully-filled cartridges); Kleczek v. Jorgensen, 767 N.E.2d 913, 920 (Ill. App. Ct. 2002) (seller, who had been told of housing code violations but had not yet gotten written notice of them, made a misleading statement by representing in sales contract that he had not "received" any notice of a dwelling code violation); Heider v. Leewards Creative Crafts, Inc., 245 Ill. App. 3d 258, 265, 613 N.E.2d 805, 811 (1993) (defendant could be liable for statement that asbestos in building was "not a problem" when, though statement was true at the time the defendant made it, defendant knew that the asbestos could cause future problems); Keefhaver v. Kimbrell, 58 S.W.3d 54 (Mo. Ct. App. 2001) (reversing directed verdict for sellers of home who understated problems with leakage, drainage, and rot); Serv. Corp. Int'l Mgmt. Corp. v. Galvan, 2001 Tex. App. LEXIS 747, at *11 (Tex. App. Jan. 18, 2001) (though cemetery plot seller initially had no duty to bury family members near each other, once it volunteered to do so, seller could be liable for negligently misrepresenting that it held title to the adjacent plots). *Compare* Johnson v. Hewlett-Packard Co., 2002 WL 1050426, at *4 (Minn. Ct. App. May 22, 2002) (computer printer seller's representation that printers included ink cartridges could mislead buyers into concluding the cartridges were standard, full cartridges and not the half-full cartridges that the seller supplied) *with* Andre Strishak & Associates, Prof'l Corp. v. Hewlett-Packard Co., 300 A.D.2d 608, 752 N.Y.S.2d 400 (2002) (when seller did not specifically describe amount of ink in included ink cartridges, buyers failed to make a deceptive advertising claim).

Page 440

11.4.4.3 Seller's Superior Means of Ascertaining the Truth

Addition to notes 246, 250.

246   *Add to Peerless Wall & Window citation*: aff'd, 234 F.3d 1265 (3d Cir. 2000); *add*: Howard Opera House Associates v. Urban Outfitters, Inc., 166 F. Supp. 2d 917, 928 (D. Vt. 2001) (affirming summary judgment for each party on grounds neither had a duty to disclose), *aff'd in part, vacated in part on other grounds*, 322 F.3d 125 (2d Cir. 2003); Adams v. NVR Homes, Inc., 135 F. Supp. 2d 675, 703 (D. Md. 2001) (plaintiff must show reliance), *modified in part on other grounds*, 142 F. Supp. 2d 649 (D. Md. 2001); Wright v. Brooke Group, Ltd., 2001 U.S. Dist. LEXIS 10525, at *17, *18 (N.D. Iowa Mar. 9, 2001) (unpublished) (denying tobacco company's motion to dismiss fraud claim based on defendants' superior knowledge of nicotine's addictive effects); Scheck Mech. Corp. v. Borden, Inc., 186 F. Supp. 2d 724 (W.D. Ky. 2001) (denying defendant's motion for summary judgment); Lanier Home Ctr., Inc. v. Underwood, 557 S.E.2d 76, 81 (Ga. Ct. App. 2001) (if builder had actual knowledge of a septic system defect he was required to disclose it to purchasers); Wilhite v. Mays, 232 S.E.2d 141, 143 (Ga. Ct. App. 1976) (recognizing "passive concealment" exception to the general rule of *caveat emptor* when builder/seller of realty has special knowledge not apparent to the buyer), *aff'd*, 235 S.E.2d 532 (Ga. 1977); Artilla Cove Resort, Inc. v. Hartley, 72 S.W.3d 291, 298 (Mo. Ct. App. 2002) (defendants, because they had superior knowledge of structural damage, had duty to disclose collapsing foundation that was hidden behind a wall); Everts v. Parkinson, 555 S.E.2d 667, 674 (N.C. Ct. App. 2001) (duty to disclose arises when vendor of property has access to facts that she knows are out of reach to the purchaser); Hermansen v. Tasulis, 48 P.3d 235, 242 (Utah 2002) (seller had duty to disclose any known defects in the subsurface conditions of home's lot); Mitchell v. Christensen, 31 P.3d 572, 576 (Utah 2001) (seller had duty to disclose latent defects in swimming pool); *see also* TVT Records v. Island Def Jam Music Group, 279 F. Supp. 2d 366, 380, 381 (S.D.N.Y. 2003) (affirming fraud judgment based on defendant's concealment of its intent not to perform contract with plaintiff); Miller v. Kennedy & Minshew, Prof'l Corp., 2003 WL 22725125, at *13, *14 (Tex. App. Nov. 20, 2003) (client could be liable for fraud when he entered into contingent fee agreement with attorney but never intended to perform his responsibilities necessary to achieve contingency; affirming jury verdict for attorney); Logue v. Flanagan, 584 S.E.2d 186, 188–191 (W. Va. 2003) (*per curiam*) (sellers of tract of land owed buyers a duty to disclose septic system problems).

250   Steigerwald v. Bradley, 136 F. Supp. 2d 460, 469 (D. Md. 2001).

Add to text at end of subsection's first paragraph:

Some courts only impose a duty to disclose on a defendant when that defendant owes some sort of a fiduciary duty to the plaintiff.[250.1]

250.1   *See, e.g.*, Ala. OB/GYN Specialists, Prof'l Corp. v. Cynosure, Inc., 2003 WL 297560 (W.D. Tenn. Feb. 7, 2003) (Tennessee recognizes duty to disclose only when a fiduciary duty existed between the parties, when the transaction was intrinsically fiduciary, or when a party to a contract expressly reposed trust in the other); Xiangyuan Zhu v. Countrywide Realty, Co., 165 F. Supp. 2d 1181, 1202 (D. Kan. 2001) (listing agent of house did not owe buyer a fiduciary duty, nonetheless agent had duty not to fraudulently misrepresent or conceal facts from buyer); Plastic Packaging Corp. v. Sun Chem. Corp., 136 F. Supp. 2d 1201, 1205 (D. Kan. 2001); *see also* Steigerwald v. Bradley, 136 F. Supp. 2d 460 (D. Md. 2001) (bank might be held a fiduciary if it (1) took on extra services for the borrowers, (2) received greater economic benefit than normal, (3) exercised extensive control over the transaction, or (4) was asked by the borrowers if there were any lien actions pending; however, bank that made initial contact between sophisticated buyer and seller, appraised the property that was the subject of the sale, and retained part of a loan as collateral was not found to owe a fiduciary duty to the buyer; citing Parker v. Columbia Bank, 91 Md. App. 346, 604 A.2d 521, 533 (1992)); Ralston Purina Co. v. McKendrick, 850 S.W.2d 629, 635, 636 (Tex. App. 1993).

Addition to note 251.	251	*Replace last sentence of note with*: For a more thorough discussion of an automobile dealer's duty to inspect the vehicles it sells, see National Consumer Law Center, Automobile Fraud § 2.6.2.3 (2d ed. 2003); *add*: *See* Underwood v. Monte Asti Buick Co., 73 Pa. D. & C.2d 773, 20 U.C.C. Rep. Serv. 657 (C.P. Allegheny County 1976) (seller did not disclose prior collision damage); Murphy v. Hewitt, 103 Wash. App. 1059, 2000 Wash. App. LEXIS 2651, at *9 (Wash. Ct. App. Dec. 26, 2000) (unpublished) (duty to disclose arises when one party is relying upon the superior and specialized knowledge and experience of the other, when a seller knows a material fact not easily discoverable by the buyer, and statute imposes a duty to disclose).

Page 441

Add note 251.1 at end of sentence following sentence containing note 251.	251.1	*See, e.g.*, Salinas v. Skelton, 249 Ga. App. 217, 547 S.E.2d 289, 292 (2001) (seller of real estate must disclose a defect that would likely influence buyer's decision if buyer is ignorant of that defect); Keefhaver v. Kimbrell, 58 S.W.3d 54, 59, 60 (Mo. Ct. App. 2001) (seller of house who knew that roof leaked and deck had rotted should have fully disclosed these defects to buyer); Rader v. Danny Darby Real Estate, Inc., 2001 Tex. App. LEXIS 6198, at *16, *18 (Tex. App. Sept. 10, 2001) (home seller's broker, who represented that seller could finance the sale, could be liable for failing to disclose that seller's mortgage had a due on sale clause).
Addition to note 260.	260	*Add after Bynum citation: See also* Smiley v. S & J Investments, Inc., 580 S.E.2d 283, 289, 290 (Ga. Ct. App. 2003) (seller's real estate experience raised inference that he knew of new home's structural problems sufficient to satisfy *scienter* element of buyer's fraud claim based on seller's non-disclosure of those problems).
Replace note 261 with:	261	Azam v. M/I Schottenstein Homes, Inc., 813 So. 2d 91 (Fla. 2002) (it was for trier of fact to determine whether seller committed fraud by not disclosing to buyers the county's plan to build a school immediately outside housing development).

11.4.4.4 Affirmative Concealment

Addition to notes 266–268.	266	*See also* Norris v. Church & Co., 63 P.3d 153 (Wash. Ct. App. 2002) (builder who told buyers that leaks were attributable to improper roof maintenance instead of construction defects could be liable for fraudulent concealment).
	267	*Replace NCLC citation with*: National Consumer Law Center, Automobile Fraud (2d ed. 2003).
	268	*But see* Curry v. Thornsberry, 2003 WL 22510425 (Ark. Nov. 6, 2003) (house sellers not liable for fraudulent concealment based on their attempts to repair cracks in foundation when buyers could see both cracks and repairs at time they bought the house); Clark v. Allen, 796 N.E.2d 965, 970–972 (Ohio Ct. App. 2003) (house sellers not liable for moisture problems when no evidence showed that modifications were made to conceal water damage or that sellers were aware that the contractor's repairs to drainage system were inadequate); Yahner v. Kerlin, 2003 WL 21714917, at *6–*8 (Ohio Ct. App. July 24, 2003) (evidence that foundation cracks had been painted and repaired did not demonstrate that sellers had concealed basement leakage problems without evidence that they took such actions to prepare the home for sale).

Page 442

11.4.4.5 Statutory Duty to Disclose

Replace note 279 with:	279	For a discussion of such statutes, see National Consumer Law Center, Automobile Fraud § 6.2.3 (2d ed. 2003). *See also* Stone v. Clifford Chrysler-Plymouth, Inc., 775 N.E.2d 92, 95 (Ill. App. Ct. 2002) (buyer of car that had been wrecked and repaired created issue of fact whether costs to repair the vehicle properly would have exceeded new car damage disclosure statute's six percent threshold).
Addition to note 283.	283	*See also* Check v. Clifford Chrysler-Plymouth of Buffalo Grove Inc., 342 Ill. App. 3d 150, 158, 794 N.E.2d 829, 835 (2003) (court reasoned in *dicta* that a jury's finding that a dealer's failure to disclose vandalism

did not violate state new car damage disclosure statute was inconsistent with its finding that the non-disclosure constituted fraud, because if damage did not trigger statute it was not a material fact).

Replace note 284 with:

284 Carter v. Chrysler Corp., 1998 Ala. Civ. App. LEXIS 734 (Nov. 6, 1998) (reversing summary judgment for defendant); Pear v. Daimler Chrysler Corp., 772 N.E.2d 712, 719 (Ohio Ct. App. 2002) (affirming award of punitive damages against dealership that sold lemon buy back without complying with state's disclosure laws); *see also* Preferred Auto. Sales v. Sisson, 44 S.W.3d 818, 821 (Ky. Ct. App. 2001) (dealer did not fulfill statutory duty to disclose that truck was rebuilt by leaving branded certificate of title in glove compartment); National Consumer Law Center, Automobile Fraud § 6.4 (2d ed. 2003).

Add to text at end of subsection:

A state's real estate agent licensing act may specifically impose a duty on agents or sellers not to engage in fraud or misrepresentation.[285.1] Many states also have real estate disclosure statutes that require sellers to list and describe defects in the property and in any improvements thereon that are being sold.[285.2]

285.1 *See, e.g.,* Kan. Stat. Ann. § 58-3062(a)(14); *see also* Xiangyuan Zhu v. Countrywide Realty, Co., 165 F. Supp. 2d 1181, 1202 (D. Kan. 2001) (real estate listing agent's duty, imposed by statute, could be basis for buyer's misrepresentation claim); Baird v. Russello, 2003 WL 203598, at *2 (Ohio Ct. App. Jan. 31, 2003) (city ordinance requiring real estate agent to schedule a pre-sale inspection and forbidding the sale of property without a certificate of no exterior zoning or housing maintenance violations created duty of disclosure). *But see* Smith v. Taylor Built Constr. Co., 782 So. 2d 793, 796 (Ala. Civ. App. 2000) (realtor not liable for fraud for merely relaying information about a house's condition if realtor is not aware the information is false).

285.2 *See, e.g.,* Alaska Stat. §§ 34.70.010 to 34.70.200 (Michie); Cal. Civ. Code §§ 1002 to 1102.17 (West); Del. Code Ann. tit. 6, §§ 2570 to 2578; D.C. Code Ann. §§ 42-1301 to 42-1311; Haw. Rev. Stat. §§ 508D-1 to 508D-20; Idaho Code §§ 55-2501 to 55-2518 (Michie); 765 Ill. Comp. Stat. §§ 77/1 to 77/99; Ind. Code §§ 24-4.6-2-1 to 24-4.6-2-13; Me. Rev. Stat. Ann. tit. 33, §§ 171 to 179 (West); Md. Code Ann., Real Prop. § 10-702; Mass. Gen. Laws ch. 255, § 121 (urea formaldehyde foam insulation); Mich. Comp. Laws §§ 565.951 to 565.966; Neb. Rev. Stat. § 76-2,120; Nev. Rev. Stat. §§ 113.100 to 113.150; N.J. Stat. Ann. §§ 46:3C-1 to 46:3C-12 (West) (off-site conditions); N.Y. Real Prop. Law §§ 460–467 (McKinney); N.C. Gen. Stat. §§ 47E-1 to 47E-10; Okla. Stat. tit. 60, §§ 831–839; Or. Rev. Stat. § 5302.30; 68 Pa. Cons. Stat. §§ 1021–1036; R.I. Gen. Laws §§ 5-20.8-1 to 5-20.8-11; S.D. Codified Laws §§ 43-4-37 to 43-4-44 (Michie); Tenn. Code Ann. §§ 66-5-201 to 66-5-210; Tex. Prop. Code Ann. § 5.008 (Vernon); Va. Code Ann. §§ 55-517 to 55-525 (Michie); Wash. Rev. Code §§ 64.06.005 to 64.06.900; *see also* Giametti v. Inspections, Inc., 76 Conn. App. 352, 362, 824 A.2d 1, 8, 9 (2003) (statutory disclosure statute did not preclude common law negligent misrepresentation claim); McLellan v. Yeager, 2003 WL 354407, at *4 (Ky. Ct. App. Feb. 14, 2003) (though disclosure statement not itself a warranty, could become one when incorporated into sales contract); Snierson v. Scruton, 145 N.H. 73, 77, 78, 761 A.2d 1046, 1049, 1050 (N.H. 2000) (representations in statutorily-required disclosure form could be basis for fraud and negligent misrepresentation actions); Malach v. Chuang, 194 Misc. 2d 651, 666, 754 N.Y.S.2d 835, 846 (Civ. Ct. 2002) (holding that though home buyers had no cause of action under disclosure statute, the representations the sellers made pursuant to that statute could be the basis for a misrepresentation action; however, disclosures merged into contract pursuant to merger and integration clause; characterizing New York's residential real property disclosure statute as "a law, Drafted by a legislature, full of sound and fury, Achieving almost nothing" (citation omitted)); Funk v. Durant, 155 Ohio App. 3d 99, 104, 105, 799 N.E.2d 221, 225, 226 (2003) (new home buyers could not claim justifiable reliance on seller's incomplete disclosure of drainage problems in statutorily-required disclosure form when signs of water damage notified buyers that seller had not disclosed the full extent of the problems); Skurnowicz v. Lucci, 798 A.2d 788, 794 (Pa. Super. Ct. 2002) (sellers who reported no flooding problems on seller's disclosure form committed an affirmative misrepresentation); Stebbins v. Wells, 818 A.2d 711, 717, 718 (R.I. 2003) (*per curiam*) (though buyer has no private right of action for violation of real estate disclosure statute, statute did create a duty in seller and agent to disclose defects in property that could support a claim of fraudulent non-disclosure based on soil erosion problems); Dentler v. Helm-Perry, 2002 WL 31557302 (Tex. App. Nov. 20, 2002) (home sellers' disclosure of only "slight seepage" in face of history of repeated flooding could be basis of fraud action); Murphy v. Hewitt, 103 Wash. App. 1059, 2000 Wash. App. LEXIS 2651, at *9 (Wash. Ct. App. Dec. 26, 2000) (unpublished) (state requires sellers to disclose material information about their property, duty can not be fulfilled by vague reference to defects); Olmsted v. Mulder, 72 Wash. App. 169, 863 P.2d 1355, 1360 (1993) (vague answers to disclosure form may amount to negligent misrepresentation).

Add new subsections to text after § 11.4.4.5.

11.4.4a Justifiable Reliance and the Buyer's Opportunity to Inspect

Regardless of whether the claim asserts intentional, negligent, or innocent misrepresentation, a plaintiff must show not just that she relied on the representation but that her reliance was reasonable.[285.3] Reliance which might otherwise be justifiable may be deemed unjustifiable if contradictory information is present but the consumer fails to investigate it.[285.4]

The circumstances that raise the duty to inquire vary. One test is whether a reasonable person in the position of the consumer would be expected to investigate the representation.[285.5] In any case, the jury—not the judge—should decide whether a consumer's failure to investigate renders her reliance on the representation unjustifiable.[285.6]

In the case of real property, the age or other obvious conditions of the property can suggest that a buyer should get the property inspected.[285.7] However, not every jurisdiction requires the buyer of real property to have had it professionally inspected in order to preserve a fraud claim, at least when the defects are sufficiently latent.[285.8]

Even when the circumstances suggest that inspection would have been prudent, if a simple inspection would not have revealed the problem—that is, if the defect is genuinely latent—the buyer's failure to inspect should not render the buyer's reliance on the representation unjustifiable.[285.9] In addition, if the seller or the seller's agent hinders the buyer's ability to inspect the property, the buyer should be considered to have been as diligent as if she had actually completed an inspection.[285.10] Furthermore, the consumer must have had an opportunity to investigate *before* the agreement is reached. If the consumer does not have sufficient opportunity to investigate representations prior to acting, the consumer may still claim justifiable reliance on the representations.[285.11] But a buyer who conducts or obtains an inspection proceeds at her own peril if that inspection reveals defects the buyer later finds to be intolerable.[285.12]

11.4.4b Remedies

Those states that have adopted the rules of the Restatement (Second) of Torts for negligent misrepresentation and damages measure damages by (1) the lesser of the cost of cure or the difference between actual and represented property value, and (2) the reasonably foreseeable consequential damages.[285.13] Similarly, the damages for innocent misrepresentation are generally limited to the difference between the amount the buyer paid and the value of the property the buyer received.[285.14]

If repairs to the product can not bring it to its represented value, a plaintiff should recover both the repair costs *and* the remaining gap between the amount paid and the value of the property received.[285.15]

In appropriate circumstances, a tort claim can also yield punitive damages.[285.16] An extensive discussion of punitive damages, including preconditions, state statutory limits, and constitutional limits, can be found in NCLC's *Automobile Fraud*.[285.17]

In the alternative to damages, most jurisdictions allow rescission as a remedy for fraud.[285.18] In addition, the UCC provides that the same remedies are available for fraud or material misrepresentation as exist for non-fraudulent breach.[285.19] Thus, a defrauded buyer has the option of pursuing rejection or revocation of acceptance under the UCC. A buyer who rescinds or rejects or returns goods on grounds of fraud may recover damages under the UCC unless the circumstances of the case make the remedies incompatible.[285.20]

285.3   *See, e.g.*, Xiangyuan Zhu v. Countrywide Realty, Co., 165 F. Supp. 2d 1181, 1201 (D. Kan. 2001); Clifford St. John & Sons v. Farley Co., 2000 Conn. Super. LEXIS 3565, at *7, *11 (Conn. Super. Ct. Dec. 14, 2000); Harrel v. Solt, 2000 Ohio App. LEXIS 6312, at *25 (Ohio Ct. App. Dec. 27, 2000); ESCA Corp. v. KPMG Peat Marwick, 135 Wash. 2d 820, 959 P.2d 651, 654 (1998).

        Under some circumstances, proof of a duty to disclose may obviate the need for proof of justifiable reliance. When, for example, a jurisdiction's test for a duty to disclose requires that the plaintiff show that the seller knew that the plaintiff did not have access to the undisclosed facts, a court may deem that the plaintiff has established justifiable reliance because the plaintiff could not have discovered the defect with reasonable diligence. Everts v. Parkinson, 555 S.E.2d 667, 674, 675 (N.C. Ct. App. 2001).

285.4   Goff v. Am. Sav. Ass'n, 1 Kan. App. 2d 75, 82, 561 P.2d 897, 903 (" 'A recipient of a fraudulent misrepresentation is justified in relying upon its truth without investigation, unless he knows or has reason to know of facts which make his reliance unreasonable.' . . .[t]he test is whether the recipient has 'information which would serve as a danger signal and a red light to any normal person of his intelligence and experience.' "); *see also* Keefhaver v. Kimbrell, 58 S.W.3d 54 (Mo. Ct. App. 2001) (fraud plaintiff must show that "the undisclosed information was beyond her reasonable reach and not discoverable in the exercise of reasonable diligence") (citing VanBooven v. Small, 938 S.W.2d 324, 328 (Mo. Ct. App. 1997)).

285.5   Wilson v. Dryvit Sys., Inc., 206 F. Supp. 2d 749, 756 (E.D.N.C. 2002) (plaintiff must show defects were not discoverable "in the exercise of diligent attention or observation" to sustain claim for nondisclosure), *aff'd*, 2003 WL 21805618 (4th Cir. Aug. 7, 2003) (*per curiam*) (unpublished); Newbern v. Mansbach, 777 So. 2d 1044, 1045, 1046 (Fla. Dist. Ct. App. 2001) (holding that the fact that land use regulations, which are public records, would have revealed defendant's representation to have been mistaken did not automatically render buyer's reliance unreasonable) (citing Gilchrist Tiber Co. v. ITT Rayonier, Inc., 696 So. 2d 334, 339 (Fla. 1997)); Azam v. M/I Schottenstein Homes, Inc., 761 So. 2d 1195, 1196 (Fla. Dist. Ct. App. 2000) (that school development plan was a matter of public record did not preclude jury from finding that buyer of home justifiably relied on seller's representation that school site would continue to be a nature preserve), *review granted*, 786 So. 2d 1186 (Fla. 2001); Merlin v. Fuselier Constr., Inc., 789 So. 2d 710, 715 (La. Ct. App. 2001) (buyer only need inspect when inspection would be reasonable under the circumstances, which include the buyer's knowledge and expertise, the opportunity for inspection, and the assurances by the seller); *see also* Swain v. Preston Falls E., Ltd. Liab. Co., 156 N.C. App. 357, 362, 363, 576 S.E.2d 699, 703 (2003) (failure of town house buyers to have property inspected after receiving a pre-closing disclosure form that stated that the synthetic stucco used on the exterior of the home had been subject to problems in other homes constituted contributory negligence as a matter of law; affirming summary judgment for builder and subcontractor); Norris v. Church & Co., 63 P.3d 153 (Wash. Ct. App. 2002) (buyers of newly constructed homes are not obligated to have them inspected).

285.6   Azam v. M/I Schottenstein Homes, Inc., 761 So. 2d 1195, 1196 (Fla. Dist. Ct. App. 2000) (for jury to decide whether buyer exercised ordinary diligence in failing to discover school development plan, which was a matter of public record), *review granted*, 786 So. 2d 1186 (Fla. 2001); Harrel v. Solt, 2000 Ohio App. LEXIS 6312, at *25 (Ohio Ct. App. Dec. 23, 2000) (for jury to decide whether buyers could have been expected to discover that land was inappropriate for development); Denaxas v. Sandstone Court of Bellevue, Ltd. Liab. Co., 2001 Wash. App. LEXIS 1982, at *10, *11 (Wash. Ct. App. Aug. 20, 2001) (reversing trial court's dismissal of negligent misrepresentation action), *review granted*, 45 P.3d 552 (Wash. 2002).

285.7   Smith v. Walden, 249 Ga. App. 757, 549 S.E.2d 750, 750 (2001) (buyer who did not receive answer to question regarding price of similar property sold by seller was on notice that seller's representation as to value may have been false, and buyer should have taken further action to ascertain the actual price); Fann v. Mills, 248 Ga. App. 460, 546 S.E.2d 853, 857, 858 (2001) (buyer of home who observed water damage and received inspection report referring to water damage could not justifiably rely on seller's alleged representation that the house had never had a water problem); Keefhaver v. Kimbrell, 58 S.W.3d 54 (Mo. Ct. App. 2001); Hearne v. Statesville Lodge No. 687, 143 N.C. App. 560, 546 S.E.2d 414, 415 (2001) (plaintiff home buyers who had right to inspect property could not maintain fraud or negligent misrepresentation action against seller's realtor for failing to disclose that septic system would not be adequate for plaintiff's purposes); Stebbins v. Wells, 766 A.2d 369, 373 (R.I. 2001) (location of property along waterfront should have notified buyer of possibility of erosion and created duty to inspect and to inquire about extent of erosion); Larsen v. Carlene Langford & Associates, 41 S.W.3d 245, 254, 255 (Tex. App. 2001) (buyers who failed to take advantage of their opportunity to have seventy-year-old home inspected after a walk-through revealed cracks and other problems could not claim justifiable reliance on the seller's representations); Rader v. Danny Darby Real Estate, Inc., 2001 Tex. App. LEXIS 6198, at *11 (Tex. App. Sept. 10, 2001) (when house showed obvious flaws, buyer could not demonstrate justifiable reliance when buyer failed to have house inspected); *see also* Mitchell v. Christensen, 31 P.3d 572, 575 (Utah 2001) (under the reasonably prudent person standard for discovery of a defect, a home buyer may be put on notice that requires additional investigation or expert inspection).

285.8   *See, e.g.*, Brown v. Johnson, 109 Wash. App. 56, 34 P.3d 1233 (2001); *see also* Groening v. Opsata, 323 Mich. 73, 34 N.W.2d 560, 563 (1948) (buyers of lakefront property were entitled to rely on seller's representation that bluffs were sound notwithstanding that they could have learned of erosion problems by investigating other sources).

285.9   *See* Lindberg v. Roseth, 46 P.3d 518, 524 (Idaho 2002) (plaintiffs were entitled to rely on seller's failure to disclose property defects on disclosure form, despite their independent inspection of the property, as defects were latent); Merlin v. Fuselier Constr., Inc., 789 So. 2d 710, 715, 716 (La. Ct. App. 2001) (when inspection did not discover that roof had been improperly installed, buyers could maintain negligent misrepresentation action against seller who had claimed the roof had not leaked); Artilla Cove Resort, Inc. v. Hartley, 72 S.W.3d 291, 298 (Mo. Ct. App. 2002) (when commonly accepted inspection practices would not have included removing plywood wall that hid collapsing foundation, plaintiffs entitled to rely on defendant's nondisclosure of damage); Brown v. Johnson, 109 Wash. App. 56, 34 P.3d 1233 (2001) (when a professional inspection did not reveal problems, buyer could justifiably rely on seller's nondisclosure of defects; while "[t]he buyer has a duty to observe what can be seen through diligent observation . . . there is no requirement that the buyer hire an expert to discover problems that she would not recognize"). *But see* Wilson v. Dryvit Sys., Inc., 206 F. Supp. 2d 749, 756 (E.D.N.C. 2002) (to sustain claim for nondisclosure, plaintiff had to show that the defects were not discoverable "in the exercise of diligent attention or observation"), *aff'd*, 2003 WL 21805618 (4th Cir. Aug. 7, 2003) (*per curiam*) (unpublished). However, in one perverse result, a court held that the plaintiff, by having the property inspected, lost the ability to claim justifiable reliance on the seller's failure to disclose termite damage notwithstanding that the damage was so latent the inspection failed to reveal it. Kashman v. Haas, 766 N.E.2d 417, 422 (Ind. Ct. App. 2002).

285.10   *See* Carter v. Mueller, 457 N.E.2d 1335, 1340 (Ill. App. Ct. 1983) (plaintiff not required to inspect when defendant had inhibited plaintiff's inquiries by creating a false sense of security or by blocking an investigation; plaintiff's failure to inspect apartment before moving in did not destroy her fraud claim based on its uninhabitability); Oakwood Mobile Homes, Inc. v. Cabler, 73 S.W.3d 363, 371 (Tex. App. 2002) (seller can not obstruct an inspection for defects in his property and still rely on "as is" clause for protection).

285.11   S Dev. Co. v. Pima Capital Mgmt. Co., 31 P.3d 123, 130 (Ariz. Ct. App. 2001) (if defect is latent, or if it is patent and the defendant did not give the buyer the opportunity to investigate, defendant may still be liable for negligent nondisclosure; buyers were not able to discover defective pipe that was buried inside walls when buyers were not allowed to inspect inside walls); William v. Miller Chevrolet/Geo, Inc., 762 N.E.2d 1, 9 (Ill. App. Ct. 2001) (when certificate of title was sole document that revealed car sold as "executive driven" had been previously owned, and it was not turned over to the plaintiff until after purchase contract was signed, it did not negate plaintiff's justifiable reliance element); Duran v. Leslie Oldsmobile, Inc., 594 N.E.2d 1355, 1363 (Ill. App. Ct. 1992) (when car buyer signed agreement before salesman filled in blanks with information that contradicted his earlier representations, her "subsequent opportunity to inform [herself] of the true facts contradicting such misrepresentation cannot render such prior reliance unreasonable"); *see also* Hummel v. Suglia, 2003 WL 22235370, at *6 (Ohio Ct. App. Sept. 30, 2003) (affirming fraud verdict based on car seller's false representation that car was roadworthy and its engine had been rebuilt when buyer could not inspect car before purchase).

285.12   Keiser v. Wecker, 2001 Conn. Super. LEXIS 1027, at *5 (Conn. Super. Ct. Apr. 12, 2001) (purchasers who conducted their own inspection of septic system in house could not maintain negligent misrepresentation claim against seller for failing to disclose alleged defects in system); Funk v. Durant, 155 Ohio App. 3d 99, 104, 105, 799 N.E.2d 221, 225, 226 (2003) (new home buyers could not claim justifiable reliance on seller's incomplete disclosure of drainage problems in statutorily-required disclosure form when signs of water damage notified buyers that seller had not disclosed the full extent of the problems); Grove v. Karlous, 2001 Wash. App. LEXIS 7, at *7 (Wash. Ct. App. Jan. 2, 2001) (buyer who had received inspection report that indicated leakage or water problems could not justifiably rely on seller's representation that seller had repaired the leaks). Even when an inspection fails to reveal the defect, a buyer who obtains an inspection on a property may lose the ability to claim justifiable reliance on the seller's failure to disclose the defect, at least when the seller urged the plaintiff to have the property inspected. Giametti v. Inspections, Inc., 76 Conn. App. 352, 364, 824 A.2d 1, 8, 9 (2003) (plaintiff could not show justifiable reliance on seller's failure to disclose carpenter ant infestation in property when buyer had property inspected and inspection did not reveal the ants, reversing judgment for buyer on negligent misrepresentation claim). The *Giametti* court may have reasoned that the plaintiff relied on the inspection, not the seller's non-disclosure of the problem. Nonetheless, in general a buyer's reliance on a clean inspection report should not preclude a finding that the buyer justifiably relied on the seller's failure to disclose a defect. *Cf.* Capiccioni v. Brennan Naperville, Inc., 339 Ill. App. 3d 927, 939, 940, 791 N.E.2d 553, 563 (2003) (plaintiffs, who bought home based on broker's misrepresentation that it was in a particular school district, showed justifiable reliance on misrepresentation notwithstanding that they confirmed the broker's statement with the school district office before buying the property).

285.13   Restatement (Second) of Torts § 552B; *see also* Beaux v. Jacob, 30 P.3d 90, 97 (Alaska 2001) (cost of cure); Economic Exterminators v. Wheeler, 576 S.E.2d 601 (Ga. Ct. App. 2003) (affirming award of repair costs plus other damages); Zanaskis-Pico v. Cutter Dodge, Inc., 47 P.3d 1222, 1234, 1235 (Haw. 2002) (recoverable damages for fraud include out-of-pocket consequential damages, including dollars spent on travel in reliance upon defendant's misleading advertisement); Artilla Cove Resort, Inc. v. Hartley, 72 S.W.3d 291, 300 (Mo. Ct. App. 2002) (benefit of the bargain damages); Smith v. Coldwell Banker Hunter Realty, 2002 WL 31060377, at *2, *3 (Ohio Ct. App. Sept. 18, 2002) (plaintiffs were entitled only to the lesser of cost of cure or diminution in value); Vahanian v. Kaylor, 2001 Wash. App. LEXIS 1519, at *21, *22 (Wash. Ct. App. July 13, 2001); Olmsted v. Mulder, 72 Wash. App. 169, 863 P.2d 1355, 1360, 1361 (1993) (damages should be cost of cure when it is less than benefit of the bargain).

285.14   Orsini Imports, Inc. v. Marciano, 2001 Conn. Super. LEXIS 1722, at *9 (Conn. Super. Ct. June 21, 2001).

285.15   *See* Harrison v. McMillan, 828 So. 2d 756 (Miss. 2002) (buyer of defectively constructed house could recover for both the repairs and the difference between the property as repaired and the fair market value of the property as represented). *But see* Klaiber v. Freemason Associates, Inc., 587 S.E.2d 555, 558, 559 (Va. 2003) (condominium buyers could not base fraud claim's damages on cost of repairing or replacing defective windows).

285.16   *See, e.g.*, Pearn v. DaimlerChrysler Corp., 772 N.E.2d 712 (Ohio Ct. App. 2002) (affirming award of punitive damages when plaintiff demonstrated "egregious fraud" in compliance with statute).

285.17   National Consumer Law Center, Automobile Fraud § 7.10 (2d ed. 2003).

285.18   *See* National Consumer Law Center, Automobile Fraud § 7.11 (2d ed. 2003).

285.19   U.C.C. § 2-721.

285.20   U.C.C. § 2-721; *see also* Official Comment to U.C.C. § 2-721.

Chapter 12

Negligence and Strict Liability in Tort

Page 445

12.1 Utility of Tort Theories in Consumer Warranty Cases

Addition to notes 3, 4.

3   *Add after Wallace citation*: *See also* Hitachi Constr. Mach. Co. v. Amax Coal Co., 737 N.E.2d 460 (Ind. Ct. App. 2000) (product liability statute does not displace warranty law). ,

4   *Replace Ex Parte Grand Manor citation with*: 778 So. 2d 173 (Ala. 2000).

12.2 Are Economic Damages Recoverable Under Negligence and Strict Liability Claims?

Page 447

12.2.1 Economic Damages Generally Not Recoverable

Addition to notes 13, 14.

13   *Add to Alabama entry*: *Ex parte* Grand Manor, Inc., 778 So. 2d 173 (Ala. 2000) (negligent manufacture of mobile home); *in Arizona entry replace In re Jackson Nat'l Life Ins. Co. citation with*: 107 F. Supp. 2d 841 (W.D. Mich. 2000); *add to California entry*: Aas v. Super. Court, 24 Cal. 4th 627, 101 Cal. Rptr. 2d 718, 12 P.3d 1125, 1130 (2000) (though tort law provides a remedy for construction defects that cause property damage or personal injury, economic loss doctrine barred plaintiff's claim that sought to recover reduction in value due to deviations from standards of quality); *add new entry*: *Colorado*: Grynberg v. Agri Tech, Inc., 10 P.3d 1267 (Colo. 2000); Town of Alma v. Azco Constr., Inc., 10 P.3d 1256, 1264 (Colo. 2000) (expressly adopting economic loss doctrine); Jardel Enterprises, Inc. v. Triconsultants, Inc., 770 P.2d 1301, 1304 (Colo. Ct. App. 1988); *add to Florida entry*: Wilson v. De Angelis, 156 F. Supp. 2d 1335, 1341 (S.D. Fla. 2001); Fla. Power & Light Co. v. Westinghouse Elec. Corp., 510 So. 2d 899 (Fla. 1987); *add to Kansas entry*: Ministic Air Ltd. v. Raytheon Aircraft Co., 2001 U.S. Dist. LEXIS 10126, at *4, *5 (D. Kan. Mar. 20, 2001); *add to Kentucky entry*: Ohio Cas. Ins. Co. v. Vermeer Mfg. Co., 2004 WL 60487 (W.D. Ky. Jan. 12, 2004) (predicting that Kentucky Supreme Court would adopt economic loss doctrine); *add to Michigan entry*: Sherman v. Sea Ray Boats, Inc., 649 N.W.2d 783 (Mich. Ct. App. 2002); *add to Minnesota entry*: Minn. Stat. § 604.10; *in New Jersey entry, add to Stewart Title Guar. Co. citation*: *aff'd*, 281 F.3d 224 (3d Cir. 2001) (table); *in New York entry add to Black Radio Network citation*: *aff'd on other grounds*, 2001 U.S. App. LEXIS 16005 (2d Cir. July 16, 2001); *add to New York entry*: Amin Realty, Ltd. Liab. Co. v. K & R Constr. Corp., 306 A.D.2d 230, 762 N.Y.S.2d 92 (2003); *add to South Carolina entry*: Sea Side Villas II Horizontal Prop. Regime v. Single Source Roofing Corp., 64 Fed. Appx. 367, 373 (4th Cir. 2003) (negligence claim); *add to Texas entry*: Trans-Gulf Corp. v. Performance Aircraft Services, Inc., 82 S.W.3d 691 (Tex. App. 2002); *add new entry*: *Washington*: Berschauer/Phillips Constr. Co. v. Seattle Sch. Dist. 1, 124 Wash. 2d 816, 881 P.2d 986 (1994); Carlson v. Sharp, 99 Wash. App. 324, 994 P.2d 851 (1999); *add to Wisconsin entry*: Ivankovic v. Wis. O'Connor Corp., 264 Wis. 2d 893, 664 N.W.2d 126 (Wis. Ct. App. 2003) (table) (text available at 2003 WL 1983485) (economic loss doctrine barred negligent misrepresentation and strict liability claims).

Page 449

14   *See also* E. River S.S. Corp. v. Transamerica Delaval, Inc., 476 U.S. 858, 866, 106 S. Ct. 2295, 90 L. Ed. 2d 865 (1986) (expressing fear that if products liability law progressed too far, "contract law would drown in a sea of tort"); Brunson Communications, Inc. v. Arbitron, Inc., 266 F. Supp. 2d 377, 383–385 (E.D. Pa. 2003) (citing policy concern that allowing tort claims for economic losses would burden the economic system); Calloway v. City of Reno, 993 P.2d 1259, 1265, 1266 (Nev. 2000) (contract law is designed to enforce standards of quality, while tort law is designed to enforce standards of conduct); Hermansen v. Tasulis, 48 P.3d 235, 239 (Utah 2002) (economic loss rule separates contract law, which entails expectancy interests arising from agreements, from tort law, which protects individuals and their property from physical harm).

Add to text following sentence containing note 14:

Supporters also reason that parties to a contract may allocate their risks in their agreement and do not need tort law to give them additional protection and compensation for a breach of contract.[14.1] A third argument in favor of the economic loss rule is that it encourages the purchaser to assume or to insure against the risk of economic loss.[14.2] These rationales assume the parties can negotiate their agreement clause by clause; they fail if a consumer is faced with a boilerplate, take-it-or-leave-it deal. Other courts look to the source of the duty breached, examining the tort action to find whether the duty alleged to have been breached was the contract promise itself, or some larger, social duty,[14.3] on the grounds that tort law is an appropriate remedy for breaches of the latter.

14.1   E. River S.S. Corp. v. Transamerica Delaval, Inc., 476 U.S. 858, 872, 873, 106 S. Ct. 2295, 90 L. Ed. 2d 865 (1986) ("[c]ontract law, and the law of warranty in particular, is well suited to commercial controversies of the sort involved in this case because the parties may set the terms of their own agreements"); Werwinski v. Ford Motor Co. 286 F.3d 661, 680 (3d Cir. 2002) (arguing that plaintiffs do not need additional tort remedies if they can be made whole under contract law); *In re* StarLink Corn Products Liab. Litig., 212 F. Supp. 2d 828, 839 (N.D. Ill. 2002); Prent Corp. v. Martek Holdings, Inc., 618 N.W.2d 201, 207, 46 U.C.C. Rep. Serv. 2d 68 (Wis. Ct. App. 2000) (buyers of software could have bargained for recovery of consequential damages).

14.2   *See, e.g., In re* StarLink Corn Products Liab. Litig., 212 F. Supp. 2d 828, 839 (N.D. Ill. 2002); Budgetel Inns, Inc. v. Micros Sys., Inc., 8 F. Supp. 2d 1137, 1149 (E.D. Wis. 1998); Kailin v. Armstrong, 643 N.W.2d 132, 144 (Wis. Ct. App. 2002).

14.3   Mut. Serv. Cas. Ins. Co. v. Elizabeth State Bank, 265 F.3d 601, 615, 616 (7th Cir. 2001) (bank's duty toward depositor, though it depended on existence of contract, arose independently from contract through common law, and therefore presented an action in tort); Air Products & Chemicals, Inc. v. Eaton Metal Products Co., 256 F. Supp. 2d 329, 342, 343 (E.D. Pa. 2003) (Utah law) (economic loss doctrine did not bar claim when duty breached arose from state statute imposing a duty of care); Ploog v. HomeSide Lending, Inc., 209 F. Supp. 2d 863, 875 (N.D. Ill. 2002) (rule did not bar mortgagor's breach of fiduciary duty claim against mortgagee who mispaid mortgagor's property taxes; mortgage contracts carry with them an implied duty of professional competence that arises independently of the contract); Loughridge v. Goodyear Tire & Rubber Co., 192 F. Supp. 2d 1175, 1183 (D. Colo. 2002); Hinkle Eng'g, Inc. v. 175 Jackson Ltd. Liab. Co., 2001 WL 1246757, at *3 (N.D. Ill. Oct. 18, 2001) (landlord's duty to provide quiet and peaceful enjoyment of the premises to tenant arose outside of the contract, and therefore plaintiff could recover for a negligent breach of that duty); Town of Alma v. Azco Constr., Inc., 10 P.3d 1256, 1263 (Colo. 2000) (noting that some relationships, such as that between attorney and client, automatically impose a duty of care separate and apart from the contractual relationship); Sherman v. Sea Ray Boats, Inc., 649 N.W.2d 783, 788 (Mich. Ct. App. 2002); Flynn Co. v. Peerless Door & Glass, Inc., 2002 WL 1018937 (Pa. C.P. May 15, 2002) (alleged duty to use ordinary and reasonable care in installing windows arose from contract, and not social policy, and therefore fraud claim barred by rule); Hermansen v. Tasulis, 48 P.3d 235, 240 (Utah 2002) (proper focus is on the source of the duties alleged to have been breached).

Addition to notes 15, 18.

15   *See also* Indemnity Ins. Co. of N. Am. v. Am. Aviation, Inc., 344 F.3d 1136, 1148 (11th Cir. 2003) *(per curiam)* (certifying to Florida Supreme Court question of whether state's economic loss doctrine applies when parties have no contractual relationship). *But see* Higginbotham v. Dryvit Sys., Inc., 2003 WL 1528483, at *5 (M.D.N.C. Mar. 20, 2003) (mag.) (plaintiffs' lack of contract and U.C.C. remedies against subcontractor did not prevent application of economic loss rule to bar their tort claims); *In re* StarLink Corn Products Liab. Litig., 212 F. Supp. 2d 828, 839 (N.D. Ill. 2002) (even though plaintiffs had no viable contract remedy, economic loss doctrine barred their tort claims); Carstens v. City of Phoenix, 75 P.3d 1081, 1082, 1083 (Ariz. Ct. App. 2003) (that plaintiff could not seek contract claims against alleged tortfeasor, as opposed to another party, did not prevent the economic loss doctrine from barring plaintiff's tort claims); Anderson Elec., Inc. v. Ledbetter Erection Corp., 503 N.E.2d 246, 249 (Ill. 1986) (limitation on tort recovery holds true regardless of the plaintiff's ability to recover in contract); Mequon Med. Associates v. S.T.O. Indus., Inc., 671 N.W.2d 717 (Wis. Ct. App. 2003) (table) (text available at 2003 WL 22093818) (that buyer had no contractual relationship with product's manufacturer did not preclude economic loss doctrine from barring products liability claims).

18   *Add to Florida entry: Compare* CSIR Enterprises, Inc. v. Sebrite Agency, Inc., 214 F. Supp. 2d 1276 (M.D. Fla. 2002) (doctrine did not bar conversion or RICO claims); *in Illinois entry replace Voyles citation with:* 311 Ill. App. 3d 649, 244 Ill. Dec. 192, 724 N.E.2d 1276 (2000), *rev'd on other grounds*, 196 Ill. 2d 288, 256 Ill. Dec. 289, 751 N.E.2d 1126 (2001); *add to Massachusetts entry:* Arthur D. Little Int'l., Inc. v. Dooyang Corp., 928 F. Supp. 1189, 1203 (D. Mass. 1996) (economic loss doctrine did not bar claim for negligent breach of contract, but recovery limited by the contract's damages clause); *in Ohio entry replace In re Jackson Nat'l Life Ins. Co. citation with:* 107 F. Supp. 2d 841 (W.D. Mich. 2000); *in Wisconsin entry add to Douglas-Hanson Co. citation: aff'd*, 233 Wis. 2d 276, 607 N.W.2d 621 (Wis. 2000).

Page 450

*Add new subsection to text
after § 12.2.1.*

12.2.1a Fraud, Intentional Misrepresentation, and Duties Arising Outside of the Contract

Most courts do not apply the economic loss rule to bar claims that the defendant fraudulently induced the transaction,[19.1] or intentionally defrauded the plaintiff.[19.2] These courts reason that the purpose of the rule, to limit parties to contract remedies, is not promoted when fraud has undermined the consumer's ability to freely negotiate the terms and remedies of the contract.[19.3] Other courts do not issue a blanket exception, but allow fraud claims to proceed only if the fraud is "extraneous to the contract," rather than "interwoven with the breach of contract."[19.4] These courts disallow claims based on a misrepresentation about the quality or character of the goods sold, on the reasoning that the buyer could have negotiated for a warranty or other remedy to protect against the risk of defects.[19.5] However, when the duty alleged to have been breached arose independently from the specific terms of the contract, the claim may proceed.[19.6] One test these courts use is whether the factual allegations necessary to prove the fraudulent inducement claim are the same as those necessary to prove a breach of contract.[19.7] Accordingly, to avoid application of the rule in courts adopting this position, a tort claim should be framed as arising not from the defendant's performance of the agreement but rather from some act occurring outside the four corners of the contract. Courts have used similar reasoning to allow negligence claims between parties based on a duty that arose outside the terms of the contract itself.[19.8]

Nonetheless, a significant number of cases have held that the economic loss rule bars even those tort claims based on a contract induced by fraud, especially when the statements made to induce the contract are embodied in the contract itself.[19.9] Courts of this school apparently expect parties to negotiate their agreements under the assumption that every word and action leading up to the agreement was false,[19.10] no matter how discordant such expectations are with both reality and a marketplace of comity.

In a hybrid approach, Florida courts have limited application of the doctrine to products liability-type cases, finding that the reasons that support the rule do not apply outside that context. So, for example, a claim alleging negligence in the provision of professional services would not be barred by the rule.[19.11]

19.1   *See, e.g.*, O'Keefe v. Mercedes-Benz USA, Ltd. Liab. Co., 214 F.R.D. 266, 275–278 (E.D. Pa. 2003) (economic loss doctrine did not bar fraudulent inducement claim; court declines to follow Werwinski v. Ford Motor Co., 286 F.3d 661 (3d Cir. 2002), in a thoroughly reasoned opinion); McKesson Medical-Surgical, Inc. v. Kearney, 271 F. Supp. 2d 827, 829 (E.D. Va. 2003) (doctrine did not bar constructive fraud claim arising from representations made before the contract was formed); Medline Indus. Inc. v. Maersk Med. Ltd., 230 F. Supp. 2d 857, 867, 868 (N.D. Ill. 2002) (economic loss doctrine did not bar claim based on fraudulent inducement, notwithstanding that allegedly false statement was also in the contract); Geneva Pharm. Tech. Corp. v. Barr Laboratories, Inc., 201 F. Supp. 2d 236, 287, 288 (S.D.N.Y. 2002); HTP, Ltd. v. Lineas Aereas Costarricenses, S.A., 685 So. 2d 1238, 1239, 1240 (Fla. 1996); D & M Jupiter, Inc. v. Friedopfer, 853 So. 2d 485, 487, 488 (Fla. Dist. Ct. App. 2003) (doctrine did not bar fraudulent inducement claim based on misrepresentation made in sale of commercial property); Hinton v. Brooks, 820 So. 2d 325, 328 (Fla. Dist. Ct. App. 2001) (allowing home buyers' fraud counterclaim in foreclosure action); *In re* Chicago Flood Litig., 680 N.E.2d 265, 275 (Ill. 1997) (listing exceptions to economic loss rule); Tietsworth v. Harley-Davidson, Inc., 2003 WL 116123 (Wis. Ct. App. Jan. 13, 2003) (purchaser of defective motorcycle could recover purely economic damages for fraud); Phoenix Controls, Inc. v. Eisenmann Corp., 644 N.W.2d 293 (Wis. Ct. App. 2002) (table) (text available at 2002 WL 436367, at *4); Kailin v. Armstrong, 643 N.W.2d 132, 145 (Wis. Ct. App. 2002); Douglas-Hanson Co. v. BF Goodrich Co., 598 N.W.2d 262, 268 (Wis. Ct. App. 1999), *aff'd*, 233 Wis. 2d 276, 607 N.W.2d 621 (Wis. 2000); *see also* Minn. Stat. § 604.10(e) (economic loss rule does not bar tort actions based on fraud or intentional misrepresentation).

19.2   *See, e.g.*, Digicorp, Inc. v. Bacher Communications, Inc., 650 N.W.2d 321 (Wis. Ct. App. 2002) (table) (text available at 2002 WL 1277220). *But see* Mequon Med. Associates v. S.T.O. Indus., Inc., 671 N.W.2d 717 (Wis. Ct. App. 2003) (table) (text available at 2003 WL 22093818) (economic loss doctrine bars intentional fraud claim unless the fraud induced the transaction).

19.3   *See, e.g.*, Budgetel Inns, Inc. v. Micros Sys., Inc., 8 F. Supp. 2d 1137, 1138 (E.D. Wis. 1998) ("[d]ue diligence cannot ensure against intentional dishonesty"); HTP, Ltd. v. Lineas Aereas Costarricenses, S.A., 685 So. 2d 1238, 1239, 1240 (Fla. 1996) (arguing that "the interest protected by fraud is society's need for true factual statements in important human relationships, primarily commercial or business relationships"); Digicorp, Inc. v. Bacher Communications, Inc., 650 N.W.2d 321 (Wis. Ct. App. 2002) (table) (text available at 2002 WL 1277220, at *7) (finding plaintiff was "unable to properly and fairly assess the risks of the contract" as a result of the defendant's misrepresentations); Kailin v. Armstrong, 643 N.W.2d 132, 145 (Wis. Ct. App. 2002); Douglas-Hanson Co. v. BF Goodrich Co., 598 N.W.2d 262, 268 (Wis. Ct. App. 1999), aff'd, 233 Wis. 2d 276, 607 N.W.2d 621 (2000).

19.4   Huron Tool & Eng'g Co. v. Precision Consulting Services, Inc., 209 Mich. App. 365, 532 N.W.2d 541, 545 (1995) (holding that rule barred claim based on alleged fraud regarding the quality and characteristics of the software sold); *see also* AKA Distrib. Co. v. Whirlpool Corp., 137 F.3d 1083, 1087 (8th Cir. 1993) (economic loss rule barred distributor's claim regarding alleged length of contract, as that was a term to be governed by the agreement, but did not bar claim that manufacturer had fraudulently misrepresented its business development plans to induce plaintiff into contract, which was a collateral matter); Convergent Group Corp. v. County of Kent, 266 F. Supp. 2d 647, 660 (W.D. Mich. 2003) (economic loss doctrine barred fraud claim based on defendant's representations about its performance of a contract); Rosa v. Amoco Oil Co., 262 F. Supp. 2d 1364, 1368 (S.D. Fla. 2003) (economic loss doctrine barred fraudulent inducement claim based on representations that were directly contradicted by the terms of the contract itself, as such representations were not independent of the contract); Bracco Diagnostics, Inc. v. Bergen Brunswig Drug Co., 226 F. Supp. 2d 557, 563, 564 (D.N.J. 2002) (rule barred fraud claim that was not extrinsic to underlying contract claim); Excess Risk Underwriters, Inc. v. Lafayette Life Ins. Co., 208 F. Supp. 2d 1310, 1315, 1316 (S.D. Fla. 2002) (economic loss rule precluded claim based on breach of defendant's fiduciary duty when duty arose from the terms of the contract, a confidentiality agreement, itself); Wright Tool Co., v. ChemChamp N. Am. Corp., 185 F. Supp. 2d 781, 785 (E.D. Mich. 2002) (disallowing tort claim when fraud alleged was identical to the factual allegations supporting plaintiff's breach of contract claim); Premix-Marbletite Mfg. Corp. v. SKW Chemicals, Inc., 145 F. Supp. 2d 1348, 46 U.C.C. Rep. Serv. 2d 77 (S.D. Fla. 2001) (when actions complained of relate directly to the subject matter of the parties' agreement, economic loss rule bars a tort action); Rich Products Corp. v. Kemutec, Inc. 66 F. Supp. 2d 937, 978 (E.D. Wis. 1999) (rule barred claim alleging intentional misrepresentations regarding advertisements and brochures for the product, because these representations went to the quality of the product sold); Budgetel Inns, Inc. v. Micros Sys., Inc., 34 F. Supp. 2d 720, 728 (E.D. Wis. 1999) ("intentional misrepresentation that induces one party to enter into an agreement draws into the question the validity of the agreement itself; no party, commercial or individual, should be limited solely to remedies under a contract that perhaps should be rescinded altogether").

19.5   Marvin Lumber & Cedar Co. v. PPG Indus., Inc., 223 F.3d 873, 885 (8th Cir. 2000) (fraud claim based on efficacy of wood preservative barred by rule); TIBCO Software, Inc. v. Gordon Food Serv., Inc., 2003 WL 21683850, at *5 (W.D. Mich. July 3, 2003) (when software buyer's fraud claim was based on allegations that software lacked the character for which buyer bargained, fraud was interwoven with the breach of contract claim and was accordingly barred by the economic loss doctrine); Gen. Elec. Co. v. Latin Am. Imports, S.A., 214 F. Supp. 2d 758, 764 (W.D. Ky. 2002) (when fraud alleged goes to terms of the contract itself, the fraud is inseparable from the contract claims and is barred by the economic loss rule); Reilly Foam Corp. v. Rubbermaid Corp., 206 F. Supp. 2d 643, 659 (E.D. Pa. 2002) (claim based on defendant's failure to make its requirements purchases exclusively from plaintiff related to quantity terms that were directly covered by the contract); Huron Tool & Eng'g Co. v. Precision Consulting Services, Inc., 209 Mich. App. 365, 532 N.W.2d 541, 545 (1995).

19.6   Air Products & Chemicals, Inc. v. Eaton Metal Products Co., 256 F. Supp. 2d 329, 338, 339 (E.D. Pa. 2003) (economic loss doctrine did not bar claim contract induced by fraud regarding a subject outside the terms of the contract itself, distinguishing Werwinski v. Ford Motor Co., 286 F.3d 661 (3d Cir. 2002), on grounds that the fraud alleged in that case related to the defective goods themselves whereas in this case the representation concerned the seller's industry certification to produce the goods sold); Ohio Bell Tel. Co. v. CoreComm Newco, Inc., 214 F. Supp. 2d 810, 820 (N.D. Ohio 2002) (promise relating to defendant's business intentions that was not a contract term could be basis of fraudulent inducement claim); Gen. Elec. Co. v. Latin Am. Imports, S.A., 214 F. Supp. 2d 758, 764 (W.D. Ky. 2002) (misrepresentations regarding defendant's intent to award an exclusive distributorship to plaintiff were distinct from the terms of the contract between the parties, and therefore could be the basis of a tort action); Loughridge v. Goodyear Tire & Rubber Co., 192 F. Supp. 2d 1175, 1183 (D. Colo. 2002) (when defendant had duty to act reasonably outside of its contractual duties, economic loss rule did not preclude tort claims); Am. Express Travel Related Services, Co. v. Symbiont Software, 837 So. 2d 434 (Fla. Dist. Ct. App. 2002) (claims by buyer of software systems against seller based on employee of seller's theft of buyer's information was not barred by economic loss rule as duty at issue arose completely outside the contract between the parties); Pendleton Yacht Yard, Inc. v. Smith, 2003 WL 21714927, at *4, *5 (Me. Super. Ct. Mar. 24, 2003) (economic loss rule did not bar negligent misrepresentation claim based on duty arising outside the contract); Cooper v. Berkshire Life Ins. Co., 810 A.2d 1045, 1069, 1070 (Md. Ct. Spec. App. 2002) (insurance agents and brokers have an independent duty to perform professionally); Farm Bureau Mut. Ins. Co. v. Combustion Research Corp., 255 Mich. App. 715, 726, 727, 662 N.W.2d 439, 445 (2003) (*per curiam*) (while economic loss doctrine barred claim based on sale of goods itself, buyers could base a tort claim on the breach of an independent duty to properly inspect the goods that may have arisen from visit by defendant's employee).

19.7   *See, e.g.,* Excess Risk Underwriters, Inc. v. Lafayette Life Ins. Co., 208 F. Supp. 2d 1310, 1320 (S.D. Fla. 2002); Geneva Pharm. Tech. Corp. v. Barr Laboratories, Inc., 201 F. Supp. 2d 236, 287, 288 (S.D.N.Y. 2002) (when allegations in plaintiff's breach of contract claim were same as in negligence and negligent misrepresentation claims, rule barred tort actions).

19.8   *See, e.g.,* Me. Rubber Int'l v. Envtl. Mgmt. Group, Inc., 216 F.R.D. 222, 224, 225 (D. Me. 2003) (doctrine would not bar negligence and negligent misrepresentation claims that were based on professional malpractice, granting leave to plaintiff to amend complaint); Air Products & Chemicals, Inc. v. Eaton Metal Products Co., 329, 342, 343 (E.D. Pa. 2003) (Utah law) (economic loss doctrine did not bar claim when duty breached arose independently of the contract; duty imposed by state statute); Harger v. Spirit Airlines, Inc., 2003 WL 21218968, at *10 (N.D. Ill. May 22, 2003) (statement by agent of defendant, an airline, that passenger's bag would be safe did not create a duty outside of the carriage contract to protect bag, therefore economic loss doctrine barred passenger's negligence claim); *see also* Indemnity Ins. Co. of N. Am. v. Am. Aviation, Inc., 344 F.3d 1136, 1148 (11th Cir. 2003) (*per curiam*) (certifying to Florida Supreme Court question of whether certified mechanical services fell within the "professional services" exception to the economic loss doctrine); Florida State Bd. of Admin. v. Eng'g & Envtl. Services, Inc., 262 F. Supp. 2d 1004, 1018, 1019 (D. Minn. 2003) (Fla. law) (economic loss doctrine barred breach of fiduciary duty and negligence claims that arose solely as a result of the contract between the parties, but did not bar negligent misrepresentation claim).

19.9   *See, e.g.,* Werwinski v. Ford Motor Co., 286 F.3d 661, 680 (3d Cir. 2002) (economic loss doctrine applies to fraudulent concealment claims); Hoseline, Inc. v. U.S.A. Diversified Products, Inc., 40 F.3d 1198, 1200 (11th Cir. 1994) (rule barred buyer's civil theft and fraud claims alleging that seller had misrepresented the amount of product); Excess Risk Underwriters, Inc. v. Lafayette Life Ins. Co., 208 F. Supp. 2d 1310, 1318, 1319 (S.D. Fla. 2002) (ruling that defendant's fraudulent inducement claim was not separate and distinct from the terms of the contract itself); Nelson Distrib., Inc. v. Stewart Warner Indus. Balancers, 808 F. Supp. 684, 688 (D. Minn. 1992) (rule barred buyer's fraudulent inducement claim); Robinson Helicopter Co. v. Dana Corp., 129 Cal. Rptr. 2d 682 (Cal. Ct. App.) (fraud allegations were so intertwined with contract performance that plaintiff could not allege separate damages, therefore economic loss ruled applied to intentional fraud claim), *review granted, opinion superseded by* 68 P.3d 344 (Cal. 2003); Duncan v. Kasim, Inc., 810 So. 2d 968, 970 (Fla. Dist. Ct. App. 2002) (conversion and civil theft claims arose outside the terms of the contract and therefore were not barred by the rule).

19.10   *See* Werwinski v. Ford Motor Co., 286 F.3d 661, 679 (3d Cir. 2002). *Werwinski* rejected policy reasons for an intentional fraud exception to the economic loss rule. The court accepted Ford's argument that its intent to defraud did not increase the amount of damages the plaintiff suffered by virtue of the breach of contract. The decision ignored the potential deleterious effects of ignoring Ford's malice and giving sellers a free pass to defraud, because without the risk of tort damages they would have no incentive not to lie, cheat and steal at every opportunity, with nothing more to fear than routine contract remedies.

19.11   Moransais v. Heathman, 744 So. 2d 973 (Fla. 1996) (professional engineers); Susan Fixel, Inc. v. Rosenthal & Rosenthal, Inc., 842 So. 2d 204, 209 (Fla. Dist. Ct. App. 2003) (doctrine did not bar claim of negligent misrepresentation that alleged a duty to disclose arising from a fiduciary duty, when fiduciary duty arose independently of underlying contract); *see also* Carolina Indus. Products, Inc. v. Learjet, Inc., 189 F. Supp. 2d 1147, 1176 (D. Kan. 2001) (rule did not bar claim for damage caused by defendant's negligent work, as opposed to a defective product). *But see* Florida State Bd. of Admin. v. Eng'g & Envtl. Services, Inc., 262 F. Supp. 2d 1004, 1017, 1019 (D. Minn. 2003) (Fla. law) (*Moransais* did not prevent economic loss rule from barring breach of fiduciary duty and negligence claims that depended upon a breach of the contract).

12.2.2 *Economic Damages May Be Allowed in Consumer, But Not Commercial Cases*

Addition to notes 20–22.

20   *See* Mt. Lebanon Personal Care Home v. Hoover Universal, Inc., 276 F.3d 845 (6th Cir. 2002) (predicting that Kentucky Supreme Court would apply economic loss rule to bar tort claims in business cases, in contrast to consumer cases); Blackward v. Simplex Products Div., 2001 WL 1255924, at *3, 46 U.C.C. Rep. Serv. 2d 397 (Mich. Ct. App. 2001) (economic loss rule did not apply to bar tort claims of plaintiffs, who bought defective exterior cladding system for their home, because they were not a commercial business and had no "commercial or economic expectations" with regard to the system). *But see* Werwinski v. Ford Motor Co. 286 F.3d 661, 674 (3d Cir. 2002) (predicting that Pennsylvania Supreme Court would apply economic loss rule to consumers as well as commercial entities); Sherman v. Sea Ray Boats, Inc., 649 N.W.2d 783, 788 (Mich. Ct. App. 2002) (rejecting commercial/consumer distinction).

Page 451

21   Mt. Lebanon Personal Care Home v. Hoover Universal, Inc., 276 F.3d 845 (6th Cir. 2002); Cook Associates, Inc. v. PCS Sales (USA) Inc., 271 F. Supp. 2d 1343, 1359 (D. Utah 2003) (describing parties as "sophisticated merchants able to anticipate the risks of their transactions and contract accordingly").

22   *See also* HDM Flugservice GmbH v. Parker Hannifin Corp., 332 F.3d 1025, 1032 (6th Cir. 2003) (Ohio law) (attributing to commercial purchaser the ability to allocate the risk of loss of the defective helicopter, distinguishing "a consumer purchasing a product from a store, who does not negotiate warranties or allocate the risk of loss").

12.2.3 Recovery of Economic Injury Where Damage Linked to Accident, Personal Injury, or Property Damage

Addition to notes 24, 25.

24 Menard, Inc. v. U.S. Equities Dev., Inc., 2002 WL 31050160, at *8, *9 (N.D. Ill. Sept. 13, 2002) (exception applied to allow party that had contracted for store to be built to sue in tort for defective retaining wall). *But see* Full Faith Church of Love W., Inc. v. Hoover Treated Wood Products, Inc., 224 F. Supp. 2d 1285, 1291 (D. Kan. Sept. 26, 2002) (rejecting exception); Mars, Inc. v. Heritage Builders of Effingham, Inc., 763 N.E.2d 428, 436–439 (Ill. App. Ct. 2002) (though thunderstorm that caused warehouse frame to collapse was a "sudden and dangerous" occurrence, economic loss rule still applied because plaintiff failed to show that the frame was "other property"; court confusingly conflates the sudden and dangerous exception with the other property exception).

Page 452

25 *Delete 532 Madison Ave. Gourmet Foods citation*; *add to note's first paragraph*: Hinkle Eng'g, Inc. v. 175 Jackson Ltd. Liab. Co., 2001 WL 1246757, at *3 (N.D. Ill. Oct. 18, 2001) (when damage was caused by sudden event, as opposed to slow deterioration, rule did not apply); T.H.S. Northstar Associates, Ltd. v. W.R. Grace & Co., 767 F. Supp. 969 (D. Minn. 1991) (risk of injury from asbestos was not one that would ordinarily be contemplated by parties to a commercial transaction); Indep. Sch. Dist. No. 197 v. W.R. Grace & Co., 752 F. Supp. 286 (D. Minn. 1990) (same); Council of Co-Owners Atlantis Condominium, Inc. v. Whiting-Turner Contracting Co., 308 Md. 18, 517 A.2d 336, 344, 345 (1986) (homeowners may recover in tort costs of correcting construction defects that present "a clear danger of death or personal injury"). *But see* Mt. Lebanon Personal Care Home, Inc. v. Hoover Universal, Inc., 276 F.3d 845, 853 (6th Cir. 2002) (rejecting a serious risk of injury exception to the economic loss rule); Aas v. Superior Court, 24 Cal. 4th 627, 101 Cal. Rptr. 2d 718, 12 P.3d 1125, 1140 (2000) (whether economic loss rule applies depends on whether property damage has occurred rather than on the possible gravity of damages that have not yet occurred); Restatement (Third) of Torts § 21 cmt. d (rejecting exception from economic loss rule for product defects that raise a serious risk of injury).

Add to text at end of subsection:

The distinction between damage to the product sold itself, which is not recoverable in tort, and damage to other property, which is recoverable, is examined in § 12.2.6, *infra*.

12.2.4 Repairs and Services

Addition to note 27.

27 Heidtman Steel Products, Inc. v. Compuware Corp., 168 F. Supp. 2d 743 (N.D. Ohio 2001) (economic loss rule does not apply to claim of fraud in services contract); Carolina Indus. Products, Inc. v. Learjet, Inc., 189 F. Supp. 2d 1147, 1176 (D. Kan. 2001) (rule did not bar claim for damage caused by defendant's negligent work, as opposed to a defective product); *see also* Indemnity Ins. Co. of N. Am. v. Am. Aviation, Inc., 344 F.3d 1136, 1148 (11th Cir. 2003) (*per curiam*) (certifying to Florida Supreme Court question of whether state's economic loss doctrine applies to torts if the defendant has provided services to a product rather than has sold a product); SICK, Inc. v. Motion Control Corp., 2003 WL 21448864, at *6 (D. Minn. June 19, 2003) (employing "predominant purpose test" to find that distributorship agreement was primarily for the sale of goods and therefore the economic loss doctrine barred distributor's tort claims). *But see* Fox Associates, Inc. v. Robert Half Int'l, Inc., 777 N.E.2d 603 (Ill. App. Ct. 2002) (economic loss doctrine applies to services as well as products); Farm Bureau Mut. Ins. Co. v. Combustion Research Corp., 255 Mich. App. 715, 722, 723, 662 N.W.2d 439, 443, 444 (*per curiam*) (2003) (buyers could not avoid economic loss rule by claiming that tort claim was based on seller's failure to properly inspect and install heater as opposed to defects in the heater itself, when the purpose of the buyers' contract with seller was to purchase the heater, not to acquire services).

Page 453

12.2.5 Breach of Statutory Duty or Where Special Relationship

Addition to note 31.

31 *Add to Benevento citation*: rev'd on other grounds sub nom. In re LifeUSA Holding Inc., 242 F.3d 136 (3d Cir. 2001); *add*: Biakanja v. Irving, 49 Cal. 2d 647, 320 P.2d 16, 19 (1958) (listing six factors to consider); Cooper v. Berkshire Life Ins. Co., 810 A.2d 1045, 1068, 1069 (Md. Ct. Spec. App. 2002) (an "intimate nexus" between the parties will avoid the economic loss doctrine; nexus element may be satisfied by contractual privity or by the defendant's supplying of false information for the guidance of the plaintiff in the plaintiff's business transactions); E. Steel Constructors, Inc. v. City of Salem, 209 W. Va. 392, 549 S.E.2d 266 (2001) (construction contractor may recover purely economic damages for negligence from a design professional because contractors belong to a special class of plaintiffs particularly foreseeable to the defendant).

12.2.6 Distinguishing Economic Loss from Property Damage

Addition to note 36.   36   *Add*: *See, e.g.*, Erie Ins. Group v. Ford Motor Co., 51 Pa. D. & C.4th 220, 223 (C.P. Adams County 2001) (plaintiff could recover economic damages suffered when insured's personal property within car was destroyed when car burned up); *add new paragraph to end of note*: See also Restatement (Third) of Torts § 21, which provides:

> For purposes of this Restatement, harm to persons or property includes economic loss if caused by harm to:
>> (a) the plaintiff's person; or
>> (b) the person of another when harm to the other interferes with an interest of the plaintiff protected by tort law; or
>> *(c) the plaintiff's property other than the defective product itself.*

(Emphasis added).

Add to text at end of subsection's first paragraph: In some jurisdictions the "other property" injured must have belonged to the buyer, and not some third party, to escape the rule.[36.1]

36.1   *See, e.g.*, Am. Specialty Sys., Inc. v. Chicago Metallic Corp., 47 U.C.C. Rep. Serv. 2d 949 (N.D. Ill. Mar. 15, 2002) (plaintiff, who bought defendant's system to incorporate into its own product, which it then placed in a third party's manufacturing plants, could not rely on damage the system did to the plants to escape economic loss rule); *In re* StarLink Corn Products Liab. Litig., 212 F. Supp. 2d 828, 841 (N.D. Ill. 2002) (plaintiff must have an ownership interest in the "other property").

Page 454

Addition to note 40.   40   *Add to Rich Prods. Corp. citation*: *aff'd*, 241 F.3d 915 (7th Cir. 2001); *add*: *See, e.g.*, Irish Venture, Inc. v. Fleetguard, Inc., 270 F. Supp. 2d 84, 85–87 (D. Mass. 2003) (economic loss doctrine did not bar negligence claim to recover damage to engine caused by defective oil filter sold by defendant); Jiminez v. Super. Ct., 127 Cal. Rptr. 2d 614, 623 (Cal. 2002) (manufacturer of a defective window installed in a mass-produced home may be held strictly liable in tort for damage the window causes to other parts of the home; "the duty of a product manufacturer to prevent property damage does not necessarily end when the product is incorporated into a larger product"); Shoreline Care Ltd. P'ship v. Jansen & Rogan Consulting Engineers, Prof'l Corp., 31 Conn. L. Rptr. 223, 2002 WL 173155, at *2 (Conn. Super. Ct. 2002) (allowing plaintiff to assert negligence claim for property damage resulting from defective HVAC system); Berish v. Bornstein, 770 N.E.2d 961, 975 (Mass. 2002) (vacating dismissal of negligence count against builder when condominium association claimed that construction defects caused property damage beyond the defects themselves); Aldrich v. Add Inc., 770 N.E.2d 447, 455 (Mass. 2002) (economic loss rule did not bar negligence claim against architect based on structural defects in condominium); Stonhard v. Advanced Glassfiber Yarns, Inc., 2001 WL 1807359, at *2 (Pa. C.P. Nov. 21, 2001) (original flooring damaged by defective flooring installed over it was "other property" for purposes of rule; court focused on what the defendant put "into the stream of commerce"); Messer Griesheim Indus., Inc. v. Cryotech of Kingsport, Inc., 2003 WL 21634392, at *7 (Tenn. Ct. App. July 10, 2003) (buyer's carbon dioxide that was contaminated by seller's feedgas carbon dioxide was "other property"; granting summary judgment to seller on other grounds); *see also* Indemnity Ins. Co. of N. Am. v. Am. Aviation, Inc., 344 F.3d 1136, 1148 (11th Cir. 2003) (*per curiam*) (certifying to Florida Supreme Court question of whether aircraft that was damaged by a defective landing gear was damage to "other property" under state's economic loss doctrine); KB Home v. Super. Ct., 112 Cal. App. 4th 1076, 1087, 1088, 5 Cal. Rptr. 3d 587, 597 (2003) (whether defective component is separate from damaged property depends on whether it is a "sufficiently discrete element of the larger product that it is not reasonable to expect its failure invariably to damage other portions of the finished product"; granting writ of mandate to builder who had brought products liability claims against manufacturer of furnaces for damages caused to furnaces by defective emissions control device). *But see* Mt. Lebanon Personal Care Home v. Hoover Universal, Inc., 276 F.3d 845 (6th Cir. 2002) (applying economic loss rule to bar claim for damages to building caused by failure of trusses when commercial parties had allocated the risks by their contract and when the buyer's contract was with the builder for construction of the building, not with the manufacturer of the trusses); Delmarva Power & Light v. Meter-Treater, Inc., 218 F. Supp. 2d 564, 570, 571 (D. Del. July 31, 2002) (damage to vehicles caused by meters sold by defendant, measured at $171.36, were too tiny to support "other property" exception to economic loss rule given the millions of dollars plaintiff sought); Premix-Marbletite Mfg. Corp. v. SKW Chems., Inc., 145 F. Supp. 2d 1348, 1359, 1360 (S.D. Fla. 2001) (discoloring of pools by defective coating was not damage to other property but damage to the finished product of which defective product was a part).

*Add to text following
sentence containing note 40:*
Nonetheless, when the proffered "other property" is a system of which the failing product was a part or a component, many courts will still deny recovery on the basis of the economic loss rule.[40.1]

> 40.1   *See, e.g.*, HDM Flugservice GmbH v. Parker Hannifin Corp., 332 F.3d 1025, 1027–1032 (6th Cir. 2003) (Ohio law) (damage to rest of helicopter caused by defect in landing gear not recoverable in tort); Kice Indus., Inc. v. AWC Coatings, Inc., 255 F. Supp. 2d 1255, 1258, 1259 (D. Kan. 2003) (damage caused to equipment by paint not recoverable in tort); Higginbotham v. Dryvit Sys., Inc., 2003 WL 1528483, at *4 (M.D.N.C. Mar. 20, 2003) (mag.) (economic loss rule barred home owner's tort claims for damage to house based on defective synthetic stucco applied to house—rejecting argument that because stucco would be treated as a separate product under the U.C.C. it should be treated as a separate component of the house for purposes of the other property exception to the economic loss rule); Full Faith Church of Love W., Inc. v. Hoover Treated Wood Products, Inc., 224 F. Supp. 2d 1285, 1290 (D. Kan. 2002) (defective roof trusses were integrated into roof, therefore plaintiff could not recover in tort for damage trusses caused to roof); Wilson v. Dryvit Sys., Inc., 206 F. Supp. 2d 749, 754 (E.D.N.C. 2002) (new home damaged by defective external cladding system was not other property because the cladding was an "integral component" of the house), *aff'd*, 2003 WL 21805618 (4th Cir. Aug. 7, 2003) (*per curiam*) (unpublished); Mars, Inc. v. Heritage Builders of Effingham, Inc., 763 N.E.2d 428, 436–439 (Ill. App. Ct. 2002) (plaintiff could not recover in tort for warehouse frame that was to become integrated into warehouse being built by defendant); Gunkel v. Renovations, Inc., 797 N.E.2d 841, 845 (Ind. Ct. App. 2003) (damage caused to home's walls, ceilings, floors, carpets, and drywall by defective facade work was not damage to other property, economic loss doctrine barred home owners' negligence claim against stone mason); Norris v. Church & Co., 108 Wash. App. 1050, 2001 WL 1301337, at *9 (2001) (home purchasers could not recover in negligence for damage done to home by defects in materials and workmanship that caused structure to deteriorate); Mequon Med. Associates v. S.T.O. Indus., Inc., 671 N.W.2d 717 (Wis. Ct. App. 2003) (table) (text available at 2003 WL 22093818) (once exterior insulation finish system applied to building the building was no longer "other property" and economic loss doctrine barred buyer's products liability claims); Selzer v. Brunsell Bros., Ltd., 652 N.W.2d 806, 818 (Wis. Ct. App. 2002) (defective windows were integrated into the house, therefore siding damaged by rot was not "other property" for which plaintiff could recover); Bay Breeze Condo. Ass'n, Inc. v. Norco Windows, Inc., 651 N.W.2d 738, 745, 746 (Wis. Ct. App. 2002) (holding that economic loss doctrine bars tort action based on building construction defects when defective product, such as a window, is a component part of an integrated structure or finished product).

Addition to note 41.
> 41   *See, e.g.*, Longport Ocean Plaza Condo., Inc. v. Robert Cato & Associates, 2002 WL 2013925 (E.D. Pa. Aug. 29, 2002) (condominium's owner could not recover in tort for damage done to building by faulty renovation); Radford v. Daimler Chrysler Corp., 168 F. Supp. 2d 751 (N.D. Ohio 2001) (economic loss rule barred tort action for damages for destruction of car caused by faulty instrument panel; car, into which panel had been integrated, was not "other property"); Premix-Marblelite Mfg. Corp. v. SKW Chems., Inc., 145 F. Supp. 2d 1348, 1359 n.13 (S.D. Fla. 2001); Mars, Inc. v. Heritage Builders of Effingham, Inc., 763 N.E.2d 428, 438 (Ill. App. Ct. 2002) (when plaintiff had bargained for a completed warehouse, plaintiff could not recover in tort for damage to warehouse frame that was to become an integrated part of the warehouse); Fennell v. Green, 77 P.3d 339, 344 (Utah Ct. App. 2003) (damage to landscaping caused by landslide on unstable portion of lot was not damage to "other property" when home owner had purchased whole lot as a single package); *see also* Alcan Aluminum Corp. v. BASF Corp., 133 F. Supp. 2d 482, 504 (N.D. Tex. 2001) (when plaintiff assembled defective component into an integrated product, damage extending beyond component was not damage to "other property," reasoning that, in the context of a commercial transaction, damage to other components was clearly foreseeable and therefore covered by contract principles).

*Add to text at end of
subsection's third paragraph:*
A recent Sixth Circuit decision has broadened the scope of the property covered by the economic loss rule by holding that it includes "the entire unit for which a party to a complex commercial transaction has the ability to distribute risk by contract and insure against loss."[41.1] In theory, this principle would expand the rule to the limits of the widest possible insurance policy, however disconnected the defective product might be from the other property it damaged. Even if the plaintiff was not in privity with the seller of the defective product—and therefore could not have negotiated risk allocation with the seller—the rule as framed would nonetheless shield the seller from tort liability.[41.2] Another court focused on the buyer's expectations, suggesting that if a buyer could have foreseen that the failure of the defective product would have caused the damage, the damage does not constitute harm to other property.[41.3]

> 41.1   Mt. Lebanon Personal Care Home, Inc. v. Hoover Universal, Inc., 276 F.3d 845, 848 (6th Cir. 2002) (Ky. law) ("product" was entire nursing home that plaintiff had contracted to have built, so the rule precluded

plaintiff from recovering damages caused to the structure by defective fire retardant chemical used to treat lumber in building's trusses).

41.2   *Id*. The court reasoned that the plaintiff could have negotiated a comprehensive warranty with the general contractor with whom it directly contracted. *See also* Excess Risk Underwriters, Inc. v. Lafayette Life Ins. Co., 208 F. Supp. 2d 1310, 1314 (S.D. Fla. 2002) (privity not required to raise economic loss doctrine as a defense).

41.3   *In re* StarLink Corn Products Liab. Litig., 212 F. Supp. 2d 828, 841 (N.D. Ill. 2002).

12.3 Elements of Strict Liability in Tort

12.3.1 Introduction

Page 455

Addition to note 47.

47   Smith v. Bryco Arms, 33 P.3d 638, 644 (N.M. 2001); *see also* Green v. Smith & Nephew AHP, Inc., 629 N.W.2d 727, 750 (Wis. 2001).

Add to text at end of subsection's first paragraph:

In contrast to negligence, strict products liability imposes liability without regard to the concepts of duty, or care, or foreseeability.[48.1]

48.1   *See, e.g.*, Green v. Smith & Nephew AHP, Inc., 629 N.W.2d 727, 746 (Wis. 2001).

Page 456

Add to text at end of subsection:

A number of states have codified their products liability laws into statutes.[48.2] These statutes are the first source to examine when considering a products liability claim. Note that North Carolina[48.3] and Virginia[48.4] do not yet recognize strict liability in products liability cases, and Michigan courts may not allow such claims to be asserted in conjunction with negligence and implied warranty claims.[48.5]

48.2   Ala. Code §§ 6-5-525 (limitations periods, evidence); Ariz. Rev. Stat. §§ 12-681 to 12-687; Ark. Code Ann. §§ 16-116-101 to 16-116-107 (Michie); Cal Civ Code § 17-14-45 (West) (consumer products known to be inherently unsafe); Colo. Rev. Stat. § 30-80-106 (limitations period); Conn. Gen. Stat. §§ 52-572m to 52-572q; Ga. Code Ann. §§ 51-1-11.1, 51-1-22.1; 735 Ill. Comp. Stat. §§ 5/2-621 (pleading), 5/2-623 (certificate of merit required), 5/2-2101 to 5/2-2109, 5/13-213 (statute of repose) (note that portions of the Illinois provisions were declared unconstitutional by Best v. Taylor Mach. Works, 689 N.E.2d 1057 (Ill. 1997)); Ind. Code §§ 34-20-1-1 to 34-20-9-1; Iowa Code §§ 613.18 (limitation on liability of non-manufacturer), 668.12 (state of the art defense); Kan. Stat. Ann. §§ 60-3301 to 60-5307; Ky. Rev. Stat. Ann. §§ 411.300 to 411.350 (Michie); La. Rev. Stat. Ann. §§ 9:2800.51 to 9:2800.60 (West); Me. Rev. Stat. Ann. tit. 14, § 221 (West) (defective or unreasonably dangerous goods); Md. Code Ann., Cts. & Jud. Proc. § 5-405 (product liability, sealed receptacle defense); Mich. Comp. Laws §§ 600.2946 to 600.2949a; Minn. Stat. § 544.41 (limit on liability of non-manufacturers); Miss. Code Ann. § 11-1-63; Mo. Rev. Stat. §§ 537.760 to 537.765; Mont. Code Ann. § 27-1-719; N.H. Rev. Stat. Ann. §§ 507-D:1 to 507-D:5; N.J. Stat. Ann. §§ 2A:58C-1 to 2A:58C-11 (West); N.C. Gen. Stat. §§ 99B-1 to 99B-11 (§ 99B-1.1 abolishes strict liability in tort for products liability actions); N.D. Cent. Code §§ 28-01.3-01 to 28-01.3-09; Ohio Rev. Code Ann. §§ 2307.71 to 2307.801 (West); Or. Rev. Stat. §§ 30.900 to 30.927; S.C. Code Ann. §§ 15-73-10 to 15-73-40 (Law. Co-op.); Tenn. Code Ann. §§ 29-28-101 to 29-28-108; Tex. Civ. Prac. & Rem. Code Ann. §§ 82.001 to 82.006 (Vernon); Utah Code Ann. §§ 78-15-1 to 78-15-7; Wash. Rev. Code §§ 7.72.010 to 7.72.060.

48.3   Holley v. Burroughs Wellcome Co., 330 S.E.2d 228, 232 (N.C. Ct. App. 1985) (1980), *aff'd*, 348 S.E.2d 772 (N.C. 1986).

48.4   Harris v. T.I., Inc., 413 S.E.2d 605, 609, 610 (Va. 1992).

48.5   Johnson v. Chrysler Corp., 254 N.W.2d 569, 571 (Mich. Ct. App. 1979).

12.3.2 Strict Liability Can Apply to Retailers, Manufacturers, and Lessors

Addition to notes 51–53.

51   *See, e.g.*, Md. Code Ann., Cts. & Jud. Proc. § 5-405 (product liability, sealed receptacle defense); Minn. Stat. § 544.41; N.C. Gen. Stat. § 99B-2 (sealed container defense); N.D. Cent. Code § 28-01.3-04; Ohio Rev. Code Ann. § 2307.78 (West); Tenn. Code Ann. § 29-28-106; *see also In re* Bridgestone/Firestone, Inc. Products Liab. Litig., 204 F. Supp. 2d 1149 (S.D. Ind. 2002) (citing Georgia statute barring strict liability claims against sellers who are not manufacturers).

52   *Add to beginning of note*: Smith v. Bryco Arms, 33 P.3d 638, 644 (N.M. 2001) (supplier is liable to persons the supplier can reasonably expect to use the product and to be in the vicinity during the use of the product).

53   Ritchie v. Glidden Co., 242 F.3d 713, 726, 727 (7th Cir. 2001) (holding that supplier could be liable for failure to warn of dangers of pump, reversing summary judgment for defendant); *see also* Restatement (Second) of Torts § 388 (imposing liability on a supplier of goods that are known to be dangerous for an intended use if the supplier does not use reasonable care to warn the buyer of the dangers).

Page 458

12.3.3 Products Covered

Addition to note 62.

62   *See, e.g.*, Mangual v. Abdul, Inc., 2002 WL 819060, at *3 (Conn. Super. Ct. Apr. 2, 2002) (Connecticut products liability statute does not allow claim for services); Romeo v. Pittsburgh Associates, 787 A.2d 1027, 1032 (Pa. Super. Ct. 2001) (sale of ticket to a baseball game is sale of a service, not a product, therefore strict products liability does not apply).

Add to text at end of subsection:

The Consumer Product Safety Commission regulates certain consumer products under the authority of the Consumer Products Safety Act,[64.1] which may raise preemption issues when that product becomes the subject of a products liability suit. The Ninth Circuit has recently held, however, that the preemption clause of the Act, which specifies that a federal safety standard for a particular product preempts a state safety standard or regulation, did not preclude strict liability and negligence claims against the manufacturer of a shower door that was subject to a federal product safety standard.[64.2] The court ruled not only that the Act does not preempt common law claims premised on violations of the federal safety standards, but that the Act does not preempt claims that rely on a state-established standard of care which exceeds the federal safety standard.[64.3] There was no conflict, reasoned the court, because it would be possible for a manufacturer to meet both federal and state requirements; furthermore, state common law tort actions would not conflict with the goal of the Act, which is to minimize conflicting regulations.[64.4] Rather, the Act merely created a minimum level of safety standards, leaving states free to create higher non-conflicting standards, whether through common law or otherwise.[64.5]

64.1   15 U.S.C. §§ 2051–2084.
64.2   Leipart v. Guardian Indus., 234 F.3d 1063, 1067 (9th Cir. 2000).
64.3   *Id.* at 1069, 1070.
64.4   *Id.* at 1070. The court applied the conflict analysis of Hines v. Davidowitz, 312 U.S. 52 (1941).
64.5   *Leipart*, 234 F.3d at 1070.

12.3.4 Defective Condition

Addition to notes 67, 69, 71.

67   *Add to beginning of note*: Beneway v. Superwinch, Inc., 216 F. Supp. 2d 24, 29 (N.D.N.Y. 2002); McCroy v. Coastal Mart, Inc., 207 F. Supp. 2d 1265, 1271 (D. Kan. 2002); Chapman v. Bernard's Inc., 167 F. Supp. 2d 406, 416 (D. Mass. 2001) (to prove defective design, consumer must show that due to a defect that made product unreasonably dangerous, it was not fit for ordinary uses, which include those that the manufacturer intended and those that are reasonably foreseeable); Shreve v. Sears, Roebuck & Co., 166 F. Supp. 2d 378, 407 (D. Md. 2001); Carballo-Rodriguez v. Clark Equip. Co., 147 F. Supp. 2d 66, 71 (D. P.R. 2001); Vautour v. Body Masters Sports Indus., Inc., 784 A.2d 1178, 1182 (N.H. 2001); Smith v. Bryco Arms, 33 P.3d 638, 644 (N.M. 2001).

69   *Add before McCarthy citation: See also* Chapman v. Maytag Corp., 297 F.3d 682, 289 (7th Cir. 2002) (Ind. law) (adequate warnings can not cure a product with a manufacturing defect, regardless of whether the consumer failed to comply with the warnings); *add*: E.g., Beneway v. Superwinch, Inc., 216 F. Supp. 2d 24, 28 (N.D.N.Y. 2002); McCroy v. Coastal Mart, Inc., 207 F. Supp. 2d 1265, 1271 (D. Kan. 2002); Huffine v. Kawasaki Motors Corp., 2002 WL 459933, at *4 (N.D. Tex. Jan. 31, 2002); Shreve v. Sears, Roebuck & Co., 166 F. Supp. 2d 378, 413 (D. Md. 2001) (plaintiff must show that defendant knew or should have known of the danger in order to demonstrate a duty to warn of such danger); Marshall v. Sheldahl, Inc., 150 F. Supp. 2d 400, 405 (N.D.N.Y. 2001) (manufacturer must anticipate reasonably foreseeable uses of a product in making warnings); Chandler v. Gene Messer Ford, Inc., 81 S.W.3d 493, 504 (Tex. App. 2002) (listing five elements for a marketing defect, or failure to warn, claim, and noting that plaintiff is entitled to a presumption that proper warnings would have been followed if provided); Coleman v. Cintas Sales Corp., 40 S.W.3d 544, 551 (Tex. App. 2001) (reversing summary judgment for manufacturer on marketing defect claim); *add new paragraph at end of note*: The Restatement (Third) of Torts specifies circumstances when a seller should be liable for failing to give a post-sale warning. Restatement (Third) of Torts: Products Liability § 10.

Page 459

71   Rudd v. GMC, 127 F. Supp. 2d 1330, 1345 (M.D. Ala. 2001) (under Alabama doctrine, plaintiff can show product was defective or unreasonably dangerous despite a lack of direct evidence identifying a specific defect).

12.3.5 *The Unreasonably Dangerous Requirement*

Addition to notes 72, 73.

72   *See, e.g.*, Harris v. Gen. Motors Corp., 34 Fed. Appx. 487, 489 (7th Cir. 2002); Giles v. Miners, Inc., 242 F.3d 810, 813 (8th Cir. 2001); McCroy v. Coastal Mart, Inc., 207 F. Supp. 2d 1265, 1271 (D. Kan. 2002) (noting that plaintiff must prove that the product is both defective *and* unreasonably dangerous); Epler v. Jansport, Inc., 2001 U.S. Dist. LEXIS 1890, at *5 (E.D. Pa. Feb. 22, 2001) (for court to decide as an initial matter of law whether product is unreasonably dangerous); Chandler v. Gene Messer Ford, Inc., 81 S.W.3d 493, 503 (Tex. App. 2002).

73   *Add to note's first paragraph: See also* Ford v. GACS, Inc., 265 F.3d 670 (8th Cir. 2001) (for jury to determine what is unreasonably dangerous, without reference to any specific test); Wheeler v. Ho Sports, Inc., 232 F.3d 754, 758 (10th Cir. 2000); McCroy v. Coastal Mart, Inc., 207 F. Supp. 2d 1265, 1274 (D. Kan. 2002) (plaintiff failed to show convenience store's hot chocolate was so hot as to be unreasonably dangerous for a heated beverage).

Add to text at end of subsection's first paragraph:

However, if a particular danger is so open and obvious that no reasonable consumer would take that risk, the danger may not be considered a design defect.[73.1]

73.1   *See, e.g.*, Ford v. GACS, Inc., 265 F.3d 670, 676 (8th Cir. 2001) (Mo. law); Huffine v. Kawasaki Motors Corp., 2002 WL 459933, at *4 (N.D. Tex. Jan. 31, 2002) (no duty to warn when risks are ordinary knowledge, and supplier may rely on expertise of user in creating warning); Marshall v. Sheldahl, Inc., 150 F. Supp. 2d 400, 405 (N.D.N.Y. 2001) (dangers of putting fingers in running machine so open and obvious that failure to provide hand shield was not a design defect); *see also* McCroy v. Coastal Mart, Inc., 207 F. Supp. 2d 1265, 1277, 1278 (D. Kan. 2002) (even if the resulting injury was more serious than an average consumer would expect, if the expectation was mistaken only as to degree of injury and not as to kind, no liability will arise).

Page 460

Addition to notes 74, 77.

74   *Replace McCathern citation with*: 332 Or. 59, 23 P.3d 320 (2001); *add to note's first paragraph: See, e.g.*, Shreve v. Sears, Roebuck & Co., 166 F. Supp. 2d 378, 416 (D. Md. 2001) (listing seven factors considered in risk/utility test); Carballo-Rodriguez v. Clark Equip. Co., 147 F. Supp. 2d 66, 72 (D. P.R. 2001) (factors to be considered include gravity of the danger, likelihood it would occur, feasibility of alternative design, and adverse consequences of alternate design); Epler v. Jansport, Inc., 2001 U.S. Dist. LEXIS 1890, at *7, *8 (E.D. Pa. Feb. 22, 2001) (listing seven factors for court to consider in employing risk/utility test); Vautour v. Body Masters Sports Indus., Inc., 784 A.2d 1178, 1182 (N.H. 2001); *add to second sentence of note's second paragraph: see also* U.S. Xpress, Inc. v. Great N. Ins. Co., 2003 WL 124021, at *3 (D. Minn. Jan. 8, 2003) (citing seven factors to be evaluated that include both consumer expectations and risk/utility factors).

77   *Add following citation to Restatement (Third) of Torts § 2(b)*: Burt v. Makita USA, Inc., 212 F. Supp. 2d 893, 900 (N.D. Ind. 2002) (entering summary judgment against plaintiff who failed to show a feasible alternative design for table saw that would have reduced the risk of injury); *see, e.g.*, Giles v. Miners, Inc., 242 F.3d 810 (8th Cir. 2001); Marshall v. Sheldahl, Inc., 150 F. Supp. 2d 400, 403 (N.D.N.Y. 2001) (plaintiff must show that item could feasibly have been designed more safely); Rudd v. Gen. Motors Corp., 127 F. Supp. 2d 1330, 1347 (M.D. Ala. 2001) (plaintiff must show that injuries would have been reduced by the alternative design and that the utility of the alternative design, including styling and cost, would have outweighed the utility of the design used); *add to end of note: See, e.g., In re* Methyl Tertiary Butyl Ether Products Liab. Litig., 175 F. Supp. 2d 593 (S.D.N.Y. 2001) (citing Third Restatement); Vautour v. Body Masters Sports Indus., Inc., 784 A.2d 1178, 1182 (N.H. 2001) (plaintiff did not need to prove a safer, alternative design in addition to the risk-utility factors); Green v. Smith & Nephew AHP, Inc., 629 N.W.2d 727, 752 (Wis. 2001) (rejecting Restatement (Third) of Torts: Products Liability § 2(b), criticizing it for adding a "considerable" element of proof, an excessive burden on injured persons).

Add to text at end of subsection's second paragraph:

Some jurisdictions, such as Missouri, have declined to define "unreasonably dangerous," leaving it for the jury to determine on a case-by-case basis.[78.1]

78.1   *See, e.g.*, Ford v. GACS, Inc., 265 F.3d 670, 677 (8th Cir. 2001) (Mo. law), *cert. denied*, 535 U.S. 954 (2002).

Addition to note 83.

83   *See also* Wheeler v. Ho Sports, Inc., 232 F.3d 754, 759 (10th Cir. 2000) (life jacket's warning that it was insufficient to float a person face-up did not adequately warn wearer that it would not float a person at all); Carballo-Rodriguez v. Clark Equip. Co., 147 F. Supp. 2d 66, 72 (D. P.R. 2001) (duty to warn extends to all reasonably foreseeable uses of a product); *add to end of note*: The court will evaluate the warning from the perspective of an ordinary user of the product, as opposed to someone completely unfamiliar with the product. *See, e.g.*, McLennan v. Am. Eurocopter Corp., 245 F.3d 403, 429 (5th Cir. 2001) (helicopter manufacturer had no duty to warn of problem that was common knowledge among experienced pilots such as the plaintiff).

Page 461

Add to text after subsection's fifth paragraph:

A product safety statute may be relevant in determining whether a product is unreasonably dangerous. *The Restatement (Third) of Torts* provides that a product's noncompliance with such a statute renders it defective with respect to those risks sought to be reduced by the statute.[87.1] On the other hand, compliance with such a statute is not determinative, although compliance should be considered when determining whether the product is defective.[87.2] A seller may also be liable for harm caused by the seller's failure to recall a product after sale.[87.3]

[87.1]   Restatement (Third) of Torts: Products Liability § 4.

[87.2]   *Id.*

[87.3]   *The Restatement (Third) of Torts* provides:

> One engaged in the business of selling or otherwise distributing products is subject to liability for harm to persons or property caused by the seller's failure to recall a product after the time of sale or distribution if:
>
> (a) (1) a governmental directive issued pursuant to a statute or administrative regulation specifically requires the seller or distributor to recall the product; or
>
> (a) (2) the seller or distributor, in the absence of a recall requirement under Subsection (a)(1), undertakes to recall the product; and
>
> (b) the seller or distributor fails to act as a reasonable person in recalling the product.

Restatement (Third) of Torts: Products Liability § 11.

12.3.6 Causation

Addition to notes 93, 95.

93   *Replace Dyson citation with*: 113 F. Supp. 2d 1093 (D.D.C. 2000) (claim dismissed), *aff'd*, 2001 WL 1297493 (D.C. Cir. Sept. 12, 2001).

95   *Replace Dyson citation with*: 113 F. Supp. 2d 35 (D.D.C. 2000) (affirming summary judgment for manufacturer because plaintiff failed to show failure to warn proximately caused her child's injuries), *aff'd*, 2001 WL 1297493 (D.C. Cir. Sept. 12, 2001); *replace entire Wright citation with*: 259 F.3d 1226 (10th Cir. 2001) (affirming summary judgment for manufacturer); *add: See, e.g.*, Wilson v. Bradlees of New Eng., Inc., 250 F.3d 10, 14, 15 (1st Cir. 2001) (affirming trial court's finding that plaintiff failed to show that a more particularized warning as to sweatshirt's flammability would have prevented child from reaching for kettle on kitchen stove, which resulted in burns).

Page 462

12.3.7 Use in a Normal or Foreseeable Manner

Addition to notes 97, 99.

97   *See also* Burt v. Makita USA, Inc., 212 F. Supp. 2d 893, 897, 898 (N.D. Ind. 2002) (consumer's misuse of a product not reasonably foreseeable and thus completely bars products liability claim); Jonas v. Isuzu Motors Ltd., 210 F. Supp. 2d 1373, 1377 (M.D. Ga. 2002) (manufacturers are liable for foreseeable misuses of property).

99   *Add to note's first paragraph: See* Boerner v. Brown & Williamson Tobacco Corp., 260 F.3d 837, 848 (8th Cir. 2001) (Ark. law) (contributory negligence does not bar recovery under strict liability theory, so existence of a filtered cigarette that consumer could have used was irrelevant to whether cigarette she did use was unreasonably dangerous); Mayor of Baltimore v. Utica Mut. Ins. Co., 802 A.2d 1070, 1089 (Md. Ct. Spec. App.) (contributory negligence defense may be asserted in failure to warn negligence actions but not in strict liability actions), *cert. granted*, 810 A.2d 961 (Md. 2002). *But see* Lienhart v. Dryvit Sys., Inc., 255 F.3d 138, 148 (4th Cir. 2001) (N.C. law) (failure of user to follow adequate warnings absolutely precludes liability under products liability theory); Burt v. Makita USA, Inc., 212 F. Supp. 2d 893, 897, 898 (N.D. Ind. 2002) (citing Indiana statute that permits misuse and incurred risk defenses); *add to note's second paragraph: See, e.g.*, Ford v. GACS, Inc., 265 F.3d 670, 676 (8th Cir. 2001) (Mo. law) (openness and obviousness of any alleged design defect does not preclude recovery).

12.4 Elements of the Negligence Claim

12.4.1 Duty to Conform to a Reasonable Standard of Conduct

Page 463

12.4.1.1 General

Addition to notes 101, 102.

101   *Add to end of note*: *The Restatement (Third) of Torts* provides:

> A person acts with negligence if the person does not exercise reasonable care under all the circumstances. Primary factors to consider in ascertaining whether the person's conduct lacks reasonable care are the foreseeable likelihood that it will result in harm, the foreseeable severity of the harm that may ensue, and the burden that would be borne by the person and others if the person takes precautions that eliminate or reduce the possibility of harm.

Restatement (Third) of Torts: Liability Physical Harm § 3.

102   *See also* Carballo-Rodriguez v. Clark Equip. Co., 147 F. Supp. 2d 66, 72 (D. P.R. 2001) (plaintiff must show duty, breach, and causation); Smith v. Bryco Arms, 33 P.3d 638, 645 (N.M. 2001) (manufacturers and suppliers have duty to use ordinary care, including duty to consider risks of injury created by foreseeable misuse of the product); E. Steel Constructors, Inc. v. City of Salem, 209 W. Va. 392, 549 S.E.2d 266 (2001).

Add to text at end of subsection's third paragraph:

A builder who fails to construct a home with the ordinary skill of a skilled builder may also be liable for negligence.[105.1]

105.1   *See, e.g.*, Greene v. Perry, 62 Conn. App. 338, 771 A.2d 196, 199 (2001) (affirming judgment of negligence against building contractor who had failed to use a steel-carrying beam despite architect's recommendation).

Add note 105.2 at end of first sentence of subsection's fourth paragraph.

105.2   *See, e.g.*, Epler v. Jansport, Inc., 2001 U.S. Dist. LEXIS 1890, at *17, *18 (E.D. Pa. Feb. 22, 2001) (duty analysis asks whether a reasonable person should have foreseen the likelihood of harm to the plaintiff from the defendant's conduct).

Addition to note 110.

110   *But see* Smiley v. S & J Investments, Inc., 580 S.E.2d 283, 287, 288 (Ga. Ct. App. 2003) (engineering firm which inspected property for seller, who requested inspection to induce buyers to purchase property, could not be liable for negligence to the buyers for failing to discover structural problems in the property because firm was not in privity with buyers).

Add to text at end of subsection:

Be careful when bringing both strict liability and negligence claims in the same action because, in some jurisdictions, a court may find that, if the claims are based on the same allegations, the claims merge into one another.[110.1]

110.1   *See, e.g.*, Giles v. Miners, Inc., 242 F.3d 810 (8th Cir. 2001); Spain v. Brown & Williamson Tobacco Corp., 230 F.3d 1300 (11th Cir. 2000); Rudd v. Gen. Motors Corp., 127 F. Supp. 2d 1330, 1347 (M.D. Ala. 2001) (plaintiff's negligence claim merged into products liability claim).

Page 464

12.4.1.3 Standard of Care as to Design and Manufacture

Addition to notes 116, 117.

116   *See also* Cigna Ins. Co. v. Oy Saunatec, Ltd., 241 F.3d 1, 15 (1st Cir. 2001) (Mass. law) (manufacturers have duty to design products according to the standard of an ordinary reasonably prudent designer in like circumstances).

117   *Add after Kinser citation*: *See also* Epler v. Jansport, Inc., 2001 U.S. Dist. LEXIS 1890, at *19, *20 (E.D. Pa. Feb. 22, 2001) (even if risk of injury to eye from elasticized draw cord was foreseeable, risk was not unreasonable under a risk/utility analysis).

Add to text at end of subsection:

A building contractor, when constructing a home, has the duty to exercise the degree of care that a skilled builder of ordinary prudence would have exercised under the same or similar conditions.[119.1]

119.1   Greene v. Perry, 62 Conn. App. 338, 771 A.2d 196, 199 (2001).

Page 465

12.4.1.4 Standard of Care as to Inspection for Defects and Preparation for Sale

Addition to note 128.

128   *Replace NCLC citation with*: National Consumer Law Center, Automobile Fraud §§ 2.6.2.4, 6.2.4 (2d ed. 2003).

Page 466

12.4.1.5 Standard of Care to Warn the Consumer of Defects or Dangers in Use

Addition to notes 138, 147.

138   Delahunt v. Cytodyne Technologies, 241 F. Supp. 2d 827, 844 (S.D. Ohio 2003) (buyers of ephedrine stated claim against manufacturer for failure to warn of drug's risks).

147   Epler v. Jansport, Inc., 2001 U.S. Dist. LEXIS 1890, at *20 (E.D. Pa. Feb. 22, 2001) (defendant can be negligent for failure to warn only if danger is not obvious; risks inherent in elasticized cord are obvious).

Page 468

12.4.5 Defenses

Addition to notes 169, 172.

169   *See, e.g.*, Jones v. Ford Motor Co., 559 S.E.2d 592, 605 (Va. 2002) (evidence supported contributory negligence instruction).

172   *See also* Cigna Ins. Co. v. Oy Saunatec, Ltd., 241 F.3d 1, 16 (1st Cir. 2001) (Mass. law).

Add to text at end of subsection's third paragraph:

Comparative negligence may be asserted in those cases in which the buyer misused a product in a foreseeable, but nonetheless arguably unreasonable, way.[172.1] The unreasonable use defense differs from the comparative negligence defense in that every unreasonable use is potential evidence of comparative negligence, but the opposite is not true.[172.2]

172.1   *See, e.g.*, Cigna Ins. Co. v. Oy Saunatec, Ltd., 241 F.3d 1, 16 (1st Cir. 2001) (Mass. law) (if plaintiff subjectively knew that product was defective and dangerous, and plaintiff's use of the product was objectively unreasonable, defense of unreasonable use has been made out).

172.2   *Id.*

Page 469

Addition to note 175.

175   *See, e.g.*, Cigna Ins. Co. v. Oy Saunatec, Ltd., 241 F.3d 1, 18 (1st Cir. 2001) (Mass. law) (ample evidence that the draping of a towel on a heater was a foreseeable use).

Add to text at end of subsection:

Foreseeability of harm is not an element of a strict liability claim.[175.1]

175.1   Green v. Smith & Nephew AHP, Inc., 629 N.W.2d 727, 745 (Wis. 2001).

Chapter 13   New Cars

Page 471

13.1 Introduction

*Replace section's last
paragraph with:*

New car sales also raise issues of unfair and deceptive pricing and sales techniques. These are outside the scope of this volume, and are covered instead by NCLC's *Unfair and Deceptive Acts and Practices*.[0.1] Financing issues are covered by NCLC's *Truth in Lending*[0.2] and *The Cost of Credit: Regulation and Legal Challenges*.[0.3]

0.1   National Consumer Law Center, Unfair and Deceptive Acts and Practices § 5.4 (5th ed. 2001 and Supp.).
0.2   National Consumer Law Center, Truth in Lending (5th ed. 2003).
0.3   National Consumer Law Center, The Cost of Credit: Regulation and Legal Challenges (2d ed. 2000 and Supp.).

13.2 Lemon Laws: Repair, Replace, or Refund

13.2.1 Introduction

Addition to note 1.

1   *Add at end of note*: Links to states' lemon law websites may be found at www.ialla.net, which is the website of the International Association of Lemon Law Administrators.

*Add to text at end of
subsection's first paragraph:*

Canada also has a lemon law.[1.1]

1.1   Information about Canada's lemon law can be found at www.camvap.ca.

Addition to notes 3, 5.

3   Genetti v. Caterpillar, Inc., 261 Neb. 98, 621 N.W.2d 529, 43 U.C.C. Rep. Serv. 2d 829 (2001); Reddin v. Toyota Motor Distributors, Inc., 1991 WL 21522 (Ohio Ct. App. Feb. 22, 1991) (unpublished); Herzberg v. Ford Motor Co., 626 N.W.2d 67, 43 U.C.C. Rep. Serv. 2d 1137 (Wis. Ct. App. 2001).

Page 472

5   Rothermel v. Safari Motor Coaches, 1994 U.S. Dist. LEXIS 21591 (N.D. Ohio July 29, 1994); *see, e.g.,* Singer v. Land Rover N. Am., 955 F. Supp. 359 (D.N.J. 1997); Harvill v. Fleetwood Enterprises, Inc., 2003 WL 21702375 (Cal. Ct. App. July 23, 2003) (unpublished); Collins v. Mullinax E., Inc., 153 Ohio App. 3d 534, 795 N.E.2d 68 (2003); Muzzy v. Chevrolet Div., Gen. Motors Corp., 153 Vt. 179, 571 A.2d 609 (Vt. 1989); Oregel v. Am. Isuzu Motors, Inc., 90 Cal. App. 4th 1094, 109 Cal. Rptr. 2d 583 (2001) (lemon law should be given construction consistent with its remedial purpose); Kwan v. Mercedes-Benz of N. Am., Inc., 23 Cal. App. 4th 174, 28 Cal. Rptr. 2d 371 (1994) (Song-Beverly Act); Harmon v. Concord Volkswagen, Inc., 598 A.2d 696 (Del. Super. Ct. 1991); King v. King Motor Co., 780 So. 2d 937 (Fla. Dist. Ct. App. 2001); *see also* Royster v. Toyota Motor Sales, 92 Ohio St. 3d 327, 750 N.E.2d 531 (2001) (lemon law must be simple and must have teeth to be effective); Sweeney v. SMC Corp., 178 Or. App. 576, 37 P.3d 244 (2002) (construing lemon law in light of its purpose to increase incentives for compliance by manufacturers).

*Add to text at end of
subsection:*

Because lemon laws were passed to overcome the inadequacies of the UCC, the shortcomings of the UCC should not be read back into them.[5.1]

5.1   Herzberg v. Ford Motor Co., 626 N.W.2d 67, 43 U.C.C. Rep. Serv. 2d 1137 (Wis. Ct. App. 2001).

13.2.2 Lemon Laws Are Constitutional

Addition to note 6.

6   *See also* Holzhauer-Mosher v. Ford Motor Co., 772 So. 2d 7 (Fla. Dist. Ct. App. 2000) (rejecting buyer's argument that refund formula was unconstitutional).

13.2.3 Scope of New Car Lemon Laws

Page 473   ### 13.2.3.1 Types of Vehicles Covered

Addition to note 12.   12   *But cf.* Nichols v. Chester Mack Sales & Serv., Inc., 1990 WL 251559 (Del. Super. Ct. Dec. 5, 1990) (commercial tractor-trailer cab is not a "passenger motor vehicle"), *aff'd without opinion*, 670 A.2d 1339 (Del. 1995).

Add to text after sentence   This term covers any vehicle designed to carry a passenger in addition to the driver.[12.1]
containing note 12:   12.1   Sweeney v. SMC Corp., 178 Or. App. 576, 37 P.3d 244 (2002).

Addition to note 14.   14   *See* Nichols v. Chester Mack Sales & Serv., Inc., 1990 WL 251559 (Del. Super. Ct. Dec. 5, 1990) (commercial tractor-trailer cab is not a "passenger motor vehicle"), *aff'd without opinion*, 670 A.2d 1339 (Del. 1995).

Add to text at end of   Many lemon laws exclude vehicles over a certain gross vehicle weight. Unless the statute
subsection's first paragraph: contains a different definition, "gross vehicle weight" is generally accepted as referring to the weight of the vehicle when unloaded. By contrast, "gross vehicle weight rating" refers to the weight of a vehicle plus the load it is carrying.[15.1]
                              15.1   *See* Tractor Supply Co. v. Pa. Bureau of Prof'l and Occupational Affairs, 752 A.2d 924 (Pa. Commw. Ct. 2000).

Addition to note 16.   16   *Accord* Robinson v. Am. Marine Holdings, Inc., 2002 WL 873185 (E.D. La. Apr. 30, 2002) (Fla. law).

Add to text after subsection's ### 13.2.3.1a Motor Homes
second paragraph:

Add to text at beginning of   Motor homes are covered by the lemon law in a majority of states.[17.1]
subsection's final paragraph: 17.1   Motor homes are covered by the lemon law in Alaska, Arizona (vehicle portions only, no more than 10,000 lbs.), Arkansas (vehicle portions only), California (chassis, chassis cab, and drive train only, if vehicle under 10,000 lbs.), Delaware (vehicle portions only), Florida (most vehicle portions only, no more than 10,000 lbs.), Georgia (vehicle portions only, no more than 10,000 lbs.), Hawaii (no more than 10,000 lbs.), Idaho (no more than 12,000 lbs.), Illinois (must be motorized), Kansas (vehicle portions only, no more than 12,000 lbs.), Louisiana (chassis and drive train only), Maine (use must be non-commercial; commercial use vehicle covered if under 8500 lbs.), Minnesota (chassis only), Mississippi (portions added by recreational vehicle company excluded), Missouri (chassis, engine, power train, and related parts), Montana (vehicle portions only), Nebraska, New Hampshire (only four-wheeled vehicles under 9000 lbs.), New Jersey (vehicle portions only), New Mexico (must be under 10,000 lbs.), New York (vehicle portions only), North Carolina (covered if under 10,000 lbs. and not a house trailer), Ohio (vehicle portions only), Oklahoma (vehicle portions only and must be under 10,000 lbs.), South Carolina (vehicle portions only), Texas, Utah (vehicle portions only), Virginia (chassis only), Washington, West Virginia (chassis only), Wisconsin, and Wyoming (if under 10,000 lbs.). *See* Appx. F, *infra* (state-by-state lemon law summaries).

Addition to note 18.   18   *Replace parenthetical in Dillow citation with*: (company that assembles motor home is liable for defects except as to living facilities excluded by statute; may be entitled to assert contribution claim against chassis manufacturer); *add*: *See* Rothermel v. Safari Motor Coaches, 1994 U.S. Dist. LEXIS 21591 (N.D. Ohio July 29, 1994) (final assembler, which also installed many parts including the brakes, is liable under lemon law for breach of its warranty and of any warranty issued by chassis manufacturer; it has recourse against manufacturers of components); Camp v. Fleetwood Motor Homes, 2003 WL 22025071 (Ohio Ct. App. June 6, 2003) (lemon law covers motor home except for components excluded by statute; when covered component's failure caused damage to non-covered components, manufacturer is responsible for both repairs); Lesjak v. Forest River, Inc., 2002 WL 1483421 (Ohio Ct. App. July 5, 2002) (lemon law covers motor homes except for components explicitly excluded by the statute); *see also* Barker v. Fleetwood Enterprises, Inc., 2002 WL 453931 (Cal. Ct. App. Mar. 26, 2002) (unpublished) (Song-Beverly Act's provisions for other consumer goods apply to coach portion of motor home; court applies substantial impairment language from motor vehicle sections to coach portion of motor home).

Add to text after sentence   An Ohio decision holds a leaky window in a motor home to be covered by the state lemon
containing note 19:   law, as windows are not part of the permanently installed facilities for cold storage, cooking, eating, and sleeping that are excluded from the statute.[19.1]
                              19.1   Lesjak v. Forest River, Inc., 2002 WL 1483421 (Ohio Ct. App. July 5, 2002).

Add to text at end of subsection:

Several Ohio decisions hold that the final manufacturer who assembles the motor home is liable under the lemon law for breach of not only its own warranty but also any separate warranty issued by the manufacturer who supplied the chassis.[20.1] An Oregon decision holds a motor home to be a passenger vehicle and therefore covered in its entirety by the lemon law.[20.2] In New York, the manufacturer of a motor home is responsible for any defect that substantially impairs value, regardless of whether its warranty covers that portion of the home.[20.3] Either manufacturing or distributing a motor home chassis is covered by the West Virginia lemon law, so a manufacturer that bought the chassis, built the rest of the motor home, and then distributed it, is covered.[20.4] State lemon laws that exclude vehicles over a certain weight may exclude some or all motor homes.

> 20.1   Rothermel v. Safari Motor Coaches, Inc., 1994 U.S. Dist. LEXIS 21591 (N.D. Ohio July 29, 1994); Camp v. Fleetwood Motor Homes, 2003 WL 22025071 (Ohio Ct. App. June 6, 2003) (consumer can also seek recovery directly from chassis manufacturer).
>
> 20.2   Sweeney v. SMC Corp., 178 Or. App. 576, 37 P.3d 244 (2002).
>
> 20.3   Safari Motor Coaches, Inc. v. Corwin, 225 A.D.2d 921, 638 N.Y.S.2d 992 (1996) (interpreting N.Y. Gen. Bus. Law § 198-a(n)(4) (McKinney)).
>
> 20.4   Boland v. Georgie Boy Mfg., Inc., 240 F. Supp. 2d 582 (S.D. W. Va. 2003).

13.2.3.2 Demonstrators and Low-Mileage Used Cars

Add to text at end of subsection's first paragraph:

Maine amended its lemon law in 2003 to delete the requirement that the vehicle be new, so any vehicle sold under warranty is covered during the first three years after its original sale or the first 18,000 miles it is operated, whichever occurs first.[22.1]

> 22.1   Me. Rev. Stat. Ann. tit. 10, § 1163 (West) (as amended by 2003 Me. Laws 337, §§ 2, 5).

Replace sentence containing note 24 with:

The Virginia Supreme Court[24] and an Ohio trial court[24.1] have reached the same conclusion about their lemon laws.

> 24   [*Retain as in main edition.*]
>
> 24.1   Browning v. Am. Isuzu Motors, Inc., 2002 WL 32063978 (Ohio C.P. Mar. 21, 2003).

Addition to note 26.

> 26   *Add to end of note*: An earlier unreported decision, Markee v. Ford Motor Co., 584 N.W.2d 235 (Wis. Ct. App. 1998) (unpublished) (text available at 1998 WL 404870) had held that the lemon law covered these vehicles.

Page 474

13.2.3.3 Leased Vehicles

Addition to notes 28, 30, 31.

> 28   *See also* Brady v. Mercedes-Benz USA, 243 F. Supp. 2d 1004, 1007 (N.D. Cal. 2002); Cato v. Am. Suzuki Motor Corp., 622 N.W.2d 486 (Iowa 2001); Varda v. Gen. Motors Corp., 242 Wis. 2d 756, 626 N.W.2d 346 (Ct. App. 2001) (lemon law covers leased vehicles, but consumer who gives notice only after purchasing vehicle at end of lease term is not entitled to relief).
>
> 30   *Add parenthetical to Pertuset citation*: (note that the Ohio statute was amended in 1999 to make coverage of leases even clearer); *add parenthetical to Industrial Valley Bank & Trust Co. citation*: (note that statute was amended, effective Feb. 11, 2002, to explicitly cover leases).
>
> 31   *Add at end of note*: Revised U.C.C. § 1-201(b)(29) makes this conclusion even clearer by adding leases to the list of examples of types of purchases. As of early 2004, revised Article 1 had been adopted by Texas, Virginia, and the Virgin Islands, and was under consideration by several other states.

13.2.3.4 Out-of-State Vehicles

Addition to notes 33–36.

> 33   Holloway v. Monaco Coach Corp., 2003 WL 21146720 (D. Del. May 14, 2003) (Delaware lemon law covers vehicles leased, bought, or registered in Delaware, so covers vehicle bought in Pennsylvania but registered in Delaware, when seller knew where vehicle would be registered).
>
> 34   *Add explanatory parenthetical to Mikula citation*: (note that a statutory amendment, effective Dec. 1, 2002, allows lemon law coverage when a vehicle is purchased or leased out of state but registered for the first time in-state); *add*: *But see* Cummins, Inc. v. Super. Ct., 1 Cal. Rptr. 3d 129 (Ct. App. 2003) (some parts of Song-Beverly Consumer Warranty Act, including requirement of repair or replacement, apply to goods that are offered for sale in state but the consumer buys out of state and then uses within state), *review granted, opinion withdrawn*, 2003 WL 22175779 (Cal. Sept. 10, 2003).
>
> 35   *Replace Sheller citation parenthetical with*: (Pennsylvania lemon law limited to vehicles which are

purchased and currently registered in the state; note that the statute was broadened somewhat, effective Dec. 1, 2002).

36   *Replace Gholson citation with*: 52 Va. Cir. 383 (2000).

Page 475

13.2.3.5 Covered Car Owners

Add to text after subsection's first sentence:

If the statute applies to "persons" or defines consumers as persons it will probably cover corporations that purchase vehicles as long as they meet the other requirements for coverage.[39.1] In many states there is a definition of person in a general section of the code that applies to all of the state's statutes which defines person to include corporations.

39.1   Results Real Estate, Inc. v. Lazy Days R.V. Ctr., Inc., 505 So. 2d 587 (Fla. Dist. Ct. App. 1987).

Addition to note 43.

43   McLaughlin v. Chrysler Corp., 262 F. Supp. 2d 671 (N.D. W. Va. 2002) (lemon law did not apply to vehicle used primarily for business purposes), *aff'd*, 2002 WL 31246891 (4th Cir. Oct. 8, 2002) (*per curiam*) (unpublished); Sweeney v. SMC Corp., 178 Or. App. 576, 37 P.3d 244 (2002); *see also* Durso v. Chrysler Corp., 41 Va. Cir. 211 (1996) (vehicle sold to corporation not covered unless complaint specifically alleges substantial consumer use).

Replace note 44 with:

44   Interpretations of similar language in some state deceptive practice statutes and in the Truth in Lending Act may serve as useful precedent. *See, e.g.*, Gallegos v. Stokes, 593 F.2d 372 (10th Cir. 1979) (truck was primarily for personal use even though plaintiff also intended to use it for a business she hoped to establish); Waterloo Leasing Co. v. McNatt, 620 S.W.2d 194 (Tex. Civ. App. 1981) (Consumer Leasing Act case; statement "this vehicle to be used for business" did not mean it was primarily so, and facts showed it was primarily for consumer purposes); *see also* National Consumer Law Center, Truth in Lending § 2.2.3 (5th ed. 2003); National Consumer Law Center, Unfair and Deceptive Acts and Practices § 2.1.8 (5th ed. 2001 and Supp.).

Addition to note 45.

45   Beckman v. Daimlerchrysler Corp., 2003 WL 892302 (Minn. Ct. App. Mar. 4, 2003) (unpublished) (lemon law inapplicable when there was no evidence that vehicle met statutory requirement of being used for personal, family, or household use at least forty percent of the time).

13.2.3.6 Defendants Covered by New Car Lemon Laws

Addition to notes 47, 48.

47   *See, e.g.*, Durso v. Chrysler Corp., 41 Va. Cir. 211 (1996); *see also* Gen. Elec. Capital Auto Lease, Inc. v. D'Agnese, 239 A.D.2d 462, 658 N.Y.S.2d 55 (1997); Laurel Bank v. Karstetter, 7 Pa. D. & C.4th 663 (C.P. 1990).

48   *See* Cal. Civ. Code § 1795 (West); *see also* Contreras v. Ford Motor Co., 2002 WL 31727261 (Cal. Ct. App. Dec. 5, 2002) (unpublished).

Add to text at end of subsection:

Van converters will also be covered by lemon laws that apply to distributors of motor vehicles.[49.1]

Sometimes it is difficult to determine which of a number of related corporations is the one that manufactured the vehicle. Lemon laws that apply to distributors as well as manufacturers minimize this problem by making the company that imported the vehicle into the United States liable along with the actual manufacturer.[49.2] Pleading a parallel claim under the Magnuson-Moss Act against the warrantor is helpful when there is uncertainty about the identity of the manufacturer,[49.3] because the Magnuson-Moss regulations require the name and mailing address of the warrantor to be clearly and conspicuously disclosed to the consumer.[49.4]

49.1   *See, e.g.*, Boland v. Georgie Boy Mfg., Inc., 240 F. Supp. 2d 582 (S.D. W. Va. 2003) (motor home manufacturer covered as distributor).

49.2   *Cf.* Luciano v. World-Wide Volkswagen Corp., 127 App. Div. 2d 1, 514 N.Y.S.2d 140 (1987) (United States distributor for foreign manufacturer not subject to lemon law when it did not issue the warranty); Miller v. Crabtree Mazda, Inc., 146 Misc. 2d 658, 552 N.Y.S.2d 526 (Civ. Ct. 1990) (distributor not covered by lemon law, so service on foreign manufacturer is necessary in lemon law suit; consumer can avoid expense of service by seeking arbitration, in which manufacturer will be compelled to participate).

49.3   15 U.S.C. § 2310(d) (making "supplier, warrantor, or service contractor" liable); *see* § 2.2.7.1, *supra*.

49.4   16 C.F.R. § 701.3(a)(5); *see* § 2.6.4.6, *supra*.

13.2.4 Defects Covered by New Car Lemon Laws

13.2.4.1 Breach of Express and Implied Warranties

Page 476

Addition to notes 50, 52.

50 Oregel v. Am. Isuzu Motors, Inc., 90 Cal. App. 4th 1094, 109 Cal. Rptr. 2d 583 (2001) (listing elements of lemon law claim, including existence of noncomformity covered by express warranty); Vanderbrook v. Coachmen Indus., 818 So. 2d 906 (La. Ct. App. 2002) (buyer must prove existence of express warranties to recover under lemon law); Rhodes v. All Star Ford, Inc., 599 So. 2d 812 (La. Ct. App. 1992) (buyer must introduce warranty into evidence to prove lemon law claim); Bevington v. Gen. Motors Corp., 2001 Ohio App. LEXIS 1888 (Ohio Ct. App. Apr. 20, 2001). *But see* Schimmer v. Jaguar Cars, Inc., 2003 WL 21518589 (N.D. Ill. July 2, 2003) (finding a repair or replace warranty not to be a warranty as defined by the U.C.C., so it does not create lemon law rights; this holding is clearly contrary to the legislative intent as it would remove all vehicles from the lemon law; it is also contrary to most interpretations of the U.C.C., see § 3.2.2.4, *supra*).

52 *Add before Reveles citation*: Swann v. DaimlerChrysler Motors Corp., 2003 WL 1818139 (Cal. Ct. App. Apr. 8, 2003) (unpublished) (service contract is express warranty and buyer of used car with service contract has lemon law cause of action), *review granted*, 2003 Cal. LEXIS 3959 (Cal. June 18, 2003) *and*; *add before Adams citation*: Gavaldon v. Daimlerchrysler Corp., 115 Cal. Rptr. 2d 732 (Ct. App. 2002) (replacement or restitution remedy applies only to breach of express warranty, not breach of service contract; confines *Reveles* to damage suits involving used goods), *review granted*, 47 P.3d 222 (Cal. 2002) *and*.

Add to text after subsection's first paragraph:

The lemon law may apply to a component of the vehicle that is covered by a warranty from the supplier of that component, even though the warranty issued by the manufacturer of the vehicle excludes that component. For example, the Wisconsin lemon law applies whenever a new vehicle fails to conform to "an applicable express warranty,"[52.1] without requiring that that warranty be one issued by the manufacturer. Thus, a truck manufacturer was liable under the lemon law when the engine could not be conformed to a separate warranty from the engine supplier, even though the manufacturer's warranty excluded the engine.[52.2]

52.1 Wis. Stat. § 218.0171(2)(a).

52.2 Schonscheck v. Paccar, Inc., 661 N.W.2d 476 (Wis. Ct. App. 2003).

Addition to notes 54, 56.

54 *See* Lesjak v. Forest River, Inc., 2003 WL 22861722 (Ohio Ct. App. Nov. 26, 2003) (unpublished) ("condition" includes design defects).

56 *Replace O'Henry citation with*: 215 F.3d 1327 (6th Cir. 2000) (unpublished) (text available at 2000 U.S. App. LEXIS 11843); *add*: Contreras v. Ford Motor Co., 2002 WL 31727261 (Cal. Ct. App. Dec. 5, 2002) (unpublished); Oregel v. Am. Isuzu Motors, Inc., 90 Cal. App. 4th 1094, 109 Cal. Rptr. 2d 583 (2001) ("We do not interpret the statute as depriving a consumer of a remedy if he cannot do what the manufacturer, with its presumably greater expertise, was incapable of doing, i.e. identify the source of the leak."); Genetti v. Caterpillar, Inc., 261 Neb. 98, 621 N.W.2d 529, 43 U.C.C. Rep. Serv. 2d 829 (2001) (consumer need not prove specific defect); Reddin v. Toyota Motor Distributors, Inc., 1991 WL 21522 (Ohio Ct. App. Feb. 22, 1991) (unpublished).

Add to text after sentence containing note 56:

A defect is actionable even if it is common to all models of a particular year.[56.1] Circumstantial evidence is sufficient.[56.2]

56.1 Mason v. Porsche Cars of N. Am., 688 So. 2d 361 (Fla. Dist. Ct. App. 1997).

56.2 Genetti v. Caterpillar, Inc., 261 Neb. 98, 621 N.W.2d 529, 43 U.C.C. Rep. Serv. 2d 829 (2001); Reddin v. Toyota Motor Distributors, Inc., 1991 WL 21522 (Ohio Ct. App. Feb. 22, 1991) (unpublished).

13.2.4.2 Manufacturer Obligation for Dealer Warranties and Actions

Page 477

Addition to note 63.

63 *See, e.g.*, Barker v. Fleetwood Enterprises, Inc., 2002 WL 453931 (Cal. Ct. App. Mar. 26, 2002) (unpublished).

Page 478

Add to text at end of subsection's seventh paragraph:

If the manufacturer's warranty covers custom alterations made by the dealer before sale to the consumer, then the lemon law covers defects attributable to those alterations.[73.1]

73.1 Gen. Motors Corp. v. Blanchard, 1998 WL 285838 (Conn. Super. Ct. May 19, 1998); Gen. Motors Corp. v. Lee, 193 A.D.2d 741, 598 N.Y.S.2d 61 (1993). *But cf.* Alston v. Gen. Motors Corp., 1997 WL 634497

(E.D. Pa. Sept. 26, 1997) (no lemon law claim as to aftermarket installed non-manufacturer component when warranty did not cover it); *see* § 13.2.4.3, *infra*.

13.2.4.3 Exceptions for Abuse, Neglect, or Unauthorized Modifications

Addition to note 77.

77 Contreras v. Ford Motor Co., 2002 WL 31727261 (Cal. Ct. App. Dec. 5, 2002) (unpublished).

Add to text after sentence following sentence containing note 77:

The jury can infer from circumstantial evidence that the defect was caused by a breach of the warranty rather than by the fault of the buyer.[77.1]

77.1 Oregel v. Am. Isuzu Motors, Inc., 90 Cal. App. 4th 1094, 109 Cal. Rptr. 2d 583 (2001).

Replace § 13.2.4.4 with:

13.2.4.4 Nonconformity Resulting in Substantial Impairment

13.2.4.4.1 When is an impairment substantial?

The typical new car lemon law applies only if the motor vehicle fails to conform to applicable warranties *and* the nonconformity results in a substantial impairment of value, use, and safety. If the statutory standard is expressed in the disjunctive, then the consumer need only show that value, use, *or* safety is substantially impaired.[80]

The requirement that the impairment be substantial injects an element of degree.[81] A California court defined a substantial impairment as one of considerable importance, pertaining to the essentials of the car.[82] It upheld a jury instruction that minor nonconformities do not trigger lemon law remedies. A Wisconsin appellate court upheld a jury instruction that equated substantial with serious and significant.[83] Some courts have held that defects that are easily correctable are not substantial.[84]

Substantial impairment under a lemon law may be different from substantial impairment under the UCC.[85] One

reason is that lemon laws usually apply if there is a substantial impairment of use, value, or safety, while the UCC allows revocation of acceptance only upon substantial impairment of value.[86] Nonetheless, cases applying the UCC implied warranty of merchantability to new cars may be relevant in interpreting substantial impairment.[87] Certainly a car that is not fit for its ordinary purpose has a defect that substantially impairs its value, use, or safety.

The buyer need not show that the defect creates a safety hazard.[88] The mere fact that the car can be driven, despite its defect, does not disprove substantial impairment.[89] The fact

---

80 Gen. Motors Corp. v. Garito, 1997 Conn. Super. LEXIS 3413 (Conn. Super. Ct. Dec. 12, 1997).

81 Lundy v. Ford Motor Co., 87 Cal. App. 4th 472, 104 Cal. Rptr. 2d 545 (2001).

82 Contreras v. Ford Motor Co., 2002 WL 31727261 (Cal. Ct. App. Dec. 5, 2002) (unpublished).

83 Morgan v. Ford Motor Co., 231 Wis. 2d 238, 604 N.W.2d 304 (Ct. App. 1999); *see also* DiVigenze v. Chrysler Corp., 345 N.J. Super. 314, 785 A.2d 37 (Super. Ct. App. Div. 2001) (upholding jury instruction that substantial impairment is one that impairs use, value, or safety in an important, essential, or significant way, not a minor, unimportant, or trivial way).

84 LaMountain v. S & S Auto Sales, Clearinghouse No. 43,063 (N.Y. Sup. Ct. Franklin County 1986) (defects correctable, did not substantially impair value).

85 Chmill v. Friendly Ford-Mercury of Janesville, Inc., 144 Wis. 2d 796, 424 N.E.2d 747 (Ct. App. 1988); *see* § 8.3.2, *supra; see also* § 13.3.3, *infra* (substantial impairment of new cars for U.C.C. revocation). *But see* Telly's, Inc. v. Land Rover N. Am., Inc., 2001 Mich. App. LEXIS 1413 (Mich. Ct. App. June 22, 2001) (finding no basis to distinguish lemon law from U.C.C. standard); Berrie v. Toyota Motor Sales, USA, Inc., 267 N.J. Super. 152, 630 A.2d 1180 (Super. Ct. App. Div. 1993); *cf.*

Lundy v. Ford Motor Co., 87 Cal. App. 4th 472, 104 Cal. Rptr. 2d 545 (2001) (suggesting U.C.C. as analogy).

86 Chmill v. Friendly Ford-Mercury of Janesville, Inc., 144 Wis. 2d 796, 424 N.E.2d 747 (Ct. App. 1988) (comparing U.C.C. § 2-608 to lemon law).

87 *See* § 13.3.3, *infra; see also* Harvill v. Fleetwood Enterprises, Inc., 2003 WL 21702375 (Cal. Ct. App. July 23, 2003) (unpublished).

88 Mooberry v. Magnum Mfg., Inc., 108 Wash. App. 654, 32 P.3d 302 (2001).

89 Jackson v. Hyundai Motor Am., 1997 WL 119794 (E.D. Pa. Mar. 6, 1997) (Del. law); Barker v. Fleetwood Enterprises, Inc., 2002 WL 453931 (Cal. Ct. App. Mar. 26, 2002) (unpublished); Jarvis v. Safari Motor Coaches, Inc., 248 A.D.2d 899, 670 N.Y.S.2d 927 (1998) (fact that consumer was still able to use the vehicle despite its "vexing defects" is no bar to substantial impairment); Royal Chrysler-Oneonta, Inc. v. Dunham, 243 A.D.2d 1007, 663 N.Y.S.2d 410 (1997) (used car lemon law); Kapel v. Ford Motor Co., 1997 WL 401532 (Ohio Ct. App. July 3, 1997) (unpublished) (fact that buyer drove vehicle 120,000 miles is no defense); Schonscheck v. Paccar, Inc., 661 N.W.2d 476 (Wis. Ct. App. 2003); Dobbratz Trucking & Excavating, Inc. v. Paccar, Inc., 647 N.W.2d 315 (Wis. Ct. App. 2002) (simply because a vehicle can be driven does not mean that it is free of nonconformities, nor does it mean that the vehicle is not substantially impaired); Vultaggio v. Gen. Motors Corp., 429 N.W.2d 93, 99 (Wis. Ct. App. 1988); Chmill v. Friendly Ford-Mercury of Janesville, Inc., 144 Wis. 2d 796, 424 N.W.2d 747 (Ct. App. 1988) (car was operable despite alignment problem and consumer drove it 78,000 miles). *But see* McLaughlin v. Chrysler Corp., 262 F. Supp. 2d 671 (N.D. W. Va. 2002) (in dicta, citing fact that plaintiff drove the vehicle a typical number of miles in support of finding of no substantial impairment), *aff'd*, 2002 WL 31246891 (4th Cir. Oct. 8, 2002) (*per curiam*) (unpublished); Hanson v. Signer Motors, Inc., 105 Or. App. 74, 803 P.2d 1207 (1990) ("relatively minor" defects which did not impair continued use of motor home for intended purposes not

that a problem occurs intermittently rather than continuously does not make it insubstantial.[90] Courts may be willing to hold luxury cars to a higher standard because the buyer's expectations are justifiably higher.[91] The fact that the vehicle has undergone a number of repairs does not, in and of itself, prove that it has a substantial impairment.[92]

Whether a number of minor defects, none of which is substantial on its own, can be a substantial impairment in the aggregate is debatable. A California decision holds that minor defects can not be aggregated to meet the standard.[93] Another California decision, however, holds that the plaintiff need not prove each defect independently, establish how much time was spent attempting to cure each such defect, and convince the trier of fact that each such defect caused a substantial impairment.[94] It is common for lemon law cases to consider all the car's defects together in determining whether there is a substantial impairment.[95]

13.2.4.4.2 Is the standard subjective or objective?

An important issue is whether substantial impairment is an objective or subjective standard. Most courts have concluded that the standard includes a subjective element.

Many lemon laws state that the defect must impair the use, safety, or value of the motor vehicle *to the consumer.* Under Ohio's statute, which includes this language,[96] the jury must be instructed that the consumer's perspective must be taken into consideration, including her diminished con-

fidence in the vehicle.[97] Michigan's statute, which is similar, is interpreted to have both a subjective element, in that the nonconformity must have a devaluing effect on the buyer, and an objective element, in that the buyer's belief in the devaluing effect must be factually correct.[98] The Florida statute formerly was similar but was amended to delete the words "to the consumer."[99]

Maine interprets its substantial impairment standard to require an objective effect on use, value, or safety.[100] West Virginia courts adopt a similar interpretation.[101] California adopts an objective test, based on what a reasonable person would understand to be a defect, but applies it within the specific circumstances of the buyer[102] and includes consideration of whether the defect shakes the buyer's confidence in the vehicle.[103] Washington adopts an objective standard, but a reasonable subjective belief that a condition impairs the safety, use, or value of a vehicle is sufficient.[104] In New Jersey the trier of fact is to apply a mixed objective/subjective test, giving consideration to whether the defects have shaken the buyer's faith in the vehicle.[104.1] A court applying Delaware law has also adopted the shaken faith standard.[104.2]

The Connecticut Supreme Court has concluded that the substantial impairment standard is both subjective and objective.[104.3] First, the fact finder must determine the subjective circumstances of the particular consumer to conclude whether the nonconformity substantially impairs the use, safety, or value to that person. Second, the fact finder must determine whether that subjective impairment is objectively reasonable. A federal court construing Nevada's lemon law

---

substantial impairment in value); *cf.* Telly's, Inc. v. Land Rover N. Am., Inc., 2001 Mich. App. LEXIS 1413 (Mich. Ct. App. June 22, 2001) (citing fact that consumer continued to drive vehicle in reversing summary judgment for consumer).

90 Gen. Motors Corp. v. Martin, 1997 WL 805137 (Conn. Super. Ct. Dec. 16, 1997).

91 Milicevic v. Mercedes-Benz USA, Ltd. Liab. Co., 256 F. Supp. 2d 1168 (D. Nev. 2003).

92 McLaughlin v. Chrysler Corp., 262 F. Supp. 2d 671 (N.D. W. Va. 2002), *aff'd*, 2002 WL 31246891 (4th Cir. Oct. 8, 2002) (*per curiam*) (unpublished).

93 Contreras v. Ford Motor Co., 2002 WL 31727261 (Cal. Ct. App. Dec. 5, 2002) (unpublished).

94 Palmer v. Fleetwood Enterprises, Inc., 2003 WL 21228864 (Cal. Ct. App. May 28, 2003) (unpublished).

95 *See, e.g.,* Milicevic v. Mercedes-Benz USA, Ltd. Liab. Co., 256 F. Supp. 2d 1168 (D. Nev. 2003); Contreras v. Ford Motor Co., 2002 WL 31727261 (Cal. Ct. App. Dec. 5, 2002); Telly's, Inc. v. Land Rover N. Am., Inc., 2001 WL 710206 (Mich. Ct. App. June 22, 2001); DiVigenze v. Chrysler Corp., 345 N.J. Super. 314, 785 A.2d 37 (Super. Ct. App. Div. 2001); Jarvis v. Safari Motor Coaches, Inc., 248 A.D.2d 899, 670 N.Y.S.2d 927 (1998).

96 Ohio Rev. Code Ann. § 1345.71(E) (West) (definition of nonconformity). Prior to a 1999 amendment, the "to the consumer" language appeared only in Ohio Rev. Code Ann. § 1345.72(B) (West), which stated the conditions under which the consumer could demand a replacement or refund. One court interpreted this former statutory structure to set an objective rather than subjective standard. Stepp v. Chrysler Corp., 1996 WL 752794 (Ohio Ct. App. Nov. 7, 1996).

97 Brinkman v. Mazda Motor of Am., Inc., 1994 Ohio App. LEXIS 2074 (Ohio Ct. App. May 13, 1994); *accord* Gray v. Chrysler Corp., 2001 Ohio App. LEXIS 1657 (Ohio Ct. App. Apr. 11, 2001).

98 Harris v. Ford Motor Co., 2000 WL 33533986 (Mich. Ct. App. Feb. 11, 2000).

99 *See* King v. King Motor Co., 780 So. 2d 937, 939 n.2 (Fla. Dist. Ct. App. 2001).

100 Jolovitz v. Alfa Romeo Distributors, 760 A.2d 625 (Me. 2000).

101 McLaughlin v. Chrysler Corp., 262 F. Supp. 2d 671 (N.D. W. Va. 2002), *aff'd*, 2002 WL 31246891 (4th Cir. Oct. 8, 2002) (*per curiam*) (unpublished).

102 Lundy v. Ford Motor Co., 87 Cal. App. 4th 472, 104 Cal. Rptr. 2d 545 (2001).

103 Schreidel v. Am. Honda Motor Co., 34 Cal. App. 4th 1242, 40 Cal. Rptr. 2d 576 (1995) (clutch problem that caused delay in shifting into first gear was dangerous and shook buyer's confidence in car).

104 Mooberry v. Magnum Mfg., Inc., 108 Wash. App. 654, 32 P.3d 302 (2001).

104.1 Divigenze v. Chrysler Corp., 345 N.J. Super. 314, 785 A.2d 37 (Super. Ct. App. Div. 2001); *accord* Suber v. Chrysler Corp., 104 F.3d 578 (3d Cir. 1997) (N.J. law).

104.2 Jackson v. Hyundai Motor Am., 1997 WL 119794 (E.D. Pa. Mar. 6, 1997) (Del. law).

104.3 Gen. Motors Corp. v. Dohmann, 247 Conn. 274, 722 A.2d 1205 (Conn. 1998).

adopts the same formulation.[104.4] Vermont's statute, which allows a lemon law claim to proceed if the consumer is not "satisfied" after the manufacturer's final repair attempt, sets a subjective standard.[104.5]

13.2.4.4.3 Specific impairments found to be substantial

Stalling and failure to start. Frequent stalling is a substantial impairment.[104.6] The occasional failure of the car to start is not only substantial but even "lethal" if the site is remote and the weather intemperate.[104.7]

Steering problems. A dump truck that could not be steered when stationary was substantially impaired as this ability was an important function for commercial use and was contrary to the general standard for dump trucks, even though the owner never actually lost work because of the malfunction.[104.8]

Brake problems. Brake failure is so clearly a safety hazard that courts have had no difficulty finding it a substantial impairment.[104.9] Shaking and shimmying upon braking is a substantial impairment,[104.10] as is an intermittent problem with grinding, a burning order, and a squealing noise.[104.11] Malfunctioning brake lights may be a substantial impairment.[104.12]

Shifting and transmission problems. Problems that cause hesitation or delay when shifting or accelerating are substantial impairments and present some danger to the driver. For example, a clutch problem that caused delay in shifting into first gear was dangerous and shook the buyer's confidence in the car.[104.13] Transmission failure is a substantial impairment.[104.14] A slipping transmission is a substantial impairment,[104.15] as is a shudder when accelerating.[104.16] A Delaware court upheld a jury verdict that stiff shifting and a clicking noise upon turning, both of which worsened over time, amounted to a substantial impairment.[104.17] A truck was substantially impaired by a transmission that overheated, discharged fluid, and emitted a burning odor when towing a trailer of a weight it was warranted to be able to

---

104.4   Milicevic v. Mercedes-Benz USA, Ltd. Liab. Co., 256 F. Supp. 2d 1168 (D. Nev. 2003).

104.5   Muzzy v. Chevrolet Div., Gen. Motors Corp., 153 Vt. 179, 571 A.2d 609 (Vt. 1989).

104.6   Gray v. Chrysler Corp., 2001 WL 358389 (Ohio Ct. App. Apr. 11, 2001); Muzzy v. Chevrolet Div., Gen. Motors Corp., 153 Vt. 179, 571 A.2d 609, 616 (Vt. 1989); *see also* Jackson v. Hyundai Motor Am., 1997 WL 119794 (E.D. Pa. Mar. 6, 1997) (Del. law) (upholding jury verdict for consumer when car had history of overheating and stalling, even though problem was successfully repaired by time of trial); United States v. Gen. Motors Corp., 417 F. Supp. 933, 938, 939 (D.D.C. 1976) (upholding National Highway Traffic Safety Administration determination that defect that could cause car to stop running is a safety hazard: "The driver must then either abandon his vehicle in the midst of oncoming traffic or, if he can, pull over to the side of the road. Both situations are dangerous."), *aff'd in relevant part, remanded in part on other grounds*, 565 F.2d 754 (D.C. Cir. 1977) (remanding for reconsideration of amount of civil penalty); Schreidel v. Am. Honda Motor Co., 34 Cal. App. 4th 1242, 40 Cal. Rptr.2d 576, 579 (1995) (delay in shifting is similar to stalling, "a dangerous condition on the highway").

104.7   Shea v. Volvo Cars of N. Am., 1991 WL 71109 (E.D. Pa. Apr. 30, 1991); *see also* Schreidel v. Am. Honda Motor Co., 34 Cal. App. 4th 1242, 40 Cal. Rptr. 2d 576 (1995) (delay in shifting into first gear is a dangerous condition similar to stalling); Reddin v. Toyota Motor Distributors, Inc., 1991 WL 21522 (Ohio Ct. App. Feb. 22, 1991) (unpublished); Abbs v. Georgie Boy Mfg., Inc., 60 Wash. App. 157, 803 P.2d 14 (1991) (affirming judgment for buyer when air conditioning malfunctioned, causing stalling and impairing comfort and defogging).

104.8   Dobbratz Trucking & Excavating, Inc. v. Paccar, Inc., 647 N.W.2d 315 (Wis. Ct. App. 2002).

104.9   O'Henry v. Chrysler Corp., 215 F.3d 1327 (6th Cir. 2000) (unpublished) (text available at 2000 U.S. App. LEXIS 11843) (leaking brake fluid is substantial impairment when even defendant's expert stated he would not drive car for extended periods); Gen. Motors Corp. v. Zirkel, 613 N.E.2d 30 (Ind. 1993) (affirming lemon law award when brakes failed); Adventure Travel World, Ltd. v. Gen. Motors Corp., 107 N.C. App.

573, 421 S.E.2d 173 (1992) (lay witnesses' testimony about instances of brake failure created question of fact despite defendant's expert's affidavit that brakes were normal); *see also* Jarvis v. Safari Motor Coaches, Inc., 248 A.D.2d 899, 670 N.Y.S.2d 927 (1998) (citing "mushy" brakes that had occasionally failed entirely as one of impairments supporting ruling for buyer).

104.10   Jensen v. BMW of N. Am., Inc., 35 Cal. App. 4th 112, 41 Cal. Rptr. 2d 295 (1995); *see also* Milicevic v. Mercedes-Benz USA, Ltd. Liab. Co., 256 F. Supp. 2d 1168 (D. Nev. 2003) (brakes required repeated repairs, plus car had other defects).

104.11   Baker v. Chrysler Corp., 1993 U.S. Dist. LEXIS 727 (E.D. Pa. Jan. 25, 1993) (grinding sound, burning odor, and sliding motion when brakes applied; vehicle also had problems with coolant system), *aff'd*, 9 F.3d 1539 (3d Cir. 1993) (table); Gen. Motors Corp. v. Martin, 1997 WL 805137 (Conn. Super. Ct. Dec. 16, 1997) (grinding, burning order, and squealing).

104.12   DiVigenze v. Chrysler Corp., 345 N.J. Super. 314, 785 A.2d 37 (Super. Ct. App. Div. 2001) (upholding verdict for buyer when one of defects was malfunctioning brake light).

104.13   Schreidel v. Am. Honda Motor Co., 34 Cal. App. 4th 1242, 40 Cal. Rptr. 2d 576 (1995); *see also* Contreras v. Ford Motor Co., 2002 WL 31727261 (Cal. Ct. App. Dec. 5, 2002) (unpublished) (hesitation on acceleration, plus overheating and doors that scratched the paint, could be substantial impairments).

104.14   Camp v. Fleetwood Motor Homes, 2003 WL 22025071 (Ohio Ct. App. June 6, 2003).

104.15   Green v. Ford Motor Co., 1996 WL 153214 (E.D. Pa. Apr. 1, 1986); Lundy v. Ford Motor Co., 87 Cal. App. 4th 472, 104 Cal. Rptr. 2d 545 (2001).

104.16   Mason v. Porsche Cars N. Am., Inc., 688 So. 2d 361 (Fla. Dist. Ct. App. 1997); *see also* Gen. Motors Corp. v. Martine, 213 Conn. 136, 567 A.2d 808 (1989) (affirming lemon law award when defect was hesitation and surging).

104.17   Calbert v. Volkswagen of Am., 1991 WL 215669 (Del. Super. Ct. Oct. 1, 1991), *aff'd*, 634 A.2d 938 (Del. 1993) (unpublished); *see also* Burns v. Gen. Motors Corp., 833 A.2d 934 (Conn. Ct. App. 2003) (transmission noise not substantial impairment when trier of fact believed evidence that it was normal characteristic and it had caused no mechanical problems); Royal Chrysler-Oneonta, Inc. v. Dunham, 243 A.D.2d 1007, 663 N.Y.S.2d 410 (1997) (transmission noises were substantial impairment under used car lemon law).

handle.[104.18] But transmission and engine noises, which a technician testified were normal for the model and which did not prevent the car from operating, were not a substantial impairment.[104.19]

Vibration, hesitation, and alignment problems. Intermittent severe vibration can be a substantial impairment.[104.20] An alignment problem that caused the vehicle to pull to the left and that could not be repaired despite repeated attempts was a substantial impairment.[104.21]

Fluid and fuel leaks. A persistent leak of oil[104.22] or fuel[104.23] is a substantial impairment.

Overheating. A California court held that it was a jury question whether chronic overheating, which, in combination with other impairments, could lead to cylinder damage, was a substantial impairment.[104.24] Problems with the coolant system that caused the engine to overheat, the air conditioner to blow hot air, and odors to enter the passenger compartment amounted to a substantial impairment.[104.25]

Malfunctioning warning lights. A malfunctioning oil sensor light which lit up when there was in fact no problem substantially impaired the use of a car because the driver would be forced to pull off the road to check the oil or stop at the nearest service station once it came on.[104.26] Likewise, a sensor in a motor home that erroneously warned of the presence of carbon monoxide would be a substantial impairment.[104.27] The vehicle was not drivable because, if the sensor was functioning correctly, the presence of carbon monoxide would make driving dangerous, while if the sensor was not functioning correctly, the inability to detect carbon monoxide would make driving equally unsafe.

Odors. A Washington court held that an odor of diesel fuel in a carpeted storage area of a motor home was a substantial impairment.[104.28] But an appellate court upheld a trial court's finding that an occasional "rotten egg" smell, which was a natural function of the car's European-made engine, was not a substantial impairment.[104.29]

Unexplained noises. An unexplained noise that could be heard over normal conversation met the substantial impairment standard.[104.30] A squealing noise in the brakes, coupled

---

104.18 Vultaggio v. Gen. Motors Corp., 429 N.W.2d 93, 99 (Wis. Ct. App. 1988).

104.19 Kleinman v. Chrysler Motor Corp., 1995 WL 329578 (Ohio Ct. App. May 26, 1995). *But cf.* Royal Chrysler-Oneonta, Inc. v. Dunham, 243 A.D.2d 1007, 663 N.Y.S.2d 410 (1997) (transmission noises were substantial impairment under used car lemon law).

104.20 Divigenze v. Chrysler Corp., 345 N.J. Super. 314, 785 A.2d 37 (Super. Ct. App. Div. 2001) (case also involved malfunctioning brake light); Schonscheck v. Paccar, Inc., 661 N.W.2d 476 (Wis. Ct. App. 2003); *see also* Creighbaum v. Mack Trucks, Inc., 469 N.W.2d 248 (Wis. Ct. App. 1991) (unpublished) (text available at 1991 WL 74217) (affirming lemon law award when vehicle suffered vibration, engine knocking, lack of power and low oil pressure).

104.21 Chmill v. Friendly Ford-Mercury of Janesville, Inc., 144 Wis. 2d 796, 424 N.E.2d 747 (Ct. App. 1988); *see also* Taylor v. Volvo N. Am. Corp., 339 N.C. 238, 451 S.E.2d 618 (1994) (upholding trial court's ruling for consumer when defect was unrepairable shimmying problem). *But cf.* Jolovitz v. Alfa Romeo Distributors, 760 A.2d 625 (Me. 2000) (alignment problem and defects in door and seat mechanism not substantial impairments); Boyle v. Daimler Chrysler Corp., 2002 WL 1881157 (Ohio Ct. App. Aug. 16, 2002) (upholding jury's conclusion that tendency to pull to the left was not a substantial impairment when there was evidence that repairs costing just $75 per wheel would correct the problem).

104.22 Oregel v. Am. Isuzu Motors, Inc., 90 Cal. App. 4th 1094, 109 Cal. Rptr. 2d 583 (2001) (upholding lemon law verdict when car had persistent oil leak; no dispute on appeal that this would be a nonconformity).

104.23 Safari Motor Coaches, Inc. v. Corwin, 225 A.D.2d 921, 638 N.Y.S.2d 992 (1996).

104.24 Contreras v. Ford Motor Co., 2002 WL 31727261 (Cal. Ct. App. Dec. 5, 2002) (unpublished); *see also* Jackson v. Hyundai Motor Am., 1997 WL 119794 (E.D. Pa. Mar. 6, 1997) (Del. law) (upholding jury verdict for consumer when car had history of overheating and stalling, even though problem was successfully repaired by time of trial).

104.25 Baker v. Chrysler Corp., 1993 U.S. Dist. LEXIS 727 (E.D. Pa. Jan. 25, 1993) (car also had problems with brakes and oil sensor light), *aff'd*, 9 F.3d 1539 (3d Cir. 1993) (table). *But cf.* Ahrnsbrak v. Gen. Motors Corp., 502 N.W.2d 283 (Wis. Ct. App.

1993) (unpublished) (text available at 1993 WL 82006) (affirming trial court's determination that coolant leak that required repeated repair was not substantial impairment when it never caused overheating or disablement).

104.26 Baker v. Chrysler Corp., 1993 U.S. Dist. LEXIS 727 (E.D. Pa. Jan. 25, 1993), *aff'd*, 9 F.3d 1539 (3d Cir. 1993) (table); *see also* Kwan v. Mercedes-Benz of N. Am., 23 Cal. App. 4th 174, 28 Cal. Rptr. 2d 371 (1994) (affirming jury verdict on liability when check engine light malfunctioned; appellant did not challenge this finding, however); Gen. Motors Acceptance Corp. v. Jankowitz, 216 N.J. Super. 313, 523 A.2d 695 (Super. Ct. App. Div. 1987) (reversing trial court's dismissal of U.C.C. revocation of acceptance complaint when defect was malfunctioning engine light). *But see* Labonte v. Ford Motor Co., 1999 Ohio App. LEXIS 4795 (Ohio Ct. App. Oct. 7, 1999) (phantom malfunctioning check engine light not substantial impairment when consumer testified that she knew there was no real problem or threat); *cf.* Lowe v. Mercedes Benz of N. Am., Inc., 103 F.3d 118 (4th Cir. 1996) (unpublished) (text available at 1996 U.S. App. LEXIS 31215) (fact that light that was designed to come on briefly when car was started (to remind driver to deploy roll bar when there were passengers in back seat) occasionally stayed on, was not significant impairment; note that this light, unlike oil sensor light, would not falsely indicate hazard).

104.27 Bents v. Fleetwood Motor Homes, 549 N.W.2d 287 (Wis. Ct. App. 1996) (unpublished) (text available at 1996 WL 145916).

104.28 Mooberry v. Magnum Mfg., Inc., 108 Wash. App. 654, 32 P.3d 302 (2001); *see also* Lundy v. Ford Motor Co., 87 Cal. App. 4th 472, 104 Cal. Rptr. 2d 545 (2001) (whether odor was a substantial impairment would be jury question).

104.29 Mercedes-Benz Credit Corp. v. Lotito, 328 N.J. Super. 491, 746 A.2d 480 (Super. Ct. App. Div. 2000).

104.30 Eslamieh v. Coachmen Recreational Vehicle, 2003 WL 22718870 (Cal. Ct. App. Nov. 19, 2003) (unpublished) (whistling noise and defective motor home slide-out were substantial impairments); Ford Motor Co. v. Starling, 721 So. 2d 335 (Fla. Dist. Ct. App. 1998). *But see* Miller v. DaimlerChrysler Motors Corp., 2001 Ohio App. LEXIS 2450 (Ohio Ct. App. May 31, 2001) (intermittent noise and vibration in steering column was

with a grinding sensation and a burning odor, amounted to a substantial impairment.[104.31] A clicking noise upon turning, along with stiff shifting, was an adequate basis for a lemon law verdict for the buyer.[104.32] Whether turn signal and cigarette lighter malfunctions, various rattles, and engine and brake noises amounted to a substantial impairment was a question of fact.[104.33] But an occasional "grunting" noise was not a substantial impairment when the consumer presented no evidence of diminution in value and her expert could not identify any safety concerns.[104.34] Noise may also be a substantial defect simply because it is loud enough to interfere with concentration or with the use and enjoyment of the vehicle. Videotaping the vehicle's performance, with a high-quality audio track, may help prove the extent of the noise problem. A non-profit organization makes helpful information about noise problems available on its website.[104.35]

Water leaks into vehicle. A New York appellate court upheld a lemon law award when the defect was a leak in the upper corner of the windshield.[104.36] A Wisconsin decision agrees that a persistent water leak substantially impairs the safety of a vehicle.[104.37] In that case the leak allowed water into the floor area on the driver's side of the vehicle, increasing the possibility that the driver's foot would slip on the brake or accelerator pedal. The fact that slipping could occur in other circumstances, too, and that the pedals were designed to reduce the risk of slipping when the driver's shoes were wet, did not persuade the court to ignore this increased risk. A half-measure repair to the linoleum floor of a motor home, which allowed water to penetrate into the subfloor, was a substantial impairment.[104.38]

Vehicle body. A motor home door which was often impossible to open, and which trapped the elderly consumer inside, sometimes forcing her to crawl out a window, was a substantial impairment.[104.39]

Paint. Defective or damaged paint can be a substantial impairment.[104.40] One court has found a defective paint job to be a substantial impairment even if the paint job could be easily fixed.[104.41] Expert testimony that a vehicle's paint not only performs an aesthetic function, but also protects the

---

not substantial defect without evidence of effect on vehicle's ability to function); *cf.* Sharkus v. Daimler Chrysler Corp., 2002 WL 31319119 (Ohio Ct. App. Oct. 17, 2002) (unpublished) (screeching noise that dealer could not duplicate did not breach written warranty, so Magnuson-Moss claim denied).

104.31 Gen. Motors Corp. v. Martin, 1997 WL 805137 (Conn. Super. Ct. Dec. 16, 1997); *see also* Jarvis v. Safari Motor Coaches, Inc., 248 A.D.2d 899, 670 N.Y.S.2d 927 (1998) (citing engine noises as one of impairments supporting ruling for buyer).

104.32 Calbert v. Volkswagen of Am., 1991 WL 215669 (Del. Super. Ct. Oct. 1, 1991), *aff'd*, 634 A.2d 938 (Del. 1993) (unpublished); *see also* Royal Chrysler-Oneonta, Inc. v. Dunham, 243 A.D.2d 1007, 663 N.Y.S.2d 410 (1997) (transmission noises were substantial impairment under used car lemon law).

104.33 Telly's, Inc. v. Land Rover N. Am., Inc., 2001 WL 710206 (Mich. Ct. App. June 22, 2001) (reversing summary judgment for consumer; noting that manufacturer's motion for summary judgment was also properly denied); *see also* Brinkman v. Mazda Motor, 1994 WL 193762 (Ohio Ct. App. May 13, 1994) (unpublished) (remanding case for new trial on other grounds when defect was noise in brakes plus "grabbing" in brakes).

104.34 Harris v. Ford Motor Co., 2000 WL 33533986 (Mich. Ct. App. Feb. 11, 2000); *see also* Burns v. Gen. Motors Corp., 833 A.2d 934 (Conn. Ct. App. 2003) (transmission noise not substantial impairment when trier of fact believed evidence that it was a normal characteristic and it had caused no mechanical problems; Johns v. Am. Isuzu Motors, Inc., 622 So. 2d 1208 (La. Ct. App. 1993) (sporadic rattle, which technicians could not duplicate, was not a substantial impairment; Stepp v. Chrysler Corp., 1996 WL 752794 (Ohio Ct. App. Nov. 7, 1996) (noise upon turning that could only be heard when there was no other noise in vehicle was not substantial impairment); Kleinman v. Chrysler Motor Corp., 1995 WL 329578 (Ohio Ct. App. May 26, 1995) (upholding trial court's determination that transmission and engine noises, which technician testified were normal for this model and which never prevented car from operating, were not a substantial impairment).

104.35 The Noise Pollution Clearinghouse's website is located at www.nonoise.org.

104.36 Gen. Motors Corp. v. Lee, 193 A.D.2d 741, 598 N.Y.S.2d 61 (1993) (issue on appeal was whether warranty covered this

defect); *accord* Lesjak v. Forest River, Inc., 2003 WL 22861722 (Ohio Ct. App. Nov. 26, 2003) (leak into living quarters of mobile home is substantial impairment); *see also* Milicevic v. Mercedes-Benz USA, Ltd. Liab. Co., 256 F. Supp. 2d 1168 (D. Nev. 2003) (defective weather stripping around window plus other defects constitute substantial impairment); Browning v. Am. Isuzu Motors, Inc., 2002 WL 32063978 (Ohio C.P. Mar. 21, 2003) (whether persistent leaks, which may have caused electrical problems, are a substantial impairment is question of fact to be decided at trial).

104.37 Regal v. Gen. Motors Corp., 2003 WL 21537821 (Wis. Ct. App. July 9, 2003) (unpublished).

104.38 Barker v. Fleetwood Enterprises, Inc., 2002 WL 453931 (Cal. Ct. App. Mar. 26, 2002) (unpublished).

104.39 Harvill v. Fleetwood Enterprises, Inc., 2003 WL 21702375 (Cal. Ct. App. July 23, 2003) (unpublished).

104.40 Gen. Motors Corp. v. Dohmann, 247 Conn. 274, 722 A.2d 1205 (Conn. 1998) (defective paint job is substantial impairment on basis of consumer's testimony and expert opinion); Russo v. Danbury Auto Haus, Inc., 1994 Conn. Super. LEXIS 1526 (Conn. Super. Ct. June 10, 1994); Dieter v. Chrysler Corp., 234 Wis. 2d 670, 610 N.W.2d 832 (Wis. 2000) (buyers entitled to lemon law remedies when dealer's attempts to repaint scratches left "swirls" in finish); *see also* Contreras v. Ford Motor Co., 2002 WL 31727261 (Cal. Ct. App. Dec. 5, 2002) (unpublished) (defective doors, which scratched vehicle's paint, could be substantial impairment); Pavesi v. Ford Motor Co., 155 N.J. Super. 373, 382 A.2d 954 (Super. Ct. Ch. Div. 1978) (defective paint was substantial impairment that allowed U.C.C. revocation); O'Bryant v. Reeder Chevrolet Co., 1999 Tenn. App. LEXIS 245 (Tenn. Ct. App. Apr. 15, 1999) (ding in new car, costing $200 to repair, could be substantial impairment when repainting was rough and did not match); *cf.* Chaudoir v. Porsche Cars of N. Am., 667 So. 2d 569 (La. Ct. App. 1996) (Louisiana lemon law creates requirement rather than presumption). *But see* Gen. Motors Acceptance Corp. v. Hollanshead, 105 Ohio App. 3d 17, 663 N.E.2d 663 (Ohio Ct. App. 1995) (cosmetic "fit and finish" adjustments to exterior not substantial impairment).

104.41 Williams v. Chrysler Corp., 530 So. 2d 1214 (La. Ct. App. 1988).

exterior from rust and deterioration, and about any differences between a repainted vehicle and one with a factory paint job, may be helpful.

Electrical system and accessories. Electrical system problems that drain a vehicle's battery may be a substantial impairment.[104.42] Automatic door locks that locked without warning substantially impaired a vehicle's safety because of the owners' fear that their children would get locked in or out of the car.[104.43]

Motor home living quarters: Water leaks into the living quarters of a motor home substantially impair the vehicle.[104.44] A defective bedroom "slide-out" that opened unexpectedly in traffic was a substantial impairment.[104.45]

Air conditioning system. A trial court has upheld a lemon law arbitration ruling that a malfunctioning air conditioning system was a substantial impairment.[104.46] The court cited the buyer's testimony that the air conditioning was important because the vehicle would be used to transport an infant in the summertime.

13.2.4.4.4 Proving substantial impairment

Substantial impairment is a question of fact for the jury.[104.47] Whether the consumer or manufacturer bears the burden of proving substantial impairment depends on the structure of the particular lemon law. For example, the New York statute states that the manufacturer may plead as an affirmative defense that the nonconformity does not sub-

stantially impair the value.[104.48] The Maine statute takes the same approach.[104.49] Therefore, the burden of proof in those states is on the manufacturer to show the absence of substantial impairment, and a decision that improperly shifts that burden to the consumer must be vacated.[104.50] In California, the burden to prove substantial impairment is on the consumer.[104.51]

The consumer need not present expert testimony to establish a defect or nonconformity. The owner's own testimony (or anyone else's) that the vehicle does not work properly is adequate to meet the burden of proof, because the consumer is under no duty to prove the cause of the nonconformity.[104.52] Substantial impairment also need not be proven by an expert witness and may be established by the consumer's own testimony.[104.53]

104.42 Jarvis v. Safari Motor Coaches, Inc., 248 A.D.2d 899, 670 N.Y.S.2d 927 (1998) (citing battery drain as one of impairments supporting ruling for buyer).

104.43 Gen. Motors Corp. v. Garito, 1997 Conn. Super. LEXIS 3413 (Conn. Super. Ct. Dec. 12, 1997).

104.44 Lesjak v. Forest River, Inc., 2003 WL 22861722 (Ohio Ct. App. Nov. 26, 2003); *see also* Barker v. Fleetwood Enterprises, Inc., 2002 WL 453931 (Cal. Ct. App. Mar. 26, 2002) (unpublished).

104.45 Eslamieh v. Coachmen Recreational Vehicle, 2003 WL 22718870 (Cal. Ct. App. Nov. 19, 2003) (unpublished).

104.46 Gen. Motors Corp. v. Blanchard, 1998 WL 285838 (Conn. Super. Ct. May 19, 1998); *see also* Jarvis v. Safari Motor Coaches, Inc., 248 A.D.2d 899, 670 N.Y.S.2d 927 (1998) (citing air conditioning malfunction as one of impairments supporting ruling for buyer); Abbs v. Georgie Boy, 60 Wash. App. 157, 803 P.2d 14 (1991) (affirming judgment for buyer when air conditioning malfunctioned, causing stalling and impairing comfort and defogging).

104.47 Barker v. Fleetwood Enterprises, Inc., 2002 WL 453931 (Cal. Ct. App. Mar. 26, 2002) (unpublished); Schreidel v. Am. Honda Motor Co., 34 Cal. App. 4th 1242, 40 Cal. Rptr. 2d 576 (1995); Calbert v. Volkswagen of Am., Inc., 1991 WL 215669 (Del. Super. Ct. Oct. 1, 1991), *aff'd*, 634 A.2d 938 (Del. 1993) (unpublished). *But see* Schonscheck v. Paccar, Inc., 661 N.W.2d 476 (Wis. Ct. App. 2003) (mixed question of law and fact); Chmill v. Friendly Ford-Mercury of Janesville, Inc., 144 Wis. 2d 796, 424 N.E.2d 747 (Ct. App. 1988) (whether facts as found by court fulfill standard of substantial impairment is a legal conclusion).

104.48 N.Y. Gen. Bus. Law § 198-a(c)(3)(i) (McKinney).

104.49 *See* Jolovitz v. Alfa Romeo Distributors, 760 A.2d 625 (Me. 2000).

104.50 Walker v. Gen. Motors Corp., 159 Misc. 2d 651, 606 N.Y.S.2d 125 (Civ. Ct. 1993); *see also* Safari Motor Coaches, Inc. v. Corwin, 225 A.D.2d 921, 638 N.Y.S.2d 992 (1996) (manufacturer's failure to introduce any evidence at arbitration hearing precludes any claim that nonconformity did not substantially impair the value).

104.51 Schreidel v. Am. Honda Motor Co., 34 Cal. App. 4th 1242, 40 Cal. Rptr. 2d 576 (1995).

104.52 Green v. Ford Motor Co., 1996 U.S. Dist. LEXIS 4102 (E.D. Pa. Apr. 1, 1996) (jury verdict for plaintiffs upheld even though they were only witnesses to defects in transmission and defendant presented expert testimony that transmission worked properly); Baker v. Chrysler Corp., 1993 WL 18099 (E.D. Pa. Jan. 25, 1993), *aff'd*, 9 F.3d 1539 (3d Cir. 1993) (table); Schreidel v. Am. Honda Motor Co., 34 Cal. App. 4th 1242, 40 Cal. Rptr. 2d 576 (1995) (expert who testified that clutch slave cylinder was defective need not show the precise defect within the cylinder); Gen. Motors Corp. v. Martin, 1997 WL 805137 (Conn. Super. Ct. Dec. 16, 1997) (trier of fact was entitled to believe consumer's testimony about defects over manufacturer's expert); Mason v. Porsche Cars N. Am., Inc., 688 So. 2d 361 (Fla. Dist. Ct. App. 1997) (consumer need not prove existence of specific defective part; existence of problem is sufficient); Gen. Motors Corp. v. Zirkel, 613 N.E.2d 30, *aff'd on rehearing*, 617 N.E.2d 921 (Ind. 1993); Genetti v. Caterpillar, Inc., 261 Neb. 98, 621 N.W.2d 529, 43 U.C.C. Rep. Serv. 2d 829 (2001) (consumer need not prove specific defect); Christelles v. Nissan Motor Corp., 305 N.J. Super. 222, 701 A.2d 1317 (Super. Ct. App. Div. 1997); Taylor v. Volvo N. Am. Corp., 339 N.C. 238, 451 S.E.2d 618 (1994) (need not prove specific mechanical defect; evidence of shimmying is sufficient); Adventure Travel World, Ltd. v. Gen. Motors Corp., 107 N.C. App. 573, 421 S.E.2d 173 (1992) (evidence of brake failure incidents despite proper driving, plus mechanic's testimony of uneven wear and possible cause, sufficient to create issue of fact despite manufacturer's expert testimony); Dobbratz Trucking & Excavating, Inc. v. Paccar, Inc., 647 N.W.2d 315 (Wis. Ct. App. 2002); *see* § 7.4, *supra*. *But see* Vaughn v. Daimler Chrysler Corp., 2003 WL 21297310 (Tenn. Ct. App. June 4, 2003) (affirming summary judgment for manufacturer when plaintiff conceded expert testimony was necessary but failed to produce an expert to establish substantial impairment).

104.53 Green v. Ford Motor Co., 1996 WL 153214 (E.D. Pa. Apr. 1, 1996) (jury entitled to credit plaintiffs' lay testimony over

The consumer need not present evidence that quantifies the impaired value.[104.54] An impairment can be substantial even if the cost of repair is minor, especially in cases in which diagnosis of the problem has been difficult and delayed.[104.55] Impaired use may be shown simply by evidence that the consumer was prevented from using the car or chose not to drive it.[104.56] Nonetheless, when substantial impairment is a contested issue, it is helpful if an expert can testify as to the diminution in value that results from the defect. A potential buyer who knows about a defect, whether it involves safety or amenities, is likely to be unwilling to pay the same price for that car as for a car without the defect. Quantifying the effect of the defect in this way can help persuade the court that it is significant.[104.57] The owner's

manual may also be helpful, as it may instruct the driver to stop driving, or to get the vehicle serviced immediately, if a particular malfunction occurs. It should be clear that a malfunction is a substantial impairment if it means that the owner must stop driving the car.

Evidence about why a defect is important to the particular consumer can be critical in showing that a defect is substantial. As most lemon laws focus on the buyer's particular needs in determining whether an impairment is substantial, the consumer should present evidence about those needs, why the vehicle with its defects does not meet those needs, and whether the consumer would have bought the vehicle knowing of those defects.

Sometimes there is no question that the alleged defect is a serious one that, if proven, will substantially impair the value of the vehicle. Defendants may attempt to characterize other defects, such as air conditioning, noise level, and appearance problems, as minor and insubstantial. Attorneys recommend using *voir dire* to start dealing with these issues. For example, the consumer's attorney might ask jurors whether they have ever bought a car, and whether a functioning air conditioning system was important to them. Another question might be whether the juror would find it unreasonable for a buyer of a new car to insist that the air conditioning system in the car function properly. The attorney can then follow up by asking the buyer whether she would have bought the vehicle with a malfunctioning air conditioning system, and by asking the defendant's repair technicians about whether that system is important to their customers. Stressing that the buyers will be giving the vehicle back to the seller may also be helpful.

---

defendant's expert testimony); Baker v. Chrysler Corp., 1993 U.S. Dist. LEXIS 727 (E.D. Pa. Jan. 25, 1993), *aff'd*, 9 F.3d 1539 (3d Cir. 1993) (table); Gen. Motors Corp. v. Zirkel, 613 N.E.2d 30, *aff'd on rehearing*, 617 N.E.2d 921 (Ind. 1993); Christelles v. Nissan Motor Corp., 305 N.J. Super. 222, 701 A.2d 1317 (Super. Ct. App. Div. 1997).

104.54 Mason v. Porsche Cars N. Am., Inc., 688 So. 2d 361 (Fla. Dist. Ct. App. 1997).

104.55 Harvill v. Fleetwood Enterprises, Inc., 2003 WL 21702375 (Cal. Ct. App. July 23, 2003) (unpublished) (trial court did not err in excluding evidence of cost of repair).

104.56 Mason v. Porsche Cars N. Am., Inc., 688 So. 2d 361 (Fla. Dist. Ct. App. 1997); *see also* Lesjak v. Forest River, Inc., 2003 WL 22861722 (Ohio Ct. App. Nov. 26, 2003) (substantial impairment established by diminished ability to sell or trade vehicle and diminished use of it).

104.57 *See, e.g.*, Chmill v. Friendly Ford-Mercury of Janesville, Inc., 144 Wis. 2d 796, 424 N.E.2d 747 (Ct. App. 1988) (experienced car salesman testified that value of vehicle was substantially less because of defect).

Page 480

13.2.5 Notice Requirements

Addition to note 111.

111 *But cf.* Kniska v. Subaru of Am., Inc., 2003 WL 21659457 (Va. Cir. Ct. Apr. 24, 2003) (dealer's submission of warranty claims to manufacturer for reimbursement does not meet statutory notice requirement).

Add to text at end of subsection's second paragraph:

Notice need not be provided of each service visit.[113.1] Timely notice of a defect is sufficient even as to problems that occur later if those problems are related to the same defect.[113.2]

113.1 Rothermel v. Safari Motor Coaches, 1994 U.S. Dist. LEXIS 21591 (N.D. Ohio July 29, 1994).

113.2 Jackson v. Hyundai Motor Am., 1997 WL 119794 (E.D. Pa. Mar. 6, 1997) (Del. law).

Addition to note 115.

115 *See also* Cannon v. Newmar Corp., 210 F. Supp. 2d 461 (W.D.N.Y. 2003) (interpreting New York's special notice requirements for motor homes); Divigenze v. Chrysler Corp., 345 N.J. Super. 314, 785 A.2d 37 (Super. Ct. App. Div. 2001) (failure to send "last chance" letter only negates presumption, notwithstanding administrative regulation that could be interpreted to bar suit).

Page 481

Replace note 117 with:

117 *See* Gen. Motors Corp. v. Schmitz, 362 Md. 229, 764 A.2d 838 (2001) (discussing but declining to decide whether failure to comply with certified notice requirement would bar claim).

Add to text after subsection's third paragraph:

Wisconsin's lemon law requires the manufacturer, at the direction of the consumer, to offer a refund or a replacement. An intermediate appellate court has given this requirement a cramped reading, invalidating a consumer's notice to the manufacturer because it gave the manufacturer the choice between refund or replacement rather than directing one or the other.[117.1] Offering the manufacturer another opportunity to repair the vehicle also invalidates the notice, according to this decision. Another Wisconsin decision gives an excessively literal reading to the statutory requirement that the consumer's notice must offer to transfer title of the non-conforming vehicle to the manufacturer.[117.2] It holds, over a persuasive dissent, that the consumer's request for a replacement vehicle is not an implicit offer to transfer title of the non-conforming vehicle back to the manufacturer.

117.1 Berends v. Mack Truck, Inc., 643 N.W.2d 158 (Wis. Ct. App. 2002).

117.2 Garcia v. Mazda Motor of Am., Inc., 2003 WL 22207874 (Wis. Ct. App. Sept. 25, 2003).

Addition to note 119.

119 *Replace Schmitz citation with*: 362 Md. 2291, 764 A.2d 838 (2001); *add*: Ibrahim v. Ford Motor Co., 214 Cal. App. 3d 878, 263 Cal. Rptr. 64 (1989).

Replace note 120 with:

120 Gen. Motors Corp. v. Schmitz, 362 Md. 229, 764 A.2d 838 (2001).

Add note 120.1 at end of second sentence of paragraph containing note 121.

120.1 *See* Mooberry v. Magnum Mfg., Inc., 108 Wash. App. 654, 32 P.3d 302 (2001) (construing last-chance notice requirement not to apply to motor home purchased on or before June 30, 1998).

Addition to note 121.

121 *See also* Cato v. Am. Suzuki Motor Corp., 622 N.W.2d 486 (Iowa 2001) (before filing suit, consumer must give manufacturer final chance to repair).

Replace note 122 with:

122 O'Henry v. Chrysler Corp., 215 F.3d 1327 (6th Cir. 2000) (unpublished) (text available at 2000 U.S. App. LEXIS 11843).

Add to text at end of subsection's sixth paragraph:

In order to recover under Wisconsin's lemon law, a consumer who leases a vehicle must give notice to the manufacturer while still under the lease, before purchasing the vehicle at the end of the lease term.[123.1] Once timely notice is given, however, the manufacturer can not defeat the consumer's lemon law rights by delaying until the lease term expires.[123.2]

123.1 Varda v. Gen. Motors Corp., 242 Wis. 2d 756, 626 N.W.2d 346 (Ct. App. 2001).

123.2 *Id.*

13.2.6 Manufacturer's Repair Attempts

13.2.6.1 General

Page 482

Add to text at end of subsection:

Industries can not dictate the extent of their obligations under the law, and a repair can substantially impair the value of the vehicle even though it meets industry standards.[130.1]

130.1 Barker v. Fleetwood Enterprises, Inc., 2002 WL 453931 (Cal. Ct. App. Mar. 26, 2002) (unpublished).

13.2.6.2 Costs of Transporting Car to Manufacturer

Add to text at end of subsection's third paragraph:

If the warranty does not explicitly require the consumer to return the vehicle to the manufacturer, a court is unlikely to impose such a requirement.[132.1]

132.1 Harvill v. Fleetwood Enterprises, Inc., 2003 WL 21702375 (Cal. Ct. App. July 23, 2003) (unpublished).

13.2.6.3 Number of Repair Attempts Allowed

Add to text after sentence containing note 133:

The Iowa Supreme Court has held that, under its lemon law, repairs during both the initial lease of a car and after exercise by the lessor of a purchase option are to be cumulated in determining whether these thresholds have been met.[133.1]

133.1 Cato v. Am. Suzuki Motor Corp., 622 N.W.2d 486 (Iowa 2001).

Addition to notes 134, 135.

134 *See also* Safari Motor Coaches, Inc. v. Corwin, 225 A.D.2d 921, 638 N.Y.S.2d 992 (1996) (repair attempts by outside repair shop to which motor home manufacturer refers buyer count toward total).

135 Contreras v. Ford Motor Co., 2002 WL 31727261 (Cal. Ct. App. Dec. 5, 2002) (unpublished); Oregel v. Am. Isuzu Motors, Inc., 90 Cal. App. 4th 1094, 109 Cal. Rptr. 2d 583 (2001); Browning v. Am. Isuzu

Motors, Inc., 2002 WL 32063978 (Ohio C.P. Mar. 21, 2003); Regal v. Gen. Motors Corp., 2003 WL 21537821 (Wis. Ct. App. July 9, 2003) (unpublished).

Add to text after subsection's second paragraph:

The manufacturer's warranty policy and procedure manual may reveal a policy, either explicit or subtle, that discourages writing up repair orders. This policy may help the consumer persuade the court that the occasions when the car was delivered to the dealer should be counted as repair attempts even though no repair order was prepared. A California court upheld a civil penalty amounting to double damages against a manufacturer that followed a policy of not writing up repair orders, which the court held showed willfulness and a lack of good faith.[137.1]

137.1   Oregel v. Am. Isuzu Motors, Inc., 90 Cal. App. 4th 1094, 109 Cal. Rptr. 2d 583 (2001).

Page 483

Add to text after sentence containing note 139:

Periods of time when the consumer has possession of the vehicle but has been instructed to drive it only a limited amount to test the systems count as being out of service.[139.1]

139.1   Theis v. Ford Motor Co., 568 N.W.2d 786 (Wis. Ct. App. 1997) (unpublished) (text available at 1997 WL 349829).

Replace note 140 with:

140   Burke v. Pride-Chrysler-Plymouth, Inc., 1998 Mass. App. Div. 208 (Mass. Dist. Ct. 1998).

Addition to note 142.

142   Royster v. Toyota Motor Sales, 92 Ohio St. 3d 327, 750 N.E.2d 531 (2001).

Add to text at end of subsection's fifth paragraph:

The period of time that a consumer left the car with the dealer, who was waiting for parts to arrive, counted toward the total, when the dealer initially told the consumer that the parts would arrive in just a few days.[142.1] Under Nevada's lemon law, the presumption arises if the car has been out of service for more than thirty days for any one or more defects; the thirty days need not all relate to the same defect.[142.2] Providing a "loaner" car while the consumer's car is out of service does not prevent the time from counting toward the statutory period.[142.3]

142.1   Milicevic v. Mercedes-Benz USA, Ltd. Liab. Co., 256 F. Supp. 2d 1168 (D. Nev. 2003).
142.2   *Id.*
142.3   Royster v. Toyota Motor Sales, 92 Ohio St. 3d 327, 750 N.E.2d 531 (2001).

Addition to note 147.

147   *Add explanatory parenthetical to Saab Cars USA, Inc. citation:* (brake problems).

Add to text at end of subsection's seventh paragraph:

A California court interpreted its statute, which requires a reasonable number of repair "attempts," to require at least two attempts, because "attempts" is plural.[147.1]

147.1   Silvio v. Ford Motor Co., 109 Cal. App. 4th 1205, 135 Cal. Rptr. 2d 846 (2003); *see also* § 2.5.6, *supra* (interpretation of plural word "attempts" in Magnuson-Moss Act). *But see* Milicevic v. Mercedes-Benz USA, Ltd. Liab. Co., 256 F. Supp. 2d 1168, 1174, 1175 (D. Nev. 2003) (interpreting similar statute and finding that in some circumstances a single attempt, or no attempt at all, can be a reasonable number).

Addition to note 148.

148   *Replace O'Henry citation with:* 215 F.3d 1327 (6th Cir. 2000) (unpublished) (text available at 2000 U.S. App. LEXIS 11843); *add:* Brown v. Reynolds, 10 Va. Cir. 334 (1987); *see also* Fla. Stat. Ann. § 90.301(2) (West) (general provision of evidence code making all presumptions rebuttable unless statute makes them conclusive). *But see* Telly's, Inc. v. Land Rover N. Am., Inc., 2001 Mich. App. LEXIS 1413 (Mich. Ct. App. June 22, 2001) (consumer must meet either thirty days or four repair attempt requirement; when vehicle was not out of service for thirty days, court considers only those defects that persisted after four repair attempts); *cf.* Chaudoir v. Porsche Cars of N. Am., 667 So. 2d 569 (La. Ct. App. 1996) (Louisiana lemon law creates requirement rather than presumption).

Add to text at end of subsection:

The Ohio Supreme Court has expressed the same view.[150.1] But if there are not enough repair attempts to trigger the presumption, the consumer still has the opportunity to show that the repair attempts that were afforded to the manufacturer gave it a reasonable opportunity to repair the vehicle.[150.2] A few states do not use the term presumption in defining what constitutes a reasonable number of repair attempts.[150.3]

Even if a lemon law triggers the consumer's refund or replacement rights only after a certain number of repair attempts, not a certain number of days out of service, the number of days the vehicle has been out of service may still be admissible to show that the defects substantially impaired the use of the vehicle.[150.4]

150.1 Royster v. Toyota Motor Sales, 92 Ohio St. 3d 327, 750 N.E.2d 531 (2001); *accord* Camp v. Fleetwood Motor Homes, 2003 WL 22025071 (Ohio C.P. June 6, 2003) (presumption applies when motor home repairs took more than three days).

150.2 Browning v. Am. Isuzu Motors, Inc., 2002 WL 32063978 (Ohio C.P. Mar. 21, 2003).

150.3 *See* Mass. Gen. Laws ch. 90, § 7N 1/4; Wash. Rev. Code § 19.118.041; Wis. Stat. § 218.015.

150.4 Palmer v. Fleetwood Enterprises, Inc., 2003 WL 21228864 (Cal. Ct. App. May 28, 2003) (unpublished); *see also* Milicevic v. Mercedes-Benz USA, Ltd. Liab. Co., 256 F. Supp. 2d 1168 (D. Nev. 2003) (citing number of days vehicle was out of service as a factor supporting finding of substantial impairment); Schonscheck v. Paccar, Inc., 661 N.W.2d 476 (Wis. Ct. App. 2003) (same).

Page 484

13.2.7 Time Restrictions on Lemon Law Applicability

Add note 150.3 at end of subsection's first sentence.

150.3 *Cf.* Markee v. Ford Motor Co., 584 N.W.2d 235 (Wis. Ct. App. 1998) (unpublished) (text available at 1998 WL 404870) (Wisconsin requires notice within one year of first delivery of vehicle to a consumer, thus buyer of low-mileage used car had less than a year to give notice).

Addition to notes 153, 154.

153 *See* Williams v. Potamkin Motor Cars, Inc., 2002 WL 31870216 (Fla. Dist. Ct. App. Dec. 26, 2002) (applying Florida's requirement that lemon law suit be brought within three years after delivery).

154 Mills v. Forestex Co., 108 Cal. App. 4th 625, 134 Cal. Rptr. 2d 273, 287 (2003).

Add to text at end of subsection's second paragraph:

State law may allow tolling of the statute of limitations under some circumstances.[154.1]

154.1 *Cf.* Mercedes Benz of N. Am. v. Kling, 549 So. 2d 795 (Fla. 1990) (lemon law statute of limitations not tolled by assurances of repair, but court suggests that fraud or estoppel would toll it).

13.2.8 The Replacement or Refund Remedy

13.2.8.1 When Is the Remedy Triggered?

Add to text at end of subsection's second paragraph:

Nor can the manufacturer require the consumer to provide information about the condition of the vehicle if the lemon law does not require it.[165.1]

165.1 Herzberg v. Ford Motor Co., 626 N.W.2d 67, 43 U.C.C. Rep. Serv. 2d 1137 (Wis. Ct. App. 2001).

Add new subsection heading to text after subsection's second paragraph:

13.2.8.1a Must Defect Still Exist at Time of Hearing?

Addition to notes 166–168.

166 Rhodes v. All Star Ford, Inc., 599 So. 2d 812 (La. Ct. App. 1992) (defects were repaired without vehicle being out of service more than thirty days).

167 Jackson v. Hyundai Motor Am., 1997 WL 119794 (E.D. Pa. Mar. 6, 1997) (Del. law); DiVigenze v. Chrysler Corp., 345 N.J. Super. 314, 785 A.2d 37 (Super. Ct. App. Div. 2001). *But see* Kucher v. Daimlerchrysler Corp., 194 Misc. 2d 688, 754 N.Y.S.2d 512 (Civ. Ct. 2003) (presumption that four is a reasonable number of repair attempts does not apply unless defect continues to exist, but if vehicle is out of service more than thirty days presumption applies even if defect is ultimately repaired).

Page 485

168 *Delete But see* citation to Court of Appeals opinion in *Royster*; *add*: Milicevic v. Mercedes-Benz USA, Ltd. Liab. Co., 256 F. Supp. 2d 1168 (D. Nev. 2003); Kucher v. Daimlerchrysler Corp., 194 Misc. 2d 688, 754 N.Y.S.2d 512 (Civ. Ct. 2003) (if vehicle is out of service more than thirty days, presumption that there has been a reasonable number of repair attempts applies even if defect is ultimately repaired); Royster v. Toyota Motor Sales, 92 Ohio St. 3d 327, 750 N.E.2d 531 (2001).

Add to text at end of subsection:

Some lemon laws say that the presumption of a reasonable number of repairs applies if there has been a certain number of repair attempts "and the defect continues to exist." This language should be interpreted to mean that the defect must still exist after the last repair attempt, not that it must continue to exist in perpetuity.[168.1]

168.1 Krasnow v. Mercedes-Benz of N. Am., Inc., 1998 WL 437339 (Conn. Super. Ct. July 1, 1998); Gen. Motors Corp. v. Garito, 1997 WL 804876 (Conn. Super. Ct. Dec. 11, 1997).

13.2.8.3 Effect of Consumer's Inability to Return Car

Addition to notes 175, 176.

175 *Replace Schoonmaker citation with*: 1986 Conn. Super. LEXIS 241.

176   *Replace Cook citation with*: 24 Va. Cir. 377 (1991).

*Add to text at end of
subsection's fourth
paragraph:*

Another court has held that the consumer could not pursue the refund or replace remedy in this situation but could seek damages under the lemon law.[176.1]

176.1   King v. King Motor Co., 780 So. 2d 937 (Fla. Dist. Ct. App. 2001); *see* § 13.4.2, *infra.*

Page 486

13.2.8.4 Is a Replacement Vehicle Comparable?

*Add note 178.1 at end of
subsection's second sentence.*

178.1   *But see* Hynson v. Am. Motors Sales Corp., 164 A.D.2d 41, 561 N.Y.S.2d 589 (1990) ("comparable vehicle" means one with approximately the same mileage).

Replace note 179 with:

179   Dussault v. Chrysler Corp., 229 Wis. 2d 296, 600 N.W.2d 6 (Ct. App. 1999); *see also* DaimlerChrysler Corp. v. Allard, 2003 WL 22293200 (Conn. Super. Ct. Sept. 22, 2003) (unpublished) (denying manufacturer's application to revise arbitrator's award of new 2002 vehicle to replace different model 2000 vehicle).

*Add to text at end of
subsection's first paragraph:*

The replacement vehicle must include accessories and equipment comparable to what was included with the original vehicle purchased.[179.1]

179.1   Kiss v. Gen. Motors Corp., 630 N.W.2d 742 (Wis. Ct. App. 2001) (rejecting manufacturer's proposal to transfer equipment installed on the lemon to the new vehicle, which could compromise integrity of the equipment or the vehicle).

13.2.8.5 No Allowance for Use When Consumer Receives a Replacement Vehicle

Addition to note 182.

182   *Add parenthetical to Hynson citation*: (replacement vehicle must be comparable in mileage).

13.2.8.6 How to Calculate a Refund

*Add to text at beginning of
subsection:*

Lemon law refund provisions should be construed to make the consumer whole.[184.1]

184.1   Collins v. Mullinax E., Inc., 153 Ohio App. 3d 534, 795 N.E.2d 68 (2003); Willis v. Ford Motor Co., 2003 WL 21473520 (Ohio Ct. App. June 25, 2003).

*Add note 184.2 after
"optional purchases" in
sentence containing note 185.*

184.2   *See* Kiss v. Gen. Motors Corp., 630 N.W.2d 742 (Wis. Ct. App. 2001) (stating in dictum that refund probably must include all money paid by consumer on day of sale, including cost of nonmanufacturer-supplied options).

Addition to note 187.

187   *See also* Strachan v. Ford Motor Co., 1997 U.S. Dist. LEXIS 5321 (E.D. Pa. Apr. 16, 1997) (N.J. law) (ordering refund without regard to negative equity when dealer failed to show actual value of trade-in and allegedly inflated value was recorded on the documents); Dyer v. Quality Car & Truck Leasing, Inc., 1989 WL 214503 (Ohio Ct. App. June 1, 1989) (adopting value that dealer placed on trade-in at time of sale, notwithstanding later claim that it was inflated to cover negative equity). *But cf.* Meade v. Nelson Auto Group, 1997 WL 208685 (Ohio Ct. App. Mar. 31, 1997) (affirming, on other grounds, rescission award under Ohio UDAP statute that took negative equity into account).

*Add to text after sentence
containing note 187:*

Otherwise, courts would constantly be called on to go behind the documents, either at the buyer's or the seller's behest. The value stated in the contract is the value that should be assigned to the trade-in, not the private valuation that the dealer may have made but that it did not present either to the consumer or to the entity that financed the transaction.[187.1] It should be awkward for a dealer to insist that the trade-in value was inflated to cover negative equity, as the purpose can only be to deceive either the consumer or the financing entity. Knowing false statements or overvaluation of security for the purpose of influencing an action of a federally-insured financial institution is a crime.[187.2] Some state UDAP statutes or motor vehicle laws also specifically forbid jacking up the sale price to compensate for an inflated trade-in allowance.[187.3] It may be appropriate to invoke the parol evidence rule in this situation.[187.4] In Florida, however, a 1997 amendment to the lemon law provides that, if the actual trade-in allowance is not acceptable to both the manufacturer and the consumer, the NADA retail book value will be substituted, which leaves the consumer saddled with the negative equity.[187.5]

187.1 Ramirez v. Autosport, 88 N.J. 277, 440 A.2d 1345 (1982); *see also* Strachan v. Ford Motor Co., 1997 U.S. Dist. LEXIS 5321 (E.D. Pa. Apr. 16, 1997) (N.J. law) (ordering refund without regard to negative equity when dealer failed to show actual value of trade-in and allegedly inflated value was recorded on the documents).

187.2 18 U.S.C. § 1014.

187.3 *See* National Consumer Law Center, Unfair and Deceptive Acts and Practices § 5.4.4.4 (5th ed. 2001 and Supp.).

187.4 *See, e.g.,* Nelson v. Cowles Ford, Inc., 2003 WL 22293597 (4th Cir. Oct. 7, 2003) (unpublished) (no error in basing contract damage award on vehicle price stated in contract, disregarding negative equity, when contract had integration clause).

187.5 Holzhauer-Mosher v. Ford Motor Co., 772 So. 2d 7 (Fla. Dist. Ct. App. 2000).

Add to text after subsection's first paragraph:

The amount the consumer receives as a settlement with one defendant may have to be deducted from the jury's award against another defendant, unless the jury was told about the settlement and instructed to take it into account.[189.1]

189.1 Barker v. Fleetwood Enterprises, Inc., 2002 WL 453931 (Cal. Ct. App. Mar. 26, 2002) (unpublished); *see also* § 10.1.6, *supra.*

Page 487

Add to text after subsection's second paragraph:

Some lemon laws explicitly require the refund to include the finance charges the consumer incurred when purchasing the car. Ohio's statute, for example, defines the "full purchase price" that must be refunded as including all "financing charges."[190.1] The term includes any charges incurred in purchasing the vehicle, even if the buyer used a home equity loan rather than the more customary method of obtaining credit secured by the vehicle.[190.2]

190.1 Ohio Rev. Code Ann. §§ 1345.71(F)(1), 1345.72(D)(1) (West).

190.2 Collins v. Mullinax E., Inc., 153 Ohio App. 3d 534, 795 N.E.2d 68 (2003).

Add to text after sentence containing note 194:

The Vermont Supreme Court held that credit insurance premiums were included in a requirement that "credit charges or similar charges" be refunded.[194.1]

194.1 Muzzy v. Chevrolet Div., Gen. Motors Corp., 153 Vt. 179, 571 A.2d 609 (1989).

Add to text at end of subsection:

Many lemon laws cover leased vehicles.[199.1] Several courts have held that, in the case of a lease, the refund should be calculated as the actual payments the consumer has made under the lease, including vehicle registration fees.[199.2] This method of calculation makes sense as long as the consumer is able to obtain an order voiding any further obligation under the lease.[199.3]

199.1 *See* § 13.2.3.3, *supra.*

199.2 *See, e.g.,* Brady v. Mercedes-Benz USA, 243 F. Supp. 2d 1004 (N.D. Cal. 2002) (consumer can recover payments actually made, not current value of lease or payments that will come due in future); Estate of Riley v. Ford Motor Co., 635 N.W.2d 635 (Wis. Ct. App. 2001) (plaintiff is entitled to pecuniary loss, which is amount paid, not current value of lease).

199.3 *See* Brady v. Mercedes-Benz USA, 243 F. Supp. 2d 1004 (N.D. Cal. 2002).

13.2.8.7 Deduction from Refund for Reasonable Use Allowance

Addition to notes 203, 204.

203 *See also* Brady v. Mercedes-Benz USA, 243 F. Supp. 2d 1004 (N.D. Cal. 2002) (applying formula for use offset to a vehicle lease).

204 BMW of N. Am., Ltd. Liab. Co. v. Flechner, 2003 WL 1477058 (Conn. Super. Ct. Mar. 5, 2003). *But see* Saab Cars USA, Inc. v. Avidan, 1991 WL 126041 (Conn. Super. Ct. June 25, 1991) (interpreting lemon law to mandate use of statutory formula).

Page 488

Add to text at end of subsection's fourth paragraph:

It may be helpful to ask the manufacturer in discovery how many miles a consumer should expect the vehicle to last, given proper maintenance. The manufacturer is likely to claim a high figure, resulting in a lower use value per mile.

Add to text after sentence containing note 208:

The amount to be doubled or trebled is the purchase price plus other amounts, such as taxes, that are included in the refund, minus the allowance for use.[208.1]

208.1   Sweeney v. SMC Corp., 178 Or. App. 576, 37 P.3d 244 (2002).

Add note 210.1 after "UDAP statute" in sentence containing note 210.

210.1   *See* Chumbiray v. Central-Chrysler Plymouth Jeep Eagle, 1998 Mass. App. Div. 1 (Dist. Ct. 1998) (no offset for use when buyer recovered damages under UDAP statute instead of refund under lemon law).

Add to text at end of subsection:

Ohio is one of the few states that does not explicitly authorize the manufacturer to deduct a use allowance. An appellate court has concluded that manufacturers' dispute resolution boards violated the state lemon law by offering refunds that were reduced by offsets for use.[210.2] The court also held that the consumers were entitled to go to trial on their claim that the manufacturers violated the state deceptive practices statute by offering these reduced refunds.

210.2   Maitland v. Ford Motor Co., 153 Ohio App. 3d 161, 792 N.E.2d 207 (2003).

13.2.8.8 Effect of a Third Party Lender or Lessor on Replace or Refund Remedy

Addition to note 215.

215   *Replace Schoonmaker citation with*: 1986 Conn. Super. Lexis 241.

13.2.9 Informal Dispute Resolution Where Manufacturer Does Not Grant the Proper Relief

Page 489

13.2.9.1 General

Add to text at end of subsection's second paragraph:

Likewise, they are not limited by state arbitration laws.[219.1]

219.1   Kiss v. Gen. Motors Corp., 630 N.W.2d 742 (Wis. Ct. App. 2001).

13.2.9.2 Whether the Decision Is Binding on the Manufacturer and Consumer; Appellate Review

Add to text at end of subsection's second paragraph:

Wisconsin's process is not binding on the consumer, and a consumer who has accepted an award can file a lemon law suit if the manufacturer fails to implement the award.[228.1]

228.1   Kiss v. Gen. Motors Corp., 630 N.W.2d 742 (Wis. Ct. App. 2001).

Page 490

Addition to note 229.

229   Muzzy v. Chevrolet Div., Gen. Motors Corp., 153 Vt. 179, 571 A.2d 609 (Vt. 1989) (mechanism's decision may be reversed only if appellant shows clear and convincing evidence that one of four grounds applies).

Add to text after sentence containing note 230:

The court's review is de novo.[230.1]

230.1   Fla. Stat. Ann. § 681.1095 (West); Gen. Motors Corp. v. Neu, 617 So. 2d 406 (Fla. Dist. Ct. App. 1993).

Add to text at end of subsection's fourth paragraph:

Judicial review is broad, requiring that the award be in accord with due process, supported by adequate evidence in the record, rational, and not arbitrary or capricious.[233.1]

233.1   Motor Vehicle Manufacturers Ass'n v. State, 75 N.Y.2d 175, 186, 551 N.Y.S.2d 470, 550 N.E.2d 919 (1990); Safari Motor Coaches Inc. v. Corwin, 225 A.D.2d 921, 638 N.Y.S.2d 992 (1996); Gen. Motors Corp. v. Lee, 193 A.D.2d 741, 598 N.Y.S.2d 61 (1993); *accord* Lyeth v. Chrysler Corp., 929 F.2d 891 (2d Cir. 1991).

Addition to note 234.

234   Burns v. Gen. Motors Corp., 833 A.2d 934 (Conn. Ct. App. 2003).

Replace note 235 with:

235   Gen. Motors Corp. v. Dohmann, 247 Conn. 274, 722 A.2d 1205 (1998); *accord* Burns v. Gen. Motors Corp., 833 A.2d 934 (Conn. Ct. App. 2003) (upholding arbitration decision).

Add to text after sentence containing note 235:

Arbitrators have wide latitude to determine appropriate remedies.[235.1]

235.1   Chrysler Corp. v. Maiocco, 209 Conn. 579, 595, 596, 552 A.2d 1207 (1989); DaimlerChrysler Corp. v. Allard, 2003 WL 22293200 (Conn. Super. Ct. Sept. 22, 2003) (unpublished).

Page 491

13.2.9.4 Mechanism Standards

Addition to note 247.

247   *Replace "http://www.adr.bbb.org/autoline" with*: www.dr.bbb.org/autoline.

13.2.10 Judicial Enforcement of Replace or Refund Remedy

Page 493

13.2.10.1 Dispute Resolution as a Precondition

Add to text at end of subsection:

The court may, however, allow the manufacturer to raise issues and present evidence that was barred by the dispute mechanism because of non-compliance with procedural rules.[280.1] If the manufacturer does not comply with the procedural requirements for seeking review, the arbitration decision will stand.[280.2]

280.1   T.A. Enterprises v. Olarte, Inc., 835 So. 2d 1235 (Fla. Dist. Ct. App. 2003).
280.2   Quick v. Gen. Motors Corp., 1994 WL 315674 (Ohio Ct. App. June 24, 1994) (unpublished).

13.2.10.2 Availability of Judicial Replace or Refund Remedy

Add to text at end of subsection's first paragraph:

The fact that the manufacturer offered the consumer some compensation prior to suit does not preclude the buyer from suing and letting the jury decide what damages to award.[280.3]

280.3   Iuorno v. Ford Motor Co., 1996 WL 1065554 (Va. Cir. Ct. June 6, 1996).

Addition to note 281.

281   *See* Milicevic v. Mercedes-Benz USA, Ltd. Liab. Co., 256 F. Supp. 2d 1168 (D. Nev. 2003) (buyer's acceptance of $1200 payment for time when vehicle was in repair shop and loaner car was unavailable is not a waiver of lemon law remedies).

Replace first sentence of subsection's last paragraph with:

Unless the lemon law explicitly provides otherwise, the consumer can also seek damages under a lemon law, UCC Article 2, the Magnuson-Moss Act, a UDAP statute, and other claims.[281.1]

281.1   Sweeney v. SMC Corp., 178 Or. App. 576, 37 P.2d 244 (2002) (consumer can bring claims under lemon law and state and federal warranty law in same suit; lemon law recovery is then limited to amount recoverable for breach of express warranty, except that treble damages can be awarded under lemon law if plaintiff meets criteria).

Add to text after second sentence of subsection's last paragraph:

Just as the consumer can not both revoke acceptance and recover damages for breach of warranty under the UCC, the consumer can not get a refund under the lemon law while at the same time recovering damages for the breach of the warranty.[281.2] The consumer should not, however, have to make an election between revocation of acceptance under the UCC and a refund under the lemon law, as these two remedies are consistent with each other. While the consumer can not get a double recovery,[281.3] the consumer should be able to obtain the relief available under the UCC plus any non-duplicative relief available under the lemon law.

281.2   Genetti v. Caterpillar, Inc., 261 Neb. 98, 621 N.W.2d 529, 43 U.C.C. Rep. Serv. 2d 829 (2001).
281.3   Boyle v. Daimler Chrysler Corp., 2002 WL 1881157 (Ohio Ct. App. Aug. 16, 2002).

Replace note 282 with:

282   Gen. Motors Corp. v. Schmitz, 362 Md. 229, 764 A.2d 838, 841 n.2 (2001); Love v. Kenneth Hammersley Motors, Inc., 556 S.E.2d 764 (Va. 2002) (revocation of acceptance claim is a claim for money and can be filed on law side rather than equity).

Add note 282.1 at end of subsection's existing text.

282.1   *But see* Kucher v. Daimlerchrysler Corp., 194 Misc. 2d 688, 754 N.Y.S.2d 512 (Civ. Ct. 2003) (suit under N.Y. lemon law can only be filed in court with equity jurisdiction).

Add to text at end of subsection:

The Nebraska Supreme Court has held that a lemon law claim is an action at law.[282.2] Unlike equitable rescission, the replacement or refund remedy under the lemon law is not limited to cases of fraud or mistake. Rather, it is a streamlined version of revocation of acceptance, which is an action at law under the UCC.

282.2   Genetti v. Caterpillar, Inc., 261 Neb. 98, 621 N.W.2d 529, 43 U.C.C. Rep. Serv. 2d 829 (2001).

13.2.10.3 Lemon Law Attorney Fees and Expert Witness Fees

Addition to notes 283–285.

283 *See, e.g.*, Palmer v. Fleetwood Enterprises, Inc., 2003 WL 21228864 (Cal. Ct. App. May 28, 2003) (unpublished) (affirming fee award); Pifer v. DaimlerChrysler Corp., 2003 WL 22850124 (Mich. Ct. App. Dec. 2, 2003) (unpublished) (affirming award of $10,000 in fees and costs when plaintiffs won termination of lease plus $750); Willis v. Ford Motor Co., 2003 WL 21473520 (Ohio Ct. App. June 25, 2003) (awarding fees); Gray v. Chrysler Corp., 2001 Ohio App. LEXIS 1657 (Ohio Ct. App. Apr. 11, 2001); Fortner v. Ford Motor Co., 1998 WL 172862 (Ohio Ct. App. Feb. 9, 1998) (affirming fee award); O'Neil v. Chrysler Corp., 54 Va. Cir. 64 (June 6, 2000) (awarding fees and setting forth standards).

284 *See* Creighbaum v. Mack Trucks, Inc., 469 N.W.2d 248 (Wis. Ct. App. 1991) (unpublished) (text available at 1991 WL 74217).

285 Moedt v. Gen. Motors Corp., 60 P.3d 240 (Ariz. Ct. App. 2002) (fees to prevailing party are mandatory but amount is discretionary).

Replace sentence containing note 286 with:

A fee award is available even if the retainer provides that the consumer's fee obligation will be entirely satisfied by any award under the lemon law's fee-shifting provision, and the consumer has standing to seek and appeal such an award.[286] Most courts find that the award of fees is a question for the judge, not the jury.[286.1]

286 Moedt v. Gen. Motors Corp., 60 P.3d 240 (Ariz. Ct. App. 2002).

286.1 *See* § 10.1.7.1, *supra*; *see also* National Consumer Law Center, Unfair and Deceptive Acts and Practices § 8.8.10.4.6 (5th ed. 2001 and Supp.).

Replace note 287 with:

287 *See* National Consumer Law Center, Unfair and Deceptive Acts and Practices § 8.8 (5th ed. 2001 and Supp.).

Add to text after sentence containing note 287:

Appellate courts are likely to vest considerable discretion in the trial courts.[287.1]

287.1 *See* Smith v. Fox Hills Buick, 2001 WL 1511271 (Cal. Ct. App. Nov. 28, 2001) (unpublished) (affirming trial court's reduction of fees from $53,211.02 to $18,545.35 when time appeared excessive).

Addition to notes 289, 291.

289 Schreidel v. Am. Honda Motor Co., 34 Cal. App. 4th 1242, 40 Cal. Rptr. 2d 576 (1995). *But see* Moedt v. Gen. Motors Corp., 60 P.3d 240 (Ariz. Ct. App. 2002) (exercising discretion to deny appellate fees when both parties appealed unsuccessfully).

291 Moedt v. Gen. Motors Corp., 60 P.3d 240 (Ariz. Ct. App. 2002); Reveles v. Toyota By the Bay, 57 Cal. App. 4th 1139, 67 Cal. Rptr. 2d 543 (1997). *But see* § 2.7.6.5, *supra*.

Add to text at end of subsection's second paragraph:

The consumer's attorney should also be aware of the U.S. Supreme Court's interpretation of federal fee-shifting statutes in *Buckhannon Board & Care Home, Inc. v. West Virginia Department of Health and Human Resources*[292.1] to preclude fee awards for "private settlements" that are not incorporated into an enforceable court order. This decision must be considered when seeking fees under the Magnuson-Moss Act, but state courts are free to reject it when interpreting their own laws. An Arizona appellate court found fees available for a lemon law settlement even though *Buckhannon* might have precluded fees for a Magnuson-Moss claim.[292.2] The court noted that its interpretation comported with the statutory goals of encouraging settlements without extensive litigation and strengthening Arizona consumers' ability to enforce consumer protection laws.

292.1 532 U.S. 598, 121 S. Ct. 1835, 149 L. Ed. 2d 855 (2001); *see* § 2.7.6.5, *supra*.

292.2 Moedt v. Gen. Motors Corp., 60 P.3d 240 (Ariz. Ct. App. 2002); *see also* Dewan v. Ford Motor Co., 2002 WL 31834629 (Ill. App. Ct. Dec. 18, 2002) (plaintiff can be prevailing party under UDAP statute when filing of suit caused manufacturer to repair car).

Addition to notes 294, 295.

294 *See also* Hayward v. Ventura Volvo, 108 Cal. App. 4th 509, 133 Cal. Rptr. 2d 514 (2003) (fees properly based on actual time when retainer provided for fee consisting of all fees paid by defendant plus forty percent of civil penalty).

295 *But cf.* Jackson v. Hyundai Motor Am., 1997 WL 119794 (E.D. Pa. Mar. 6, 1997) (Del. law) (taking amount of recovery into account); Hilferty v. Chevrolet Motor Div., 1996 WL 287276 (E.D. Pa. May 30, 1996), *aff'd*, 116 F.3d 468 (3d Cir. 1997) (table).

Add to text at end of subsection's third paragraph:

Arizona courts use a number of factors to determine the amount of the award.[295.1] It is important to document all settlement attempts, and to break down time spent to show how many hours were made necessary by defendant's motions or other pre-trial tactics. The court may be especially favorably disposed if the consumer proposed a reasonable settlement at an early stage of the proceeding in a letter that pointed out that drawing out the litigation would result in a significant increase in the fees and the possibility of the application of a multiplier.

295.1   Moedt v. Gen. Motors Corp., 60 P.3d 240 (Ariz. Ct. App. 2002).

Replace note 296 with:

296   *See* Milicevic v. Mercedes-Benz USA, Ltd. Liab. Co., 256 F. Supp. 2d 1168 (D. Nev. 2003). *See generally* § 13.4.4, *infra*; § 2.7.6, *supra*.

Page 495

Add to text at end of subsection:

Some manufacturers hire "fee auditors" to act as expert witnesses in opposing consumers' fee petitions. Often these fee auditors have very limited experience practicing law in the jurisdiction. Useful questions in cross-examining a fee auditor include whether the witness is licensed in the jurisdiction; has ever practiced in the jurisdiction; has ever tried a civil case; has ever tried a lemon law case; knows what elements are necessary to prove a lemon law case; knows whether standard jury instructions and practice aids are available to reduce the amount of time necessary to prepare the case; and knows other details about lemon law practice. Many of these questions are useful for examining any defense fee expert who does not have a consumer law practice.

Add new subsection to text after § 13.2.10.3.

13.2.10.3a Multiple Damages and Civil Penalties

A number of states provide for multiple damages or a civil penalty for certain lemon law violations. Most require a showing of willfulness or unreasonableness.

California allows a civil penalty of two times actual damages in two circumstances: 1) if the failure to comply was willful, or 2) if the manufacturer has violated the refund-or-replace requirement, has been notified by the buyer after a presumptively reasonable number of repair attempts, and has not maintained a qualified third-party dispute resolution process.[300.1] These are alternative tests. Willfulness is not required as part of the second test.[300.2] Conversely, if a manufacturer acts willfully it is liable for civil penalties even if it maintains a dispute resolution system.[300.3] Willfulness is a jury question.[300.4] The trial court must instruct the jury on both alternate theories if the consumer presents evidence to support an award under each.[300.5] Only one civil penalty can be awarded, however, even if the consumer qualifies under both tests.[300.6] The actual damages on which the civil penalty is based include reimbursement of the purchase price but not litigation fees and expenses.[300.7] One decision holds that a consumer can not recover both civil penalties and punitive damages.[300.8]

California courts have interpreted the term "willful" on several occasions. The term means intentional, and does not require any additional blameworthiness.[300.9] A manufacturer does not act willfully if it reasonably and in good faith believes that the facts creating liability were not present.[300.10] Willfulness is shown if the manufacturer's refusal to provide a refund or replacement was either in bad faith or unreasonable in light of the facts.[300.11] The plaintiff need not prove that the defendant had actual knowledge of the facts, however, as such a requirement would only encourage deliberate ignorance.[300.12] When high level employees of the manufacturer's authorized repair agent knew that proposed repairs would be inadequate, the jury was within its rights to impose the statutory penalty.[300.13] There is no requirement that the manufacturer's managing agents engage in or ratify the willful conduct.[300.14] The amount to be doubled is the buyer's actual damages before any set-offs to account for settlements with other defendants.[300.15]

Oregon allows up to treble the amount of any damages, with a cap of $50,000, if the consumer is entitled to certain lemon law remedies and the court finds that the manufacturer did not act in good faith.[300.16] Maryland allows damages of up to $10,000 if a manufacturer, factory branch, or other distributor is found to have acted in bad faith.[300.17] North Carolina allows damages to be trebled if the manufacturer unreasonably refuses to make or arrange for repairs necessitated by nonconformities, or refuses to provide a refund or replacement.[300.18] In Virginia, the consumer may recover treble damages and attorney fees if the manufacturer fails to comply with an informal dispute resolution decision.[300.19] Wisconsin allows double damages if the consumer prevails on a lemon law damage claim, without any need to show some aggravated conduct on the part of the manufacturer.[300.20] Two state lemon laws, Idaho's[300.21] and Washington's,[300.22] allow treble damages if either party files a bad faith appeal or, in Idaho, asserts a frivolous claim or defense.

Courts are unlikely to allow punitive damages or bad faith claims if the lemon law does not explicitly provide for these remedies.[300.23] However, in many states the lemon law provides that a violation is also a UDAP violation, so multiple damages or minimum damages may be available under the UDAP statute.[300.24]

300.1   Cal. Civ. Code § 1794(c), (e) (West); *see* Suman v. BMW of N. Am., Inc., 23 Cal. App. 4th 1, 28 Cal. Rptr. 2d 133 (1994) (upholding constitutionality of penalty provision).

300.2   Suman v. BMW of N. Am., Inc., 23 Cal. App. 4th 1, 28 Cal. Rptr. 2d 133 (1994).

300.3   Jernigan v. Ford Motor Co., 24 Cal. App. 4th 488, 29 Cal. Rptr. 2d 348 (1994).

300.4   Swann v. DaimlerChrysler Motors Corp., 2003 WL 1818139 (Cal. Ct. App. Apr. 8, 2003) (unpublished), *review granted*, 2003 Cal. LEXIS 3959 (Cal. June 18, 2003).

300.5   Suman v. BMW of N. Am., Inc., 23 Cal. App. 4th 1, 28 Cal. Rptr. 2d 133 (1994).

300.6   *Id.*

300.7   Harvill v. Fleetwood Enterprises, Inc., 2003 WL 21702375 (Cal. Ct. App. July 23, 2003) (unpublished).

300.8   Troensegaard v. Silvercrest Indus., Inc., 175 Cal. App. 3d 218, 220 Cal. Rptr. 712 (1985).

300.9   Ibrahim v. Ford Motor Co., 214 Cal. App. 3d 878, 263 Cal. Rptr. 64 (1989); *see also* Eslamieh v. Coachmen Recreational Vehicle, 2003 WL 22718870 (Cal. Ct. App. Nov. 19, 2003) (unpublished) (approving specific jury instructions).

300.10   Kwan v. Mercedes-Benz of N. Am., 23 Cal. App. 4th 174, 28 Cal. Rptr. 2d 371 (1994); *see also* Jensen v. BMW of N. Am., Inc., 35 Cal. App. 4th 112, 41 Cal. Rptr. 2d 295 (1995) (penalties upheld when manufacturer failed to offer realistic refund).

300.11   Harvill v. Fleetwood Enterprises, Inc., 2003 WL 21702375 (Cal. Ct. App. July 23, 2003) (unpublished).

300.12   Barker v. Fleetwood Enterprises, Inc., 2002 WL 453931 (Cal. Ct. App. Mar. 26, 2002) (unpublished); Kwan v. Mercedes-Benz of N. Am., 23 Cal. App. 4th 174, 28 Cal. Rptr. 2d 371 (1994).

300.13   Barker v. Fleetwood Enterprises, Inc., 2002 WL 453931 (Cal. Ct. App. Mar. 26, 2002) (unpublished).

300.14   *Id.*

300.15   *Id.*

300.16   Or. Rev. Stat. § 646.359.

300.17   Md. Code Ann., Com. Law § 14-1504(b).

300.18   N.C. Gen. Stat. § 20-351.8.

300.19   Va. Code Ann. § 59.1-207.15(C) (Michie).

300.20   Wis. Stat. § 218.0171(7); *see* Creighbaum v. Mack Trucks, Inc., 469 N.W.2d 248 (Wis. Ct. App. 1991) (unpublished) (text available at 1991 WL 74217) (no need to show negligence, malice, or ill will).

300.21   Idaho Code § 48-908 (Michie).

300.22   Wash. Rev. Code § 19.118.100(3) (court may triple, but shall at least double, the award).

300.23   Willis v. Ford Motor Co., 2003 WL 21473520 (Ohio Ct. App. June 25, 2003).

300.24   *See* Hilferty v. Chevrolet Motor Div., 1996 WL 287276 (E.D. Pa. May 30, 1996) (treble damages available under UDAP statute for lemon law violation, but trebling is discretionary and amount to be trebled is refund minus value of the vehicle that the buyer returns), *aff'd*, 116 F.3d 468 (3d Cir. 1997) (table).

13.3 Revocation under the UCC as Alternative to Lemon Law Remedy

13.3.2 New Car Defects That Breach Merchantability Warranty

Add to text after bulleted item containing note 308:

- Difficulty starting;[308.1]

308.1   Christopher v. Larson Ford Sales, Inc., 557 P.2d 1009 (Utah 1976) (engine also overheated, transmission slipped, auxiliary motor was inoperable, and motor home appliances malfunctioned).

Addition to notes 311, 312.

Page 496

311   Christopher v. Larson Ford Sales, Inc., 557 P.2d 1009 (Utah 1976) (transmission slipped in and out of gear, plus vehicle had other defects).

312   Christopher v. Larson Ford Sales, Inc., 557 P.2d 1009 (Utah 1976) (engine overheated, plus vehicle had other defects).

Add to text after bulleted item containing note 315:

- Failure to provide the spare tire the buyer had ordered, when the buyer had to travel extensively on business, often in early morning hours, and feared being stranded;[315.1]

315.1   Colonial Dodge, Inc. v. Miller, 420 Mich. 452, 362 N.W.2d 704, 40 U.C.C. Rep. Serv. 1 (1984).

Addition to note 317.

317   *See also* Vanderbrook v. Coachmen Indus., 818 So. 2d 906 (La. Ct. App. 2002) (problems with electrical system that prevented motor home battery from recharging, so appliances did not work on long trips, were sufficient basis for redhibition).

Add to text after bulleted item containing note 317:

- Defective paint;[317.1]

317.1   *In re* Ford Motor Co. Vehicle Paint Litig., 1996 U.S. Dist. LEXIS 11063 (E.D. La. July 30, 1996); Check v. Clifford Chrysler-Plymouth, 342 Ill. App. 3d 150, 794 N.E.2d 829 (2003) (paint scratch had been repaired so defectively that fixing it would require stripping and repainting half of vehicle).

Add to text after bulleted item containing note 319:

A defect that causes the vehicle to violate traffic laws, such as a malfunctioning turn signal, should make the vehicle unmerchantable even if it operates properly in all other respects. A vehicle that can not be operated in conformity with the laws does not pass without objection in the trade and is not fit for its ordinary purpose.

Add to text after bulleted item containing note 321:

- Intermittent noise and vibration in the steering column that did not affect the vehicle's ability to function;[321.1]
- Occasional squeaks, problems with the compact disc player and uneven brake wear, all of which were controverted and none of which prevented the owner from driving the car 100,000 miles;[321.2]
- Misalignment and an occasional odor of gasoline;[321.3]
- Sporadic noise and vibration in the steering column;[321.4]

321.1   Miller v. DaimlerChrysler Motors Corp., 2001 Ohio App. LEXIS 2450 (Ohio Ct. App. May 31, 2001).
321.2   Bevington v. Gen. Motors Corp., 2001 Ohio App. LEXIS 1888 (Ohio Ct. App. Apr. 20, 2001).
321.3   Jolovitz v. Alfa Romeo Distributors, 760 A.2d 625 (Me. 2000) (court's opinion is unclear about whether these problems were successfully repaired).
321.4   Sharkus v. Daimler Chrysler Corp., 2002 WL 31319119 (Ohio Ct. App. Oct. 17, 2002) (unpublished).

13.3.3 Is the Impairment Substantial Enough to Allow Revocation?

13.3.3.1 Serious Defects

Page 497

Add to text at end of subsection's third paragraph:

A persistent water leak into the passenger compartment is a substantial impairment.[333.1] A court upheld a jury verdict that a clicking noise upon turning and stiff shifting, both of which worsened over time, amounted to a substantial impairment.[333.2]

333.1   Rhodes v. All Star Ford, Inc., 599 So. 2d 812 (La. Ct. App. 1992) (denying redhibition claim on other grounds).
333.2   Calbert v. Volkswagen of Am., Inc., 1991 WL 215669 (Del. Super. Ct. Oct. 1, 1991), *aff'd*, 634 A.2d 938 (Del. 1993) (unpublished).

Add to text after sentence containing note 338:

The tendency of a motor home's third axle to lock up, causing excess wear on its tires, was a substantial impairment.[338.1] A defect that causes the vehicle to violate traffic laws should be considered a substantial impairment even if it has little other effect on the operation of the vehicle.

338.1   Luppert v. Leisure Living, Inc., 2003 WL 22293178 (Conn. Super. Ct. Sept. 24, 2003) (unpublished).

Add to text at end of subsection:

But an occasional "grunting" noise was not a substantial impairment when the consumer presented no evidence of diminution in value and her expert could not identify any safety concerns.[339.1]

Even a faulty paint job can be a substantial enough impairment to allow revocation.[339.2] Paint is not merely cosmetic but protects the metal surface of the vehicle from corrosion. If it appears that the paint suffered damage in transit to the dealership due to pollution, the attorney should investigate whether the manufacturer's franchise agreement with the dealer requires the dealer to inspect and treat vehicles for this type of damage as soon as they arrive on the lot. If the dealer did not do so, the consumer may also have a claim against the dealer.[339.3]

339.1   Harris v. Ford Motor Co., 2000 Mich. App. LEXIS 2713 (Mich. Ct. App. Feb. 11, 2000).
339.2   Pavesi v. Ford Motor Co., 155 N.J. Super. 373, 382 A.2d 954 (Super. Ct. Ch. Div. 1978); *see also* Chaudoir

v. Porsche Cars of N. Am., 667 So. 2d 569 (La. Ct. App. 1996) (affirming redhibition when one of defects was acid rain damage to paint).

339.3   Daigle v. Robinson Bros., Inc., 368 So. 2d 186 (La. Ct. App. 1979).

13.3.3.2 Cumulative Effect of Minor Defects

Addition to note 342.

342   *See also* Bland v. Freightliner Ltd. Liab. Co., 206 F. Supp. 2d 1202, 49 U.C.C. Rep. Serv. 2d 524 (M.D. Fla. 2002) (cumulative effect of several defects and twenty-one repair attempts sufficient); Morrison v. Allstar Dodge, Inc., 792 So. 2d 9 (La. Ct. App. 2001).

Page 498

Add to text at end of subsection:

On the other hand, a sporadic rattle, which technicians could not duplicate, was not a significant enough impairment.[350.1]

350.1   Johns v. Am. Isuzu Motors, Inc., 622 So. 2d 1208 (La. Ct. App. 1993) (redhibition claim).

13.3.3.4 Defect Need Not Interfere with Car's Operation

Addition to note 352.

352   Sumner v. Fel-Air, Inc., 680 P.2d 1109 (Alaska 1984); Gawlick v. Am. Builders Supply, 519 P.2d 313 (N.M. Ct. App. 1974).

13.4 The Damage Remedy Under the Lemon Law and/or Alternative Theories

13.4.2 Damages Under a Lemon Law Claim

Page 499

13.4.2.1 Where Statute Only Authorizes Consumer to "Enforce" Lemon Law

Addition to note 359.

359   *Add after Jackson citation*: *See also* King v. King Motor Co., 780 So. 2d 937 (Fla. Dist. Ct. App. 2001) (giving examples of situations in which damages may be available).

Add to text after subsection's second paragraph:

The replace or refund remedy may also be unavailable because the defects did not substantially impair the use, value or safety of the vehicle. A damages remedy would be helpful to the consumer in this situation.[359.1] Consumers may also suffer damage due to violations of provisions of the lemon law for which repair or replacement is irrelevant, such as title branding provisions, and damages should be available for these violations.[359.2]

359.1   King v. King Motor Co., 780 So. 2d 937 (Fla. Dist. Ct. App. 2001) (listing this circumstance as an example of a situation in which damages may be available).

359.2   *Id.*

Replace "another case has" in sentence containing note 361 with:

two other courts have

Addition to note 361.

361   King v. King Motor Co., 780 So. 2d 937 (Fla. Dist. Ct. App. 2001).

Page 500

13.4.2.2 Lemon Laws That Provide for Damages

The Wisconsin lemon law allows a damages remedy when the dealer has not, can not, or will not repair a nonconformity.[367.1] It also

Replace first four words of sentence containing note 368 with:

367.1   Vultaggio v. Gen. Motors Corp., 429 N.W.2d 93, 99 (Wis. Ct. App. 1988); *see also* Jennings v. Ford Motor Co., 129 F.3d 119 (7th Cir. 1997) (unpublished) (text available at 1997 WL 632589) (requirement that consumer sign release before manufacturer would repair the vehicle was not a refusal to repair).

Replace note 372 with:

372   *See* National Consumer Law Center, Unfair and Deceptive Acts and Practices § 3.2.7.3 (5th ed. 2001 and Supp.).

13.4.3 Lemon Law Does Not Preempt Other Damage Claims

Add to text at end of subsection's first paragraph:

The consumer can not, however, recover the same damages twice, once on a lemon law theory and once on another theory.[381.1]

381.1   Sweeney v. SMC Corp., 178 Or. App. 576, 37 P.3d 244 (2002).

13.5 Latent Defects Discovered After Lemon Law Remedy Expires

13.5.3 Defects Discovered After Warranty Period Has Expired

Page 505

13.5.3.5 Strict Liability and Negligence

Add note 417.1 after "under the statute" in sentence containing note 418.

417.1   Ayres v. Gen. Motors Corp., 234 F.3d 514 (11th Cir. 2000) (no private cause of action to enforce federal recall law).

Addition to note 420.

420   *Cf.* Kagan v. Carwell Corp., 2001 U.S. Dist. LEXIS 4544 (C.D. Cal. Mar. 30, 2001) (Motor Vehicle Safety Act does not completely preempt UDAP claim that is based in part on violation of NHTSA regulations).

13.6 Undisclosed Damage to New Cars Before Delivery to the Consumer

Addition to notes 422, 423, 425.

422   *Replace Arizona citation with*: Ariz. Rev. Stat. § 28-4411 (disclosure of vehicle repairs costing more than 3% of suggested retail price); *replace Florida citation with*: 2001 Fla. Laws ch. 196, §§ 28, 29 (to be codified as part VI of Fla. Stat. ch. 501) (disclosure of known damage when the dealer's actual cost of repairs exceeds 3% of manufacturer's suggested list price or $650, whichever is less); *replace parenthetical following Oregon citation with*: (disclosure of repair costs exceeding $400); *replace Wisconsin citation with*: Wis. Stat. § 218.0122 (manufacturer must disclose to dealer damage costing more than 6% of manufacturer's suggested retail price or be liable for dealer's liability for failure to disclose); *add*: N.M. Stat. Ann. § 57-16-6 (Michie) (disclosure when cost of repairs exceeds six percent of retail value); S.D. Codified Laws § 32-3-51.8 (Michie) (damage in excess of $3000).

423   Neal Pope, Inc. v. Garlington, 245 Ga. App. 49, 537 S.E.2d 179 (2000).

425   *See also* Morrison v. Allstar Dodge, Inc., 792 So. 2d 9 (La. Ct. App. 2001) (undisclosed wreck damage to new vehicle allows redhibition regardless of whether plaintiff shows non-compliance with damage disclosure law).

Page 506

Add note 425.1 at end of section's third paragraph.

425.1   *But see* Morrison v. Allstar Dodge, Inc., 792 So. 2d 9 (La. Ct. App. 2001) (undisclosed wreck damage to new vehicle allows redhibition regardless of whether plaintiff shows non-compliance with damage disclosure law).

Add note 425.2 at end of section's fourth paragraph.

425.2   *But cf.* Check v. Clifford Chrysler-Plymouth, 342 Ill. App. 3d 150, 794 N.E.2d 829 (2003) (improperly repaired damage to new car is breach of implied warranty of merchantability even though cost of repair fell below damage disclosure law's threshold).

Add to text at end of section's fifth paragraph:

The consumer may still be able to bring a UDAP claim, however, based on other aspects of the repair of the damage, such as defective repairs.[426.1]

426.1   *See, e.g.*, Check v. Clifford Chrysler-Plymouth, 342 Ill. App. 3d 150, 794 N.E.2d 829 (2003).

Addition to note 427.

427   *See also* Check v. Clifford Chrysler-Plymouth, 342 Ill. App. 3d 150, 794 N.E.2d 829 (2003) (substandard repair of damage to vehicle's paint, and selling vehicle as new without inspecting the repairs, is a UDAP violation even though cost of repair fell below damage disclosure law's threshold).

Add to text at end of section:

It may also identify records of pre-sale damage that the manufacturer keeps or requires the dealer to keep.

13.7 Warranty Issues In Gray Market Vehicle Sales

Add to text at end of section's first paragraph:

Sometimes manufacturers set lower prices when they sell cars to dealers in other countries, as a way of encouraging dealerships there. This creates an incentive for U.S. dealers to buy cars in the other country and sell them in the United States.

Replace note 433 with:

433   Cal. Civ. Code §§ 1797.8 to 1797.86 (West) (violation is a UDAP violation); Conn. Gen. Stat. § 42-210 (violation is a UDAP violation); N.H. Rev. Stat. Ann. § 357-C:3 (must disclose if vehicle is "direct import," give details as to modifications performed to comply with federal or state law, and state whether manufacturer's warranty and state lemon law apply); N.Y. Gen. Bus. Law § 218-aa (McKinney); *see also* 75 Pa. Con. Stat. § 1106(b)(9) (requiring title to be branded if vehicle was originally manufactured for distribution outside U.S.).

Add to text after sentence containing note 434:

It may be impossible to get a certificate of title for a gray market vehicle because of its noncompliance with these standards. This failure will be a breach of the implied warranty of title.[434.1]

434.1   *See* Elmore v. Doenges Bros. Ford, Inc., 21 P.3d 65 (Okla. Ct. App. 2001). *See generally* § 4.5, *supra.*

Addition to note 435.

435   *See* Elmore v. Doenges Bros. Ford, Inc., 21 P.3d 65 (Okla. Ct. App. 2001) (accepting evidence that gray market vehicle purchased for $10,500 actually had only salvage value because it could not be titled).

Add new section to text after § 13.7.

13.7a Special Problems in Recreational Vehicle Cases

Cases involving defective recreational vehicles pose special problems. First is the question of coverage under the state's lemon law. Most lemon laws cover recreational vehicles to at least some extent, but even these states often exclude certain portions of the vehicle or vehicles over a certain weight. Lemon law coverage of recreational vehicles is discussed in another section.[435.1]

If the lemon law covers a recreational vehicle, it offers a number of advantages. In most states there will be a presumption that an impairment is substantial if there have been a certain number of repair attempts or the vehicle has been out of service for a certain number of days.[435.2] These presumptions establish a more favorable standard than that required for revocation of acceptance under the UCC. Because recreational vehicles are complex and their repair is often beyond the capacity of the selling dealer, it is particularly common to find that the vehicle has been out of service for the requisite number of days. Many attorneys prefer, however, to bring recreational vehicle lemon law cases only after the vehicle has been out of service the requisite number of days and has had the requisite number of repair attempts.

Another advantage of a lemon law claim is that many lemon laws provide for attorney fees to the prevailing consumer. While the Magnuson-Moss Warranty Act also provides for attorney fees, pleading a Magnuson-Moss claim in a recreational vehicle case may allow the defendant to remove the case to federal court, as discussed below. If the consumer wants to stay in state court, it may be better to plead a lemon law claim instead of a Magnuson-Moss claim.

A common problem in recreational vehicle cases is that many recreational vehicle manufacturers give written warranties only on certain parts of the vehicle. As to the remaining parts, they pass along to the consumer the written warranties issued by the manufacturers of those parts. This situation leaves the consumer with no single entity willing to take responsibility for fixing the vehicle.

There are a number of approaches to this problem. If the final manufacturer's or assembler's limitations on its warranty were not clearly disclosed, the consumer may have a claim under the Magnuson-Moss Act[435.3] or a state deceptive practices (UDAP) statute.[435.4] In addition, most courts hold that the implied warranty of merchantability arises not just against the immediate seller but also against the remote manufacturer.[435.5] The implied warranty of merchantability should cover the vehicle as a whole, as that is the product that the final manufacturer sold to the consumer through the dealer. In this respect, recreational vehicles are no different from other products, from shoes to toasters, that a final manufacturer assembles from components manufactured by many other companies.

Assuming that the implied warranty of merchantability arises against the manufacturer under state law, the Magnuson-Moss Act will prohibit the manufacturer from disclaiming it unless the manufacturer provides no written warranties on any part of the vehicle.[435.6] The selling dealer is also prohibited from disclaiming implied warranties in a number of states.[435.7]

For express warranty claims, it is critical to obtain all of the warranties that relate to the vehicle. Even though the final manufacturer arguably has implied warranty liability for everything that is wrong with the vehicle, adding claims against the manufacturers of the defective components may increase the consumer's chances of recovery. There may be separate warranties on the engine, the transmission, the chassis, and each appliance in the living area of the home. Each of these warranties may have separate time limits and notice requirements. An early discovery request should seek all warranty documents given to the buyer, just in case the buyer's collection of warranty documents is incomplete.

A component manufacturer will be liable on its express warranty for the defects in that component. In addition, if the failure of that component makes the entire motor home unusable, the component manufacturer may be liable for the diminution in value of the rest of the vehicle as consequential damages.[435.8] The component manufacturer's express warranty will almost certainly seek to exclude consequential damages, but such clauses are unenforceable if the limitation causes the remedy to fail of its essential purpose.[435.9]

Another approach is to seek revocation of acceptance against either the manufacturer or the selling dealer or both. A number of cases hold that revocation is available whenever the product is nonconforming, even if the seller itself has not given a warranty.[435.10] Thus, revocation of acceptance should be available against the dealer if the vehicle fails to conform to any of the warranties issued by the manufacturers, even if the dealer has disclaimed warranties. If the state allows revocation of acceptance against a remote manufacturer,[435.11] the buyer should be able to pursue this remedy against the final manufacturer regardless of whether the defects relate to parts that the final manufacturer has expressly warranted.

Another question to ask early in discovery is whether the entity named in the complaint as the final manufacturer actually meets that description. Many motor home manufacturers are subsidiaries of other companies. The parent company may be liable as the manufacturer's *alter ego*, but if there is any doubt that the right corporation has been sued it is best to find this fact out early and add the subsidiary to the suit.

The consumer's attorney should keep jurisdictional issues in mind when framing a complaint about a recreational vehicle. Because recreational vehicles are so expensive, the amount in controversy will usually be $50,000 or more, allowing suit in federal court if a Magnuson-Moss claim is raised.[435.12] Even without a Magnuson-Moss claim, if there is diversity of citizenship between the plaintiff and the defendants, and the amount in controversy exceeds $75,000, a federal court will have original jurisdiction over the claim.[435.13] In either case, if the suit is filed in state court, the defendant will have the right to remove it to federal court.[435.14]

When trying a motor home case, the attorney should take care to prepare the jury for any terms used in the motor home industry that are not common knowledge. The consumer's attorney should also carefully prepare the evidence that shows that the impairment is substantial. Many owners experience some problems with their motor homes. A jury that has some familiarity with motor home problems will want to know why the problems with the plaintiff's home were so substantial as to justify the relief sought.

435.1   *See* § 13.2.3.1aS, *supra.*
435.2   *See* § 13.2.6.3, *supra.*
435.3   *See* § 2.6, *supra.*
435.4   *See* § 11.1.6, *supra.*
435.5   *See* § 4.2.2.1, *supra.*
435.6   15 U.S.C. § 2308(a); *see* § 2.3.2, *supra.*
435.7   *See* § 5.4, *supra.*
435.8   *See* § 10.6.3, *supra.*
435.9   *See* § 9.5, *supra.*

435.10   *See* § 5.14, *supra.*
435.11   *See* § 8.3.8, *supra.*
435.12   15 U.S.C. § 2310(d)(3)(B); *see* § 2.7.3.1, *supra.*
435.13   28 U.S.C. § 1332(a); *see* § 2.7.3.2, *supra.*
435.14   28 U.S.C. § 1441.

13.8 Practice Pointers

13.8.1 *Investigation of the Car Defect*

Page 507

Add to text after sentence containing note 437:

Even if the manufacturer has produced TSBs in response to discovery, it is always worthwhile to check the NHTSA website to make sure that all of them have been produced.

Add after third item in first bulleted list:

- www.ialla.net. This is the website of the International Association of Lemon Law Administrators. One of its features is links to every state's lemon law website, as well as to Canada's. Some of the websites include on-line complaint forms.

Add note 441.1 at end of last item in first bulleted list.

441.1   The organization's address is Consumers for Auto Reliability and Safety, 926 J Street, Suite 522, Sacramento, CA 95814.

Page 508

Addition to note 443.

443   *Replace NCLC citation with*: National Consumer Law Center, Automobile Fraud § 2.3 (2d ed. 2003).

Add to text after sentence containing note 445:

If the consumer no longer has the owner's manual, copies are available through commercial services.[445.1]

445.1   One commercial service is TMC Publications Automobile Literature, 5817 Park Heights Ave., Baltimore, MD 21215; telephone: (410) 367-4490; website: www.tmcpubl.com. J & L Warranty Pros, whose telephone number is (800) 852-6298 and whose website is located at www.jlwarranty.com, publishes an annual Official Warranty Guide. Other sources are listed at www.AA1Car.com (click on "Links").

Add to text after sentence containing note 447:

Former webpages that a dealer, creditor, or manufacturer has deleted can often be found on a website that archives old webpages.[447.1] The Securities and Exchange Commission's EDGAR database[447.2] has a wealth of information about corporate structure and interrelationships, and the risks and inside operations of businesses.

447.1   *See* http://web.archive.org/collections/web.html.
447.2   *See* www.sec.gov (go to "filings and forms" link).

13.8.4 *Discovery*

Page 509

13.8.4.1 Document Requests, Interrogatories and Requests for Admissions

Addition to note 452.

452   *Replace second sentence of note with*: A second set of lemon law case interrogatories may be found on the CD-Rom accompanying this volume and in National Consumer Law Center, Consumer Law Pleadings No. 2, §§ 5.2–5.7 (2003 Cumulative CD-Rom and Index Guide).

Add to text after second sentence of subsection's last paragraph:

The manufacturer is likely to keep detailed records of all warranty repairs on one or more databases, to which the dealer may also have access. Ask for the shop notes and the folder that the original repair orders are kept in as well as the repair orders themselves. Often service technicians write notes about the vehicle—including repair visits for which no repair order was prepared—on the folder.

Add to text after third sentence of subsection's last paragraph:

The manufacturer may also have records, usually electronic, showing the parts that were installed on the vehicle and the inspections done as part of the manufacturing process, although the latter usually are not retained for very long. It is also a good idea to request any policy manuals, whether prepared by the dealer, the manufacturer, or a state or national organization, that deal with the issues raised in the suit. Such manuals may document a policy of evading warranty compliance, or may contain a policy that the dealer chose to ignore. If nothing else, the manual may help prove that the dealer was on notice of certain facts or laws.

Replace subsection's final sentence with:

Sample discovery in a new car lemon case is available in NCLC's *Consumer Law Pleadings*,[452.1] including interrogatories and document requests to the selling dealer, the manufacturer, and the repairing dealer.

452.1 National Consumer Law Center, Consumer Law Pleadings No. 2, Ch. 5 (2003 Cumulative CD-Rom and Index Guide).

Page 511

13.8.5 Trial

Add to text at end of subsection:

In some states, the lemon law has a clear formula for damages once liability is established. In this situation, it may be advantageous to stipulate before trial as to the damages award that will be made if the jury finds liability. This simplifies the trial and allows the jury to focus on liability. It is usually impossible to stipulate to a figure for attorney fees before trial, but the stipulation can provide that the amount of any attorney fee award will be determined by the court if the parties can not agree.

13.8.6 Evidence and Proof Issues

Add to text at end of subsection's third paragraph:

TSBs also provide a benchmark to assess whether or not the dealership has taken all possible steps to repair a problem with the vehicle, and can be useful in cases claiming negligent repair.

Add new subsection to text after § 13.8.6.

13.8.7 Collecting the Judgment

If a manufacturer fails to pay a judgment, one way to collect it is to issue a judgment attachment against the equipment in any of the manufacturer's plants in the state. Another approach is to garnish a local dealership, which will probably owe the manufacturer for vehicles and parts.

If a dealer fails to pay a judgment, there may be a state-mandated bond against which the judgment can be enforced. It may also be effective to garnish the entities that finance the vehicles that the dealer sells. Those entities may owe the dealer money for vehicle sales they are financing. In addition, the dealer's floor plan financer, or the auction where the dealer buys vehicles, may be holding money of the dealer's in reserve accounts.

Chapter 14   Used Cars

14.2 Avoiding "As Is" Used Car Sales By Finding Express Warranties

14.2.2 Manufacturer Warranties

Page 513

Add to text after subsection's first paragraph:

In one case, the consumer bought a used car with eighteen months of the manufacturer's warranty remaining.[2.1] The vehicle required repeated repairs, which the manufacturer covered. After the consumer filed suit, the manufacturer claimed that the warranty had been voided because of an accident which occurred while the previous owner owned the car. The manufacturer had reason to know of this accident before the consumer bought the vehicle but did not choose to pursue further investigation. The court held that the manufacturer's previous repairs estopped it from denying warranty coverage.

    2.1   Price v. Chevrolet Motor Div., 765 A.2d 800, 43 U.C.C. Rep. Serv. 2d 593 (Pa. Super. Ct. 2000).

Page 514

Add to text at end of subsection:

The manufacturer's and dealer's websites may have information about their involvement in these certifications and about the criteria used in the certifications.

14.2.3 The Dealer's Express Warranties

14.2.3.2 Written Warranties from Dealer

Add to text after subsection's first sentence:

A statement on the bill of sale that the vehicle is in "undamaged condition" creates an express warranty that is breached if the transmission has been improperly repaired.[5.1] Writing "Safety, air/cond., Compressor, passenger side window" under "WRITTEN PROMISES MADE TO CONSUMER" on the buyer's order created an express warranty that the vehicle would be safe and that the listed items would be repaired.[5.2]

    5.1   Sass v. Spradlin, 66 Ill. App. 3d 976, 23 Ill. Dec. 670, 384 N.E.2d 464 (1978).
    5.2   Earls v. Condor Capital Corp., 2001 Conn. Super. LEXIS 2595 (Conn. Super. Ct. Aug. 30, 2001).

Addition to note 6.

    6   *Add at end of note: See also* Palumbo v. Land Rover N. Am., Inc., 2003 WL 1962516 (Mass. Super. Ct. Mar. 3, 2003) (describing certified used car warranty program, and finding that manufacturer issuing such a warranty may be liable as a dealer under state used car lemon law).

Replace sentence containing note 7 with:

In 1999, in connection with a review of its interpretations of the Magnuson-Moss Act, the FTC published a statement that these "50-50" warranties likely violate the Magnuson-Moss Act's prohibition against tie-ins, because they restrict the consumer's choice for obtaining warranty service.[7] However, at the end of 2002 the Commission issued a letter disavowing its previous statement.[7.1] The FTC reasoned that, unlike a warranty that is conditioned on the consumer's purchase of a separate product, a 50-50 warranty can not be severed into two parts, one that the warrantor performs and a second that another repair shop performs. The Commission stressed, however, that it would likely be a deceptive practice and a breach of warranty if the dealer inflated the cost of warranted repairs in order to impose all or most of the repair costs on the consumer. As many 50-50 warranties are simply scrawled on the front of a purchase order, it is also likely that they will violate the disclosure requirements of the Magnuson-Moss Act.[7.2]

> 7   Final Action Concerning Review of Interpretations of Magnuson-Moss Warranty Act § B(1)(d), 64 Fed. Reg. 19,700 (Apr. 22, 1999); *see* § 2.4.1, *supra*. This interpretation is reprinted in Appx. B.2, *infra*.
>
> 7.1   Letter from the Fed. Trade Comm'n to Keith E. Whann (Dec. 31, 2002), *available at* www.ftc.gov/os/ 2003/01/niadaresponseletter.htm. The letter is also included on the CD-Rom accompanying this volume.
>
> 7.2   *See* § 2.6, *supra*.

Add to text after subsection's second paragraph:

The dealer may also give an express written warranty because of a statutory mandate in a used car lemon law or similar statute.[7.3] Unless the statute explicitly provides otherwise, the buyer can treat the statutory warranty as a UCC warranty and bring suit for damages or revocation of acceptance.[7.4] The statutorily-mandated warranty should also qualify as a written warranty for Magnuson-Moss Act purposes.[7.5]

> 7.3   *See* §§ 14.8, 14.9, *infra*.
>
> 7.4   Williams v. Planet Motor Car, Inc., 190 Misc. 2d 22, 738 N.Y.S.2d 170, 47 U.C.C. Rep. Serv. 2d 1000 (Civ. Ct. 2001).
>
> 7.5   *See* § 2.2.5, *supra*. *But see* Laznovsky v. Hyundai Motor Am., Inc., 190 Misc. 2d 537, 738 N.Y.S.2d 820 (Dist. Ct. 2002) (written warranty required by New York Used Car Lemon Law is not Magnuson-Moss written warranty; court relies solely on silence by an intermediate appellate court in another decision).

Addition to note 8.

> 8   *See, e.g.*, Cuesta v. Classic Wheels, Inc., 358 N.J. Super. 512, 818 A.2d 448, 50 U.C.C. Rep. Serv. 2d 791 (Super. Ct. App. Div. 2003). *See generally* National Consumer Law Center, Automobile Fraud § 8.2.3.2.1 (2d ed. 2003).

Add to text at end of subsection:

The seller's oral statements can also be introduced to explain or supplement the writing.[13.1]

> 13.1   *See, e.g.*, Earls v. Condor Capital Corp., 2001 Conn. Super. LEXIS 2595 (Conn. Super. Ct. Aug. 30, 2001). *See generally* §§ 3.7.8, 3.7.9, *supra*.

14.2.3.3 The Dealer's Oral Warranties

Addition to note 14.

> 14   McGregor v. Dimou, 101 Misc. 2d 756, 422 N.Y.S.2d 806 (Civ. Ct. 1979) ("in very good condition" and had not been in accident). *But see* Bagley v. Mazda Motor Corp., 2003 WL 21040506 (Ala. May 9, 2003) (statements that car was "good car" and "about the best one" on the lot were not express warranties).

Page 515

Add to text at end of subsection's first paragraph:

A promise to repair any problems found within the first thirty days is an express warranty.[24.1]

> 24.1   Fassi v. Auto Wholesalers, 145 N.H. 404, 762 A.2d 1034 (2000).

Addition to note 26.

> 26   *Replace Morehouse citation with*: 31 S.W.3d 55 (Mo. Ct. App. 2000).

14.3 Preserving and Enforcing Implied Warranties

14.3.1 Creation of Implied Warranties in Used Car Sales

Page 516

Add to text at end of subsection:

Some courts have held that transportation on the roads, or safe and reliable transportation, is a particular enough purpose for the warranty to arise.[35.1]

> 35.1   Earls v. Condor Capital Corp., 2001 Conn. Super. LEXIS 2595 (Conn. Super. Ct. Aug. 30, 2001) (safe and reliable transportation); Thomas v. Ford Motor Credit Co., 48 Md. App. 617, 429 A.2d 277, 31 U.C.C. Rep. Serv. 1265 (1981); Stickney v. Fairfield's Motors, Inc., 9 U.C.C. Rep. Serv. 236 (N.H. Super. Ct. 1970); *see also* Karczewski v. Ford Motor Co., 382 F. Supp. 1346 (N.D. Ind. 1974) ("particular purpose of a passenger automobile is to drive on the public streets and highways safely without uncontrolled and unsafe behavior"), *aff'd*, 515 F.2d 511 (7th Cir. 1975) (table).

14.3.2 Standards of Merchantability for Used Cars

Addition to note 45.

> 45   *See also* Berney v. Rountree Olds-Cadillac Co., 763 So. 2d 799 (La. Ct. App. 2000) (defects, primarily a persistent malfunctioning engine warning light, violate statutory implied warranty).

Add to text after bulleted item containing note 45:

- Excessive oil consumption;[45.1]
- A wheel that came off while the car was being driven;[45.2]
- Frequent stalling;[45.3]
- A suspension system that broke, causing the front of the vehicle to rise up in the air while the rear sat on its frame, plus a battery that would not start the car unless it was disconnected and reconnected each time;[45.4]
- A car that could not pass state inspection;[45.5]

45.1 Lipinski v. Martin J. Kelly Oldsmobile, Inc., 325 Ill. App. 3d 1139, 259 Ill. Dec. 586, 759 N.E.2d 66 (2001).

45.2 Bagley v. Mazda Motor Corp., 2003 WL 21040506 (Ala. May 9, 2003).

45.3 Rose v. Kemp Ford, 2003 WL 21495081 (Cal. Ct. App. June 30, 2003) (unpublished).

45.4 Earls v. Condor Capital Corp., 2001 Conn. Super. LEXIS 2595 (Conn. Super. Ct. Aug. 30, 2001).

45.5 Kimpel v. Del. Pub. Auto Auction, 2001 WL 1555932 (Del. Ct. Com. Pl. Mar. 6, 2001).

Page 517

Add to text at end of subsection's second paragraph:

One questionable decision holds that repeated stalling did not make a used car unmerchantable.[55.1] The court did not consider the extent to which stalling is a safety hazard.[55.2]

55.1 Filipovic v. Fairchild Chevrolet, 2001 Ohio App. LEXIS 4340 (Ohio Ct. App. Sept. 27, 2001).

55.2 *Cf.* Shea v. Volvo Cars of No. Am, 1991 U.S. Dist. LEXIS 5752 (E.D. Pa. Apr. 30, 1991) (occasional failure to start is dangerous).

Add to text at end of subsection:

Courts may also be willing to find that a used vehicle is not merchantable if a defect exists at delivery that causes the vehicle to violate traffic laws. A vehicle that can not be operated in conformity with the law does not pass without objection in the trade and is not fit for its ordinary purpose.

14.3.3 No Disclaimer of Implied Warranties When Dealer Provides Written Warranty or Service Contract

Addition to note 60.

60 *Add to end of note*: This opinion is included on the CD-Rom accompanying this volume.

Page 518

14.3.5 Effect of FTC Used Car Rule on Implied Warranty Disclaimers

Add to text at end of subsection:

When the dealer sells a service contract along with the vehicle, the FTC Used Car Rule requires the dealer to check the box marked "WARRANTY" on the Buyers Guide and also a box stating that state law implied warranties may give the buyer additional rights.[79.1] Regardless of whether the Magnuson-Moss Act invalidates a disclaimer of implied warranties when a service contract is sold, by checking the WARRANTY box the dealer is probably making it impossible to disclaim implied warranties successfully under the UCC.

79.1 16 C.F.R. § 455.3(b)(3); *see* Appx. D, *infra.*

Page 519

Add new subsection to text after § 14.3.6.

14.3.6a Revocation of Acceptance of Used Cars

A buyer may revoke acceptance under UCC section 2-608 if a defect substantially impairs the value of a used vehicle[79.2] or a demonstrator, whether sold as new or used.[79.3] Generally, courts look to the impact that the impairment has on the consumer,[79.4] although courts differ in characterizing the standard as subjective or objective. Most courts apply both an objective and a subjective test.[79.5] For example, one court has stated that evaluation of a consumer's "needs and circumstances" is a subjective test, while the substantial impairment issue "requires evidence from which it can be inferred that the plaintiff's needs were not met because of the nonconformity."[79.6] Another court has stated that the issue of substantial impairment is a question of fact "determined with reference to the objective needs and expectations of the buyer, not on the latter's unarticulated subjective desires."[79.7]

Courts have had little difficulty concluding that defects that render a car inoperable or unsafe are substantial enough to warrant revocation.[79.8] A buyer may revoke acceptance on this ground when the vehicle is merely on the verge of failure.[79.9] Courts also find frame damage and other incompletely repaired collision damage sufficient.[79.10] Other cases have allowed revocation when the vehicle overheated and had difficulty starting.[79.11] A buyer established grounds for revocation when the engine turned out to be five or six years older than the vehicle.[79.12] A rolled-back odometer is a substantial impairment.[79.13]

Minor defects and ones that can be easily repaired will not justify revocation of acceptance.[79.14] But substantial impairment may be established by the cumulative effect of minor defects.[79.15]

79.2   Herbert v. Harl, 757 S.W.2d 585 (Mo. 1988); Worthey v. Specialty Foam Prods., Inc., 591 S.W.2d 145 (Mo. Ct. App. 1979); Richardson v. Mast, 252 Neb. 114, 560 N.W.2d 488 (1997); Woods v. Secord, 122 N.H. 323, 444 A.2d 539 (1982); Sudol v. Rudy Papa Motors, 175 N.J. Super. 238, 417 A.2d 1133 (Dist. Ct. 1980); Tuttle v. Rolfes, 1981 Ohio App. LEXIS 14309 (Ohio Ct. App. Aug. 31, 1981); Murray v. D & J Motor Co., 958 P.2d 823 (Okla. Ct. App. 1998); Patton v. McHone, 822 S.W.2d 608 (Tenn. Ct. App. 1991); Thomas v. Ruddell Lease-Sales, Inc., 43 Wash. App. 208, 716 P.2d 911 (1986); *cf.* Berney v. Rountree Olds-Cadillac Co., 763 So. 2d 799 (La. Ct. App. 2000) (sale rescinded under non-U.C.C. analog of "action in redhibition"). *See generally* § 8.3, *supra.*

79.3   Black v. Don Schmid Motor, Inc., 232 Kan. 458, 657 P.2d 517 (1983); Inniss v. Methot Buick-Opel, Inc., 506 A.2d 212 (Me. 1986); Thomas v. Ford Motor Credit Co., 48 Md. App. 617, 429 A.2d 277 (1981); Rester v. Morrow, 491 So. 2d 204 (Miss. 1986); Seaton v. Lawson Chevrolet-Mazda, Inc., 1990 Tenn. App. LEXIS 644 (Tenn. Ct. App. Sept. 30, 1990).

79.4   Overland Bond & Inv. Corp. v. Howard, 9 Ill. App. 3d 348, 292 N.E.2d 168 (1972).

79.5   *See* § 8.3.2, *supra.*

79.6   Black v. Don Schmid Motor, Inc., 232 Kan. 458, 657 P.2d 517 (1983); *see also* Inniss v. Methot Buick-Opel, Inc., 506 A.2d 212, 219 (Me. 1986) (any defect that undermines buyer's confidence in vehicle's reliability and integrity); Murray v. D & J Motor Co., 958 P.2d 823 (Okla. Ct. App. 1998) (standard is more subjective than breach of warranty case because revocation permitted when non-conformity substantially impairs value of the goods to the buyer); Harper v. Mitchell, 1985 Tenn. App. LEXIS 3368 (Tenn. Ct. App. Dec. 4, 1985) (standard is subjective to the extent that requirements of a particular buyer are examined, but the evidence regarding the substantial impairment to a particular buyer is measured in objective terms).

79.7   Thomas v. Ruddell Lease-Sales, Inc., 43 Wash. App. 208, 716 P.2d 911 (1986).

79.8   Overland Bond & Inv. Corp. v. Howard, 9 Ill. App. 3d 348, 292 N.E.2d 168 (1972) (transmission fell out and brakes failed); Worthey v. Specialty Foam Prods., Inc., 591 S.W.2d 145 (Mo. Ct. App. 1979) (damaged bearings, bad crankshaft, car stopped running); Stream v. Sportscar Salon, Ltd., 91 Misc. 2d 99, 397 N.Y.S.2d 677 (Civ. Ct. 1977) (low compression, car would not start); Rose v. Epley Motor Sales, 288 N.C. 53, 215 S.E.2d 573 (1975) (car exploded). *But see* Green v. Benson & Gold Chevrolet, 811 So. 2d 970 (La. Ct. App. 2002) (transmission's failure eight months after purchase not grounds for redhibition when no proof of defect at time of purchase, even though Federal Trade Commission had required dealers to disclose defects Commission found in this type of transmission; strong dissent).

79.9   Murray v. D & J Motor Co., 958 P.2d 823 (Okla. Ct. App. 1998) (knocking rods, blown head gasket, and engine on verge of total failure).

79.10   Patton v. McHone, 822 S.W.2d 608 (Tenn. Ct. App. 1991) (cracked engine block and damaged frame); Thomas v. Ruddell Lease-Sales, Inc., 43 Wash. App. 208, 716 P.2d 911 (1986) (shimmying, vibration, engine problems, and misalignment due to collision).

79.11   Christopher v. Larson Ford Sales, Inc., 557 P.2d 1009 (Utah 1976) (motor home had trouble starting, engine overheated, transmission slipped, auxiliary motor did not work, appliances malfunctioned); Testo v. Russ Dunmire Oldsmobile, 16 Wash. App. 39, 554 P.2d 349 (1976) (engine overheated and had starting problems).

79.12   Tuttle v. Rolfes, 1981 Ohio App. LEXIS 14309 (Ohio Ct. App. Aug. 31, 1981).

79.13   Cuesta v. Classic Wheels, Inc., 358 N.J. Super. 512, 818 A.2d 448, 50 U.C.C. Rep. Serv. 2d 791 (Super. Ct. App. Div. 2003).

79.14   Rester v. Morrow, 491 So. 2d 204 (Miss. 1986) (demonstrator with soiled carpet, unrepaired fuse panel, and missing piece of chrome); Harper v. Mitchell, 1985 Tenn. App. LEXIS 3368 (Tenn. Ct. App. Dec. 4, 1985) (balky transmission).

79.15   Black v. Don Schmid Motor, Inc., 232 Kan. 458, 657 P.2d 517 (1983) (minor defects including problems with accelerator, radio, air conditioner, and warning light, and a transmission leak requiring daily service by the consumer; most defects continued after five attempts to have car repaired); Berney v. Rountree Olds-Cadillac Co., 763 So. 2d 799 (La. Ct. App. 2000) (minor defects alone insufficient, but multiple minor defects requiring repair may support cause of action); *see also* § 13.3.2, *supra.*

The Consumer Credit and Sales Legal Practice Series

Precise, easy-to-follow practice manuals for lawyers in *all 50 states*.

"A monumental undertaking ... should become a standard reference set."
— American Bar Association Journal

NCLC Consumer Law Manuals with Companion CD-Roms

Written by the Nation 's Experts
The National Consumer Law Center, a nonprofit corporation, has offered technical assistance, publications, and training for lawyers since 1969. NCLC is widely consulted as the nation's consumer law authority.

The Consumer Law "Bibles"
Consumer and industry lawyers tell us they view the NCLC manuals as their indispensable bibles for consumer law.

Designed for Use in All 50 States
The manuals detail state legislation and case law in all 50 states, in addition to comprehensive analysis of federal laws, regulations, cases, agency interpretations, and even informal letters. Available individually, by subject library discount, or as a complete 16-volume set discount.

Highly Practical
Sample pleadings, checklists, forms, and practice pointers make each manual a powerful tool for the practitioner. Each manual provides guidance to spot multiple claims in a case, maximizing client recovery and attorney fees.

The Series is Continuously Updated

NCLC Manuals Are as Current as Possible
NCLC manuals reliably predict trends and advise on novel legal strategies, so that our readers are always at least one step ahead.

We Keep Our Manuals Current in Three Ways
- Annual cumulative supplements with cumulative CD-Roms
- Periodic revised editions
- The NCLC REPORTS newsletter is issued 24 times a year.

Order securely online at
www.consumerlaw.org

We Make Upkeep Affordable
- Four months FREE supplements, CD-Roms, and revised editions
- Companion CD-Roms come FREE with all supplements and revised editions and include all manual appendices and many extra features
- FREE shipping
- Our supplement prices are among the lowest in legal publishing today
- 20% discounts off our already low prices for revised editions
- Set subscribers receive 30% discount on all future supplements and revised editions
- New manual purchasers automatically receive a FREE four month, 8-issue NCLC REPORTS newsletter trial subscription, your hotline to new ideas, trends and tactics in the practice of consumer law.

Keyword Search All NCLC Manuals at Our Website

NCLC's CD-Roms and our website do not include the text of the book chapters, but you can pinpoint in seconds the number of times on every page in every manual where a particular term appears. Search by case name, party name, statutory or regulatory citation, or any other terms. Just type in the search term or terms at:

www.consumerlaw.org/keyword

The tables of contents, CD-Rom contents, and indexes for all our manuals are also found at www.consumerlaw.org.

National Consumer Law Center
77 Summer Street • 10th Floor • Boston MA 02110 • (617) 542-9595 • Fax (617) 542-8028 • www.consumerlaw.org

---

FOLLOW THE EXPERTS

The Consumer Credit and Sales Legal Practice Series of manuals with companion CD-Roms are designed to be the primary — and often only — resource an attorney or advocate needs to understand the rights of consumers under federal and state law:

DEBTOR RIGHTS LIBRARY
- ☐ Consumer Bankruptcy Law and Practice
- ☐ Fair Debt Collection
- ☐ Repossessions and Foreclosures
- ☐ Student Loan Law
- ☐ Access to Utility Service

CONSUMER LITIGATION LIBRARY
- ☐ Consumer Arbitration Agreements
- ☐ Consumer Class Actions
- ☐ Consumer Law Pleadings

CREDIT AND BANKING LIBRARY
- ☐ Truth in Lending
- ☐ Fair Credit Reporting
- ☐ Consumer Banking and Payments Law
- ☐ The Cost of Credit
- ☐ Credit Discrimination

DECEPTION AND WARRANTIES LIBRARY
- ☐ Unfair and Deceptive Acts and Practices
- ☐ Automobile Fraud
- ☐ Consumer Warranty Law

OTHER NCLC PUBLICATIONS
- ☐ The Practice of Consumer Law with CD-Rom
- ☐ Stop Predatory Lending with CD-Rom
- ☐ Consumer Law in A Box CD-Rom
- ☐ NCLC Reports Newsletter
- ☐ Return to Sender: Getting a Refund or Replacement for Your Lemon Car
- ☐ NCLC Guide to Surviving Debt
- ☐ NCLC Guide to Mobile Homes
- ☐ NCLC Guide to Consumer Rights for Immigrants

ORDER TODAY! For Faster Service, Call (617) 542-9595

FREE SHIPPING

04S

☐ Please send me more information on the titles checked above.

Name/Organization _____

Address_____ City _____ State _____ Zip _____

Fax (_____) _____ E-mail _____

Order securely online at
www.consumerlaw.org

National Consumer Law Center
77 Summer Street • 10th Floor • Boston MA 02110 • (617) 542-9595 • Fax (617) 542-8028 • www.consumerlaw.org

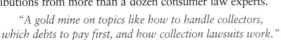

14.3.7 Cancellation Despite Disclaimer

Replace note 81 with:

81   *See* National Consumer Law Center, Unfair and Deceptive Acts and Practices § 9.5.9 (5th ed. 2001 and Supp.).

Replace note 84 with:

84   These laws are summarized at § 16.7.1, *infra*, and described in more detail at National Consumer Law Center, Unfair and Deceptive Acts and Practices § 5.8.2 (5th ed. 2001 and Supp.).

Replace NCLC citation in subsection's next-to-last paragraph with:

Unfair and Deceptive Acts and Practices § 5.8.2 (5th ed. 2001 and Supp.)

Addition to note 87.

87   *Replace NCLC citation with*: National Consumer Law Center, Fair Credit Reporting Appx. B (5th ed. 2002 and Supp.).

Replace note 88 with:

88   *See* National Consumer Law Center, Fair Credit Reporting Ch. 15 (5th ed. 2002 and Supp.) (general discussion of credit repair organization laws). *But see* Midstate Siding & Window Co. v. Rogers, 204 Ill. 2d 314, 789 N.E.2d 1248 (2001) (state credit repair law not intended to apply to retailers); Cannon v. William Chevrolet/Geo, Inc., 794 N.E.2d 843 (Ill. App. Ct. 2003) (legislature did not intend to cover car dealers; this transaction not covered because consumer's payment, even the documentary service fee, was not specifically for credit services); Snook v. Ford Motor Co., 142 Ohio App. 3d 212, 755 N.E.2d 380 (2001) (no coverage unless consumer paid fee specifically for arranging credit or the cost of this service was included in price of vehicle).

14.4 UDAP, Fraud, Tort, and Good Faith Claims

14.4.1 UDAP Claims

Page 520

Replace note 91 with:

91   *See* § 11.1.5, *supra*; National Consumer Law Center, Unfair and Deceptive Acts and Practices §§ 5.4.6, 5.4.7 (5th ed. 2001 and Supp.).

Replace note 98 with:

98   *See* National Consumer Law Center, Automobile Fraud § 6.2.1 (2d ed. 2003).

14.4.3 Good Faith Duty to Disclose Known Defects

Page 521

Replace note 112 with:

112   *See* § 14.10, *infra*; National Consumer Law Center, Automobile Fraud §§ 2.6.2.3, 2.6.2.4, 6.5 (2d ed. 2003).

Replace note 114 with:

114   *See* National Consumer Law Center, Repossessions and Foreclosures § 13.3.1 (5th ed. 2002 and Supp.).

14.4.4 Special Disclosure Requirements for Demonstrator Vehicles

Add new subsection to text after § 14.4.3.

About half the states have enacted new car damage disclosure laws.[114.1] These laws require disclosure of damage exceeding a certain percentage of a new vehicle's price that occurs while it is in the control of the manufacturer or dealer. Courts have interpreted these statutes to require disclosure of repairs necessitated not only by accidents but also by mechanical breakdowns.[114.2]

Demonstrator vehicles may qualify as "new" for purposes of these statutes because they have not previously been titled to a buyer.[114.3] The new car damage disclosure laws thus require disclosure of any significant damage or repair history for this category of used cars. Most of the statutes provide for a private cause of action but, in addition, the violation of a statutory duty of disclosure can greatly strengthen a fraud or UDAP claim.

114.1   *See* § 13.6, *supra*; *see also* National Consumer Law Center, Automobile Fraud § 6.2.3 (2d ed. 2003).

114.2   Neal Pope, Inc. v. Garlington, 245 Ga. App. 49, 537 S.E.2d 179 (2000); Smith v. Gen. Motors Corp., 979 S.W.2d 127 (Ky. Ct. App. 1998).

114.3   Neal Pope, Inc. v. Garlington, 245 Ga. App. 49, 537 S.E.2d 179 (2000).

14.5 Warranty Claims Where Car's True History Not Disclosed: Odometer Tampering, Lemon Laundering, Salvage Vehicles, Bad Title

14.5.2 Inaccurate Odometer Readings

Replace note 117 with:

117   49 U.S.C. § 32705(a)(2). Beginning June 9, 1998, and perhaps earlier, this requirement does not apply to vehicles over ten years old. *See* 49 C.F.R. § 580.17. While this exemption had existed in the regulations for a number of years before 1998, the courts had found that the National Highway Transportation Agency did not have authority to promulgate the exemption. That authority was explicitly granted to the agency by Congress, effective June 9, 1998. *See generally* National Consumer Law Center, Automobile Fraud § 3.6.4 (2d ed. 2003). Nevertheless, many transferors still provide the odometer disclosure statement for older cars and, when they do, it creates an express warranty.

Add note 118.1 at end of first sentence of subsection's second paragraph.

118.1   *See* National Consumer Law Center, Automobile Fraud § 8.2.3.2.1 (2d ed. 2003).

Replace final sentence of subsection's third paragraph with:

Another NCLC manual, *Automobile Fraud*,[118.2] examines techniques to determine if an odometer reading is inaccurate.

118.2   National Consumer Law Center, Automobile Fraud (2d ed. 2003).

Page 522

Replace final sentence of subsection's sixth paragraph with:

The federal and analogous state statutes are examined in detail in NCLC's *Automobile Fraud*.[118.3]

118.3   *Id.*

Replace subsection's next-to-last sentence with:

The applicability of state UDAP statutes to odometer misrepresentations is examined in NCLC's *Unfair and Deceptive Acts and Practices*[118.4] and *Automobile Fraud*.[118.5]

118.4   National Consumer Law Center, Unfair and Deceptive Acts and Practices § 5.4.6.5 (5th ed. 2001 and Supp.).

118.5   National Consumer Law Center, Automobile Fraud § 8.4 (2d ed. 2003).

14.5.3 Lemon Laundering

14.5.3.1 Lemon Laundering as a Breach of Warranty

Replace second sentence of subsection's second paragraph with:

A summary of state lemon laundering laws is found in another NCLC manual, *Automobile Fraud*.[119.1]

119.1   National Consumer Law Center, Automobile Fraud (2d ed. 2003).

14.5.3.2 Other Causes of Action

Addition to note 120.

120   National Consumer Law Center, Automobile Fraud Chs. 7, 8 (2d ed. 2003); National Consumer Law Center, Unfair and Deceptive Acts and Practices § 5.4.6.7 (5th ed. 2001 and Supp.).

Replace third sentence of subsection's first paragraph with:

In addition, sample complaints, interrogatories, and document requests in a lemon laundering case are found in NCLC's *Consumer Law Pleadings*,[120.1] and on the CD-Rom accompanying this volume.

120.1   National Consumer Law Center, Consumer Law Pleadings No. 2, § 6.1 (2003 Cumulative CD-Rom and Index Guide).

Replace note 121 with:

121   *See* National Consumer Law Center, Automobile Fraud § 6.3, Appx. C (2d ed. 2003).

Page 523

14.5.3.3 Determining if a Vehicle Is a Laundered Lemon

Replace last sentence of subsection's third paragraph with:

A complaint, interrogatories, and requests for documents from the manufacturer and the dealer in a lemon laundering case are provided on the CD-Rom accompanying another NCLC manual,[122] and on the CD-Rom accompanying this volume.

    122   National Consumer Law Center, Consumer Law Pleadings No. 2, § 6.1 (2003 Cumulative CD-Rom and Index Guide).

Replace last sentence of subsection's fourth paragraph with:

Interrogatories and requests for documents from a servicing dealer in a lemon laundering case are provided on the CD-Rom accompanying another NCLC manual,[123] and on the CD-Rom accompanying this volume.

    123   *Id.*

14.5.4 Salvage Vehicles

Replace note 124 with:

    124   *See* National Consumer Law Center, Automobile Fraud Appx. C (2d ed. 2003).

Replace note 125 with:

    125   National Consumer Law Center, Unfair and Deceptive Acts and Practices § 5.4.6.6.3 (5th ed. 2001 and Supp.).

Replace note 126 with:

    126   *See* National Consumer Law Center, Automobile Fraud Appx. C (2d ed. 2003).

Replace note 127 with:

    127   National Consumer Law Center, Unfair and Deceptive Acts and Practices § 5.4.6.6.3 (5th ed. 2001 and Supp.).

Replace subsection's final paragraph with:

More detailed discussions on salvage vehicles are found in NCLC's *Automobile Fraud*[127.1] and *Unfair and Deceptive Acts and Practices.*[127.2] A good example of a complaint, discovery requests, an expert's report, pretrial disclosures, a trial brief, and jury instructions concerning the undisclosed sale of a salvaged vehicle is found in NCLC's *Consumer Law Pleadings*[127.3] and on the CD-Rom accompanying this volume.

    127.1   National Consumer Law Center, Automobile Fraud (2d ed. 2003).
    127.2   National Consumer Law Center, Unfair and Deceptive Acts and Practices § 5.4.6.6 (5th ed. 2001 and Supp.).
    127.3   National Consumer Law Center, Consumer Law Pleadings No. 2, § 6.2 (2003 Cumulative CD-Rom and Index Guide).

Page 524

14.5.5 Good Title

Replace note 129 with:

    129   *See* Green v. Arcadia Fin. Ltd., 174 Misc. 2d 411, 663 N.Y.S.2d 944, 36 U.C.C. Rep. Serv. 2d 89 (Sup. Ct. 1997), *aff'd.*, 261 A.D.2d 896 (1999).

14.6 Warranty Law and Repossession of Used Cars

Page 525

14.6.4 Revocation of Acceptance After Seizure May Prevent a Deficiency

Replace subsection's first three words with:

Section 8.4.5

14.7 FTC Used Car Rule

Page 526

14.7.2 Scope

Add to text after subsection's first paragraph:

    The Rule is not explicit as to whether it applies to leases of used vehicles or only to sales of used vehicles. When the Rule was enacted used vehicles were rarely leased. Whether or not courts interpret the Rule as applying to leases of used vehicles, as a practical matter dealers will have to comply with the Rule for vehicles that are leased.

Typically when a dealer offers a vehicle it is willing to sell it or lease it. Rarely would a dealer offer a vehicle only for lease. Because the Rule requires a sticker "before you offer a used vehicle for sale," the sticker must be posted on a vehicle that is offered for sale, even if it is later leased.

In addition, when a vehicle is leased with a purchase option, then an offer to sell the vehicle to the lessee at a future time is involved. If the dealer does not provide a copy of the window sticker to the lessee at the time of the lease signing, and incorporates the sticker language into the lease, then the dealer must certainly provide a copy of the window sticker when the consumer exercises the purchase option. Finally, the federal Consumer Leasing Act will be violated if any manufacturer or dealer warranties are not disclosed in the lease.[157.1]

157.1   *See* § 19.2.5, *infra.*

14.7.3 The Buyers Guide

Page 527

14.7.3.1 General

Addition to note 174.

174   *Replace NCLC citation with*: National Consumer Law Center, Automobile Fraud § 6.2 (2d ed. 2003).

Page 529

14.7.5 Buyers Guide Disclosures Must Be Repeated in Other Documents

Add to text after sentence containing note 203:

The disclosure that the Buyers Guide is incorporated into the contract must be conspicuously displayed,[203.1] and it is a violation of the rule if it is included only in the fine print boilerplate of the contract.[203.2]

203.1   16 C.F.R. § 455.3(b).

203.2   Lawhorn v. Joseph Toyota, Inc., 141 Ohio App. 3d 153, 750 N.E.2d 610 (2001); Hachet v. Smedley's Chevrolet Sales, Inc., Clearinghouse No. 54,571 (Ohio C.P. Sept. 5, 2002); Brown v. P.A. Days, Inc., Clearinghouse No. 54,572 (Ohio C.P. Aug. 27, 2002).

Page 530

Replace note 213 with:

213   *See* National Consumer Law Center, Unfair and Deceptive Acts and Practices §§ 5.2.7.3, 5.2.8 (5th ed. 2001 and Supp.).

Add to text after sentence containing note 213:

The ambiguity created by the Buyers Guide in this situation may also lead a court to conclude that implied warranties have not been effectively disclaimed.[213.1]

213.1   *See* Berney v. Rountree Olds-Cadillac Co., 763 So. 2d 799 (La. Ct. App. 2000) (non-U.C.C. case). *See generally* §§ 5.8, 5.10, *supra.*

Replace note 214 with:

214   *See* National Consumer Law Center, Unfair and Deceptive Acts and Practices § 5.2.8 (5th ed. 2001 and Supp.).

14.7.6 Spanish Disclosures

Addition to note 216.

216   *See also* Martinez v. Rick Case Cars, Inc., 278 F. Supp. 2d 1371 (S.D. Fla. 2003).

Page 531

Replace § 14.7.8 heading with:

14.7.8 Remedies for Rule Violation

Addition to note 225.

225   *Replace NCLC citation with*: National Consumer Law Center, Unfair and Deceptive Acts and Practices § 3.4.5.6 (5th ed. 2001 and Supp.); *add*: Martinez v. Rick Case Cars, Inc., 278 F. Supp. 2d 1371 (S.D. Fla. 2003); Crowe v. Joliet Dodge, 2001 U.S. Dist. LEXIS 10066 (N.D. Ill. July 17, 2001) (denial of motion

to dismiss) (failure to provide Buyers Guide may be UDAP violation); Cummins v. Dave Fillmore Car Co., 1987 WL 19186 (Ohio Ct. App. Oct. 27, 1987) (omission of statement that information on Buyers Guide was part of contract was UDAP violation, but no actual damages shown and buyer not entitled to rescission); Rubin v. Gallery Auto Sales, 1997 WL 1068459 (Ohio C.P. June 23, 1997); Milton v. Riverside Auto Exch., Clearinghouse No. 55,453 (Ohio County Ct. Aug. 27, 1991).

Replace note 226 with:

226   National Consumer Law Center, Unfair and Deceptive Acts and Practices § 8.7 (5th ed. 2001 and Supp.).

Add to text at end of subsection's second paragraph:

The state UDAP statute may also allow rescission of the sale.[227.1]

Failure to comply with the Used Car Rule should also result in invalidation of any disclaimers. The UCC gives effect to a disclaimer of implied warranties only if it is conspicuous.[227.2] A disclaimer should not be considered conspicuous if it was not disclosed in the manner required by the Used Car Rule. Limitations on warranties that are not disclosed in compliance with the Magnuson-Moss Act are ineffective.[227.3]

227.1   *See, e.g.*, Milton v. Riverside Auto Exch., Clearinghouse No. 55,453 (Ohio County Ct. Aug. 27, 1991) (ordering rescission). *But cf.* Cummins v. Dave Fillmore Car Co., 1987 WL 19186 (Ohio Ct. App. Oct. 27, 1987) (buyer lost right to rescind by making repairs on his own that amounted to substantial change in condition of car).

227.2   U.C.C. § 2-316; *see* § 5.8, *supra.*

227.3   *See, e.g.*, Callas v. Trane CAC, Inc., 12 U.C.C. Rep. Serv. 2d 72 (W.D. Va. 1990) (remedy limitation clause unenforceable when not disclosed in compliance with Magnuson-Moss Act), *aff'd*, 940 F.2d 651 (4th Cir. 1991).

Add note 229.1 at end of sentence containing note 229.

229.1   *See also* Holley v. Gurnee Volkswagen & Oldsmobile, Inc., 2001 U.S. Dist. LEXIS 7274 (N.D. Ill. Jan. 4, 2001) (denying seller's motion for summary judgment on claim that it violated Magnuson-Moss Act by failing to give buyer a copy of Buyers Guide).

Add to text at end of subsection:

Proving that the dealer did not display the Buyers Guide on the car that the consumer bought can be tricky. Once the consumer raises this claim, the dealer is likely to put window stickers on all the cars in the lot and claim that it was standard practice that every car, including the consumer's, have a window sticker. Videotaping or photographing the cars on the dealer's lot at an early stage of the investigation can help prove that the cars did not have window stickers. A non-digital camera is best because of the greater difficulty in altering the photos. Each car should be photographed from every angle. Establishing the date by photographing the day's newspaper in front of the first car is a helpful precaution. A consumer who undertakes to photograph the lot should be advised about the laws of trespass and what to do if there is a confrontation with dealership personnel. Visiting the lot after hours but during daylight is less likely to provoke a confrontation.

14.8 Used Car Lemon Laws

14.8.1 Introduction

Add to text at end of subsection:

The New York used car lemon law specifically states that it does not preclude other remedies,[233.1] so a consumer who has won a purchase price refund through a lemon law arbitration may sue under the UCC for incidental and consequential damages that the lemon law does not cover.[233.2]

233.1   N.Y. Gen. Bus. Law § 198-b(d)(2) (McKinney).

233.2   Williams v. Planet Motor Car, Inc., 190 Misc. 2d 22, 738 N.Y.S.2d 170, 47 U.C.C. Rep. Serv. 2d 1000 (Civ. Ct. 2001).

14.8.2 Scope

Add to text at end of subsection's first paragraph:

When a used car is sold at a retail auto auction, a separate New York law forbids "as is" clauses and requires the auctioneer to disclose the identity of the seller and inform the buyer of the used car lemon law.[235.1]

235.1   N.Y. Gen. Bus. Law § 23 (McKinney).

Addition to note 239.

239   *Replace last sentence of note with*: N.Y. Gen. Bus. Law § 198-b(a)(2) (McKinney) excludes motorcycles, motor homes, and off-road vehicles until Sept. 1, 2004. After that date, it excludes only motor homes and off-road vehicles.

Page 532

Add to text at end of subsection's fourth paragraph:

A Massachusetts decision holds that a manufacturer may meet the definition of a dealer when it issues a warranty under its certified used car program.[247.1]

247.1   Palumbo v. Land Rover N. Am., Inc., 2003 WL 1962516 (Mass. Super. Ct. Mar. 3, 2003).

Addition to note 249.

249   *Replace NCLC citation with*: National Consumer Law Center, Unfair and Deceptive Acts and Practices § 6.6 (5th ed. 2001 and Supp.).

Replace note 250 with:

250   *See* National Consumer Law Center, Unfair and Deceptive Acts and Practices § 6.6 (5th ed. 2001 and Supp.).

14.8.4 Statutory Warranty Coverage

Add to text after subsection's first sentence:

The fact that a vehicle can be driven does not mean that its value is not impaired.[254.1]

254.1   Bay Ridge Toyota, Inc. v. Lyons, 272 A.D.2d 397, 707 N.Y.S.2d 205 (2000); *In re* Arbitration Between Royal Chrysler-Oneonta, Inc. v. Dunham, 243 A.D.2d 1007, 663 N.Y.S.2d 410 (1997).

Addition to note 255.

255   *Add to first sentence of note: See In re* Arbitration Between Royal Chrysler-Oneonta, Inc. v. Dunham, 243 A.D.2d 1007, 663 N.Y.S.2d 410 (1997) (recurring noises, locking up of transmission, and problems shifting triggered lemon law remedies).

Add to text at end of subsection's first paragraph:

Persistent strong vibration is a breach of the warranty required by New York's law.[255.1]

255.1   Williams v. Planet Motor Car, Inc., 190 Misc. 2d 22, 738 N.Y.S.2d 170, 47 U.C.C. Rep. Serv. 2d 1000 (Civ. Ct. 2001).

Page 533

Add to text after bulleted item containing note 256:

These matters are affirmative defenses that the seller must prove.[256.1]

256.1   Marcelin v. Motor Outlet, 2003 WL 21730040 (N.Y. App. Term. June 4, 2003).

Page 534

14.8.5 Omission or Disclaimer of Statutory Warranties

Addition to note 259.

259   *See* Williams v. Planet Motor Car, Inc., 190 Misc. 2d 22, 738 N.Y.S.2d 170, 47 U.C.C. Rep. Serv. 2d 1000 (Civ. Ct. 2001) (court will imply warranty if dealer does not provide it).

14.8.6 The Consumer's Notice and the Dealer's Attempt to Cure

Addition to notes 270, 271, 274.

270   Laznovsky v. Hyundai Motor Am., Inc., 190 Misc. 2d 537, 738 N.Y.S.2d 820 (Dist. Ct. 2002).

271   *Add to first sentence of note: See* Bay Ridge Toyota, Inc. v. Lyons, 272 A.D.2d 397, 707 N.Y.S.2d 205 (2000) (presumption applies after vehicle has been out of service due to repairs or malfunction for fifteen days, whether or not it is presently operable).

Page 535

274   Williams v. Planet Motor Car, Inc., 190 Misc. 2d 22, 738 N.Y.S.2d 170, 47 U.C.C. Rep. Serv. 2d 1000 (Civ. Ct. 2001).

Add to text at end of subsection:

In Massachusetts, the three repair attempts must occur within the warranty period.[274.1]

274.1   Deranian v. 128 Sales, Inc., 2002 WL 31174437 (Mass. Dist. Ct. Sept. 23, 2002).

14.8.7 Replacement Cars, Refunds

Add to text at end of subsection:

Unless the state statute explicitly provides otherwise, the buyer can also treat the statutory warranty as a UCC warranty and bring suit for damages or revocation of acceptance.[289.1]

289.1   Williams v. Planet Motor Car, Inc., 190 Misc. 2d 22, 738 N.Y.S.2d 170, 47 U.C.C. Rep. Serv. 2d 1000 (Civ. Ct. 2001).

14.8.9 *Coverage of Used Cars Under New Car Lemon Laws*

Page 536

Add to text after sentence containing note 299:

An Ohio decision reaches the same conclusion.[299.1] Maine's lemon law has been amended to delete the requirement that the vehicle be new, so any vehicle that is sold under warranty is covered during the first three years after its original sale or the first 18,000 miles it is operated, whichever occurs first.[299.2]

299.1 Browning v. Am. Isuzu Motors, Inc., 2002 WL 32063978 (Ohio C.P. Mar. 21, 2003) (declining to use dealer licensing law's definition of "new motor vehicle" as one that has never been transferred to an ultimate purchaser).

299.2 Me. Rev. Stat. Ann. tit. 10, § 1163 (West) (as amended by 2003 Me. Laws 337, §§ 2, 5).

Replace "One court has" in sentence containing note 300 with:

Two courts have

Addition to note 301.

301 *But see* Schey v. Chrysler Corp., 228 Wis. 2d 483, 597 N.W.2d 457 (Ct. App. 1999) (construing Wisconsin lemon law not to apply to used car sold with balance on manufacturer's warranty; vigorous dissent).

14.9 Other Minimum Statutory Standards for Used Cars

Add to text at end of section's third paragraph:

The cost of the repairs necessary to bring the car up to warranty is an appropriate measure of damages for breach of the statutory warranty.[306.1]

306.1 Altberg v. Paul Kovacs Tire Shop, Inc., 31 Conn. App. 634, 626 A.2d 804 (1993).

Page 537

Add to text after section's sixth paragraph:

New Mexico prohibits dealers from excluding, modifying, or disclaiming the implied warranty of merchantability or limiting the remedies for its breach before midnight of the fifteenth calendar day after delivery or the vehicle has been driven 500 miles, whichever occurs first. Any attempt to exclude, modify, disclaim, or limit remedies for breach of this warranty renders the sale voidable at the option of the buyer. The consumer must give the dealer reasonable notice of breach within thirty days after the breach and afford the dealer a reasonable opportunity to repair the vehicle, with the consumer paying half of the cost of the first two repairs, up to $25 each. A consumer can waive the implied warranty only as to specific defects that are fully, accurately, and conspicuously disclosed in a document the consumer signs prior to the sale.[320.1]

320.1 N.M. Stat. Ann. § 57-16A-3.1 (Michie) (added by 2003 N.M. Laws 216, effective Jan. 1, 2004).

14.10 State Inspection Laws

Delete Oklahoma citation from note 323.

Page 538

Replace note 329 with:

329 *See* § 11.1, *supra.*

Addition to note 333.

333 *See also* N.Y. Gen. Bus. Law § 23 (McKinney) (requiring retail used car auto auctions to disclose the buyer's rights under the inspection law).

Add to text after sentence containing note 335:

Compliance is determined not by specific parts but by performance.[335.1] Persistent strong vibration is a violation of this requirement.[335.2]

335.1 Williams v. Planet Motor Car, Inc., 190 Misc. 2d 22, 738 N.Y.S.2d 170, 47 U.C.C. Rep. Serv. 2d 1000 (Civ. Ct. 2001).

335.2 *Id.*

Addition to note 337.

337 *But cf.* Laznovsky v. Hyundai Motor Am., Inc., 190 Misc. 2d 537, 738 N.Y.S.2d 820 (Dist. Ct. 2002) (no

damage claim when all repairs were covered under remainder of manufacturer's warranty; loss of use not compensable when buyer did not give seller opportunity to repair).

Add to text after sentence containing note 337:

Proof of a defect raises a presumption that it existed at delivery.[337.1]

337.1   Williams v. Planet Motor Car, Inc., 190 Misc. 2d 22, 738 N.Y.S.2d 170, 47 U.C.C. Rep. Serv. 2d 1000 (Civ. Ct. 2001).

Replace note 346 with:

346   Conn. Gen. Stat. § 14-16a. The statute applies to vehicles that are ten models years old or older. A 2001 amendment rephrased the statute to allow the state agency to require inspection of these vehicles, rather than making inspection mandatory.

Page 539

Delete "Oklahoma" and note 355 from section's fifth paragraph.

14.11   State-by-State Summary of Used Car Warranty and Condition Standards

Replace note 362 with:

362   Ariz. Rev. Stat. § 28-4412; *see* § 14.9, *supra*.

Add to text after sentence following sentence containing note 366:

The definition of express warranty includes service contracts.[366.1]

366.1   Reveles v. Toyota by the Bay, 57 Cal. App. 4th 1139, 67 Cal. Rptr. 2d 543 (1997).

Replace note 372 with:

372   Conn. Gen. Stat. § 14-16a. A 2001 amendment rephrased the statute to allow the state agency to require inspection of these vehicles, rather than making inspection mandatory.

Page 540

Delete sentence containing note 378 and note 378.

Replace note 379 with:

379   Haw. Rev. Stat. §§ 481J-1 to 481J-7; *see* § 14.8, *supra*.

Addition to notes 383, 386, 390.

383   *Replace Kansas statutory citation with*: Kan. Stat. Ann. § 50-639(a)(1).
386   *Replace Louisiana statutory citation with*: La. Civ. Code Ann. art. 2520 (West).
390   *Add at end of note*: Note that this statute was amended in 2003 to create an exception for vehicles a dealer buys through an out-of-state dealer-only auction when seller is not a Maine resident or licensed as a dealer in Maine, as long as the dealer clearly discloses on the required statement that the vehicle was acquired at an out-of-state auction and historical information regarding defects and damage is not available.

Page 541

Replace note 396 with:

396   Mass. Gen. Laws ch. 90, § 7N 1/4; *see* § 14.8, *supra*.

Replace note 401 with:

401   Minn. Stat. § 325F.662; *see* § 14.8, *supra* (more detailed discussion of this statute).

Addition to note 406.

406   *Replace Missouri statutory citation with*: Mo. Rev. Stat. § 307.380.

Replace note 413 with:

413   N.J. Stat. Ann. § 56:8-69 (West); *see* § 14.8, *supra*.

Page 542

Add to text at end of New Mexico entry:

Effective January 1, 2004, New Mexico prohibits dealers from excluding, modifying, or disclaiming the implied warranty of merchantability or limiting the remedies for its breach before midnight of the fifteenth calendar day after delivery or the vehicle has been driven 500 miles, whichever occurs first, except for specific defects that are disclosed prior to the sale.[417.1]

417.1   N.M. Stat. Ann. § 57-16A-3.1 (Michie) (added by 2003 N.M. Laws 216, effective Jan. 1, 2004); *see* § 14.9, *supra.*

Replace note 418 with: 418   N.Y. Gen. Bus. Law § 198-b (McKinney); *see* § 14.8, *supra.*

Delete Oklahoma entry.

Replace note 422 with: 422   37 Pa. Code § 301.2(5); *see* § 14.9, *supra.*

Replace note 423 with: 423   R.I. Gen. Laws § 31-5.4-2; *see* § 14.8, *supra.*

Addition to note 433.   433   *See* Wolfe v. Welton, 210 W. Va. 563, 558 S.E.2d 363 (2001) (prohibition of disclaimers applies to used as well as new goods).

Add to text after sentence containing note 433:   This prohibition preserves implied warranties even when the seller gives a short-term, limited express warranty.[433.1]

433.1   Wolfe v. Welton, 210 W. Va. 563, 558 S.E.2d 363 (2001).

Replace note 434 with: 434   Wis. Admin. Code § Trans 139.06.

Replace note 435 with: 435   Wis. Admin. Code § Trans 139.04.

Replace note 436 with: 436   Wis. Admin. Code § Trans 139.04.

Page 543

14.12 Used Car Dealer Bonding

Replace note 437 with: 437   *See* National Consumer Law Center, Automobile Fraud § 9.13.4, Appx. C (2d ed. 2003).

Replace § 14.13 with:

14.13 Used Car Pleadings in This and Other NCLC Manuals

A sample complaint is found at Appendix K.3, *infra.* Three more specialized complaints are available in another NCLC publication.[451] The three complaints deal with the undisclosed sale of a lemon buyback, the undisclosed sale of a salvaged vehicle, and the sale of a used car with undisclosed defects and at an excessive price. In addition *Consumer Law Pleadings*[452] contains two complaints against banks for a used car dealer's fraud. A sample set of interrogatories for a used car sale is found at Appendix L.5, *infra.* All of these pleadings are also found on the CD-Rom accompanying this volume.

451   National Consumer Law Center, Consumer Law Pleadings No. 2, Ch. 6 (2003 Cumulative CD-Rom and Index Guide).

452   National Consumer Law Center, Consumer Law Pleadings No. 1, §§ 3.1, 4.3 (2003 Cumulative CD-Rom and Index Guide).

Chapter 15   Mobile Home Sales

15.1 Introduction

Page 545

15.1.1 Nature of the Mobile Home Market

Replace note 6 with:

6   *Id.* at 6. A 1999 AARP-sponsored survey found that, in 1995, median income for households living in mobile homes was $22,578, compared to $28,807 for all households. Am. Assoc. of Retired Persons, National Survey of Mobile Home Owners, 14, 34 (July 21, 1999), *available at* http://research.aarp.org.

Replace note 7 with:

7   U.S. Dep't of Housing & Urban Development, Ninth Report to Congress on the Manufactured Housing Program § I(A), at 2 (1996). In a 1999 AARP-sponsored national survey of mobile home owners, fifteen percent of respondents had annual household incomes under $15,000. Am. Assoc. of Retired Persons, National Survey of Mobile Home Owners, 14, 34 (July 21, 1999), *available at* http://research.aarp.org.

Addition to note 8.

8   *Add at end of note*: A 2001 AARP Research Institute report cites HUD information that forty-one percent of mobile homes occupied as a primary residence were owned or rented by a person age fifty or over. AARP Research Inst., Issues in Manufactured Housing (2002), *available at* http://research.aarp.org.

Page 546

15.1.3 Eleven Common Mobile Home Defects

Addition to notes 15, 16.

15   *Add to end of note*: Other sources of information on the nature and frequency of various problems with mobile homes include: *NCLC Guide to Mobile Homes* (2002); Am. Ass'n of Retired Persons, National Survey of Mobile Home Owners 14, 34 (July 21, 1999), *available at* http://research.aarp.org; Consumers Union, Paper Tiger, Missing Dragon: Poor Warranty Service and Worse Enforcement Leave Manufactured Home Owners in the Lurch (Nov. 2002), *available at* www.consumersunion.org/other/mh/owners.htm.

16   *Add to cases involving problems with roofs*: *See* Garner v. La. Hous., 798 So. 2d 295 (La. Ct. App. 2001) (water intrusion due to failure of marriage wall to seal properly); *add at end of note*: In a 1999 AARP national survey of mobile home owners, 23% of respondents reported problems with leaks from the roof, ceiling, or skylights. Am. Ass'n of Retired Persons, National Survey of Mobile Home Owners 14, 34 (July 21, 1999), *available at* http://research.aarp.org. Of those who paid less than $25,000 for the home, 30% reported this problem. *Id.* at 15.

Add to text after sentence containing note 17:

In a 1999 national survey of mobile home owners, 35% reported problems with windows and doors. Of those who paid less than $25,000 for the home, 46% reported these problems.[17.1]

17.1   Am. Ass'n of Retired Persons, National Survey of Mobile Home Owners 14, 15 (July 21, 1999), *available at* http://research.aarp.org. A Consumers Union report shows that 40% of surveyed Texas mobile home buyers reported problems with windows and doors. Consumers Union, Paper Tiger, Missing Dragon: Poor Warranty Service and Worse Enforcement Leave Manufactured Home Owners in the Lurch (Nov. 2002), *available at* www.consumersunion.org/other/mh/owners.htm.

Page 547

Addition to note 21.

21   *Add at end of note*: In a 1999 AARP national survey of mobile home owners, 12% of respondents reported problems with the heating or cooling system. Am. Ass'n of Retired Persons, National Survey of Mobile Home Owners 14 (July 21, 1999), *available at* http://research.aarp.org.

Add note 23.1 at end of first sentence of subsection's sixteenth paragraph.

23.1   In a 1999 AARP national survey of mobile home owners, 12% of respondents reported problems with the electrical system. Am. Ass'n of Retired Persons, National Survey of Mobile Home Owners 14 (July 21, 1999), *available at* http://research.aarp.org.

Page 548

Addition to notes 26, 29.

26   *Add at end of note*: In a 1999 AARP national survey of mobile home owners, 30.1% of respondents reported problems with plumbing. Am. Ass'n of Retired Persons, National Survey of Mobile Home Owners 14 (July 21, 1999), *available at* http://research.aarp.org.

29   *Add at end of note*: In a 1999 AARP national survey of mobile home owners, 14% of respondents reported problems with appliances. Am. Ass'n of Retired Persons, National Survey of Mobile Home Owners 14 (July 21, 1999), *available at* http://research.aarp.org.

Page 550

Add to text at end of subsection:

A much more detailed analysis of these and other mobile home defects is presented in a new book by Bill J. White, *The National Consumer Law Center Guide to Mobile Homes* (2002).[42.1] Written for potential purchasers, the volume examines in great detail potential defects and problems in a mobile home. It includes more than thirty instructive photographs and also includes:

- Tips on how to purchase a home from a dealer and ways the dealer can engage in deception;
- What types of systematic defects to look for in a new home;
- What types of problems to check for when purchasing a used home;
- Potential problems in the delivery of the home to its site;
- Signs of defective installation of a single-wide home;
- Signs of defective installation of a multi-wide home;
- Instructions on how to obtain warranty service; and
- Tips on maintaining and caring for the home.

42.1   The book costs $12, including shipping and handling, and is available by sending a check (made payable to "National Consumer Law Center") to Publications, National Consumer Law Center, 77 Summer Street, 10th Floor, Boston, Massachusetts 02110, or by calling (617) 542-9595 for credit card orders.

15.2 Applicability of Uniform Commercial Code and Magnuson-Moss Warranty Act

15.2.1 *Uniform Commercial Code*

Addition to notes 44, 46, 47.

44   *Replace Joswick citation with*: 362 Md. 261, 765 A.2d 90 (2001); *add*: Hensley v. Ray's Motor Co., 580 S.E.2d 721, 50 U.C.C. Rep. Serv. 2d 695 (N.C. Ct. App. 2003).

46   State v. Bohne, 63 P.3d 63, 49 U.C.C. Rep. Serv. 2d 59 (Utah 2002) (recognizing that modular homes are goods under U.C.C., but adopting different definition for construction trade licensing law).

47   Helterbrand v. Five Star Mobile Home Sales, Inc., 48 S.W.3d 649 (Mo. Ct. App. 2001) (site work and construction of garage not goods); *see* Ch. 17, *infra* (discussion of the law regarding services).

Add note 47.1 at end of first sentence of subsection's third paragraph.

47.1   *See* Helterbrand v. Five Star Mobile Home Sales, Inc., 48 S.W.3d 649 (Mo. Ct. App. 2001) (mobile home is converted to real property upon its attachment to a permanent foundation).

Add to text after second sentence of subsection's third paragraph:

For example, a North Carolina appellate court has stated that a mobile home can be considered realty if it is annexed to the land with the intent that it be permanent or the circumstances surrounding the association between the land and the home or the relationship between the parties otherwise justifies treating the home as realty.[47.2]

47.2   Hensley v. Ray's Motor Co., 580 S.E.2d 721, 50 U.C.C. Rep. Serv. 2d 695 (N.C. Ct. App. 2003).

Page 551

15.2.2 *Magnuson-Moss Warranty Act*

Addition to notes 51, 53.

51   *Replace In re Van Balrcum citation with*: *In re* Van Blarcum, 19 S.W.3d 484 (Tex. App. 2000) (mobile home is a "consumer product"), *vacated on other grounds sub nom. In re* Am. Homestar of Lancaster, Inc., 50 S.W.3d 480 (Tex. 2001).

53   *Add to Miller citation*: *aff'd on other grounds*, 249 F.3d 629 (7th Cir. 2001) (court states in dictum that it is doubtful that it would disagree with trial court).

Replace note 54 with:

54 Miller v. Showcase Homes, 2000 U.S. Dist. LEXIS 6028 (N.D. Ill. Mar. 14, 2000), *aff'd on other grounds*, 249 F.3d 629 (7th Cir. 2001) (court states in dictum that it is doubtful that it would disagree with trial court).

15.2.3 What Law Applies If the UCC and Magnuson-Moss Warranty Act Do Not Apply

Replace note 58 with:

58 *See* § 11.1, *supra*; National Consumer Law Center, Unfair and Deceptive Acts and Practices § 2.2.6 (5th ed. 2001 and Supp.).

15.3 National Manufactured Housing Construction and Safety Standards Act

15.3.1 Overview

Replace title of statute in subsection's second sentence with:

National Manufactured Housing Construction and Safety Standards Act of 1974

Page 552

Add note 75.1 at end of subsection's seventh paragraph.

75.1 42 U.S.C. § 5422(g); *see* Manufactured Housing Dispute Resolution Program, Advance Notice of Proposed Rulemaking, 68 Fed. Reg. 11,452 (Mar. 10, 2003) (requesting comments on structure of dispute resolution system).

Addition to note 76.

76 *See* Manufactured Housing Installation Program: Standards, Training, Licensing, and Inspection, Advance Notice of Proposed Rulemaking, 68 Fed. Reg. 11,448 (Mar. 10, 2003) (calling for comments on structure and requirements of installation program); 67 Fed. Reg. 53,007 (Aug. 14, 2002) (announcing appointment of members of consensus committee).

Page 553

15.3.3 Construction Standards

Replace note 87 with:

87 HUD adopted revisions to its smoke alarm regulations in 2002. 67 Fed. Reg. 12,812 (Mar. 19, 2002); 67 Fed. Reg. 49,794 (July 31, 2002). The regulations as amended may be found at 24 C.F.R. §§ 3280.202, 3280.208.

Add to text after sentence containing note 91:

As a result, it is particularly clear that a buyer claiming noncompliance need not prove the underlying cause of the defects: the noncompliance is sufficiently shown by the home's defective performance.[91.1]

91.1 Dalme v. Blockers Manufactured Homes, Inc., 779 So. 2d 1014 (La. Ct. App. 2001) (decided under La. Civil Code).

Page 556

15.3.5 Effect of Federal Standards Upon State Law

Addition to notes 116, 120.

116 Gianakakos v. Commodore Home Sys., Inc., 285 A.D.2d 907, 727 N.Y.S.2d 806 (2001).

120 Burton v. City of Alexander City, 2001 U.S. Dist. LEXIS 6651 (M.D. Ala. Mar. 20, 2001) (zoning laws not preempted even under the broader preemption language added in 2000); *see also* Manufactured Hous. Consensus Comm.—Rejection of Land Use Proposal, 68 Fed. Reg. 42,327 (proposed July 17, 2003) (rejecting proposed regulation that would have preempted zoning laws, on ground that it exceeds statutory authority).

Page 557

Replace note 129 with:

129 24 C.F.R. §§ 3280.208, 3280.202 (definition of smoke detector). HUD adopted revisions to these regulations in 2002. 67 Fed. Reg. 12,812 (Mar. 19, 2002); 67 Fed. Reg. 49,794 (July 31, 2002).

Page 559

15.3.6 Consumer Enforcement of Federal Standards

Addition to notes 146, 150.

146   *See also* Dalme v. Blockers Manufactured Homes, Inc., 779 So. 2d 1014 (La. Ct. App. 2001) (redhibition allowed when home did not comply with federal standards).

150   *See, e.g.*, S.C. Code Ann. §§ 40-29-190, 40-29-260(A)(2) (Law. Co-op.); *see also* Dalme v. Blockers Manufactured Homes, Inc., 779 So. 2d 1014 (La. Ct. App. 2001) (buyer may also seek redhibition on grounds other than noncompliance with HUD code).

15.4 Express Warranties for Mobile Homes

15.4.1 Introduction

Replace subsection's second sentence with:

Mobile home manufacturers typically provide a one-year express written warranty,[154] although a substantial number of warranties are for longer periods.[154.1]

154   Nat'l Comm'n on Manufactured Hous., Final Report 43 (1994); *see* S. Energy Homes v. Washington, 774 So. 2d 505, 40 U.C.C. Rep. Serv. 2d 986 (Ala. Feb. 4, 2000) (affirming $375,000 judgment for breach of express warranty); Estate of Southerland v. Oakwood Mobile Homes, Inc., 1997 Del. C.P. LEXIS 29 (Del. C.P. Sept. 8, 1997) (manufacturer's standard is to offer one-year limited warranty).

154.1   A 1999 survey found that 95% of mobile home owners received a warranty with the purchase. 39% of the warranties were for one year, 36% for two to five years, and 11% for six or more years (14% of respondents did not know how long their warranties ran). The median length of warranty coverage was 3.9 years. Am. Ass'n of Retired Persons, National Survey of Mobile Home Owners 12 (July 21, 1999), *available at* http://research.aarp.org.

Add to text after sentence containing note 156:

In a 1999 AARP national survey of mobile home owners, over 40% of respondents reported that attempts to get warranty coverage for a problem were unsuccessful.[156.1] In 21% of these cases, the owner did not get a response to calls or the dealer did not honor the warranty. In 17%, the problem recurred or was not properly fixed the first time and, in an additional 5%, the owner was told that the problem could not be fixed. Over 49% of respondents who reported a problem with their mobile home reported a less than satisfactory resolution of the problem.

156.1   Am. Ass'n of Retired Persons, National Survey of Mobile Home Owners 21, 22, 24 (July 21, 1999), *available at* http://research.aarp.org.

Addition to notes 158–160.

158   *See also* Osburn v. Bendix Home Sys., Inc., 613 P.2d 445 (Okla. 1980) (water leakage constitutes breach of warranty that home is free of defects in material or workmanship).

159   *See also* Estate of Cattano v. High Touch Homes, Inc., 2002 WL 1290411 (Ohio Ct. App. May 24, 2002) (unpublished) (failure of modular home to conform to model was UDAP violation).

Page 560

160   Oakwood Mobile Homes, Inc. v. Cabler, 73 S.W.3d 363 (Tex. App. 2002).

Add to text at end of subsection's fourth paragraph:

Express warranties can and usually do go beyond the standards required by HUD.[163.1]

163.1   Oakwood Mobile Homes, Inc. v. Cabler, 73 S.W.3d 363 (Tex. App. 2002).

Addition to note 167.

167   Osburn v. Bendix Home Sys., Inc., 613 P.2d 445 (Okla. 1980).

15.4.2 State Mobile Home Warranty Laws

Addition to notes 168–170, 174.

168   *Replace Arkansas citation with*: Ark. Code Ann. §§ 20-25-101 to 20-25-113 (Michie); *replace Louisiana citation with*: La. Rev. Stat. Ann. §§ 51.911.22(6), 51.911.22(7), 51.911.25 (West); *delete Oklahoma citation*; *replace Texas citation with*: Tex. Occ. Code Ann. §§ 1201.351 to 1201.361 (Vernon); *replace Washington citation with*: Wash. Rev. Code §§ 46.70.132 to 46.70.136; *add to New Mexico citation*: (sunsets July 1, 2006); *add*: S.C. Code Ann. § 40-29-260 (Law. Co-op); *see also* Cal. Health & Safety Code § 18046 (West) (requiring inspection and disclosure statement when used mobile home is sold); Mo. Rev. Stat. § 700.015 (does not require warranty but prohibits sale of homes that do not comply with code adopted by commission); Mo. Code Regs. Ann. tit. 4, § 240-120.100 (adopting HUD standards as state code); Okla Stat. tit. 47, § 582 (requiring Used Motor Vehicles and Parts Commission to enact regulations requiring warranties).

169   *Replace Texas citation with*: Tex. Occ. Code Ann. § 1201.351 (Vernon); *replace Majestic Indus., Inc.*

citation explanatory parenthetical with: (rejecting claim that previous Texas statute violated equal protection by applying only to dealers and manufacturers, and not to banks and finance companies selling repossessed mobile homes); *add*: *See also* Twin Town Homes, Inc. v. Molley, 2002 WL 32068353 (Me. Super. Ct. Nov. 14, 2002) (statute does not apply to modular building purchased for commercial purposes).

170   *Delete Texas citation.*

Page 561   174   *Replace Gem Homes, Inc. citation explanatory parenthetical with*: (previous state statute required seller to set up and anchor mobile home if it transported the home, even if contract did not require setup); *add*: S.C. Code Ann. § 40-29-260 (Law. Co-op.) (requiring one-year warranty for installation performed by dealer); *see also* Mo. Rev. Stat. § 700.100(3)(6) (licensing law requiring dealer to arrange for proper initial setup of new mobile home unless buyer signs written waiver).

Replace note 178 with: 178   Tex. Occ. Code Ann. § 1201.455 (Vernon).

Addition to notes 179–182.   179   *Replace Texas citation with*: Tex. Occ. Code Ann. § 1201.005 (Vernon).

180   *Replace Texas citation with*: Tex. Occ. Code Ann. § 1201.106 (Vernon).

181   *See, e.g.*, S.C. Code Ann. § 40-29-250 (Law. Co-op.).

182   *Replace Texas citation with*: Tex. Occ. Code Ann. § 1201.404 (Vernon).

Add to text after sentence containing note 185:

Therefore, UDAP remedies, which often include treble damages and attorney fees, will be available.[185.1] Even without such an explicit provision, many courts find that a violation of a consumer protection law is a per se UDAP violation.[185.2]

185.1   *See* Aguilera v. Palm Harbor Homes, Inc., 54 P.3d 993 (N.M. 2002) (affirming trial court's entry of arbitrator's award of $100,000 punitive damages under state UDAP statute for violation of mobile home warranty law).

185.2   *See* National Consumer Law Center, Unfair and Deceptive Acts and Practices § 8.8 (5th ed. 2001 and Supp.).

Add to text after subsection's third paragraph:

Many state mobile home warranty statutes create administrative bodies with enforcement authority, which can include inspecting homes[187.1] and issuing orders requiring sellers to make repairs.[187.2] A state may also provide for the same or similar authority under a separate statute,[187.3] or may provide such authority even in the absence of a mobile home warranty statute.[187.4] The West Virginia Supreme Court has held that the administrative agency charged with the responsibility to conduct inspections in response to consumer complaints has a further duty to inspect for the existence of "serious defects or imminent safety hazards which present an unreasonable risk of death or severe personal injury to the occupants," in addition to evaluating the defects or noncompliance alleged by the consumer.[187.5]

187.1   *See, e.g.*, Alaska Stat. § 45.30.040 (Michie); Ark. Code Ann. § 20-25-106 (Michie); Idaho Code § 39-4003A (Michie); La. Rev. Stat. Ann. §§ 51.911.26, 51.911.32 (West); Mich. Comp. Laws. § 125.2301; N.C. Gen. Stat. §§ 143-143.10 to 143-143.22; Okla. Stat. tit. 47, § 582; S.C. Code Ann. § 40-29-250 (Law. Co-op.); Tex. Occ. Code Ann. §§ 1201.355, 1201.356 (Vernon); Va. Code Ann. §§ 36-85.5(3), 36-85.17 (Michie); Wis. Stat. § 101.94(4).

187.2   *See, e.g.*, Alaska Stat. § 45.30.040(c)(1) (Michie); Ark. Code Ann. § 20-52-106(d) (Michie); La. Rev. Stat. Ann. § 51.911.36 (West); S.C. Code Ann. § 40-29-300 (Law. Co-op.).

187.3   *Compare* Me. Rev. Stat. Ann. tit. 10, §§ 1401–1406 (West) *with* Me. Rev. Stat. Ann. tit. 10, §§ 9001–9012 (West).

187.4   *See, e.g.*, W. Va. Code §§ 21-9-1 to 21-9-13.

187.5   Conseco Fin. Servicing Corp. v. Meyers, 211 W. Va. 631, 567 S.E.2d 641, 649 (2002).

Addition to notes 188, 189.   188   *See, e.g.*, N.M. Stat. Ann. § 60-14-19(C) (Michie); *see also* Aguilera v. Palm Harbor Homes, Inc., 54 P.3d 993 (N.M. 2002) (affirming trial court's entry of arbitrator's award of $100,000 punitive damages under state UDAP statute for violation of mobile home warranty law). *See generally* § 13.2.3.1, *supra.*

189   Pitchford v. Oakwood Mobile Homes, Inc., 2001 U.S. Dist. LEXIS 4992 (W.D. Va. Apr. 11, 2001); *see* § 16.4.1, *supra*; *see also* Lopez v. Willow Tree Homes & Commercial, Inc., 2003 WL 21213245 (Cal. Ct. App. May 27, 2003) (unpublished) (applying California's real estate disclosure statement law to sale of used mobile home; seller's inspection of railing was sufficient even though it did not reveal the defect). *But see* Garner v. La. Hous., 798 So. 2d 295 (La. Ct. App. 2001); Simmons v. S. Energy Homes, Inc., 783 So. 2d 636 (La. Ct. App. 2001); Dalme v. Blockers Manufactured Homes, Inc., 779 So. 2d 1014 (La. Ct. App. 2001).

15.5 Implied Warranties for Mobile Homes

Page 562

15.5.2 *Implied Warranty of Merchantability*

Add to text at end of subsection's first paragraph:

In some states, implied warranties do not normally arise against a manufacturer but do when the product has been specially manufactured for a particular customer, as is often the case with mobile homes.[198.1]

198.1   *See, e.g.*, Horton Homes, Inc. v. Brooks, 2001 Ala. LEXIS 431 (Ala. Nov. 30, 2001).

Page 563

Add to text after bulleted item containing note 213:

• Gaps in the roof and walls due to improper set up, loose and misaligned sheetrock, loose trim, non-level floors, a 1 inch bow in a wall, and other defects;[213.1]

213.1   Chavarria v. Fleetwood Retail Corp., Clearinghouse No. 54,576 (N.M. Dist. Ct. Aug. 29, 2002).

Addition to note 217.

217   *See also* Forest River, Inc. v. Posten, 847 So. 2d 957 (Ala. Civ. App. 2002) (leaks in motor home that damaged floor and created sour smell, plus malfunctioning leveling jacks, made home unmerchantable).

Page 564

15.5.4 *Disclaimer of Implied Warranties*

Add to text at end of subsection's first paragraph:

Even if the state mobile home warranty law does not prohibit disclaimer of implied warranties, if it requires that the home have a written warranty then the Magnuson-Moss Act precludes the disclaimer of implied warranties.[228.1]

228.1   *See* Pitchford v. Oakwood Mobile Homes, Inc., 2001 U.S. Dist. LEXIS 4992 (W.D. Va. Apr. 11, 2001).

15.6 Revocation of Acceptance of Mobile Homes

Page 565

15.6.1 *Right to Revoke Acceptance*

Add to text after subsection's first paragraph:

Revocation is allowed for defects of which the buyer was unaware at the time of sale or which the buyer reasonably assumed the seller would repair.[236.1] Many mobile home defects reveal themselves only under certain conditions, such as rain or high winds. Furthermore, even when superficial defects are visible, the typical buyer will have no way of knowing whether they are caused by underlying structural defects.[236.2]

236.1   *See* § 8.3.3, *supra.*
236.2   *See* McGough v. Oakwood Mobile Homes, Inc., 779 So. 2d 793 (La. Ct. App. 2000) (fact that buyer saw water stains did not mean she was aware that roof leaked, especially when salesman gave alternate explanation).

Addition to notes 242, 244, 245.

242   Garner v. La. Hous., 798 So. 2d 295 (La. Ct. App. 2001) (water intrusion due to failure of marriage wall to seal properly); *see also* Carpenter v. Lafayette Woodworks, 653 So. 2d 1187 (La. Ct. App. 1995) (persistent roof leaks justified redhibition of motor home).
244   *See also* Van Bibber Homes Sales v. Marlow, 778 N.E.2d 852 (Ind. Ct. App. 2002) (weaknesses caused by bad setup, plus leaks, buckling, and other problems, justify rescission); McGough v. Oakwood Mobile Homes, Inc., 779 So. 2d 793 (La. Ct. App. 2000) (these problems and a multitude of other defects).
245   Jaramillo v. Gonzales, 50 P.3d 554 (N.M. Ct. App. 2002) (affirming trial court award of revocation).

Add to text after bulleted item containing note 247:

• Noncompliance with the HUD standards;[247.1]

247.1   Dalme v. Blockers Manufactured Homes, Inc., 779 So. 2d 1014 (La. Ct. App. 2001) (decided under La. Civil Code).

Add to text after sentence containing note 250:

An improper repair to the linoleum floor of the living quarters of a motor home, which would allow water to get into the subfloor, was a substantial impairment under California's warranty law.[250.1]

250.1   Barker v. Fleetwood Enterprises, Inc., 2002 WL 453931 (Cal. Ct. App. Mar. 26, 2002) (unpublished).

Addition to note 252. 252   McGough v. Oakwood Mobile Homes, Inc., 779 So. 2d 793 (La. Ct. App. 2000).

Page 566

15.6.2 Time for Revocation

Add to text after "four" in sentence containing note 260:

or even five

Addition to note 260. 260   Jaramillo v. Gonzales, 50 P.3d 554 (N.M. Ct. App. 2002) (five years for latent plumbing defect).

15.6.3 Use of the Home After Revocation

Add to text after sentence following sentence containing note 263:

It may also lead the jury to conclude that the problems with the home are less severe than the buyers claim.

Add to text at end of subsection's second paragraph:

The buyers should also document whether their homeowner's insurance would be canceled if they moved out. Meeting the requirements to keep insurance coverage in place may be a sufficient justification in and of itself for continuing to live in the home.

Page 567

15.6.4 Sale of the Home by the Buyer After Revocation

Addition to note 273. 273   *See also* Jaramillo v. Gonzales, 50 P.3d 554 (N.M. Ct. App. 2002) (bank's refusal to acknowledge liability under FTC Holder Rule for mobile home's defective plumbing was UDAP violation).

15.7 Defects Caused By Transportation and Setup

Page 568

15.7.1 How Transportation and Setup Can Damage Mobile Homes

Addition to notes 286, 291. 286   *Add at end of note*: In a 1999 AARP national survey of mobile home owners, 15% of respondents reported problems with installation and setup. Am. Ass'n of Retired Persons, National Survey of Mobile Home Owners 14 (July 21, 1999), *available at* http://research.aarp.org.

291   *See also* Michaud v. Dow Road Associates, 2003 WL 22480193 (Conn. Super. Ct. Oct. 8, 2003) (unpublished) (defective setup caused flooring to buckle and foundation and drywall to crack); Van Bibber Homes Sales v. Marlow, 778 N.E.2d 852 (Ind. Ct. App. 2002) (weaknesses caused by bad setup); Prather v. Crane, 2004 WL 51115 (Wis. Ct. App. Jan. 13, 2004) (defects caused by misalignment of units of modular home during set up).

Add to text at end of subsection:

Even if the dealer took responsibility for setup, it may claim that site preparation was the consumer's responsibility.

Page 569

15.7.2 Responsibility for Defects Caused by Transportation and Setup

Addition to note 295. 295   *Replace entire Grand Manor citation with*: 778 So. 2d 167 (Ala. Civ. App. 1998), *rev'd on other grounds*, 778 So. 2d 173 (Ala. 2000).

Add to text at end of subsection's fourth paragraph:

Amendments made to the National Manufactured Housing Construction and Safety Standards Act in 2000 require HUD to establish and implement a manufactured housing installation program by 2005.[297.1]

297.1   *See* § 15.3.1, *supra*.

15.7.3 Liability of Manufacturer

Add to text at end of subsection's second paragraph:

When the dealer provided setup and transportation, it may be possible to argue that the manufacturer negligently selected and retained the dealer as an authorized dealer.[302.1]

302.1   Cook v. Skyline Corp., 135 Idaho 26, 13 P.3d 857 (Idaho 2000) (finding that it was not error to submit such a claim to the jury).

Page 570

15.7.4 Liability of Dealer

Addition to note 307.

307   *See* Hensley v. Ray's Motor Co., 580 S.E.2d 721, 50 U.C.C. Rep. Serv. 2d 695 (N.C. Ct. App. 2003) (U.C.C. applies to contract for sale and installation of mobile home). *But cf.* New Welton Homes v. Eckman, 786 N.E.2d 1172 (Ind. Ct. App. 2003) (applying non-U.C.C. law to retailer's contract to prepare site for the modular home it sold), *transfer granted*, 2003 Ind. LEXIS 742 (Ind. Sept. 4, 2003).

Page 571

Add to text at end of subsection's sixth paragraph:

Furthermore, the regulation provides that the dealer can not complete the sale of a home that it knows does not comply with the HUD standards.[321.1] If the dealer knows the home was damaged during transportation or setup, this portion of the regulation prohibits its sale.

321.1   24 C.F.R. § 3282.252(a)(2).

Add note 324.1 at end of subsection.

324.1   *See, e.g.*, Radenbaugh v. Farm Bureau Gen. Ins. Co., 240 Mich. App. 134, 610 N.W.2d 272 (2000) (holding dealer's insurer responsible for losses caused by defective setup and site preparation instructions).

15.7.5 Liability of Independent Transportation and Setup Company

Replace note 326 with:

326   *See* Michaud v. Dow Road Associates, 2003 WL 22480193 (Conn. Super. Ct. Oct. 8, 2003) (contractor who prepared site and installed home breached common law duty of good substantial workmanlike construction). *See generally* §§ 17.2.3, 17.4, *infra*.

Addition to note 327.

327   *See, e.g.*, Colo. Rev. Stat. §§ 24-32-3315 to 24-32-3322 (note that license can be revoked under § 24-32-3317(3) if installer does not pay for repairs and inspections necessary to bring installation into compliance with manufacturer's instructions and state standards); S.C. Code Ann. § 40-29-30 (Law. Co-op.).

Add to text after sentence containing note 327:

In the alternative, a general home improvement or construction contractor law may apply.[327.1]

327.1   *See, e.g.* Michaud v. Dow Road Associates, 2003 WL 22480193 (Conn. Super. Ct. Oct. 8, 2003) (applying new home construction statute to contractor who prepared site and installed home); *see also* Ch. 16, *infra* (discussion of new home warranty laws).

Replace note 328 with:

328   *See* National Consumer Law Center, Unfair and Deceptive Acts and Practices § 4.9.8 (5th ed. 2001 and Supp.).

15.8 Litigating Mobile Home Breach of Warranty Cases

15.8.1 Pleading Causes of Action in Mobile Home Cases

Page 572

15.8.1.2 UDAP Claims

Addition to notes 334, 340.

334   *See* Estate of Cattano v. High Touch Homes, Inc., 2002 WL 1290411 (Ohio Ct. App. May 24, 2002) (unpublished) (failure of modular home to conform to model was UDAP violation).

340   *Replace NCLC citation with*: National Consumer Law Center, Unfair and Deceptive Acts and Practices §§ 6.2–6.5 (5th ed. 2001 and Supp.).

15.8.1.3 Tort Claims

Addition to note 345.

345   *Replace Ex parte Grand Manor citation with*: 778 So. 2d 173 (Ala. 2000).

Page 573

Add note 348.1 at end of first sentence of subsection's final paragraph.

348.1   *See, e.g.,* Estate of Cattano v. High Touch Homes, Inc., 2002 WL 1290411 (Ohio Ct. App. May 24, 2002) (unpublished) (reversing dismissal of fraud claim which alleged that seller concealed modular home's noncompliance with building code).

Addition to note 349.

349   *Replace entire Grand Manor citation with*: 778 So. 2d 167 (Ala. Civ. App. 1998), *rev'd on other grounds*, 778 So. 2d 173 (Ala. 2000).

15.8.1.4 Claims Under Federal and State Credit Statutes

Replace note 354 with:

354   15 U.S.C. § 1641; *see* National Consumer Law Center, Truth in Lending § 7.3.2 (5th ed. 2003).

Replace note 355 with:

355   *See* National Consumer Law Center, Truth in Lending § 2.3.5 (5th ed. 2003).

Page 574

Replace note 361 with:

361   15 U.S.C. § 1602(aa)(1) (excluding "residential mortgage transactions"). *See generally* National Consumer Law Center, Truth in Lending § 9.2.4 (5th ed. 2003).

Replace subsection's seventh paragraph with:

The Truth in Lending Act and HOEPA are thoroughly discussed in NCLC's *Truth in Lending*.[362.1] The sample home improvement complaint included as Appx. K.4, *infra*, contains a Truth in Lending count.

362.1   National Consumer Law Center, Truth in Lending (5th ed. 2003).

15.8.1.5 Claims Against Creditor That Financed the Sale

Addition to note 368.

368   *Replace NCLC citation with*: National Consumer Law Center, Unfair and Deceptive Acts and Practices § 6.6 (5th ed. 2001 and Supp.); *add*: *See* Green Tree Acceptance, Inc. v. Pierce, 768 S.W.2d 416 (Tex. App. 1989) (assignee liable on buyer's revocation claim).

Replace note 371 with:

371   *See* National Consumer Law Center, Repossessions and Foreclosures (5th ed. 2002 and Supp.).

Add to text at end of subsection's second paragraph:

It may be so closely connected to the dealer that the dealer will be treated as its agent, making it responsible in its own right for the dealer's misdeeds.[371.1]

371.1   Oakwood Mobile Homes, Inc. v. Cabler, 73 S.W.3d 363 (Tex. App. 2002).

Page 575

15.8.2 Proof of Defective Condition at Delivery

Addition to note 375.

375   *Replace S. Energy Homes citation with*: 774 So. 2d 505, 40 U.C.C. Rep. Serv. 2d 986 (Ala. 2000).

Page 576

Add to text after sixth sentence of paragraph containing note 385:

The appearance of defects soon after setup of a mobile home is strong circumstantial evidence that they existed at the time of delivery.[385.1]

385.1   McGough v. Oakwood Mobile Homes, Inc., 779 So. 2d 793 (La. Ct. App. 2000); *see* § 7.5.1.2, *supra*.

15.8.3 Discovery

Replace note 390 with:

390   *See Ex parte* Horton Homes, Inc., 774 So. 2d 536 (Ala. 2000) (upholding on jurisdictional grounds a trial court's order that defendant produce compliant documents).

Page 577

15.8.4 Damages and Attorney Fees

Addition to note 403.

403   *Replace S. Energy Homes citation with*: 774 So. 2d 505, 40 U.C.C. Rep. Serv. 2d 986 (Ala. 2000); *add*: *Accord* Horton Homes, Inc. v. Brooks, 2001 Ala. LEXIS 431 (Ala. Nov. 30, 2001) (affirming award that included $138,000 in mental anguish damages for defective mobile home); *see also* Cook v. Skyline Corp., 135 Idaho 26, 13 P.3d 857 (Idaho 2000) (such damages allowed if buyers prove physical manifestations of emotional distress).

Chapter 16   New Home Sales

16.2 Applicability of Uniform Commercial Code and Magnuson-Moss Warranty Act

16.2.1 Uniform Commercial Code

Page 580

Addition to note 10.

> 10   *Compare* Keck v. Dryvit Sys., Inc., 830 So. 2d 1, 8 (Ala. 2002) (because exterior insulation finish system could not be detached from the home without causing material harm, it was not a good but rather an integral part of the home, and U.C.C. warranties did not attach); MacConkey v. F.J. Matter Design, Inc., 54 Va. Cir. 1, 6 (2000) (exterior insulation finish system ceased being goods once it was incorporated into home) *and* Providence Vill. Townhouse Condo. Ass'n v. Amurcon-Loudoun Corp., 24 U.C.C. Rep. Serv. 2d 864 (Va. Cir. Ct. 1994) (condominium owners could not assert U.C.C. warranty claim against manufacturer of wood incorporated into units) *with* Gables CVF, Inc. v. Bahr, Vermeer & Haecker Architect, Ltd., 506 N.W.2d 706, 712 (Neb. 1993) (plaintiff presented sufficient evidence of condominium siding's defects to raise fact issue of whether it breached U.C.C.'s implied warranty of merchantability) *and* Stoney v. Franklin, 2001 WL 683963, at *8 (Va. Cir. Ct. June 18, 2001) (allowing U.C.C. claim against manufacturer and supplier of exterior insulation finish system because at time those parties sold the materials, the materials were movable).

Add to text at end of subsection's first paragraph:

Any express warranties that may have accompanied the component should also be considered as a basis for potential claims.[11.1]

> 11.1   *See* Ch. 3, *supra.*

Addition to note 12.

> 12   *See, e.g.,* Brewer v. Poole Constr. Co., 13 Mass. L. Rptr. 97, 2001 Mass. Super. LEXIS 151, at *12, *13 (Super. Ct. May 3, 2001) (applying implied warranty by application through analogy to Article 2).

Page 581

16.2.3 Magnuson-Moss Warranty Act

Addition to note 16.

> 16   *Add to Miller citation: aff'd on other grounds sub nom.* Miller v. Willow Creek Homes, Inc., 249 F.3d 629 (7th Cir. 2001).

16.3 Common Law Implied Warranties of Quality in the Sale of a New Home

16.3.1 Introduction

Addition to notes 23, 32–34.
Page 582

> 23   *See also* Albrecht v. Clifford, 767 N.E.2d 42, 46 (Mass. 2002) (citing various rationales for warranty).
>
> 32   Wawak v. Stewart, 247 Ark. 1093, 1100, 449 S.W.2d 922, 926 (Ark. 1970); Albrecht v. Clifford, 767 N.E.2d 42, 46 (Mass. 2002); Brewer v. Poole Constr. Co., 13 Mass. L. Rptr. 97, 2001 Mass. Super. LEXIS 151, at *16, *17 (Super. Ct. May 3, 2001) (holding that a nondisclaimable warranty of habitability arises in the sale of a completed dwelling by its builder/vendor); Kishmarton v. William Bailey Constr., 93 Ohio St. 3d 226, 754 N.E.2d 785 (2001); Humber v. Morton, 426 S.W.2d 554 (Tex. 1968); *see also* Centex Homes v. Buecher, 95 S.W.3d 266 (Tex. 2002) (distinguishing the warranty of habitability from the warranty of good workmanship, recognizing both).
>
> 33   *See, e.g.,* Michaud v. Dow Road Associates, Inc., 2003 WL 22480193, at *3 (Conn. Super. Ct. Oct. 8, 2003) (modular home); Forton v. Laszar, 239 Mich. App. 711, 609 N.W.2d 850 (2000); Mullen v. Byers, 2001 Ohio App. LEXIS 4414 (Ohio Ct. App. Sept. 28, 2001); *see also* Mann v. Clowser, 59 S.E.2d 78 (Va. 1950)

(in every contract for the performance of a service there is a presumption that the work will be done in a workmanlike manner). *But see* Urban Dev., Inc. v. Evergreen Bldg. Products, Ltd. Liab. Co., 59 P.3d 112, 117 (Wash. Ct. App. 2002) (holding that construction contracts do not automatically include an implied warranty of workmanlike construction).

34   *Delete Humber citation*; *add*: *See, e.g.*, Ezzell v. Gervais, 2003 WL 22482055, at *2 (Conn. Super. Ct. Oct. 23, 2003) (construction includes "warranties that the dwelling is free from faulty materials, constructed according to sound engineering standards, constructed in a workmanlike manner, and fit for habitation at the time of completion of the dwelling"); Becker v. Graber Builders, Inc., 561 S.E.2d 905, 909 (N.C. Ct. App. 2002); Rothberg v. Olenik, 128 Vt. 295, 262 A.2d 461 (1970) (recognizing both warranty of habitability and warranty of workmanship).

Replace note 36 with:

36   *See* § 16.3.5, *infra*; *see also* Cont'l Dredging, Inc. v. De Kaizered, Inc., 2003 WL 22214293, at *6 (Tex. App. Sept. 26, 2003) (dredging company's failure to dredge to depth required by contract breached implied warranty that work would be done in a good and workmanlike manner).

Page 583

Addition to note 41.

41   *Replace Kishmarton citation and parenthetical with*: 93 Ohio St. 3d 226, 754 N.E.2d 785 (2001); *add*: Mullen v. Byers, 2001 Ohio App. LEXIS 4414 (Ohio Ct. App. Sept. 28, 2001).

Add to text following sentence containing note 42:

Likewise, Virginia has ameliorated its common law *caveat emptor* rule[42.1] with a statutory warranty.

42.1   Bruce Farms, Inc. v. Coupe, 247 S.E.2d 400, 403 (Va. 1978) (sale of new home did not carry an implied warranty of fitness for intended use).

Replace note 43 with:

43   While Utah recognizes a warranty of habitability for residential leased property, Utah's Supreme Court has reasoned that such a warranty does not need to be implied in home sale transactions because home buyers have greater bargaining power and more opportunity to inspect the premises than do tenants. Am. Towers Owners Ass'n, Inc. v. CCI Mech., Inc., 930 P.2d 1182, 1193 (Utah 1996); Fennell v. Green, 77 P.3d 339, 345 (Utah Ct. App. 2003) (affirming summary judgment for builder); *see also* Snow Flower Homeowners Ass'n v. Snow Flower, Ltd., 31 P.3d 576, 583 (Utah Ct. App. 2001) (no implied warranties in sale of condominium unit); Maack v. Res. Design & Constr., Inc., 875 P.2d 570 (Utah Ct. App. 1994) (declining to recognize warranty).

Page 584

16.3.2 Which Buyers Can Assert the Warranty?

Addition to notes 52–54.

52   Wagner Constr. Co. v. Noonan, 403 N.E.2d 1144, 1146, 1147 (Ind. Ct. App. 1980); *see also* Smith v. Miller Builders, Inc., 741 N.E.2d 731, 741 (Ind. Ct. App. 2000) (implied warranty of habitability arose when developer improved real estate and sold it for the particular purpose of the construction of a home; ultimate purchaser did not have to show they relied on developer's skill or expertise).

53   Wagner Constr. Co. v. Noonan, 403 N.E.2d 1144, 1146, 1147 (Ind. Ct. App. 1980).

54   *See also* Johnson v. Constr. & Consulting, Inc., 2003 WL 21500719, at *2, *3 (Wash. Ct. App. June 30, 2003) (declining to extend warranty to subsequent tenant).

Add to text at end of subsection:

In such jurisdictions a subsequent purchaser may be able to bring a claim for negligent construction instead.[54.1]

54.1   *See, e.g.*, Cosmopolitan Homes, Inc. v. Weller, 663 P.2d 1041, 1044, 1045 (Colo. 1983) (subsequent purchaser could bring claim of negligent construction against builder, distinguishing warranty of habitability); Coburn v. Lenox Homes, Inc., 173 Conn. 567, 574, 378 A.2d 599, 602 (Conn. 1977) (subsequent purchaser stated claim of negligence against builder); Terlinde v. Neely, 275 S.C. 395, 399, 271 S.E.2d 768, 770 (S.C. 1980) (subsequent purchasers could state claim in tort against builder for latent defects); Moxley v. Laramie Builders, Inc., 600 P.2d 733, 736 (Wyo. 1979) (same).

16.3.3 Who Gives the Warranty?

Replace note 55 with:

55   *See* Sousa v. Albino, 120 R.I. 461, 388 A.2d 804 (1978); *see also* Bynum v. Prudential Residential Services, Ltd. P'ship, 2003 WL 22456111, at *9 (Tex. App. Oct. 30, 2003) (buyers had no cause of action for breach of implied warranty of habitability against sellers or broker when neither had built nor renovated the house).

Page 585

Add to text after sentence containing note 57:

Furthermore, the form of the contract may determine whether a warranty arises. At least one court has held that a cost-plus contract does not grant an implied warranty of habitability.[57.1]

57.1   Hickman v. Kralicek Realty & Constr. Co., 2003 WL 22723484 (Ark. Ct. App. Nov. 19, 2003) (holding buyer responsible for all unforeseeable costs associated with the contract).

Addition to notes 66, 67, 72, 76–78.

66   *Add to Ramapo Brae Condo Ass'n citation*: *aff'd*, 167 N.J. 155, 770 A.2d 253 (2001) (per curiam).

67   *See also* Albrecht v. Clifford, 767 N.E.2d 42, 47 (Mass. 2002) (warranty attaches to sale of new homes by a builder-vendor).

Page 586

72   *Cf.* Beeftu v. Creekside Ventures Ltd. Liab. Co., 37 P.3d 526, 528 (Colo. Ct. App. 2001) (developer not liable for breach of warranty based on basement flooding when builder was the party who decided to build home with a basement, notwithstanding soil tests that indicated a water table problem).

76   *But see* Codner v. Arellano, 40 S.W.3d 666, 674 (Tex. App. 2001) (no implied warranty runs from a subcontractor to the benefit of the home owner; home owner's recourse is directly against the contractor).

77   J.M. Krupar Constr. Co. v. Rosenberg, 95 S.W.3d 322 (Tex. App. 2002) (no action for breach of warranty against subcontractor).

78   *But cf.* Kirkman v. Parex, Inc., 2003 WL 22887934, at *3, *4 (S.C. Ct. App. Dec. 8, 2003) (developer's lender did not become sufficiently involved in construction of house to justify imposing liability for breach of implied warranty of habitability, notwithstanding that lender spent over $40,000 to complete the construction after foreclosure; court emphasized the buyers' ability to recover from other parties).

Page 587

16.3.4 What Property Does the Warranty Cover?

Addition to notes 79, 82, 85.

79   Fretschel v. Burbank, 351 N.W.2d 403, 404 (Minn. Ct. App. 1984) (buyers of used house had no implied warranty claim against sellers who had not built the home).

82   *See, e.g.*, Gable v. Silver, 258 So. 2d 11, 18 (Fla. Dist. Ct. App. 1972); Berish v. Bornstein, 770 N.E.2d 961, 972 (Mass. 2002) (extending implied warranty of habitability to purchase of a new condominium unit and also holding that an organization of unit owners could bring a breach of warranty claim based on latent defects in the common areas that implicate the habitability of units); Everts v. Parkinson, 555 S.E.2d 667, 678 (N.C. Ct. App. 2001); *see also* Michaud v. Dow Road Associates, Inc., 2003 WL 22480193, at *3, *4 (Conn. Super. Ct. Oct. 8, 2003) (good and workmanlike construction warranty arose on sale of modular home (described in the opinion as a "manufactured home")).

85   Overton v. Kingsbrooke Dev., Inc., 788 N.E.2d 1212, 1217 (Ill. App. Ct. 2003) (implied warranty arose from developer that sold vacant lot on which it had improperly compacted fill, affirming judgment of rescission).

Add to text after "for example," in sentence containing note 87:

a retaining wall,[86.1]

86.1   Hershewe v. Perkins, 102 S.W.3d 73, 78 (Mo. Ct. App. 2003).

16.3.5 Standards and Breach

Page 588

16.3.5.1 The Standards

Addition to notes 95, 96, 100.

95   Hershewe v. Perkins, 102 S.W.3d 73, 78 (Mo. Ct. App. 2003) (buyer continuing to live in house did not preclude finding that collapsed retaining wall breached implied warranty). *But see* Klos v. Gockel, 87 Wash. 2d 567, 570, 571, 554 P.2d 1349, 1352, 1353 (1976) (no breach for mudslide and settling of fill-damaged patio and backyard when house suffered minimal damage, noting that home owners never moved out of the house) (*dicta*).

96   Overton v. Kingsbrooke Dev., Inc., 788 N.E.2d 1212, 1218 (Ill. App. Ct. 2003) (warranty breached in sale of a vacant lot sold to be part of a residential community when developer inadequately compacted fill such that it could not support a house); Wagner Constr. Co. v. Noonan, 403 N.E.2d 1144, 1148 (Ind. Ct. App. 1980) (warranty breached by a defect that "substantially impairs the enjoyment of the residence").

100   *See* Satterfield v. Medlin, 59 P.3d 33, 36 (Mont. 2002) (warranty limited to those defects that are so substantial as to reasonably preclude use of the dwelling as a residence); Centex Homes v. Buecher, 95 S.W.3d 266 (Tex. 2002) (implied warranty of habitability protects against only those conditions "that are so defective that the property is unsuitable for its intended use as a home," distinguishing implied warranty of good workmanship).

Add to text at end of subsection's third paragraph:

The home owner may have to show how the builder's work caused or was connected to the defect; in contrast, a home owner may show a breach of an express warranty by the mere existence of the defect itself.[100.1]

> 100.1　*See, e.g.*, Buckley v. JR Builders, Inc., 16 Mass. L. Rptr. 19 (Super. Ct. 2003) (denying summary judgment to home owners on implied warranty of habitability claim because they failed to show the cause of basement leaks, but granting summary judgment on express warranty claim).

Addition to note 105.

> 105　Albrecht v. Clifford, 767 N.E.2d 42 (Mass. 2002); Mullen v. Byers, 2001 Ohio App. LEXIS 4414, at *7 (Ohio Ct. App. Sept. 28, 2001).

Page 589

Add to text after sentence containing note 107:

Failing to comply with the construction contract may also breach the warranty.[107.1]

> 107.1　*See* Cont'l Dredging, Inc. v. De Kaizered, Inc., 2003 WL 22214293, at *6 (Tex. App. Sept. 26, 2003) (dredging company's failure to dredge to depth required by contract breached implied warranty that work would be done in a good and workmanlike manner).

Addition to note 109.

> 109　*See, e.g.*, Centex Homes v. Buecher, 95 S.W.3d 266 (Tex. 2002).

Add to text at end of subsection's fifth paragraph:

The implied warranty of good workmanship may also be the basis for a claim when the defect arises in an area of the property not intended to be habitable and therefore not within the habitability warranty.[109.1]

> 109.1　*See, e.g.*, Aronsohn v. Mandara, 484 A.2d 675 (N.J. 1984) (while implied warranty of habitability did not apply to defect in patio, home buyers created question of fact with respect to workmanship warranty); Meadowbrook Condo. Ass'n v. S. Burlington Realty Corp., 565 A.2d 238, 241 (Vt. 1989) (implied warranty of habitability did not cover defects in condominium's common areas that were not intended for living space, but court affirmed verdict that developer had breached workmanship warranty).

Addition to note 113.

> 113　*See, e.g.*, Albrecht v. Clifford, 767 N.E.2d 42, 48 (Mass. 2002) (buyers must demonstrate that defects are latent).

16.3.5.2　Common Defects That Breach the Warranty

Addition to notes 116, 118–120.

> 116　*See, e.g.*, Snyder v. Wernecke, 813 So. 2d 213, 215 (Fla. Dist. Ct. App. 2002) (cracks caused by foundation improperly set in "muck").
>
> 118　*See, e.g.*, Krol v. York Terrace Bldg., Inc., 370 A.2d 589 (Md. Ct. Spec. App. 1977) (a home without usable water would breach statutory warranty); Forbes v. Mercado, 583 P.2d 552 (Or. 1978) (well water that was undrinkable due to its high iron content breached warranty).
>
> 119　Smith v. Taylor Built Constr. Co., 782 So. 2d 793, 796 (Ala. Civ. App. 2000) (reversing summary judgment in favor of builder on claims alleging breach of contract and breach of express and implied warranties); *see also* Lanier Home Ctr., Inc. v. Underwood, 557 S.E.2d 76 (Ga. Ct. App. 2001) (failure of septic system justified rescission of home purchase contract).

Page 590

> 120　*See also* Ezzell v. Gervais, 2003 WL 22482055, at *2 (Conn. Super. Ct. Oct. 23, 2003) (misalignment of dormer and faulty Sheetrock installation breached warranty).

Add to text following sentence containing note 121:

A plaintiff may only have to show that the home contains an inherent structural defect which is almost certain to cause damage, rather than showing actual completed damage.[121.1]

> 121.1　*See, e.g.*, Hicks v. Kaufman & Broad Home Corp., 89 Cal. App. 4th 908, 107 Cal. Rptr. 2d 761, 770 (2001) (reversing denial of motion to certify class); Callander v. Sheridan, 546 N.E.2d 850 (Ind. Ct. App. 1989) (defect does not need to render home totally uninhabitable to breach warranty; upholding finding that defects in covered porch and pillar which presented imminent danger of collapse breached warranty); *see also* J.M. Krupar Constr. Co. v. Rosenberg, 95 S.W.3d 322 (Tex. App. 2002) (while buyers did not have to wait for defective foundation to buckle before bringing claim, damages for reduction in value due to the repair were recoverable only if structure actually failed, citing state residential construction liability statute).

Addition to notes 122–124, 126.

> 122　*See, e.g.*, Pontiere v. James Dinert, Inc., 627 A.2d 1204 (Pa. Super. Ct. 1993) (upholding verdict that builder had breached both implied warranty of habitability and condominium statute's warranty).
>
> 123　*See, e.g.*, *In re* Gordon Urmson Builder & Sons, Inc., 295 B.R. 546, 551 (Bankr. W.D. Pa. 2003) (leaking skylights breached warranty).
>
> 124　*See also* Adams v. NVR Homes, Inc., 135 F. Supp. 2d 675, 690 (D. Md. 2001) (mere threat of methane gas from solid waste dump underlying purchased homes did not violate statutory warranty of habitability), *modified in part on other grounds*, 142 F. Supp. 2d 649 (D. Md. 2001).

126 *See, e.g.*, Thorn v. Caskey, 745 So. 2d 653, 661 (La. Ct. App. 1999) (roof structure of garage that was built on 24 inch rather than 16 inch centers, contrary to contract and in violation of building code, breached statutory warranty).

16.3.6 Duration

Addition to note 128.

128 Wagner Constr. Co. v. Noonan, 403 N.E.2d 1144, 1148 (Ind. Ct. App. 1980) (warranty extends for a reasonable length of time under the circumstances; for defective septic system, five years fell within warranty period); Point E. Condo. Owners' Ass'n v. Cedar House Associates Co., 663 N.E.2d 343, 356 (Ohio Ct. App. 1995) (describing implied warranty as "indefinite").

16.4 Statutory Implied Warranties

16.4.1 Homes

Add to text at beginning of subsection:

California,[132.1]

132.1 Cal. Civ. Code §§ 896 to 945.5 (West) (applying to purchase contracts for residential units executed after January 1, 2003).

Addition to notes 133–135, 137, 138, 140, 141–144, 146, 147.

133 *Add to end of note*: *See also* Cashman v. Calvo, 493 A.2d 891 (Conn. 1985) (upholding verdict that defective exterior siding violated warranty); Beckman v. Jalich Homes, Inc., 460 A.2d 488 (Conn. 1983) (president of builder-vendor not personally liable for breach of statutory warranty); Cafro v. Brophy, 774 A.2d 206 (Conn. Ct. App. 2001) (builder did not effectively disclaim statutory warranty); Greene v. Perry, 771 A.2d 196 (Conn. Ct. App. 2001) (statute did not apply when builder built home on lot already owned by plaintiff, however, plaintiff's negligence claim upheld); Krawiec v. Blake Manor Dev. Corp., 602 A.2d 1062 (Conn. Ct. App. 1992) (implied warranty statute covered lot as well as home; affirming verdict that drainage defects breached statutory warranty); Fava v. Arrigoni, 402 A.2d 356 (Conn. Super. Ct. 1979) (subcontractors met definition of builder-vendor under terms of statute); Graveline v. Posin, 329 A.2d 368 (Conn. C.P. 1974) (certificate of occupancy provision of implied warranty statute did not apply to two-family house).

134 *See also* Choung v. Iemma, 708 N.E.2d 7 (Ind. Ct. App. 1999) (neither seller, who had not built home, nor real estate brokerage or agent were builder-vendors deemed by the statute to have given an implied warranty); Weber v. Costin, 654 N.E.2d 1130 (Ind. Ct. App. 1995) (construing statute's definition of builder-vendor).

135 *See also* Austin Homes, Inc. v. Thibodeaux, 821 So. 2d 10 (La. Ct. App. 2002) (applying warranty); Craig v. Adams Interior, Inc., 785 So. 2d 997 (La. Ct. App. 2001) (finding contractor breached statutory warranty by failing to properly install fireplace); Sowers v. Dixie Shell Homes of Am., Inc., 762 So. 2d 186 (La. Ct. App. 2000) (applying warranty); Thorn v. Caskey, 745 So. 2d 653 (La. Ct. App. 1999) (New Home Warranty Act was not home buyers' exclusive remedy; they could also assert breach of contract claim against builder who abandoned project before completing it); Graf v. Jim Walter Homes, Inc., 713 So. 2d 682 (La. Ct. App. 1998) (applying warranty); *add at end of note*: ; Louisiana also has a redhibition statute that provides that a seller warrants against those defects that "render the thing useless, or its use so inconvenient that it must be presumed that a buyer would not have bought the thing had he known of the defect." La. Civ. Code Ann. art. 2520 (West). However, if the transaction is covered by the New Home Warranty Act, a buyer must instead make a claim under that statute. La. Civ. Code Ann. art. 2520 (West) cmt. 3; *see also* Ory v. A.V.I. Constr., Inc., 848 So. 2d 115, 116 (La. Ct. App. 2003); Royer v. V.P. Pierret Constr. Co., 834 So. 2d 1078, 1081 (La. Ct. App. 1996) (holding that because New Home Warranty Act did not apply retroactively, redhibition article applied to house purchased before effective date of the Act). However, the redhibition article may apply to sales not covered by the Act, such as the sale of a used home. *See, e.g.*, Tarifa v. Riess, 856 So. 2d 21 (La. Ct. App. 2003) (awarding buyers damages for termite damage).

137 *See also* Lumsden v. Design Tech Builders, Inc., 749 A.2d 796, 799 (Md. 2000) (limitations period began to run when owners discovered defect in driveway, not later time when they learned the source of the defect); Morris v. Osmose Wood Preserving, 667 A.2d 624 (Md. 1995) (home owners could not bring statutory warranty suit against manufacturer of defective building materials because statute only applied to home sellers and real estate brokers); Andrulis v. Levin Constr. Corp., 628 A.2d 197 (Md. 1993) (statutory warranty extended to retaining walls in yard); Antigua Condo. Ass'n v. Melba Investors Atl., Inc., 517 A.2d 75 (Md. 1986) (interpreting limitations provisions of statute); Starfish Condo. Ass'n v. Yorkridge Serv. Corp., 458 A.2d 805 (Md. 1983) (interpreting the definition of purchaser under the statutory warranty); Potterton v. Ryland Group, Inc., 424 A.2d 761 (Md. 1981) (reversing lower court's dismissal of case on limitations grounds); Loch Hill Constr. Co. v. Fricke, 399 A.2d 883 (Md. 1979) (home without potable water breached warranty statute); Milton Co. v. Council of Unit Owners of Bentley Place Condo., 708 A.2d 1047 (Md. Ct. Spec. App. 1998) (applying statute to allow condominium association to

recover for builders' breach of warranty), *aff'd*, 729 A.2d 981 (Md. 1999); Krol v. York Terrace Bldg., Inc., 370 A.2d 589 (Md. Ct. Spec. App. 1977) (interpreting warranty duration provision in case in which home's water system failed); Bay State Ins. Co. v. Hill, 368 A.2d 1024 (Md. Ct. Spec. App. 1977) (interpreting statute's limitations period).

138   *See also* Koes v. Advanced Design, Inc., 636 N.W.2d 352 (Minn. Ct. App. 2001) (interpreting limitations period).

140   *See also* McDonald v. Mianecki, 398 A.2d 1283 (N.J. 1979) (applying statute); Lakhani v. Bureau of Homeowner's Prot., 811 A.2d 918 (N.J. Super. Ct. App. Div. 2002); Ingraham v. Trowbridge Builders, 687 A.2d 785 (N.J. Super. Ct. App. Div. 1997) (applying statute); *In re* Appeal of Adoption of N.J.A.C. 5:25A-1.1, 630 A.2d 383 (N.J. Super. Ct. App. Div. 1993) (interpreting warranty's durational period); Glaum v. Bureau of Constr. Code Enforcement, 533 A.2d 986 (N.J. Super. Ct. App. Div. 1987) (home that had been rehabilitated following fire damage was not new and therefore was not covered by warranty statute); Lloyd v. Bureau of Homeowners Prot., 95 N.J. Admin. 2d 71, 1995 WL 425218 (Dep't of Cmty. Affairs May 8, 1995) (interpreting notice requirements of administrative regulations pertaining to warranty program); Testa v. Edgewood Properties, Inc., 95 N.J. Admin. 2d 19, 1994 WL 760482 (Dep't of Cmty. Affairs Nov. 19, 1994); Shost v. Renz, 95 N.J. Admin. 2d 66, 1994 WL 814820 (Dep't of Cmty. Affairs Sept. 29, 1994) (applying statute and administrative regulations to cover some of the defects complained of, but not others); Carchia v. Bureau of Homeowner Prot., 91 N.J. Admin. 2d 1, 1991 WL 403148 (Dep't of Cmty. Affairs Aug. 6, 1991) (lack of support for the space over the garage was not a major structural defect remediable by the warranty statute).

Page 591

141   *See also* Taggart v. Martano, 723 N.Y.S.2d 211 (App. Div. 2001) (dismissing claims of home buyers who failed to comply with statute's notice provision); Watt v. Irish, 708 N.Y.S.2d 264 (Sup. Ct. 2000) (statutory warranty did not apply to house built on site the home buyer already owned).

142   *See also* Vaughn, Inc. v. Beck, 554 S.E.2d 88 (Va. 2001) (home owners were not required to notify builder of well defect within one year period of warranty's duration); Grogg v. Massey & Leonard Constr., Inc., 39 Va. Cir. 522 (1996) (determining point at which limitations period starts to run); Ell v. Moss, 31 Va. Cir. 8 (1995) (determining point at which limitations period starts to run); Johnson v. Jones, 37 Va. Cir. 590 (1994) (warranty statute does not apply to used home); Colodny v. Wines Constr., Inc., 33 Va. Cir. 321 (1994) (wife of home buyer, who was not a party to the original real estate contract, could not maintain statutory warranty action); Newton v. Burch, 30 Va. Cir. 391 (1993) (defective water system could breach warranty provided by statute).

143   *See* Glaum v. Bureau of Constr. Code Enforcement, 533 A.2d 986 (N.J. Super. Ct. App. Div. 1987) (home that had been rehabilitated following fire damage was not new and therefore was not covered by warranty statute).

144   *See also* Milton Co. v. Council of Unit Owners of Bentley Place Condo., 708 A.2d 1047 (Md. Ct. Spec. App. 1998) (rejecting argument that subsequent purchasers of condominium units had no standing to sue under warranty statute).

146   *Add to end of note*: Maryland's statute also provides that if a vendor sells to an intermediary in order to avoid the warranty, the sham sale will be ignored and the vendor will be treated as having sold directly to the ultimate user. Md. Code Ann., Real Prop. § 10-205.

147   *Add after statutory citations*: *See, e.g.*, Scott v. Regency Developers, 2000 Conn. Super. LEXIS 2943, at *8–*11 (Conn. Super. Ct. Nov. 8, 2000) (statute did not apply to a builder who built upon land already owned by plaintiffs); Carroll's Mobile Homes v. Hedegard, 744 N.E.2d 1049 (Ind. Ct. App. 2001) (implied warranty of habitability did not apply to a mere vendor, as opposed to a builder/vendor).

Replace note 150 with:

150   Va. Code Ann. § 55-70.1 (Michie); *see* Weiss v. Cassidy Dev. Corp., 2003 WL 22519650, at *3 (Va. Cir. Ct. Aug. 18, 2003) (principal of corporate joint venturer that constructed the home could be liable when corporation terminated before date of construction agreement).

Addition to notes 151–153.

151   *Add to end of note*: New York courts have split on whether the statutory implied warranties cover a home built on land already owned by the buyers. *Compare* Gorsky v. Triou's Custom Homes, Inc., 755 N.Y.S.2d 197 (Sup. Ct. 2002) (statute applies) *with* Watt v. Irish, 708 N.Y.S.2d 264, 267 (N.Y. Sup. Ct. 2000) (statute does not apply).

152   *See, e.g.*, Rizzo Pool Co. v. Del Grosso, 232 Conn. 666, 657 A.2d 1087, 1093, 1094 (1995) (as swimming pool was not installed as part of the contract for the new home, it was not covered by the home warranty statute but was instead covered by the state's home improvement act).

153   *But see* Andrulis v. Levin Constr. Corp., 628 A.2d 197, 200 (Md. 1993) (statutory warranty extended to retaining walls in yard).

Add to text at end of subsection's third paragraph:

Jurisdictions are divided on whether a statutory warranty attaches to the sale of a mobile home.[153.1]

153.1   *Compare* Pitchford v. Oakwood Mobile Homes, Inc., 2001 U.S. Dist. LEXIS 4992 (W.D. Va. Apr. 11, 2001) (Virginia's statutory implied warranty attached to sale of mobile home) *with* Carroll's Mobile Homes v. Hedegard, 744 N.E.2d 1049 (Ind. Ct. App. 2001) (statutory implied warranty of habitability did not attach to sale of mobile home) *and* Dalme v. Bockers Manufactured Homes, Inc., 779 So. 2d 1014 (La.

Ct. App. 2001) (new home warranty act did not apply to mobile homes, which were instead covered by Louisiana's Uniform Standards Code for Mobile Homes and Manufactured Housing). For a discussion of the U.C.C.'s warranties as they apply to the sale of a mobile home, see § 15.5, *supra*.

Addition to note 154.

154 *See also* Craig v. Adams Interior, Inc., 785 So. 2d 997 (La. Ct. App. 2001) (improperly installed fireplace could be basis of statutory warranty claim because it was part of the heating system; home need not be "almost falling down" to establish breach); Sowers v. Dixie Shell Homes of Am., Inc., 762 So. 2d 186 (La. Ct. App. 2000) (home that was built out of level and "framed up crooked" breached warranty); Thorn v. Caskey, 745 So. 2d 653, 661 (La. Ct. App. 1999) (roof structure of garage that was built on 24 inch rather than 16 inch centers, contrary to contract and in violation of building code, breached statutory warranty); Graf v. Jim Walter Homes, Inc., 713 So. 2d 682, 688 (La. Ct. App. 1998) (numerous construction defects that met neither contractual plans and specifications nor building code breached statutory warranty); Vlahos v. R & I Constr. of Bloomington, Inc., 658 N.W.2d 917, 922 (Minn. Ct. App. 2003) (structural damage caused by repeated water infiltration did not show breach of statutory warranty because it occurred after home was completed and sold to plaintiffs), *review granted* (June 17, 2003); Carchia v. Bureau of Homeowner Prot., 91 N.J. Admin. 2d 1, 1991 WL 403148 (Dep't of Cmty. Affairs Aug. 6, 1991) (lack of support for the space over the garage that was not intended to be living space was not a major structural defect remediable by the warranty statute).

Add to text after sentence containing note 159:

Minnesota's statute protects against those defects that are attributable to noncompliance with the state's building code.[159.1] Similarly, Louisiana's statute protects buyers against the builder's failure to comply with the local building code.[159.2]

159.1 Minn. Stat. §§ 327A.01 to 327A.02 (defining "building standards" to mean the State Building Code).

159.2 La. Rev. Stat. Ann. § 9:3144(1) (West); *see also* Davis v. Seghers, 860 So. 2d 261, 265, 266 (La. Ct. App. 2003) (buyer could claim breach of the statutory warranty for improper grading, which violated the local building code—rejecting builder's argument that statutory exclusion of landscaping from the builder's warranty precluded buyer's action).

Addition to note 161.

161 *But see* Graveline v. Posin, 329 A.2d 368 (Conn. C.P. 1974) (certificate of occupancy provision of implied warranty statute did not apply to two-family house).

Page 592

Add to text at end of subsection's sixth paragraph:

California has recently enacted a construction statute that sets out detailed standards for many features of new homes, including water resistance, structural integrity, soil engineering, fire protection, and plumbing and electrical systems.[163.1]

163.1 Cal. Civ. Code §§ 896 to 945.5 (West). While the statute provides that the standards are "intended to address every function or component of a structure," they are not exclusive. Cal. Civ. Code § 896 (West). Home owners may make a claim for a defect in a non-listed component if it causes damage. Cal. Civ. Code § 896 (West). The statute also describes a pre-litigation procedure for home owners and builders that home owners must comply with in order to maintain a claim. Cal. Civ. Code § 910 (West). The owner, to make a claim, need only show that the home does not meet the applicable standards, subject to some specified affirmative defenses. Cal. Civ. Code § 941(e) (West). The owner need not show any further causation or damages. Cal. Civ. Code § 941(e) (West).

Add to text at end of subsection's seventh paragraph:

New Jersey uses a government agency to enforce its warranty. The agency has established a registration process for builders, a security fund to provide a source of payment to correct builders' deficiencies, and its own administrative arbitration procedure to handle warranty claims.[166.1] Its regulations provide extensive detail about the precise nature of the warranty's coverage.[166.2]

166.1 N.J. Stat. Ann. § 46:3B-6 (West); N.J. Admin. Code tit. 5, §§ 25-1.1 to 25-5.5; *see also* Lakhani v. Bureau of Homeowner's Prot., 811 A.2d 918 (N.J. Super. Ct. App. Div. 2002).

166.2 N.J. Admin. Code tit. 5, §§ 25-3.1 to 25-3.10.

Add to text before bulleted item containing note 168:

- *California*: One year for defects in the fit and finish of specified building components; four years for defects in plumbing and sewer systems, electrical systems, and certain defects in exterior walkways, driveways, and patios.[167.1]

167.1 Except with regard to the fit and finish warranty, Cal. Civ. Code § 900 (West), these time limits are phrased as time limitations on actions brought based on the breach of the statutory standard, rather than as the duration of a warranty. Cal. Civ. Code § 896 (West). Additional limitation periods, ranging from two to four years, apply to some other, more specific, building standards. Cal. Civ. Code § 896 (West).

Replace note 170 with:

170   La. Rev. Stat. Ann. § 9:3144 (West). The Louisiana legislature recently revised the home warranty statute to specifically exclude mold and mold damage from the builder's warranty. 2003 La. Acts 333, § 1.

Addition to notes 171, 172, 174, 177, 178, 180, 181.

171   *See also* Lumsden v. Design Tech Builders, Inc., 749 A.2d 796, 799 (Md. 2000) (limitations period began to run when owners discovered defect in driveway, not later time when they learned the source of the defect); Antigua Condo. Ass'n v. Melba Investors, 517 A.2d 75 (Md. 1986) (interpreting limitations provisions of statute); Potterton v. Ryland Group, Inc., 424 A.2d 761, 764 (Md. 1981) (letter by builder acknowledging responsibility to repair defects extended limitations period); Gensler v. Korb Roofers, Inc., 378 A.2d 180, 182 (Md. Ct. Spec. App. 1977) (holding limitations period had expired); Bay State Ins. Co. v. Hill, 368 A.2d 1024 (Md. Ct. Spec. App. 1977) (interpreting statute's limitations period).

172   *See also* Koes v. Advanced Design, Inc., 636 N.W.2d 352, 357 (Minn. Ct. App. 2001) (home owners could bring a claim for breach of statutory home warranties after two year warranty period expired, so long as they brought suit within general limitations period applicable to warranty actions).

174   N.J. Admin. Code tit. 5, §§ 25-1.1 to 25-5.5; *see also In re* Appeal of Adoption of N.J.A.C. 5:25A-1.1, 630 A.2d 383, 386 (N.J. Super. Ct. App. Div. 1993) (statute extended to plywood that showed inevitable premature failure within the warranty period, even if it had not actually failed within the period); Harborview Condo. Ass'n v. Bureau of Homeowner Prot., 95 N.J. Admin. 2d 38, 1994 WL 809579 (Dep't of Cmty. Affairs Oct. 19, 1994) (plaintiffs' claims either fell outside of the applicable durational period or failed to meet administrative prerequisites for filing); Bridgewaters Townhouse Condo. Ass'n v. New Home Warranty Program, 92 N.J. Admin. 2d 24, 1992 WL 252269 (Dep't of Cmty. Affairs Jan. 13, 1992) (water penetration defect was merely a construction defect, not a major structural defect, and therefore plaintiff's claim filed beyond the applicable time period).

177   *Add to parenthetical following Thorn citation*: ; letter which listed only thirty-three defective items did not fail to meet notice requirement even though buyers proved additional defects at trial); *add*: Cal. Civ. Code §§ 910, 912–930, 937 (West) (for new homes sold after January 1, 2003, owner required not only to give notice of the claim to builder but also, at builder's election, to comply with specified pre-litigation procedures that allow owner to acquire certain designated documents from the builder and to have a mediator hear the dispute, and allow the builder to inspect the property, provide a detailed offer to repair the problem or to pay the cash equivalent, and complete those repairs (or, at owner's election, have an alternative builder complete them); any failure by the builder to comply with the procedures releases the owner from having to complete them); *see also* Graf v. Jim Walter Homes, Inc., 713 So. 2d 682, 689 (La. Ct. App. 1998) (notice sufficient notwithstanding buyer's later testimony at trial as to additional defects); Taggart v. Martano, 723 N.Y.S.2d 211 (App. Div. 2001) (dismissing claims of home buyers who failed to comply with statute's notice provision).

178   The statute limits the types of damages a home owner can obtain from a contractor for a construction defect to:

> (1) the reasonable cost of repairs necessary to cure any construction defect, including any reasonable and necessary engineering or consulting fees required to evaluate and cure the construction defect, that the contractor is responsible for repairing under this chapter;
> (2) the reasonable expenses of temporary housing reasonably necessary during the repair period;
> (3) the reduction in market value, if any, to the extent the reduction is due to structural failure; and
> (4) reasonable and necessary attorney's fees.

Id. at § 27.004(h). The statute further provides that, before bringing suit, a home owner must notify the contractor of any construction defect discovered and give the contractor forty-five days in which to make an offer of settlement. *Id*. at § 27.004(a), (b). If a home owner unreasonably rejects the offer, or fails to give the contractor a reasonable opportunity to repair the defect, then the statute limits the amount of damages the home owner can recover to the cost of repairs and attorney fees and costs incurred prior to the settlement offer. *Id*. at § 27.004(g). In the home owner's favor, however, the statute provides that, if the contractor fails to make a reasonable settlement offer, the contractor loses the benefit of *all* limitations on damages *and* the defenses to liability provided by section 27.004. A Texas court recently held that the limitations on damages lost include not only the limitation in subsection 27.004(i) on the amount of damages recoverable by a home owner, but also the limitation in subsection 27.004(h) on the types of damages recoverable. Perry Homes v. Alwattari, 33 S.W.3d 376, 384 (Tex. App. 2001) (overruling, in part, O'Donnell v. Roger Bullivant of Texas, Inc., 940 S.W.2d 411 (Tex. App. 1997)). The court upheld the jury's finding that the contractor's offer of settlement, which required the plaintiffs to pay forty percent of the repair costs (though with a promise of later reimbursement) and to execute a full release of all claims, was not reasonable. 33 S.W.3d at 383. Accordingly, the home owners could pursue a UDAP claim that sought types of damages not provided for by the Texas statute. *Id*. at 383, 384.

180   *See, e.g.*, Cal. Civ. Code § 901 (West) (prohibiting builder from limiting the building standards' protections through a limited warranty, though builder may offer greater protection); Cal. Civ. Code §§ 901–906 (West) ("enhanced protection agreement" provisions); *see also* Cafro v. Brophy, 62 Conn. App. 113, 774 A.2d 206, 212, 213 (2001) (purported disclaimer failed to meet statutory requirements and therefore was ineffective); Hughes v. Potter Homes, Inc., 53 Va. Cir. 416 (2000) (upholding disclaimer of warranty).

Page 593

181 *Add to Cafro citation: rev'd on other grounds*, 62 Conn. App. 113 (2001); *add: See, e.g.*, McKibben Constr., Inc. v. Longshore, 788 N.E.2d 452, 460 (Ind. Ct. App. 2003) (buyer's waiver of right to inspect home did not waive statutory implied warranty because waiver did not meet statute's requirements); Starfish Condo. Ass'n v. Yorkridge Serv. Corp., 458 A.2d 805, 810 (Md. 1983) ("as is" disclaimer that did not meet statutory requirements was ineffective); Latiuk v. Faber Constr. Co., 269 A.D.2d 820, 703 N.Y.S.2d 645 (2000) (when builder's express warranty did not meet or exceed standards provided by statutory warranty, defendant builder could not rely on the shorter period in its own warranty); Weiss v. Cassidy Dev. Corp., 2003 WL 1563425, at *6, *7 (Va. Cir. Ct. Feb. 21, 2003) (disclaimer ineffective).

Replace note 182 with:

182 *See* § 16.6.1, *infra.*

Addition to notes 183, 186, 187, 189.

183 McKibben Constr., Inc. v. Longshore, 788 N.E.2d 452, 460 (Ind. Ct. App. 2003) (disclaimer ineffective when builder did not produce evidence that it complied with the statute); Latiuk v. Faber Constr. Co., 703 N.Y.S.2d 645 (App. Div. 2000) (builder who failed to comply with statute's disclaimer provision did not effectively limit warranty); Speier v. Renaissance at Victoria Farms, Ltd. Liab. Co., 58 Va. Cir. 90, 2001 WL 1830005, at *2 (Dec. 3, 2001) (disclaimer that was not in enlarged type, as called for by statute, ineffective to limit statutory warranties).

186 *See* Terrace Condo. Ass'n v. Midwest Nat'l Bank, 633 A.2d 1060, 1066 (N.J. Super. Ct. Law Div. 1993) (warranty statute's durational periods did not affect plaintiff's implied warranty claims based on common law); Postizzi v. Leisure + Tech., Inc., 235 N.J. Super. 285, 562 A.2d 232, 234, 235 (Super. Ct. App. Div. 1989) (participation in informal conciliation proceeding was not an election of remedies under New Home Warranty Act that foreclosed home buyers from bringing suit against builder).

187 *Replace Louisiana statutory citation with*: La. Rev. Stat. Ann. § 9:3150 (West); *add: See also* Ory v. A.V.I. Constr., Inc., 848 So. 2d 115, 118–120 (La. Ct. App. 2003) (exclusive remedy).

189 *See, e.g.*, Squyres v. Nationwide Hous. Sys., Inc., 715 So. 2d 538 (La. Ct. App. 1998); Melancon v. Sunshine Constr., 712 So. 2d 1011, 1015 (La. Ct. App. 1998) (vandalism of floors was not a construction defect, therefore owners were not limited to statutory warranty claim); *add at end of note*: In such a case in Louisiana, a buyer may be able to state a claim under Louisiana's redhibition statute. La. Civ. Code Ann. art. 2520 (West); *see* Tarifa v. Riess, 856 So. 2d 21, 24, 25 (La. Ct. App. 2003) (holding termite damage was a redhibitory defect and finding vendors liable for difference between purchase price and home's actual value).

16.4.2 Condominium-Specific Statutes

Add to text at end of subsection:

While home buyers are not limited to New Jersey's statutory warranty, they must choose one of two mutually exclusive enforcement mechanisms: arbitration/conciliation under the statute or a lawsuit.[189.1] A plaintiff's ability to seek compensation in the courts after the New Home Warranty and Builders' Registration Act arbitration process has been completed is not clear.[189.2]

189.1 N.J. Admin. Code tit. 5, § 25-3.10; *see also* Yaroshefsky v. ADM Builders, Inc., 793 A.2d 25 (N.J. Super. Ct. App. Div. 2002); Nolan v. Homes by Brinkerhoff, Inc., 553 A.2d 392 (N.J. Super. Ct. Law Div. 1988) (home buyer did not elect remedy under warranty act by participating in conciliation with builder pursuant to private home owner warranty insurance program).

189.2 *See* Yaroshefsky v. ADM Builders, Inc., 793 A.2d 25, 33, 34 (N.J. Super. Ct. App. Div. 2002) (plaintiffs could pursue those remedies remaining once arbitration completed); Konieczny v. Micciche, 702 A.2d 831 (N.J. Super. Ct. App. Div. 1997) (though home buyers could not pursue additional relief against builder, exclusive remedy provision would not bar a negligence claim against home inspector for failing to discover defects); Spolitback v. Cyr Corp., 684 A.2d 1021 (N.J. Super. Ct. App. Div. 1996) (home buyer would not be held to have made preclusive choice to arbitrate those defects of which he was unaware at the time he submitted known claims); Rzepiennik v. U.S. Home Corp., 534 A.2d 89 (N.J. Super. Ct. App. Div. 1987) (New Home Warranty Program remedies exclusive as to defects claimed).

Page 594

Replace note 196 with:

196 Unif. Condo. Act § 4-114 cmt. 5; *see also* Park Ave. Condo. Owners Ass'n v. Buchan Developments, Ltd. Liab. Co., 117 Wash. App. 369, 380, 71 P.3d 692, 697 (2003) (statute's quality construction warranty broader than U.C.C.'s warranty of suitability).

Add to text after "Alabama,[200]" in first sentence of subsection's fourth paragraph:

Connecticut,[200.1]

200.1 Conn. Gen. Stat. § 47-74e (replacing Uniform Act's warranty provisions with a one year implied warranty of fitness and merchantability for roof, structural components, mechanical, electrical and plumbing systems, and other elements); *see also* Old Town Common Condo. Ass'n v. O Corp., 1990 WL 283756

(Conn. Super. Ct. Oct. 16, 1990); Greentree Condo. Ass'n v. RSP Corp., 415 A.2d 248 (Conn. Super. Ct. 1980) (condominium association could assert common law implied warranty claims; condominium statute's warranty not exclusive).

Addition to notes 201, 202.

201   *See also* Dunelawn Owners' Ass'n v. Gendreau, 750 A.2d 591 (Me. 2000) (interpreting statute of limitations to find condominium owners' implied warranty claims time-barred).

202   *See also* Hyland Hill N. Condo. Ass'n v. Hyland Hill Co., 549 N.W.2d 617, 623 (Minn. 1996) (breach of condominium act warranties governed by that statute's six year limitations period, not two year period applicable to other warranty claims); Chapman Place Ass'n v. Prokasky, 507 N.W.2d 858, 862, 863 (Minn. Ct. App. 1993) (association could recover damages attributable to breach of warranty for all units, even those that were purchased after defects appeared); Tara Hills Condo. Ass'n v. Gaughan, 399 N.W.2d 638, 642 (Minn. Ct. App. 1987) (developer's disclosure statement met statute's disclosure requirements by referring to statutory warranties without fully setting them forth).

Add to text after "form),[204]" in first sentence of subsection's fourth paragraph:

New Hampshire,[204.1]

204.1   N.H. Rev. Stat. Ann. § 356-B:41 (providing a one year warranty for structural defects); *see also* Gilmore v. Bradgate Associates, Inc., 1990 WL 614628 (D.N.H. July 27, 1990) (addressing limitations issue); Border Brook Terrace Condo. Ass'n v. Gladstone, 622 A.2d 1248 (N.H. 1993) (association had standing to sue for defects that arose prior to association's creation); Terren v. Butler, 597 A.2d 69 (N.H. 1991) (holding that six year limitations period applied to actions based on breach of statutory warranty).

Addition to notes 205, 206.

205   *See also* Roanoke Properties Ltd. P'ship v. Dewberry, 201 F.3d 437 (4th Cir. 1999) (table) (text available at 1999 WL 1032605, at *3) (N.C. law) (disclaimer of statutory warranties effective).

206   *See also* Pontiere v. James Dinert, Inc., 627 A.2d 1204 (Pa. Super. Ct. 1993) (upholding verdict that builder had breached both implied warranty of habitability and condominium statute's warranty).

Replace "and Vermont[208]" in first sentence of subsection's fourth paragraph with:

Vermont,[208] and Washington[208.1]

208   [*Retain as in main edition.*]

208.1   Wash. Rev. Code §§ 64.34.443 to 64.34.445; *see also* Park Ave. Condo. Owners Ass'n v. Buchan Developments, Ltd. Liab. Co., 117 Wash. App. 369, 376, 71 P.3d 692, 695 (2003) (holding that warranty disclaimer was ineffective when it did not comply with the statute's requirements, and that statutory warranty that construction was in compliance with all laws imposed liability for violation of building code, rejecting argument that violation had to be material, and affirming liability of builder for costs to repair improperly installed exterior insulation and finish system); Marina Cove Condo. Owners Ass'n v. Isabella Estates, 34 P.3d 870 (Wash. Ct. App. 2001) (warranty disclaimer could effectively limit warranty for defects not known at time of contracting); Eagle Point Condo. Owners Ass'n v. Coy, 9 P.3d 898 (Wash. Ct. App. 2000) (applying statute's warranty provision); Lanza v. Bd. of Directors of Providence Point Umbrella Ass'n, 2000 WL 264019, at *3 (Wash. Ct. App. Mar. 6, 2000) (pool was not a common element with respect to individual unit owner, therefore owner did not have standing to sue for breach of statutory warranty).

Addition to note 209.

209   *See also* Towers Tenant Ass'n v. Towers Ltd. P'ship, 563 F. Supp. 566 (D.D.C. 1983) (applying statute).

Add to text after "Columbia,[209]" in second sentence of subsection's fourth paragraph:

Florida,[209.1]

209.1   Fla. Stat. Ann. § 718.203 (West) (three year implied warranty of fitness and merchantability); *see also* Leisure Resorts, Inc. v. Frank J. Rooney, Inc., 654 So. 2d 911, 914 (Fla. 1995) (pursuant to statutory condominium warranty, contractor warranted that air conditioner would conform to generally accepted standards of workmanship and performance); Charley Toppino & Sons, Inc. v. Seawatch at Marathon Condo. Ass'n, 658 So. 2d 922 (Fla. 1994) (determining applicable limitations period); Stroshein v. Harbour Hall Inlet Club II Condo. Ass'n, 418 So. 2d 473, 474 (Fla. Dist. Ct. App. 1982) (upholding verdict that deteriorated tennis courts breached statutory condominium warranty).

Addition to notes 210–214.

210   *See also* Milton Co. v. Council of Unit Owners of Bentley Place Condo., 729 A.2d 981, 990, 991 (Md. 1999) (condominium association entitled to assert both statutory warranties applicable to condominiums and those applicable to newly constructed private dwellings); Antigua Condo. Ass'n v. Melba Investors Atl., Inc., 517 A.2d 75 (Md. 1986) (applying statute).

211   *See also* Gilmore v. Bradgate Associates, Inc., 1990 WL 614628 (D.N.H. July 27, 1990) (addressing limitations issue); Border Brook Terrace Condo. Ass'n v. Gladstone, 622 A.2d 1248 (N.H. 1993) (association had standing to sue for defects that arose prior to association's creation); Terren v. Butler, 597 A.2d 69 (N.H. 1991) (holding that six year limitations period applied to actions based on breach of statutory warranty).

212   *See also* Ohio Rev. Code Ann. § 5311.26 (West) (developer must disclose to potential purchasers warranties for structural elements and for mechanical and other systems); Wolf v. Southwestern Place Condo. Ass'n, 2002 WL 31163660 (Ohio Ct. App. Sept. 27, 2002) (holding that six year limitations period

applied to warranty claims arising under condominium statute); Fugo v. White Oak Condo. Ass'n, 1993 WL 317445 (Ohio Ct. App. Aug. 19, 1993) (applying statute); Springer v. Koehler Bros., 591 N.E.2d 316 (Ohio Ct. App. 1990) (awarding damages for developer's violation of disclosure provision); Kruse v. Holzer, 518 N.E.2d 961, 963, 964 (Ohio Ct. App. 1986) (prospective purchasers can receive damages for violation of disclosure provision, regardless of whether they ultimately purchase a unit).

213   *See also* Ass'n of Unit Owners of Bridgeview Condominiums v. Dunning, 187 Or. App. 595, 611, 612, 69 P.3d 788, 797, 798 (2003) (condominium association could bring action for breach of express warranties, citing Or. Rev. Stat. § 100.405).

214   *See also* Harbour Gate Owners' Ass'n v. Berg, 348 S.E.2d 252 (Va. 1986) (applying warranty, determining applicable limitations period).

Replace note 215 with:

215   *See also* Cal. Civ. Code § 1375 (West) (establishing pre-litigation dispute procedures for actions for damages brought against common interest development builders); Mass. Gen. Laws ch. 183B, § 46 (time share units only).

Addition to note 216.

216   *See, e.g.*, Park Ave. Condo. Owners Ass'n v. Buchan Developments, Ltd. Liab. Co., 117 Wash. App. 369, 377, 71 P.3d 695 (2003) (rejecting builder's argument that list of express warranties together with general disclaimers amounted to a list of specific disclaimers that satisfied the statute's requirements); *see also* Ass'n of Unit Owners of Bridgeview Condominiums v. Dunning, 187 Or. App. 595, 614, 69 P.3d 788, 799 (2003) (though condominium statute provides that the statutory warranty precludes an implied warranty of habitability, such preclusion only occurs when the declarant complies with the statute by providing warranties that conform to its terms; reversing dismissal of implied warranty claim).

Page 595

Add new subsection to text after § 16.4.3.

16.4.4 Home Warranty Programs

A seller or third party may provide a home warranty service agreement in connection with the sale of the home. One of the largest issuers of such agreements is the Home Owner's Warranty Corporation, which runs the HOW program through which participating home builders issue a "Home Warranty" to the initial purchaser of a home.[220.1] Such an agreement typically provides that the issuer promises to repair or replace any structural component or appliance in the home that fails for specified reasons, such as wear and tear; deterioration or defect; failure of an inspection to detect a defect; or substandard material or workmanship. Although, on the surface, the agreement may resemble the warranties implied by common law or statute, it more closely resembles a service agreement such as one might purchase with a new or used car. At least one jurisdiction has ruled that these service agreements are forms of insurance and that, therefore, the home buyers are entitled to all the protections that cover insureds, such as strict construction of the policy in favor of the insured.[220.2]

A handful of states regulate home warranty programs and those that issue home warranty service agreements.[220.3] Typically, such statutes require those who issue home warranty service agreements to obtain a license from the state[220.4] and to maintain a bond or some other form of security to secure performance under the warranty agreement.[220.5] Some states specifically define certain acts, such as false advertising of the program, to be unfair and deceptive acts or practices.[220.6] Most of these states do not require any specific protections to be included in the service agreements. Maryland, however, has enacted a comprehensive statute that requires such agreements to include, at a minimum, a five-year warranty against structural defects, a two-year warranty against defects in systems and appliances, and a one-year warranty against defects in materials and workmanship.[220.7]

Two states give consumers a ten-day period in which to cancel a home warranty agreement if the agreement was issued in connection with a loan.[220.8]

220.1   HOW Insurance Company and its subsidiary corporations, Home Warranty Corporation and Home Owner's Warranty Corporation, have been put into receivership by a Virginia court, and claims must now be filed with the deputy receiver, the Virginia Commissioner of Insurance. *See* Commonwealth of Virginia v. HOW Ins. Co., Case No. Ins 940218 (Va. State Corp. Comm'n Nov. 29, 1994) (directive of deputy receiver imposing suspension and moratorium). Additional information may be found at www.howcorp.com.

220.2   Riffe v. Home Finders Assocs., 205 W. Va. 216, 517 S.E.2d 313 (1999).

220.3   *See* Ariz. Rev. Stat. §§ 20-1095 to 20-1095.10; Colo. Rev. Stat. §§ 12-61-602 to 12-61-615 (applies to contracts issued with respect to pre-owned homes); Conn. Gen. Stat. § 38a-20 (defines home warranty service contract to be a form of insurance, but specifically excludes an agreement of a seller guaranteeing workmanship to a purchaser); Fla. Stat. Ann. §§ 634.301 to 634.348 (West); Md. Code Ann., Real Prop. §§ 10-604 to 10-610; Mass. Gen. Laws ch. 175, §§ 149F to 149L; Miss. Code Ann. §§ 83-57-1 to 83-57-79; N.J. Stat. Ann. §§ 46:3B-8 to 46:3B-20 (West); Okla. Stat. tit. 36, §§ 6601 to 6639; Or. Rev. Stat. §§ 3957.01 to 3957.99.

220.4 *See, e.g.*, Ariz. Rev. Stat. § 20-1095.01; Fla. Stat. Ann. § 634.306 (West); Mass. Gen. Laws ch. 175, § 149G; Miss. Code Ann. § 83-57-7; Okla. Stat. tit. 36, § 6604; Or. Rev. Stat. § 3957.02.

220.5 *See, e.g.*, Ariz. Rev. Stat. § 20-1095.03; Fla. Stat. Ann. § 634.305 (West); Md. Code Ann., Real Prop. § 10-606; Mass. Gen. Laws ch. 175, § 149I; Miss. Code Ann. § 83-57-13 (funding and reserve requirements); Okla. Stat. tit. 36, § 6606.

220.6 *See* Ariz. Rev. Stat. § 20-1095.09; Miss. Code Ann. § 83-57-99; Okla. Stat. tit. 36, §§ 6632, 6633.

220.7 Md. Code Ann., Real Prop. § 10-604; *see also* Or. Rev. Stat. § 3957.12 (requiring contract to specify the services to be performed, any fees, the period of the contract, that all services shall be rendered within a reasonable time, and any exclusions for defects existing prior to the date of the contract).

220.8 Fla Stat. Ann. § 634.345 (West); Miss. Code Ann. § 83-57-3.

16.5 Express Warranties

Addition to notes 222, 223, 225.

222 *But see* Everts v. Parkinson, 555 S.E.2d 667, 677 (N.C. Ct. App. 2001) (express warranty claims are governed by the U.C.C., which does not apply to sales of realty, therefore home buyers are limited to breach of contract claims, for breach of contractual warranty).

223 *But see* Farley v. Gary Nichols Builders, 2000 Ohio App. LEXIS 6172, at *9, *10 (Ohio Ct. App. Dec. 27, 2000) (as oral warranty contract could not be performed in less than a year, it fell within the statute of frauds and was not enforceable).

225 *See, e.g.*, Imperia v. Marvin Windows of N.Y., Inc., 747 N.Y.S.2d 35, 36 (App. Div. 2002) (brochure's language suggesting that special coating would extend life of window could create an express warranty, notwithstanding that warranty period was not precisely defined).

Add to text at end of section's first paragraph:

A statutory disclosure form may serve as an express warranty if it is incorporated into the purchase contract.[226.1]

226.1 McLellan v. Yeager, 2003 WL 354407, at *3, *4 (Ky. Ct. App. Feb. 14, 2003) (because disclosure form was incorporated into contract it created an express warranty notwithstanding statute's explicit provision that the form itself was not a warranty).

Add to text at end of section's second paragraph:

However, given that an express warranty is contractual, conditions placed on it, such as a requirement that the buyer notify the seller of a breach of the warranty within a specific period of time, will be enforced.[228.1]

228.1 *See, e.g.*, Dryvit Sys., Inc. v. Stein, 568 S.E.2d 569, 570 (Ga. Ct. App. 2002) (buyers lost benefit of warranty by failing to give required thirty day written notice); Albrecht v. Clifford, 767 N.E.2d 42, 45 (Mass. 2002) (express warranty claim barred by agreement's limitations period); Rothstein v. Equity Ventures, Ltd. Liab. Co., 750 N.Y.S.2d 625, 627, 628 (App. Div. 2002) (failure to provide notice of warranty claim precluded action); Allen v. Roberts Constr. Co., 138 N.C. App. 557, 532 S.E.2d 534, 543 (2000) (complaint that did not specifically allege that the house failed to meet the terms of the warranty was insufficient to meet the contractual requirement that buyers give notice of the breach within one year); *see also* Plymouth Pointe Condo. Ass'n v. Delcor Homes-Plymouth Pointe, Ltd., 2003 WL 22439654, at *4 (Mich. Ct. App. Oct. 28, 2003) (express warranty that limited warranty for defects in materials and workmanship for new condominium to one year was not unconscionable, even though part of an adhesion contract, when warranty was explained to each buyer and other buyers testified that they understood the terms of the warranty).

Page 596

Addition to notes 233, 235.

233 *See also* Ware v. Uhl, 2002 WL 1332775 (Iowa Ct. App. June 19, 2002) (statement that plumbing was "in working condition" could have created an express warranty).

235 *See also* Hartford Accident & Indem. Co. v. Scarlett Harbor Associates, Ltd., 674 A.2d 106 (Md. Ct. Spec. App. 1996) (addressing express warranties in contract for construction of condominium), *aff'd on other grounds*, 695 A.2d 153 (Md. 1997).

16.6 Defenses

16.6.1 As-Is, Disclaimers and Merger Doctrine

Addition to notes 237, 238.

237   *See, e.g.*, Brewer v. Poole Constr. Co., 13 Mass. L. Rptr. 97, 2001 Mass. Super. LEXIS 151, at *8, *9 (Super. Ct. May 3, 2001). *But see* Fennell v. Green, 77 P.3d 339, 345 (Utah Ct. App. 2003) (finding builder disclaimed implied warranty of habitability, but as Utah does not recognize such a warranty the case should not have much precedential effect).

238   *But see* Centex Homes v. Buecher, 95 S.W.3d 266 (Tex. 2002) (while warranty of habitability may only be waived as to defects that are fully disclosed, warranty of good workmanship may be waived when the agreement "provides sufficient detail on the manner and quality of the desired construction").

Replace note 239 with:

239   Crawford v. Whittaker Constr., Inc., 772 S.W.2d 819 (Mo. Ct. App. 1989); *see also* Norris v. Church & Co., 2001 WL 1301337, at *3 (Wash. Ct. App. Oct. 26, 2001) (warranty disclaimers are ineffectual unless parties explicitly negotiate them).

Add to text at end of subsection's second paragraph:

In Massachusetts the implied warranty may not be waived or disclaimed at all.[239.1]

239.1   Albrecht v. Clifford, 767 N.E.2d 42 (Mass. 2002).

Addition to notes 240–242, 244–246, 248, 254.

240   *But see* Bullington v. Palangio, 345 Ark. 320, 45 S.W.3d 834, 839 (Ark. 2001) (express warranty in a contract excludes an implied warranty on the same subject, but express warranty as to workmanship does not exclude implied warranties of habitability and proper construction).

241   Brevorka v. Wolfe Constr., Inc., 2003 WL 22518805 (N.C. Nov. 7, 2003) (limited warranty agreement that was separate from the contract with the builder did not supplant builder's warranties of habitability and workmanlike construction), *rev'g* 155 N.C. App. 353, 573 S.E.2d 656 (2002). *But see* Plymouth Pointe Condo. Ass'n v. Delcor Homes-Plymouth Pointe, Ltd., 2003 WL 22439654, at *2–*4 (Mich. Ct. App. Oct. 28, 2003) (one-year limit on express warranty against latent defects was not unconscionable).

242   Riverfront Lofts Condo. Owners Ass'n v. Milwaukee/Riverfront Properties Ltd. P'ship, 236 F. Supp. 2d 918 (E.D. Wis. 2002) (holding disclaimer ineffective); Hughes v. Potter Homes, Inc., 53 Va. Cir. 416, 418 (2000) (upholding disclaimer).

Page 597

244   *See, e.g.*, Bullington v. Palangio, 345 Ark. 320, 45 S.W.3d 834, 839 (Ark. 2001) (express warranty in a contract excludes an implied warranty on the same subject, but express warranty as to workmanship does not exclude implied warranties of habitability and proper construction).

245   Brevorka v. Wolfe Constr., Inc., 2003 WL 22518805 (N.C. Nov. 7, 2003) (disclaimer language that referenced implied warranties of merchantability and fitness for particular purpose did not disclaim warranties of habitability and workmanlike construction), *rev'g* 155 N.C. App. 353, 573 S.E.2d 656 (2002).

246   *Add to Buecher citation: aff'd on other grounds*, 95 S.W.3d 266 (Tex. 2002); *add: But see* Bynum v. Prudential Residential Services, Ltd. P'ship, 2003 WL 22456111, at *4, *5 (Tex. App. Oct. 30, 2003) ("as is" clause barred buyers from recovering for breach of an express warranty made prior to the sale).

248   *But see* Costello v. 44 Bliss Mine Road Prop., 1991 WL 789888 (R.I. Super. Ct. Sept. 6, 1991) (enforcing "as is" clause that specifically referenced inhabitability); Bynum v. Prudential Residential Services, Ltd. P'ship, 2003 WL 22456111, at *4, *5 (Tex. App. Oct. 30, 2003) (enforcing "as is" clause despite buyers' argument that it was "boilerplate," emphasizing buyers' sophistication and understanding of the clause, and their representation by a broker; holding clause barred buyers from recovering for breach of an express warranty and also for fraudulent misrepresentation when buyers could not show the defendants knew that their representation that remodeling work was done with proper permits was false).

Page 598

254   Coughlin v. Gustafson, 772 N.E.2d 864, 868, 869 (Ill. App. Ct. 2002) (merger doctrine did not extinguish express warranty in sales contract because warranty was independent from the deed's purpose of transferring title); Brewer v. Poole Constr. Co., 13 Mass. L. Rptr. 97, 2001 Mass. Super. LEXIS 151, at *9, *10 (Super. Ct. May 3, 2001) (doctrine of merger does not apply when seller promises to build on property sold); Davis v. Tazewell Place Associates, 492 S.E.2d 162, 165 (Va. 1997) (express warranty did not merge into deed because it did not pertain to title); Brown v. Johnson, 109 Wash. App. 56, 34 P.3d 1233 (2001) (when buyer's misrepresentation action did not relate to title or any other terms in the deed, merger doctrine did not preclude action). *But see* Albrecht v. Clifford, 767 N.E.2d 42, 51 (Mass. 2002) (paragraph describing conditions on which buyers could have refused to close purchase of home was not a warranty, did not survive buyers' acceptance of the deed).

16.6.2 Notice of Defects to the Builder

Addition to note 261.

261   Deckard v. Ratcliff, 553 N.E.2d 523, 523 (Ind. Ct. App. 1990) (before purchaser may seek damages under warranty statute, purchaser must notify builder of defect and give the builder an opportunity to repair it); Wagner Constr. Co. v. Noonan, 403 N.E.2d 1144, 1150 (Ind. Ct. App. 1980) (same).

16.7 Litigating New Home Breach of Warranty Cases

16.7.1 *Proof of Defects*

Page 599

Addition to note 265.

265   *See, e.g.*, Greene v. Perry, 62 Conn. App. 338, 771 A.2d 196, 199 (2001) (affirming judgment of negligence against home builder when court relied on testimony of a structural and civil engineer, a building contractor, and a building official with respect to defendant's breach of duty to exercise the degree of care applicable to a skilled builder); Wilkinson v. Dwiggins, 80 S.W.3d 849 (Mo. Ct. App. 2002); Mondelli v. Kendel Homes Corp., 262 Neb. 263, 631 N.W.2d 846, 854–857 (2001) (trial court erred in not permitting environmental toxicologist to testify regarding mold found in house); Mullen v. Byers, 2001 Ohio App. LEXIS 4414, at *8 (Ohio Ct. App. Sept. 28, 2001) (plaintiff presented two witnesses to testify regarding measures builder should have taken to deal with water hazard inherent in the building site).

Add note 265.1 at end of subsection's first paragraph.

265.1 *See, e.g.*, Sowers v. Dixie Shell Homes of Am., Inc., 762 So. 2d 186, 190 (La. Ct. App. 2000) (expert witness testimony supported court's finding that builder breached warranty); Thorn v. Caskey, 745 So. 2d 653, 661 (La. Ct. App. 1999) (expert testimony regarding roof structure's noncompliance with building code was sufficient to support finding that builder breached statutory warranty); Hartford Accident & Indem. Co. v. Scarlett Harbor Associates, Ltd., 674 A.2d 106, 126, 127 (Md. Ct. Spec. App. 1996) (plaintiffs needed expert testimony to support claims that elevator shaft's heating system was defective and that poor grading had resulted in water ponding, but not for claimed construction defect of excessive noise and vibration from HVAC system), *aff'd on other grounds*, 695 A.2d 153 (Md. 1997).

16.7.2 *Remedies*

16.7.2.2 Repair or Replacement

Addition to notes 268, 269.

268   *See, e.g.*, *In re* Gordon Urmson Builder & Sons, Inc., 295 B.R. 546, 551 (Bankr. W.D. Pa. 2003) (entering credit to buyers on trustee's claim for building contract sums); Plymouth Pointe Condo. Ass'n v. Delcor Homes-Plymouth Pointe, Ltd., 2003 WL 22439654, at *8 (Mich. Ct. App. Oct. 28, 2003) (proper measure of damages when defects are repairable is the cost of repair, regardless of defect's effect on fair market value of condominium); Mullen v. Byers, 2001 Ohio App. LEXIS 4414, at *9 (Ohio Ct. App. Sept. 28, 2001) (proper measure is the reasonable cost of placing the building in the condition the parties contemplated at the time of contract); Atrium Companies v. Bethke, 2002 WL 31892204 (Tex. App. Dec. 31, 2002) (upholding award of replacement costs supported by evidence of submitted bids); *see also* Klaiber v. Freemason Associates, Inc., 266 Va. 478, 487, 488, 587 S.E.2d 555, 560 (2003) (former condominium owners could claim damages from breach of warranty based on their continuing liability to purchasers for costs to repair units, as that was an appropriate measure of recoverable damages).

269   Forton v. Laszar, 239 Mich. App. 711, 609 N.W.2d 850 (2000) (trial court was entitled to select plaintiff's estimate of cost of repairs ($15,000) over defendant's ($4700)); Mullen v. Byers, 2001 Ohio App. LEXIS 4414 (Ohio Ct. App. Sept. 28, 2001).

16.7.2.6 Specific Performance and Rescission

Page 601

Addition to note 284.

284   *See, e.g.*, Henley v. Britton, 2003 WL 22271499, at *3 (Ark. Ct. App. Oct. 1, 2003) (affirming grant of rescission); Lanier Home Ctr., Inc. v. Underwood, 557 S.E.2d 76 (Ga. Ct. App. 2001) (affirming remedy of rescission when septic system failure rendered home uninhabitable); Overton v. Kingsbrooke Dev., Inc., 788 N.E.2d 1212, 1219 (Ill. App. Ct. 2003) (rescission an appropriate remedy for breach of warranty of habitability, rejecting vendor's argument that parties could not be returned to status quo on grounds that vendor was the party who had created that impossibility).

16.7.3 *Failure to Mitigate*

Addition to notes 286, 288.

286   *See, e.g.*, Callander v. Sheridan, 546 N.E.2d 850, 854 (Ind. Ct. App. 1989) (home buyers had no duty to make repairs that they could not afford); Ingraham v. Trowbridge Builders, 687 A.2d 785, 791, 792 (N.J. Super. Ct. App. Div. 1997) (builder did not sufficiently prove that buyers had failed to mitigate their damages).

288   Ingraham v. Trowbridge Builders, 687 A.2d 785, 791, 792 (N.J. Super. Ct. App. Div. 1997) (buyer was entitled to refuse builder's fourth attempt to repair defect when previous three repairs had failed).

Page 602

16.7.4 Consequential Damages

Add to text at end of subsection:

A plaintiff should also be able to recover as remedial damages any costs incurred in an attempt to repair the defect.[293.1]

293.1   *See, e.g.*, Mullen v. Byers, 2001 Ohio App. LEXIS 4414, at *11 (Ohio Ct. App. Sept. 28, 2001).

16.7.5 Attorney Fees

Replace note 298 with:

298   *See* § 11.1, *supra. See generally* National Consumer Law Center, Unfair and Deceptive Acts and Practices (5th ed. 2001 and Supp.).

16.8 Pleading Causes of Action

Replace note 302 with:

302   *See* National Consumer Law Center, Unfair and Deceptive Acts and Practices (5th ed. 2001 and Supp.).

Addition to notes 308, 313.

308   Beaux v. Jacob, 30 P.3d 90, 95 (Alaska 2001) (affirming judgment that home sellers negligently failed to fully disclose the proper use of sump pump on statutorily-required form); Coughlin v. Gustafson, 772 N.E.2d 864, 872 (Ill. App. Ct. 2002) (used home case); Barrett v. Akin Bldg. Ctr., 2002 WL 1973038, at *3 (Iowa Ct. App. Aug. 28, 2002) (upholding verdict that builder was negligent in constructing the house); Becker v. Graber Builders, Inc., 561 S.E.2d 905, 910 (N.C. Ct. App. 2002) (reversing dismissal of plaintiff's negligence claim based on inadequate septic system).

Page 603

313   *See, e.g.*, Becker v. Graber Builders, Inc., 561 S.E.2d 905, 910 (N.C. Ct. App. 2002); Norris v. Church & Co., 2001 WL 1301337, at *4, *5 (Wash. Ct. App. Oct. 26, 2001).

Chapter 16a
new chapter

Laws for Assistive Technological Devices

16a.1 Introduction

Lemon laws are not only applicable to cars. Numerous states have passed "wheelchair lemon laws," a misnomer because many such laws' coverage has been expanded beyond wheelchairs to include other types of devices intended to assist persons with disabilities in daily life activities. A more accurate description for these laws is assistive technological (AT) device warranty laws. These laws follow the classic motor vehicle lemon law model in that they provide consumers with certain remedies when an assistive device can not be fixed within a certain number of attempts or after a certain numbers of days. Many also include provisions which require that certain warranties be given on assistive devices.

Consumers with disabilities are a growing segment of the general population who are often adversely affected by defective or malfunctioning products. Many such consumers are sold assistive technological devices that fail to meet appropriate performance standards or that fail to operate as promised by the manufacturer or dealer. Moreover, purchasers of assistive technological devices often have limited choices for vendors or suppliers and thus they have little bargaining power when purchasing such devices.

With advances in technology, improved community inclusion, and increases in the number of persons with disabilities has come an increase in the number and types of assistive devices available in the marketplace. In addition, such devices are no longer limited to medical products. Examples of such devices include manual and motorized wheelchairs, seating and positioning aids, telephone communication devices for persons with hearing impairments (TTY devices), optical scanners, talking software, computers, and Braille printers.

The variety of such devices and the problems consumers have experienced with them due to some defect or other nonconformity has prompted a majority of states and Puerto Rico to pass Assistive Technological (AT) device warranty laws.[1] These laws have many similar general requirements,

but differ with respect to: scope of coverage; warranty requirements; procedures for obtaining repairs or replacements; and remedies. Only nine states (Alabama, Delaware, Illinois, Mississippi, New Hampshire, North Carolina, Tennessee, Texas, and Wyoming) and the District of Columbia have no AT device warranty law.[2]

This Chapter focuses on several components of AT device warranty laws, including the scope of coverage; how AT device lemons are defined; the types of warranties provided; who can bring claims; the remedies available; and potential defenses. While there is little case law under these statutes, decisions interpreting motor vehicle lemon laws are likely to be persuasive because of the similarities in the statutes.[3]

---

1 Alaska Stat. §§ 45.45.600 to 45.45.690 (Michie); Ariz. Rev. Stat. §§ 44-1351 to 44-1355; Ark. Code Ann. § 4-105-201 (Michie); Cal. Civ. Code §§ 1792.2, 1793.02, 1793.025 (West); Colo. Rev. Stat. §§ 6-1-401 to 6-1-412; Conn. Gen. Stat. §§ 42-330 to 42-336; Fla. Stat. Ann. §§ 427.801 to 427.806 (West);

Ga. Code Ann. §§ 10-1-870 to 10-1-875; Haw. Rev. Stat. §§ 481K-1 to 481K-6; Idaho Code §§ 48-1401 to 48-1407 (Michie); Ind. Code §§ 24-5-20-1 to 24-5-20-14; Iowa Code §§ 216E.1 to 216E.7; Kan. Stat. Ann. §§ 50-696 to 50-6,102; Ky. Rev. Stat. Ann. §§ 151B.300 to 151B.335 (Michie); La. Rev. Stat. Ann. §§ 51:2761 to 51:2767 (West); Me. Rev. Stat. Ann. tit. 10, §§ 1500 to 1500-F (West); Md. Code Ann., Com. Law §§ 14-2701 to 14-2706; Mass. Gen. Laws ch. 93, § 107; Mich. Comp. Laws §§ 445.1081 to 445.1087; Minn. Stat. §§ 325G.203 to 325G.208; Mo. Rev. Stat. §§ 407.950 to 407. 970; Mont. Code Ann. §§ 30-14-1201 to 30-14-1207; Neb. Rev. Stat. §§ 69-2601 to 69-2619; Nev. Rev. Stat. §§ 597.264 to 597.2667; N.J. Stat. Ann. §§ 56:12-75 to 56:12-86 (West); N.M. Stat. Ann. §§ 57-27-1 to 57-27-5 (Michie); N.Y. Gen. Bus. Law § 670 (McKinney); N.D. Cent. Code §§ 51-24-01 to 51-24-08; Ohio Rev. Code Ann. §§ 1345.90 to 1345.95 (West); Okla. Stat. tit. 15, §§ 910 to 910.5; Or. Rev. Stat. §§ 646.482 to 646.498; Pa. Stat. Ann. tit. 73, §§ 2231–2237 (West); 8 P.R. Laws Ann. §§ 851–859; R.I. Gen. Laws §§ 6-45-1 to 6-45-7; S.C. Code Ann. §§ 39-54-10 to 39-54-60 (Law. Co-op.); S.D. Codified Laws §§ 37-31-1 to 37-31-9 (Michie); Utah Code Ann. §§ 70A-2-801 to 70A-2-807; Vt. Stat. Ann. tit. 9, §§ 2467–2470; Va. Code. Ann. §§ 59.1-470 to 59.1-474 (Michie); Wash. Rev. Code §§ 19.184.010 to 19.184.060; W. Va. Code §§ 46A-6E-1 to 46A-6E-7; Wis. Stat. § 134.87.

2 Alabama, Delaware, the District of Columbia, New Hampshire, and North Carolina have modest protections for hearing aids only. *See* Ala. Code §§ 34-14-1 to 34-14-14 (licensing statute); Del. Code Ann. tit. 24, §§ 3701–3720 (licensing statute); D.C. Code Ann. § 28-4004 (thirty-day trial period); N.H. Rev. Stat. Ann. § 137-F:26 (thirty-day trial period); N.C. Gen. Stat. § 93D-3 (right to refund if consumer presents opinion of otolaryngologist that hearing can not be improved by hearing aid).

3 *See* Ch. 13, § 14.8, *supra*.

16a.2 Scope of Coverage

States differ as to how they define assistive technological devices. Each statute should be researched to determine the full scope of its coverage. Some states limit the definition to wheelchairs,[4] while others cover a host of devices, including wheelchairs, hearing aids, TTY devices, computer equipment, and Braille printers.[5] Others even include environmental control devices.[6] Michigan's law covers a used or refurbished wheelchair for a period of sixty days from the date of purchase.[7] California requires an implied warranty for all assistive devices, except for catalog sales, items costing less than fifteen dollars, and surgical implants.[8] Express warranties are required for new and used wheelchairs, except for those manufactured for competitive, athletic, or off-road use.[9]

A number of states exclude certain specificied types of medical devices from coverage under their statute.[10] In some states hearing aids or other assistive listening devices are specifically excluded from the definition.[11] This exclusion is likely due to pressure from the hearing aid industry. Batteries and "nonfunctional accessories" are also often excluded.[12] Some states also require that the AT device meet a minimum purchase price. For example, Utah's statute only covers devices which cost more than $1000 and are still under warranty.[13]

16a.3 Are AT Device Warranty Laws Preempted by Federal Law?

The Medical Device Amendments to the Food, Drug and Cosmetics Act require the Food and Drug Administration (FDA) to review and regulate medical devices.[14] Medical devices are subject to varying levels of review depending upon their classification. Class I devices, such as canes,[15] manually-operated wheelchairs,[16] and hearing aids that do not use bone conduction,[17] are subject only to minimal regulation by "general controls," which are general requirements for manufacturing, labeling, and so forth.[18] Class II devices, such as motorized wheelchairs[19] and hearing aids that use bone conduction,[20] must comply with federal performance standards known as "special controls."[21] Class III devices, which are potentially dangerous, are subject to the most rigorous level of review, and must go through a pre-market approval process or an equivalent procedure.[22] Almost all devices covered by AT warranty laws fall into either Class I or Class II.[23]

The Medical Device Amendments preclude the states from establishing or continuing in effect any requirement which is different from, or in addition to, any requirement applicable under the Act, and which relates to the safety or effectiveness of the device or to any other matter included in a requirement applicable to the device under the Act.[24] A number of cases have held that this provision preempts state warranty and tort claims involving Class III medical devices in at least some circumstances, as the review procedure

---

4 Mass. Gen. Laws ch. 93, § 107; N.J. Stat. Ann. § 56:12-75 (West); N.Y. Gen. Bus. Law § 670 (McKinney); Or. Rev. Stat. § 646.482 (includes scooters); Pa. Stat. Ann. tit. 73, § 2232 (West); Wis. Stat. § 134.87.

5 Alaska Stat. § 45.45.600 (Michie); Ariz. Rev. Stat. § 44-1351; Cal. Civ. Code § 1793.02 (West); Conn. Gen. Stat. § 42-330; Fla. Stat. Ann. § 427.802 (West); Idaho Code § 48-1402 (Michie); Minn. Stat. § 325G.203; Neb. Rev. Stat. § 69-2603; N.D. Cent. Code § 51-24-01; Ohio Rev. Code Ann. § 1345.90 (West); R.I. Gen. Laws § 6-45-1; S.C. Code Ann. § 39-54-20 (Law. Co-op.); S.D. Codified Laws § 37-31-1 (Michie); Utah Code Ann. § 70A-2-802; Vt. Stat. Ann. tit. 9, § 2467; Va. Code Ann. § 59.1-470 (Michie); W. Va. Code § 46A-6E-1.

6 Ariz. Rev. Stat. § 44-1351; Fla. Stat. Ann. § 427.802 (West); Idaho Code § 48-1402 (Michie); Minn. Stat. § 325G.203; Neb. Rev. Stat. § 69-2603; N.D. Cent. Code § 51-24-01; Ohio Rev. Code Ann. § 1345.90 (West); R.I. Gen. Laws § 6-45-1.

7 Mich. Comp. Laws § 445.1081.

8 *See* Cal. Civ. Code § 1793.02 (West); Fender v. Medtronic, Inc., 887 F. Supp. 1326 (E.D. Cal. 1995) (no cognizable claim against manufacturer of pacemaker based on exemption of surgical implant performed by physician or surgeon).

9 Cal. Civ. Code §§ 1791, 1792.2, 1793.02, 1793.025 (West).

10 Cal. Civ. Code § 1793.02 (West) (excludes surgical implant performed by a physician or surgeon and restoration or dental prosthesis provided by a dentist); Idaho Code § 48-1402(1) (Michie); Ind. Code § 24-5-20-2 (excluding surgical implants, dental or other prostheses, batteries, tires, and nonfunctional accessories); Iowa Code § 216E.1 (excluding any medical device, surgical device, or organ implanted or transplanted into or attached directly to an individual); Minn. Stat. § 325G.203(2) (excluding transcutaneous electrical nerve stimulator, neuromuscular electrical stimulator, or a dynamic range of motion splint, if the stimulator or splint is already covered by a warranty); N.D. Cent. Code § 51-24-01(1)(b) (excluding devices that are modified, hearing instruments, eyeglasses, surgical implant performed by physician or surgeon, or a restoration by dentist); Ohio Rev. Code Ann. § 1345.90 (West) (excluding an invasive or non-invasive medical device that attempts to treat a medical condition or a hearing aid).

11 *See, e.g.,* Idaho Code § 48-1402 (Michie); N.D. Cent. Code § 51-24-01; Ohio Rev. Code Ann. § 1345.90 (West).

12 *See, e.g.,* La Rev. Stat. Ann. § 51:2762 (West).

13 Utah Code Ann. § 70A-2-802.

14 Medical Device Amendments of 1976, Pub. L. No. 94-295, 90 Stat. 539 (codified in scattered sections of 21 U.S.C. §§ 301–395).

15 21 C.F.R. § 890.3075.

16 21 C.F.R. § 890.3850.

17 21 C.F.R. § 874.330.

18 21 U.S.C. § 360c(a)(1)(A).

19 21 C.F.R. §§ 890.3860, 890.3800, 880.3900.

20 21 C.F.R. § 874.330.

21 21 U.S.C. § 360c(a)(1)(B).

22 21 U.S.C. § 360c(a)(1)(C); *see* Medtronic, Inc. v. Lohr, 518 U.S. 470, 116 S. Ct. 2240, 135 L. Ed. 2d 700 (1996).

23 One exception is stair-climbing wheelchairs, which are classified as Class III. 21 C.F.R. § 890.3890.

24 21 U.S.C. § 360k(a).

which such a device must go through produces specific and detailed requirements regulating the device.[25] The Supreme Court, however, has held that the Medical Device Amendments only preempt state requirements that conflict with a specific federal requirement.[26] The Court also held that the FDA's general regulations concerning labeling and good manufacturing practices were too generic to preempt state claims raised with respect to a Class III device that had gone through an abbreviated form of review.[27] Because Class I and Class II devices are mostly subject to generic requirements and do not go through the FDA review process that generates specific requirements, it is unlikely that there will be grounds for preemption of state claims concerning such devices.[28]

16a.4 What Is an AT Device Lemon?

As with automobiles, a "lemon" in the context of assistive technological devices usually means a device that fails to work and requires a certain number of repair attempts be made within a stated time period. The time period and number of repairs necessary to trigger a claim varies from state to state.[29] Some state AT device warranty laws require

two repair attempts, with the device being out of service for at least thirty days.[30] Others require three repair attempts and thirty days during which the device is out of service.[31] In Montana only two repair attempts are required, but the device must be out of service for forty-five days.[32] New Jersey requires that the device be out of service for only twenty days.[33] In Massachusetts a consumer must show four repair attempts or that the wheelchair was out of service for thirty days during the warranty period in order to assert a claim.[34]

16a.5 Warranties Under AT Device Lemon Laws

Warranties provided by AT device lemon laws also vary. Most provide for a one-year express warranty and require the repair of any defect at no cost to the consumer. In some states the period may be tolled based on the number of days the device is out of service or being repaired.[35] Alaska's law requires a warranty that the "device is free from any nonconformity."[36] If the nonconforming device is made available through the dealer, lessor, or manufacturer, it must be repaired and the manufacturer must pay "collateral costs" incurred by the consumer.[37] Arizona provides that, in the absence of an express warranty, the manufacturer is deemed

---

25 *See* § 1.4.9, *supra.*

26 Medtronic, Inc. v. Lohr, 518 U.S. 470, 495, 501, 116 S. Ct. 2240, 135 L. Ed. 2d 700 (1996). The FDA also takes a narrow view of the preemptive scope of the statute. 21 C.F.R. § 808.1(d).

27 Medtronic, Inc. v. Lohr, 518 U.S. 470, 500–503, 116 S. Ct. 2240, 135 L. Ed. 2d 700 (1996). This holding is in Part V of the plurality opinion, which commanded a majority of the Court.

28 A number of cases prior to *Lohr* dealt with preemption of claims regarding Class I and Class II devices, and most rejected preemption. *See* Kealoha v. E.I. du Pont de Nemours & Co., 82 F.3d 894 (9th Cir. 1996) (no preemption when FDA had not issued regulations relating to safety or efficiency of Class II device); Anguiano v. E.I. du Pont de Nemours & Co., 44 F.3d 806 (9th Cir. 1995) (same); La Montagne v. E.I. du Pont de Nemours & Co., 41 F.3d 846 (2d Cir. 1994) (no preemption when FDA had no regulations specific to Class II device). Because *Lohr* took a narrow view of preemption under the Medical Device Amendments, cases finding preemption, such as the following, are of doubtful precedential value: Maslar v. Johnson & Johnson Prof'l, Inc., 1996 WL 162302 (E.D. Pa. Apr. 4, 1996) (preemption applies to claims concerning manufacturing defects for Class II device that was subject to general regulations concerning good manufacturing practices, but not design defects; because *Lohr* held that the good manufacturing practice regulations were not specific enough to preempt state claims concerning a Class III device, this holding is no longer good law); Bateman v. Gen. Med. Corp., 29 Pa. D. & C.4th 1 (Pa. C.P. Mar. 1, 1996) (claims regarding Class I device not preempted except those that relate to inadequate labeling, as FDA regulated labeling specifically; because *Lohr* held that general labeling requirements did not preempt state claims concerning a Class III device, this holding is no longer good law).

29 Alaska Stat. § 45.45.620 (Michie); Ariz. Rev. Stat. § 44-1351(12)(a), (b); Ark. Code Ann. § 4-105-201 (Michie); Cal. Civ. Code § 1793.025 (West); Colo. Rev. Stat. § 6-1-402; Conn.

Gen. Stat. § 42-331(d); Fla. Stat. Ann. § 427.802(12)(a), (b) (West); Ga. Code Ann. § 10-1-871(11)(a), (b); Haw. Rev. Stat. § 481K-3(b)(3); Idaho Code § 48-1402(12)(a), (b) (Michie); Ind. Code § 24-5-20-09; Iowa Code § 216E.1(12)(a), (b); Kan. Stat. Ann. § 50-696(k)(1), (2); Ky. Rev. Stat. Ann. § 151B.300(12)(a), (b) (Michie); La. Rev. Stat. Ann. § 51:2762(11) (West); Me. Rev. Stat. Ann. tit. 10, § 1500-C (West); Md. Code Ann., Com. Law § 14-2701(*l*)(1), (2); Mass. Gen. Laws ch. 93, § 107(A)(1); Mich. Comp. Laws § 445.1081(i); Minn. Stat. § 325G.203(12); Mo. Rev. Stat. § 407.950(11)(a), (b); Mont. Code Ann. § 30-14-1205; Neb. Rev. Stat. §§ 69-2601 to 69-2619; Nev. Rev. Stat. § 597.266(1)(a), (b); N.J. Stat. Ann. § 56:12-78 (West); N.M. Stat. Ann. § 57-27-2(K)(1), (2) (Michie); N.Y. Gen. Bus. Law § 670 (McKinney); N.D. Cent. Code § 51-24-01(8)(a), (b); Ohio Rev. Code Ann. § 1345.91(C)(1), (2) (West); Okla. Stat. tit. 15, § 910.1(11)(a), (b); Or. Rev. Stat. § 646.482(15)(a); Pa. Stat. Ann. tit. 73, § 2232 (West); 8 P.R. Laws Ann. § 851(8)(a)–(c); R.I. Gen. Laws § 6-45-4(a); S.C. Code Ann. § 39-54-20(12)(a), (b) (Law. Co-op.); S.D. Codified Laws § 37-31-1(11)(a), (b) (Michie); Utah Code Ann. § 70A-2-804(3)(a); Vt. Stat. Ann. tit. 9, § 2467(12)(a), (b); Va. Code. Ann. § 59.1-470 (Michie); Wash. Rev. Code § 19.184.010(8)(a), (b); W. Va. Code § 46A-6E-1(m)(1), (2); Wis. Stat. § 134.87(k)(1), (2).

30 *See, e.g.*, Ariz. Rev. Stat. § 44-1351.

31 *See, e.g.*, Col. Rev. Stat. § 6-1-402; Conn. Gen. Stat. § 42-330; Fla. Stat. Ann. § 427.804 (West).

32 Mont. Code Ann. § 30-14-1205.

33 N.J. Stat. Ann. § 56:12-75 (West).

34 Mass. Gen. Laws ch. 93, § 107.

35 *See, e.g.*, Haw. Rev. Stat. § 481K-6.

36 Alaska Stat. § 45.45.600 (Michie).

37 Alaska Stat. § 45.45.600 (Michie).

to have expressly warranted that the device will be free from a defect, malfunction, or condition that substantially impairs the use, safety, or value of the device.[38] If the device is made available through the manufacturer, the manufacturer must repair it at no charge.[39] Maine mandates an implied warranty that the device is fit for the particular needs of the buyer.[40] Florida's law requires a one-year express warranty that the device is free from any condition or defect that substantially impairs the value of the device.[41] Any nonconformity must be repaired without charge to the consumer.[42] Louisiana's law provides that the manufacturer must give a one-year express warranty and that the manufacturer, lessor, or dealer must attempt to repair nonconformities.[43] If the repairs take more than ten days, or the defect was subject to two prior repair attempts, the manufacturer must provide a loaner device or a replacement allowance of up to $20.00 per day.[44]

Some AT device lemon law warranties depend on the type of device involved or take into account the buyer's particular needs. For example, Colorado requires a six-month warranty on new wheelchairs if there are dealer modifications and a ninety-day warranty on specialty control modules.[45] In Georgia, the AT device lemon law requires a one-year warranty that the device has no defect.[46] The manufacturer must correct any nonconformity. Additionally, if the manufacturer or dealer recommends a particular device it may be returned within thirty days if it does not meet the needs of the consumer.[47] In Puerto Rico, the manufacturer, supplier, or lessor must install equipment and provide training for the consumer on the use and handling of the device.[48]

Maryland's AT device lemon law provides that warranty rights thereunder are not limited by Article 2A of the UCC.[49] Many states also prohibit waiver of these warranties.[50]

16a.6 Who Can Bring Claims Under AT Device Warranty Laws?

Nearly all AT device warranty law statutes cover those who acquire, purchase, lease, or have the ability to enforce the warranty on the device.[51] Some states also cover the agent for the purchaser or lessor.[52] In Virginia, only persons with disabilities, as the term is defined under the Americans with Disabilities Act,[53] or their legal representatives may bring claims. Virginia also covers any entity that purchases or leases an assistive device for a person with a disability using state or federal funds.[54]

It is very common for insurance companies and for state and federal agencies like Medicaid or Medicare to purchase AT devices for persons with disabilities. This practice may cause some defendants to question whether the user of an AT device purchased by Medicaid or Medicare has standing to bring a claim based on a defect or some other nonconformity. There is no case law on this issue under any state AT device lemon law, but the issue has been addressed by the Wyoming Supreme Court based on claims under Wyoming's Uniform Commercial Code.[55] In the Wyoming case, the plaintiff was a recipient of Medicaid whose nursing services provider sold her a custom-made wheelchair. Medicaid purchased the wheelchair from the provider for the benefit of the plaintiff. The plaintiff brought claims against the provider under the Wyoming UCC for breach of contract and breach of warranty, as well as a separate negligence claim. When the plaintiff filed suit, the provider asserted that

---

38 Ariz. Rev. Stat. § 44-1352.

39 Ariz. Rev. Stat. § 44-1352.

40 Me. Rev. Stat. Ann. tit. 10, § 1500-A (West).

41 Fla. Stat. Ann. § 427.803 (West).

42 Fla. Stat. Ann. § 427.803 (West).

43 La. Rev. Stat. Ann. § 51:2763 (West).

44 La. Rev. Stat. Ann. § 51:2763 (West).

45 Colo. Rev. Stat. § 6-1-403.

46 Ga. Code Ann. §§ 10-1-872, 10-1-892.

47 Ga. Code Ann. §§ 10-1-872, 10-1-892.

48 8 P.R. Laws Ann. § 854.

49 Md. Code Ann., Com. Law § 14-2704.

50 *See* Alaska Stat. § 45.45.660 (Michie); Ariz. Rev. Stat. § 44-1355(B); Cal. Civ. Code § 1793.02 (West); Colo. Rev. Stat. § 6-1-408; Conn. Gen. Stat. § 42-336; Fla. Stat. Ann. § 427.805 (West); Ga. Code Ann. § 10-1-875; Haw. Rev. Stat. § 481K-5(b); Idaho Code § 48-1407(3) (Michie); Iowa Code § 216E.6; Ky. Rev. Stat. Ann. § 151B.330 (Michie); La. Rev. Stat. Ann. § 51:2767 (West); Me. Rev. Stat. Ann. tit. 10, § 1500-F (West); Md. Code Ann., Com. Law § 14-2704(b); Mass. Gen. Laws ch. 93, § 107(E); Mich. Comp. Laws § 445.1087; Minn. Stat. § 325G.207; Mont. Code Ann. § 14-1207(2); N.J. Stat. Ann. § 56:12-84 (West); N.Y. Gen. Bus. Law § 670 (McKinney); N.D. Cent. Code § 51-24-08; Ohio Rev. Code Ann. § 1345.95 (West); Okla. Stat. tit. 15, § 910.5; Pa. Stat. Ann. tit. 73, § 2236 (West); R.I. Gen. Laws § 6-45-7; Utah Code Ann. § 70A-2-807; Va.

Code Ann. § 59.1-474 (Michie); Wash. Rev. Code § 19.184.050; W. Va. Code § 46A-6E-7; Wis. Stat. § 134.87.

51 Ariz. Rev. Stat. § 44-1351; Ark. Code Ann. § 4-105-201 (Michie); Cal. Civ. Code § 1791 (West); Colo. Rev. Stat. § 6-1-402; Conn. Gen. Stat. § 42-330; Fla. Stat. Ann. § 427.802 (West); Ga. Code Ann. § 10-1-871; Haw. Rev. Stat. § 481K-1; Idaho Code § 48-1402 (Michie); Ind. Code § 24-5-20-4; Iowa Code § 216E.1; Kan. Stat. Ann. § 50-696; Ky. Rev. Stat. Ann. § 151B.300 (Michie); La. Rev. Stat. Ann. § 51:2762 (West); Me. Rev. Stat. Ann. tit. 10, § 1500 (West); Md. Code Ann., Com. Law § 14-2701; Mass. Gen. Laws ch. 93, § 107; Mich. Comp. Laws § 445.1081; Minn. Stat. § 325G.203; Mo. Rev. Stat. § 407.950; Mont. Code Ann. § 30-14-1202; Neb. Rev. Stat. § 69-2607; Nev. Rev. Stat. § 597.264; N.J. Stat. Ann. § 56:12-75 (West); N.M. Stat. Ann. § 57-27-1 (Michie); N.Y. Gen. Bus. Law § 670 (McKinney); N.C. Gen. Stat. § 93D-3; N.D. Cent. Code § 51-24-01; Ohio Rev. Code Ann. § 1345.90 (West); Okla. Stat. tit. 15, § 910; Or. Rev. Stat. § 646.482; Pa. Stat. Ann. tit. 73, § 2231 (West); 8 P.R. Laws Ann. § 851; R.I. Gen. Laws § 6-45-1; S.C. Code Ann. § 39-54-10 (Law. Co-op.); S.D. Codified Laws § 37-31-1 (Michie); Utah Code Ann. § 70A-2-801; Vt. Stat. Ann. tit. 9, § 2467; Va. Code Ann. § 59.1-470 (Michie); Wash. Rev. Code § 19.184.010; W. Va. Code § 46A-6E-1; Wis. Stat. § 134.87.

52 *See, e.g.*, La. Rev. Stat. Ann. § 51:2762 (West).

53 Va. Code. Ann. § 59.1-470 (Michie).

54 Va. Code. Ann. § 59.1-470 (Michie).

55 Kirby v. NMC/Continue Care, 993 P. 2d 951 (Wyo. 1999) (Wyoming has no state AT device warranty law).

the plaintiff was not a "buyer" under Wyoming's UCC and prevailed in the trial court. However, the Wyoming Supreme Court reversed the trial court, finding that the plaintiff, who allocated her limited Medicaid benefits for the purchase of the wheelchair, was a "buyer," even though the payment came directly from Medicaid.[56] The court concluded that it was inconsequential that the actual payment came from Medicaid and not the plaintiff.[57]

16a.7 Remedies for Consumers

16a.7.1 Remedies Provided by AT Device Warranty Laws

In addition to providing rights to repairs, returns, and refunds, many AT device warranty laws provide for private enforcement and the right to recover pecuniary damages, costs, and attorney fees.[58] Many also provide for multiple pecuniary damages and equitable relief.[59] In addition, many AT device warranty laws do not limit the consumers' rights under other statutes, and some specifically provide that a violation of the state AT device warranty law also constitutes a violation of its UDAP law.[60]

16a.7.2 Affirmative Defenses

Affirmative defenses are included in some of the AT device warranty laws. These include exclusions from coverage of any condition or defect that is caused by abuse or alteration of the device by the consumer,[61] including neglect.[62] In Maine it is also an affirmative defense if the seller did not know of the intended use of the device.[63] Nebraska's AT device lemon law does not apply if the defect or condition is the result of abuse, neglect, or unauthorized modification or alteration by the consumer, or if the condition is the result of normal use, which could be resolved through appropriate adjustments, proper care, and cleaning.[64]

Pleading claims for violations of AT device warranty laws should be carefully considered, especially if additional claims are made. For example, some state products liability statutes contain exclusivity provisions, precluding other claims, including negligence, strict liability, and warranty for harm caused by a product.[65] A Connecticut trial court held that the exclusivity provision in its products liability statute precludes all common law and statutory claims that are co-extensive with or functionally equivalent to the product liability claim. It concluded that an unfair and deceptive practices claim for personal injuries caused by a defective wheelchair could not be brought along with a products liability claim.[66]

16a.7.3 Prohibitions and Limitations on Laundering of AT Device Lemons

Many states specifically prohibit the laundering of AT device lemons. Most AT device warranty laws state that a returned device may not be resold or leased without full disclosure of the reasons for the return of the device.[67] Such

---

56 *Id.*

57 *Id.* at 953.

58 Alaska Stat. § 45.45.680 (Michie); Ariz. Rev. Stat. § 44-1351; Ark. Code Ann. § 4-105-206 (Michie); Cal. Civ. Code § 1793.02 (West); Colo. Rev. Stat. § 6-1-410; Conn. Gen. Stat. § 42-335; Fla. Stat. Ann. § 427.806 (West); Ga. Code Ann. § 10-1-878; Haw. Rev. Stat. § 481K-5; Idaho Code § 48-1407 (Michie); Ind. Code § 24-5-20-13; Iowa Code § 216E.6; Kan. Stat. Ann. § 50-6,101; Ky. Rev. Stat. Ann. § 151B.330 (Michie); La. Rev. Stat. Ann. § 51:2767 (West); Me. Rev. Stat. Ann. tit. 10, § 1500-E (West); Md. Code Ann., Com. Law § 14-2705; Mass. Gen. Laws ch. 93, § 107(F); Mich. Comp. Laws § 445.1087; Minn. Stat. § 325G.207; Mo. Rev. Stat. § 407.967; Mont. Code Ann. § 30-14-1207; Neb. Rev. Stat. § 69-2616; Nev. Rev. Stat. § 597.2665; N.J. Stat. Ann. § 56:12-85 (West); N.M. Stat. Ann. § 57-27-5 (Michie); N.Y. Gen. Bus. Law § 670 (McKinney); N.D. Cent. Code § 51-24-08; Ohio Rev. Code Ann. § 1345.09 (West); Okla. Stat. tit. 15, § 910.5; Or. Rev. Stat. § 646.498; Pa. Stat. Ann. tit. 73, § 2237 (West); 8 P.R. Laws Ann. § 855; R.I. Gen. Laws § 6-45-7; S.C. Code Ann. § 39-54-60 (Law. Co-op.); S.D. Codified Laws § 37-31-7 (Michie); Utah Code Ann. § 70A-2-807; Vt. Stat. Ann. tit. 9, § 2470(j); Va. Code. Ann. § 59.1-473 (Michie); Wash. Rev. Code § 19.184.060; W. Va. Code § 46A-6E-6; Wis. Stat. § 134.87.

59 Alaska Stat. § 45.45.680 (Michie); Fla. Stat. Ann. § 427.806 (West); Ga. Code Ann. § 10-1-875; Haw. Rev. Stat. § 481K-5; Idaho Code § 48-1407 (Michie); Iowa Code § 216E.6; N.Y. Gen. Bus. Law § 670 (McKinney); Or. Rev. Stat. § 646.498; S.D. Codified Laws § 37-31-7 (Michie); Wash. Rev. Code § 19.184.060; W. Va. Code § 46A-6E-7.

60 Haw. Rev. Stat. § 481K-5; Md. Code Ann., Com. Law § 14-2705.

61 N.D. Cent. Code § 51-24-01.

62 Ariz. Rev. Stat. § 44-1351(11); Ark. Code Ann. § 4-105-201(11) (Michie); Colo. Rev. Stat. § 6-1-401; Conn. Gen. Stat. §§ 743q, 42-330; Ga. Code Ann. § 10-1-871; Idaho Code § 48-1402 (Michie); Iowa Code § 216E.1; Kan. Stat. Ann. § 50-696; La. Rev. Stat. Ann. § 51:2762 (West); Mont. Code Ann. § 30-14-1202; Utah Code Ann. § 70A-2-802.

63 Me. Rev. Stat. Ann. tit. 10, §§ 1500 to 1500-F (West).

64 Neb. Rev. Stat. § 69-2603.

65 Conn. Gen. Stat. § 52-572n(a).

66 Fitzgerald v. Pawtuxet Valley Prescription & Surgical, Inc., 2002 WL 31662341 (Conn. Super. Ct. Nov. 7, 2002) (unpublished).

67 Alaska Stat. § 45.45.650 (Michie); Ariz. Rev. Stat. § 44-1351; Cal. Civ. Code § 1794 (West); Colo. Rev. Stat. § 6-1-407; Conn. Gen. Stat. § 42-333; Fla. Stat. Ann. § 427.804 (West); Ga. Code Ann. § 10-1-873; Haw. Rev. Stat. § 481K-4; Idaho Code § 48-1405 (Michie); Ind. Code § 24-5-20-12; Iowa Code § 216E.5; Kan. Stat. Ann. § 50-699; Ky. Rev. Stat. Ann. § 151B.300 (Michie); La. Rev. Stat. Ann. § 51:2765 (West); Me. Rev. Stat. Ann. tit. 10, § 1500-D (West); Md. Code Ann., Com.

provisions are intended to prevent defective devices from being passed on to unsuspecting consumers.

16a.7.4 Other Causes of Action

In addition to claims under state AT device warranty laws, there are many other causes of action consumer advocates can bring on behalf of consumers with disabilities who have

Law § 14-2703(h); Mass. Gen. Laws ch. 93, § 107; Mich. Comp. Laws § 445.1086; Minn. Stat. § 325G.206; Mo. Rev. Stat. § 407.963; Mont. Code Ann. § 30-14-1204; Neb. Rev. Stat. § 69-2604; Nev. Rev. Stat. § 597.263; N.J. Stat. Ann. § 56:12-82 (West); N.M. Stat. Ann. § 57-27-3 (Michie); N.Y. Gen. Bus. Law § 670 (McKinney); N.D. Cent. Code § 51-24-07; Ohio Rev. Code Ann. § 1345.93 (West); Okla. Stat. tit. 15, § 910.4; Or. Rev. Stat. § 646.492; Pa. Stat. Ann. tit. 73, § 2234 (West); 8 P.R. Laws Ann. § 852; R.I. Gen. Laws § 6-45-6; S.C. Code Ann. § 39-54-40 (Law. Co-op.); S.D. Codified Laws § 37-31-8 (Michie); Utah Code Ann. § 70A-2-806; Vt. Stat. Ann. tit. 9, § 2470(f); Va. Code. Ann. § 59.1-472 (Michie); Wash. Rev. Code § 19.184.03; W. Va. Code § 46A-6E-5; Wis. Stat. § 134.87.

devices that are defective or do not perform as promised. These would include claims under Article 2 of the UCC, the Magnuson-Moss Warranty Act,[68] and other traditional warranty claims.

Unfair and deceptive acts and practices (UDAP) claims may be important in cases involving AT devices. In addition, UDAP statutes prohibit oral deception, failure to disclose material information, and other related practices. UDAP claims are not dependent on other claims but may be stand-alone claims based on the deceptive practices of the dealer or manufacturer. Some states also provide that a violation of their AT device lemon law is a UDAP violation.[69] For further discussion of UDAP claims see NCLC's *Unfair and Deceptive Acts and Practices* manual.[70]

68 *See* Ch. 2, *supra*.
69 Haw. Rev. Stat. § 481K-5; Md. Code Ann., Com. Law § 14-2705.
70 National Consumer Law Center, Unfair and Deceptive Acts and Practices (5th ed. 2001 and Supp.).

Chapter 17

Automobile Repair, Home Improvements, and Other Services

17.2 Applicability of UCC Article 2 and Magnuson-Moss Warranty Act to Service Transactions

17.2.2 UCC Article 2 Applicability

Addition to notes 5, 10.

5   *See, e.g.,* Smith v. Skone & Connors Produce, Inc., 107 Wash. App. 199, 26 P.3d 981 (2001) (agreement to harvest, clean, pack and sell agricultural produce on commission is a service contract).

10   *Replace entire Rosetti citation with*: Rossetti v. Busch Entm't Corp., 87 F. Supp. 2d 415, 40 U.C.C. Rep. Serv. 2d 960 (E.D. Pa. 2000).

17.2.3 UCC Applicability by Analogy

Addition to note 12.

12   *E.g.,* Group One, Ltd. v. Hallmark Cards, Inc., 254 F.3d 1041, 45 U.C.C. Rep. Serv. 2d 88 (Fed. Cir. 2001) (U.C.C. useful, although not authoritative, in patent dispute); Emerson Radio Corp. v. Orion Sales, Inc., 253 F.3d 159, 44 U.C.C. Rep. Serv. 2d 681 (3d Cir. 2001) (applying U.C.C. definition of good faith to trademark licensing agreement); Clark v. Orkin Exterminating Co., 147 F. Supp. 2d 458 (W.D. Va. 2001) (analogizing to U.C.C. and relying on public policy to disregard clauses that immunize seller of services from breach of common law warranties); Mitsui O.S.K. Lines v. Consol. Rail Corp., 327 N.J. Super. 343, 743 A.2d 362, 43 U.C.C. Rep. Serv. 2d 897 (Super. Ct. App. Div. 2000) (Pa. law); Smith v. Skone & Connors Produce, Inc., 107 Wash. App. 199, 26 P.3d 981 (2001) (following U.C.C. as guidance on definition of written contract).

17.3 UCC Applicability to Mixed Goods and Services Transactions

17.3.1 Introduction

Add to text at end of subsection:

Whether goods or services predominate in a mixed transaction is a question of fact.[13.1]

13.1   Busch v. Dyno Nobel, Inc., 48 U.C.C. Rep. Serv. 2d 874 (6th Cir. 2002) (unpublished) (Mich. law).

17.3.3 Does the UCC Apply to the Service Component if Sale of Services Is Predominant Purpose?

Add note 22.1 at end of subsection's first sentence.

22.1   IMI Norgren Inc. v. D & D Tooling & Mfg., Inc., 2003 WL 21501783 (N.D. Ill. June 25, 2003) (contract to apply heat treatment to machine parts was predominantly services so UCC does not apply).

17.3.4 Does UCC Apply to Incidental Services Where Goods Component Predominates?

Addition to notes 37, 38.

37   Richard A. Rosenblatt & Co. v. Davidge Data Sys. Corp., 295 A.D.2d 168, 743 N.Y.S.2d 471, 47 U.C.C. Rep. Serv. 2d 1390 (2002); *see also* Busch v. Dyno Nobel, Inc., 48 U.C.C. Rep. Serv. 2d 874 (6th Cir. 2002) (unpublished) (Mich. law) (applying U.C.C. to transaction as a whole when goods predominate); ePresence, Inc. v. Evolve Software, Inc., 190 F. Supp. 2d 159, 47 U.C.C. Rep. Serv. 2d 132 (D. Mass. 2002)

(applying U.C.C. to entire contract when goods predominated); Analysts Int'l Corp. v. Recycled Paper Products, Inc., 45 U.C.C. Rep. Serv. 2d 747, 1987 WL 12917 (N.D. Ill. June 19, 1987) (Illinois uses dominant purpose test for contracts involving both goods and services); Hensley v. Ray's Motor Co., 580 S.E.2d 721, 50 U.C.C. Rep. Serv. 2d 695 (N.C. Ct. App. 2003) (applying U.C.C. to contract as a whole; claim arising from contract for sale and installation of mobile home is barred by U.C.C. statute of limitations); Kietzer v. Land O'Lakes, 47 U.C.C. Rep. Serv. 2d 918 (Wis. Ct. App. 2002) (unpublished) (applying U.C.C. to entire contract when goods predominated); *cf.* Farm Bureau Mut. Ins. Co. v. Combustion Research Corp., 662 N.W.2d 439, 50 U.C.C. Rep. Serv. 2d 67 (Mich. Ct. App. 2003) (when purchaser's ultimate goal is to acquire goods, UCC applies to service aspects, but not to services that seller performed on a visit twenty-two months after sale and that were not required by the sales contract).

38   SMR Technologies, Inc. v. Aircraft Parts Int'l Combs, Inc., 141 F. Supp. 2d 923 (W.D. Tenn. 2001).

17.3.5 Does UCC Apply to Incidental Goods Where Services Component Predominates?

Addition to note 39.

39   Palmer v. Espey Huston & Associates, 84 S.W.2d 345, 49 U.C.C. Rep. Serv. 2d 48 (Tex. App. 2002) (when buyer's complaint related to services component, U.C.C. does not apply). *But cf.* Satterwhite v. Image Bank, 48 U.C.C. Rep. Serv. 2d 1307 (S.D.N.Y. 2002) (applying non-U.C.C. law to contract as a whole when services predominated).

Page 609

Add to text at end of subsection's first paragraph:

Even if the UCC does not apply to the provider of the services, it may apply to the manufacturer or supplier of the goods.[42.1]

42.1   *See, e.g.,* Stoney v. Franklin, 44 U.C.C. Rep. Serv. 2d 1211 (Va. Cir. Ct. 2001); *see also* Hicks v. Kaufman & Broad Home Corp., 89 Cal. App. 4th 908, 107 Cal. Rptr. 2d 761 (2001) (applying U.C.C. to component of foundation of home).

Addition to note 43.

43   *See* Lucid, Inc. v. DiSanto Tech., 43 U.C.C. Rep. Serv. 2d 1083 (Conn. Super. Ct. 2000); Homer v. J.M. Burman, 743 N.E.2d 1144 (Ind. Ct. App. 2001) (applying U.C.C. to entire transaction when services predominated); *see also* Heart of Tex. Dodge, Inc. v. Star Coach, 255 Ga. App. 801, 567 S.E.2d 61, 48 U.C.C. Rep. Serv. 2d 48 (2002) (applying U.C.C. to contract as a whole when services predominated); Fox v. Mountain W. Elec., Inc., 137 Idaho 703, 52 P.3d 848, 48 U.C.C. Rep. Serv. 2d 505 (Idaho 2002).

17.3.6 Determining the Predominant Purpose

17.3.6.1 Parties' Intent as Determining Predominant Purpose

Add note 44.1 at end of subsection's first sentence.

44.1   Brandt v. Boston Scientific Corp., 204 Ill. 2d 640, 792 N.E.2d 296, 50 U.C.C. Rep. Serv. 2d 701 (2003) (adopting predominant purpose test); Hensley v. Ray's Motor Co., 580 S.E.2d 721, 50 U.C.C. Rep. Serv. 2d 695 (N.C. Ct. App. 2003) (endorsing predominant purpose test). *But cf.* Thorn's Diesel Serv., Inc. v. Houston Ship Repair, Inc., 253 F. Supp. 2d 1332, 49 U.C.C. Rep. Serv. 2d 380 (N.D. Ala. 2002) (expressing doubt about whether Alabama courts would adopt predominant purpose test).

Addition to notes 45–48.

45   Controlled Environments Constr., Inc. v. Key Indus. Refrigeration Co., 670 N.W.2d 771, 785 (Neb. 2003) (buyer's written proposal shows that contract was predominantly for goods); Smart Online, Inc. v. Opensite Technologies, Inc., 51 U.C.C. Rep. Serv. 2d 47 (N.C. Super. Ct. 2003).

46   True N. Composites, Ltd. Liab. Co. v. Trinity Indus., Inc., 50 U.C.C. Rep. Serv. 2d 683 (4th Cir. 2003) (unpublished); *see also* Donatelle Plastics Inc. v. Stonhard, Inc., 48 U.C.C. Rep. Serv. 2d 1399 (D. Minn. 2002) (contract's description of transaction as a "project" tends to show that services predominate).

Page 610

47   Donatelle Plastics Inc. v. Stonhard, Inc., 48 U.C.C. Rep. Serv. 2d 1399 (D. Minn. 2002); *see also* True N. Composites, Ltd. Liab. Co. v. Trinity Indus., Inc., 50 U.C.C. Rep. Serv. 2d 683 (4th Cir. 2003) (unpublished) (fact that contract price was a certain amount per unit of goods produced tends to show that it was contract for goods).

48   Brandt v. Boston Scientific Corp., 204 Ill. 2d 640, 792 N.E.2d 296, 50 U.C.C. Rep. Serv. 2d 701 (2003); Smart Online, Inc. v. Opensite Technologies, Inc., 51 U.C.C. Rep. Serv. 2d 47 (N.C. Super. Ct. 2003).

Add to text immediately following note 48:

whether the buyer's primary purpose was to buy the seller's skill and knowledge,[48.1]

48.1   Wharton Mgmt. Group v. Sigma Consultants, Inc., 50 U.C.C. Rep. Serv. 2d 678 (Del. Super. Ct. 1990), *aff'd,* 582 A.2d 936 (Del. 1990); Brandt v. Boston Scientific Corp., 204 Ill. 2d 640, 792 N.E.2d 296, 50 U.C.C. Rep. Serv. 2d 701 (2003) (contract for surgical implantation of medical devices is for services).

17.4 Common Law Warranties

Page 611

17.4.2 Common Law Express Warranties

Addition to note 57.

57   *See, e.g.,* Livchak v. Logsdon Sons, Inc., 2002 WL 31423656 (Ohio Ct. App. Oct. 30, 2002) (unpublished).

Add to text at end of subsection's first paragraph:

As the claim is based on breach of the contractual warranty, it is not necessary for the consumer to prove what the standard of care is or that the contractor deviated from it.[57.1]

57.1   Livchak v. Logsdon Sons, Inc., 2002 WL 31423656 (Ohio Ct. App. Oct. 30, 2002) (unpublished).

17.4.3 Common Law Implied Warranties

Addition to notes 61–63.

61   *But see* Pearl Investments, Ltd. Liab. Co. v. Standard I/O, Inc., 257 F. Supp. 2d 326, 50 U.C.C. Rep. Serv. 2d 377 (D. Me. 2003) (finding no implied warranty for services); Urban Dev., Inc. v. Evergreen Bldg. Products, 59 P.3d 112, 49 U.C.C. Rep. Serv. 2d 372 (Wash. Ct. App. 2002) (commercial case) (implied warranties do not arise in construction contracts), *review granted,* 149 Wash. 2d 1027 (2003).

62   Armstrong v. Nationwide Mortgage Plan/Trust (*In re* Armstrong), 288 B.R. 404 (Bankr. E.D. Pa. 2003) (finding home improvement contractor's substandard work to be breach of contract); Nulite Indus. Co. v. Horne, 252 Ga. App. 378, 556 S.E.2d 255 (2001) (installation of siding and replacement windows on mobile home); Homer v. J.M. Burman, 743 N.E.2d 1144 (Ind. Ct. App. 2001); Hernandez v. Martinez, 781 So. 2d 815 (La. Ct. App. 2001) (home improvement contract); Cannan v. Bob Chambers Ford, 432 A.2d 387 (Me. 1981) (duty to perform diligently, skillfully, and in workmanlike manner); Helterbrand v. Five Star Mobile Home Sales, Inc., 48 S.W.3d 649 (Mo. Ct. App. 2001) (mobile home dealer that acted as general contractor for construction of garage impliedly warranted that it would be done in workmanlike manner); Earl v. Leiffer Constr., Inc., 2001 Ohio App. LEXIS 3857 (Ohio Ct. App. Aug. 31, 2001) (roof repair); Snyder v. Cooper, 2001 Ohio App. LEXIS 1407 (Ohio Ct. App. Mar. 20, 2001) (failure to perform in workmanlike manner using ordinary care is breach of implied duty imposed by law); Szabo v. Rosenberg, 1998 Ohio App. LEXIS 2790 (Ohio Ct. App. June 24, 1998) (construction services); City of Springfield v. Hobson Cleaning, Inc., 2001 Tenn. App. LEXIS 474 (Tenn. Ct. App. July 5, 2001). *But see* Pearl Investments, Ltd. Liab. Co. v. Standard I/O, Inc., 257 F. Supp. 2d 326, 50 U.C.C. Rep. Serv. 2d 377 (D. Me. 2003) (finding no implied warranty for services); Trans-Gulf Corp. v. Performance Aircraft Services, Inc., 82 S.W.3d 691 (Tex. App. 2002) (refusing to extend Texas's limited implied warranty in service transactions to work on aircraft fuel tanks when negligence claims would be barred by economic loss rule).

63   Jones v. Star Houston, Inc., 45 S.W.3d 350 (Tex. App. 2001) (repair shop breached warranty when it damaged hood when repairing dashboard light).

Add to text at end of subsection's first paragraph:

Courts may analogize to the UCC and use public policy to restrict limitations on damages and disclaimer of these warranties.[63.1]

63.1   Clark v. Orkin Exterminating Co., 147 F. Supp. 2d 458 (W.D. Va. 2001).

Page 612

Add to text after sentence containing note 64:

However, the seller may not have a right to cure under the common law.[64.1]

64.1   Heart of Tex. Dodge, Inc. v. Star Coach, 255 Ga. App. 801, 567 S.E.2d 61, 48 U.C.C. Rep. Serv. 2d 48 (2002); *see* § 8.2.7, *supra* (right to cure when buyer rejects goods).

Add note 64.2 at end of subsection's second paragraph.

64.2   *See, e.g.,* Jones v. Star Houston, Inc., 45 S.W.3d 350 (Tex. App. 2001) (party to repair contract has common law duty to perform with ordinary care and skill, and negligent omission or commission is both a tort and a breach of contract).

Add to text at end of subsection's second paragraph:

If the seller has held itself out as an expert, it may be held to a higher standard of care, one requiring performance in a professional manner, using the skills and expertise of others providing the same services.[64.3]

64.3   City of Springfield v. Hobson Cleaning, Inc., 2001 Tenn. App. LEXIS 474 (Tenn. Ct. App. July 5, 2001).

Replace note 67 with:

67   Interstate Contracting Corp. v. City of Dallas, 2000 U.S. Dist. LEXIS 13111 (N.D. Tex. Sept. 8, 2000) (concluding that there is still no implied warranty for purely professional services in Texas); Melody Home Mfg. Co. v. Barnes, 741 S.W.2d 349 (Tex. 1987); *see also* Rocky Mountain Helicopters v. Lubbock County Hosp. Dist., 987 S.W.2d 50 (Tex. 1998) (implied warranty that services will be performed in a good and

workmanlike manner arises when services relate to repair or modification of tangible goods or property, not to helicopter maintenance); Parkway Co. v. Woodruff, 901 S.W.2d 434 (Tex. 1995); Humble Nat'l Bank v. DCV, Inc., 933 S.W.2d 224 (Tex. App. 1996) (in case involving commercial parties, no implied warranty of reasonably safe and sound banking services; plaintiff has adequate alternative remedies to redress the alleged wrong).

Add to text at end of subsection:

The consumer has the burden of proving that the provider failed to use ordinary care and skill in performing the work and that this failure proximately caused the consumer's damages.[68.1] Sometimes the consumer will have to present expert testimony that establishes what the common standards of workmanship are and that the provider deviated from them. But expert testimony is unnecessary if the question is not highly technical or scientific, or not beyond the experience or knowledge of the average trier of fact.[68.2] For example, expert testimony was unnecessary when a home suffered interior water damage despite steps that a contractor took to protect the interior from rain during roof repairs.[68.3] The jury could infer from these facts that the contractor did not use ordinary care.

68.1　Earl v. Leiffer Constr., Inc., 2001 Ohio App. LEXIS 3857 (Ohio Ct. App. Aug. 31, 2001).
68.2　*Id.*
68.3　*Id.*

17.4.4 Damages for Breach of Common Law Warranties

Addition to notes 70, 72.

70　*See, e.g.*, Brooks v. Ibsen, 2001 Tenn. App. LEXIS 630 (Tenn. Ct. App. Aug. 24, 2001) (awarding expectancy damages).
72　*See* Sampson v. Winnie, 2001 Tenn. App. LEXIS 894 (Tenn. Ct. App. Dec. 11, 2001) (awarding cost of improvements necessary to make heating unit work); Brooks v. Ibsen, 2001 Tenn. App. LEXIS 630 (Tenn. Ct. App. Aug. 24, 2001) (awarding cost of replacing defective swimming pool).

17.5 Negligence in Service Transactions

Page 613

17.5.1 Advantages and Disadvantages of the Negligence Claim

Add to text at end of subsection's first paragraph:

While negligent performance of a contract may give rise to both a contract claim and a negligence claim, the consumer is entitled to only one recovery.[82.1]

82.1　Bonan v. Goldring Home Inspections, Inc., 68 Conn. App. 862, 794 A.2d 997 (2002).

Page 614

17.5.2 The Negligence Cause of Action in Service Transactions

Addition to notes 88, 91, 93, 98.

88　*But see* Jones v. Star Houston, Inc., 45 S.W.3d 350 (Tex. App. 2001) (either omission or commission can give rise to negligence claim in contract for repairs).
91　*See, e.g.*, Ussery Printing Co. v. Heidelberg USA, Inc., 2001 U.S. Dist. LEXIS 2882, at *11 (N.D. Tex. Mar. 16, 2001) (plaintiff failed to show that repairer did not act as a reasonable service technician would act under the same or similar circumstances); Bonan v. Goldring Home Inspectors, Inc., 794 A.2d 997, 1002 (Conn. Ct. App. 2002) (affirming award against negligent home inspector who failed to find termite damage).
93　*Add to Dow Chemical citation: aff'd in relevant part, vacated in part on other grounds*, 753 N.E.2d 633 (Ind. 2001); *add*: Weathersby Chevrolet Co. v. Redd Pest Control Co., 778 So. 2d 130 (Miss. 2001) (faulty repair of air conditioner that led to destruction of truck).

Page 615

98　*But see* Boyian v. Harbor Lights Marina, 286 A.D.2d 904, 730 N.Y.S.2d 636 (2001) (granting summary judgment to defendant boat repairman who had informed plaintiffs that, to prevent damage to the boat, he would not inspect concealed portions of fuel system unless a problem was indicated).

Page 616

17.5.4 Proving Damages

Addition to note 111.

111　*See, e.g.*, Anderson v. Gengras Motors, 141 Conn. 688 (1954) (damages for tort that deprives owner of use of vehicle include rental value minus wear and tear and depreciation).

Page 617

17.6 UDAP, Fraud, Three Day Cooling-Off Periods, and TIL Rescission

Replace NCLC citation in section's first paragraph with:

Unfair and Deceptive Acts and Practices §§ 4.9.7, 5.4.1, 5.6.1 (5th ed. 2001 and Supp.)

Replace note 116 with:

116   *See* National Consumer Law Center, Unfair and Deceptive Acts and Practices § 5.8.2 (5th ed. 2001 and Supp.); National Consumer Law Center, Truth in Lending Ch. 6 (5th ed. 2003).

17.7 Special Issues Concerning Home Improvement Contracts

17.7.1 Cancelling the Contract

17.7.1.1 UCC Revocation and Cancellation Based Upon Misrepresentation

Replace note 121 with:

121   *See* National Consumer Law Center, Unfair and Deceptive Acts and Practices § 9.5.9 (5th ed. 2001 and Supp.).

Replace note 122 with:

122   *See* National Consumer Law Center, Unfair and Deceptive Acts and Practices § 8.7.2 (5th ed. 2001 and Supp.).

Page 618

17.7.1.2 Truth in Lending Rescission

Replace note 125 with:

125   *See generally* National Consumer Law Center, Truth in Lending Ch. 6 (5th ed. 2003).

Replace NCLC citation in subsection's third paragraph with:

NCLC's *Truth in Lending*[125.1]

125.1   National Consumer Law Center, Truth in Lending Ch. 6 (5th ed. 2003).

Replace note 127 with:

127   *Id.* Appx. D (sample notice).

Replace note 128 with:

128   *Id.* Ch. 6.

Replace note 129 with:

129   *See* National Consumer Law Center, Truth in Lending Ch. 9 (5th ed. 2003).

17.7.1.3 FTC Cooling-Off Rule for Off-Premises Sales

Replace NCLC citation in subsection's first paragraph with:

Unfair and Deceptive Acts and Practices § 5.8.2 (5th ed. 2001 and Supp.)

Replace note 131 with:

131   National Consumer Law Center, Unfair and Deceptive Acts and Practices § 5.8.2.6 (5th ed. 2001 and Supp.).

17.7.1.4 State Home Solicitation Statutes

Replace note 134 with:

134   National Consumer Law Center, Unfair and Deceptive Acts and Practices § 5.8.2.3 (5th ed. 2001 and Supp.).

Page 619

17.7.1.5 Credit Repair Organization Statutes

Addition to note 136.

136   *Replace NCLC citation with*: National Consumer Law Center, Unfair and Deceptive Acts and Practices § 5.1.17.6 (5th ed. 2001 and Supp.); *add*: *But see* Wojcik v. Courtesy Auto Sales, Inc., 2002 WL 31663298 (D. Neb. Nov. 25, 2002) (finding that car dealer was not a credit repair organization when it did not charge

additional fee for credit repair service and buyers had not gone to it in response to credit repair advertisements); *add at end of note*: *See also* National Consumer Law Center, Fair Credit Reporting Ch. 15 (5th ed. 2002 and Supp.).

17.7.3 Special Relevance of Building Codes and Permits

Addition to note 138.

138   *See, e.g.*, Homer v. J.M. Burman, 743 N.E.2d 1144 (Ind. Ct. App. 2001) (compliance with electrical code was implied term in home improvement transaction); Becker v. Graber Builders, Inc., 561 S.E.2d 905, 909 (N.C. Ct. App. 2002).

Page 620

Add note 140.1 at end of sentence preceding sentence containing note 141.

140.1   *See, e.g.*, Homer v. J.M. Burman, 743 N.E.2d 1144 (Ind. Ct. App. 2001) (failure to obtain permit was breach of contract).

Replace § 17.7.4 heading with:

17.7.4 State Home Improvement Statutes and Regulations

Addition to notes 143, 150, 151, 153.

143   *Replace "$1400" in Maine citation with*: $3000; *add*: *See also* Haw. Rev. Stat. §§ 444-1 to 444-36 (licensing of contractors; also requires disclosures to consumers and sets up recovery fund); Code Haw. R. §§ 16-77-1 to 16-77-117 (requires disclosures, written contract, and workmanlike work conforming to trade standards).

150   *See* Brace v. Titcomb, 2002 WL 1335871 (Me. Super. Ct. May 17, 2002) (contract's failure to conform to statute is UDAP violation, but no damages shown).

151   Homer v. J.M. Burman, 743 N.E.2d 1144 (Ind. Ct. App. 2001) (violation was UDAP violation); *see also* Hiraga v. Baldonado, 31 P.3d 222 (Haw. Ct. App. 2001) (contract void when it complied with most but not all requirements, but contractor can recover in *quantum meruit*); *see also* Scott v. Mayflower Home Improvement Co., 363 N.J. Super. 145, 831 A.2d 564 (Super. Ct. Law Div. 2001) (failure to comply with home improvement contractor licensing and other requirements renders contract void and contractor is not entitled to *quantum meruit* recovery); Frank v. Feiss, 266 A.D.2d 825, 698 N.Y.S.2d 363 (1999) (failure to give signed contract bars contract recovery, but *quantum meruit* allowed).

Page 621

153   *See also* Bentivegna v. Powers Steel & Wire Products, Inc., 81 P.3d 1040 (Ariz. Ct. App. 2004) (unlicensed contractor may not recover affirmatively, but may retain funds already collected).

Add to text at end of subsection's fifth paragraph:

The existence of a complaint procedure administered by the licensing board should not have any effect on the consumer's ability to sue the contractor.[153.1]

153.1   Bentivegna v. Powers Steel & Wire Products, Inc., 81 P.3d 1040 (Ariz. Ct. App. 2004).

Page 622

Addition to note 168.

168   *Replace NCLC citation with*: National Consumer Law Center, Unfair and Deceptive Acts and Practices § 5.6.1 (5th ed. 2001 and Supp.); *add*: *See, e.g.*, Forton v. Laszar, 239 Mich. App. 711, 609 N.W.2d 850 (2000) (deviation from blueprints was UDAP violation).

17.7.5 Damage Claims Against an Insolvent Home Improvement Contractor

Replace note 169 with:

169   For more detail on these theories, see National Consumer Law Center, Unfair and Deceptive Acts and Practices Ch. 6 (5th ed. 2001 and Supp.).

Page 623

17.7.6 Refusing to Pay the Balance Due as a Consumer Remedy

Replace note 171 with:

171   National Consumer Law Center, Unfair and Deceptive Acts and Practices § 6.6 (5th ed. 2001 and Supp.).

17.7.7 Dealing with Mortgages and Liens on the Consumer's Home

Replace NCLC citation in subsection's first sentence with:

Repossessions and Foreclosures[172.1]

172.1   National Consumer Law Center, Repossessions and Foreclosures Chs. 15, 16 (5th ed. 2002 and Supp.).

17.7.8 Lender Liability for Punitive Damages

Replace first sentence of subsection's third paragraph with:

NCLC's *Consumer Law Pleadings*[173.1] contains copies of a complaint in a successful home improvement case, in which the consumers recovered twenty-eight million dollars in punitive damages from a major bank.

173.1   National Consumer Law Center, Consumer Law Pleadings No. 1, Ch. 5 (2003 Cumulative CD-Rom and Index Guide).

17.7.9 Home Improvement Contract Litigation Tips

Page 625

17.7.9.1 Investigating the Case

Replace subsection's second sentence with:

A sample client interview sheet for a home improvement case is found in Appendix H.2, *infra*, and on the CD-Rom accompanying this volume.

17.7.9.2 Pleading

Replace note 176 with:

176   *See* National Consumer Law Center, Repossessions and Foreclosures Chs. 16, 17, 20 (5th ed. 2002 and Supp.).

Replace third and fourth sentences of subsection's final paragraph with:

Another complaint that asserts breach of implied warranties by a home improvement contractor is found in NCLC's *Consumer Law Pleadings*.[176.1] This complaint is also available on the CD-Rom accompanying this volume.

176.1   National Consumer Law Center, Consumer Law Pleadings No. 2, § 4.4 (2003 Cumulative CD-Rom and Index Guide).

Replace note 177 with:

177   National Consumer Law Center, Consumer Law Pleadings No. 1, Ch. 5 (2003 Cumulative CD-Rom and Index Guide); National Consumer Law Center, Consumer Law Pleadings No. 2, § 4.3 (2003 Cumulative CD-Rom and Index Guide). These pleadings are also found on NCLC's comprehensive CD-Rom *Consumer Law in a Box.*

17.7.9.3 Discovery

Replace note 178 with:

178   In addition, NCLC's *Consumer Law Pleadings* contains copies of discovery in a successful case involving fraud in the financing of home improvements, in which the consumers recovered twenty-eight million dollars in punitive damages. National Consumer Law Center, Consumer Law Pleadings No. 1, Ch. 5 (2003 Cumulative CD-Rom and Index Guide). Other discovery dealing with lenders' participation in home improvement fraud is also available in National Consumer Law Center, Consumer Law Pleadings No. 2, § 4.3 (2003 Cumulative CD-Rom and Index Guide). These documents are also found on NCLC's comprehensive CD-Rom *Consumer Law in a Box.*

17.8 Special Issues Concerning Automobile Repair

17.8.1 Repair Shop Refusal to Return Car Until Repair Bill Paid

Page 626

17.8.1.1 Consumer's Remedy Where Repair Shop Has No Right to Retain the Car

Replace note 179 with:

179 For a more detailed discussion of statutory liens, see National Consumer Law Center, Repossessions and Foreclosures Ch. 15 (5th ed. 2002 and Supp.).

17.8.3 State Automobile Repair Laws

Page 627

17.8.3.1 General

Add to text at end of subsection:

A sample jury verdict form that includes claims under a state automobile repair law is included on the CD-Rom accompanying this volume.

17.8.3.2 Disclosure and Regulation Laws

Page 628

17.8.3.2.2 Required disclosures

Addition to note 200.

200 *See also* Testan v. Carlsen Motor Cars, Inc., 2002 Cal. App. Unpub. LEXIS 1837 (Cal. Ct. App. Feb. 19, 2002) (unpublished) (not a violation to use clearly disclosed flat rates rather than hourly rates for estimates).

Page 631

17.8.3.3 Repair Shop or Mechanic Licensing

Replace note 274 with:

274 *See* National Consumer Law Center, Unfair and Deceptive Acts and Practices § 4.9.8 (5th ed. 2001 and Supp.).

Page 632

17.8.4 State UDAP Statutes

Addition to note 279.

279 *See, e.g.,* Perkins v. Stapleton Buick-GMC Truck, Inc., 2001 Ohio App. LEXIS 2651 (Ohio Ct. App. June 15, 2001) (misrepresentation that repairs had been made when they had not been successful).

Replace NCLC citation in subsection's last paragraph with:

Unfair and Deceptive Acts and Practices § 5.4.1 (5th ed. 2001 and Supp.)

Chapter 18

Service Contracts, Extended Warranties and Mechanical Breakdown Insurance

18.1 Getting Started

Page 635

18.1.1 Introduction

Replace note 2 with:

2 *See* National Consumer Law Center, Unfair and Deceptive Acts and Practices §§ 5.2.7.2, 5.4.3.5, 5.4.3.6 (5th ed. 2001 and Supp.).

Replace note 3 with:

3 *See* National Consumer Law Center, Truth in Lending § 3.6.5.2 (5th ed. 2003).

Page 636

18.2 Distinguishing Service Contracts From Warranties

Addition to note 6.

6 *See also* Gavaldon v. DaimlerChrysler Corp., 115 Cal. Rptr. 2d 732 (Ct. App.), *review granted, opinion superseded by* 47 P.3d 222 (Cal. 2002).

Page 637

18.3 Is a Service Contract Regulated as Insurance?

Replace note 14 with:

14 308 Op. Vt. Att'y Gen. 46 (1959); *see also In re* Griffin Sys., 117 F.T.C. 515 (Fed. Trade Comm'n 1994) (A.L.J.).

Add note 14.1 after second sentence of section's fifth paragraph.

14.1 *See In re* Griffin Sys., 117 F.T.C. 515 (Fed. Trade Comm'n 1994) (A.L.J.).

18.4 Contract Coverage

18.4.1 General

Add to text after subsection's fourth paragraph:

Another way that service contracts limit coverage is by a restrictive definition of the time period that the contract will be in effect. For example, one company sold service contracts for "60 Months/60,000 Miles" on used cars and disclosed that "mechanical coverage" began on the date the service contract was purchased. A later part of the contract, however, stated that the time and mileage limits began to run on the same day as the new vehicle warranty, when the odometer read zero, thus ensuring that no buyer would ever receive sixty months or 60,000 miles of coverage.[16.1]

16.1 Oldendorf v. Gen. Motors Corp., 322 Ill. App. 3d 825, 256 Ill. Dec. 161, 751 N.E.2d 214 (2001) (reversing grant of motion to dismiss).

Replace note 17 with:

17 *See* Morehouse v. Behlmann Pontiac-GMC Truck Serv., Inc., 31 S.W.3d 55 (Mo. Ct. App. 2000).

Add to text at end of subsection:

A service contract administrator may deny coverage when the consumer did not obtain prior approval for repairs, as required by the agreement. But this practice has been found to be unfair and deceptive when the service contract administrator had a practice of not responding to consumer requests for prior approval.[18.1] It is similarly unfair and deceptive for the administrator to cancel a policy when the consumer has made a number of claims, when such cancelation is not authorized in the contract, and to then refuse to perform work under the "canceled" contract.[18.2]

18.1   *See In re* Griffin Sys., 117 F.T.C. 515 (Fed. Trade Comm'n 1994) (A.L.J.).
18.2   *Id.*

Page 638

18.4.3 Terms Not Clearly Disclosed or at Variance With Prior Representations

Add to text after subsection's first sentence:

More and more service contracts are also advertised on the Internet. For example, Ford's service contracts are described in detail at www.qualitycareservice.com. `

Addition to notes 20, 22.

20   *See also* Oldendorf v. Gen. Motors Corp., 322 Ill. App. 3d 825, 256 Ill. Dec. 161, 751 N.E.2d 214 (2001) (deliberate obfuscation of terms of coverage through vague, contradictory language and concealed clauses may be UDAP violation).
22   *See* Paul v. Timco, Inc., 811 A.2d 948 (N.J. Super. Ct. App. Div. 2002).

Replace note 30 with:

30   National Consumer Law Center, Unfair and Deceptive Acts and Practices § 4.2.14.3 (5th ed. 2001 and Supp.).

Add to text at end of subsection:

It may also be fruitful to determine if the service contract company ever in fact mailed the service contract to the consumer. Dealerships often view the service contract as just a profit center, without expecting consumers to actually file claims. In this environment, the parties involved in the service contract may not even think it worthwhile to send the contract to the consumer.[31.1] If that is the case, it is hard to see how a contract can be binding on a consumer who never saw it.

One area in which service contract provisions may be at variance with a dealer's representations is the time period during which the service contract is to be in effect, particularly when that time period is based on the duration of the written warranty. For example, a service contract may state that it applies for only one year after the written warranty expires or 100,000 miles, whichever comes sooner. The written warranty may last for four years or 50,000 miles, whichever comes sooner. The dealer may represent this service contract as expiring in five years or 100,000 miles. But such a description is confusing because in fact the service contract will expire after three years if the owner drives 50,000 miles in the first two years.

31.1   *Cf.* Paul v. Timco, Inc., 811 A.2d 948 (N.J. Super. Ct. App. Div. 2002).

18.5 Remedies for a Contractor's Failure to Pay a Covered Claim

Page 639

18.5.2 Shaping the Consumer's Legal Claim

Add note 33.1 at end of first sentence of subsection's second paragraph.

33.1   *See, e.g.,* Morehouse v. Behlmann Pontiac-GMC Truck Serv., Inc., 31 S.W.3d 55 (Mo. Ct. App. 2000).

Add to text at end of second sentence of subsection's second paragraph:

On the other hand, a breach of contract claim may have a longer statute of limitations than other claims. For example, it will often be longer than even the UCC's four-year limitations period for warranty claims.[33.2]

33.2   Brainard v. Freightliner Corp., 2002 WL 31207467 (W.D.N.Y. Oct. 1, 2002).

18.5.3 Magnuson-Moss Warranty Act Remedies

18.5.3.1 General

Addition to note 36.

36 *See also* Lysek v. Elmhurst Dodge, Inc., 2001 Ill. App. LEXIS 823 (Ill. App. Ct. Oct. 25, 2001).

Page 640

18.5.4 UDAP Statutes

Replace note 46 with:

46 *See* National Consumer Law Center, Unfair and Deceptive Acts and Practices §§ 5.2.5, 5.3.3 (5th ed. 2001 and Supp.).

Add to text after sentence containing note 47:

Other UDAP claims may be more complicated. For example, when a franchise dealer denies a service contract claim on behalf of a manufacturer obligated on the service contract, is the manufacturer guilty of an unfair trade practice because of the incentive structure it creates for its franchise dealers to deny the claim? It has been alleged that manufacturers give dealers with a history of denying claims the authority to authorize repairs on their own, while requiring other dealers to obtain the manufacturer's prior approval. Does this policy encourage dealers to be stingy in their claims processing, and is that therefore a UDAP violation? A manufacturer's incentives concerning service contract claims may be stated in the manufacturer's warranty administration manual.

18.5.6 Insurance Regulation

Replace note 54 with:

54 *See* National Consumer Law Center, Unfair and Deceptive Acts and Practices § 2.3.1 (5th ed. 2001 and Supp.).

18.5.7 State Service Contract Statutes

Addition to note 56.

56 *But cf.* Gavaldon v. DaimlerChrysler Corp., 115 Cal. Rptr. 2d 732 (Ct. App. 2002) (Song-Beverly Act does not apply to service contract because service contract is not an express warranty).

Add new subsections to text after § 18.5.7.

18.5.8 State Lemon Laws or Other Warranty Statutes May Apply to Service Contracts

California's lemon law, like many such state laws, provides that written warranty violations can be grounds for a court to order the manufacturer to replace a defective vehicle or offer a full refund of the purchase price, plus attorney fees.[57.1] In legislative action that offers consumers important protections, the California lemon law has been amended to explicitly provide these remedies for breaches of new vehicle service contracts as well.[57.2]

The California lemon law is ambiguous whether these remedies for new vehicle service contract violations also apply to used vehicle service contracts. But the California courts have applied the lemon law to breaches of used vehicle service contracts as well, considering that to be the legislature's intent.[57.3]

18.5.9 Effect of Arbitration Clause on Consumer's Remedies

Service contract agreements may require that disputes concerning the contract be submitted to binding arbitration. Because of the expense of arbitration and because the consumer's remedies may be limited in arbitration, consumers often want to avoid this forum.[57.4] A number of theories to use to avoid such an arbitration requirement are set out earlier in this volume.[57.5]

Of special relevance to service contracts is the question of whether the consumer ever agreed to the arbitration clause found in the service contract. Service contracts are usually sold by auto dealers using a one-sentence, written description of the policy (for example, five years or 100,000 miles). The actual terms of the service contract are not sent to the consumer until later, if they are sent at all.

If the arbitration clause is found in the service contract agreement sent to the consumer after the agreement has been consummated, the question is whether the consumer has agreed to this provision. The service contract policy, when sent to the consumer, typically does not require the consumer to signify agreement to the policy terms, or provide an option for the consumer to cancel if the consumer is dissatisfied with the terms. The terms are just presented unilaterally or the policy is never sent at all. At least one court in the context of a service contract has found such a unilateral imposition of an arbitration requirement not to be enforceable,[57.6] and other courts have reached the same conclusion in other contexts.[57.7]

57.1   Cal. Civ. Code §§ 1793.1 to 1793.5 (West).

57.2   Cal. Civ. Code §§ 1793.1 to 1793.5 (West). *But cf.* Adams v. Nissan Motor Corp., 387 S.E.2d 288 (W. Va. 1989) (West Virginia lemon law not so interpreted).

57.3   Swann v. DaimlerChrysler Motors Corp., 2003 WL 1818139 (Cal. Ct. App. May 5, 2003); Reveles v. Toyota by the Bay, 57 Cal. App. 4th 1139 (1997).

57.4   *See* § 10.2S, *supra.*

57.5   *See* § 10.2S, *supra.*

57.6   *See* Paul v. Timco, Inc., 811 A.2d 948 (N.J. Super. Ct. App. Div. 2002).

57.7   *See* § 10.2S, *supra.*

18.7 Third Parties Liable for Service Contract Obligor's Failure to Pay on a Claim

18.7.2 *Liability of the Service Contract Administrator*

Page 641

Add note 57.8 at the end of the first sentence of the subsection's second paragraph.

57.8   *See* Kimpel v. Del. Pub. Auto Auction, 2001 Del. C.P. LEXIS 35 (Del. Ct. Com. Pl. Mar. 6, 2001).

Page 642

18.7.3 *Selling Dealer's Obligations When Service Contractor Is Insolvent*

Replace note 63 with:

63   *See* Toyota Town, Inc. v. Comm'r, 2000 Tax Ct. Memo LEXIS 40 (Tax Ct. 2000), *aff'd on other grounds,* 268 F.3d 1156 (9th Cir. 2001).

18.7.4 *Reimbursement Insurance, State Insurance Guaranty Funds, and Bonds*

Replace note 69 with:

69   *See* Toyota Town, Inc. v. Comm'r, 2000 Tax Ct. Memo LEXIS 40 (Tax Ct. 2000), *aff'd on other grounds,* 268 F.3d 1156 (9th Cir. 2001).

18.7.5 *Raising Service Contract Defenses to Claims by a Related Creditor or Lessor*

Replace note 71 with:

71   16 C.F.R. pt. 433; *see also* National Consumer Law Center, Unfair and Deceptive Acts and Practices § 6.6 (5th ed. 2001 and Supp.).

Page 643

18.8 Refunds Upon Service Contract Cancellation

Replace note 77 with:

77   *See* National Consumer Law Center, Repossessions and Foreclosures § 11.3.4 (5th ed. 2002 and Supp.).

Chapter 19   Leases

Page 645

19.1 Introduction

Replace section's last paragraph with:

The discussion in this chapter is limited to consumer warranty rights in lease transactions. Disclosure of lease terms as required by the Federal Consumer Leasing Act and state law is examined in NCLC's *Truth in Lending*.[0.1] Repossession of leased property and early termination of automobile leases are detailed in NCLC's *Repossessions and Foreclosures*.[0.2] Unfair and deceptive automobile leasing and rent-to-own practices are described in NCLC's *Unfair and Deceptive Acts and Practices*.[0.3] Regulation of rent-to-own transactions is treated in NCLC's *The Cost of Credit: Regulation and Legal Challenges*.[0.4]

   0.1   National Consumer Law Center, Truth in Lending Ch. 10 (5th ed. 2003).

   0.2   National Consumer Law Center, Repossessions and Foreclosures Ch. 14 (5th ed. 2002 and Supp.).

   0.3   National Consumer Law Center, Unfair and Deceptive Acts and Practices §§ 5.4.9, 5.7.4 (5th ed. 2001 and Supp.).

   0.4   National Consumer Law Center, The Cost of Credit: Regulation and Legal Challenges (2d ed. 2000 and Supp.).

19.2 Sources of Lease Warranty Law

19.2.1 UCC Article 2A on Leases

19.2.1.1 States Enacting Article 2A

Delete "South Carolina" from sentence containing note 4.

Add to text at end of subsection:

South Carolina has now enacted Article 2A.[4.1]

   4.1   *See* 2001 S.C. Acts 67.

Page 646

19.2.1.2 Article 2A Scope

Replace note 8 with:

   8   Revised Article 1, which the National Conference of Commissioners on Uniform State Laws (NCCUSL) approved in 2001 for adoption by the states, redesignates the portions of U.C.C. § 1-201(37) that distinguish between leases and security interests as U.C.C. § 1-203 without substantive change. *See* National Consumer Law Center, Repossessions and Foreclosures § 14.1 (5th ed. 2002 and Supp.).

19.2.1.3 Finance Leases Distinguished From Other Leases

Add note 8.1 at end of subsection.

   8.1   *See* Cooper v. Lyon Fin. Services, Inc., 65 S.W.3d 197 (Tex. App. 2001) (lease meets definition of finance lease).

Page 647

19.2.1.4 Applicable Law When Article 2A Does Not Apply

Add note 10.1 after "section 1-102" in subsection's second paragraph.

   10.1   Revised Article 1, which NCCUSL approved in 2001 for adoption by the states, redesignates this comment as U.C.C. § 1-103 cmt. 1 without substantive change.

Page 648

Replace note 13 with:

13   Revised Article 1, which NCCUSL approved in 2001 for adoption by the states, redesignates U.C.C. § 1-102 cmt. 1 as U.C.C. § 1-103 cmt. 1 without substantive change. *See* § 1.6, *supra*.

19.2.3 Magnuson-Moss Warranty Act

Replace entire subsection with:

The issue of whether the Magnuson-Moss Warranty Act remedies for breach of warranty are available to consumer lessees is now analyzed at § 2.2.2.5 (Supp.), *supra*. Assuming that the Act applies, consumers have a claim for actual damages and attorney fees, as set out in more detail in Chapter 2, *supra*.

Page 649

19.2.4 State Lemon Laws

Add to text at end of subsection's third paragraph:

Revised Article 1, approved by the National Conference of Commissioners on Uniform State Laws (NCCUSL) in 2001 for adoption by the states, makes this conclusion even clearer by adding leases to the list of examples of types of purchases.[29.1]

29.1   Revised U.C.C. § 1-201(b)(29). As of early 2004, revised Article 1 had been adopted by Texas, Virginia, and the Virgin Islands, and was under consideration by several other states.

19.2.5 Federal Consumer Leasing Act

Replace note 31 with:

31   Reg. M, 12 C.F.R. § 213.4(p). *See generally* 15 U.S.C. § 1667; National Consumer Law Center, Truth in Lending Ch. 10 (5th ed. 2003).

Replace note 32 with:

32   National Consumer Law Center, Truth in Lending Ch. 10 (5th ed. 2003).

Replace note 34 with:

34   *See* National Consumer Law Center, Truth in Lending § 10.7 (5th ed. 2003).

Page 650

19.2.6 UCC Article 2A Unconscionability Claims

Addition to note 47.

47   *Replace NCLC citation with*: National Consumer Law Center, Unfair and Deceptive Acts and Practices § 8.8.11.4 (5th ed. 2001 and Supp.).

Page 651

19.2.7 UDAP Statutes, Tort Law, and State Leasing Acts

Addition to note 49.

49   *See also* Gadula v. Gen. Motors Corp, 2001 Mich. App. LEXIS 692 (Mich. Ct. App. Jan. 5, 2001) (UDAP claim allowed for lessor's breach of warranty).

Replace note 51 with:

51   *See* National Consumer Law Center, Repossessions and Foreclosures Ch. 14 (5th ed. 2002 and Supp.).

Add to text at end of subsection:

A notable exception is the Connecticut leasing statute, patterned after the Uniform Consumer Leasing Act, which states: "A term in a consumer lease that attempts to exclude or modify an implied warranty of merchantability or fitness or to exclude or modify a remedy for breach of such warranties is not enforceable."[51.1] The provision also essentially tracks Magnuson-Moss's limitations on disclaimers of implied warranties when a supplier offers written warranties or a service contract.[51.2]

51.1   Conn Gen. Stat. § 42-416(e) (effective July 1, 2003).
51.2   Conn Gen. Stat. § 42-416(b), (c), (d) (effective July 1, 2003).

19.3 Dealer-Lessor's Warranty Obligations

19.3.2 Dealer's Obligations as a Lessor

Add note 52.1 at end of first sentence of subsection's last paragraph.

52.1 *See* Gadula v. Gen. Motors Corp, 2001 Mich. App. LEXIS 692 (Mich. Ct. App. Jan. 5, 2001) (lessee did not present evidence of damages to support a breach of warranty claim but did present a valid claim for revocation of acceptance).

Add note 52.2 at end of second sentence of subsection's last paragraph.

52.2 For example, the lessee can sue for damages even when the lessee has not revoked acceptance or rejected the goods. Fuego Cubano Corp. v. Equip. Sales & Serv., Inc., 49 U.C.C. Rep. Serv. 2d 1234 (Cal. Ct. App. 2003).

Add to text at end of subsection:

The revised version of Article 2A, approved by the National Conference of Commissioners on Uniform State Laws in 2003 for consideration by state legislatures, clarifies that for consumer transactions this four year limitation period can not be shortened in the lease.[53.1]

53.1 Revised U.C.C. § 2A-506(1). Selected portions of revised Article 2A are reproduced in Appx. E.8S, *infra*, and on the CD-Rom accompanying this volume.

19.3.3 Disclaimer of Dealer-Lessor's Implied Warranties

Add to text at end of subsection's first paragraph:

The revised version of Article 2A, approved by the National Conference of Commissioners on Uniform State Laws in 2003 for consideration by state legislatures, somewhat strengthens consumer protections as to disclaimers of the implied warranty of merchantability for both sales and leases. The disclaimer, instead of mentioning "merchantability," must state for consumer leases that: "The lessor undertakes no responsibility for the quality of the goods except as otherwise provided in this contract."[53.2]

53.2 Revised U.C.C. § 2A-214(2). Selected portions of revised Article 2A are reproduced in Appx. E.8S, *infra*, and on the CD-Rom accompanying this volume.

Add to text at end of sentence containing note 55:

, or have otherwise enacted legislation limiting disclaimers of implied warranties.[55.1]

55.1 *See* Conn. Gen. Stat. § 42-158f (limits on implied warranties or modifications of remedies for breach are unenforceable).

Page 652

Add new subsections to text after § 19.3.3.

19.3.4 Rejection, Revocation, and Withholding of Payments

19.3.4.1 Comparison to Sales Transactions

Lessees have similar but somewhat different rights than buyers when it comes to rejecting goods, revoking acceptance, and withholding payments for breaches of contract. Buyers' rights in this regard are set out in Chapter 8, *supra*. Lessees' different rights flow from the different natures of leases and sales.

A buyer becomes owner of the goods upon acceptance, and the seller's obligations after that point are limited. Revocation is principally based on nonconformity of the goods. On the other hand, in a lease, ownership of the goods always rests with the lessor, and the lessor and lessee have continuing obligations under the lease. Revocation under a lease can be based not only on nonconformity of the goods but on nonconformities relating to other aspects of the lease agreement, including lessor obligations that continue for years after the lease's inception.

19.3.4.2 Lessee's Rights to Reject and Revoke

When goods fail in any respect to conform to the lease contract the lessee may reject the goods, if the rejection is within a reasonable time after tender of delivery[57.1] and the lessee seasonably notifies the lessor.[57.2] The lessor can then seasonably notify the lessee of the intent to cure and may make a conforming delivery within the time period provided for in the lease agreement.[57.3]

The lessee may revoke acceptance for any default under the lease contract that substantially impairs the value of the goods to the lessee.[57.4] This right relates both to nonconformity in the goods and to any default in any of the lessor's other obligations under the lease agreement.

The lessee may revoke acceptance when acceptance was made without discovery of the nonconformity, if the lessee's acceptance was induced by the lessor's assurances or occurred because of the difficulty of discovering the nonconformity before acceptance.[57.5] A lessee may revoke acceptance even if the lessee knew about the nonconformity at acceptance if the lessee had the reasonable assumption that the nonconformity would be cured and it has not been seasonably cured.[57.6]

Revocation must occur within a reasonable time after the lessee discovers or should have discovered any default, and before any substantial change in the condition of the goods which is not caused by the nonconformity.[57.7] Article 2A clearly assumes that a lessee may revoke acceptance after the goods have been in use for some time.[57.8] The revised version of Article 2A, approved by the National Conference of Commissioners on Uniform State Laws in 2003 for consideration by state legislatures, has a new subsection dealing with this issue. If use of the goods is reasonable, then the use is not acceptance, but the lessee in appropriate cases will be liable for the value of the use. Use that is unreasonable is acceptance only if ratified by the lessor or supplier.[57.9] But revocation is not effective until the consumer notifies the lessor.[57.10] The revised version of Article 2A provides that the lessee's failure to provide notice bars the lessee from a remedy only to the extent that the lessor or supplier is prejudiced by that failure.[57.11]

As with revocation in the sales context, courts have yet to fully resolve whether revocation applies just to the immediate dealer or whether the lessee can revoke acceptance as against the manufacturer.[57.12] As the dealer (or its assignee) owns the vehicle, difficulties arise if the lessee wants to return the dealer's vehicle to the manufacturer.

The burden of establishing the default is upon the lessee.[57.13] As is usual with the UCC, the parties can vary these rights by agreement except as otherwise provided in the UCC and except that the obligations of good faith, diligence, reasonableness and care may not be disclaimed.[57.14]

19.3.4.3 Grounds Leading to Revocation

Article 2A's grounds for revocation are broader than under Article 2. Article 2A considers any lessor default in the lease agreement to be grounds for revocation. Article 2, in contrast, refers only to nonconformity in the goods themselves. Consequently, grounds for lease revocation could include:

- The goods failing to comply with any description or characteristic specified in the lease agreement;
- The lessor failing to provide the manufacturer's warranty specified in the lease agreement (the federal Consumer Leasing Act requires disclosure of all manufacturer warranties);[57.15]
- Breach of a service contract sold in conjunction with the lease agreement, if that contract is viewed as incorporated into the lease agreement;
- The dealer failing to respond properly to claims under the manufacturer's warranty, when the manufacturer's warranty is viewed as incorporated into the lease agreement;
- The lessor assessing additional charges not specified in the lease agreement;
- The lessor quoting an early termination charge in excess of the amount specified in the lease agreement;
- The lessor failing to maintain the goods, if that is the lessor's responsibility under the lease agreement; and

- The lessor failing to pay taxes or other fees, if those are the lessor's responsibility under the lease agreement.

The test is simply whether the lessor has defaulted in any aspect of the lease agreement, and whether that default substantially impairs the value of the goods to the lessee.

19.3.4.4 Consumer Remedies for Lessor Default

Whenever the lessor fails to deliver goods in conformity to the lease or the lessee rightfully rejects the goods or justifiably revokes acceptance, the lessor is in default under the lease contract.[57.16] Based on this default (or any other lessor default under the lease),[57.17] the consumer may cancel the lease[57.18] and recover so much of the rent and security deposit as has been paid and is just under the circumstances.[57.19]

While in a sales transaction revocation requires the seller to return all payments made by the buyer, in a lease transaction such is not always the case. The Official Comments indicate that if the goods are rejected immediately then the lessee should recover all payments, but if, after one year, the lessor breaches an obligation to maintain the goods in an equipment lease, it may be just to return only a small portion or none of the rental payments the lessee has already made.[57.20]

The rationale for the lessee not recovering all rental payments in this example is that the lessee has had full use of the equipment for the first year, and it is thus reasonable that the lessee pay as rent for that use something close to the actual rental payments. This example is quite distinct from the situation in which the consumer continues to take a vehicle in for repairs, and finally gives up and revokes acceptance after a year. During that year the consumer did not have full use of the vehicle and, in fact, incurred extensive inconvenience. In that case it would not be "just under the circumstances" for the consumer to pay full rent for the vehicle, as the consumer did not have full use of the vehicle.[57.21] In any event, the burden of showing the amount of an offset that is justified against the amount already paid should be placed on the lessor, and not on the consumer.[57.22]

The lessee can also cover by leasing substitute goods and recover consequential damages.[57.23] Of course, after revocation of acceptance, the consumer has no obligation for further rental payments and is not subject to an early termination penalty.

As with a sales transaction, when a lessee rightfully rejects or justifiably revokes acceptance, the lessee has a security interest in the goods in the lessee's possession for any rent or security deposit that has been paid and any expenses incurred to inspect, transport, and care for the goods. This security interest arises even though the lessee never owned the goods. The lessee may hold the goods and dispose of them in a commercially reasonable manner.[57.24] A purchaser who purchases in good faith from a lessee in such a sale takes the goods free of any rights of the lessor.[57.25]

A lessee, after notifying the lessor, may deduct all or any part of the damages resulting from any default under the lease contract from any part of the rent still due under the lease contract.[57.26] Article 2A makes exceptions to this right for finance leases that are not consumer leases,[57.27] but there are no exceptions for consumer leases. The Official Comments state: "No attempt is made to state how the set-off should occur; this is to be determined by the facts of each case."[57.28]

All of these lessee remedies are cumulative. "Use of multiple remedies is barred only if the effect is to put the lessee in a better position than it would have been in had the lessor fully performed under the lease."[57.29]

57.1   *Cf.* Santiago v. DaimlerChrysler Corp., 292 A.D.2d 226, 47 U.C.C. Rep. Serv. 2d 596 (2002).

57.2   U.C.C. § 2A-509.

57.3   U.C.C. § 2A-513(1).

57.4   U.C.C. § 2A-517(2); *see also* Cuesta v. Classic Wheels, Inc., 818 A.2d 448 (N.J. Super. Ct. App. Div. 2003).

57.5   U.C.C. § 2A-517(1)(b).

57.6   U.C.C. §§ 2A-517(1)(a), 2A-516(2).

57.7   U.C.C. § 2A-517(4); *see also* U.C.C. § 2A-516(3)(a).

57.8   Official Comment 2 to U.C.C. § 2A-508; *see also* Cuesta v. Classic Wheels, Inc., 818 A.2d 448 (N.J. Super. Ct. App. Div. 2003).

57.9   Revised U.C.C. § 2A-517(6). Selected portions of revised Article 2A are reproduced in Appx. E.8S, *infra*, and on the CD-Rom accompanying this volume.

57.10 U.C.C. § 2A-517(4); *see also* U.C.C. § 2A-516(3)(a).

57.11 Revised U.C.C. § 2A-516(3)(a). Selected portions of revised Article 2A are reproduced in Appx. E.8S, *infra*, and on the CD-Rom accompanying this volume.

57.12 *Cf.* Santiago v. DaimlerChrysler Corp., 292 A.D.2d 226, 47 U.C.C. Rep. Serv. 2d 596 (2002).

57.13 U.C.C. § 2A-516(3)(c).

57.14 U.C.C. § 1-102(3); *see also* U.C.C. § 2A-103(4); Official Comment 1 to U.C.C. § 2A-508.

57.15 *See* 12 C.F.R. § 213.4(p).

57.16 U.C.C. § 2A-508(1).

57.17 U.C.C. § 2A-508(3).

57.18 U.C.C. § 2A-508(1)(a); *see also* Me. Rev. Stat. Ann. tit. 10, § 1168 (West).

57.19 U.C.C. § 2A-508(1)(b); *see also* Cuesta v. Classic Wheels, Inc., 818 A.2d 448 (N.J. Super. Ct. App. Div. 2003).

57.20 Official Comment 2 to U.C.C. § 2A-508; *see also* Cuesta v. Classic Wheels, Inc., 818 A.2d 448 (N.J. Super. Ct. App. Div. 2003).

57.21 *Cf.* Pifer v. DaimlerChrysler Corp., 2003 WL 22850124 (Mich. Ct. App. Dec. 2, 2003) (jury awards offset reflecting use until defects arose).

57.22 *See* Cuesta v. Classic Wheels, Inc., 818 A.2d 448 (N.J. Super. Ct. App. Div. 2003).

57.23 U.C.C. §§ 2A-508(1)(c), 2A-518.

57.24 U.C.C. § 2A-508(5).

57.25 U.C.C. § 2A-511(4).

57.26 U.C.C. § 2A-508(6).

57.27 U.C.C. § 2A-407.

57.28 Official Comment 9 to U.C.C. § 2A-508.

57.29 Official Comment 2 to U.C.C. § 2A-508; *see also* U.C.C. §§ 2A-103(4), 2A-501(4), 1-106(1).

19.4 Manufacturer Liability Under Non-Finance Lease

19.4.1 Liability Under the Written Warranty

Add to text after sentence containing note 59:

The revised version of Article 2, approved by the National Conference of Commissioners on Uniform State Laws in 2003 for consideration by state legislatures, explicitly provides that lessees have warranty-like rights as to promises that the manufacturer or other remote seller puts in writing inside or accompanying the product, or disseminates in advertising.[59.1]

59.1   Revised U.C.C. §§ 2-313A, 2-313B. Selected portions of revised Article 2 are reproduced in Appx. E.7S, *infra*, and on the CD-Rom accompanying this volume.

Add to text at end of subsection's fourth paragraph:

State law may also provide that the lessee has all the rights of a lessor on a written warranty,[61.1] or state law may provide that the lessee has the same rights against the manufacturer as does a consumer buyer.[61.2]

61.1   *See* Cal. Civ. Code § 1795.4 (West).

61.2   *See* Me. Rev. Stat. Ann. tit. 10, § 1168 (West).

19.4.2 Breach of Non-Written Express Warranties

Add to text after subsection's second sentence:

The revised version of Article 2, approved by the National Conference of Commissioners on Uniform State Laws in 2003 for consideration by state legislatures, explicitly provides that lessees have warranty-like rights as to promises that the manufacturer or other remote seller puts in writing inside or accompanying the product, or disseminates in advertising.[63.1]

63.1   Revised U.C.C. §§ 2-313A, 2-313B. Selected portions of revised Article 2 are reproduced in Appx. E.7S, *infra*, and on the CD-Rom accompanying this volume.

Page 653

19.5 Subsequent Lessor's Liability If Seller Was the Original Lessor (Liability of the Assignee Lessor)

Replace note 71 with:

71   *See* National Consumer Law Center, Unfair and Deceptive Acts and Practices § 6.6.2.2 (5th ed. 2001 and Supp.); *see also* Marchionna v. Ford Motor Co., 1995 U.S. Dist. LEXIS 11408 (N.D. Ill. Aug. 9, 1995) (magistrate's opinion); Bescos v. Bank of Am., 129 Cal. Rptr. 2d 423 (Ct. App. 2003) (does not apply to leases); LaChappelle v. Toyota Motor Credit Corp., 126 Cal. Rptr. 2d (Ct. App. 2002); Jarvis v. S. Oak Dodge, 747 N.E.2d 383 (Ill. App. Ct. 2001) (does not apply to leases), *rev'd on other grounds*, 773 N.E.2d 641 (Ill. 2002).

Add to text at end of section's fourth paragraph:

But as a result the consumer may only be able to raise defenses against an assignee's collection action, and not be able to raise affirmative claims against the assignee lessor, claims which could be raised utilizing the FTC Holder Notice.[71.1]

State law may also be relevant. For example, Connecticut's new leasing statute, patterned after the Uniform Consumer Leasing Act, provides that consumers can raise against holders the claims that they could raise against the dealer or originating lessors.[71.2] Illinois has a state holder rule that applies explicitly to leases, but only applies when the violation was apparent on the face of the lease.[71.3]

71.1   *See* Bescos v. Bank of Am., 129 Cal. Rptr. 2d 423 (Ct. App. 2003).
71.2   Conn. Gen. Stat. § 42-411(b) (effective July 1, 2003).
71.3   *See* 815 Ill. Comp. Stat. § 636/70; *see also* Jarvis v. S. Oak Dodge, Inc., 773 N.E.2d 641 (Ill. 2002).

19.6 Manufacturer and Dealer Liability Under Finance Leases

19.6.1 Consumer Has All Rights Provided to Lessor

Replace note 75 with:

75   One Stop Pet, Inc. v. E. Bus. Mach., Inc., 49 Va. Cir. 221, 40 U.C.C. Rep. Serv. 2d 497 (1999).

Page 654

Replace § 19.7 heading with:

19.7 Lessor's Warranty Obligations When Dealer Was Not the Original Lessor

Page 655

19.7.4 Lessor's Warranty Obligations in a Finance Lease

Addition to note 84.

84   *Replace entire One Stop Pet, Inc. citation with*: 49 Va. Cir. 221, 40 U.C.C. Rep. Serv. 2d 497 (1999).

Page 656

19.7.5 Can an Affiliated Lessor Cut Off Consumer Defenses?

Replace note 87 with:

87   *See* National Consumer Law Center, Unfair and Deceptive Acts and Practices § 6.6.2.2.1 (5th ed. 2001 and Supp.); *see also* Marchionna v. Ford Motor Co., 1995 U.S. Dist. LEXIS 11408 (N.D. Ill. Aug. 9, 1995) (magistrate's opinion); Bescos v. Bank of Am., 129 Cal. Rptr. 2d 423 (Ct. App. 2003) (does not apply to leases); LaChappelle v. Toyota Motor Credit Corp., 126 Cal. Rptr. 2d (Ct. App. 2002); Jarvis v. S. Oak Dodge, 747 N.E.2d 383 (Ill. App. Ct. 2001) (does not apply to leases), *rev'd on other grounds*, 773 N.E.2d 641 (Ill. 2002).

Replace note 95 with:

95   *See* National Consumer Law Center, Unfair and Deceptive Acts and Practices § 5.2.3.2 (5th ed. 2001 and Supp.).

Page 657

19.7.6 Lessor Liable Under the CLA If Lease Inaccurately Discloses Manufacturer Warranty

Addition to notes 98, 99.

98   *Replace Tarnoff citation with*: 1997 U.S. Dist. LEXIS 11792 (N.D. Ill. Aug. 5, 1997).

99   *Replace* Tarnoff *citation with*: 1997 U.S. Dist. LEXIS 11792 (N.D. Ill. Aug. 5, 1997).

Replace § 19.8 heading with: **19.8 Consumer Lessee's Damages for Breach of Warranty in a Lease**

Uniform Commercial Code Warranty Provisions

Page 701

Add to end of introductory text:

E.1 Listing of UCC Sections Reprinted in This Appendix

In 2001, NCCUSL and ALI approved a revised version of Article 1. As of early 2004, several states were considering revised Article 1 and Texas, Virginia, and the Virgin Islands had adopted it. Two subsections of note are reprinted here.

In 2003, NCCUSL and ALI approved a revised version of Articles 2 and 2A for consideration by state legislatures. The revisions have not yet been introduced in any state legislature. The provisions that affect UCC consumer warranty law are reprinted here.

Page 703

Add to text at end of list of sections:

Article 1 General Provisions

Part 3 Territorial Applicability and General Rules
    1-301. Territorial Applicability; Parties' Power to Choose Applicable Law.
    1-303. Course of Performance, Course of Dealing, and Usage of Trade.

Article 2 Sales

Prefatory Note
Part 1 Short Title, General Construction and Subject Matter
    2-103. Definitions and Index of Definitions.
    2-108. Transactions Subject to Other Law.
Part 2 Form, Formation, Terms and Readjustment of Contract; Electronic Contracting
    2-201. Formal Requirements; Statute of Frauds.
    2-202. Final ~~Written~~ Expression in a Record: Parol or Extrinsic Evidence.
    2-204. Formation in General.
    2-207. ~~Additional Terms in Acceptance or~~ Terms of Contract; Effect of Confirmation.
    2-211. Legal Recognition of Electronic Contracts, Records, and Signatures.
    2-212. Attribution.
    2-213. Electronic Communication.
Part 3 General Obligation and Construction of Contract
    2-312. Warranty of Title and Against Infringement; Buyer's Obligation Against Infringement.
    2-313. Express Warranties by Affirmation, Promise, Description, Sample; Remedial Promise.
    2-313a. Obligation to Remote Purchaser Created by Record Packaged with or Accompanying Goods.
    2-313b. Obligation to Remote Purchaser Created by Communication to the Public.
    2-314. Implied Warranty: Merchantability; Usage of Trade.
    2-316. Exclusion or Modification of Warranties.
    2-318. ~~Third Party~~ Third-Party Beneficiaries of Warranties ~~Express or Implied~~ and Obligations.
Part 5 Performance
    2-508. Cure by Seller of Improper Tender or Delivery; Replacement.

Replace Appx. E.2 heading with:

E.2 Article 1—Selected Provisions and Official Comments

Add note 1.1 at end of heading for § 1-101.

1.1 *Editor's note*: In 2001, the National Conference of Commissioners on Uniform State Laws (NCCUSL) approved a major revision to Article 1. As of early 2004, several states were considering the revised Article and Texas, Virginia, and the Virgin Islands had adopted it. It would add a statement to U.C.C. § 1-101 that Article 1 may be cited as the "Uniform Commercial Code—General Provisions." Significant substantive changes that revised Article 1 would make to the provisions reprinted here are highlighted in footnotes. Revised Article 1 is reproduced on the CD-Rom accompanying this volume.

Add note 1.2 at end of heading for § 1-102.

1.2 *Editor's note*: In 2001, NCCUSL approved a major revision to Article 1. As of early 2004, Texas, Virginia, and the Virgin Islands had adopted the revised Article and several states were considering it. It would transfer existing U.C.C. § 1-102(1) and (2) to revised U.C.C. § 1-103; transfer a somewhat rephrased version of U.C.C. § 1-102(5) to revised U.C.C. § 1-106; and transfer U.C.C. § 1-102(3) and (4) to revised U.C.C. § 1-302.

Page 705

Add note 1.3 at end of heading for § 1-103.	1.3 *Editor's note*: Revised Article 1, approved by NCCUSL in 2001, preserves this provision as revised U.C.C. § 1-103(b). As of early 2004, several states were considering revised Article 1 and Texas, Virginia, and the Virgin Islands had adopted it.
Add note 1.4 at end of heading for § 1-106.	1.4 *Editor's note*: Revised Article 1, approved by NCCUSL in 2001 and adopted by Texas, Virginia, and the Virgin Islands, preserves this provision as revised U.C.C. § 1-305.
Add note 1.5 at end of heading for § 1-107.	1.5 *Editor's note*: Revised Article 1, approved by NCCUSL in 2001 and adopted by Texas, Virginia, and the Virgin Islands, preserves this provision as revised U.C.C. § 1-306.

Page 706

Addition to note 2.	2 *Add new paragraph at end of note*: Revised Article 1, approved by NCCUSL in 2001, was under consideration by several states and had been adopted by Texas, Virginia, and the Virgin Islands as of early 2004. It would delete the U.C.C. § 1-201(19) definition of "good faith" in favor of an expanded definition found at revised U.C.C. § 1-201(b)(2) that would apply to all Articles except Article 5. The expanded definition includes both honesty in fact and the observance of reasonable commercial standards of fair dealing. Revised Article 1 also moves the definitions of notice, notify, knowledge, and related terms in U.C.C. § 1-201(25), (26), and (27) to revised U.C.C. § 1-202 without substantive change. It simplifies the definition of organization to "a person other than an individual," and makes a corresponding simplification in the definition of person. It expands the definition of purchase to include creating an interest in property by lease. It moves most of the definition of "security interest" to a separate section, revised U.C.C. § 1-203. It revises the definition of send to be consistent with revised U.C.C. § 9-102(a)(74). It moves the definition of value to revised U.C.C. § 9-204. It also revises the definition of conspicuous.

Page 711

Add note 2.1 at end of heading for § 1-203.	2.1 *Editor's note*: Revised Article 1, approved in 2001 by NCCUSL, would transfer this provision to revised U.C.C. § 1-304 and rephrase it to say that the duty applies to the "performance and enforcement" of all contracts.
Add note 2.2 at end of heading for § 1-204.	2.2 *Editor's note*: Revised Article 1, approved in 2001 by NCCUSL, would transfer this provision to revised U.C.C. §§ 1-205 and 1-302(b) without substantive change.

Page 712

Add note 2.3 at end of heading for § 1-205.	2.3 *Editor's note*: Revised Article 1, approved in 2001 by NCCUSL, would transfer this provision to revised U.C.C. § 1-303, along with the provision about course of performance that is currently found in U.C.C. §§ 2-208 and 2A-207. As a result, the rules about course of performance would apply to all U.C.C. Articles, not just Articles 2 and 2A, and the treatment of course of performance would be more consistent with the treatment of course of dealing and usage of trade. As of early 2004, several states were considering revised Article 1 and Texas, Virginia, and the Virgin Islands had adopted it. Revised U.C.C. § 1-303 is reprinted in Appx. E.6, *infra*.

Page 713

E.3   Article 2—Selected Provisions and Official Comments

Addition to note 3.	3 *Add at end of note*: Revised Article 1, approved in 2001 by NCCUSL, expands the definition of good faith to include both honesty in fact and the observance of reasonable commercial standards of fair dealing, whether or not the actor is a merchant. This definition, found in revised U.C.C. § 1-201(b)(2), would apply to all U.C.C. Articles except Article 5. A conforming amendment deletes the definition of good faith at U.C.C. § 2-103(1)(b) as redundant. As of early 2004, several states were considering revised Article 1 and Texas, Virginia, and the Virgin Islands had adopted it.

Page 719

Add note 3.1 at end of heading for § 2-208.	3.1 *Editor's note*: Revised Article 1, approved in 2001 by NCCUSL, would transfer this provision to revised U.C.C. § 1-303, along with the rules about course of dealing and usage of trade that are currently found in U.C.C. § 1-205. As a result, the rules about course of performance would apply to all U.C.C. Articles. Revised Article 1's treatment of course of performance is also somewhat more consistent with its treatment of course of dealing and usage of trade. As of early 2004, several states were considering revised Article

1 and Texas, Virginia, and the Virgin Islands had adopted it. Revised U.C.C. § 1-303 is reprinted in Appx. E.6, *infra*.

Page 753

E.4 Article 2A—Selected Provisions and Official Comments

Add note 5.1 at end of heading for § 2A-207.

5.1 *Editor's note*: Revised Article 1, approved in 2001 by NCCUSL, would transfer this provision to revised U.C.C. § 1-303, along with the rules about course of dealing and usage of trade that are currently found in U.C.C. § 1-205. As a result, the rules about course of performance would apply to all U.C.C. Articles. Revised Article 1's treatment of course of performance is also somewhat more consistent with its treatment of course of dealing and usage of trade. As of early 2004, several states were considering revised Article 1 and Texas, Virginia, and the Virgin Islands had adopted it. Revised U.C.C. § 1-303 is reprinted in Appx. E.6, *infra*.

Page 769

Add new appendices after Appx. E.5:

E.6 Revised Article 1—Selected Provisions and Official Comments[7]

ARTICLE 1

GENERAL PROVISIONS

* * *

PART 3

TERRITORIAL APPLICABILITY AND GENERAL RULES

§ 1-301. Territorial Applicability; Parties' Power to Choose Applicable Law.

(a) In this section:

(1) "Domestic transaction" means a transaction other than an international transaction.

(2) "International transaction" means a transaction that bears a reasonable relation to a country other than the United States.

(b) This section applies to a transaction to the extent that it is governed by another article of the [Uniform Commercial Code].

(c) Except as otherwise provided in this section:

(1) an agreement by parties to a domestic transaction that any or all of their rights and obligations are to be determined by the law of this State or of another State is effective, whether or not the transaction bears a relation to the State designated; and

(2) an agreement by parties to an international transaction that any or all of their rights and obligations are to be determined by the law of this State or of another State or country is effective, whether or not the transaction bears a relation to the State or country designated.

(d) In the absence of an agreement effective under subsection (c), and except as provided in subsections (e) and (g), the rights and obligations of the parties are determined by the law that would be selected by application of this State's conflict of laws principles.

(e) If one of the parties to a transaction is a consumer, the following rules apply:

(1) An agreement referred to in subsection (c) is not effective unless the transaction bears a reasonable relation to the State or country designated.

---

7 © Copyright 2001 by the American Law Institute and the National Conference of Commissioners on Uniform State Laws. Reproduced with the permission of the Permanent Editorial Board for the Uniform Commercial Code. All rights reserved.

(2) Application of the law of the State or country determined pursuant to subsection (c) or (d) may not deprive the consumer of the protection of any rule of law governing a matter within the scope of this section, which both is protective of consumers and may not be varied by agreement:

(A) of the State or country in which the consumer principally resides, unless subparagraph (B) applies; or

(B) if the transaction is a sale of goods, of the State or country in which the consumer both makes the contract and takes delivery of those goods, if such State or country is not the State or country in which the consumer principally resides.

(f) An agreement otherwise effective under subsection (c) is not effective to the extent that application of the law of the State or country designated would be contrary to a fundamental policy of the State or country whose law would govern in the absence of agreement under subsection (d).

(g) To the extent that [the Uniform Commercial Code] governs a transaction, if one of the following provisions of [the Uniform Commercial Code] specifies the applicable law, that provision governs and a contrary agreement is effective only to the extent permitted by the law so specified:

(1) Section 2-402;

(2) Sections 2A-105 and 2A-106;

(3) Section 4-102;

(4) Section 4A-507;

(5) Section 5-116;

[(6) Section 6-103;]

(7) Section 8-110;

(8) Sections 9-301 through 9-307.

Official Comment

Source: Former Section 1-105.

Summary of changes from former law: Section 1-301, which replaces former Section 1-105, represents a significant rethinking of choice of law issues addressed in that section. The new section reexamines both the power of parties to select the jurisdiction whose law will govern their transaction and the determination of the governing law in the absence of such selection by the parties. With respect to the power to select governing law, the draft affords greater party autonomy than former Section 1-105, but with important safeguards protecting consumer interests and fundamental policies.

Section 1-301 addresses contractual designation of governing law somewhat differently than does former Section 1-105. Former law allowed the parties to any transaction to designate a jurisdiction whose law governs if the transaction bears a "reasonable relation" to that jurisdiction. Section 1-301 deviates from this approach by providing different rules for transactions involving a consumer than for non-consumer transactions, such as "business to business" transactions.

In the context of consumer transactions, the language of Section 1-301, unlike that of former Section 1-105, protects consumers against the possibility of losing the protection of consumer protection rules applicable to the aspects of the transaction governed by the Uniform Commercial Code. In most situations, the relevant consumer protection rules will be those of the consumer's home

jurisdiction. A special rule, however, is provided for certain face-to-face sales transactions. (See Comment 3.)

In the context of business-to-business transactions, Section 1-301 generally provides the parties with greater autonomy to designate a jurisdiction whose law will govern than did former Section 1-105, but also provides safeguards against abuse that did not appear in former Section 1-105. In the non-consumer context, following emerging international norms, greater autonomy is provided in subsections (c)(1) and (c)(2) by deleting the former requirement that the transaction bear a "reasonable relation" to the jurisdiction. In the case of wholly domestic transactions, however, the jurisdiction designated must be a State. (See Comment 4.)

An important safeguard not present in former Section 1-105 is found in subsection (f). Subsection (f) provides that the designation of a jurisdiction's law is not effective (even if the transaction bears a reasonable relation to that jurisdiction) to the extent that application of that law would be contrary to a fundamental policy of the jurisdiction whose law would govern in the absence of contractual designation. Application of the law designated may be contrary to a fundamental policy of the State or country whose law would otherwise govern either because of the nature of the law designated or because of the "mandatory" nature of the law that would otherwise apply. (See Comment 6.)

In the absence of an effective contractual designation of governing law, former Section 1-105(1) directed the forum to apply its own law if the transaction bore "an appropriate relation to this state." This direction, however, was frequently ignored by courts.

Section 1-301(d) provides that, in the absence of an effective contractual designation, the forum should apply the forum's general choice of law principles, subject to certain special rules in consumer transactions. (See Comments 3 and 7).

1. **Applicability of section.** This section is neither a complete restatement of choice of law principles nor a free-standing choice of law statute. Rather, it is a provision of Article 1 of the Uniform Commercial Code. As such, the scope of its application is limited in two significant ways.

First, this section is subject to Section 1-102, which states the scope of Article 1. As that section indicates, Article 1, and the rules contained therein, apply to transactions to the extent that they are governed by one of the other Articles of the Uniform Commercial Code. Thus, this section does not apply to matters outside the scope of the Uniform Commercial Code, such as a services contract, a credit card agreement, or a contract for the sale of real estate. This limitation was implicit in former Section 1-105, and is made explicit in Section 1-301(b).

Second, subsection (g) provides that this section is subject to the specific choice of law provisions contained in other Articles of the Uniform Commercial Code. Thus, to the extent that a transaction otherwise within the scope of this section also is within the scope of one of those provisions, the rules of that specific provision, rather than of this section, apply.

The following cases illustrate these two limitations on the scope of Section 1-301:

> **Example 1:** A, a resident of Indiana, enters into an agreement with Credit Card Company, a Delaware corporation with its chief executive office located in New York, pursuant to which A agrees to pay Credit Card Company for purchases charged to A's credit card. The agreement contains a provision stating that it is governed by the law of South Dakota. The choice of law rules in Section 1-301 do not apply to this agreement because the agreement is not governed by any of the other Articles of the Uniform Commercial Code.
>
> **Example 2:** A, a resident of Indiana, maintains a checking account with Bank B, an Ohio banking corporation located in Ohio. At the time that the account was established, Bank B and A entered into a "Bank-Customer Agreement" governing their relationship with respect to the account. The Bank-Customer Agreement contains some provisions that purport to limit the liability of Bank B with respect to its decisions whether to honor or dishonor checks purporting to be drawn on A's account. The Bank-Customer Agreement also contains a provision stating that it is governed by the law of Ohio. The provisions purporting to limit the liability of Bank B deal with issues governed by Article 4. Therefore, determination of the law applicable to those issues (including determination of the effectiveness of the choice of law clause as it applies to those issues) is within the scope of Section 1-301 as provided in subsection (b). Nonetheless, the rules of Section 1-301 would not apply to that determination because of subsection (g), which states that

the choice of law rules in Section 4-102 govern instead.

2. **Contractual choice of law.** This section allows parties broad autonomy, subject to several important limitations, to select the law governing their transaction, even if the transaction does not bear a relation to the State or country whose law is selected. This recognition of party autonomy with respect to governing law has already been established in several Articles of the Uniform Commercial Code (see Sections 4A-507, 5-116, and 8-110) and is consistent with international norms. See, e.g., Inter-American Convention on the Law Applicable to International Contracts, Article 7 (Mexico City 1994); Convention on the Law Applicable to Contracts for the International Sale of Goods, Article 7(1) (The Hague 1986); EC Convention on the Law Applicable to Contractual Obligations, Article 3(1) (Rome 1980).

There are three important limitations on this party autonomy to select governing law. First, a different, and more protective, rule applies in the context of consumer transactions. (See Comment 3). Second, in an entirely domestic transaction, this section does not validate the selection of foreign law. (See Comment 4.) Third, contractual choice of law will not be given effect to the extent that application of the law designated would be contrary to a fundamental policy of the State or country whose law would be applied in the absence of such contractual designation. (See Comment 6).

This Section does not address the ability of parties to designate non-legal codes such as trade codes as the set of rules governing their transaction. The power of parties to make such a designation as part of their agreement is found in the principles of Section 1-302. That Section, allowing parties broad freedom of contract to structure their relations, is adequate for this purpose. This is also the case with respect to the ability of the parties to designate recognized bodies of rules or principles applicable to commercial transactions that are promulgated by intergovernmental organizations such as UNCITRAL or Unidroit. See, e.g., Unidroit Principles of International Commercial Contracts.

3. **Consumer transactions.** If one of the parties is a consumer (as defined in Section 1-201(b)(11)), subsection (e) provides the parties less autonomy to designate the State or country whose law will govern.

First, in the case of a consumer transaction, subsection (e)(1) provides that the transaction must bear a reasonable relation to the State or country designated. Thus, the rules of subsection (c) allowing the parties to choose the law of a jurisdiction to which the transaction bears no relation do not apply to consumer transactions.

Second, subsection (e)(2) provides that application of the law of the State or country determined by the rules of this section (whether or not that State or country was designated by the parties) cannot deprive the consumer of the protection of rules of law which govern matters within the scope of Section 1-301, are protective of consumers, and are not variable by agreement. The phrase "rule of law" is intended to refer to case law as well as statutes and administrative regulations. The requirement that the rule of law be one "governing a matter within the scope of this section" means that, consistent with the scope of Section 1-301, which governs choice of law only with regard to the aspects of a transaction governed by the Uniform Commercial Code, the relevant consumer rules are those that govern those aspects of the transaction. Such rules may be found in the Uniform Commercial Code itself, as are the consumer-protective rules in Part 6 of Article 9, or in other law if that other law governs the UCC aspects of the transaction. See, for example, the rule in Section 2.403 of the Uniform Consumer Credit Code which prohibits certain sellers and lessors from taking negotiable instruments other than checks and provides that a holder is not in good faith if the holder takes a negotiable instrument with notice that it is issued in violation of that section.

With one exception (explained in the next paragraph), the rules of law the protection of which the consumer may not be deprived are those of the jurisdiction in which the consumer principally resides. The jurisdiction in which the consumer principally resides is determined at the time relevant to the particular issue involved. Thus, for example, if the issue is one related to formation of a contract, the relevant consumer protective rules are rules of the jurisdiction in which the consumer principally resided at the time the facts relevant to contract formation occurred, even if the consumer no longer principally resides in that jurisdiction at the time the dispute arises or is litigated. If, on the other hand, the issue is one relating to enforcement of obligations, then the relevant consumer protective rules are those of the jurisdiction in which the consumer principally resides at the time enforcement is sought, even if the consumer did not principally reside in that jurisdiction at the time the transaction was entered into.

In the case of a sale of goods to a consumer, in which the consumer both makes the contract and takes possession of the goods in the same jurisdiction and that jurisdiction is not the consumer's principal residence, the rule in subsection (e)(2)(B) applies. In that situation, the relevant consumer protective rules, the protection of which the consumer may not be deprived by the choice of law rules of subsections (c) and (d), are those of the State or country in which both the contract is made and the consumer takes delivery of the goods. This rule, adapted from Section 2A-106 and Article 5 of the EC Convention on the Law Applicable to Contractual Obligations, enables a seller of goods engaging in face-to-face transactions to ascertain the consumer protection rules to which those sales are subject, without the necessity of determining the principal residence of each buyer. The reference in subsection (e)(2)(B) to the State or country in which the consumer makes the contract should not be read to incorporate formalistic concepts of where the last event necessary to conclude the contract took place; rather, the intent is to identify the state in which all material steps necessary to enter into the contract were taken by the consumer.

The following examples illustrate the application of Section 1-301(e)(2) in the context of a contractual choice of law provision:

> **Example 3:** Seller, located in State A, agrees to sell goods to Consumer, whose principal residence is in State B. The parties agree that the law of State A would govern this transaction. Seller ships the goods to Consumer in State B. An issue related to contract formation subsequently arises. Under the law of State A, that issue is governed by State A's uniform version of Article 2. Under the law of State B, that issue is governed by a non-uniform rule, protective of consumers and not variable by agreement, that brings about a different result than would occur under the uniform version of Article 2. Under Section 1-301(e)(2)(A), the parties' agreement that the law of State A would govern their transaction cannot deprive Consumer of the protection of State

B's consumer protective rule. This is the case whether State B's rule is codified in Article 2 of its Uniform Commercial Code or is found elsewhere in the law of State B.

> **Example 4:** Same facts as Example 3, except that (i) Consumer takes all material steps necessary to enter into the agreement to purchase the goods from Seller, and takes delivery of those goods, while on vacation in State A and (ii) the parties agree that the law of State C (in which Seller's chief executive office is located) would govern their transaction. Under subsections (c)(1) and (e)(1), the designation of the law of State C as governing will be effective so long as the transaction is found to bear a reasonable relation to State C (assuming that the relevant law of State C is not contrary to a fundamental policy of the State whose law would govern in the absence of agreement), but that designation cannot deprive Consumer of the protection of any rule of State A that is within the scope of this section and is both protective of consumers and not variable by agreement. State B's consumer protective rule is not relevant because, under Section 1-301(e)(2)(B), the relevant consumer protective rules are those of the jurisdiction in which the consumer both made the contract and took delivery of the goods—here, State A—rather than those of the jurisdiction in which the consumer principally resides.

It is important to note that subsection (e)(2) applies to all determinations of applicable law in transactions in which one party is a consumer, whether that determination is made under subsection (c) (in cases in which the parties have designated the governing law in their agreement) or subsection (d) (in cases in which the parties have not made such a designation). In the latter situation, application of the otherwise-applicable conflict of laws principles of the forum might lead to application of the laws of a State or country other than that of the consumer's principal residence. In such a case, however, subsection (e)(2) applies to preserve the applicability of consumer protection rules for the benefit of the consumer as described above.

4. **Wholly domestic transactions.** While this Section provides parties broad autonomy to select governing law, that autonomy is limited in the case of wholly domestic transactions. In a "domestic transaction," subsection (c)(1) validates only the designation of the law of a State. A "domestic transaction" is a transaction that does not bear a reasonable relation to a country other than the United States. (See subsection (a)). Thus, in a wholly domestic non-consumer transaction, parties may (subject to the limitations set out in subsections (f) and (g)) designate the law of any State but not the law of a foreign country.

5. **International transactions.** This section provides greater autonomy in the context of international transactions. As defined in subsection (a)(2), a transaction is an "international transaction" if it bears a reasonable relation to a country other than the United States. In a non-consumer international transaction, subsection (c)(2) provides that a designation of the law of any State or country is effective (subject, of course, to the limitations set out in subsections (f) and (g)). It is important to note that the transaction need

not bear a relation to the State or country designated if the transaction is international. Thus, for example, in a non-consumer lease of goods in which the lessor is located in Mexico and the lessee is located in Louisiana, a designation of the law of Ireland to govern the transaction would be given effect under this section even though the transaction bears no relation to Ireland. The ability to designate the law of any country in non-consumer international transactions is important in light of the common practice in many commercial contexts of designating the law of a "neutral" jurisdiction or of a jurisdiction whose law is well-developed. If a country has two or more territorial units in which different systems of law relating to matters within the scope of this section are applicable (as is the case, for example, in Canada and the United Kingdom), subsection (c)(2) should be applied to designation by the parties of the law of one of those territorial units. Thus, for example, subsection (c)(2) should be applied if the parties to a non-consumer international transaction designate the laws of Ontario or Scotland as governing their transaction.

6. **Fundamental policy.** Subsection (f) provides that an agreement designating the governing law will not be given effect to the extent that application of the designated law would be contrary to a fundamental policy of the State or country whose law would otherwise govern. This rule provides a narrow exception to the broad autonomy afforded to parties in subsection (c). One of the prime objectives of contract law is to protect the justified expectations of the parties and to make it possible for them to foretell with accuracy what will be their rights and liabilities under the contract. In this way, certainty and predictability of result are most likely to be secured. See Restatement (Second) Conflict of Laws, Section 187, comment *e*.

Under the fundamental policy doctrine, a court should not refrain from applying the designated law merely because application of that law would lead to a result different than would be obtained under the local law of the State or country whose law would otherwise govern. Rather, the difference must be contrary to a public policy of that jurisdiction that is so substantial that it justifies overriding the concerns for certainty and predictability underlying modern commercial law as well as concerns for judicial economy generally. Thus, application of the designated law will rarely be found to be contrary to a fundamental policy of the State or country whose law would otherwise govern when the difference between the two concerns a requirement, such as a statute of frauds, that relates to formalities, or general rules of contract law, such as those concerned with the need for consideration.

The opinion of Judge Cardozo in *Loucks v. Standard Oil Co. of New York*, 120 N.E. 198 (1918), regarding the related issue of when a state court may decline to apply the law of another state, is a helpful touchstone here:

> Our own scheme of legislation may be different. We may even have no legislation on the subject. That is not enough to show that public policy forbids us to enforce the foreign right. A right of action is property. If a foreign statute gives the right, the mere fact that we do not give a like right is no reason for refusing to help the plaintiff in getting what belongs to him. We are not so provincial as to say that every solution of a problem is wrong because we deal with it otherwise at home. Similarity of legislation has indeed this importance;

its presence shows beyond question that the foreign statute does not offend the local policy. But its absence does not prove the contrary. It is not to be exalted into an indispensable condition. The misleading word "comity" has been responsible for much of the trouble. It has been fertile in suggesting a discretion unregulated by general principles.

* * *

> The courts are not free to refuse to enforce a foreign right at the pleasure of the judges, to suit the individual notion of expediency or fairness. They do not close their doors, unless help would violate some fundamental principle of justice, some prevalent conception of good morals, some deep-rooted tradition of the common weal.

120 N.E. at 201-02 (citations to authorities omitted).

Application of the designated law may be contrary to a fundamental policy of the State or country whose law would otherwise govern either (i) because the substance of the designated law violates a fundamental principle of justice of that State or country or (ii) because it differs from a rule of that State or country that is "mandatory" in that it *must* be applied in the courts of that State or country without regard to otherwise-applicable choice of law rules of that State or country and without regard to whether the designated law is otherwise offensive. The mandatory rules concept appears in international conventions in this field, *e.g.*, EC Convention on the Law Applicable to Contractual Obligations, although in some cases the concept is applied to authorize the *forum* state to apply *its* mandatory rules, rather than those of the State or country whose law would otherwise govern. The latter situation is not addressed by this section. (See Comment 9.)

It is obvious that a rule that is freely changeable by agreement of the parties under the law of the State or country whose law would otherwise govern cannot be construed as a mandatory rule of that State or country. This does not mean, however, that rules that cannot be changed by agreement under that law are, for that reason alone, mandatory rules. Otherwise, contractual choice of law in the context of the Uniform Commercial Code would be illusory and redundant; the parties would be able to accomplish by choice of law no more than can be accomplished under Section 1-302, which allows variation of otherwise applicable rules by agreement. (Under Section 1-302, the parties could agree to vary the rules that would otherwise govern their transaction by substituting for those rules the rules that would apply if the transaction were governed by the law of the designated State or country without designation of governing law.) Indeed, other than cases in which a mandatory choice of law rule is established by statute (see, *e.g.*, Sections 9-301 through 9-307, explicitly preserved in subsection (g)), cases in which courts have declined to follow the designated law solely because a rule of the State or country whose law would otherwise govern is mandatory are rare.

7. **Choice of law in the absence of contractual designation.** Subsection (d), which replaces the second sentence of former Section 1-105(1), determines which jurisdiction's law governs a transaction in the absence of an effective contractual choice by the parties. Former Section 1-105(1) provided that the law of the forum (*i.e.*, the Uniform Commercial Code) applied if the transaction bore "an appropriate relation to this state." By using an "appropriate

relation'' test, rather than, for example, a "most significant relationship" test, Section 1-105(1) expressed a bias in favor of applying the forum's law. This bias, while not universally respected by the courts, was justifiable in light of the uncertainty that existed at the time of drafting as to whether the Uniform Commercial Code would be adopted by all the states; the pro-forum bias would assure that the Uniform Commercial Code would be applied so long as the transaction bore an "appropriate" relation to the forum. Inasmuch as the Uniform Commercial Code has been adopted, at least in part, in all U.S. jurisdictions, the vitality of this point is minimal in the domestic context, and international comity concerns militate against continuing the pro-forum, pro-UCC bias in transnational transactions. Whether the choice is between the law of two jurisdictions that have adopted the Uniform Commercial Code, but whose law differs (because of differences in enacted language or differing judicial interpretations), or between the Uniform Commercial Code and the law of another country, there is no strong justification for directing a court to apply different choice of law principles to that determination than it would apply if the matter were not governed by the Uniform Commercial Code. Similarly, given the variety of choice of law principles applied by the states, it would not be prudent to designate only one such principle as the proper one for transactions governed by the Uniform Commercial Code. Accordingly, in cases in which the parties have not made an effective choice of law, Section 1-301(d) simply directs the forum to apply its ordinary choice of law principles to determine which jurisdiction's law governs, subject to the special rules of Section 1-301(e)(2) with regard to consumer transactions.

8. **Primacy of other Uniform Commercial Code choice of law rules.** Subsection (g), which is essentially identical to former Section 1-105(2), indicates that choice of law rules provided in the other Articles govern when applicable.

9. **Matters not addressed by this section.** As noted in Comment 1, this section is not a complete statement of conflict of laws doctrines applicable in commercial cases. Among the issues this section does not address, and leaves to other law, three in particular deserve mention. First, a forum will occasionally decline to apply the law of a different jurisdiction selected by the parties when application of that law would be contrary to a fundamental policy of the forum jurisdiction, even if it would not be contrary to a fundamental policy of the State or country whose law would govern in the absence of contractual designation. Standards for application of this doctrine relate primarily to concepts of sovereignty rather than commercial law and are thus left to the courts. Second, in determining whether to give effect to the parties' agreement that the law of a particular State or country will govern their relationship, courts must, of necessity, address some issues as to the basic validity of that agreement. These issues might relate, for example, to capacity to contract and absence of duress. This section does not address these issues. Third, this section leaves to other choice of law principles of the forum the issues of whether, and to what extent, the forum will apply the same law to the non-UCC aspects of a transaction that it applies to the aspects of the transaction governed by the Uniform Commercial Code.

* * *

§ 1-303. Course of Performance, Course of Dealing, and Usage of Trade.

(a) A "course of performance" is a sequence of conduct between the parties to a particular transaction that exists if:

(1) the agreement of the parties with respect to the transaction involves repeated occasions for performance by a party; and

(2) the other party, with knowledge of the nature of the performance and opportunity for objection to it, accepts the performance or acquiesces in it without objection.

(b) A "course of dealing" is a sequence of conduct concerning previous transactions between the parties to a particular transaction that is fairly to be regarded as establishing a common basis of understanding for interpreting their expressions and other conduct.

(c) A "usage of trade" is any practice or method of dealing having such regularity of observance in a place, vocation, or trade as to justify an expectation that it will be observed with respect to the transaction in question. The existence and scope of such a usage must be proved as facts. If it is established that such a usage is embodied in a trade code or similar record, the interpretation of the record is a question of law.

(d) A course of performance or course of dealing between the parties or usage of trade in the vocation or trade in which they are engaged or of which they are or should be aware is relevant in ascertaining the meaning of the parties' agreement, may give particular meaning to specific terms of the agreement, and may supplement or qualify the terms of the agreement. A usage of trade applicable in the place in which part of the performance under the agreement is to occur may be so utilized as to that part of the performance.

(e) Except as otherwise provided in subsection (f), the express terms of an agreement and any applicable course of performance, course of dealing, or usage of trade must be construed whenever reasonable as consistent with each other. If such a construction is unreasonable:

(1) express terms prevail over course of performance, course of dealing, and usage of trade;

(2) course of performance prevails over course of dealing and usage of trade; and

(3) course of dealing prevails over usage of trade.

(f) Subject to Section 2-209, a course of performance is relevant to show a waiver or modification of any term inconsistent with the course of performance.

(g) Evidence of a relevant usage of trade offered by one party is not admissible unless that party has given the other party notice that the court finds sufficient to prevent unfair surprise to the other party.

Official Comments

Source: Former Sections 1-205, 2-208, and Section 2A-207.

Changes from former law: This section integrates the "course of performance" concept from Articles 2 and 2A into the principles of former Section 1-205, which deals with course of dealing and usage of trade. In so doing, the section slightly modifies the articulation of the course of performance rules to fit more comfortably with the approach and structure of former Section 1-205. There are also slight modifications to be more consistent with the definition of "agreement" in former Section 1-201(3). It should be noted that a course of performance that might otherwise establish a defense to the obligation of a party to a negotiable instrument is not available as a defense against a holder in due course who took the instrument without notice of that course of performance.

1. The Uniform Commercial Code rejects both the "lay-dictionary" and the "conveyancer's" reading of a commercial agreement. Instead the meaning of the agreement of the parties is to be determined by the language used by them and by their action, read and interpreted in the light of commercial practices and other surrounding circumstances. The measure and background for interpretation are set by the commercial context, which may explain and supplement even the language of a formal or final writing.

2. "Course of dealing," as defined in subsection (b), is restricted, literally, to a sequence of conduct between the parties previous to the agreement. A sequence of conduct after or under the agreement, however, is a "course of performance." "Course of dealing" may enter the agreement either by explicit provisions of the agreement or by tacit recognition.

3. The Uniform Commercial Code deals with "usage of trade" as a factor in reaching the commercial meaning of the agreement that the parties have made. The language used is to be interpreted as meaning what it may fairly be expected to mean to parties involved in the particular commercial transaction in a given locality or in a given vocation or trade. By adopting in this context the term "usage of trade," the Uniform Commercial Code expresses its intent to reject those cases which see evidence of "custom" as representing an effort to displace or negate "established rules of law." A distinction is to be drawn between mandatory rules of law such as the Statute of Frauds provisions of Article 2 on Sales whose very office is to control and restrict the actions of the parties, and which cannot be abrogated by agreement, or by a usage of trade, and those rules of law (such as those in Part 3 of Article 2 on Sales) which fill in points which the parties have not considered and in fact agreed upon. The latter rules hold "unless otherwise agreed" but yield to the contrary agreement of the parties. Part of the agreement of the parties to which such rules yield is to be sought for in the usages of trade which furnish the background and give particular meaning to the language used, and are the framework of common understanding controlling any general rules of law which hold only when there is no such understanding.

4. A usage of trade under subsection (c) must have the "regularity of observance" specified. The ancient English tests for "custom" are abandoned in this connection. Therefore, it is not required that a usage of trade be "ancient or immemorial," "universal," or the like. Under the requirement of subsection (c) full recognition is thus available for new usages and for usages currently observed by the great majority of decent dealers, even though dissidents ready to cut corners do not agree. There is room also for proper recognition of usage agreed upon by merchants in trade codes.

5. The policies of the Uniform Commercial Code controlling explicit unconscionable contracts and clauses (Sections 1-304, 2-302) apply to implicit clauses that rest on usage of trade and carry forward the policy underlying the ancient requirement that a custom or usage must be "reasonable." However, the emphasis is shifted. The very fact of commercial acceptance makes out a *prima facie* case that the usage is reasonable, and the burden is no longer on the usage to establish itself as being reasonable. But the anciently established policing of usage by the courts is continued to the extent necessary to cope with the situation arising if an unconscionable or dishonest practice should become standard.

6. Subsection (d), giving the prescribed effect to usages of which the parties "are or should be aware," reinforces the provision of subsection (c) requiring not universality but only the described "regularity of observance" of the practice or method. This subsection also reinforces the point of subsection (c) that such usages may be either general to trade or particular to a special branch of trade.

7. Although the definition of "agreement" in Section 1-201 includes the elements of course of performance, course of dealing, and usage of trade, the fact that express reference is made in some sections to those elements is not to be construed as carrying a contrary intent or implication elsewhere. Compare Section 1-302(c).

8. In cases of a well established line of usage varying from the general rules of the Uniform Commercial Code where the precise amount of the variation has not been worked out into a single

standard, the party relying on the usage is entitled, in any event, to the minimum variation demonstrated. The whole is not to be disregarded because no particular line of detail has been established. In case a dominant pattern has been fairly evidenced, the party relying on the usage is entitled under this section to go to the trier of fact on the question of whether such dominant pattern has been incorporated into the agreement.

9. Subsection (g) is intended to insure that this Act's liberal recognition of the needs of commerce in regard to usage of trade shall not be made into an instrument of abuse.

E.7 Revised Article 2—Selected Provisions and Official Comments[8]

PREFATORY NOTE

After over a decade of analysis and discussion, a set of amendments to Article 2 has been adopted. For the most part, the changes update the article to accommodate electronic commerce, which is desirable to avoid questions of interrelation with federal law, and also to reflect the development of business practices, changes in other law, and to resolve some interpretive difficulties of practical significance. The amendments reflect the fact that, overall, Article 2 continues to serve well. This is largely a result of the approach of the Article, which relies to a large extent on the ability of the parties to adapt its provisions by agreement, including course of performance, course of dealing and usage of trade, and on the courts to apply the provisions sensibly. A summary of the amendments includes:

Good Faith

Consistent with the other articles of the Uniform Commercial Code, other than Article 5, the definition of good faith, which is in Section 2-103(1)(j), is amended to cover both "honesty in fact and observance of reasonable commercial standards of fair dealing".

Scope

Although the scope of Article 2 remains unchanged, three amendments affect its application. First, "information," which is an undefined term, is excluded from the definition of "goods" in Section 2-103(1)(k). Second, the subject matter of "foreign exchange transactions," a term defined in Section 2-103(1)(i) in a manner that distinguishes transactions crediting and debiting trading balances from transactions for the physical exchange of money, is also excluded from the definition of "goods." Finally, Section 2-108 addresses the relationship between Article 2 and other laws relating to transactions in goods.

Electronic Commerce

There are a number of changes designed to accommodate electronic commerce. These include the change of the term "writing" to "record" throughout the article, a redefinition of the terms "sign" and "conspicuous," and definitions and use of the new terms "electronic," "electronic agent," and "electronic record." Section 2-204, which is concerned with formation generally, has been amended to provide that a contract may be formed by the interaction of electronic agents or the interaction of an individual and an electronic agent. New Section 2-211 provides that a record, signature, or contract cannot be denied legal effect and enforce-

ability merely because it is electronic in form. New Section 2-212 provides a rule to determine whether an electronic record or electronic signature is attributable to a person. New Section 2-213 provides that if receipt of an electronic communication has a legal effect, that effect is not changed merely because no individual is aware of the receipt. This section also provides that receipt of an electronic communication does not establish the content of the communication.

Formation and Terms

The statute-of-frauds provision, contained in Section 2-201, has been amended to change the jurisdictional amount from $500 to $5,000 to reflect over 50 years of inflation. The exception for admissions in court has been broadened to include out-of-court admissions "under oath." The amended section also implicitly recognizes the application of nonstatutory exceptions such as promissory estoppel. The section also expressly excludes application of a statute-of-frauds provision from other law which is predicated on the passage of time.

Section 2-202, which sets out the rules on parol or extrinsic evidence, has been amended to clarify that a finding of ambiguity is not a prerequisite to an admission of evidence of a course of dealing, course of performance, or usage of trade for the purpose of explaining a term.

Section 2-207 has been thoroughly revised. The section no longer addresses issues of offer and acceptance. The principle that a definite and seasonable expression of acceptance on terms other than those of the offer may operate as an acceptance, which was contained previously in Section 2-207(1), has been moved to Section 2-206(3), and Section 2-207 is now only concerned with the terms of the contract. Section 2-207 applies to all contracts, not just those formed by a "battle of the forms". The amended section now provides that terms that appear in the records of both parties, terms to which both parties agree, and supplemental terms under the UCC constitute the contract.

Former Sections 2-319 through 2-324 that dealt with shipping and delivery have been deleted. Those sections dealt with standard shipping terms in a manner inconsistent with modern commercial usage.

Clarifying what was unclear in the prior law, Section 2-503 now provides that, when goods are in the bailee's possession and are to be delivered without movement by tender of delivery, a bailee's acknowledgment must be to the buyer. This section now explicitly provides that the effect of a bailee's receipt of notice on third-party rights is subject to Article 9. Section 2-504 has also been changed to clarify that compliance with the requirements for a shipping contract requires a seller to put "conforming" goods in the carrier's possession.

Section 2-513 now provides explicitly that the parties may by agreement fix a standard of inspection, and Section 2-309 now

---

provides explicitly that the parties may by agreement specify a standard for the nature and timing of a notice of termination.

Sections 2-325, 2-506, and 2-514 have been amended to coordinate with Article 5.

Warranties

Section 2-312 has been amended to bring into the text what was formerly in the comments; that is, the warranty of title is breached if the sale "unreasonably exposes the buyer to litigation because of a colorable claim or interest in the goods."

Section 2-313, which is subject to Section 2-318, has been amended to make it clear that the section applies only to parties in privity. The section has also been amended to provide that a "remedial promise," which is defined in Section 2-103(1)(n) as a promise by a seller to repair, replace, or refund upon the happening of an agreed event, is enforceable without reference to the basis-of-the-bargain test. "Remedial promise" as a distinct category of promise was created to deal with a statute-of-limitations problem. New Section 2-725(2)(c) provides that a cause of action accrues if a remedial promise is not performed when performance is due.

New Sections 2-313A and 2-313B, which are also subject to Section 2-318, create statutory obligations in the nature of express warranties that run directly from a seller to a remote purchaser that is not in privity. Each section applies only to "new goods or goods sold or leased as new goods in a transaction of purchase in the normal chain of distribution," excludes liability for statements that are mere opinion, permits the seller to modify or limit remedies as long as the modification or limitation is provided to the remote purchaser at or before the time of purchase, and excludes recovery for consequential damages in the form of lost profits. Liability under Section 2-313A arises only if the seller "makes an affirmation of fact or promise that relates to the goods, provides a description that relates to the goods, or makes a remedial promise," the affirmation, promise, description or remedial promise is "in a record packaged with or accompanying the goods," and the seller "reasonably expects the record to be, and the record is, furnished to the remote purchaser." Section 2-313B differs from Section 2-313A in that it is predicated on an affirmation of fact, promise, description or remedial promise made "in advertising or a similar communication to the public." In addition to the tests for liability set forth in Section 2-313A, under Section 2-313B the remote purchaser must also enter into the transaction "with knowledge of and with the expectation that the goods will conform to the affirmation of fact, promise, or description, or that the seller will perform the remedial promise."

Section 2-316, which deals with the exclusion or modification of warranties, has been amended to provide that a disclaimer of the implied warranty of merchantability in a consumer contract, which is defined in Section 2-103(1)(d) as a contract between a merchant seller and a consumer, must be in a record, must be conspicuous, and must use understandable language that states "[T]he seller undertakes no responsibility for the quality of the goods except as otherwise provided in this contract." The section as amended also provides that a disclaimer of the implied warranty of fitness for a particular purpose in a consumer contract must be in a record, be conspicuous, and use understandable language that states "[T]he seller assumes no responsibility that the goods will be fit for any particular purpose for which you may be buying these goods,

except as otherwise provided in this contract." The amendments also now provide that an "as is" or "with all faults" disclaimer in a consumer contract must be conspicuously set forth in a record if the consumer contract is evidenced by a record. The amended section also clarifies that a buyer's refusal to inspect must be predicated on a demand by the seller.

Section 2-318 retains the three alternatives of the former article but is revised to extend to the class of persons designated in each alternative the benefits of remedial promises and statutory obligations in the nature of express warranties under Sections 2-313A and 2-313B.

Performance and Breach

Several provisions on acceptance, rejection, and revocation of acceptance have been amended. The test for rejection of a single installment in Section 2-612 is now consistent with the test for revocation of acceptance under Section 2-608. The test is that the installment may be rejected if the installment's value to the buyer is substantially impaired. Section 2-602 has been amended to clarify that the buyer must take reasonable care of the goods in both rightful and wrongful rejection cases. Sections 2-602 and 2-608 have been amended in light of many cases to provide that a buyer's reasonable use of goods after rejection or revocation of acceptance is not an acceptance of the goods, but the buyer may be obligated to pay for the value of the use to the buyer. Unreasonable use remains wrongful against the seller and is an acceptance if ratified.

Section 2-508 has been revised to provide that, in a nonconsumer contract, the seller has a right to cure if the buyer justifiably revokes acceptance under Section 2-608(2). The section now predicates the right to cure on good-faith performance by the seller and, when the time for performance has expired, on the cure being appropriate and timely under the circumstances. Another amendment to this section imposes liability on the seller for the buyer's reasonable expenses caused by the breach and subsequent cure.

Section 2-605 has been amended to provide that a buyer that fails to state with particularity a defect ascertainable by reasonable inspection that justifies revocation of acceptance suffers the same consequences as a buyer that similarly fails to particularize a defect in connection with a rejection. The particularity requirement applies only if the seller has a right to cure the defect, not merely the ability to cure. Failure to state a defect with particularity bars the buyer from predicating a rightful rejection or justifiable revocation of acceptance on the defect but no longer bars the buyer from using the defect to establish breach. Section 2-607 has been amended to provide that failure to give timely notice of breach in the case of accepted goods bars a remedy only to the extent the seller is prejudiced by the untimely notice.

Section 2-509, which governs risk of loss, has been amended to provide that if the goods are to be delivered through a bailee and tender is based on notification to the bailee, for risk of loss to pass, the bailee must acknowledge to the buyer that the buyer has a right to possess the goods. In the case of a noncarrier, nonbailee delivery, the section has been amended so that risk of loss for both merchant and nonmerchant passes upon the buyer's receipt of the goods.

The terminology in the excuse provisions, Sections 2-614 through 2-616, has been changed to govern all performance issues and not just delivery issues.

Remedies

Sections 2-703 and 2-711 contain a comprehensive indexing, respectively, of seller's and buyer's remedies.

A credit seller's right to reclaim the goods under Section 2-702 has been changed to provide that demand must be made within a "reasonable time" based on the circumstances instead of the former fixed period of 10 days after delivery or a longer reasonable time if there has been a misrepresentation of solvency. A cash seller's right to reclaim goods under Section 2-507 is now parallel to the credit seller's right under Section 2-702.

For a stoppage in transit in cases other than insolvency, Section 2-705 has been broadened by eliminating the requirement that the goods be by the "carload, truckload, planeload or larger shipments of express or freight" as this is no longer necessary due to modern tracking technology.

The amendments incorporate the change to Section 2-502(1) that were promulgated as part of the revision of Article 9 which provide a consumer buyer with a right to possession if the seller repudiates or fails to deliver the goods as required by the contract. The vesting rule of subsection (2) has been broadened to cover all rights of buyer under the section. The change to Section 2-716 promulgated as part of the revision of Article 9 is also included in the amendments with the vesting rule in this section broadened so that it applies to all buyers that seek replevin. In addition, Section 2-716 has been expanded to give courts discretion in nonconsumer contracts to enforce the parties' agreement for specific performance unless the sole remaining obligation is the payment of money.

Several provisions governing sellers' damages have been clarified or amended. Section 2-706 now explicitly provides that a seller's failure to resell in accordance with the section does not bar the seller from other remedies. Under Section 2-707, the remedies available to a person in the position of a seller include all remedies available to sellers generally. Under Section 2-708, the market price of goods in the case of an anticipatory repudiation is measured at the "expiration of a commercially reasonable time after the seller learned of the repudiation" and Section 2-723 has been amended to be consistent. Section 2-708(2) now explicitly provides that the lost-profit measure of damages is available when the resale remedy is not adequate and the troublesome language in former 2-708(2) that provided for "due allowance for costs reasonably incurred and due credit for payments or proceeds of resale" has been deleted. Moreover, sellers may now recover consequential damages in nonconsumer contracts subject to a test set out in Section 2-710(2) that parallels the test for buyers' consequential damages in Section 2-715(2)(a). Sellers may not recover consequential damages in consumer contracts.

Consistent with Section 2-708(1), Section 2-713 on buyers' market damages has been amended to provide that the market price in the case of an anticipatory repudiation is measured at the "expiration of a commercially reasonable time after the seller learned of the repudiation." The market price in cases other than anticipatory repudiation is now measured at the time for tender.

Section 2-718 has been amended to provide that, in a nonconsumer contract, the test for enforceability of a liquidated damage clause is limited to the reasonableness of the clause in light of the actual or anticipated harm. The former language that indicated that a clause that provided for an unreasonably large amount of liquidated damages was void as a penalty has been deleted because it might cause some to infer, incorrectly, that a clause setting an unreasonably small amount of liquidated damages cannot constitute a penalty. Language has also been added to clarify that the enforceability of a clause that limits remedies is to be determined under Section 2-719.

Section 2-718(3) has been amended to expand a buyer's right to restitution of the price paid to all circumstances in which the seller stops performance because of the buyer's breach or insolvency. The statutory liquidated-damages deduction from the breaching buyer's restitution remedy has also been eliminated.

The general limitations period of Section 2-725(1) has been amended from a flat four years to "one year after the breach was or should have been discovered, but no longer than five years after the right of action accrued." The limitation period may not be reduced in a consumer contract. In addition to retaining the accrual rules from current law, the section now provides specific accrual rules for breach by repudiation, breach of a remedial promise, a claim over (indemnity), breach of a warranty of title, breach of a warranty against infringement, and breach of a statutory obligation arising under Section 2-313A or Section 2-313B.

A Note Regarding the CISG

When parties enter into an agreement for the international sale of goods, because the United States is a party to the United Nations Convention on Contracts for the International Sale of Goods (CISG), the Convention may be the applicable law. Since many of the provisions of the CISG appear similar to provisions of Article 2, the committee drafting the amendments considered making references in the Official Comments to provisions in the CISG. However, upon reflection, it was decided that this would not be done because the inclusion of such references might suggest a greater similarity between Article 2 and the CISG than in fact exists.

The principle concern was the possibility of an inappropriate use of cases decided under one law to interpret provisions of the other law. This type of interpretation is contrary to the mandate of both the Uniform Commercial Code and the CISG. Specifically, Section 1-103(b) of the Code directs courts to interpret it in light of its common-law history. This was an underlying principle in original Article 2, and these amendments do not change this in any way. On the other hand, the CISG specifically directs courts to interpret its provisions in light of international practice with the goal of achieving international uniformity. *See* CISG art. 7. This approach specifically eschews the use of domestic law, such as Article 2, as a basis for interpretation.

AMENDMENTS TO ARTICLE 2

SALES

PART 1

SHORT TITLE, GENERAL CONSTRUCTION AND SUBJECT MATTER

§ 2-103. Definitions and Index of Definitions.

(1) In this article unless the context otherwise requires:

(a) "Buyer" means a person ~~who~~ that buys or contracts to buy goods.

(b) "Conspicuous", with reference to a term, means so written, displayed, or presented that a reasonable person against which it is to operate ought to have noticed it. A term in an electronic record intended to evoke a response by an electronic agent is conspicuous if it is presented in a form that would enable a reasonably configured electronic agent to take it into account or react to it without review of the record by an individual. Whether a term is "conspicuous" or not is a decision for the court. Conspicuous terms include the following:

  (i) for a person:

   (A) a heading in capitals equal to or greater in size than the surrounding text, or in contrasting type, font, or color to the surrounding text of the same or lesser size; and

   (B) language in the body of a record or display in larger type than the surrounding text, or in contrasting type, font, or color to the surrounding text of the same size, or set off from surrounding text of the same size by symbols or other marks that call attention to the language; and

  (ii) for a person or an electronic agent, a term that is so placed in a record or display that the person or electronic agent may not proceed without taking action with respect to the particular term.

(c) "Consumer" means an individual who buys or contracts to buy goods that, at the time of contracting, are intended by the individual to be used primarily for personal, family, or household purposes.

(d) "Consumer contract" means a contract between a merchant seller and a consumer.

(e) "Delivery" means the voluntary transfer of physical possession or control of goods.

(f) "Electronic" means relating to technology having electrical, digital, magnetic, wireless, optical, electromagnetic, or similar capabilities.

(g) "Electronic agent" means a computer program or an electronic or other automated means used independently to initiate an action or respond to electronic records or performances in whole or in part, without review or action by an individual.

(h) "Electronic record" means a record created, generated, sent, communicated, received, or stored by electronic means.

(i) "Foreign exchange transaction" means a transaction in which one party agrees to deliver a quantity of a specified money or unit of account in consideration of the other party's agreement to deliver another quantity of a different money or unit of account either currently or at a future date, and in which delivery is to be through funds transfer, book entry accounting, or other form of payment order, or other agreed means to transfer a credit balance. The term includes a transaction of this type involving two or more moneys and spot, forward, option, or other products derived from underlying moneys and any combination of these transactions. The term does not include a transaction involving two or more moneys in which one or both of the parties is obligated to make physical delivery, at the time of contracting or in the future, of banknotes, coins, or other form of legal tender or specie.

[(j) Reserved]

[(j) "Good faith" means honesty in fact and the observance of reasonable commercial standards of fair dealing .]

Legislative Note: The definition of "good faith" should not be adopted if the jurisdiction has enacted this definition as part of Article 1.

(k) "Goods" means all things that are movable at the time of identification to a contract for sale. The term includes future goods, specially manufactured goods, the unborn young of animals, growing crops, and other identified things attached to realty as described in Section 2-107. The term does not include information, the money in which the price is to be paid, investment securities under Article 8, the subject matter of foreign exchange transactions, or choses in action.

(*l*) "Receipt of goods" means taking physical possession of goods.

(m) "Record" means information that is inscribed on a tangible medium or that is stored in an electronic or other medium and is retrievable in perceivable form.

Legislative Note: The definition of "record" should not be adopted if the jurisdiction has enacted revised Article 1.

(n) "Remedial promise" means a promise by the seller to repair or replace goods or to refund all or part of the price of goods upon the happening of a specified event.

(d) (*o*) "Seller" means a person ~~who~~ that sells or contracts to sell goods.

(p) "Sign" means, with present intent to authenticate or adopt a record:

    (i) to execute or adopt a tangible symbol; or

    (ii) to attach to or logically associate with the record an electronic sound, symbol, or process.

(2) Other definitions applying to this Article or to specified Parts thereof, and the sections in which they appear are:

"Acceptance". Section 2-606.

~~"Banker's credit". Section 2-325.~~

"Between merchants". Section 2-104.

"Cancellation". Section 2-106(4).

"Commercial unit". Section 2-105.

"Confirmed credit". Section 2-325.

"Conforming to contract". Section 2-106.

"Contract for sale". Section 2-106.

"Cover". Section 2-712.

"Entrusting". Section 2-403.

"Financing agency". Section 2-104.

"Future goods". Section 2-105.

"Goods". Section 2-103.

"Identification". Section 2-501.

"Installment contract". Section 2-612.

~~"Letter of credit". Section 2-325.~~

"Lot". Section 2-105.

"Merchant". Section 2-104.

~~"Overseas". Section 2-323.~~

"Person in position of seller". Section 2-707.

"Present sale". Section 2-106.

"Sale". Section 2-106.

"Sale on approval". Section 2-326.

"Sale or return". Section 2-326.

"Termination". Section 2-106.

(3) "Control" as provided in Section 7-106 ~~The~~ and the following definitions in other Articles apply to this Article:

"Check". Section 3-104(f).

"Consignee". Section 7-102(3).

"Consignor". Section 7-102(4).

"Consumer goods". Section 9-102(a)(23).

"Dishonor". Section 3-502.

"Draft". Section 3-104(e).

"Honor". Section 5-102(a)(8).

"Injunction against honor". Section 5-109(b).

"Letter of credit". Section 5-102(a)(10).

(4) In addition Article 1 contains general definitions and principles of construction and interpretation applicable throughout this Article.

In this Section, the original Official Comment has been substantially revised or replaced by the following 2003 Official Comment. However, the original Official Comment may remain appropriate legislative history. For that reason, the original Official Comment may be found in Appendix [___] for the convenience of those who may wish to study it. [Editor's note: *Appendix [___] is not reprinted here, but the original Official Comment is reprinted in Appendix E of the main edition.*]

Official Comment

1. The first sentence of the definition of "conspicuous" is based on Section 1-201(10) but the concept is expanded to include terms in electronic records. The general standard is, that to be conspicuous, a term ought to be noticed by a reasonable person. The second sentence states a special rule for situations where the sender of an electronic record intends to evoke a response from an electronic agent. In that case, the presentation of the term must be capable of evoking a response from a reasonably configured electronic agent. Whether a term is conspicuous is an issue for the court.

Paragraphs (i) and (ii) set out several methods for making a term conspicuous. The requirement that a term be conspicuous functions both as notice (the term ought to be noticed) and as a basis for planning (giving guidance to the party that relies on the term about how that result can be achieved).

Paragraph (i), which relates to the general standard for conspicuousness, is based on original Section 1-201(10) but it is intended to give more guidance than was given in the prior version of this definition. Paragraph (ii) is new and it relates to the special standard for electronic records that are intended to evoke a response from an electronic agent. Although these paragraphs indicate some of the methods for calling attention to a term, the test is whether notice of the term can reasonably be expected. The statutory language should not be construed to permit a result that is inconsistent with that test.

2. A "consumer" is a natural person (*cf.* Section 1-201(27)) who enters into a transaction for a purpose typically associated with consumers—*i.e.*, a personal, family or household purpose. The requirement that the buyer intend that the goods be used "primarily" for personal, family or household purposes is generally consistent with the definition of consumer goods in revised Article 9. *See* Section 9-102(a)(23).

3. The term "consumer contract" is limited to a contract for sale between a seller that is a "merchant" and a buyer that is a

"consumer". Thus, neither a sale by a consumer to a consumer nor a sale by a merchant to an individual who intends that the goods be used primarily in a home business qualify as a consumer contract.

4. "Delivery" with respect to documents of title is defined in Section 1-201(15) as the voluntary transfer of possession of the document. This Article defines "delivery" with respect to goods to mean the voluntary transfer of physical possession or control of the goods.

5. The electronic contracting provisions, including the definitions of "electronic," "electronic agent," "electronic record," and "record" are based on the provisions of the Uniform Electronic Transactions Act and are consistent with the federal Electronic Signatures in Global and National Commerce Act (15 U.S.C. § 7001 *et seq.*).

6. The term "foreign exchange transaction" is used in the definition of goods in Section 2-103(1)(k). That definition excludes "the subject matter of foreign exchange transactions."

7. The definition of "goods" in this article has been amended to exclude information not associated with goods. Thus, this article does not directly apply to an electronic transfer of information, such as the transaction involved in *Specht v. Netscape*, 150 F. Supp. 2d 585 (S.D.N.Y. 2001), *aff'd*, 306 F.3d 17 (2d. Cir. 2002). However, transactions often include both goods and information: some are transactions in goods as that term is used in Section 2-102, and some are not. For example, the sale of "smart goods" such as an automobile is a transaction in goods fully within this article even though the automobile contains many computer programs. On the other hand, an architect's provision of architectural plans on a computer disk would not be a transaction in goods. When a transaction includes both the sale of goods and the transfer of rights in information, it is up to the courts to determine whether the transaction is entirely within or outside of this article, or whether or to what extent this article should be applied to a portion of the transaction. While this article may apply to a transaction including information, nothing in this Article alters, creates, or diminishes intellectual property rights.

The definition has also been amended to exclude the subject matter of "foreign exchange transactions." *See* Section 2-103(1)(i). Although a contract in which currency in the commodity exchanged is a sale of goods, an exchange in which delivery is "through funds transfer, book entry accounting, or other form of payment order, or other agreed means to transfer a credit balance is not a sale of goods and is not governed by this article. In the latter case, Article 4A or other law applies. On the other hand, if the parties agree to a forward transaction where dollars are to be physically delivered in exchange for the delivery of another currency, the transaction is not within the "foreign exchange" exclusion and this article applies.

8. Section 1-202(e) provides rules for determining whether a notice or notification has been received. This Article by contrast defines "receipt of goods" to mean the taking of physical possession of the goods.

9. A "remedial promise" is a promise by the seller to take a certain remedial action upon the happening of a specified event. The types of remedies contemplated by this term as used in this Article are specified in the definition—repair or replacement of the goods, or refund of all or part of the price. No other promise by a seller qualifies as a remedial promise. Furthermore, the seller is entitled to specify precisely the event that will precipitate the obligation. Typical examples include a commitment to repair any parts of the goods that are defective, or a commitment to refund the purchase price if the goods fail to perform in a certain manner. A post-sale promise to correct a problem with the goods that the seller is not obligated to correct that is made to placate a dissatisfied customer is not within the definition of remedial promise. Whether the promised remedy is exclusive, and if so whether it has failed its essential purpose, is determined under Section 2-719.

The distinction between a remedial promise and a warranty that is made in this Article resolves a statute-of-limitations problem. Under original Section 2-725, a right of action for breach of an express warranty accrued at the time the goods were tendered unless the warranty explicitly extended to the future performance of the goods. In that case, the statute of limitations began to run at the time of the discovery of the breach. By contrast, a right of action for breach of an ordinary (non-warranty) promise accrued when the promise was breached. A number of courts held that commitments by sellers to take remedial action in the event the goods proved to be defective during a specified period of time constituted a warranty, and in theses cases the courts determined that the statute of limitations began to run at the time that the goods were tendered. Other courts used strained reasoning that allowed them to apply the discovery rule even though the promise referred to the future performance of the seller and not the future performance of the goods.

Under this Article, a promise by the seller to take remedial action is not a warranty at all and therefore the statute of limitations for a breach of a remedial promise does not begin to run at either the time the goods are tendered or at the time the breach is discovered. Section 2-725(2)(c) separately addresses the accrual of a right of action for a remedial promise. *See* Official Comment 3 to Section 2-725.

10. The definition of "sign" is broad enough to cover any record that is signed within the meaning of Article 1 or that contains an electronic signature within the meaning of the Uniform Electronic Transactions Act. It is consistent with the federal Electronic Signatures in Global and National Commerce Act (15 U.S.C. § 7001 *et seq.*).

§ 2-108. Transactions Subject to Other Law.

(1) A transaction subject to this article is also subject to any applicable:

(a) [list any certificate of title statutes of this State covering automobiles, trailers, mobile homes, boats, farm tractors, or the like], except with respect to the rights of a buyer in ordinary course of business under Section 2-403(2) which arise before a certificate of title covering the goods is effective in the name of any other buyer;

(b) rule of law that establishes a different rule for consumers; or

(c) statute of this state applicable to the transaction, such as a statute dealing with:

    (i)   the sale or lease of agricultural products;

    (ii) the transfer of human blood, blood products, tissues, or parts;

    (iii) the consignment or transfer by artists of works of art or fine prints;

    (iv) distribution agreements, franchises, and other relationships through which goods are sold;

    (v) the misbranding or adulteration of food products or drugs; and

    (vi) dealers in particular products, such as automobiles, motorized wheelchairs, agricultural equipment, and hearing aids.

(2) Except for the rights of a buyer in ordinary course of business under subsection (1)(a), in the event of a conflict between this article and a law referred to in subsection (1), that law governs.

(3) For purposes of this article, failure to comply with a law referred to in subsection (1) has only the effect specified in that law.

(4) This article modifies, limits, and supersedes the federal Electronic Signatures in Global and National Commerce Act, 15 U.S.C. Section 7001 et seq., except that nothing in this article modifies, limits, or supersedes Section 7001(c) of that Act or authorizes electronic delivery of any of the notices described in Section 7003(b) of that Act.

Official Comment

1. Section 2-108, which was not in the prior version of this Article, follows the form of Section 2A-104(1).

2. In subsection (1), it is assumed that this article is subject to any applicable federal law, such as the United Nations Convention on Contracts for the International Sale of Goods, 15 U.S.C. App., or the Magnuson-Moss Warranty Act, 15 U.S.C. Sections 2301–2312.

3. Subsection (1)(a) permits the states to list any applicable certificate-of-title statutes. It also provides that Article 2 is subject to their provisions on the transfer and effect of title except for the rights of a buyer in ordinary course of business in certain limited situations. In entrustment situations, the exception in subsection (1)(a) overrides those certificate-of-title statutes that provide that a person cannot qualify as an owner unless a certificate has been issued in the person's name. In those cases where an owner in whose name a certificate has been issued entrusts a titled asset to a dealer that then sells it to a buyer in ordinary course of business, this section provides that the priority issue between the owner and the buyer is to be resolved by reference to the certificate-of-title statute.

> Illustration #1. A used car is stolen from the owner by a thief and the thief, by fraud, is able to obtain a clean certificate of title from State X. The thief sells the car to the buyer, a good faith purchaser for value but not a buyer in ordinary course of business, and the thief transfers the certificate of title to the buyer. The exception in subsection (1)(a) does not apply to protect the buyer. Furthermore, under Section 2-403(1), the buyer does not get good title from the thief, regardless of the certificate. The

same result follows if the applicable state certificate of title law makes the certificate prima facie evidence of ownership. The buyer will prevail, however, if the applicable certificate of title law conflicts with the result obtained under this Article by making issuance of the certificate conclusive on title.

> Illustration #2. The dealer sells a new car to buyer #1 and the dealer signs a form permitting buyer #1 to apply for a certificate of title. Buyer #1 leaves the car with the dealer so that the dealer can finish the preparation work on the car. While the car remains in the dealer's possession and before the state issues a certificate of title in buyer #1's name, buyer #2 makes the dealer a better offer on the car, which the dealer accepts. Buyer #1 entrusted the car to the dealer, and if buyer #2 qualifies as a buyer in ordinary course of business, buyer #2's title to the car will be superior to that of buyer #1.

> Illustration #3. An owner in whose name a certificate of title has been issued leaves a car with a dealer for repair. The dealer sells the car to a buyer, who qualifies as a buyer in ordinary course of business. If the certificate-of-title law in the state resolves the priority contest between the owner and the buyer, that solution should be implemented. Otherwise, the buyer prevails under Section 2-403(2).

4. This section also deals with the effect of a conflict or failure to comply with any other state law that might apply to a transaction governed by this Article. Subsection (1) provides that a transaction

subject to this Article is also subject to other applicable law, and subsection (2) provides that in the event of a conflict the other law governs (except for the rights of a buyer in ordinary course of business under subsection (1)(a)).

Subsection (1)(b) provides that this Article is also subject to any rule of law that establishes a different rule for consumers. "Rule of law" includes a statute, an administrative rule properly promulgated under the statute, and a final court decision.

The relationship between Article 2 and federal and state consumer laws will vary from transaction to transaction and from State to State. For example, the Magnuson-Moss Warranty Act, 15 U.S.C.A. §§ 2301 *et. seq.*, may or may not apply to the consumer dispute in question and the applicable state "lemon law" may provide more or less protection than Magnuson-Moss. To the extent that the other law applies and there is a conflict with this Article, that law controls.

Subsection (1)(c) provides an illustrative but not exhaustive list of other applicable state statutes that may preempt all or part of Article 2. For example, franchise contracts may be regulated by state franchise acts, the seller of unmerchantable blood or human tissue may be insulated from warranty liability and disclaimers of the implied warranty of merchantability may be invalidated by non-uniform amendments to Article 2. The existence, scope, and effect of these statutes must be assessed from State to State.

Assuming that there is a conflict, subsection (3) deals with the failure of parties to the contract to comply with the applicable law. The failure has the "effect specified" in the law. Thus, the failure to obtain a required license may make the contract illegal, and therefore unenforceable, while the nonnegligent supply of unmerchantable blood under a "blood shield" statute may mean only that the supplier is insulated from liability for injury to person or property.

5. Subsection (4) takes advantage of a provision of the federal Electronic Signatures in Global and National Commerce Act (E-Sign). E-Sign permits state law to modify, limit or supersede its provisions if the state law is consistent with Titles I and II of E-Sign, gives no special legal effect or validity to and does not require the implementation or application of specific technologies or technical specifications, and if enacted subsequent to E-Sign makes specific reference to E-Sign. Subsection (4) does not apply to section 101(c) of E-Sign, nor does it authorize electronic delivery of the notices described in section 103(b) of E-Sign.

Cross References:

Point 3: Section 2-403.

Definitional Cross References:

"Lease". Section 2A-103.

PART 2

FORM, FORMATION, TERMS AND READJUSTMENT OF CONTRACT; ELECTRONIC CONTRACTING

§ 2-201. Formal Requirements; Statute of Frauds.

(1) ~~Except as otherwise provided in this section a~~ A contract for the sale of goods for the price of ~~$500~~ $5,000 or more is not enforceable by way of action or defense unless there is some ~~writing~~ record sufficient to indicate that a contract for sale has been made between the parties and signed by the party against ~~whom~~ which enforcement is sought or by ~~his~~ the party's authorized agent or broker. A ~~writing~~ record is not insufficient because it omits or incorrectly states a term agreed upon, but the contract is not enforceable under this ~~paragraph~~ subsection beyond the quantity of goods shown in ~~such~~ the ~~writing~~ record.

(2) Between merchants if within a reasonable time a ~~writing~~ record in confirmation of the contract and sufficient against the sender is received and the party receiving it has reason to know its contents, it satisfies the requirements of subsection (1) against ~~such party~~ the recipient unless ~~written~~ notice of objection to its contents is given in a record within 10 days after it is received.

(3) A contract ~~which~~ that does not satisfy the requirements of subsection (1) but which is valid in other respects is enforceable:

(a) if the goods are to be specially manufactured for the buyer and are not suitable for sale to others in the ordinary course of the seller's business and the seller, before notice of repudiation is received and under circumstances ~~which~~ that reasonably indicate that the goods are for the buyer, has made either a substantial beginning of their manufacture or commitments for their procurement; ~~or~~

(b) if the party against ~~whom~~ which enforcement is sought admits in ~~his~~ the party's pleading, or in the party's testimony or otherwise ~~in court~~ under oath that a contract for sale was made, but the contract is not enforceable under this ~~provision~~ paragraph beyond the quantity of goods admitted; or

(c) with respect to goods for which payment has been made and accepted or which have been received and accepted (Sec. 2-606).

(4) A contract that is enforceable under this section is not unenforceable merely because it is not capable of being performed within one year or any other period after its making.

In this Section, the original Official Comment has been substantially revised or replaced by the following 2003 Official Comment. However, the original Official Comment may remain appropriate legislative history. For that reason, the original Official Comment may be found in Appendix [___] for the convenience of those who may wish to study it. [Editor's note: Appendix [___] is not reprinted here, but the original Official Comment is reprinted in Appendix E of the main edition.]

Official Comment

1. The record required by subsection (1) need not contain all of the material terms of the contract, and the material terms that are stated need not be precise or accurate. All that is required is that the record afford a reasonable basis to determine that the offered oral evidence rests on a real transaction. The record may be written on a piece of paper or entered into a computer. It need not indicate which party is the buyer and which party is the seller. The only term which must appear is the quantity term. A term indicating the manner by which the quantity is determined is sufficient. Thus, for example, a term indicating that the quantity is based on the output of the seller or the requirements of the buyer satisfies the requirement. *See e.g., Advent Systems v. Unisys*, 925 F.2d 670 (3rd Cir. 1991); *Gestetner Corp. v. Case Equip. Co.*, 815 F.2d 806 (1st Cir. 1987). The same reasoning can be extended to a term that indicates that the contract is similar to, but does not qualify as, an output or requirement contract. *See e.g., PMC Corp. v. Houston Wire and Cable Co.* 797 A.2d 125 (N.H. 2002). Similarly, a term that refers to a master contract that provides a basis for determining a quantity satisfies this requirement. *See e.g., Reigel Fiber Corp. v. Anderson Gin Co.*, 512 F.2d 784 (5th Cir.1975). If a specific amount is stated in the record, even if not accurately stated, recovery is limited to the stated amount. However, the price, time and place of payment or delivery, the general quality of the goods, or any particular warranties need not be included.

Special emphasis must be placed on the permissibility of omitting the price term. In many valid contracts for sale the parties do not mention the price in express terms. The buyer is bound to pay and the seller to accept a reasonable price, which the trier of the fact will determine. Frequently the price is not mentioned at all since the parties have based their agreement on a price list or catalogue known to both of them, and the list or catalogue serves as an efficient safeguard against perjury. Also, "market" prices and valuations that are current in the vicinity constitute a similar check. Of course, if the "price" consists of goods rather than money, the quantity of goods must be stated.

There are only three definite and invariable requirements for the memorandum made by subsection (1). First, the memorandum must evidence a contract for the sale of goods; second, the memorandum must be signed; and third, the memorandum must have a quantity term or a method to determine the quantity.

2. The prior version of subsection (1) began with the phrase "Except as otherwise provided in this section." This language has been deleted. This change was made to provide that the statement of the three statutory exceptions in subsection (3) should not be read as limiting under subsection (1) the possibility that a promisor will be estopped to raise the statute-of-frauds defense in appropriate cases.

3. "Partial performance" as a substitute for the required record can validate the contract only for the goods which have been accepted or for which payment has been made and accepted.

Receipt and acceptance either of goods or of the price constitutes an unambiguous overt admission by both parties that a contract exists. If the court can make a just apportionment, therefore, the agreed price of any goods actually delivered can be recovered without a writing or, if the price has been paid, the seller can be forced to deliver an apportionable part of the goods. The overt actions of the parties make admissible evidence of the other terms of the contract necessary to a just apportionment. This is true even though the actions of the parties are not in themselves inconsistent with a different transaction such as a consignment for resale or a mere loan of money.

Part performance by the buyer requires that the buyer deliver something that is accepted by the seller as the performance. Thus, part payment may be made by money or check accepted by the seller. If the agreed price consists of goods or services, then they must also have been delivered and accepted. When the seller accepts partial payment for a single item the statute is satisfied as to that item. *See Lockwood v. Smigel,* 18 Cal App.3d 800, 99 Cal Rept. 289 (1971).

4. Between merchants, failure to answer a confirmation of a contract in a record that satisfies the requirements of subsection (1) against the sender within ten days of receipt renders the record sufficient against the recipient. The only effect, however, is to take away from the party that fails to answer the defense of the Statute of Frauds. The burden of persuading the trier of fact that a contract was in fact made orally prior to the record confirmation is unaffected.

A merchant includes a person "that by occupation purports to have knowledge or skill peculiar to the *practices* or goods involved in the transaction." Section 2-104(1)(emphasis supplied). Thus, a professional or a farmer should be considered a merchant because the practice of objecting to an improper confirmation ought to be familiar to any person in business.

5. Failure to satisfy the requirements of this section does not render the contract void for all purposes, but merely prevents it from being judicially enforced in favor of a party to the contract. For example, a buyer that takes possession of goods provided for in an oral contract which the seller has not meanwhile repudiated is not a trespasser. Nor would the statute-of-frauds provisions of this section be a defense to a third person that wrongfully induces a party to refuse to perform an oral contract, even though the injured party cannot maintain an action for damages against the party that refuses to perform.

6. It is not necessary that the record be delivered to anybody, nor is this section intended to displace decisions that have given effect to lost records. It need not be signed by both parties, but except as stated in subsection (2), it is not sufficient against a party that has not signed it. Prior to a dispute, no one can determine which party's signature may be necessary, but from the time of contracting each party should be aware that it is the signature of the other which is important.

7. If the making of a contract is admitted in court, either in a written pleading, by stipulation or by oral statement before the court, or is admitted under oath but not in court, as by testimony in a deposition or an affidavit filed with a motion, no additional record is necessary. Subsection (3)(b) makes it impossible to admit the contract in these contexts, and assert that the Statute of Frauds is still a defense. However, in these circumstances, the contract is not conclusively established. The admission is evidential only against the maker and only for the facts admitted. As against the other party, it is not evidential at all.

8. Subsection (4), which was not in prior versions of this Article, repeals the "one year" provision of the Statute of Frauds for contracts for the sale of goods. The phrase "any other applicable period" recognizes that some state statutes apply to periods longer than one year. The confused and contradictory interpretations under the so-called "one year" clause are illustrated by *C.R. Klewin, Inc. v. Flagship Properties, Inc.*, 600 A.2d 772 (Conn. 1991).

Cross References:

See Sections 1-201, 2-202, 2-207, 2-209 and 2-304.
Point 1: Sections 2-211 thru 2-213.
Point 4: Section 2-104

Definitional Cross References:

"Action". Section 1-201.
"Between merchants". Section 2-104.
"Buyer". Section 2-103.
"Contract". Section 1-201.
"Contract for sale". Section 2-106.
"Goods". Section 2-103.
"Notice". Section 1-202.
"Party". Section 1-201.
"Reasonable time". Section 1-205.
"Record". Section 2-103.
"Sale". Section 2-106.
"Seller". Section 2-103.
"Sign". Section 2-103.

§ 2-202. Final ~~Written~~ Expression in a Record: Parol or Extrinsic Evidence.

(1) Terms with respect to which the confirmatory ~~memoranda~~ records of the parties agree or which are otherwise set forth in a ~~writing~~ record intended by the parties as a final expression of their agreement with respect to such terms as are included therein may not be contradicted by evidence of any prior agreement or of a contemporaneous oral agreement but may be ~~explained or~~ supplemented by evidence of:

(a) ~~by course of dealing or usage of trade (Section 1-205) or by course of performance (Section 2-208)~~ course of performance, course of dealing, or usage of trade (Section 1-303); and

(b) ~~by evidence of~~ consistent additional terms unless the court finds the ~~writing~~ record to have been intended also as a complete and exclusive statement of the terms of the agreement.

(2) Terms in a record may be explained by evidence of course of performance, course of dealing, or usage of trade without a preliminary determination by the court that the language used is ambiguous.

Legislative Note: The cross-references in subsection (1)(a) should not be changed if the jurisdiction has not adopted revised Article 1.

In this Section, the original Official Comment has been substantially revised or replaced by the following 2003 Official Comment. However, the original Official Comment may remain appropriate legislative history. For that reason, the original Official Comment may be found in Appendix [__] for the convenience of those who may wish to study it. [Editor's note: Appendix [__] is not reprinted here, but the original Official Comment is reprinted in Appendix E of the main edition.]

Official Comment

1. Subsection (1) codifies the parol evidence rule. The operation of this rule depends on the intention of both parties that the terms in a record are the "final expression of their agreement with respect to the included terms." Without this mutual intention to integrate the record, the parol evidence rule does not apply to exclude evidence of other terms allegedly agreed to prior to or contemporaneously with the record. Unless there is a final record, these alleged terms are provable as part of the agreement by relevant evidence from any credible source. When each party sends a confirmatory record, mutual intention to integrate the agreement is presumed for terms "with respect to which the confirmatory records of the parties agree."

2. Because a record is final for the included terms (an integration), this does not mean that the parties intended that the record contain all the terms of their agreement (a total integration). If a record is final but not complete and exclusive, it cannot be contradicted by evidence of prior agreements reflected in a record or prior or contemporaneous oral agreements, but it can be supplemented by other evidence, drawn from any source, of consistent additional terms. Even if the record is final, complete and exclusive, it can be supplemented by evidence of noncontradictory terms drawn from an applicable course of performance, course of dealing, or usage of trade unless those sources are carefully negated by a term in the record. If the record is final, complete and exclusive it cannot be supplemented by evidence of terms drawn from other sources, even terms that are consistent with the record.

3. Whether a writing is final, and whether a final writing is also complete, are issues for the court. This section rejects any assumption that because a record has been worked out which is final on

some matters, it is to be taken as including all the matters agreed upon. If the additional terms are those that, if agreed upon, would certainly have been included in the document in the view of the court, then evidence of their alleged making must be kept from the trier of fact. This section is not intended to suggest what should be the evidentiary strength of a merger clause as evidence of the mutual intent that the record be final and complete. That determination depends upon the particular circumstances of each case.

4. This section does not exclude evidence introduced to show that the contract is avoidable for misrepresentation, mistake, or duress, or that the contract or a term is unenforceable because of unconscionability. This section also does not operate to exclude evidence of a subsequent modification or evidence that, for the purpose of claiming excuse, both parties assumed that a certain event would not occur.

5. Issues of interpretation are generally left to the courts. In interpreting terms in a record, subsection (2) permits either party to introduce evidence drawn from a course of performance, a course of dealing, or a usage of trade without any preliminary determination by the court that the term at issue is ambiguous. This article takes no position on whether a preliminary determination of ambiguity is a condition to the admissibility of evidence drawn from any other source or on whether a contract clause can exclude an otherwise applicable implied-in-fact source.

Cross References:

Point 2: Sections 2-206 and 2-207.
Point 3: Section 2-207.
Point 4: Section 2-302.

Definitional Cross References:

"Agreement". Section 1-201.
"Course of dealing". Section 1-303.
"Course of performance". Section 1-303.
"Parties". Section 1-201.
"Record". Section 2-103.
"Term". Section 1-201.
"Usage of trade". Section 1-303.

§ 2-204. Formation in General.

(1) A contract for sale of goods may be made in any manner sufficient to show agreement, including offer and acceptance, conduct by both parties which recognizes the existence of ~~such~~ a contract, the interaction of electronic agents, and the interaction of an electronic agent and an individual.

(2) An agreement sufficient to constitute a contract for sale may be found even ~~though~~ if the moment of its making is undetermined.

(3) Even ~~though~~ if one or more terms are left open, a contract for sale does not fail for indefiniteness if the parties have intended to make a contract and there is a reasonably certain basis for giving an appropriate remedy.

(4) Except as otherwise provided in Sections 2-211 through 2-213, the following rules apply:

(a) A contract may be formed by the interaction of electronic agents of the parties, even if no individual was aware of or reviewed the electronic agents' actions or the resulting terms and agreements.

(b) A contract may be formed by the interaction of an electronic agent and an individual acting on the individual's own behalf or for another person. A contract is formed if the individual takes actions that the individual is free to refuse to take or makes a statement, and the individual has reason to know that the actions or statement will:

(i) cause the electronic agent to complete the transaction or performance; or

(ii) indicate acceptance of an offer, regardless of other expressions or actions by the individual to which the electronic agent cannot react.

In this Section, the original Official Comment has been substantially revised or replaced by the following 2003 Official Comment. However, the original Official Comment may remain appropriate legislative history. For that reason, the original Official Comment may be found in Appendix [__] for the convenience of those who may wish to study it. [Editor's note: Appendix [__] is not reprinted here, but the original Official Comment is reprinted in Appendix E of the main edition.]

Official Comment

1. Subsection (1) sets forth the basic policy to recognize any manner of expression of agreement. In addition to traditional contract formation by oral or written agreement, or by performance, subsection (1) provides that an agreement may be made by electronic means. Regardless of how the agreement is formed under this section, the legal effect of the agreement is subject to the other provisions of this Article.

2. Under subsection (1), appropriate conduct by the parties may be sufficient to establish an agreement. Subsection (2) is directed primarily when the correspondence does not disclose the exact point at which the agreement was formed, but the conduct of the parties indicate that a binding obligation has been undertaken.

3. Subsection (3) states the principle for "open terms" which underlies later sections of this Article. If the parties intend to enter

into a binding agreement, this subsection recognizes the agreement as valid in law, despite missing terms, if there is any reasonably certain basis for granting a remedy based on commercial standards of indefiniteness. Neither certainty for what the parties were to do nor a finding of the exact amount of damages is required. Neither is the fact that one or more terms are left to be agreed upon enough by itself to defeat an otherwise adequate agreement. This Act makes provision elsewhere for missing terms needed for performance, open price, remedies and the like.

The more terms the parties leave open, the less likely it is that the parties have intended to conclude a binding agreement, but their actions may be conclusive on the matter despite the omissions.

4. Subsections (4)(a) and (b) are derived from Sections 14(a) and (b) of the Uniform Electronic Transactions Act. Subsection (4)(a) confirms that contracts may be formed by machines functioning as electronic agents for the parties to a transaction. This subsection is intended to negate any claim that lack of human intent, at the time of contract formation, prevents contract formation. When machines are involved, the requisite intention to contract flows from the programing and use of the machine. This provision, along with sections 2-211, 2-212, and 2-213, is intended to remove barriers to electronic contract formation.

5. When the requisite intent to enter into a contract exists, subsection (4)(b) validates contracts formed by an individual and an electronic agent. This subsection validates an anonymous click-through transaction. As with subsection (4)(a), the intent to contract by means of an electronic agent comes from the programing and use of the machine. The requisite intent to contract by the individual is found by the acts of the individual that the individual has reason to know will be interpreted by the machine as allowing the machine to complete the transaction or performance, or that will be interpreted by the machine as signifying acceptance on the part of the individual. This intent is only found, though, when the individual is free to refuse to take the actions that the machine will interpret as acceptance or allowance to complete the transaction. For example, if A goes to a website that provides for purchasing goods over the Internet, and after choosing items to be purchased is confronted by a screen which advises her that the transaction will be completed if A clicks "I agree," then A will be bound by the click if A knew or had reason to know that the click would be interpreted as signifying acceptance and A was also free to refuse to take the final action. This provision does not, however, provide for a determination of what terms exist in the agreement. That question is governed by Section 2-207.

6. Nothing in this section is intended to restrict equitable defenses, such as fraud or mistake, in electronic contract formation. However, because the law of electronic mistake is not well developed, and because factual issues may arise that are not easily resolved by legal standards developed for nonelectronic transactions, courts should not automatically apply standards developed in other contexts. The specific differences between electronic and nonelectronic transactions should also be factored in to resolve equitable claims in electronic contracts.

Cross References:

Point 1: Sections 1-103, 2-201, 2-211 thru 2-213. and 2-302.
Point 2: Sections 2-205 through 2-209.
Point 3: See Part 3.
Point 4: Sections 2-211 thru 2-213.
Point 5: Sections 2-211 thru 2-213.

Definitional Cross References:

"Agreement". Section 1-201.
"Contract". Section 1-201.
"Contract for sale". Section 2-106.
"Electronic". Section 2-103.
"Electronic agent". Section 2-103.
"Goods". Section 2-103.
"Party". Section 1-201.
"Remedy". Section 1-201.
"Term". Section 1-201.

§ 2-207. ~~Additional Terms in Acceptance or~~ Terms of Contract; Effect of Confirmation.

~~(1) A definite and seasonable expression of acceptance or a written confirmation which is sent within a reasonable time operates as an acceptance even though it states terms additional to or different from those offered or agreed upon, unless acceptance is expressly made conditional on assent to the additional or different terms.~~

~~(2) The additional terms are to be construed as proposals for addition to the contract. Between merchants such terms become part of the contract unless:~~

~~(a) the offer expressly limits acceptance to the terms of the offer;~~

~~(b) they materially alter it; or~~

~~(c) notification of objection to them has already been given or is given within a reasonable time after notice of them is received.~~

~~(3) Conduct by both parties which recognizes the existence of a contract is sufficient to establish a contract for sale although the writings of the parties do not otherwise establish a contract. In such case the terms of the particular contract consist of those terms on which the writings of the parties agree, together with any supplementary terms incorporated under any other provisions of this Act.~~

Subject to Section 2-202, if (i) conduct by both parties recognizes the existence of a contract although their records do not otherwise establish a contract, (ii) a contract is formed by an offer and acceptance, or (iii) a contract formed in any manner is confirmed by a record that contains terms additional to or different from those in the contract being confirmed, the terms of the contract are:

(a) terms that appear in the records of both parties;

(b) terms, whether in a record or not, to which both parties agree; and

(c) terms supplied or incorporated under any provision of this Act.

In this Section, the original Official Comment has been substantially revised or replaced by the following 2003 Official Comment. However, the original Official Comment may remain appropriate legislative history. For that reason, the original Official Comment may be found in Appendix [__] for the convenience of those who may wish to study it. [Editor's note: Appendix [__] is not reprinted here, but the original Official Comment is reprinted in Appendix E of the main edition.]

Official Comment

1. This section applies to all contracts for the sale of goods, and it is not limited only to those contracts where there has been a "battle of the forms."

2. This section applies only when a contract has been created under another section of this Article. The purpose of this section is solely to determine the terms of the contract. When forms are exchanged before or during performance, the result from the application of this section differs from the prior Section 2-207 of this Article and the common law in that this section gives no preference to either the first or the last form; the same test is applied to the terms in each. Terms in a record that insist on all of that record's terms and no other terms as a condition of contract formation have no effect on the operation of this section. When one party insists in that party's record that its own terms are a condition to contract formation, if that party does not subsequently perform or otherwise acknowledge the existence of a contract, if the other party does not agree to those terms, the record's insistence on its own terms will keep a contract from being formed under Sections 2-204 or 2-206, and this section is not applicable. As with original Section 2-207, the courts will have to distinguish between "confirmations" that are addressed in this section and "modifications" that are addressed in Section 2-209.

3. Terms of a contract may be found not only in the consistent terms of records of the parties but also from a straightforward acceptance of an offer, and an expression of acceptance accompanied by one or more additional terms might demonstrate the offeree's agreement to the terms of the offer. If, for example, a buyer sent a purchase order with technical specifications and the seller responded with a record stating "Thank you for your order. We will fill it promptly. Note that we do not make deliveries after 3:00 p.m. on Fridays." it might be reasonable to conclude that both parties agreed to the technical specifications.

Similarly, an offeree's performance is sometimes the acceptance of an offer. If, for example, a buyer sends a purchase order, there is no oral or other agreement, and the seller delivers the goods in response to the purchase order—but the seller does not send the seller's own acknowledgment or acceptance—the seller should normally be treated as having agreed to the terms of the purchase order.

If, however, parties exchange records with conflicting or inconsistent terms, but conduct by both parties recognizes the existence of a contract, subsection (a) provides that the terms of the contract are terms that appear in the records of both parties. But even when both parties send records, there could be nonverbal agreement to additional or different terms that appear in only one of two records. If, for example, both parties' forms called for the sale of 700,000 nuts and bolts but the purchase order or another record of the buyer conditioned the sale on a test of a sample to see if the nuts and bolts would perform properly, the seller's sending a small sample to the buyer might be construed to be an agreement to the buyer's condition. It might also be found that the contract called for arbitration when both forms provided for arbitration but each contained immaterially different arbitration provisions.

In a rare case the terms in the records of both parties might not become part of the contract. This could be the case, for example, when the parties contemplated an agreement to a single negotiated record, and each party submitted to the other party similar proposals and then commenced performance, but the parties never reached a negotiated agreement because of the differences over crucial terms. There is a variety of verbal and nonverbal behavior that may be suggest agreement to another's record. This section leaves the interpretation of that behavior to the discretion of the courts.

4. An "agreement" may include terms derived from a course of performance, a course of dealing, and usage of trade. *See* Sections 1-201(a)(2) and 1-303. If the members of a trade, or if the contracting parties, expect to be bound by a term that appears in the record of only one of the contracting parties, that term is part of the agreement. However, repeated use of a particular term or repeated failure to object to a term on another's record is not normally sufficient in itself to establish a course of performance, a course of dealing or a trade usage.

5. The section omits any specific treatment of terms attached to the goods, or in or on the container in which the goods are delivered. This article takes no position on whether a court should follow the reasoning in Step-Saver Data Systems, Inc. v. Wyse Technology, 939 F.2d 91 (3d Cir. 1991) and Klocek v. Gateway, Inc. 104 F. Supp. 2d 1332 (D. Kan. 2000) (original 2-207 governs) or the contrary reasoning in Hill v. Gateway 2000, 105 F. 3d 1147 (7th Cir. 1997) (original 2-207 inapplicable).

Cross References:

Point 1: Sections 2-204 and 2-206.
Point 2: Sections 2-204, 2-206, and 2-209.
Point 3: Sections 1-303, 2-204, 2-206, and 2-209.
Point 4: Sections 1-201, and 1-303.

Definitional Cross References:

"Acceptance". Section 2-206.
"Agree". Section 1-201.
"Contract". Section 1-201.
"Offer". Section 2-204.

"Parties". Section 1-201.
"Records". Section 2-103.
"Terms". Section 1-201.

§ 2-211. Legal Recognition of Electronic Contracts, Records, and Signatures.

(1) A record or signature may not be denied legal effect or enforceability solely because it is in electronic form.

(2) A contract may not be denied legal effect or enforceability solely because an electronic record was used in its formation.

(3) This article does not require a record or signature to be created, generated, sent, communicated, received, stored, or otherwise processed by electronic means or in electronic form.

(4) A contract formed by the interaction of an individual and an electronic agent under Section 2-204(4)(b) does not include terms provided by the individual if the individual had reason to know that the agent could not react to the terms as provided.

Official Comment

1. Subsections (1) and (2) are derived from Section 7(a) and (b) of the Uniform Electronic Transactions Act (UETA), and subsection (3) is derived from Section 5(b) of UETA. Subsection (4) is based on Section 206(c) of the Uniform Computer Information Transactions Act (UCITA). Each subsection conforms to the federal Electronic Signatures in Global and National Commerce Act (15 U.S.C. § 7001 *et seq.*).

2. This section sets forth the premise that the medium in which a record, signature, or contract is created, presented or retained does not affect its legal significance. Subsections (1) and (2) are designed to eliminate the single element of medium as a reason to deny effect or enforceability to a record, signature, or contract. The fact that the information is set forth in an electronic, as opposed to paper, medium is irrelevant.

3. A contract may have legal effect and yet be unenforceable. *See* Restatement 2d Contracts Section 8. To the extent that a contract in electronic form may have legal effect but be unenforceable, because it is in electronic form, subsection (2) validates its legality. Likewise, to the extent that a record or signature in electronic form may have legal effect but be unenforceable, because it is in electronic form, subsection (1) validates the legality of the record or signature.

For example, though a contract may be unenforceable, the parties' electronic records may have collateral effects, as in the case of a buyer that insures goods purchased under a contract that is unenforceable under Section 2-201. The insurance company may not deny a claim on the ground that the buyer is not the owner, though the buyer may have no direct remedy against the seller for failure to deliver. *See* Restatement 2d Contracts, Section 8, Illustration 4. Whether an electronic record or signature is valid under other law is not addressed by this Act.

4. While subsection (2) validates the legality of an electronic contract, it does not in any way diminish the requirements for the formation of contracts under Sections 2-204 and 2-206.

Cross References:

Point 3: Section 2-201.
Point 4: Section 2-204 and 2-206.

Definitional Cross References:

"Contract". Section 1-201.
"Electronic". Section 2-103.
"Electronic agent". Section 2-103.
"Electronic record". Section 2-103.
"Record". Section 2-103.
"Signature". Section 2-103.

§ 2-212. Attribution.

An electronic record or electronic signature is attributable to a person if it was the act of the person or the person's electronic agent or the person is otherwise legally bound by the act.

Official Comment

1. This section is based on Section 9 of the Uniform Electronic Transactions Act (UETA).

2. As long as an electronic record is created by a person or the electronic signature results from a person's action it is attributed to that person. The legal effect of the attribution is derived from other provisions of this Act or from other law. This section simply assures that these rules will be applied in the electronic environment. A person's actions include actions taken by a human agent of the person as well as actions taken by an electronic agent, of the person. Although this section may appear to state the obvious, it assures that the record or signature is not ascribed to a machine, as opposed to the person operating or programming the machine.

3. In each of the following cases, both the electronic record and electronic signature would be attributable to a person under this section:

A. The person types his or her name as part of an e-mail purchase order;

B. The person's employee, pursuant to authority, types the person's name as part of an e-mail purchase order;

C. The person's computer, programmed to order goods upon receipt of inventory information within particular parameters, issues a purchase order which includes the person's name, or other identifying information, as part of the order.

In each of these cases, law other than this Act would ascribe both the signature and the action to the person if done in a paper medium. This section provides that the same result will occur when an electronic medium is used.

4. Nothing in this section affects the use of an electronic signature as a means of attributing a record to a person. Once an electronic signature is attributed to the person, the electronic record with which it is associated would also be attributed to the person unless the person established fraud, forgery, or other invalidating cause. However, an electronic signature is not the only method for attribution of a record.

5. In the context of attribution of records, normally the content of the record will provide the necessary information for a finding of attribution. It is also possible that an established course of dealing between parties may result in a finding of attribution. Just as with a paper record, evidence of forgery or counterfeiting may be introduced to rebut the evidence of attribution. The use of facsimile transmissions provides a number of examples of attribution using information other than a signature. A facsimile may be attributed to a person because of the information printed across the top of the page that indicates the machine from which it was sent. Similarly, the transmission may contain a letterhead which identifies the sender. Some cases have held that the letterhead actually constituted a signature because it was a symbol adopted by the sender with intent to sign the record. *See Cox Engineering v. Funston Mach. & Supply*, 749 S.W.2d 508, 511 (Tex. App.1988) (plaintiff's letterhead, including address, appearing at top of invoice, provides authentication that identifies the party to be charged and thus satisfies the statute of frauds' signature requirement); *Owen v. Kroger Co.*, 936 F. Supp. 579 (S.D. Ind. 1996)(determining that a letterhead satisfies the signature requirement of the UCC). However, the signature determination resulted from the necessary finding of intention in that case. Other cases have found letterheads not to be signatures because the requisite intention was not present. *See First National Bank in Alamosa v. Ford Motor Credit Co.*, 748 F. Supp 1464 (D. Colo, 1990)(determining that a pre-printed name on a draft was not a signature for the purpose of accepting a draft). The critical point is that with or without a signature, information within the electronic record may well suffice to provide the facts resulting in attribution of an electronic record to a particular party.

6. Certain information may be present in an electronic environment that does not appear to attribute but which clearly links a person to a particular record. Numerical codes, personal identification numbers, public and private key combinations, all serve to establish the party to which an electronic record should be attributed. Security procedures will be another piece of evidence available to establish attribution.

7. Once it is established that a record or signature is attributable to a particular person, the legal significance of the record or signature is determined by the context and surrounding circumstances in which the recorder signature is created, including the parties' agreement, if any. This will primarily be governed by other sections of this article. *See, e.g.*, Sections 2-201, 2-202, 2-204, 2-206, 2-207, and 2-209.

Cross References:

Point 3: Section 2-201.
Point 5: Section 1-303.
Point 7: Sections 2-201, 2-202, 2-204, 2-206, and 2-209.

Definitional Cross References:

"Electronic". Section 2-103.
"Electronic agent". Section 2-103.
"Electronic record". Section 2-103.
"Record". Section 2-103.
"Signature". Section 2-103.

§ 2-213. Electronic Communication.

(1) If the receipt of an electronic communication has a legal effect, it has that effect even if no individual is aware of its receipt.

(2) Receipt of an electronic acknowledgment of an electronic communication establishes that the communication was received but, in itself, does not establish that the content sent corresponds to the content received.

Official Comment

1. This section is adapted from Sections 15(e) and (f) of the Uniform Electronic Transactions Act (UETA).

2. This section deals with electronic communications generally, and it is not limited to electronic records which must be retrievable in perceivable form. The section does not resolve the questions of when or where electronic communications are determined to be sent or received, nor does it indicate that a communication has any particular substantive legal effect.

3. Under subsection (1), receipt is not dependent on a person having notice of the communication. An analogy in a paper based transaction is the recipient that does not read a notice received in the mail. Although "receipt" as defined in Article 1 applies by its terms only to notices, the same concept would apply equally to a communication that is not a notice.

4. Subsection (2) provides legal certainty about the effect of an electronic acknowledgment. This subsection only addresses the fact of the receipt, and it does not set forth the legal significance of the quality of the content, nor whether the electronic communication was read or "opened."

5. This section does not address the question of whether the exchange of electronic communications constitutes the formation of a contract. Those questions are addressed by Sections 2-204 and 2-206.

Cross References:

Point 5: Section 2-204 and 2-206.

Definitional Cross References:

"Electronic". Section 2-103.
"Sent". Section 1-201.

PART 3

GENERAL OBLIGATION AND CONSTRUCTION OF CONTRACT

§ 2-312. Warranty of Title and Against Infringement; Buyer's Obligation Against Infringement.

(1) Subject to subsection ~~(2)~~(3), there is in a contract for sale a warranty by the seller that:

(a) the title conveyed shall be ~~good,~~ good and its transfer rightful and shall not unreasonably expose the buyer to litigation because of any colorable claim to or interest in the goods; and

(b) the goods shall be delivered free from any security interest or other lien or encumbrance of which the buyer at the time of contracting has no knowledge.

~~(2) A warranty under subsection (1) will be excluded or modified only by specific language or by circumstances which give the buyer reason to know that the person selling does not claim title in himself or that it is purporting to sell only such right or title as it or a third person may have.~~

~~(3) Unless otherwise agreed a seller who is a merchant regularly dealing in goods of the kind warrants that the goods shall be delivered free of the rightful claim of any third person by way of infringement or the like but a buyer who furnishes specifications to the seller must hold the seller harmless against any such claim which arises out of compliance with the specifications.~~

(2) Unless otherwise agreed, a seller that is a merchant regularly dealing in goods of the kind warrants that the goods shall be delivered free of the rightful claim of any third person by way of infringement or the like but a buyer that furnishes specifications to the seller must hold the seller harmless against any such claim that arises out of compliance with the specifications.

(3) A warranty under this section may be disclaimed or modified only by specific language or by circumstances that give the buyer reason to know that the seller does not claim title, that the seller is purporting to sell only the right or title as the seller or a third person may have, or that the seller is selling subject to any claims of infringement or the like.

In this Section, the original Official Comment has been substantially revised or replaced by the following 2003 Official Comment. However, the original Official Comment may remain appropriate legislative history. For that reason, the original Official Comment may be found in Appendix [__] for the convenience of those who may wish to study it. [Editor's note: Appendix [__] is not reprinted here, but the original Official Comment is reprinted in Appendix E of the main edition.]

Official Comment

1. Subsection (1) provides for a buyer's basic needs for a title which the buyer in good faith expects to acquire by the purchase, namely, that the buyer receive a good, clean title transferred also in a rightful manner so that the buyer will not be exposed to a lawsuit to protect the title. Under subsection (1), the seller warrants that (1) the title conveyed is good, (2) the transfer is rightful, and (3) the transfer does not unreasonably expose the buyer to litigation because a third person has or asserts a "colorable claim" to or interest in the goods.

In addition to sales in which there is an actual cloud on the title, a warranty that the "title conveyed is good and its transfer rightful"

also covers cases when the title is good but the transfer is not rightful. For example, a wrongful transfer with good title occurs where a merchant bailee to which goods are entrusted for repair sells them without authority to a buyer in the ordinary course of business. *See* Section 2-403(2); *Sumner v. Fel-Air, Inc.*, 680 P.2d 1109 (Alaska 1984).

The subsection now expressly states what the courts have long recognized; further protection for the buyer is needed when the title is burdened by colorable claims that affect the value of the goods. *See Frank Arnold KRS, Inc. v. L.S. Meier Auction Co., Inc.*, 806 F.2d 462 (3d Cir. 1986) (two lawsuits contest title); *Jeanneret v. Vichey*, 693 F.2d 259 (2d Cir. 1982) (export restrictions in country from which painting was taken affect value); Colton v. Decker, 540 N.W.2d 172 (S.D. 1995) (conflicting vehicle identification numbers). Therefore, not only is the buyer entitled to a good title, but the buyer is also entitled to a marketable title, and until the colorable claim is resolved the market for the goods is impaired. *See Wright v. Vickaryous*, 611 P.2d 20 (Alaska 1980).

The justification for this rule is that the buyer of goods that are warranted for title has a right to rely on the fact that there will be no need later to have to contest ownership. The mere casting of a substantial shadow over the buyer's title, regardless of the ultimate outcome, violates the warranty of good title. *See American Container Corp. v. Hanley Trucking Corp.*, 111 N.J. Super. 322, 268 A.2d 313,318 (1970). It should be noted that not any assertion of a claim by a third party will constitute a breach of the warranty of title. The claim must be reasonable and colorable. *See C.F. Sales, Inc. v. Amfert*, 344 N.W.2d 543 (Iowa 1983).

The warranty of title extends to a buyer whether or not the seller was in possession of the goods at the time the sale or contract to sell was made.

Consistent with original Article 2, this section does not provide for a separate warranty of quiet possession in addition to the warranty of title. Disturbance of quiet possession, although not mentioned specifically, is one way, among many, in which the breach of the warranty of title might be established.

2. "Knowledge" as referred to in subsection (1)(b) is actual knowledge as distinct from notice.

3. The provisions of this Article that require notification to the seller within a reasonable time after the buyer's discovery of a breach (Section 2-607(3)(a)) apply to notice of a breach of the warranty of title when the seller's breach was innocent. However, if the seller's breach were in bad faith, the seller cannot claim prejudice by the delay in giving notice.

4. Subsection (2) provides the warranty against infringement. Unlike the warranty of title, this warranty is limited to sellers that are merchants that "regularly dealing in goods of the kind" sold.

When the goods are part of the seller's normal stock, and are sold in the normal course of business, it is the seller's duty to see that no claim of infringement of a patent or trademark by a third party will impair the buyer's title. A sale by a person other than a dealer, however, raises no implication in its circumstances of the warranty. Nor is there an implication when the buyer orders goods to be assembled, prepared or manufactured on the buyer's own specifications. If, in such a case, the resulting product infringes a patent or trademark, the liability will run from buyer to seller. There is, under these circumstances, a tacit representation on the part of the buyer that the seller will be safe in manufacturing according to the specifications, and the buyer is under an obligation in good faith to indemnify the seller for any loss suffered.

5. Under this section, the cases which recognize the principle that infringements violate the warranty of title but deny the buyer a remedy unless he has been expressly prevented from using the goods are rejected. Under this Article "eviction" is not a necessary condition to the buyer's remedy since the buyer's remedy arises immediately upon receipt of notice of infringement; it is merely one way of establishing the fact of breach.

6. Subsection (3) is concerned with the disclaimer or modification of the warranties of title or against infringement. This is a self-contained provision that govern the modification or disclaimer of warranties under this section. The warranties in this section are not designated as "implied" warranties, and hence these warranties are not subject to the modification and disclaimer provisions of Section 2-316(2) and (3). Unlike Section 2-316, subsection (3) of this section does not create any specific requirements that the disclaimer or modification be contained in a record or be conspicuous.

Under subsection (3), sales by sheriffs, executors, certain foreclosing lienors and persons similarly situated are recognized as possibly being so out of the ordinary commercial course that their peculiar character is immediately apparent to the buyer, and therefore no personal obligation is imposed upon the seller that is purporting to sell only an unknown or limited right. This subsection is not intended to touch upon, and it leaves open, all questions of restitution that arise in these cases, such as when a unique article that is sold is reclaimed by a third party as the rightful owner.

For a foreclosure sale under Article 9, Section 9-610 of revised Article 9 provides that a disposition of collateral under that section includes warranties such as those imposed by this section on a voluntary disposition of property. Consequently, unless properly excluded under subsection (3) or under the special provisions for exclusion in Section 9-610, a disposition under that section of collateral consisting of goods includes the warranties imposed by subsection (1) and, if applicable, subsection (2).

7. The statute of limitations for a breach of warranty under this section is determined under the provisions set out in Section 2-725(1) and (3)(c).

Cross References:

Point 1: Section 2-403.
Point 3: Sections 2-607 and 2-725.
Point 4: Section 1-203.
Point 6: Sections 2-316, 2-609, 2-610 and 2-725.
Point 7: Section 2-316 and 2-725.

Definitional Cross References:

"Agreement". Section 1-201.
"Buyer". Section 2-103.
"Contract for sale". Section 2-106.
"Goods". Section 2-103.
"Merchant". Section 2-104.
"Person". Section 1-201.
"Right". Section 1-201.
"Seller". Section 2-103.

§ 2-313. Express Warranties by Affirmation, Promise, Description, Sample; Remedial Promise.

(1) In this section, "immediate buyer" means a buyer that enters into a contract with the seller.

(1) (2) Express warranties by the seller to the immediate buyer are created as follows:

(a) Any affirmation of fact or promise made by the seller to the buyer which relates to the goods and becomes part of the basis of the bargain creates an express warranty that the goods shall conform to the affirmation or promise.

(b) Any description of the goods which is made part of the basis of the bargain creates an express warranty that the goods shall conform to the description.

(c) Any sample or model ~~which~~ that is made part of the basis of the bargain creates an express warranty that the whole of the goods shall conform to the sample or model.

~~(2)~~ (3) It is not necessary to the creation of an express warranty that the seller use formal words such as ''warrant'' or ''guarantee'' or that ~~he~~ the seller have a specific intention to make a warranty, but an affirmation merely of the value of the goods or a statement purporting to be merely the seller's opinion or commendation of the goods does not create a warranty.

(4) Any remedial promise made by the seller to the immediate buyer creates an obligation that the promise will be performed upon the happening of the specified event.

In this Section, the original Official Comment has been substantially revised or replaced by the following 2003 Official Comment. However, the original Official Comment may remain appropriate legislative history. For that reason, the original Official Comment may be found in Appendix [__] for the convenience of those who may wish to study it. [Editor's note: Appendix [__] is not reprinted here, but the original Official Comment is reprinted in Appendix E of the main edition.]

Official Comment

1. In subsections (2) and (4) the term ''immediate buyer'' is used to make clear that the section is limited to express warranties and remedial promises made by a seller to a buyer with which the seller has a contractual relationship. Sections 2-313A and 2-313B address obligations that run directly from a seller to a remote purchaser.

2. Subsection (4) uses the term ''remedial promise,'' which was not used in original Article 2. This section deals with remedial promises to immediate buyers. Sections 2-313A and 2-313B deal with remedial promises running directly from a seller to a remote purchaser. Remedial promise is defined in Section 2-103(1)(n).

3. ''Express'' warranties rest on ''dickered'' aspects of the individual bargain, and go so clearly to the essence of that bargain that words of disclaimer in a form are repugnant to the basic dickered terms. ''Implied'' warranties rest so clearly on a common factual situation or set of conditions that no particular language or action is necessary to evidence them and they will arise in such a situation unless unmistakably negated. As with original Article 2, warranties of description and sample are designated ''express'' rather than ''implied.''

4. This section is limited in its scope and direct purpose to express warranties and remedial promises made by the seller to the immediate buyer as part of a contract for sale. It is not designed in any way to disturb those lines of case law which have recognized that warranties need not be confined to contracts within the scope of this Article.

Under Section 2-313B, a seller may incur an obligation to a remote purchaser through a medium for communication to the public such as advertising. An express warranty to an immediate buyer may also arise through a medium for communication to the public if the elements of this section are satisfied.

The fact that a buyer has rights against an immediate seller under this section does not preclude the buyer from also asserting rights against a remote seller under Section 2-313A or 2-313B.

5. The present section deals with affirmations of fact or promises made by the seller, descriptions of the goods, or exhibitions of samples or models, exactly as it deals with any other part of a negotiation which ends in a contract. No specific intention to make a warranty is necessary if any of these factors is made part of the basis of the bargain. In actual practice affirmations of fact and promises made by the seller about the goods during a bargain are regarded as part of the description of those goods; hence no particular reliance on these statements need be shown in order to weave them into the fabric of the agreement. Rather, any fact which is to take these affirmations or promises, once made, out of the agreement requires clear affirmative proof. The issue normally is one of fact.

6. In view of the principle that the whole purpose of the law of warranty is to determine what it is that the seller has in essence agreed to sell, the policy is adopted of those cases which refuse except in unusual circumstances to recognize a material deletion of the seller's obligation. Thus, a contract is normally a contract for a sale of something describable and described. A clause generally disclaiming ''all warranties, express or implied'' cannot reduce the seller's obligation for the description and therefore cannot be given literal effect under Section 2-316(1).

This is not intended to mean that the parties, if they consciously desire, cannot make their own bargain as they wish. But in determining what they have agreed upon good faith is a factor and consideration should be given to the fact that the probability is small that a real price is intended to be exchanged for a pseudo-obligation.

7. Subsection (2)(b) makes specific some of the principles set forth above when a description of the goods is given by the seller.

A description need not be by words. Technical specifications, blueprints and the like can afford more exact description than mere language and if made part of the basis of the bargain goods must conform with them. Past deliveries may set the description of quality, either expressly or impliedly by course of dealing. Of course, all descriptions by merchants must be read against the applicable trade usages with the general rules as to merchantability resolving any doubts.

8. The basic situation as to statements affecting the true essence of the bargain is no different when a sample or model is involved in the transaction. This section includes both a ''sample'' actually drawn from the bulk of goods which is the subject matter of the sale, and a ''model'' which is offered for inspection when the subject matter is not at hand and which has not been drawn from the bulk of the goods.

Although the underlying principles are unchanged, the facts are often ambiguous when something is shown as illustrative, rather than as a straight sample. In general, the presumption is that any sample or model, just as any affirmation of fact, is intended to become a basis of the bargain. But there is no escape from the question of fact. When the seller exhibits a sample purporting to be drawn from an existing bulk, good faith of course requires that the sample be fairly drawn. But in mercantile experience the mere exhibition of a "sample" does not of itself show whether it is merely intended to "suggest" or to "be" the character of the subject-matter of the contract. The question is whether the seller has so acted with reference to the sample as to become responsible that the whole shall have at least the values shown by it. The circumstances aid in answering this question. If the sample has been drawn from an existing bulk, it must be regarded as describing values of the goods contracted for unless it is accompanied by an unmistakable denial of responsibility. If, on the other hand, a model of merchandise not on hand is offered, the mercantile presumption that it has become a literal description of the subject matter is not so strong, and particularly so if modification on the buyer's initiative impairs any feature of the model.

9. The precise time when words of description or affirmation are made or samples are shown is not material. The sole question is whether the language or samples or models are fairly to be regarded as part of the contract. If language that would otherwise create an obligation under this section is used after the closing of the deal (as when the buyer when taking delivery asks and receives an additional assurance), an obligation will arise if the requirements for a modification are satisfied. *See Downie v. Abex Corp.*, 741 F.2d 1235 (10th Cir. 1984).

10. Concerning affirmations of value or a seller's opinion or commendation under subsection (3), the basic question remains the same: What statements of the seller have in the circumstances and in objective judgment become part of the basis of the bargain? As indicated above, all of the statements of the seller do so unless good reason is shown to the contrary. The provisions of subsection (3) are included, however, since common experience discloses that some statements or predictions cannot fairly be viewed as entering into the bargain. Even as to false statements of value, however, the possibility is left open that a remedy may be provided by the law relating to fraud or misrepresentation.

There are a number of factors relevant to determine whether an expression creates a warranty under this section or is merely puffing. For example, the relevant factors may include whether the seller's representations taken in context, (1) were general rather than specific, (2) related to the consequences of buying rather than the goods themselves, (3) were "hedged" in some way, (4) were related to experimental rather than standard goods, (5) were concerned with some aspects of the goods but not a hidden or unexpected nonconformity, (6) were informal statements made in a formal contracting process, (7) were phrased in terms of opinion rather than fact, or (8) were not capable of objective measurement.

11. The use of the word "promise" in subsection (2)(a) refers to statements about the quality or performance characteristics of the goods. For example, a seller might make an affirmation of fact to the buyer that the goods are of a certain quality, or may promise that the goods when delivered will be of a certain quality, or may promise that the goods will perform in a certain manner after delivery. In normal usage, "promise" refers to a what a person, not goods, will do; that is, a promise is a commitment to act, or refrain from acting, in a certain manner in the future. A promise about the quality or performance characteristics of the goods creates an express warranty if the other elements of a warranty are present whereas a promise by which the seller commits itself to take remedial action upon the happening of a specified event is a remedial promise. The distinction has meaning in the context of the statute of limitations. A right of action for breach of an express warranty accrues when the goods are tendered to the immediate buyer (Section 2-725(3)(a)) unless the warranty consists of a promise that explicitly extends to the future performance of the goods and discovery must await the time for performance, in which case accrual occurs when the immediate buyer discovers or should have discovered the breach (Section 2-725(3)(d)). Section 2-725(2)(c) separately addresses the accrual of a right of action for breach of a remedial promise.

The concept of remedial promise is dealt with in a separate subsection to make clear that it is a concept separate and apart from express warranty and that the elements of an express warranty, such as basis of the bargain, are not applicable.

Cross References:

Point 1: Sections 2-313A and 2-313B.
Point 2: Sections 2-103, 2-313A and 2-313B.
Point 3: Section 2-316(2)(b).
Point 4: Section 2-316.
Point 5: Sections 1-205(4) and 2-314.
Point 6: Section 2-316.
Point 7: Section 2-209.
Point 8: Section 1-103.
Point 11: Section 2-313 and 2-725.

Definitional Cross References:

"Buyer". Section 2-103.
"Conforming". Section 2-106.
"Goods". Section 2-103.
"Remedial promise". Section 2-103.
"Seller". Section 2-103.
"Tender of delivery". Sections 2-503 and 2-507.

---

§ 2-313a. Obligation to Remote Purchaser Created by Record Packaged with or Accompanying Goods.

(1) In this section:

(a) "Immediate buyer" means a buyer that enters into a contract with the seller.

(b) "Remote purchaser" means a person that buys or leases goods from an immediate buyer or other person in the normal chain of distribution.

(2) This section applies only to new goods and goods sold or leased as new goods in a transaction of purchase in the normal chain of distribution.

(3) If in a record packaged with or accompanying the goods the seller makes an affirmation of fact or promise that relates to the goods, provides a description that relates to the goods, or makes a remedial promise, and the seller reasonably expects the record to be, and the record is, furnished to the remote purchaser, the seller has an obligation to the remote purchaser that:

(a) the goods will conform to the affirmation of fact, promise, or description unless a reasonable person in the position of the remote purchaser would not believe that the affirmation of fact, promise, or description created an obligation; and

(b) the seller will perform the remedial promise.

(4) It is not necessary to the creation of an obligation under this section that the seller use formal words such as "warrant" or "guarantee" or that the seller have a specific intention to undertake an obligation, but an affirmation merely of the value of the goods or a statement purporting to be merely the seller's opinion or commendation of the goods does not create an obligation.

(5) The following rules apply to the remedies for breach of an obligation created under this section:

(a) The seller may modify or limit the remedies available to the remote purchaser if the modification or limitation is furnished to the remote purchaser no later than the time of purchase or if the modification or limitation is contained in the record that contains the affirmation of fact, promise, or description.

(b) Subject to a modification or limitation of remedy, a seller in breach is liable for incidental or consequential damages under Section 2-715, but not for lost profits.

(c) The remote purchaser may recover as damages for breach of a seller's obligation arising under subsection (3) the loss resulting in the ordinary course of events as determined in any reasonable manner.

(6) An obligation that is not a remedial promise is breached if the goods did not conform to the affirmation of fact, promise, or description creating the obligation when the goods left the seller's control.

Legislative Note: To maintain their relative positions in this Act, Sections 2-313A and 2-313B may have to be renumbered according to the convention used by a particular state. For example, in some states they may be designated as 2-313.1 and 2-313.2.

Official Comment

1. Sections 2-313A and 2-313B are new, and they follow case law and practice in extending a seller's obligations regarding new goods to remote purchasers. Section 2-313A deals with what are commonly called "pass-through warranties". The usual transaction in which this obligation arises is when a manufacturer sells goods in a package to a retailer and include in the package a record that sets forth the obligations that the manufacturer is willing to undertake in favor of the final party in the distributive chain, who is the person that buys or leases the goods from the retailer. If the manufacturer had sold the goods directly to the final party in the distributive chain, whether the manufacturer would incur liability is determined by Section 2-313 and this section is inapplicable.

No direct contract exists between the seller and the remote purchaser, and thus the seller's obligation under this section is not referred to as an "express warranty." Use of "obligation" rather than "express warranty" avoids any inference that the obligation arises as part of the basis of the bargain as would be required to create an express warranty under section 2-313. The test for whether an obligation other than a remedial promise arises is similar in some respects to the basis of the bargain requirement in section 2-313, but the test set forth in this section is exclusive. Because "remedial promise" in Section 2-313 is not subject to the

requirement that it arise as part of the basis of the bargain, the term is used in this section.

2. The party to which an obligation runs under this section may either buy or lease the goods, and thus the term "remote purchaser" is used. The term is more limited than "purchaser" in Article 1, however, and does not include a donee or any voluntary transferee who is not a buyer or lessee. Moreover, the remote purchaser must be part of the normal chain of distribution for the particular product. That chain will, by definition, include at least three parties and may well include more. For example, the manufacturer might sell first to a wholesaler that would then resell the goods to a retailer for sale or lease to the public. A buyer or lessee from the retailer would qualify as a remote purchaser and could invoke this section against either the manufacturer or the wholesaler (if the wholesaler provided a record to the retailer to be furnished to the final party in the distribution chain), but no subsequent transferee, such as a used-goods buyer or sublessee, would qualify. The law governing assignment and third-party beneficiary, including Section 2-318, should be consulted to determine whether a party other than the remote purchaser can enforce an obligation created under this section.

3. The application of this section is limited to new goods and goods sold or leased as new goods within the normal chain of distribution. It does not apply to goods that are sold outside the

normal chain, such as "gray" goods or salvaged goods, nor does it apply if the goods are unused but sold as seconds. The concept is flexible, and to determine whether goods have been sold or leased in the normal chain of distribution requires consideration of the seller's expectations for the manner in which its goods will reach the remote purchaser. For example, a car manufacturer may be aware that certain of its dealers transfer cars among themselves, and under the particular circumstances of the case a court might find that a new car sold initially to one dealer but leased to the remote purchaser by another dealer was leased in the normal chain of distribution. The concept may also include such practices as door-to-door sales and distribution through a nonprofit organization.

The phrase "goods sold or leased as new goods" refers to goods that in the normal course of business would be considered new. There are many instances in which goods might be used for a limited purpose yet be sold or leased in the normal chain of distribution as new goods. For example, goods that have been returned to a dealer by a purchaser and placed back into the dealer's inventory might be sold or leased as new goods in the normal chain of distribution. Other examples might include goods that have been used for the purpose of inspection (*e.g.*, a car that has been test-driven) and goods that have been returned by a sale-or-return buyer (Section 2-326).

4. This section applies only to obligations set forth in a record that is packaged with the goods or otherwise accompanies them (subsection (2)). Examples include a label affixed to the outside of a container, a card inside a container, or a booklet handed to the remote purchaser at the time of purchase. In addition, the seller must be able to anticipate that the remote purchaser will acquire the record, and therefore this section is limited to records that the seller reasonably expects to be furnished, and that are in fact furnished, to the remote purchaser.

Neither this section nor Section 2-313B are intended to overrule cases that impose liability on facts outside the direct scope of one of the sections. For example, the sections are not intended to overrule a decision imposing liability on a seller that distributes a sample to a remote purchaser.

5. Obligations other than remedial promises created under this section are analogous to express warranties and are subject to a test that is akin to the basis of the bargain test of Section 2-313(2). The seller is entitled to shape the scope of the obligation, and the seller's language tending to create an obligation must be considered in context. If a reasonable person in the position of the remote purchaser, reading the seller's language in its entirety, would not believe that an affirmation of fact, promise or description created an obligation, there is no liability under this section.

6. There is no difference between remedial promise as used in this section (and Section 2-313B) and the same term as used in Section 2-313.

7. Subsection (5)(a) makes clear that the seller may employ the provisions of Section 2-719 to modify or limit the remedies available to the remote purchaser for breach of the seller's obligation in this section. The modification or limitation may appear on the same record as the one which creates the obligation, or it may be provided to the remote purchaser separately, but in no event may it be furnished to the remote purchaser any later than the time of purchase.

The requirements and limitations set forth in Section 2-719, such as the requirement of an express statement of exclusivity and the tests for failure of essential purpose (Section 2-719(2)) and unconscionability (Section 2-719(3)) are applicable to a modification or limitation of remedy under this section.

8. As with express warranties, no specific language or intention is necessary to create an obligation, and whether an obligation exists is normally an issue of fact. Subsection (3) is virtually identical to Section 2-313(3), and the tests developed under the common law and under that section to determine whether a statement creates an obligation or is mere puffing are applicable to this section.

Just as a seller can limit the extent to which its language creates an express warranty under Section 2-313 by placing that language in a broader context, a seller under this section or Section 2-313B can limit the extent of its liability to a remote purchaser (subsection(4)(a)). In other words, the seller, in undertaking an obligation under these sections, can control the scope and limits of that obligation.

9. As a rule, a remote purchaser may recover monetary damages measured in the same manner as in the case of an aggrieved buyer under Section 2-714 as well as incidental and consequential damages under Section 2-715 to the extent they would be available to an aggrieved buyer. Subsection (5)(c) parallels Section 2-714(1) in allowing the buyer to recover for loss resulting in the ordinary course of events as determined in any manner which is reasonable. In the case of an obligation that is not a remedial promise, the normal measure of damages would be the difference between the value of the goods if they had conformed to the seller's statements and their actual value, and the normal measure of damages for breach of a remedial promise would be the difference between the value of the promised remedial performance and the value of the actual performance received.

Subsection (5)(b) precludes a remote purchaser from recovering consequential damages in the form of lost profits.

Cross References:

Point 1: Sections 2-313, 2-313A and 2-313B.
Point 2: Section 2-318.
Point 3: Section 2-326.
Point 4: Section 2-313B.
Point 5: Section 2-313.
Point 6: Section 2-313 and 2-313B.
Point 7: Section 2-719.
Point 8: Section 2-313 and 2-313B.
Point 9: Sections 2-714 and 2-715.

Definitional Cross References:

"Buyer". Section 2-103.
"Conforming". Section 2-106.
"Goods". Section 2-103.
"Lease". Section 2A-103.
"Purchase". Section 1-201.
"Record". Section 2-103.
"Remedial promise". Section 2-103.
"Remedy". Section 1-201.
"Sale". Section 2-106.
"Seller". Section 2-103.

§ 2-313b. Obligation to Remote Purchaser Created by Communication to the Public.

(1) In this section:

(a) "Immediate buyer" means a buyer that enters into a contract with the seller.

(b) "Remote purchaser" means a person that buys or leases goods from an immediate buyer or other person in the normal chain of distribution.

(2) This section applies only to new goods and goods sold or leased as new goods in a transaction of purchase in the normal chain of distribution.

(3) If in an advertisement or a similar communication to the public a seller makes an affirmation of fact or promise that relates to the goods, provides a description that relates to the goods, or makes a remedial promise, and the remote purchaser enters into a transaction of purchase with knowledge of and with the expectation that the goods will conform to the affirmation of fact, promise, or description, or that the seller will perform the remedial promise, the seller has an obligation to the remote purchaser that:

(a) the goods will conform to the affirmation of fact, promise, or description unless a reasonable person in the position of the remote purchaser would not believe that the affirmation of fact, promise, or description created an obligation; and

(b) the seller will perform the remedial promise.

(4) It is not necessary to the creation of an obligation under this section that the seller use formal words such as "warrant" or "guarantee" or that the seller have a specific intention to undertake an obligation, but an affirmation merely of the value of the goods or a statement purporting to be merely the seller's opinion or commendation of the goods does not create an obligation.

(5) The following rules apply to the remedies for breach of an obligation created under this section:

(a) The seller may modify or limit the remedies available to the remote purchaser if the modification or limitation is furnished to the remote purchaser no later than the time of purchase. The modification or limitation may be furnished as part of the communication that contains the affirmation of fact, promise, or description.

(b) Subject to a modification or limitation of remedy, a seller in breach is liable for incidental or consequential damages under Section 2-715, but not for lost profits.

(c) The remote purchaser may recover as damages for breach of a seller's obligation arising under subsection (3) the loss resulting in the ordinary course of events as determined in any reasonable manner.

(6) An obligation that is not a remedial promise is breached if the goods did not conform to the affirmation of fact, promise, or description creating the obligation when the goods left the seller's control.

Legislative Note: In order to maintain their relative positions in this Act, Sections 2-313A and 2-313B may have to be renumbered according to the convention used by a particular state. For example, in some states they may be designated as 2-313.1 and 2-313.2.

Official Comment

1. Sections 2-313B and 2-313A are new, and they follow case law and practice in extending a seller's obligations for new goods to remote purchasers. This section deals with obligations to a remote purchaser created by advertising or a similar communication to the public. The normal situation where this obligation will arise is when a manufacturer engages in an advertising campaign directed towards all or part of the market for its product and will make statements that if made to an immediate buyer would amount to an express warranty or remedial promise under Section 2-313.

The goods, however, are sold to someone other than the recipient of the advertising and are then resold or leased to the recipient. By imposing liability on the seller, this section adopts the approach of cases such as *Randy Knitwear, Inc. v. American Cyanamid Co.*, 11 N.Y.2d 5, 226 N.Y.S.2d 363, 181 N.E.2d 399 (Ct. App. 1962).

If the seller's advertisement is made to an immediate buyer, whether the seller incurs liability is determined by Section 2-313 and this section is inapplicable.

2. This section parallels Section 2-313A in most respects, and the Official Comments to that section should be consulted. In

particular, the reasoning of Comment 1 (scope and terminology), Comment 2 (definition of remote purchaser), Comment 3 (new goods and goods sold as new goods in the normal chain of distribution), Comment 4 (reasonable person in the position of the remote purchaser), Comment 7 (modification or limitation of remedy), Comment 8 (puffing and limitations on extent of obligation) and Comment 9 (damages) is adopted here.

3. This section provides an additional test for enforceability not found in Section 2-313A. For the obligation to be created the remote purchaser must, at the time of purchase, have knowledge of the affirmation of fact, promise, description or remedial promise and must also have an expectation that the goods will conform or that the seller will comply. This test is entirely subjective, while the reasonable person test in subsection (3)(a) is objective in nature. Both tests must be met.

Thus, the seller will incur no liability to the remote purchaser if: i) the purchaser did not have knowledge of the seller's statement at the time of purchase; ii) the remote purchaser knew of the seller's statement at the time of purchase but did not expect the goods to conform or the seller to comply; iii) a reasonable person in the position of the remote purchaser would not believe that the seller's statement created an obligation (this test does not apply to remedial promises), or iv) the seller's statement is puffing.

4. To determine whether the tests set forth in this section are satisfied the temporal relationship between the communication and the purchase should be considered by the court. For example, the remote purchaser may acquire the goods years after the seller's advertising campaign. In this circumstance, it would be highly unusual for the advertisement to have created the level of expectation in the remote purchaser or belief in the reasonable person in the position of the remote person necessary for the creation of an obligation under this section.

5. To determine whether an obligation arises under this Section, all information known to the remote purchaser at the time of contracting must be considered. For example, a news release by a manufacturer limiting the statements made in its advertising and which are known by the remote purchaser, or a communication to the remote purchaser by the immediate seller limiting the statements made in the manufacturer's advertising must be considered to determine whether the expectation requirement applicable to the remote purchaser and the belief requirement applicable to the reasonable person in the position of the remote purchaser are satisfied.

6. The remedies for breach of an obligation arising under this section may be modified or limited as set forth in Section 2-719. The modification or limitation may be contained in the advertisement that creates the obligation, or it may be separately furnished to the remote purchaser no later than the time of purchase.

7. Section 2-318 deals with the extension of obligations to certain third-party beneficiaries. Of course, no extension is necessary if the goods are purchased by an agent. In this case, the knowledge and expectation of the principal, not the agent, are relevant in determining whether an obligation arises under this section. Nothing in this Act precludes a court from determining that a household operates as a buying unit under the law of agency.

Cross References:

Point 1: Sections 2-313, 2-313A and 2-313B.
Point 2: Section 2-313A.
Point 3: Section 2-313A.
Point 6: Section 2-719.
Point 7: Section 2-318.

Definitional Cross References:

"Buyer". Section 2-103.
"Conforming". Section 2-106.
"Goods". Section 2-103.
"Lease". Section 2A-103.
"Purchase". Section 1-201.
"Record". Section 2-103.
"Remedial promise". Section 2-103.
"Remedy". Section 1-201.
"Sale". Section 2-106.
"Seller". Section 2-103.

§ 2-314. Implied Warranty: Merchantability; Usage of Trade.

(1) Unless excluded or modified (Section 2-316), a warranty that the goods shall be merchantable is implied in a contract for their sale if the seller is a merchant with respect to goods of that kind. Under this section the serving for value of food or drink to be consumed either on the premises or elsewhere is a sale.

(2) Goods to be merchantable must be at least such as:

(a) pass without objection in the trade under the contract description; ~~and~~

(b) in the case of fungible goods, are of fair average quality within the description; ~~and~~

(c) are fit for the ordinary purposes for which ~~such~~ goods of that description are used; ~~and~~

(d) run, within the variations permitted by the agreement, of even kind, quality and quantity within each unit and among all units involved; ~~and~~

(e) are adequately contained, packaged, and labeled as the agreement may require; and

(f) conform to the promise or affirmations of fact made on the container or label if any.

(3) Unless excluded or modified (Section 2-316) other implied warranties may arise from course of dealing or usage of trade.

In this Section, the original Official Comment has been substantially revised or replaced by the following 2003 Official Comment. However, the original Official Comment may remain appropriate legislative history. For that reason, the original Official Comment may be found in Appendix [__] for the convenience of those who may wish to study it. [Editor's note: Appendix [__] is not reprinted here, but the original Official Comment is reprinted in Appendix E of the main edition.]

Official Comment

1. The phrase "goods of that description" rather than the language from the original Article 2 "for which such goods are used" is used in subsection (2)(c). This change emphasizes the importance of the agreed description in determining fitness for ordinary purposes.

2. The seller's obligation applies to present sales as well as to contracts to sell subject to the effects of any examination of specific goods. *See* Section 2-316(3)(b). The warranty of merchantability also applies to sales for use as well as to sales for resale.

3. The question when the warranty is imposed turns basically on the meaning of the terms of the agreement as recognized in the trade. Goods delivered under an agreement made by a merchant in a given line of trade must be of a quality comparable to that generally acceptable in that line of trade under the description or other designation of the goods used in the agreement. The responsibility imposed rests on any merchant-seller.

4. A specific designation of goods by the buyer does not exclude the seller's obligation that they be fit for the general purposes appropriate to the goods. A contract for the sale of second-hand goods, however, involves only an obligation as is appropriate to the goods according to their contract description. A person making an isolated sale of goods is not a "merchant" within the meaning of the full scope of this section and, thus, no warranty of merchantability would apply. The seller's knowledge of any defects not apparent on inspection would, however, without need for express agreement and in keeping with the underlying reason of the present section and the provisions on good faith, impose an obligation that known material but hidden defects be fully disclosed.

5. Although a seller may not be a "merchant" for the goods in question, if the seller states generally that the goods are "guaranteed," the provisions of this section may furnish a guide to the content of the resulting express warranty. This has particular significance in the case of second-hand sales, and has further significance in limiting the effect of fine-print disclaimer clauses where their effect would be inconsistent with large-print assertions of "guarantee."

6. The second sentence of subsection (1) covers the warranty for food and drink. The serving for value of food or drink for consumption on the premises or elsewhere is treated as a sale.

7. Suppose that an unmerchantable lawn mower causes personal injury to the buyer, who is operating the mower. Without more, the buyer can sue the seller for breach of the implied warranty of merchantability and recover for injury to person "proximately resulting" from the breach. Section 2-715(2)(b).

This opportunity does not resolve the tension between warranty law and tort law where goods cause personal injury or property damage. The primary source of that tension arises from disagreement over whether the concept of defect in tort and the concept of merchantability in Article 2 are coextensive where personal injuries are involved, *i.e.,* if goods are merchantable under warranty law, can they still be defective under tort law, and if goods are not defective under tort law, can they be unmerchantable under warranty law? The answer to both questions should be no, and the tension between merchantability in warranty and defect in tort where personal injury or property damage is involved should be resolved as follows:

> When recovery is sought for injury to person or property, whether goods are merchantable is to be determined by applicable state products liability law. When, however, a claim for injury to person or property is based on an implied warranty of fitness under Section 2-315 or an express warranty under Section 2-313 or an obligation arising under Section 2-313A or 2-313B, this Article determines whether an implied warranty of fitness or an express warranty was made and breached, as well as what damages are recoverable under Section 2-715.
>
> To illustrate, suppose that the seller makes a representation about the safety of a lawn mower that becomes part of the basis of the buyer's bargain. The buyer is injured when the gas tank cracks and a fire breaks out. If the lawnmower without the representation is not defective under applicable tort law, it is not unmerchantable under this section. On the other hand, if the lawnmower did not conform to the representation about safety, the seller made and breached an express warranty and the buyer may sue under Article 2.

8. Subsection (2) does not purport to exhaust the meaning of "merchantable" nor to negate any of its attributes not specifically mentioned in the text of the statute but that arise by usage of trade or through case law. The language used is "must be at least such as . . . ," and the intention is to leave open other possible attributes of merchantability.

9. Paragraphs (a) and (b) of subsection (2) are to be read together. Both refer to the standards of that line of the trade which fits the transaction and the seller's business. "Fair average" is a term directly appropriate to agricultural bulk products and means goods centering around the middle belt of quality, not the least or the worst that can be understood in the particular trade by the designation, but such as can pass "without objection." Of course a fair percentage of the least is permissible but the goods are not "fair average" if they are all of the least or worst quality possible under the description. In cases of doubt about what quality is intended, the price at which a merchant closes a contract is an excellent indication of the nature and scope of the merchant's obligation under the present section.

10. Fitness for the ordinary purposes for which goods of the type are used is a fundamental concept of the present section and is covered in paragraph (2)(c). As stated above, merchantability is also a part of the obligation owing to the buyer for use. Correspondingly, protection, under this aspect of the warranty, of the person buying for resale to the ultimate consumer is equally necessary, and merchantable goods must therefore be "honestly" resalable in the normal course of business because they are what they purport to be.

11. Paragraph (2)(d) on evenness of kind, quality and quantity follows case law. But precautionary language has been added as a remainder of the frequent usages of trade which permit substantial variations both with and without an allowance or an obligation to replace the varying units.

12. Paragraph (2)(e) applies only where the nature of the goods and of the transaction require a certain type of container, package or label. Paragraph (2)(f) applies, on the other hand, wherever there is a label or container on which representations are made, even though the original contract, either by express terms or usage of trade, may not have required either the labeling or the representation. This follows from the general obligation of good faith which requires that a buyer should not be placed in the position of reselling or using goods delivered under false representations appearing on the package or container. No problem of extra consideration arises in this connection since, under this Article, an obligation is imposed by the original contract not to deliver mislabeled articles, and the obligation is imposed where mercantile good faith so requires and without reference to the doctrine of consideration.

13. Exclusion or modification of the warranty of merchantability, or of any part of it, is dealt with in Section 2-316. That section must be read with particular reference to subsection (4) on limitation of remedies. The warranty of merchantability, wherever it is normal, is so commonly taken for granted that its exclusion from the contract is a matter threatening surprise and therefore requiring special precaution.

14. Subsection (3) is to make explicit that usage of trade and course of dealing can create warranties and that they are implied rather than express warranties and thus subject to exclusion or modification under Section 2-316. A typical instance would be the obligation to provide pedigree papers to evidence conformity of the animal to the contract in the case of a pedigreed dog or blooded bull.

15. In an action based on breach of warranty, it is of course necessary to show not only the existence of the warranty but the fact that the warranty was broken and that the breach of the warranty was the proximate cause of the loss sustained. An affirmative showing by the seller that the loss resulted from some action or event following the seller's delivery of the goods can operate as a defense. Equally, evidence indicating that the seller exercised care in the manufacture, processing or selection of the goods is relevant to the issue of whether the warranty was in fact broken. An action by the buyer following an examination of the goods which ought to have indicated the defect complained of can be shown as matter bearing on whether the breach itself was the cause of the injury.

Cross References:

Point 1: Section 2-316.
Point 2: Section 2-316.
Point 3: Sections 1-203 and 2-104.
Point 5: Section 2-315.
Point 7: Section 2-715.
Point 11: Section 2-316.
Point 12: Sections 1-201, 1-205 and 2-316.
Point 13: Section 2-316.
Point 14: Section 2-316.

Definitional Cross References:

"Agreement". Section 1-201.
"Contract". Section 1-201.
"Contract for sale". Section 2-106.
"Goods". Section 2-103.
"Merchant". Section 2-104.
"Seller". Section 2-103.

§ 2-316. Exclusion or Modification of Warranties.

(1) Words or conduct relevant to the creation of an express warranty and words or conduct tending to negate or limit warranty shall be construed wherever reasonable as consistent with each other; but subject to ~~the provisions of this Article on parol or extrinsic evidence (Section 2-202)~~ Section 2-202, negation or limitation is inoperative to the extent that such construction is unreasonable.

(2) Subject to subsection (3), to exclude or modify the implied warranty of merchantability or any part of it in a consumer contract the language must be in a record, be conspicuous, and state "The seller undertakes no responsibility for the quality of the goods except as otherwise provided in this contract," and in any other contract the language must mention merchantability and in case of a ~~writing~~ record must be conspicuous~~, and to~~. Subject to subsection (3), to exclude or modify the implied warranty of fitness, the exclusion must be ~~by a writing~~ in a record and be conspicuous. Language to exclude all implied warranties of fitness in a consumer contract must state "The seller assumes no responsibility that the goods will be fit for any particular purpose for which you may be buying these goods, except as otherwise provided in the contract," and in any other contract the language is sufficient if it states, for example, that "There are no warranties ~~which~~ that extend beyond the description on the face hereof." Language that satisfies the requirements of this subsection for the exclusion or modification of a warranty in a consumer contract also satisfies the requirements for any other contract.

(3) Notwithstanding subsection (2):

(a) unless the circumstances indicate otherwise, all implied warranties are excluded by expressions like "as is", "with all faults" or other language ~~which~~ that in common understanding calls the buyer's attention to the exclusion of warranties ~~and~~, makes plain that there is no implied warranty, and, in a consumer contract evidenced by a record, is set forth conspicuously in the record; ~~and~~

(b) ~~when~~ if the buyer before entering into the contract has examined the goods or the sample or model as fully as ~~he~~ desired or has refused to examine the goods after a demand by the seller there is no implied warranty with regard to defects ~~which~~ that an examination ~~ought~~ in the circumstances ~~to~~ should have revealed to ~~him~~ the buyer; and

(c) an implied warranty ~~can~~ may also be excluded or modified by course of dealing or course of performance or usage of trade.

(4) Remedies for breach of warranty ~~can~~ may be limited in accordance with ~~the provisions of this article on liquidation or limitation of damages and on contractual modification of remedy (Sections 2-718 and 2-719)~~ Sections 2-718 and 2-719.

In this Section, the original Official Comment has been substantially revised or replaced by the following 2003 Official Comment. However, the original Official Comment may remain appropriate legislative history. For that reason, the original Official Comment may be found in Appendix [__] for the convenience of those who may wish to study it. [Editor's note: Appendix [__] is not reprinted here, but the original Official Comment is reprinted in Appendix E of the main edition.]

Official Comment

1. Subsection (1) is designed principally to deal with those frequent clauses in sales contracts which seek to exclude "all warranties, express or implied." It seeks to protect a buyer from unexpected and unbargained language of disclaimer by denying effect to this language when inconsistent with language of express warranty and permitting the exclusion of implied warranties only by language or other circumstances which protect the buyer from surprise.

The seller is protected against false allegations of oral warranties by this Article's provisions on parol and extrinsic evidence and against unauthorized representations by the customary "lack of authority" clauses. This Article treats the limitation or avoidance of consequential damages as a matter of limiting remedies for breach, separate from the matter of creation of liability under a warranty. If no warranty exists, there is of course no problem of limiting remedies for breach of warranty. Under subsection (4), the question of limitation of remedy is governed by the sections referred to rather than by this section.

2. The general test for disclaimers of implied warranties remains in subsection (3)(a), and the more specific tests are in subsection (2). A disclaimer that satisfies the requirements of subsection (3)(a) need not also satisfy any of the requirements of subsection (2).

3. Subsection (2) distinguishes between commercial and consumer contracts. In a commercial contract, language that disclaims the implied warranty of merchantability need not be in a record, but if it is in a record it must be conspicuous. Under this subsection, a conspicuous record is required to disclaim the implied warranty of merchantability in a consumer contract and to disclaim the implied warranty of fitness in any contract. Use of the language required by this subsection for consumer contracts satisfies the language requirements for other contracts governed by this subsection.

4. Subsection (2) presupposes that the implied warranty in question exists unless excluded or modified. Whether or not language of disclaimer satisfies the requirements of this section, the language may be relevant under other sections to the question of whether the warranty was ever in fact created. Thus, unless the provisions of this Article on parol and extrinsic evidence prevent its introduction, oral language of a disclaimer may raise issues of fact about whether reliance by the buyer occurred and whether the seller had "reason to know" under the section on implied warranty of fitness for a particular purpose.

5. Subsection (3)(a) deals with general terms such as "as is," "as they stand," "with all faults," and the like. These terms in ordinary commercial usage are understood to mean that the buyer takes the entire risk as to the quality of the goods involved. The terms covered by the subsection are in fact merely a particularization of subsection (3)(c), which provides for exclusion or modification of implied warranties by usage of trade. Nothing in subsection (3)(a) prevents a term such as "there are no implied warranties" from being effective in appropriate circumstances, as when the term is a negotiated term between commercial parties.

Satisfaction of subsection (3)(a) does not require that the language be set forth in a record, but if there is a record the language must be conspicuous if the contract is a consumer contract.

6. The exceptions to the general rule set forth in subsections (3)(b) and (3)(c) are common factual situations in which the circumstances surrounding the transaction are in themselves sufficient to call the buyer's attention to the fact that no implied warranties are made or that a certain implied warranty is being excluded.

Under subsection (3)(b), warranties may be excluded or modified by the circumstances when the buyer examines the goods or a sample or model of them before entering into the contract. "Examination" as used in this paragraph is not synonymous with inspection before acceptance or at any other time after the contract has been made. Of course if the buyer discovers the defect and uses the goods anyway, or if the buyer unreasonably fails to examine the goods before using them, the resulting injuries may be found to have resulted from the buyer's own action rather than have been proximately caused by a breach of warranty. *See* Sections 2-314 and 2-715.

To bring the transaction within the scope of "refused to examine" in subsection (3)(b), it is not sufficient that the goods are available for inspection. There must in addition be an actual examination by the buyer or a demand by the seller that the buyer examine the goods fully. The seller's demand must place the buyer on notice that the buyer is assuming the risk of defects which the examination ought to reveal.

Application of the doctrine of "caveat emptor" in all cases where the buyer examines the goods regardless of statements made by the seller is, however, rejected by this Article. Thus, if the offer of examination is accompanied by words about their merchantability or specific attributes, and the buyer indicates clearly a reliance on those words rather than on the buyer's examination, the words give rise to an "express" warranty. In these cases, the question is one of fact about whether a warranty of merchantability has been expressly incorporated in the agreement.

The particular buyer's skill and the normal method of examining goods in the circumstances determine what defects are excluded by the examination. A failure to notice defects which are obvious cannot excuse the buyer because of the lack of notice. However, an examination under circumstances which do not permit chemical or other testing of the goods does not exclude defects which could be ascertained only by testing. Nor can latent defects be excluded by a simple examination. A professional buyer examining a product in the buyer's field will be held to have assumed the risk for all defects which a professional in the field ought to observe, while a nonprofessional buyer will be held to have assumed the risk only for the defects as a layperson might be expected to observe.

7. The situation in which the buyer gives precise and complete specifications to the seller is not explicitly covered in this section, but this is a frequent circumstance by which the implied warranties may be excluded. The warranty of fitness for a particular purpose would not normally arise since in this situation there is usually no reliance on the seller by the buyer. The warranty of merchantability in a transaction of this type, however, must be considered in connection with the next section on the cumulation and conflict of warranties. Under paragraph(c) of that section in case of an inconsistency the implied warranty of merchantability is displaced by the express warranty that the goods will comply with the specifications. Thus, where the buyer gives detailed specifications as to the goods, neither of the implied warranties as to quality will normally apply to the transaction unless consistent with the specifications.

Cross References:

Point 1: Sections 2-202, 2-718 and 2-719.
Point 6: Sections 1-205, 2-314 and 2-715.

Definitional Cross References:

"Agreement". Section 1-201.
"Buyer". Section 2-103.
"Conspicuous". Section 2-103.
"Consumer contract". Section 2-103.
"Contract". Section 1-201.
"Course of dealing". Section 1-303.
"Goods". Section 2-103.
"Record". Section 2-103.
"Remedy". Section 1-201.
"Seller". Section 2-103.
"Usage of trade". Section 1-303.

§ 2-318. ~~Third Party~~ Third-Party Beneficiaries of Warranties ~~Express or Implied~~ and Obligations.

(1) In this section:

(a) "Immediate buyer" means a buyer that enters into a contract with the seller.

(b) "Remote purchaser" means a person that buys or leases goods from an immediate buyer or other person in the normal chain of distribution.

Alternative A to subsection (2)

(2) ~~A seller's warranty whether express or implied extends to any natural person who is in the family or household of his buyer or who is a guest in his home if it is reasonable to expect that such person may use, consume or be affected by the goods and who is injured in person by breach of the warranty.~~ A seller's warranty to an immediate buyer, whether express or implied, a seller's remedial promise to an immediate buyer, or a seller's obligation to a remote purchaser under Section 2-313A or 2-313B extends to any individual who is in the family or household of the immediate buyer or the remote purchaser or who is a guest in the home of either if it is reasonable to expect that the person may use, consume, or be affected by the goods and who is injured in person by breach of the warranty, remedial promise, or obligation. A seller may not exclude or limit the operation of this section.

Alternative B to subsection (2)

(2) ~~A seller's warranty whether express or implied extends to any natural person who may reasonably be expected to use, consume or be affected by the goods and who is injured in person by breach of the warranty.~~ A seller's warranty to an immediate buyer, whether express or implied, a seller's remedial promise to an immediate buyer, or a seller's obligation to a remote purchaser under Section 2-313A or 2-313B extends to any

individual who may reasonably be expected to use, consume, or be affected by the goods and who is injured in person by breach of the warranty, remedial promise, or obligation. A seller may not exclude or limit the operation of this section.

Alternative C to subsection (2)

(2) ~~A seller's warranty whether express or implied extends to any person who may reasonably be expected to use, consume or be affected by the goods and who is injured by breach of the warranty.~~ A seller's warranty to an immediate buyer, whether express or implied, a seller's remedial promise to an immediate buyer, or a seller's obligation to a remote purchaser under Section 2-313A or 2-313B extends to any person that may reasonably be expected to use, consume, or be affected by the goods and that is injured by breach of the warranty, remedial promise, or obligation. A seller may not exclude or limit the operation of this section with respect to injury to the person of an individual to whom the warranty, remedial promise, or obligation extends.

In this Section, the original Official Comment has been substantially revised or replaced by the following 2003 Official Comment. However, the original Official Comment may remain appropriate legislative history. For that reason, the original Official Comment may be found in Appendix [__] for the convenience of those who may wish to study it. [Editor's note: *Appendix [__] is not reprinted here, but the original Official Comment is reprinted in Appendix E of the main edition.*]

Official Comment

1. This section retains original Article 2's alternative approaches but expands each alternative to cover obligations arising under Sections 2-313A and 2-313B and remedial promises.

2. The last sentence of each alternative to subsection (2) is not meant to suggest that a seller is precluded from excluding or disclaiming a warranty which might otherwise arise in connection with the sale provided the exclusion or modification is permitted by Section 2-316. Nor is it intended to suggest that the seller is precluded from limiting the remedies of the immediate buyer or remote purchaser in any manner provided in Sections 2-718 or 2-719. *See also* Section 2-313A(4) and Section 2-313B(4). To the extent that the contract of sale contains provisions under which warranties are excluded or modified, or remedies for breach are limited, the provisions are equally operative against beneficiaries of warranties under this section. What this last sentence forbids is exclusion of liability by the seller to the persons to whom the warranties, obligations and remedial promises accruing to the immediate buyer or remote purchaser would extend under this section.

Alternative A extends protection to a third party beneficiaries who is a guest in the home of the immediate buyer or remoter purchaser. The status of "guest in the home" describes the category of beneficiaries covered by this provision, and it does not limit the situs of the breach. Thus, a guest in the home that would otherwise have rights under this section could be injured in the automobile of the immediate buyer or remote purchaser. Beyond this, the section is neutral and is not intended to enlarge or restrict the developed or developing case law on whether the seller's warranties, given to his buyer who resells, extend to other persons in the distributive chain.

The last sentence of Alternative C permits a seller to reduce its obligations to third-party beneficiaries to a level commensurate with that imposed on the seller under Alternative B—that is, to eliminate liability to persons that are not individuals and to eliminate liability for damages other than personal injury.

3. As used in this section, the term "remote purchaser" refers to the party to whom an obligation initially runs under Section 2-313A or 2-313B. It does not refer to any subsequent purchaser of the goods.

4. As applied to warranties and remedial promises arising under Sections 2-313, 2-314 and 2-315, the purpose of this section is to give certain beneficiaries the benefit of the warranties and remedial promises which the immediate buyer received in the contract of sale, thereby freeing any beneficiaries from any technical rules as to "privity." It seeks to accomplish this purpose without any derogation of any right or remedy arising under the law of torts. Implicit in the section is that any beneficiary of a warranty may bring a direct action for breach of warranty against the seller whose warranty extends to the beneficiary.

Obligations and remedial promises under Sections 2-313A and 2-313B arise initially in a non-privity context but are extended under this section to the same extent as warranties and remedial promises running to a buyer in privity.

Cross References:

Point 1: Sections 2-313A, 2-313B.
Point 2: Sections 2-313A, 2-313B, 2-316, 2-718 and 2-719.
Point 3: Sections 2-313A, 2-313B.
Point 4: Section 2-313, 2-313A, 2-313B, 2-314, 2-315.

Definitional Cross References:

"Buyer". Section 2-103.
"Contract". Section 1-201.
"Goods". Section 2-103.
"Lease". Section 2A-103.
"Remedial promise". Section 2-103.
"Seller". Section 2-103.

PART 5

PERFORMANCE

§ 2-508. Cure by Seller of Improper Tender or Delivery; Replacement.

~~(1) Where any tender or delivery by the seller is rejected because non-conforming and the time for performance has not yet expired, the seller may seasonably notify the buyer of his intention to cure and may then within the contract time make a conforming delivery.~~

~~(2) Where the buyer rejects a non-conforming tender which the seller had reasonable grounds to believe would be acceptable with or without money allowance the seller may if he seasonably notifies the buyer have a further reasonable time to substitute a conforming tender.~~

(1) If the buyer rejects goods or a tender of delivery under Section 2-601 or 2-612 or, except in a consumer contract, justifiably revokes acceptance under Section 2-608(1)(b) and the agreed time for performance has not expired, a seller that has performed in good faith, upon seasonable notice to the buyer and at the seller's own expense, may cure the breach of contract by making a conforming tender of delivery within the agreed time. The seller shall compensate the buyer for all of the buyer's reasonable expenses caused by the seller's breach of contract and subsequent cure.

(2) If the buyer rejects goods or a tender of delivery under Section 2-601 or 2-612 or, except in a consumer contract, justifiably revokes acceptance under Section 2-608(1)(b) and the agreed time for performance has expired, a seller that has performed in good faith, upon seasonable notice to the buyer and at the seller's own expense, may cure the breach of contract, if the cure is appropriate and timely under the circumstances, by making a tender of conforming goods. The seller shall compensate the buyer for all of the buyer's reasonable expenses caused by the seller's breach of contract and subsequent cure.

Official Comment

1. Subsection (1) permits a seller that has made a nonconforming tender in any case to make a conforming tender within the contract time upon seasonable notification to the buyer. It presumes that the buyer has rightfully rejected or justifiably revoked acceptance under Section 2-608(1)(b) through timely notification to the seller and has complied with any particularization requirements imposed by Section 2-605(1). This subsection also applies where the seller has taken back the nonconforming goods and refunded the purchase price. The seller may still make a good tender within the contract period. The closer, however, it is to the contract date, the greater is the necessity for extreme promptness on the seller's part in notifying of the intention to cure, if the notification is to be "seasonable" under this subsection.

The rule of this subsection, moreover, is qualified by its underlying reasons. Thus if, after contracting for June delivery, a buyer later makes known to the seller a need for shipment early in the month and the seller ships accordingly, the "contract time" has been cut down by the supervening modification and the time for cure of tender must reflect this modified time term.

2. Cure after a justifiable revocation of acceptance is not available as a matter of right in a consumer contract. Furthermore, even in a nonconsumer contract, cure is not available if the revocation is predicated on Section 2-608(1)(a). If the buyer is revoking because of a known defect that the seller has not been willing or able to cure, there is no justification for giving the seller a second chance to cure.

3. Subsection (2) expands the seller's right to cure after the time for performance has expired. As under subsection (1), the buyer's rightful rejection or in a nonconsumer contract justifiable revocation of acceptance under Section 2-608(1)(b) trigger the seller's right to cure. Original Section 2-508(2) was designed to prevent surprise rejections by requiring the seller to have "reasonable grounds to believe" the nonconforming tender was acceptable. Although this test has been abandoned, the requirement that the initial tender be made in good faith prevents a seller from deliberately tendering goods that the seller knows the buyer cannot use in order to save the contract and then, upon rejection, insisting on a second right to cure. The good faith standard applies under both subsection (1) and subsection (2).

4. The seller's cure under both subsection (1) and subsection (2) must be of conforming goods. Conforming goods includes not only conformity to the contracted-for quality but also as to quantity or assortment or other similar obligations under the contract. Since the time for performance has expired in a case governed by subsection (2), however, the seller's tender of conforming goods required to effect a cure under this section could not conform to the contracted time for performance. Thus, subsection (1) requires that cure be tendered "within the agreed time" while subsection (2) requires that the tender be "appropriate and timely under the circumstances."

The requirement that the cure be "appropriate and timely under the circumstances" provides important protection for the buyer. If the buyer is acquiring inventory on a just-in-time basis and needs to procure substitute goods from another supplier to keep the buyer's process moving, the cure would not be timely. If the seller knows from the circumstances that strict compliance with the contract obligations is expected, the seller's cure would not be appropriate. If the seller attempts to cure by repair, the cure would not be appropriate if the attempted cure resulted in goods that did not conform in every respect to the requirements of the contract. The standard for quality on the second tender is governed by Section 2-601. Whether a cure is appropriate and timely is based upon the circumstances and needs of the buyer. A seasonable notice to the buyer and timely cure are predicated on the requirement that the notice and offered cure would be untimely if the buyer has reasonably changed its position in good faith reliance on the nonconforming tender.

5. Cure is at the seller's expense, and the seller is obligated to compensate the buyer for all of the buyer's reasonable expenses caused by the breach and the cure. The term "reasonable expenses" is not limited to expenses that would qualify as incidental damages. The seller's compensation of the buyer's expenses provided in both subsections (1) and (2) is not controlled by remedy limitations that the parties may have agreed to as provided in Section 2-719. A remedy limitation under Section 2-719 is based upon compensation to the aggrieved party for a breach. The reasonable expenses contemplated under this section are designed to cure the breach in conjunction with the seller's provision of a conforming tender or conforming goods. If the seller is not attempting to cure its breach, a remedy limitation agreed to by the parties under Section 2-719 is an effective way to provide compensation for breach.

Cross References:

Point 1: Sections 2-605 and 2-608.
Point 2: Section 2-608.
Point 3: Section 2-608.
Point 4: Section 2-511.
Point 5: Section 2-719.

Definitional Cross References:

"Agreement". Section 1-201.
"Buyer". Section 2-103.
"Conforming". Section 2-106.
"Consumer contract". Section 2-103.
"Contract". Section 1-201.
"Delivery". Section 2-103.
"Goods". Section 2-103.
"Good faith". Section 2-103.
"Notice". Section 1-202.
"Reasonable time". Section 1-205.
"Seasonable". Section 1-205.
"Seller". Section 2-103.

PART 6

BREACH, REPUDIATION, AND EXCUSE

§ 2-605. Waiver of Buyer's Objections by Failure to Particularize.

(1) ~~The~~ A buyer's failure to state in connection with rejection a particular defect or in connection with revocation of acceptance a defect that justifies revocation ~~which is ascertainable by reasonable inspection~~ precludes ~~him~~ the buyer from relying on the unstated defect to justify rejection or ~~to establish breach~~ revocation of acceptance if the defect is ascertainable by reasonable inspection:

(a) ~~where~~ if the seller had a right to cure the defect and could have cured it if stated seasonably; or

(b) between merchants, ~~when~~ if the seller has after rejection or revocation of acceptance made a request in ~~writing~~ a record ~~and~~ for a full and final ~~written~~ statement in a record of all defects on which the buyer proposes to rely.

(2) ~~Payment~~ A buyer's payment against documents tendered to the buyer made without reservation of rights precludes recovery of the payment for defects apparent ~~on the face of~~ in the documents.

In this Section, the original Official Comment has been substantially revised or replaced by the following 2003 Official Comment. However, the original Official Comment may remain appropriate legislative history. For that reason, the original Official Comment may be found in Appendix [__] for the convenience of those who may wish to study it. [Editor's note: Appendix [__] is not reprinted here, but the original Official Comment is reprinted in Appendix E of the main edition.]

Official Comment

1. This section rests upon a policy of permitting the buyer to give a quick and informal notice of defects in a tender without penalizing the buyer for omissions, while at the same time protecting a seller that is reasonably misled by the buyer's failure to state curable defects. When the defect in a tender is one which could have been cured by the seller, a buyer that merely rejects the delivery without stating any objections to the tender is probably acting in commercial bad faith and is seeking to get out of a agreement which has become unprofitable. Following the general policy of this Article to preserve the deal wherever possible, subsection (1)(a) requires that the seller's right to correct the tender in the circumstances be protected.

Subsection (1) as amended makes three substantive changes. First, the failure to particularize affects only the buyer's right to reject or revoke acceptance. It does not affect the buyer's right to establish a breach of the agreement. Waiver of a right to damages for breach because of a failure properly to notify the seller is governed by Section 2-607(3).

Second, subsection (1) now requires the seller to have had a right to cure under Section 2-508 in addition to having the ability to cure. This point was perhaps implicit in the original provision, but it is now expressly stated to avoid any question of whether this section creates a seller's right to cure independent of the right enumerated in Section 2-508. Thus, if the defect is one that could be cured under Section 2-508, the buyer will have waived that defect as a basis for rejecting the goods or revoking acceptance if the buyer fails to state the defect with sufficient particularity to facilitate the seller's exercise of its right to cure as provided in Section 2-508.

Subsection (1) as revised has been extended to include a notice requirement not only as to rejection but also as to revocation of acceptance. This is necessitated by the expansion of the right to cure (Section 2-508) to cover revocation of acceptance in nonconsumer contracts. The application of the subsection to revocation cases is limited in the following ways: 1) because a revocation under Section 2-608(1)(a) does not activate a right to cure under Section 2-508, the revocation does not activate subsection (1); 2) because Section 2-608(1)(b) involves defects that are by definition difficult to discover, there is no waiver under subsection (1) unless the defect justifies the revocation and the buyer has notice of it; and 3) because the right to cure following revocation of acceptance is restricted under Section 2-508 to nonconsumer contracts, this notice requirement does not apply to a consumer who is seeking to revoke acceptance.

2. When the time for cure has passed, subsection (1)(b) provides that a merchant seller is entitled upon request to a final statement of objections by a merchant buyer upon which the seller can rely. What is needed is a clear statement to the buyer of exactly what is being sought. A formal demand will be sufficient in the case of a merchant-buyer.

3. Subsection (2) has been amended to make clear that a buyer that makes payment upon presentation of the documents to the buyer may waive defects, but that a person that is not the buyer, such as the issuer of a letter of credit that pays as against documents, is not waiving the buyer's right to assert defects in the documents as against the seller.

Subsection (2) applies to documents the same principle contained in Section 2-606(1)(a) for the acceptance of goods; that is, if the buyer accepts documents that have apparent defects, the buyer is presumed to have waived the defects as a basis for rejecting the documents. Subsection (2) is limited to defects which are apparent on the face of the documents. When payment is required against documents, the documents must be inspected before the payment, and the payment constitutes acceptance of the documents. When the documents are delivered without requiring a contemporary payment by the buyer, the acceptance of the documents by non-objection is postponed until after a reasonable time for the buyer to inspect the documents. In either situation, however, the buyer "waives" only what is apparent on the face of the documents. Moreover, in either case, the acceptance of the documents does not constitute an acceptance of the goods and does not impair any options or remedies of the buyer for improper delivery of the goods. *See* Section 2-512(2).

Cross References:

Point 1: Sections 2-508, 2-607 and 2-608.
Point 3: Sections 2-512, 2-606 and 2-607.

Definitional Cross References:

"Between merchants". Section 2-104.
"Buyer". Section 2-103.
"Record". Section 2-103.
"Seasonably". Section 1-205.
"Seller". Section 2-103.

§ 2-607. Effect of Acceptance; Notice of Breach; Burden of Establishing Breach After Acceptance; Notice of Claim or Litigation to Person Answerable Over.

(1) The buyer must pay at the contract rate for any goods accepted.

(2) Acceptance of goods by the buyer precludes rejection of the goods accepted and if made with knowledge of a ~~non-conformity cannot~~ nonconformity may not be revoked because of it unless the acceptance was on the reasonable assumption that the ~~non-conformity~~ nonconformity would be seasonably cured, but acceptance does not of itself impair any other remedy provided by this Article for ~~non-conformity~~ nonconformity.

(3) ~~Where~~ If a tender has been accepted:

    (a) the buyer must within a reasonable time after ~~he~~ the buyer discovers or should have discovered any breach notify the seller ~~of breach or be barred from any remedy.~~, but failure to give timely notice bars the buyer from a remedy only to the extent that the seller is prejudiced by the failure; and

    (b) if the claim is one for infringement or the like ~~(subsection (3) of Section 2-312)~~ under Section 2-312(2) and the buyer is sued as a result of such a breach, ~~he~~ the buyer must so notify the seller within a reasonable time after ~~he~~ the buyer receives notice of the litigation or be barred from any remedy over for liability established by the litigation.

(4) The burden is on the buyer to establish any breach with respect to the goods accepted.

(5) ~~Where~~ If the buyer is sued for indemnity, breach of a warranty, or other obligation for which ~~his seller~~ another party is answerable over:

(a) ~~he~~ the buyer may give ~~his seller~~ the other party ~~written~~ notice of the ~~litigation. If~~ litigation in a record, and if the notice states that the ~~seller~~ other party may come in and defend and that if the ~~seller~~ other party does not do so ~~he~~ the other party will be bound in any action against ~~him~~ the other party by ~~his~~ the buyer by any determination of fact common to the two litigations, then unless the ~~seller~~ other party after seasonable receipt of the notice does come in and defend ~~he~~ the other party is so bound.

(b) if the claim is one for infringement or the like ~~(subsection (3) of Section 2-312)~~ under Section 2-312(2), the original seller may demand in ~~writing~~ a record that ~~his~~ its buyer turn over to ~~him~~ it control of the litigation including settlement or else be barred from any remedy over and if ~~he~~ it also agrees to bear all expense and to satisfy any adverse judgment, ~~then the buyer is so barred~~ unless the buyer after seasonable receipt of the demand does turn over control ~~the buyer is so barred~~.

(6) ~~The provisions of subsections~~ Subsections (3), (4), and (5) apply to any obligation of a buyer to hold the seller harmless against infringement or the like ~~(subsection (3) of Section 2-312)~~ under Section 2-312(2).

In this Section, the original Official Comment has been substantially revised or replaced by the following 2003 Official Comment. However, the original Official Comment may remain appropriate legislative history. For that reason, the original Official Comment may be found in Appendix [__] for the convenience of those who may wish to study it. [Editor's note: Appendix [__] is not reprinted here, but the original Official Comment is reprinted in Appendix E of the main edition.]

Official Comment

1. Under subsection (1), once the buyer accepts a tender the seller acquires a right to its price on the contract terms. In cases of partial acceptance, the price of any part accepted is, if possible, to be reasonably apportioned. Usually this is to be determined in terms of "the contract rate," which is the rate determined from the agreement based on the rules and policies of this Article.

2. Under subsection (2) acceptance of goods precludes their subsequent rejection of the goods. Any return of the goods thereafter must be by way of revocation of acceptance under Section 2-608. Revocation is unavailable for a non-conformity known to the buyer at the time of acceptance, except where the buyer has accepted on the reasonable assumption that the non-conformity would be seasonably cured.

3. All other remedies of the buyer remain unimpaired under subsection (2). This is intended to include the buyer's full rights for future installments despite the buyer's acceptance of any earlier non-conforming installment.

4. Subsection (3)(a) provides that the buyer must, within a reasonable time of the discovery, or when the buyer should have discovered any breach, give the seller notification of the breach. A failure to give this notice to the seller bars the buyer from a remedy for breach of contract if the seller suffers prejudice due to the failure to notify. *See* Restatement (Second) of Contracts § 229, which provides for an excuse of a condition where the failure is not material and implementation would result in a disproportionate forfeiture.

The time of notification is to be determined by applying commercial standards to a merchant buyer. "A reasonable time" for notification from a retail consumer is to be judged by different standards so that in that case it could be extended beyond what would be a "commercially" reasonable time in appropriate circumstances because the requirement of notification is meant to defeat commercial bad faith, not to deprive a good faith consumer of a remedy.

The content of the notification need merely be sufficient to let the seller know that the transaction is still troublesome and must be watched. There is no reason to require that the notification which saves the buyer's rights under this section must include a clear statement of all the objections that will be relied on by the buyer, as is required for statements of defects upon rejection (Section 2-605). Nor is there reason to require the notification to be a claim for damages or of any threatened litigation or other resort to a remedy. The notification which preserves the buyer's rights under this Article need only be one that informs the seller that the transaction is claimed to involve a breach, and thus opens the way for normal settlement through negotiation.

5. Under this Article various beneficiaries are given rights for injuries sustained by them because of the seller's breach of warranty. Such a beneficiary does not fall within the reason of the present section in regard to discovery of defects and the giving of notice within a reasonable time after acceptance, since he has nothing to do with acceptance. However, the reason of this section does extend to requiring the beneficiary to notify the seller that an injury has occurred. What is said above, with regard to the extended time for reasonable notification from the lay consumer after the injury is also applicable here; but even a beneficiary can be properly held to the use of good faith in notifying, once he has had time to become aware of the legal situation.

6. Subsection (4) unambiguously places the burden of proof to establish breach on the buyer after acceptance. However, this rule becomes one purely of procedure when the tender accepted was non-conforming and the buyer has given the seller notice of breach under subsection (3). For subsection (2) makes it clear that acceptance leaves unimpaired the buyer's right to be made whole, and that right can be exercised by the buyer not only by way of cross-claim for damages, but also by way of recoupment in diminution or extinction of the price.

7. The vouching-in procedure in subsection (5) includes indemnity actions, and it includes any other party that is answerable over, not just the immediate seller.

Vouching-in does not confer on the notified seller a right to intervene, does not confer jurisdiction of any kind on the court over the seller, and does not create a duty to defend on the part of the seller. Those matters continue to be governed by the applicable rules of civil procedure and substantive law outside this section.

Vouching in is based upon the principle that the seller is liable for its contractual obligations for quality or title to the goods which the buyer is being forced to defend.

8. Subsections (3)(b) and (5)(b) give a warrantor against infringement an opportunity to defend or compromise third-party claims or be relieved of liability. Subsection (5)(a) codifies for all warranties the practice of voucher to defend. Subsection (6) makes these provisions applicable to the buyer's liability for infringement under Section 2-312.

9. All of the provisions of this section are subject to any explicit reservation of rights. Section 1-308.

Cross References:

Point 1: Section 1-201.
Point 2: Section 2-608.
Point 4: Sections 1-204 and 2-605.

Point 5: Section 2-318.
Point 6: Sections 2-312 and 3-803.
Point 8: Section 2-312.
Point 9: Section 1-308.

Definitional Cross References:

"Burden of establishing". Section 1-201.
"Buyer". Section 2-103.
"Conform". Section 2-106.
"Contract". Section 1-201.
"Goods". Section 2-103.
"Notice". Section 1-202.
"Reasonable time". Section 1-205.
"Remedy". Section 1-201.
"Seasonably". Section 1-205.

§ 2-608. Revocation of Acceptance in Whole or in Part.

(1) ~~The~~ A buyer may revoke ~~his~~ acceptance of a lot or commercial unit whose ~~non-conformity~~ nonconformity substantially impairs its value to ~~him~~ the buyer if ~~he~~ the buyer has accepted it:

(a) on the reasonable assumption that its ~~non-conformity~~ nonconformity would be cured and it has not been seasonably cured; or

(b) without discovery of ~~such non-conformity~~ the nonconformity if ~~his~~ the buyer's acceptance was reasonably induced either by the difficulty of discovery before acceptance or by the seller's assurances.

(2) Revocation of acceptance must occur within a reasonable time after the buyer discovers or should have discovered the ground for it and before any substantial change in condition of the goods which is not caused by their own defects. ~~It~~ The revocation is not effective until the buyer notifies the seller of it.

(3) A buyer ~~who~~ that so revokes has the same rights and duties with regard to the goods involved as if ~~he~~ the buyer had rejected them.

(4) If a buyer uses the goods after a rightful rejection or justifiable revocation of acceptance, the following rules apply:

(a) Any use by the buyer that is unreasonable under the circumstances is wrongful as against the seller and is an acceptance only if ratified by the seller.

(b) Any use of the goods that is reasonable under the circumstances is not wrongful as against the seller and is not an acceptance, but in an appropriate case the buyer is obligated to the seller for the value of the use to the buyer.

Comment 8 added in 2003. The original official comment has not been amended to reflect the change from "writing" to "record."

Official Comment

Prior Uniform Statutory Provision: Section 69(1)(d), (3), (4) and (5), Uniform Sales Act.

Changes: Rewritten.

Purposes of Changes: To make it clear that:

1. Although the prior basic policy is continued, the buyer is no longer required to elect between revocation of acceptance and recovery of damages for breach. Both are now available to him. The non-alternative character of the two remedies is stressed by the terms used in the present section. The section no longer speaks of "rescission," a term capable of ambiguous application either to transfer of title to the goods or to the contract of sale and susceptible also of confusion with cancellation for cause of an executed or executory portion of the contract. The remedy under this section is instead referred to simply as "revocation of acceptance" of goods tendered under a contract for sale and involves no suggestion of "election" of any sort.

2. Revocation of acceptance is possible only where the non-conformity substantially impairs the value of the goods to the buyer. For this purpose the test is not what the seller had reason to know at the time of contracting; the question is whether the non-conformity is such as will in fact cause a substantial impairment of value to the buyer though the seller had no advance knowledge as to the buyer's particular circumstances.

3. "Assurances" by the seller under paragraph (b) of subsection (1) can rest as well in the circumstances or in the contract as in explicit language used at the time of delivery. The reason for recognizing such assurances is that they induce the buyer to delay discovery. These are the only assurances involved in paragraph (b). Explicit assurances may be made either in good faith or bad faith. In either case any remedy accorded by this Article is available to the buyer under the section on remedies for fraud.

4. Subsection (2) requires notification of revocation of acceptance within a reasonable time after discovery of the grounds for such revocation. Since this remedy will be generally resorted to only after attempts at adjustment have failed, the reasonable time period should extend in most cases beyond the time in which notification of breach must be given, beyond the time for discovery of non-conformity after acceptance and beyond the time for rejection after tender. The parties may by their agreement limit the time for notification under this section, but the same sanctions and considerations apply to such agreements as are discussed in the comment on manner and effect of rightful rejection.

5. The content of the notice under subsection (2) is to be determined in this case as in others by considerations of good faith, prevention of surprise, and reasonable adjustment. More will generally be necessary than the mere notification of breach required under the preceding section. On the other hand the requirements of the section on waiver of buyer's objections do not apply here. The fact that quick notification of trouble is desirable affords good ground for being slow to bind a buyer by his first statement. Following the general policy of this Article, the requirements of the content of notification are less stringent in the case of a non-merchant buyer.

6. Under subsection (2) the prior policy is continued of seeking substantial justice in regard to the condition of goods restored to the seller. Thus the buyer may not revoke his acceptance if the goods have materially deteriorated except by reason of their own defects. Worthless goods, however, need not be offered back and minor defects in the articles reoffered are to be disregarded.

7. The policy of the section allowing partial acceptance is carried over into the present section and the buyer may revoke his acceptance, in appropriate cases, as to the entire lot or any commercial unit thereof.

8. Subsection (4) deals with the problem of post-rejection or revocation use of the goods. The courts have developed several alternative approaches. Under original Article 2, a buyer's post-rejection or revocation use of the goods could be treated as an acceptance, thus undoing the rejection or revocation, could be a violation of the buyer's obligation of reasonable care, or could be a reasonable use for which the buyer must compensate the seller. Subsection (4) adopts the third approach.

In general, a buyer that either rejects or revokes acceptance of the goods should not subsequently use the goods in a manner that is inconsistent with the seller's ownership. In some instances, however, the use may be reasonable. For example, a consumer buyer may have incurred an unavoidable obligation to a third-party financier and, if the seller fails to refund the price as required by this Article, the buyer may have no reasonable alternative but to use the goods (e.g., a rejected mobile home that provides needed shelter). Another example might involve a commercial buyer that is unable immediately to obtain cover and must use the goods to fulfill its obligations to third parties. If circumstances change so that the buyer's use after an effective rejection or a justified revocation of acceptance is no longer reasonable, the continued use of the goods is unreasonable and is wrongful against the seller. This gives the seller the option of ratifying the use, thereby treating it as an acceptance, or pursuing a non-Code remedy for conversion.

If the buyer's use is reasonable under the circumstances, the buyer's actions cannot be treated as an acceptance. The buyer must compensate the seller for the value of the use of the goods to the buyer. Determining the appropriate level of compensation requires a consideration of the buyer's particular circumstances and should take into account the defective condition of the goods. There may be circumstances, such as where the use is solely for the purpose of protecting the buyer's security interest in the goods, where no compensation is due the seller under this section. If the seller has a right to compensation under this section that compensation must be netted out against any right of the buyer to damages for the seller's breach of contract.

Cross References:

Point 3: Section 2-721.
Point 4: Sections 1-204, 2-602 and 2-607.
Point 5: Sections 2-605 and 2-607.
Point 7: Section 2-601.

Definitional Cross References:

"Buyer". Section 2-103.
"Commercial unit". Section 2-105.
"Conform". Section 2-106.
"Goods". Section 2-103.
"Notifies". Section 1-202.
"Reasonable time". Section 1-205.
"Rights". Section 1-201.
"Seasonably". Section 1-205.
"Seller". Section 2-103.
"Value". Section 1-204.

PART 7

REMEDIES

§ 2-710. Seller's Incidental and Consequential Damages.

(1) Incidental damages to an aggrieved seller include any commercially reasonable charges, expenses or commissions incurred in stopping delivery, in the transportation, care, and custody of goods after the buyer's breach, in connection with return or resale of the goods or otherwise resulting from the breach.

(2) Consequential damages resulting from the buyer's breach include any loss resulting from general or particular requirements and needs of which the buyer at the time of contracting had reason to know and which could not reasonably be prevented by resale or otherwise.

(3) In a consumer contract, a seller may not recover consequential damages from a consumer.

In this Section, the original Official Comment has been substantially revised or replaced by the following 2003 Official Comment. However, the original Official Comment may remain appropriate legislative history. For that reason, the original Official Comment may be found in Appendix [__] for the convenience of those who may wish to study it. [Editor's note: Appendix [__] is not reprinted here, but the original Official Comment is reprinted in Appendix E of the main edition.]

Official Comment

1. Subsection (1) provides for reimbursement by the seller for the expenses reasonably incurred as a result of the buyer's breach. The section sets forth as examples the usual and normal types of damages that may arise from the breach but the provision is intended intends to provide for all commercially reasonable expenditures made by the seller.

2. Subsection (2) permits an aggrieved seller to recover consequential damages. Under this section the loss must result from general or particular requirements of the seller of which the buyer had reason to know at the time of contracting. As with Section 2-715, the "tacit agreement" test is rejected. (*See* Official Comment 2 to Section 2-715). The buyer is not liable for losses that could have been mitigated.

Sellers rarely suffer compensable consequential damages. A buyer's usual default is failure to pay. In normal circumstances, the disappointed seller will be able to sell to another buyer, borrow to replace the breaching buyer's promised payment, or otherwise adjust the seller's affairs to avoid consequential loss. *cf. Afram Export Corp. v. Metallurgiki Halyps, S.A.*, 772 F.2d 1358, 1368 (7th Cir. 1985).

3. Subsection (3) precludes a seller from recovering consequential damages from a consumer. This is a nonwaivable provision.

Cross References:

Point 1: Section 2-710, 2-711 and 2-715.
Point 2: Section 2-103.

Definitional Cross References:

"Aggrieved party". Section 1-201.
"Buyer". Section 2-103.
"Consumer contract". Section 2-103.
"Delivery". Section 2-103.
"Goods". Section 2-103.
"Seller". Section 2-103.

§ 2-711. Buyer's Remedies in General; Buyer's Security Interest in Rejected Goods.

(1) Where the seller fails to make delivery or repudiates or the buyer rightfully rejects or justifiably revokes acceptance then with respect to any goods involved, and with respect to the whole if the breach goes to the whole contract (Section 2-612), the buyer may cancel and whether or not he has done so may in addition to recovering so much of the price as has been paid

(a) "cover" and have damages under the next section as to all the goods affected whether or not they have been identified to the contract; or

(b) recover damages for non-delivery as provided in this Article (Section 2-713).

(2) Where the seller fails to deliver or repudiates the buyer may also

(a) if the goods have been identified recover them as provided in this Article (Section 2-502); or

(b) in a proper case obtain specific performance or replevy the goods as provided in this Article (Section 2-716).

(1) A breach of contract by the seller includes the seller's wrongful failure to deliver or to perform a contractual obligation, making of a nonconforming tender of delivery or performance, and repudiation.

(2) If the seller is in breach of contract under subsection (1), the buyer, to the extent provided for by this Act or other law, may:

(a) in the case of rightful cancellation, rightful rejection, or justifiable revocation of acceptance, recover so much of the price as has been paid;

(b) deduct damages from any part of the price still due under Section 2-717;

(c) cancel;

(d) cover and have damages under Section 2-712 as to all goods affected whether or not they have been identified to the contract;

(e) recover damages for nondelivery or repudiation under Section 2-713;

(f) recover damages for breach with regard to accepted goods or breach with regard to a remedial promise under Section 2-714;

(g) recover identified goods under Section 2-502;

(h) obtain specific performance or obtain the goods by replevin or similar remedy under Section 2-716;

(i) recover liquidated damages under Section 2-718;

(j) in other cases, recover damages in any manner that is reasonable under the circumstances.

(3) On rightful rejection or justifiable revocation of acceptance a buyer has a security interest in goods in ~~his~~ the buyer's possession or control for any payments made on their price and any expenses reasonably incurred in their inspection, receipt, transportation, care and custody and may hold such goods and resell them in like manner as an aggrieved seller (Section 2-706).

In this Section, the original Official Comment has been substantially revised or replaced by the following 2003 Official Comment. However, the original Official Comment may remain appropriate legislative history. For that reason, the original Official Comment may be found in Appendix [__] for the convenience of those who may wish to study it. [Editor's note: *Appendix [__] is not reprinted here, but the original Official Comment is reprinted in Appendix E of the main edition.*]

Official Comment

1. Despite the seller's breach proper re-tender of delivery as a cure under Section 2-508 effectively precludes the buyer's remedies under this section except for damages for any delay.

2. Under subsection (3), the buyer may hold and resell rejected goods if the buyer has paid a part of the price or incurred expenses of the type specified. "Paid," as used here, includes acceptance of a draft or other time negotiable instrument or the signing of a negotiable note. The buyer's freedom of resale is coextensive with that of a seller under this Article except that the buyer may not keep any profit resulting from the resale and the buyer is limited to retaining only the amount of the price paid and the costs involved in the inspection and handling of the goods. The buyer's security interest in the goods is intended to be limited to the items listed in subsection (3), and the buyer is not permitted to retain funds that the buyer might believe adequate for the damages. The buyer's right to cover, or to have damages for non-delivery, is not impaired by the buyer's exercise of the right of resale.

3. This Act requires its remedies to be liberally administered and provides that any right or obligation which it declares is enforceable by action unless a different effect is specifically prescribed (Section 1-103).

Cross References:

Point 1: Sections 2-502, 2-508, 2-601 and 2-712 through 2-718.
Point 2: Section 2-706.
Point 3: Section 1-103.

Definitional Cross References:

"Aggrieved party". Section 1-201.
"Buyer". Section 2-103.
"Cancellation". Section 2-106.
"Conforming". Section 2-106.
"Contract". Section 1-201.
"Cover". Section 2-712.
"Delivery". Section 2-103.
"Goods". Section 2-103.
"Notifies". Section 1-202.
"Receipt of goods". Section 2-103.
"Remedial promise". Section 2-103.
"Remedy". Section 1-201.
"Security interest". Section 1-201.
"Seller". Section 2-103.

§ 2-713. Buyer's Damages for ~~Non-Delivery~~ Nondelivery or Repudiation.

(1) Subject to ~~the provisions of this Article with respect to proof of market price (Section 2-723),~~ Section 2-723, if the seller wrongfully fails to deliver or repudiates or the buyer rightfully rejects or justifiably revokes acceptance:

(a) the measure of damages ~~for non-delivery or repudiation~~ in the case of wrongful failure to deliver by the seller or rightful rejection or justifiable revocation of acceptance by the buyer is the difference between the market price at the time ~~when the buyer learned of the breach~~ for tender under the contract and the contract price together with any incidental ~~and~~ or consequential damages ~~provided in this Article (Section 2-715)~~ under Section 2-715, but less expenses saved in consequence of the seller's ~~breach.~~ breach; and

(b) the measure of damages for repudiation by the seller is the difference between the market price at the expiration of a commercially reasonable time after the buyer learned of the repudiation, but no later than the time stated in paragraph (a), and the contract price together with any incidental or consequential damages provided in this Article (Section 2-715), less expenses saved in consequence of the seller's breach.

(2) Market price is to be determined as of the place for tender or, in cases of rejection after arrival or revocation of acceptance, as of the place of arrival.

In this Section, the original Official Comment has been substantially revised or replaced by the following 2003 Official Comment. However, the original Official Comment may remain appropriate legislative history. For that reason, the original Official Comment may be found in Appendix [__] for the convenience of those who may wish to study it. [Editor's note: Appendix [__] is not reprinted here, but the original Official Comment is reprinted in Appendix E of the main edition.]

Official Comment

1. This section provides a rule for anticipatory repudiation cases. This is consistent with the new rule for sellers in Section 2-708(1)(b). In a case not involving repudiation, the buyer's damages will be based on the market price at the time for tender under the agreement. This changes the former rule where the time for measuring damages was at the time the buyer learned of the breach.

2. This section provides for a buyer's expectancy damages when the seller wrongfully fails to deliver the goods or repudiates the contract or the buyer rightfully rejects or justifiably revokes acceptance. This section provides an alternative measure of damages to the cover remedy provided for in Section 2-712.

3. Under subsection (1)(a), the measure of damages for a wrongful failure to deliver the goods by the seller or a rightful rejection or justifiable revocation of acceptance by the buyer is the difference between the market price at the time for tender under the agreement and the contract price.

4. Under subsection (1)(b), in the case of an anticipatory repudiation by the seller the market price should be measured at the place where the buyer would have covered at a commercially reasonable time after the buyer learned of the repudiation, but no later than the time of tender under the agreement. This time approximates the market price at the time the buyer would have covered even though the buyer has not done so under Section 2-712. This subsection is designed to put the buyer in the position the buyer would have been in if the seller had performed by approximating the harm the buyer has suffered without allowing the buyer an unreasonable time to speculate on the market at the seller's expense.

5. The market price to be used in comparison with the contract price under this section is the price for goods of the same kind and in the same branch of trade.

When the market price under this section is difficult to prove, Section 2-723 on the determination and proof of market price is available to permit a showing of a comparable market price. When no market price is available, evidence of spot sale prices may be used to determine damages under this section. When the unavailability of a market price is caused by a scarcity of goods of the type involved, a good case may be made for specific performance under Section 2-716. *See* the Official Comment to that Section.

6. In addition to the damages provides in this section, the buyer is entitled to incidental and consequential damages under Section 2-715.

7. A buyer that has covered under Section 2-712 may not recover the contract price market price difference under this section, but instead must base the damages on those provided in Section 2-712. To award an additional amount because the buyer could show the market price was higher than the contract price would put the buyer in a better position than performance would have. Of course, the seller would bear the burden of proving that cover had the economic effect of limiting the buyer's actual loss to an amount less than the contract price-market price difference.

An apparent cover, which does not in fact replace the goods contracted for, should not foreclose the use of the contract price-market price measure of damages. If the breaching seller cannot prove that the new purchase is in fact a replacement for the one not delivered under the contract, the "cover" purchase should not foreclose the buyer's recovery under 2-713 of the market contract difference.

Cross References:

Point 2: Section 2-712.
Point 4: Section 2-712.
Point 5: Sections 1-106, 2-708, 2-716 and 2-723.
Point 6: Section 2-715.
Point 7: Section 2-708, 2-712 and 2-713.

Definitional Cross References:

"Buyer". Section 2-103.
"Contract". Section 1-201.
"Delivery". Section 2-103.
"Reasonable time". Section 1-205.
"Seller". Section 2-103.

§ 2-714. Buyer's Damages for Breach in Regard to Accepted Goods.

(1) ~~Where~~ If the buyer has accepted goods and given notification ~~(subsection (3) of Section 2-607)~~ ~~he~~ pursuant to Section 2-607(3), the buyer may recover as damages for any ~~non-conformity~~ nonconformity of tender the loss resulting in the ordinary course of events from the seller's breach as determined in any reasonable manner ~~which is reasonable~~.

(2) The measure of damages for breach of warranty is the difference at the time and place of acceptance between the value of the goods accepted and the value they would have had if they had been as warranted, unless special circumstances show proximate damages of a different amount.

(3) In a proper case any incidental and consequential damages under ~~the next section~~ Section 2-715 may also be recovered.

In this amended Section in 2003, the original Official Comments have not been amended and continue to be an effective discussion of the Section as amended. The original Official Comment has not been amended to reflect the change from "writing" to "record."

Official Comment

Prior Uniform Statutory Provision: Section 69(6) and (7), Uniform Sales Act.

Changes: Rewritten.

Purposes of Changes:

1. This section deals with the remedies available to the buyer after the goods have been accepted and the time for revocation of acceptance has gone by. In general this section adopts the rule of the prior uniform statutory provision for measuring damages where there has been a breach of warranty as to goods accepted, but goes further to lay down an explicit provision as to the time and place for determining the loss.

The section on deduction of damages from price provides an additional remedy for a buyer who still owes part of the purchase price, and frequently the two remedies will be available concurrently. The buyer's failure to notify of his claim under the section on effects of acceptance, however, operates to bar his remedies under either that section or the present section.

2. The "non-conformity" referred to in subsection (1) includes not only breaches of warranties but also any failure of the seller to perform according to his obligations under the contract. In the case of such non-conformity, the buyer is permitted to recover for his loss "in any manner which is reasonable."

3. Subsection (2) describes the usual, standard and reasonable method of ascertaining damages in the case of breach of warranty but it is not intended as an exclusive measure. It departs from the measure of damages for non-delivery in utilizing the place of acceptance rather than the place of tender. In some cases the two may coincide, as where the buyer signifies his acceptance upon the tender. If, however, the non-conformity is such as would justify revocation of acceptance, the time and place of acceptance under this section is determined as of the buyer's decision not to revoke.

4. The incidental and consequential damages referred to in subsection (3), which will usually accompany an action brought under this section, are discussed in detail in the comment on the next section.

Cross References:

Point 1: Compare Section 2-711; Sections 2-607 and 2-717.
Point 2: Section 2-106.
Point 3: Sections 2-608 and 2-713.
Point 4: Section 2-715.

Definitional Cross References:

"Buyer". Section 2-103.
"Conform". Section 2-106.
"Goods". Section 2-103.
"Notification". Section 1-202.
"Seller". Section 2-103.

§ 2-725. Statute of Limitations in Contracts for Sale.

~~(1) An action for breach of any contract for sale must be commenced within four years after the cause of action has accrued. By the original agreement the parties may reduce the period of limitation to not less than one year but may not extend it.~~

~~(2) A cause of action accrues when the breach occurs, regardless of the aggrieved party's lack of knowledge of the breach. A breach of warranty occurs when tender of delivery is made, except that where a warranty explicitly extends to future performance of the goods and discovery of the breach must await the time of such performance the cause of action accrues when the breach is or should have been discovered.~~

(1) Except as otherwise provided in this section, an action for breach of any contract for sale must be commenced within the later of four years after the right of action has accrued under subsection (2) or (3) or one year after the breach was or should have been discovered, but no longer than five years after the right of action accrued. By the original agreement the parties may reduce the period of limitation to not less than one year but may not extend it. However, in a consumer contract, the period of limitation may not be reduced.

(2) Except as otherwise provided in subsection (3), the following rules apply:

(a) Except as otherwise provided in this subsection, a right of action for breach of a contract accrues when the breach occurs, even if the aggrieved party did not have knowledge of the breach.

(b) For breach of a contract by repudiation, a right of action accrues at the earlier of when the aggrieved party elects to treat the repudiation as a breach or when a commercially reasonable time for awaiting performance has expired.

(c) For breach of a remedial promise, a right of action accrues when the remedial promise is not performed when performance is due.

(d) In an action by a buyer against a person that is answerable over to the buyer for a claim asserted against the buyer, the buyer's right of action against the person answerable over accrues at the time the claim was originally asserted against the buyer.

(3) If a breach of a warranty arising under Section 2-312, 2-313(2), 2-314, or 2-315, or a breach of an obligation, other than a remedial promise, arising under Section 2-313A or 2-313B, is claimed, the following rules apply:

(a) Except as otherwise provided in paragraph (c), a right of action for breach of a warranty arising under Section 2-313(2), 2-314, or 2-315 accrues when the seller has tendered delivery to the immediate buyer, as defined in Section 2-313, and has completed performance of any agreed installation or assembly of the goods.

(b) Except as otherwise provided in paragraph (c), a right of action for breach of an obligation, other than a remedial promise, arising under Section 2-313A or 2-313B accrues when the remote purchaser, as defined in Section 2-313A or 2-313B, receives the goods.

(c) If a warranty arising under Section 2-313(2) or an obligation, other than a remedial promise, arising under Section 2-313A or 2-313B explicitly extends to future performance of the goods and discovery of the breach must await the time for performance, the right of action accrues when the immediate buyer as defined in Section 2-313 or the remote purchaser as defined in Section 2-313A or 2-313B discovers or should have discovered the breach.

(d) A right of action for breach of warranty arising under Section 2-312 accrues when the aggrieved party discovers or should have discovered the breach. However, an action for breach of the warranty of noninfringement may not be commenced more than six years after tender of delivery of the goods to the aggrieved party.

(3) (4) Where If an action commenced within the time limited by subsection (1) is so terminated as to leave available a remedy by another action for the same breach, such the other action may be commenced after the expiration of the time limited and within six months after the termination of the first action unless the termination resulted from voluntary discontinuance or from dismissal for failure or neglect to prosecute.

(4) (5) This section does not alter the law on tolling of the statute of limitations nor does it apply to causes of action which have that accrued before this Act becomes effective.

In this Section, the original Official Comment has been substantially revised or replaced by the following 2003 Official Comment. However, the original Official Comment may remain appropriate legislative history. For that reason, the original Official Comment may be found in Appendix [__] for the convenience of those who may wish to study it. [Editor's note: Appendix [__] is not reprinted here, but the original Official Comment is reprinted in Appendix E of the main edition.]

Official Comment

1. Original Section 2-725 has been changed as follows: 1) The basic four-year limitation period in subsection (1) has been supplemented by a discovery rule that permits a cause of action to be brought within one year after the breach was or should have been discovered, although no later than five years after the time the cause would otherwise have accrued; 2) The applicable limitation period cannot be reduced in a consumer contract (subsection (1)); 3) Subsection (2) contains specific rules for cases of repudiation,

breach of a remedial promise, and actions where another person is answerable over; 4) Subsection (3)(a) provides that the limitation period for breach of warranty accrues when tender of delivery has occurred and the seller has completed any agreed installation or assembly of the goods; 5) Subsection (3) contains specific rules for breach of an obligation arising under Section 2-313A or 2-313B, for breach of a warranty arising under Section 2-312, and for breach of a warranty against infringement.

2. Subsection (1) continues the four-year limitation period of original Article 2 but provides for a possible one-year extension to accommodate a discovery of the breach late in the four year period after accrual. The four year period under this Article is shorter than many other statutes of limitation for breach of contract and it provides a period which is appropriate given the nature of the contracts under this Article and modern business practices. As under original Article 2, the period of limitation can be reduced to one year by an agreement in a commercial contract, but the amended section does not permit this reduction in consumer contracts.

3. Subsections (2) and (3) provide rules for accrual of the various types of action that this Article allows. Certainty of commercial relationships is advanced when the rules are clearly set forth. Subsection (2) sets out the accrual rules for actions other than for breach of a warranty, which includes actions based on repudiation or breach of a remedial promise and actions where another person is answerable over. Subsection (3) sets out the accrual rules for the various claims based on a warranty, including a warranty of title and a warranty against infringement, or on an obligation other than a remedial promise arising under Section 2-313A or 2-313B.

Subsection (2)(a) states the general rule from prior law that a right of action for breach of contract accrues when the breach occurs without regard to the aggrieved party's knowledge of the breach. This general rule is then subject to the three more explicit rules in subsection (2) and to the rules for breach of warranty stated in subsection (3).

Subsection (2)(b) provides an explicit rule for repudiation. In a repudiation, the aggrieved party may await performance for a commercially reasonable time or resort to any remedy for breach. Section 2-610. The accrual rule for breach of contract in a repudiation case is based on the earlier of those two time periods.

Subsection (2)(c) provides that a cause of action for breach of a remedial promise accrues when the promise is not performed at the time performance is due.

Subsection (2)(d) addresses the problem that has arisen in the cases when an intermediary party is sued for a breach of obligation for which its seller or another person is answerable over, but the limitations period in the upstream lawsuit has already expired. This subsection allows a party four years, or if reduced in the agreement, not less than one year, from when the claim is originally asserted against the buyer for the buyer to sue the person that is answerable over. Whether a party is in fact answerable over to the buyer is not addressed in this section.

4. Subsection (3) addresses the accrual rules for breach of a warranty arising under Section 2-312, 2-313(2), 2-314 or 2-315, or of an obligation other than a remedial promise arising under Section 2-313A or 2-313B. The subsection does not apply to remedial promises arising under Section 2-313(4); the limitation for all remedial promises are governed by subsection 2(c). The accrual rules explicitly incorporate the definitions of "immediate buyer" and "remote purchaser" in Sections 2-313, 2-313A and 2-313B. Any cause of action brought by another person to which

the warranty or obligation extends is derivative in nature. Thus, the time period applicable to the immediate buyer or remote purchaser governs even if the action is brought by a person to which the warranty or obligation extends under Section 2-318.

Subsection (3)(a) continues the general rule that an action for breach of warranty accrues in the case of an express or implied warranty to an immediate buyer upon completion of tender of delivery of nonconforming goods to the immediate buyer but makes explicit that accrual is deferred until the completion of any installation or assembly that the seller has agreed to undertake. This extension of the time of accrual in the case of installation or assembly applies only in the case of a seller that promises to install or assemble and not in the case of a third party, independent of the seller, undertaking the action.

Subsection (3)(b) addresses the accrual of a cause of action for breach of an obligation other than a remedial promise arising under Section 2-313A or 2-313B. In these cases, the cause of action accrues when the remote purchaser (as defined in those sections) receives the goods. This accrual rule balances the rights of the remote buyer or remote lessee to be able to have a cause of action based upon the warranty obligation the seller has created against the rights of the seller to have some limit on the length of time the seller is liable.

Both of these accrual rules are subject to the exception in subsection (3)(c) for a warranty or obligation that explicitly extends to the future performance of the goods and discovery of the breach must await the time for performance. In this case, the cause of action does not accrue until the buyer or remote purchaser discovers or should have discovered the breach.

For a warranty of title or a warranty of non-infringement under Section 2-312, subsection (3)(d) provides that a cause of action accrues when the aggrieved party discovers or should have discovered the breach. In a typical case, the aggrieved party will not discover the breach until it is sued by a party that asserts title to the goods or that asserts an infringement, either event which could be many years after the buyer acquired the goods. This accrual rule allows the aggrieved party appropriate leeway to then bring a claim against the person that made the warranty. In recognition of a need to have a time of repose in an infringement case, a party may not bring an action based upon a warranty of non-infringement more than six years after tender of delivery.

5. Subsection (4) states the saving provision included in many state statutes and permits an additional short period for bringing new actions where suits begun within the four year period have been terminated so as to leave a remedy still available for the same breach.

6. Subsection (5) makes it clear that this Article does not purport to alter or modify in any respect the law on tolling of the Statute of Limitations as it now prevails in the various jurisdictions.

Cross References:

Point 1: Sections 2-312, 2-313A, and 2-313B.
Point 3: Sections 2-313A, 2-313B, and 2-610.
Point 4: Sections 2-312, 2-313, 2-313A, 2-313B, 2-314, 2-315 and 2-318.

Definitional Cross References:

"Action". Section 1-201.
"Aggrieved party". Section 1-201.
"Agreement". Section 1-201.

"Buyer". Section 2-103.
"Consumer contract". Section 2-103.
"Contract". Section 1-201.
"Contract for sale". Section 2-106.
"Delivery". Section 2-103.
"Goods". Section 2-103.

"Party". Section 1-201.
"Reasonable time". Section 1-205.
"Remedial promise". Section 2-103.
"Remedy". Section 1-201.
"Term". Section 1-201.
"Termination". Section 2-106.

E.8 Revised Article 2A—Selected Provisions and Official Comments[9]

AMENDMENTS TO ARTICLE 2A

LEASES

PART 1

GENERAL PROVISIONS

§ 2A-101. Short Title.

* * *

Official Comment

* * *

2003 AMENDMENTS TO
UNIFORM COMMERCIAL CODE ARTICLE 2A—LEASES

The Drafting Committee was charged with making changes to Article 2A where appropriate to incorporate amendments to Article 2, also being considered at this time, and also with making changes to the Article necessitated by the recent revision of Article 9. It is anticipated that the amendments to Articles 2 and 2A will be presented to the state legislatures as a single package.

As with original Article 2A, these amendments are intended to reflect the distinctive nature of leasing as a commercial transaction. Therefore the following principles should be considered in applying this Article:

Leasing Is Distinctive from Other Commercial Transactions

Leasing is a distinct commercial transaction which is different in many respects from either the sale or the secured financing of goods. A true lease of goods involves the payment for the temporary possession, use and enjoyment of goods, and a lease is entered into with an expectation that the goods will be returned to the owner at the end of the lease term. In contrast, a sale of goods involves a transfer of title for a price, and a security interest involves an interest in the goods that is limited to the remaining secured debt. The separation of ownership and possession in a lease of goods as well as other considerations can result in many differences between the law of leases and the law for the sale of goods. These differences include remedies and, to some extent, contract formation and warranties.

Lease Contract Formation

Leases often involve complex, on-going, multi-faceted obligations. Ownership of the residual remains with the lessor, and for

that reason the lessor has a continuing economic interest in the goods that is not present in a sale. Therefore, lease contracts commonly cover many matters other than the lessor's duty to provide the goods and the lessee's duty to pay rent. These include where and when the goods will be returned to the lessor; options to renew the lease or purchase the goods; maintenance and repairs; restrictions on use of the goods; taxes, insurance; and record keeping. For these reasons, leasing custom and practice favors formal, structured rules of contract formation and greater usage, particularly in commercial leases, of a record of the parties' agreement embodying their understanding.

Warranties

Because of the manner in which leased goods are promoted and distributed—for example, lessors generally do not engage in mass-market advertising aimed at, or make representations in materials to be delivered to, remote lessees—amended Article 2A does not contain provisions analogous to Sections 2-313A and 2-313B of amended Article 2. Though nothing in this Article precludes, in an appropriate case, the application of the principles contained in those sections to a lease transaction, a lessor is responsible only for the lessor's representations and those of the lessor's agents and the lessor is not for the representations made by a third party, such as the supplier or manufacturer of the goods. In addition, a lessee may have the right as a "remote purchaser" under Article 2 to assert claims under Sections 2A-313A and 2-313B directly against a manufacturer or supplier that has engaged in advertising.

Damages

The typical measure of damages for breach of a lease differs from that applied in the law that governs the sale of goods in that, for breach of a lease contract by the lessee, the present value of an ongoing stream of rental payments normally must be taken into consideration as well as the lessor's rights to return of the goods with a certain residual value. As a result, if the goods are sold following a default by the lessee, in calculating the lessee's deficiency, the value of the lessor's residual interest should be excluded from the disposition proceeds that are credited to the lessee.

---

§ 2A-103. Definitions and Index of Definitions.

(1) In this Article, unless the context otherwise requires:

* * *

~~(b)~~ (a) "Cancellation" occurs when either party puts an end to the lease contract for default by the other party.

* * *

~~(d)~~ (c) "Conforming" goods or performance under a lease contract means goods or performance that are in accordance with the obligations under the lease contract.

(d) "Conspicuous", with reference to a term, means so written, displayed, or presented that a reasonable person against which it is to operate ought to have noticed it. A term in an electronic record intended to evoke a response by an electronic agent is conspicuous if it is presented in a form that would enable a reasonably configured electronic agent to take it into account or react to it without review of the record by an individual. Whether a term is "conspicuous" or not is a decision for the court. Conspicuous terms include the following:

  (i) for a person:

   (A) a heading in capitals equal to or greater in size than the surrounding text, or in contrasting type, font, or color to the surrounding text of the same or lesser size; and

   (B) language in the body of a record or display in larger type than the surrounding text, or in contrasting type, font, or color to the surrounding text of the same size, or set off from surrounding text of the same size by symbols or other marks that call attention to the language; and

  (ii) for a person or an electronic agent, a term that is so placed in a record or display that the person or electronic agent cannot proceed without taking action with respect to the particular term.

(e) "Consumer" means an individual who leases or contracts to lease goods that, at the time of contracting, are intended by the individual to be used primarily for personal, family, or household purposes.

~~(e)~~ (f) "Consumer lease" means a lease that a lessor regularly engaged in the business of leasing or selling makes to ~~a lessee who is an individual and who takes under the lease primarily for a personal, family, or household purpose [, if the total payments to be made under the lease contract, excluding payments for options to renew or buy, do not exceed $_____]~~ a consumer.

Legislative Note: Present Article 2A has a bracketed provision allowing States to insert a dollar cap on leases designated as consumer leases, amended Article 2 defines "consumer contract" and does not include a dollar cap in the definition. Some States have not included a dollar cap in present Article 2A and States which have adopted a dollar cap have stated varying amounts. If a State wishes to include a dollar cap, the cap should be inserted here. Any cap probably should be set high enough to bring within the definition most automobile leasing transactions for personal, family, or household use.

(g) "Delivery" means the voluntary transfer of physical possession or control of goods.

(h) "Electronic" means relating to technology having electrical, digital, magnetic, wireless, optical, electromagnetic, or similar capabilities.

(i) "Electronic agent" means a computer program or an electronic or other automated means used independently to initiate an action or respond to electronic records or performances in whole or in part, without review or action by an individual.

(j) "Electronic record" means a record created, generated, sent, communicated, received, or stored by electronic means.

(f) (k) "Fault" means wrongful act, omission, breach, or default.

(g) ~~"Finance lease" means a lease with respect to which:~~

~~(i) the lessor does not select, manufacture, or supply the goods;~~

~~(ii) the lessor acquires the goods or the right to possession and use of the goods in connection with the lease; and~~

~~(iii) one of the following occurs:~~

~~(A) the lessee receives a copy of the contract by which the lessor acquired the goods or the right to possession and use of the goods before signing the lease contract;~~

~~(B) the lessee's approval of the contract by which the lessor acquired the goods or the right to possession and use of the goods is a condition to effectiveness of the lease contract;~~

~~(C) the lessee, before signing the lease contract, receives an accurate and complete statement designating the promises and warranties, and any disclaimers of warranties, limitations or modifications of remedies, or liquidated damages, including those of a third party, such as the manufacturer of the goods, provided to the lessor by the person supplying the goods in connection with or as part of the contract by which the lessor acquired the goods or the right to possession and use of the goods; or~~

~~(D) if the lease is not a consumer lease, the lessor, before the lessee signs the lease contract, informs the lessee in writing (a) of the identity of the person supplying the goods to the lessor, unless the lessee has selected that person and directed the lessor to acquire the goods or the right to possession and use of the goods from that person, (b) that the lessee is entitled under this Article to the promises and warranties, including those of any third party, provided to the lessor by the person supplying the goods in connection with or as part of the contract by which the lessor acquired the goods or the right to possession and use of the goods, and (c) that the lessee may communicate with the person supplying the goods to the lessor and receive an accurate and complete statement of those promises and warranties, including any disclaimers and limitations of them or of remedies.~~

(*l*) "Finance lease" means a lease with respect to which:

(i) the lessor does not select, manufacture, or supply the goods;

(ii) the lessor acquires the goods or the right to possession and use of the goods in connection with the lease or, in the case of goods that have been leased previously by the lessor and are not being leased to a consumer, in connection with another lease; and

(iii) one of the following occurs:

(A) the lessee receives a copy of the agreement by which the lessor acquired, or proposes to acquire, the goods or the right to possession and use of the goods before signing the lease agreement;

(B) the lessee's approval of the agreement or of the general contractual terms under which the lessor acquired or proposes to acquire the goods or the right to possession and use of the goods is a condition to the effectiveness of the lease contract;

(C) the lessee, before signing the lease agreement, receives an accurate and complete statement designating the promises and warranties, and any disclaimers of warranties, limitations or modifications of remedies, or liquidated damages, including those of a third party, such as the manufacturer of the goods, provided to the lessor by the person supplying the goods in connection with or as part of the contract by which the lessor acquired the goods or the right to possession and use of the goods; or

(D) if the lease is not a consumer lease, before the lessee signs the lease agreement, the lessor informs the lessee in a record:

(I)   of the identity of the person supplying the goods to the lessor, unless the lessee has selected that person and directed the lessor to acquire the goods or the right to possession and use of the goods from that person;

(II)   that the lessee is entitled under this article to the promises and warranties, including those of any third party, provided to the lessor by the person supplying the goods in connection with or as part of the contract by which the lessor acquired the goods or the right to possession and use of the goods; and

(III)   that the lessee may communicate with the person supplying the goods to the lessor and receive an accurate and complete statement of those promises and warranties, including any disclaimers and limitations of them, or a statement of remedies.

(m) "Good faith" means honesty in fact and the observance of reasonable commercial standards of fair dealing.

Legislative Note: Definition (m) should not be adopted if the jurisdiction has enacted the equivalent provision in the 2001 Revised Article 1.

(h) (n) "Goods" means all things that are movable at the time of identification to a lease contract or that are fixtures (Section 2A-309) but the term does not include money, documents, instruments, accounts, chattel paper, general intangibles, or minerals and the like, including oil and gas, before extraction. The term includes future goods, specially manufactured goods, and the unborn young of animals. The term does not include information, the money in which the price is to be paid, investment securities under Article 8, or choses in action. The term also includes the unborn young of animals.

* * *

(j) (p) "Lease" means a transfer of the right to possession and use of goods for a term period in return for consideration, but a sale, including a sale on approval or a sale or return, or retention or creation of a security interest, or license of information is not a lease. Unless the context clearly indicates otherwise, the term includes a sublease.

(k) (q) "Lease agreement", as distinguished from "lease contract", means the bargain, with respect to the lease, of the lessor and the lessee in fact as found in their language or inferred by implication from other circumstances including course of performance, course of dealing , or usage of trade dealing or usage of trade or course of performance as provided in Section 1-303. this Article. Unless the context clearly indicates otherwise, the term includes a sublease agreement.

(l) (r) "Lease contract", as distinguished from "lease agreement", means the total legal obligation that results from the lease agreement as determined by the [Uniform Commercial Code] as supplemented by affected by this Article and any other applicable rules of law. Unless the context clearly indicates otherwise, the term includes a sublease contract.

(m) (s) "Leasehold interest" means the interest of the lessor or the lessee under a lease contract.

(n) (t) "Lessee" means a person who that acquires the right to possession and use of goods under a lease. Unless the context clearly indicates otherwise, the term includes a sublessee.

* * *

(p) (v) "Lessor" means a person who that transfers the right to possession and use of goods under a lease. Unless the context clearly indicates otherwise, the term includes a sublessor.

* * *

(v) (bb) "Purchase" includes taking by sale, lease, mortgage, security interest, pledge, gift, or any other voluntary transaction creating an interest in goods.

Legislative Note: Definition (bb) should not be adopted if the jurisdiction has enacted the equivalent provision in the 2001 Revised Article 1.

(cc) "Record" means information that is inscribed on a tangible medium or that is stored in an electronic or other medium and is retrievable in perceivable form.

Legislative Note: Definition (cc) should not be adopted if the jurisdiction has enacted the equivalent provision in the 2001 Revised Article 1.

(dd) "Sign" means, with present intent to authenticate or adopt a record,

    (i) to execute or adopt a tangible symbol; or

    (ii) to attach to or logically associate with the record an electronic sound, symbol, or process.

* * *

~~(x)~~ (ff) "Supplier" means a person from ~~whom~~ which a lessor buys or leases goods to be leased under a finance lease.

~~(y)~~ (gg) "Supply contract" means a contract under which a lessor buys or leases goods to be leased.

~~(z)~~ (hh) "Termination" occurs when either party pursuant to a power created by agreement or law puts an end to the lease contract otherwise than for default.

* * *

Official Comment

* * *

[*Editor's note*: The prior comment (g) on finance leases is deleted.]

(g) For a transaction to qualify as a finance lease it must first qualify as a lease. Unless the lessor is comfortable that the transaction will qualify as a finance lease, the lease agreement should include provisions giving the lessor the benefits created by the subset of rules applicable to the transaction that qualifies as a finance lease under this Article.

A finance lease is the product of a three party transaction. The supplier manufactures or supplies the goods pursuant to the lessee's specification, perhaps even pursuant to a purchase order, sales agreement or lease agreement between the supplier and the lessee. After the prospective finance lease is negotiated, a purchase order, sales agreement, or lease agreement is entered into by the lessor (as buyer or prime lessee) or an existing order, agreement or lease is assigned by the lessee to the lessor, and the lessor and the lessee then enter into a lease or sublease of the goods. Due to the limited function usually performed by the lessor, the lessee looks almost entirely to the supplier for representations, covenants and warranties. If a manufacturer's warranty carries through, the lessee may also look to that. Yet, this definition does not restrict the lessor's function solely to the supply of funds; if the lessor undertakes or performs other functions, express warranties, covenants and the common law will protect the lessee.

This definition focuses on the transaction, not the status of the parties; to avoid confusion it is important to note that in other contexts, *e.g.*, tax and accounting, the term finance lease has been used to connote different types of lease transactions, including leases that are disguised secured transactions. M. Rice, *Equipment Financing*, 62-71 (1981). A lessor who is a merchant with respect to goods of the kind subject to the lease may be a lessor under a finance lease. Many leases that are leases back to the seller of goods (Section 2A-308(3)) will be finance leases. This conclusion is easily demonstrated by a hypothetical. Assume that B has bought goods from C pursuant to a sales contract. After delivery to and acceptance of the goods by B, B negotiates to sell the goods to A and simultaneously to lease the goods back from A, on terms and conditions that, we assume, will qualify the transaction as a lease. In documenting the sale and lease back, B assigns the original sales contract between B, as buyer, and C, as seller, to A. A review of these facts leads to the conclusion that the lease from A to B qualifies as a finance lease, as all three conditions of the definition are satisfied. Subparagraph (A) is satisfied as A, the lessor, had nothing to do with the selection, manufacture, or supply of the equipment. Subparagraph (B) is satisfied as A, the lessor, bought the equipment at the same time that A leased the equipment to B, which certainly is in connection with the lease. Finally, subparagraph (C)(i) is satisfied as A entered into the sales contract with B at the same time that A leased the equipment back to B. B, the lessee, will have received a copy of the sales contract in a timely fashion.

Subsection (A) requires the lessor to remain outside the selection, manufacture and supply of the goods; that is the rationale for releasing the lessor from most of its traditional liability. The lessor is not prohibited from possession, maintenance or operation of the goods, as policy does not require such prohibition. To insure the lessee's reliance on the supplier, and not on the lessor, subsection (B) requires that the goods (where the lessor is the buyer of the goods) or that the right to possession and use of the goods (where the lessor is the prime lessee and the sublessor of the goods) be acquired in connection with the lease (or sublease) to qualify as a finance lease. The scope of the phrase "in connection with" is to be developed by the courts, case by case. Finally, as the lessee generally relies almost entirely upon the supplier for representations and covenants, and upon the supplier or a manufacturer, or both, for warranties with respect to the goods, subsection (C) requires that one of the following occur: (A) the lessee receive a copy of the supply contract before signing the lease contract; (B) the lessee's approval of the supply contract is a condition to the effectiveness of the lease contract; (C) the lessee receive a statement describing the promises and warranties and any limitations relevant to the lessee before signing the lease contract; or (D) before signing the lease contract and except in a consumer lease, the lessee receive a writing identifying the supplier (unless the supplier was selected and required by the lessee) and the rights of the lessee under Section 2A-303, and advising the lessee a statement of promises and warranties is available from the supplier. Thus, even where oral supply orders or computer placed supply orders are compelled by custom and usage the transaction may still qualify as a finance lease if the lessee approves the supply contract before the lease contract is effective and such approval was a condition to the effectiveness of the lease contract. Moreover, where the lessor does not want the lessee to see the entire supply contract, including price information, the lessee may be provided with a separate statement of the terms of the supply contract relevant to the lessee; promises between the supplier and the lessor that do not affect the lessee need not be included. The statement can be a restatement of those terms or a copy of portions of the supply contract with the relevant terms clearly designated. Any implied warranties need not be designated, but a disclaimer or modification of remedy must be designated. A copy of any manufacturer's warranty is sufficient if that is the warranty provided. However, a copy of any Regulation M disclosure given pursuant to 12 C.F.R. § 213.4(g) concerning warranties in itself is not sufficient since those disclosures need only briefly identify express warranties and need not include any disclaimer of warranty.

Under subsections (B) and (C), except when the new lease is to a consumer lessee, a finance lessor can have that status on releasing the property after it is returned from an original lease. However, in that case, the other elements required for the lease to be a finance lessee must be complied with.

If a transaction does not qualify as a finance lease, the parties may achieve the same result by agreement; no negative implications are to be drawn if the transaction does not qualify. Further, absent the application of special rules (fraud, duress, and the like), a lease that qualifies as a finance lease and is assigned by the lessor or the lessee to a third party does not lose its status as a finance lease under this Article. Finally, this Article creates no special rule where the lessor is an affiliate of the supplier; whether the transaction qualifies as a finance lease will be determined by the facts of each case.

* * *

§ 2A-104. Leases Subject to Other Law.

(1) A lease, ~~although~~ subject to this Article~~,~~ is also subject to any applicable:

(a) ~~certificate of title statute of this State:~~ ([list any certificate of title statutes covering automobiles, trailers, mobile homes, boats, farm tractors, or ~~and~~ the like);]

(b) certificate of title statute of another jurisdiction (Section 2A-105); or

(c) ~~consumer protection statute of this State, or final consumer protection decision of a court of this State existing on the effective date of this Article~~ rule of law that establishes a different rule for consumers.

(2) To the extent there is a ~~In case of~~ conflict between this Article, other than Sections 2A-105, 2A-304(3), and 2A-305(3), and a ~~statute or decision~~ law referred to in subsection (1), that law governs ~~the statute or decision controls~~.

(3) ~~Failure to comply with an applicable law has only the effect specified therein~~ For purposes of this Article, failure to comply with a law referred to in subsection (1) has only the effect specified in that law.

(4) This article modifies, limits, and supersedes the federal Electronic Signatures in Global and National Commerce Act, 15 U.S.C. Section 7001 et seq., except that nothing in this article modifies, limits, or supersedes Section 7001(c) of that Act or authorizes electronic delivery of any of the notices described in Section 7003(b) of that Act.

Comment 6 added in 2003. The original Official Comment has not been amended to reflect the change from "writing" to "record."

Official Comment

* * *

6. Subsection (4) takes advantage of a provision of the federal Electronic Signatures in Global and National Commerce Act (E-Sign). E-Sign permits state law to modify, limit or supersede its provisions if the state law is consistent with Titles I and II of E-Sign, gives no special legal effect or validity to and does not require the implementation or application of specific technologies or technical specifications, and if enacted subsequent to E-Sign makes specific reference to E-Sign. Subsection (4) does not apply to section 101(c) of E-Sign, nor does it authorize electronic delivery of the notices described in section 103(b) of E-Sign.

* * *

§ 2A-107. Waiver or Renunciation of Claim or Right After Default.

~~Any~~ A claim or right arising out of an alleged default or breach of warranty may be discharged in whole or in part without consideration by ~~a written waiver or renunciation signed and delivered by~~ the aggrieved party in a signed record.

In this amended Section in 2003, the original Official Comments have not been amended and continue to be an effective discussion of the Section as amended. The original Official Comment has not *been amended to reflect the change from "writing" to "record."*

* * *

§ 2A-108. Unconscionability.

* * *

(4) In an action in which the lessee claims unconscionability with respect to a consumer lease:

* * *

(b) If the court does not find unconscionability and the lessee claiming unconscionability has brought or maintained an action ~~he [or she]~~ the lessee knew to be groundless, the court shall award reasonable attorney's fees to the party against ~~whom~~ which the claim is made.

* * *

In this amended Section in 2003, the original Official Comments have not been amended and continue to be an effective discussion of the Section as amended. The original Official Comment has not *been amended to reflect the change from "writing" to "record."*

* * *

PART 2

FORMATION AND CONSTRUCTION OF LEASE CONTRACT; ELECTRONIC CONTRACTING

§ 2A-202. Final ~~Written~~ Expression in a Record: Parol or Extrinsic Evidence.

(1) Terms with respect to which the confirmatory memoranda of the parties agree or which are otherwise set forth in a ~~writing~~ record intended by the parties as a final expression of their agreement with respect to such terms as are included therein may not be contradicted by evidence of any prior agreement or of a contemporaneous oral agreement but may be ~~explained or~~ supplemented by evidence of :

(a) ~~by course of dealing or usage of trade or by course of performance~~ course of performance, course of dealing, or usage of trade (Section 1-303); and

(b) ~~by evidence of~~ consistent additional terms unless the court finds the ~~writing~~ record to have been intended also as a complete and exclusive statement of the terms of the agreement.

(2) Terms in a record may be explained by evidence of course of performance, course of dealing, or usage of trade without a preliminary determination by the court that the language used is ambiguous.

Comment amended in 2003.

Official Comment

Uniform Statutory Source: Section 2-202.

This section is based on and conforms to amended Article 2, Section 2-202. The Official Commentary to that Section may be of aid in the interpretation of this section.

* * *

§ 2A-207. [Reserved.] [Course of Performance or Practical Construction.]

[(1) If a lease contract involves repeated occasions for performance by either party with knowledge of the nature of the performance and opportunity for objection to it by the other, any course of performance accepted or acquiesced in without objection is relevant to determine the meaning of the lease agreement.

(2) The express terms of a lease agreement and any course of performance, as well as any course of dealing and usage of trade, must be construed whenever reasonable as consistent with each other; but if that construction is unreasonable, express terms control course of performance, course of performance controls both course of dealing and usage of trade, and course of dealing controls usage of trade.

(3) Subject to the provisions of Section 2A-208 on modification and waiver, course of performance is relevant to show a waiver or modification of any term inconsistent with the course of performance.]

Legislative Note: Section 2A-207 should not be repealed if a jurisdiction has not enacted the 2001 Revised Article 1.

In this amended Section in 2003, the original Official Comments have not been amended and continue to be an effective discussion of the Section as amended. The original Official Comment has not been amended to reflect the change from "writing" to "record."

* * *

§ 2A-212. Implied Warranty of Merchantability.

* * *

(2) Goods to be merchantable must be at least such as

* * *

(c) are fit for the ordinary purposes for which goods of that ~~type~~ description are used;

* * *

Official Comment

1. The question when the warranty is imposed turns basically on the meaning of the terms of the agreement as recognized in the trade. Goods delivered under an agreement made by a merchant in a given line of trade must be of a quality comparable to that generally acceptable in that line of trade under the description or other designation of the goods used in the agreement. The responsibility imposed rests on any merchant-lessor.

2. If an unmerchantable good causes personal injury to the lessee who is injured while using the good, the lessee can sue the lessor for breach of the implied warranty of merchantability and recover for injury to person "proximately resulting" from the breach. Section 2A-520(2)(b). Because the lessee has an action for breach of warranty and probably an action in tort as well, there is a tension between warranty law and tort law where goods cause personal injury or property damage. The primary source of that tension comes from the disagreement over whether the concept of defect in tort and the concept of merchantability in Article 2A are coextensive when a personal injury is caused by the defective good: *i.e.,* if goods are merchantable under warranty law can they still be defective under tort law, and if goods are not defective under tort law can they be unmerchantable under warranty law? The answer to both questions should be no, and the tension between merchantability in warranty and defect in tort where personal injury or property damage is involved should be resolved as follows:

> When recovery is sought for injury to person or property, whether goods are merchantable is to be determined by applicable state products liability law. When, however, a claim for injury to person or property is based on an implied warranty of fitness under Section 2A-213 or an express warranty under Section 2A-210 this Article determines whether an implied warranty of fitness or an express warranty was made and breached, as well as what damages are recoverable under Section 2A-530.

Thus, if a lessor makes a representation about the safety of a product that becomes part of the basis of the lessee's bargain and the lessee is injured by the product, the product without the representation is not defective under applicable tort law, it is not unmerchantable under this section. On the other hand, if the product did not conform to the representation about safety, then the lessor made and breached an express warranty and the lessee may recover under Article 2A.

3. Subsection (2) does not purport to exhaust the meaning of "merchantable" nor to negate any of its attributes not specifically mentioned in the text of the statute but that arise by usage of trade or through case law. The language used is "must be at least such as . . . ," and the intention is to leave open other possible attributes of merchantability.

4. Paragraphs (a) and (b) of subsection (2) are to be read together. Both refer to the standards of that line of the trade which fits the transaction and the lessor's business. "Fair average" is a term directly appropriate to agricultural bulk products and means goods centering around the middle belt of quality, not the least or the worst that can be understood in the particular trade by the designation, but such as can pass "without objection." Of course a fair percentage of the least is permissible but the goods are not "fair average" if they are all of the least or worst quality possible under the description. In cases of doubt about what quality is intended, the price at which a merchant closes a contract is an excellent indication of the nature and scope of the merchant's obligation under the present section.

5. Fitness for the ordinary purposes for which goods of the type are used is a fundamental concept of the present section and is covered in paragraph (2)(c). The phrase "goods of that descrip-

tion" rather than the language from the original Article 2A "for which goods of that type are used" is used in subsection (2)(c). This change emphasizes the importance of the agreed description to determine fitness for ordinary purposes.

6. Paragraph (2)(d) on evenness of kind, quality and quantity follows case law. But precautionary language has been added as a reminder of the frequent usages of trade which permit substantial variations both with and without an allowance or an obligation to replace the varying units.

7. Paragraph (2)(e) applies only where the nature of the goods and of the transaction require a certain type of container, package or label. Paragraph (2)(f) applies, on the other hand, wherever there is a label or container on which representations are made, even though the original contract, either by express terms or usage of trade, may not have required either the labeling or the representation. This follows from the general obligation of good faith which requires that a lessee should not be placed in the position of using goods delivered under false representations that appear on the package or container. No problem of extra consideration arises in this connection since, under this Article, an obligation is imposed by the original contract not to deliver mislabeled articles, and the obligation is imposed where mercantile good faith requires and without reference to the doctrine of consideration.

8. Exclusion or modification of the warranty of merchantability, or of any part of it, is dealt with in Section 2A-214. That section must be read with particular reference to its subsection (6) on limitation of remedies. The warranty of merchantability, wherever it is normal, is so commonly taken for granted that its exclusion from the contract is a matter threatening surprise and therefore requiring special precaution.

9. Subsection (3) makes explicit that usage of trade and course of dealing can create warranties, and that they are implied rather than express warranties, and thus subject to exclusion or modification under Section 2A-214.

10. In an action based on breach of warranty, it is of course necessary to show not only the existence of the warranty but the fact that the warranty was broken and that the breach of the warranty was the proximate cause of the loss sustained. An affirmative showing by the lessor that the loss resulted from some action or event following the lessor's delivery of the goods can operate as a defense. Equally, evidence that indicates that the lessor exercised care in the manufacture, processing or selection of the goods is relevant to the issue of whether the warranty was in fact broken. An action by the lessee following an examination of the goods which ought to have indicated the defect complained of can be shown as matter bearing on whether the breach itself was the cause of the injury.

Cross References:

Point 2: Sections 2A-210, 2A-520 and 2A-530.
Point 8: Section 2A-214.
Point 9: Section 2A-214.

Definitional Cross References:

"Conforming". Section 2A-103(1)(c).
"Course of dealing". Section 1-303.
"Finance lease". Section 2A-103(1)(*l*).
"Fungible". Section 1-201.
"Goods". Section 2A-103(1)(n).
"Lease agreement". Section 2A-103(1)(k).
"Lease contract". Section 2A-103(1)(r).
"Lessor". Section 2A-103(1)(v).
"Merchant". Section 2-104(1).
"Usage of trade". Section 1-303.

§ 2A-214. Exclusion or Modification of Warranties.

(1) Words or conduct relevant to the creation of an express warranty and words or conduct tending to negate or limit a warranty must be construed wherever reasonable as consistent with each other; but, subject to ~~the provisions of~~ Section 2A-202 ~~on parol or extrinsic evidence~~, negation or limitation is inoperative to the extent that the construction is unreasonable.

(2) Subject to subsection (3), to exclude or modify the implied warranty of merchantability or any part of it the language must be in a record and be conspicuous. In a consumer lease the language must state "The lessor undertakes no responsibility for the quality of the goods except as otherwise provided in this contract," and in any other contract the language must mention "merchantability" ~~be by a writing, and be conspicuous~~. Subject to subsection (3), to exclude or modify ~~any~~ the implied warranty of fitness the exclusion must be ~~by a writing~~ in a record and be conspicuous. Language to exclude all implied warranties of fitness in a consumer lease must state "The lessor assumes no responsibility that the goods will be fit for any particular purpose for which you may be leasing these goods, except as otherwise provided in the contract," and in any other contract the language is sufficient if it ~~is in writing, is conspicuous and~~ states, for example, that "There ~~is~~ are no ~~warranty~~ warranties that ~~the goods will be fit for a particular purpose~~ extend beyond the description on the face hereof." Language that satisfies the requirements of this subsection for a consumer lease also satisfies its requirements for any other lease contract.

(3) Notwithstanding subsection (2)~~:, but subject to subsection (4)~~

(a) unless the circumstances indicate otherwise, all implied warranties are excluded by expressions like "as is", "with all faults", or ~~by~~ other language that in common understanding calls the lessee's attention to the exclusion of warranties and makes plain that there is no implied warranty, if in ~~writing~~ a record and conspicuous;

(b) if the lessee before entering into the lease contract has examined the goods or the sample or model as fully as desired or has refused to examine the goods, after a demand by the lessor there is no implied warranty with regard to defects that an examination ought in the circumstances to have revealed to the lessee; and

(c) an implied warranty may also be excluded or modified by course of dealing, or course of performance, or usage of trade.

(4) Remedies for breach of warranty can be limited in accordance with Section 2A-503 and 2A-504.

~~(4) To exclude or modify a warranty against interference or against infringement (Section 2A-211) or any part of it, the language must be specific, be by a writing, and be conspicuous, unless the circumstances, including course of performance, course of dealing, or usage of trade, give the lessee reason to know that the goods are being leased subject to a claim or interest of any person.~~

In this Section, the original Official Comment has been substantially revised or replaced by the following 2003 Official Comment. However, the original Official Comment may remain appropriate legislative history. For that reason, the original Official Comment may be found in Appendix [__] for the convenience of those who may wish to study it. [Editor's note: *Appendix [__] is not reprinted here, but the original Official Comment is reprinted in Appendix E of the main edition.*]

Official Comment

The changes conform to amended Article 2. Former subsection (4) has been moved to Section 2-211.

1. Subsection (1) deals with clauses in lease contracts that seek to exclude "all warranties, express or implied." This section protects a lessee from unexpected and unbargained language of disclaimer by denying effect to this language when it is inconsistent with language of express warranty, and permits the exclusion of implied warranties only by language or other circumstances which protect the lessee from surprise.

The lessor is protected against false allegations of oral warranties by this Article's provisions on parol and extrinsic evidence and against unauthorized representations by the customary "lack of authority" clauses. This Article treats the limitation or avoidance of consequential damages as a matter of limiting remedies for breach, separate from the matter of creation of liability under a warranty. If no warranty exists, there is of course no problem of limiting remedies for breach of warranty. Under subsection (4), the question of limitation of remedy is governed by the sections referred to rather than by this section.

2. The general test for disclaimers of implied warranties remains in subsection (3)(a), and the more specific tests are in subsection (2). A disclaimer that satisfies the requirements of subsection (3)(a) need not also satisfy any of the requirements of subsection (2).

3. Subsection (2) distinguishes between commercial and consumer leases. However, unlike the parallel provision in Article 2 (Section 2-316), under this section all exclusions under subsection (2) must be in a record and the language must be conspicuous, unlike Article 2 which only makes this mandatory for consumer contracts. Thus in both commercial and consumer leases, language that disclaims the implied warranty of merchantability must be in a record, and must be conspicuous. Subsection (2) presupposes that the implied warranty in question exists unless excluded or modified.

4. Subsection (3)(a) deals with general terms such as "as is," "as they stand," "with all faults," and the like. These terms in ordinary commercial usage are understood to mean that the lessee takes the entire risk as to the quality of the goods involved. The terms covered by the subsection are in fact merely a particularization of subsection (3)(c), which provides for exclusion or modification of implied warranties by usage of trade. Nothing in subsection (3)(a) prevents a term such as "there are no implied warranties" from being effective in appropriate circumstances, as when the term is a negotiated term between commercial parties.

Satisfaction of subsection (3)(a) requires that the language be set forth in a record and the language must be conspicuous. This is a variance with the parallel provision in Article 2 that makes these requirements mandatory only in consumer contracts.

5. The exceptions to the general rule set forth in subsections (3)(b) and (3)(c) are common factual situations in which the circumstances surrounding the transaction are in themselves sufficient to call the lessee's attention to the fact that no implied warranties are made or that a certain implied warranty is being excluded.

Under subsection (3)(b), warranties may be excluded or modified by the circumstances when the lessee examines the goods or a sample or model of them before entering into the contract. "Examination" as used in this paragraph is not synonymous with inspection before acceptance or at any other time after the lease has been made. Of course if the lessee discovers the defect and uses the goods anyway, or if the lessee unreasonably fails to examine the goods before using them, the resulting injuries may be found to have resulted from the lessee's own action rather than have been proximately caused by a breach of warranty.

To bring the transaction within the scope of "refused to examine" in subsection (3)(a), it is not sufficient that the goods are available for inspection. There must in addition be an actual examination by the lessee or a demand by the lessor that the lessee examine the goods fully. The lessor's demand must place the lessee on notice that the lessee is assuming the risk of defects which the examination ought to reveal.

The particular lessee's skill and the normal method of examining goods in the circumstances determine what defects are excluded by the examination. A failure to notice defects which are obvious cannot excuse the lessee because of the lack of notice. However, an examination under circumstances which do not permit chemical or other testing of the goods does not exclude defects which could be ascertained only by testing. Nor can latent defects be excluded by a simple examination. A professional lessee examining a product in the lessee's field will be held to have assumed the risk for all defects which a professional in the field ought to observe, while a nonprofessional lessee will be held to have assumed the risk only for the defects as a layperson might be expected to observe.

Definitional Cross References:

"Conspicuous". Section 2A-103(1)(d).
"Course of dealing". Section 1-303.
"Fault". Section 2A-103(1)(k).
"Goods". Section 2A-103(1)(n).
"Knows". Section 1-201.
"Lease". Section 2A-103(1)(p).
"Lease contract". Section 2A-103(1)(r).
"Lessee". Section 2A-103(1)(t).
"Person". Section 1-201.
"Record". Section 2A-103(1)(cc).
"Usage of trade". Section 1-303.

PART 5

DEFAULT

A. IN GENERAL

§ 2A-506. Statute of Limitations.

(1) An action for default under a lease contract, including breach of warranty or indemnity, must be commenced within ~~four~~ 4 years after the cause of action accrued. ~~By the original lease contract the parties may reduce the period of limitation to not less than one year~~ Except in a consumer lease or an action for indemnity, the original lease agreement may reduce the period of limitations to not less than one year.

* * *

Official Comment

1. Subsection (1) does not incorporate the limitation found in Section 2-725(1) prohibiting the parties from extending the period of limitation. Breach of warranty and indemnity claims often arise in a lease transaction; with the passage of time such claims often diminish or are eliminated. To encourage the parties to commence litigation under these circumstances makes little sense.

2. As amended, subsection (1) now contains the similar limitations contained in amended Section 2-725, which restricts the parties' right to reduce the four year limitation period in the consumer lease.

3. Subsection (2) states two rules for determining when a cause of action accrues. With respect to default, the rule of Section 2-725(2) is not incorporated in favor of a more liberal rule of the later of the date when the default occurs or when the act or omission on which it is based is or should have been discovered. With respect to indemnity, a similarly liberal rule is adopted.

* * *

B. DEFAULT BY LESSOR

§ 2A-508. Lessee's Remedies.

~~(1) If a lessor fails to deliver the goods in conformity to the lease contract (Section 2A-509) or repudiates the lease contract (Section 2A-402), or a lessee rightfully rejects the goods (Section 2A-509) or justifiably revokes acceptance of the goods (Section 2A-517), then with respect to any goods involved, and with respect to all of the goods if under an installment lease contract the value of the whole lease contract is substantially impaired (Section 2A-510), the lessor is in default under the lease contract and the lessee may:~~

~~(a) cancel the lease contract (Section 2A-505(1));~~

~~(b) recover so much of the rent and security as has been paid and is just under the circumstances;~~

~~(c) cover and recover damages as to all goods affected whether or not they have been identified to the lease contract (Sections 2A-518 and 2A-520), or recover damages for nondelivery (Sections 2A-519 and 2A-520);~~

~~(d) exercise any other rights or pursue any other remedies provided in the lease contract.~~

~~(2) If a lessor fails to deliver the goods in conformity to the lease contract or repudiates the lease contract, the lessee may also:~~

~~(a) if the goods have been identified, recover them (Section 2A-522); or~~

~~(b) in a proper case, obtain specific performance or replevy the goods (Section 2A-521).~~

(1) If a lessor fails to deliver the goods in conformity to the lease contract or repudiates the contract, or a lessee rightfully rejects the goods or justifiably revokes acceptance of the goods, the lessor is in default under the lease contract, and the lessee may do one or more of the following:

(a) cancel the lease contract under Section 2A-505(1);

(b) recover so much of the rent and security as has been paid and is just under the circumstances;

(c) cover and obtain damages under Section 2A-518;

(d) recover damages for nondelivery under Section 2A-519(1);

(e) if an acceptance of goods has not been justifiably revoked, recover damages for default with regard to accepted goods under Section 2A-519(3) and (4);

(f) enforce a security interest under subsection (4);

(g) recover identified goods under Section 2A-522;

(h) obtain specific performance or obtain the goods by replevin or similar remedy under Section 2A-507A;

(i) recover liquidated damages under Section 2A-504;

(j) enforce limited remedies under Section 2A-503;

(k) exercise any other right or pursue any other remedy as provided in the lease contract.

~~(3)~~ (2) If a lessor is otherwise in default under a lease contract, the lessee may exercise the rights and pursue the remedies provided in the lease contract, which may include a right to cancel the lease, and in Section 2A-519(3).

~~(4)~~ (3) If a lessor has breached a warranty, whether express or implied, the lessee may recover damages (Section 2A-519(4)).

~~(5)~~ (4) On rightful rejection or justifiable revocation of acceptance, a lessee has a security interest in goods in the lessee's possession or control for any rent and security that has been paid and any expenses reasonably incurred in their inspection, receipt, transportation, and care and custody and may hold those goods and dispose of them in good faith and in a commercially reasonable manner, subject to Section 2A-527(5).

~~6)~~ (5) Subject to the provisions of Section 2A-407, a lessee, on notifying the lessor of the lessee's intention to do so, may deduct all or any part of the damages resulting from any default under the lease contract from any part of the rent still due under the same lease contract.

In this Section, the original Official Comment has been substantially revised or replaced by the following 2003 Official Comment. However, the original Official Comment may remain appropriate legislative history. For that reason, the original Official Comment may be found in Appendix [__] for the convenience of those who may wish to study it. [Editor's note: Appendix [__] is not reprinted here, but the original Official Comment is reprinted in Appendix E of the main edition.]

Official Comment

1. This section is an index to Sections 2A-503 through 2A-505 and 2A-509 through 2A-522 which set out the lessee's rights and remedies after the lessor's default. The lessor and the lessee can agree to modify the rights and remedies available under this Article; they can, among other things, provide that for defaults other than those specified in subsection (1) the lessee can exercise the rights and remedies referred to in subsection (1); and they can create a new scheme of rights and remedies triggered by the occurrence of the default. Sections 2A-103(4) and 1-302.

2. Subsection (1), a substantially rewritten version of the provisions of Section 2-711(1), lists the cumulative remedies of the lessee where the lessor has failed to deliver conforming goods or has repudiated the contract, or the lessee has rightfully rejected or justifiably revoked. Sections 2A-501(2) and (4). Subsection (1) also allows the lessee to exercise any contractual remedy. This Article rejects any general doctrine of election of remedy. To determine if

one remedy bars another in a particular case is a function of whether the lessee has been put in as good a position as if the lessor had fully performed the lease agreement. Use of multiple remedies is barred only if the effect is to put the lessee in a better position than it would have been in had the lessor fully performed under the lease. Sections 2A-103(4), 2A-501(4). Subsection (1)(b), in recognition that no bright line can be created that would operate fairly in all installment lease cases and in recognition of the fact that a lessee may be able to cancel the lease (revoke acceptance of the goods) after the goods have been in use for some period of time, does not require that all lease payments made by the lessee under the lease be returned upon cancellation. Rather, only such portion as is just of the rent and security payments made may be recovered. If a defect in the goods is discovered immediately upon tender to the lessee and the goods are rejected immediately, then the lessee should recover all payments made. If, however, for example, a 36-month equipment lease is terminated in the 12th month because the lessor has materially breached the contract by failing to perform its maintenance obligations, it may be just to return only a small part or none of the rental payments already made.

3. Subsection (2) covers defaults which do not deprive the lessee of the goods and which are not so serious as to justify rejection or revocation of acceptance under subsection (1). It also covers defaults for which the lessee could have rejected or revoked acceptance of the goods but elects not to do so and retains the goods. In either case, a lessee which retains the goods is entitled to recover damages as stated in Section 2A-519(3). That measure of damages is "the loss resulting in the ordinary course of events from the lessor's default as determined in any manner that is reasonable together with incidental and consequential damages, less expenses saved in consequence of the lessor's breach."

4. Subsection (1)(k) and subsection (2) recognize that the lease agreement may provide rights and remedies in addition to or different from those which Article 2A provides. In particular, subsection (2) provides that the lease agreement may give the remedy of cancellation of the lease for defaults by the lessor that would not otherwise be material defaults which would justify cancellation under subsection (1). If there is a right to cancel, there is, of course, a right to reject or revoke acceptance of the goods.

5. Subsection (3) adds to the completeness of the index by including a reference to the lessee's recovery of damages upon the lessor's breach of warranty. This breach may not rise to the level of a default by the lessor justifying revocation of acceptance. If the lessee properly rejects or revokes acceptance of the goods because of a breach of warranty, the rights and remedies are those provided in subsection (1) rather than those in Section 2A-519(4).

6. Subsection (4), a revised version of the provisions of Section 2-711(3), recognizes, on rightful rejection or justifiable revocation, the lessee's security interest in goods in its possession and control. Section 9-110 recognizes security interests arising under that Article. Pursuant to Section 2A-511(4), a purchaser who purchases goods from the lessee in good faith takes free of any rights of the lessor, or in the case of a finance lease, the supplier. These goods, however, must have been rightfully rejected and disposed of pursuant to Section 2A-511 or 2A-512. However, Section 2A-517(5) provides that the lessee will have the same rights and duties with respect to goods where acceptance has been revoked as with respect to goods rejected. Thus, Section 2A-511(4) will apply to the lessee's disposition of the goods.

7. Pursuant to Section 2A-527(5), the lessee must account to the lessor for the excess proceeds of such disposition, after satisfaction of the claim secured by the lessee's security interest.

8. Subsection (5) sanctions a right of set-off by the lessee, subject to the rule of Section 2A-407 with respect to irrevocable promises in a finance lease that is not a consumer lease, and further subject to an enforceable "hell or high water" clause in the lease agreement. Section 2A-407 Official Comment. No attempt is made to state how the set-off should occur. This is to be determined by the facts of each case.

9. There is no special treatment of the finance lease in this section. Absent supplemental principles of law and equity to the contrary, in the case of most finance leases, following the lessee's acceptance of the goods, the lessee will have no rights or remedies against the lessor, because the lessor's obligations to the lessee are minimal. Sections 2A-210 and 2A-211(1). Since the lessee will look to the supplier for performance, this is appropriate. Section 2A-209.

Cross References:

Point 1: Section 1-302 and Sections 2A-103, 2A- 503 through 2A-505 and 2A-509 through 2A-522.

Point 2: Section 2-711 and Section 2A-501.

Point 3: Section 2A-519.

Point 5: Section 2A-519.

Point 6: Section 2-711 and Sections 2A-511, 2A-512, 2A-517 and Section 9-110.

Point 7: Section 2A-527.

Point 8: Section 2A-407.

Point 9: Sections 2A-209, 2A-210 and 2A-211.

Definitional Cross References:

"Conforming". Section 2A-103(1)(c).

"Delivery". Section 2A-103(1)(g).

"Good faith". Sections 2A-103(1)(m).

"Goods". Section 2A-103(1)(n).

"Installment lease contract". Section 2A-103(1)(*o*).

"Lease contract". Section 2A-103(1)(r).

"Lessee". Section 2A-103(1)(t).

"Lessor". Section 2A-103(1)(v).

"Notifies". Section 1-201.

"Receipt". Section 2-103(1)(c).

"Remedy". Section 1-201.

"Rights". Section 1-201.

"Security interest". Section 1-201.

"Value". Section 1-204.

§ 2A-509. Lessee's Rights on Improper Delivery; ~~Rightful~~ Manner and Effect of Rejection.

~~(1) Subject to the provisions of Section 2A-510 on default in installment lease contracts, if the goods or the tender or delivery fail in any respect to conform to the lease contract, the lessee may reject or accept the goods or accept any commercial unit or units and reject the rest of the goods.~~

(2) Rejection of goods is ineffective unless it is within a reasonable time after tender or delivery of the goods and the lessee seasonably notifies the lessor.

(1) Subject to Sections 2A-503, 2A-504, and 2A-510, if the goods or the tender of delivery fail in any respect to conform to the contract, the lessee may:

(a) reject the whole;

(b) accept the whole; or

(c) accept any commercial unit or units and reject the rest.

(2) Rejection of goods must be within a reasonable time after their delivery or tender. It is ineffective unless the lessee seasonably notifies the lessor or supplier.

(3) Subject to Sections 2A-511, 2A-512, and 2A-517(6):

(a) after rejection any use by the lessee with respect to any commercial unit is wrongful as against the lessor or supplier; and

(b) if the lessee has before rejection taken physical possession of goods in which the lessee does not have a security interest under Section 2A-508(4), the lessee is under a duty after rejection to hold them with reasonable care at the lessor's or supplier's disposition for a time sufficient to permit the lessor or supplier to remove them; but

(c) the lessee has no further obligations with regard to goods rightfully rejected.

(d) The lessor's or supplier's remedies with respect to goods wrongfully rejected are governed by Section 2A-523.

Comment amended in 2003.

Official Comment

Uniform Statutory Source: Sections 2-601 and 2-602(1).

Changes: Revised to reflect leasing practices and terminology.

1. This section, which conforms with amended Article 2, contains the parallel rules for a sales contract that are contained in Section 2-601 and 2-602. The amendments clarify that this section is subject not only to Section 2A-510, but also Sections 2A-503 and 2A-504.

2. Subsection (3) was originally contained in the prior version of 2A-512, and this has been moved for logical clarity. This subsection sets forth the duties of the lessee upon rejection. In addition to the duty to hold the goods with reasonable care for the lessor's disposition, the lessee also has those duties, as appropriate, specified in Sections 2A-511, 2A-512 and 2A-5-17(6).

3. Elimination of the word "rightful" in the title makes it clear that a buyer can effectively reject goods even though the rejection is wrongful and constitutes a breach. The word "rightful has also been deleted from the titles to Section 2A-511 and 2A-512.

Cross References:

Point 1: Section 2-601 and 2-602 and Section 2A-510, 2A-503 and 2A-504.

Point 2: Section 2-603, 2-604 and 2-608(4).

Point 3: Section 2-603, 2-604 and 2-703.

Definitional Cross References:

"Commercial unit". Section 2A-103(1)(b).

"Conforming". Section 2A-103(1)(c).

"Delivery". Section 2A-103(1)(g).

"Goods". Section 2A-103(1)(n).

"Installment lease contract". Section 2A-103(1)(*o*).

"Lease contract". Section 2A-103(1)(r).

"Lessee". Section 2A-103(1)(t).

"Lessor". Section 2A-103(1)(v).

"Notifies". Section 1-201.

"Reasonable time". Section 1-205.

"Rights". Section 1-201.

"Seasonably". Section 1-204(3).

§ 2A-512. Lessee's Duties As to ~~Rightfully~~ Rejected Goods.

(1) Except as otherwise provided with respect to goods that threaten to decline in value speedily (Section 2A-511) and subject to any security interest of a lessee (Section 2A-508(4)),

(a) the lessee, after rejection of goods in the lessee's possession, shall hold them with reasonable care at the lessor's or the supplier's disposition for a reasonable time after the lessee's seasonable notification of rejection;

(b) if the lessor or the supplier gives no instructions within a reasonable time after notification of rejection, the lessee may store the rejected goods for the lessor's or the supplier's account or ship them to the lessor or the supplier or dispose of them for the lessor's or the supplier's account with reimbursement in the manner provided in Section 2A-511; but

(c) the lessee has no further obligations with regard to goods rightfully rejected.

(1) If the lessor or the supplier gives no instructions within a reasonable time after notification of rejection, the lessee may store the rejected goods for the lessor's or the supplier's account or ship them to the lessor or the supplier or dispose of them for the lessor's or the supplier's account with reimbursement in the manner provided in Section 2A-511.

(2) Action by the lessee pursuant to subsection (1) is not acceptance or conversion.

Comment amended in 2003.

Official Comment

Uniform Statutory Source: Sections 2-602(2)(b) and (e) and 2-604.

Changes: Substantially rewritten.

Purposes: The introduction to subsection (1) references goods that threaten to decline in value speedily and not perishables, the reference in Section 2-604, the statutory analogue. This is a change in style, not substance, as the first phrase includes the second. Subparagraphs (a) and (e) are revised versions of the provisions of Section 2-602(2)(b) and (c). Subparagraph (a) states the rule with respect to the lessee's treatment of goods in its possession following rejection; subparagraph (b) states the rule regarding such goods if the lessor or supplier then fails to give instructions to the lessee. If the lessee performs in a fashion consistent with subparagraphs (a) and (b), subparagraph (c) exonerates the lessee.

Changes: The change in the title conforms to amended Article 2. Original subsections (1)(a) and (c) have been moved to Section 2A-509(3).

Cross References:

Section 2A-509.

Definitional Cross References:

"Action". Section 1-201.
"Goods". Section 2A-103(1)(n).
"Lessee". Section 2A-103(1)(t).
"Lessor". Section 2A-103(1)(v).
"Notification". Section 1-202.
"Reasonable time". Section 1-205.
"Seasonably". Section 1-204(3).
"Security interest". Section 1-201.
"Supplier". Section 2A-103(1)(ff).
"Value". Section 1-204.

§ 2A-513. Cure by Lessor of Improper Tender or Delivery; Replacement.

(1) If any tender or delivery by the lessor or the supplier is rejected because nonconforming and the time for performance has not yet expired, the lessor or the supplier may seasonably notify the lessee of the lessor's or the supplier's intention to cure and may then make a conforming delivery within the time provided in the lease contract.

(2) If the lessee rejects a nonconforming tender that the lessor or the supplier had reasonable grounds to believe would be acceptable with or without money allowance, the lessor or the supplier may have a further reasonable time to substitute a conforming tender if he [or she] seasonably notifies the lessee.

(1) If the lessee rejects goods or a tender of delivery under Section 2A-509 or 2A-510 or, except in a consumer contract, justifiably revokes acceptance under Section 2A-517(1)(b) and the agreed time for performance has not expired, a lessor or a supplier that has performed in good faith, upon seasonable notice to the lessee, and at the lessor's or supplier's own expense, may cure the default by making a conforming tender of delivery within the agreed time. The lessor or supplier shall compensate the lessee for all of the lessee's reasonable expenses caused by the lessor's or supplier's default and subsequent cure.

(2) If the lessee rejects goods or a tender of delivery under Section 2A-509 or 2A-510 or, except in a consumer lease, justifiably revokes acceptance under Section 2A-517(1)(b) and the agreed time for performance has expired, a lessor or supplier that has performed in good faith may, upon seasonable notice to the lessee and at the lessor's or supplier's own expense, cure the default, if the cure is appropriate and timely under the circumstances, by making a tender of conforming goods. The lessor or supplier shall compensate the lessee for all of the lessee's reasonable expenses caused by the lessor's or supplier's default and subsequent cure.

Comment amended in 2003.

Official Comment

Uniform Statutory Source: Section 2-508.

Changes: Revised to reflect leasing practices and terminology.

This section is based on and conforms to amended Article 2, Section 2-508. The Official Commentary to that Section may be of aid in the interpretation of this section.

Definitional Cross References:

"Conforming". Section 2A-103(1)(c).
"Delivery". Section 2A-103(1)(g).
"Lease contract". Section 2A-103(1)(r).
"Lessee". Section 2A-103(1)(t).
"Lessor". Section 2A-103(1)(v).
"Money". Section 1-201.
"Notifies". Section 1-201.
"Reasonable time". Section 1-205.
"Seasonably". Section 1-204(3).
"Supplier". Section 2A-103(1)(ff).

§ 2A-514. Waiver of Lessee's Objections.

(1) In rejecting goods, a lessee's failure to state a particular defect that is ascertainable by reasonable inspection precludes the lessee from relying on the defect to justify rejection or to establish default:

(a) if, stated seasonably, the lessor or the supplier could have cured it (Section 2A-513); or

(b) between merchants if the lessor or the supplier after rejection has made a request in writing for a full and final written statement of all defects on which the lessee proposes to rely.

(1) A lessee's failure to state in connection with rejection a particular defect or in connection with revocation of acceptance a defect that justifies revocation precludes the lessee from relying on the unstated defect to justify rejection or revocation of acceptance if the defect is ascertainable by reasonable inspection

(a) if the lessor or supplier had a right to cure the defect and could have cured it if stated seasonably; or

(b) between merchants if the lessor or the supplier after rejection or revocation of acceptance has made a request in a record for a full and final statement in a record of all defects on which the lessee proposes to rely.

(2) A lessee's failure to reserve rights when paying rent or other consideration against documents precludes recovery of the payment for defects apparent in on the face of the documents.

Comment amended in 2003.

Official Comment

Uniform Statutory Source: Section 2-605.

Changes: Revised to reflect leasing practices and terminology.

Purposes: The principles applicable to the commercial practice of payment against documents (subsection 2) are explained in Official Comment 4 to Section 2-605, the statutory analogue to this section.

This section is based on and conforms to amended Article 2 Section 2-605. The Official Commentary to that Section may aid in the interpretation of this section.

Cross Reference:

Section 2-605 Official Comment 4.

Definitional Cross References:

"Between merchants". Section 2-104(3).
"Goods". Section 2A-103(1)(n).
"Lessee". Section 2A-103(1)(t).
"Lessor". Section 2A-103(1)(v).
"Record". Section 2A-103(1)(cc).
"Rights". Section 1-201.
"Seasonably". Section 1-204(3).
"Supplier". Section 2A-103(1)(ff).

§ 2A-515. Acceptance of Goods.

(1) Acceptance of goods occurs after the lessee has had a reasonable opportunity to inspect the goods and

(a) the lessee signifies or acts with respect to the goods in a manner that signifies to the lessor or the supplier that the goods are conforming or that the lessee will take or retain them in spite of their nonconformity; or

(b) the lessee fails to make an effective rejection of the goods (Section 2A-509(2)).

(1) Acceptance of goods occurs when the lessee:

(a) after a reasonable opportunity to inspect the goods signifies to the lessor or supplier that the goods are conforming or will be taken or retained in spite of their nonconformity;

(b) fails to make an effective rejection under Section 2A-509(2), but such acceptance does not occur until the lessee has had a reasonable opportunity to inspect them; or

(c) subject to Section 2A-517(6), uses the goods in any manner that is inconsistent with the lessor's or supplier's rights.

(2) Acceptance of a part of any commercial unit is acceptance of that entire unit.

Comment amended in 2003.

Official Comment

~~Uniform Statutory Source: Section 2-606.~~

~~Changes: The provisions of Section 2-606(1)(a) were substantially rewritten to provide that the lessee's conduct may signify acceptance. Further, the provisions of Section 2-606(1)(c) were not incorporated as irrelevant given the lessee's possession and use of the leased goods.~~

This section parallels the rules for acceptance under Article 2 (Section 2-606).

Cross Reference:

Section 2-608.

Definitional Cross References:

"Commercial unit". Section 2A-103(1)(b).
"Conforming". Section 2A-103(1)(c).
"Goods". Section 2A-103(1)(n).
"Lessee". Section 2A-103(1)(t).
"Lessor". Section 2A-103(1)(v).
"Supplier". Section 2A-103(1)(ff).

§ 2A-516. Effect of Acceptance of Goods; Notice of Default; Burden of Establishing Default After Acceptance; Notice of Claim or Litigation to Person Answerable Over.

(1) A lessee must pay rent for any goods accepted in accordance with the lease contract~~, with due allowance for goods rightfully rejected or not delivered~~.

(2) A lessee's acceptance of goods precludes rejection of the goods accepted. In the case of a finance lease, if made with knowledge of a nonconformity, acceptance may not ~~cannot~~ be revoked because of it. In any other case, if made with knowledge of a nonconformity, acceptance may not ~~cannot~~ be revoked because of it unless the acceptance was on the reasonable assumption that the nonconformity would be seasonably cured. Acceptance does not of itself impair any other remedy provided by this Article or the lease agreement for nonconformity.

(3) If a tender has been accepted:

(a) within a reasonable time after the lessee discovers or should have discovered any default, the lessee shall notify the lessor and the supplier, if any~~;, or be barred from any remedy against the party not notified~~ however, failure to give timely notice bars the lessee from a remedy only to the extent that the lessor or suppler is prejudiced by the failure;

(b) except in the case of a consumer lease, within a reasonable time after the lessee receives notice of litigation for infringement or the like (Section 2A-211) the lessee shall notify the lessor or be barred from any remedy over for liability established by the litigation; and

(c) the burden is on the lessee to establish any default.

(4) If a lessee is sued for indemnity, breach of a warranty or other obligation for which ~~a lessor or a supplier~~ another party is answerable over the following rules apply:

(a) The lessee may give ~~the lessor or the supplier, or both, written~~ the other party notice of the litigation in a record. If the notice states that the person notified may come in and defend and that if the person notified does not do so that person will be bound in any action against that person by the lessee by any determination of fact common to the two litigations, then unless the person notified after seasonable receipt of the notice does come in and defend that person is so bound.

(b) The ~~lessor or the supplier~~ other party may demand in ~~writing~~ a record that the lessee turn over control of the litigation including settlement if the claim is one for infringement or the like (Section 2A-211) or else be barred from any remedy over. If the demand states that the ~~lessor or the supplier~~ other party agrees to bear all expense and to satisfy any adverse judgment, then unless the lessee after seasonable receipt of the demand does turn over control the lessee is so barred.

(5) Subsections (3) and (4) apply to any obligation of a lessee to hold the lessor or the supplier harmless against infringement or the like (Section 2A-211).

Comment amended in 2003.

Official Comment

Uniform Statutory Source: Section 2-607.

Changes: Substantially Revised.

Purposes:

1. Subsection (2) creates a special rule for finance leases, precluding revocation if acceptance is made with knowledge of nonconformity with respect to the lease agreement, as opposed to the supply agreement; this is not inequitable as the lessee has a direct claim against the supplier. Section 2A-209(1). Revocation of acceptance of a finance lease is permitted if the lessee's acceptance was without discovery of the nonconformity (with respect to the lease agreement, not the supply agreement) and was reasonably induced by the lessor's assurances. Section 2A-517(1)(b). Absent exclusion or modification, the lessor under a finance lease makes certain warranties to the lessee. Sections 2A-210 and 2A-211(1). Revocation of acceptance is not prohibited even after the lessee's promise has become irrevocable and independent. Section 2A-407 Official Comment. Where the finance lease creates a security interest, the rule may be to the contrary. *General Elec. Credit Corp. of Tennessee v. Ger-Beck Mach. Co.*, 806 F.2d 1207 (3rd Cir. 1986).

2. Subsection (3)(a) requires the lessee to give notice of default within a reasonable time after the lessee discovered or should have discovered the default. Failure to provide the notice bars the lessee from any remedy to the extent that the lessor or supplier is prejudiced by the lack of notice. In a finance lease, notice may be given either to the supplier, the lessor, or both, but remedy is barred against ~~the party not notified~~ either party if that party is not notified and that party is prejudiced by the lack of notice. In a finance lease, the lessor is usually not liable for defects in the goods and the essential notice is to the supplier. While notice to the finance lessor will often not give any additional rights to the lessee, it would be good practice to give the notice since the finance lessor has an interest in the goods. Subsection (3)(a) does not use the term finance lease, but the definition of supplier is a person from whom a lessor buys or leases goods to be leased under a finance lease. Section 2A-103(1)(x). Therefore, there can be a "supplier" only in a finance lease. Subsection (4) applies similar notice rules ~~as to lessors and suppliers~~ if a lessee is sued for a breach of warranty or other obligation for which ~~a lessor or supplier~~ another party is answerable over.

3. Subsection (3)(b) requires the lessee to give the lessor notice of litigation for infringement or the like. There is an exception created ~~in the case of~~ for a consumer lease. While ~~such an~~ the exception was considered for a finance lease, it was not created because it was not necessary—the lessor in a finance lease does not give a warranty against infringement. Section 2A-211(2). Even though not required under subsection (3)(b), the lessee who takes under a finance lease should consider giving notice of litigation for infringement or the like to the supplier, because the lessee obtains the benefit of the suppliers' promises subject to the suppliers' defenses or claims. Sections 2A-209(1) and 2-607(3)(b).

Cross References:

Point 1: Section 2A-209, 2A-210, 2A-211 2A-407, 2A-517.

Point 2: Sections 2A-103.

Point 3: Section 2-607 and 2A- 209, 2A-211.

Definitional Cross References:

"Action". Section 1-201.

"Agreement". Section 1-201.

"Burden of establishing". Section 1-201.

"Conforming". Section 2A-103(1)(c).

"Consumer lease". Section 2A-103(1)(f).

"Delivery". Section 2A-103(1)(g).

"Discover". Section 1-201.

"Finance lease". Section 2A-103(1)(*l*).

"Goods". Section 2A-103(1)(n).

"Knowledge". Section 1-202.

"Lease agreement". Section 2A-103(1)(q).

"Lease contract". Section 2A-103(1)(r).

"Lessee". Section 2A-103(1)(t).

"Lessor". Section 2A-103(1)(v).

"Notice". Section 1-202.

"Notifies". Section 1-202.

"Person". Section 1-201.

"Reasonable time". Section 1-205.

"Receipt". Section 2-103(1)(c).

"Record". Section 2A-103(1)(cc).

"Remedy". Section 1-201.

"Seasonably". Section 1-204(3).

"Supplier". Section 2A-103(1)(ff).

§ 2A-517. Revocation of Acceptance of Goods.

* * *

(5) A lessee ~~who~~ that so revokes has the same rights and duties with regard to the goods involved as if the lessee had rejected them.

(6) If a lessee uses the goods after a rightful rejection or justifiable revocation of acceptance, the following rules apply:

(a) Any use by the lessee which is unreasonable under the circumstances is wrongful as against the lessor or supplier and is an acceptance only if ratified by the lessor or supplier under Section 2-515(1)(c).

(b) Any use of the goods which is reasonable under the circumstances is not wrongful as against the lessor or supplier and is not an acceptance, but in an appropriate case the lessee shall be obligated to the lessor or supplier for the value of the use to the lessee.

Comment amended in 2003.

Official Comment

Uniform Statutory Source: Section 2-608.

Changes: Revised to reflect leasing practices and terminology. Note that in the case of a finance lease the lessee retains a limited right to revoke acceptance. Sections 2A-517(1)(b) and 2A-516 Official Comment. New subsections (2) and (3) added.

Purposes:

* * *

3. Subsection (6) deals with the problem of post-rejection or revocation use of the goods. If the lessee's use after an effective rejection or a justified revocation of acceptance is unreasonable under the circumstances, it is inconsistent with the rejection or revocation of acceptance and is wrongful as against the lessor. This gives the lessor the option of ratifying the use, thereby treating it as an acceptance, or pursuing a non-Code remedy for conversion.

If the lessee's use is reasonable under the circumstances, the lessee's actions cannot be treated as an acceptance. The lessee must compensate the lessor for the value of the use of the goods to the lessee. Determining the appropriate level of compensation requires a consideration of the lessee's particular circumstances and should take into account the defective condition of the goods. There may be circumstances, such as where the use is solely for the purpose of protecting the lessee's security interest in the goods, where no compensation is due the lessor. In other circumstances, the lessor's right to compensation must be netted out against any right of the lessee to damages.

In general, a lessee that either rejects or revokes acceptance of the goods should not subsequently use the goods in a manner that is inconsistent with the lessor's interest. In some instances, however, the use may be reasonable. An example might involve a commercial lessee that is unable immediately to obtain cover and must use the goods to fulfill the lessee's obligations to third parties. If circumstances change so that the lessee's use is no longer reasonable, the continued use of the goods is unreasonable and is wrongful against the lessor. Of course, a lessee's rejection must be rightful, or its revocation must be justified; a lessee cannot make a false claim of nonconformity and limit the obligation to pay rent to the value of the use to the lessee.

* * *

State-by-State Analysis of New Car Lemon Laws

Page 772

ARKANSAS

Replace Persons covered *entry with:*

Persons covered: Purchaser, lessee, or any person entitled to enforce the warranty (§ 40-90-403(4)).

Add to end of Disclosure requirements *entry:*

Dealer must obtain and maintain for five years the consumer's acknowledgment of receipt of statement of rights (§ 4-90-404(b)).

Replace Required consumer notice *entry with:*

Required consumer notice: Consumer must notify manufacturer by certified or registered mail of the need to repair the nonconformity.

Add to Informal dispute resolution *entry after "otherwise":*

or unless manufacturer failed to disclose as required an explanation of the consumer's rights and obligations (§ 4-90-406(a)(1))

Add to Resale of lemon *entry after "required":*

for first resale to a retail customer

Page 774

DISTRICT OF COLUMBIA

Replace entire District of Columbia summary with:

D.C. Code Ann. §§ 50-501 to 50-510

Vehicles covered: Passenger vehicles sold or registered in D.C.; excludes buses sold for public transportation, motorcycles, motor homes, and recreational vehicles (§ 50-501(9)).

Persons covered: Purchasers or lessees, transferees during express warranty period, or any person entitled to enforce the warranty (§ 50-501(2)).

Period covered: Whichever comes first: 18,000 miles or two years (§ 50-502(a)).

Disclosure requirements: Manufacturer must give written notice to the prospective consumer of consumer rights (§ 50-504).

Required consumer notice: Must report the nonconformity to the manufacturer, its agent, or the authorized dealer (§ 50-502).

Repair requirements: It is presumed that a reasonable number of attempts have been made if the same nonconformity is subjected to four or more repairs, or the vehicle is out of service for a cumulative total of thirty or more days, or if a safety-related defect is subjected to one or more repair attempts (§ 50-502(d)).

Affirmative defenses: The nonconformity does not substantially impair the vehicle, or is the result of the consumer's abuse, neglect, or unauthorized modifications or alterations (§ 50-502(c)); statute of limitations (§ 50-507(b)).

Replace/refund: At the consumer's option, the manufacturer shall replace with a comparable vehicle, or refund the full purchase price less a reasonable use allowance (defined) (§ 50-502(b)).

Other reimbursement: Taxes, fees, and charges (§ 50-502(b)).

Other remedies: There is no limit on other consumer remedies (§ 50-507(a)).

Informal dispute resolution: For remedies under this section, a consumer must first use the government-run arbitration board's informal dispute settlement procedure (§§ 50-502(f), 50-503).

Resale of lemon: Vehicle return for reason of nonconformity noted on title; dealer must disclose to prospective buyer (§ 50-502(g)).

<table>
<tr><td>*Page 775*</td><td>**HAWAII**</td></tr>
<tr><td>*Delete "excluding interest" from* Other reimbursement *entry.*</td><td></td></tr>
<tr><td>*Page 778*</td><td>**MAINE**</td></tr>
<tr><td>*Replace* Vehicles covered *entry with:*</td><td>*Vehicles covered*: Vehicles sold or leased in-state to convey passengers or property; excludes vehicles over 8500 lbs. gross vehicle weight used primarily for commercial purposes (§ 1161(3)).</td></tr>
<tr><td>*In* Period covered *entry replace "two years" with:*</td><td>three years</td></tr>
<tr><td>*Delete "or is sent two times to the same agent," from* Repair requirements *entry.*</td><td></td></tr>
<tr><td>*Add after first sentence of* Repair requirements *entry:*</td><td>If the nonconformity has resulted in a serious failure of the braking or steering system, the presumption applies if the vehicle has been subject to one or more repair attempts (§ 1163(A-2)).</td></tr>
<tr><td>*Replace* Resale of lemon *entry with:*</td><td>*Resale of lemon*: Full disclosure required (§ 1163(7), (8)).</td></tr>
<tr><td>*Page 780*</td><td>**MONTANA**</td></tr>
<tr><td>*In* Vehicles covered *entry replace "Vehicles sold in-state" with:*</td><td>Vehicles sold or registered in-state</td></tr>
<tr><td>*Delete "and motorcycles" from* Vehicles covered *entry.*</td><td></td></tr>
<tr><td>*Page 781*</td><td>**NEBRASKA**</td></tr>
<tr><td>*Replace* Resale of lemon *entry with:*</td><td>*Resale of lemon*: Title must be branded "manufacturer buyback" (Neb. Rev. Stat. §§ 60-129, 60-130).</td></tr>
<tr><td></td><td>**NEW HAMPSHIRE**</td></tr>
<tr><td>*Replace* Vehicles covered *entry with:*</td><td>*Vehicles covered*: Vehicles as defined in § 259.60, four-wheel vehicles under 9000 lbs., and motorcycles; excludes tractors and mopeds (§ 357-D:2(X)).</td></tr>
<tr><td>*Page 782*</td><td>**NEW YORK**</td></tr>
<tr><td>*Delete "motorcycles and" from* Vehicles covered *entry.*</td><td></td></tr>
<tr><td>*Page 784*</td><td>**OHIO**</td></tr>
<tr><td>*Add to end of* Vehicles covered *entry:*</td><td>Includes leased vehicles (§ 1345.71(A)).</td></tr>
<tr><td>*Replace second sentence of* Resale of lemon *entry with:*</td><td>Twelve month or 12,000 mile warranty, or remainder of manufacturer's warranty if greater, required on resale (§ 1345.76(A)(1)).</td></tr>
</table>

OREGON

Add to Other reimbursement
*entry after "Attorney fees
and costs":*

and treble damages not to exceed $50,000 over amount of refund due.

Add to Other remedies *entry
after "treble damages
allowed":*

with cap of $50,000

Page 785

PENNSYLVANIA

Replace Vehicles covered
entry with:

Vehicles covered: New and unused vehicles purchased or leased and registered in-state, or purchased or leased elsewhere and registered for the first time in-state, including demonstrator or dealer cars which convey fewer than fifteen persons; excludes motorcycles, motor homes, off-road, and commercial vehicles (§ 1952). Leased vehicles covered effective Feb. 11, 2002.

Replace first two sentences of
Resale of lemon *entry with:*

Title must be branded as repurchase, and buyer must also be given separate disclosure (§ 1960(a)). If vehicle sold without disclosure, seller liable to state for civil penalty of $2000 and buyer may opt for refund or replacement. Vehicle that was returned because of nonconformity resulting in complete failure of braking or steering system likely to cause death or serious bodily injury may not be resold in the state (§ 1960(b)).

Page 786

TENNESSEE

In Vehicles covered *entry
replace "and registered"
with:*

and subject to registration and titling in Tennessee or another state

In Repair requirements *entry
replace "four or more
repairs" with:*

three or more repairs, and the nonconformity continues to exist,

TEXAS

*Replace entire Texas
summary with:*

Tex. Occ. Code Ann. §§ 2301.601 to 2301.613 (Vernon)
Vehicles covered: A fully self-propelled vehicle having two or more wheels whose primary purpose is transporting persons or property on public highways; also includes some other vehicles having certificates of title, towable recreational vehicles, and certain heavy vehicle components (§ 2301.002).
Persons covered: Retail purchasers who are entitled to enforce warranty; lessors, lessees, and transferees and assignees who are state residents and are entitled to enforce warranty (§ 2301.601).
Period covered: Whichever comes first: twenty-four months or 24,000 miles (§ 2301.605).
Disclosure requirements: Manufacturer must provide notice of complaint procedures and rights (§ 2301.613).
Required consumer notice: Buyer must mail written notice of defect to manufacturer, converter, or distributor before board may issue order for refund or replacement (§ 2301.606). To extend duty to repair beyond warranty period, consumer must report the nonconformity to the manufacturer, converter, distributor, agent, or dealer (§ 2301.603).
Repair requirements: It is presumed that a reasonable number of attempts have been made if the same nonconformity continues to exist after four or more repair attempts, two of which were made within the first twelve months or 12,000 miles, and the other two within twelve months or 12,000 miles after the second repair attempt. If the defect creates a serious safety hazard, the presumption applies if the defect continues to exist after two or more repairs, one of which occurred within the first twelve months or 12,000 miles, and the second within

twelve months or 12,000 miles after the first attempt. Presumption also applies if defect still exists and vehicle is out of service for thirty or more days during first twenty-four months or 24,000 miles and at least two repair attempts were made in the first twelve months or 12,000 miles (§ 2301.605). Board may not issue order for refund or replacement unless manufacturer, converter, or distributor has been given an opportunity to cure the alleged nonconformity (§ 2301.606).

Affirmative defenses: The nonconformity does not substantially impair the use or market value of the vehicle, or is the result of the consumer's abuse, neglect, or unauthorized modifications or alteration (§ 2301.606); statute of limitations (§ 2301.606).

Replace/refund: The manufacturer shall replace with a comparable vehicle, or refund the full purchase price less a reasonable use allowance (§ 2301.604).

Other reimbursement: Reasonable incidental costs (§ 2301.604).

Other remedies: There is no limit on other consumer remedies (§§ 2301.603, 2301.607).

Informal dispute resolution: For remedies under this section, a consumer must use an informal dispute settlement procedure established by the commission (§ 2301.607). Judicial review is available (§ 2301.609).

Resale of lemon: Full disclosure including toll-free telephone number; new twelve-month, 12,000 mile warranty; restoration to factory specifications (§ 2301.610).

Page 789

WISCONSIN

Replace entire Wisconsin summary with:

Wis. Stat. § 218.0171

Vehicles covered: Vehicles registered and purchased or leased in state, including demonstrator or executive vehicles; excludes mopeds, semitrailers and trailers used with trucks (§ 218.0171(1)(d)).

Persons covered: Purchasers or lessees, transferees during express warranty period, or any person entitled to enforce the warranty (§ 218.0171(1)(b)).

Period covered: Whichever comes first: expiry of term of express warranty or one year from date of delivery (§ 218.0171(2)(a)).

Disclosure requirements: None for manufacturer.

Required consumer notice: Must report nonconformity to the manufacturer or authorized dealer (§ 218.0171(2)(a)).

Repair requirements: It is presumed that a reasonable number of attempts have been made if the same nonconformity is subjected to four or more repairs, or the vehicle is out of service for thirty or more calendar days (§ 218.0171(1)(h)).

Affirmative defenses: The nonconformity is the result of the consumer's abuse, neglect, or unauthorized modifications or alterations (§ 218.0171(1)(f)). No statute of limitations specified.

Replace/refund: At the consumer's option, the manufacturer shall replace with a new comparable vehicle, or refund the full purchase price less a reasonable use allowance (defined) (§ 218.0171(2)(b)).

Other reimbursement: Collateral costs and charges; refund to the consumer and lienholder; other damages (§ 218.0171(2)(b)). Double damages, costs and attorney fees (§ 218.0171(7)). Sales tax to be returned by department of revenue (§ 218.0171(2)(f)).

Other remedies: There is no limit on other consumer remedies (§ 218.0171(5). No cause of action created against dealer by virtue of exclusion of dealers from definition of manufacturer and its agents (§ 218.0171(1)(c)).

Informal dispute resolution: For remedies under this section a consumer must first use an informal dispute settlement procedure established by the manufacturer, provided the procedure complies with 16 C.F.R. 703 (§ 218.0171(3), (4)).

Resale of lemon: Full disclosure required (§ 218.0171(2)(d)).

State-by-State Analysis of Service Contract Laws and Regulations

Page 793   **MISSISSIPPI**

Add to end of entry: Service contracts related to home repairs are not regulated as insurance, but are subject to the Mississippi Consumer Protection Act.

Page 795   **VIRGINIA**

Add to end of entry: Service contract obligors must post a bond or a letter of credit.

State-by-State Analysis of New Home and Condominium Warranty Laws

Page 797

Add new summary to text before Connecticut summary.

CALIFORNIA

New Home Warranties: Cal. Civ. Code §§ 895 to 945.5 (West)

Structures covered: Original construction intended to be sold as an individual dwelling unit, but not condominium conversions.

Eligible buyers: The original purchasers and their successors in interest.

Warrantors: The general contractors, subcontractors, material suppliers, product manufacturers, and design professionals who contribute to an original dwelling unit.

Express Warranty Provisions: Fit and finish items must come with a written, express warranty of at least one year's duration.

Implied Warranties Provided/Duration: While not providing for implied warranties, the statute sets specific standards as follows, and provides that an action for the breach of these standards must be brought within ten years of substantial completion of the structure, except when the statute provides a shorter time period:

- Doors, windows, patio doors, deck doors, roofs, roofing systems, chimney caps, ventilation components, decks, deck systems, balconies, balcony systems, exterior stairs, stair systems, foundation systems, slabs, hardscape, paths, patios, irrigation systems, landscaping systems, drainage systems, stucco, exterior siding, exterior walls, exterior wall finishes, fixtures, retaining walls, site walls, plumbing systems, sewer systems, utility systems, shower and bath enclosures, ceramic tile, and tile countertops must meet stated waterproofing standards.
- Foundations, load bearing components, and slabs must not contain significant cracks or significant vertical displacement, must not cause the structure to be structurally unsafe, and must materially comply with designated regulations for chemical deterioration or corrosion resistance, and for earthquake and wind load resistance.
- Soils and engineered retaining walls must not cause damage to the structure, must not cause the structure to be materially unsafe, and must not cause the structure to become unusable for its purpose.
- Structures must meet applicable regulations for fire protection; fireplaces, chimneys, chimney structures, chimney termination caps, electrical systems, and mechanical systems must not cause an unreasonable risk of fire outside of the fireplace enclosure or chimney; and electrical and mechanical systems must not cause an unreasonable risk of fire.
- Plumbing and sewer systems must be installed to operate properly and may not materially impair the use of the structure by its inhabitants (action must be brought within four years of the close of escrow).
- Electrical systems must be installed to operate properly and may not materially impair the use of the structure by its inhabitants (action must be brought within four years of the close of escrow).
- Exterior pathways, driveways, hardscape, sidewalls, sidewalks, and patios installed by

the original builder must not contain excessive cracks or cracks that display significant vertical displacement (action must be brought within four years of the close of escrow).
- Stucco, exterior siding, and other exterior wall finishes and fixtures must not contain significant cracks or separations.
- The installation of manufactured products must not interfere with the products' useful life (which must not be less than one year).
- Heating must be installed to maintain a temperature of seventy degrees.
- Air conditioning, if provided, must meet designated size and efficiency criteria.
- Attached structures must comply with applicable interunit noise transmission standards (action must be brought within one year from the date of occupancy of the adjacent unit).
- Irrigation systems and drainage must not damage landscaping or other external improvements (action must be brought within one year of the close of escrow).
- Untreated wood posts must be installed so that any contact with the soil does not cause unreasonable decay (action must be brought within two years of the close of escrow).
- Untreated steel fences and their adjacent components must be installed so as to prevent unreasonable corrosion (action must be brought within four years of the close of escrow).
- Paint and stain must not cause the building's surfaces to deteriorate within the manufacturers' specified time period (action must be brought within five years of the close of escrow).
- Roofing materials must be installed so as to avoid materials falling from the roof.
- Landscaping systems must be installed so as to survive at least one year (action must be brought within two years of the close of escrow).
- Ceramic tile and tile backing must be installed so that the tile does not detach.
- Dryer ducts must be installed and terminated pursuant to the manufacturer's requirements (action must be brought within two years of the close of escrow).
- Structures must be constructed so that they do not impair the occupants' safety from public health hazards.
- A defect in any function or component of a structure not addressed by the standards may lead to an action if it causes damage.

Exclusions/Restrictions: A home owner may not file an action against a party who has violated the designated standards unless the home owner (claimant) has complied with the statute's pre-litigation procedures, which require the claimant to notify the builder in writing of the defects, allow the builder to inspect the claimed defects, and allow the builder an opportunity to repair within a designated time or to pay the claimant cash in lieu of making a repair. If the builder fails to meet its obligations under the pre-litigation procedures, the claimant may then file suit. The home owner must follow all reasonable maintenance obligations and schedules and all commonly accepted maintenance practices. Except when the statute provides for a shorter period, actions must be brought within ten years of substantial completion of the improvement.

Disclaimability: The builder may not obtain any release or waiver in exchange for the required repair work.

Remedies: Limited to the reasonable value of repairing the violations and related damages, and costs and fees recoverable by contract or statute.

Exclusivity: Exclusive, as to actions to enforce the designated standards.

Add to text at end of Connecticut summary:

CONNECTICUT

Condominium Warranties: **Conn. Gen. Stat. § 47-74e**

Structures Covered: The condominium building, all improvements, and the personal property transferred with a building or improvement.
Eligible Buyers: Unit owners and their successors.
Warrantors: Declarant, contractor, subcontractors, and suppliers.
Express Warranty Provisions: No applicable provisions.

Implied Warranties Provided/Duration: The declarant, contractors, subcontractors, and suppliers are liable for a one year implied warranty of fitness and merchantability for the covered structures. The date from which the warranty runs depends upon whether the component serves a building or an individual unit, and upon whether the warrantor is the developer or another party.

Exclusions/Restrictions: Conditioned upon routine maintenance.

Disclaimability: No applicable provisions.

Remedies: No applicable provisions.

Exclusivity: No applicable provisions.

Sample Notices Triggering Self-Help Remedies

J.1 Sample Notice of Rejection or Revocation of Acceptance

Page 835

Add to text after notice's first sentence:

In addition, I am canceling my contract with you.[1.1]

    1.1   U.C.C. § 2-711(1) allows a buyer who revokes acceptance to cancel the contract.

Page 836

Replace Alternative 2 with:

[*ALTERNATIVE 2—if the buyer is returning the car to the dealer*]:

I am returning the car to [dealer] and demand the return of my $_____ at this time. I will maintain insurance on the vehicle only through [date]. After that date, you must maintain insurance on the vehicle if you wish to protect yourself from loss.

Page 837

J.2 Sample Notice That Consumer Is Deducting Damages From the Outstanding Balance

Replace note 4 with:

    4   *See* National Consumer Law Center, Unfair and Deceptive Acts and Practices § 6.6 (5th ed. 2001 and Supp.) (discussion of consumer remedies when the FTC Notice should be included in the promissory note but is not).

Sample Complaints

K.1 Introduction

Page 839

Replace Appx. K.1.1 with:

K.1.1 Warranty Complaints in This Appendix and on the CD-Rom

This appendix contains a number of sample complaints. All are also available on the CD-Rom accompanying this volume.

First, Appendix K.2 contains a set of very basic, skeletal complaints for breach of express warranty, breach of implied warranty of merchantability, breach of implied warranty of fitness for a particular purpose, and revocation of acceptance. These complaints are intended to be used more as outlines for attorneys preparing their own pleadings than as actual model pleadings. They contain allegations of the essential elements for claims under the UCC.

Next this Appendix includes a model complaint in a used car sale (Appx. K.3). This complaint contains detailed allegations regarding hypothetical facts, and sets forth not only UCC claims but also claims under the Magnuson-Moss Act and claims for fraud and UDAP violations.

The next item is a model complaint in a home improvement case (Appx. K.4). This complaint includes claims for violation of common law warranties, UDAP violations, fraud, and Truth in Lending.

The final three items are sample complaints that were actually filed in various jurisdictions: a new car lemon law complaint from Michigan (Appx. K.5), a complaint from Illinois involving defective manufacture of a mobile home (Appx. K.6), and a complaint from Virginia involving defective setup of a mobile home (Appx. K.7). These complaints are more specific to the particular jurisdiction, but even their non-federal, non-UCC claims are based largely on laws that many states have adopted in one form or another.

The CD-Rom accompanying this volume contains not only the complaints that are included in this Appendix, but also:

- A used car complaint featuring claims involving odometer rollback, breach of warranty, UDAP violations and disclosure violations. This complaint is also reproduced in National Consumer Law Center, Consumer Law Pleadings No. 1, Ch. 3 (2003 Cumulative CD-Rom and Index Guide).
- Complaints involving the undisclosed sale of a lemon buyback, the undisclosed sale of a salvaged vehicle and the sale of a defective used car, all of which include warranty claims and all of which are also reproduced in National Consumer Law Center, Consumer Law Pleadings No. 2, Ch. 6 (2003 Cumulative CD-Rom and Index Guide).
- A complaint filed by an attorney general's office against a used car dealer, raising claims involving warranty violations and deception in both sales and financing. This complaint is also found in National Consumer Law Center, Consumer Law Pleadings No. 6, Ch. 9 (2003 Cumulative CD-Rom and Index Guide).
- A complaint involving the sale of a "gray market" vehicle, which is also found in National Consumer Law Center, Consumer Law Pleadings No. 6, Ch. 11 (2003 Cumulative CD-Rom and Index Guide).

- A RICO complaint against a bank that failed to include the FTC Holder Notice in the financing documents for sales of defective cars with undisclosed wreck damage. This complaint is also reproduced in National Consumer Law Center, Consumer Law Pleadings No. 1, Ch. 4 (2003 Cumulative CD-Rom and Index Guide).
- A complaint involving disclaimers and breach of warranties in an automobile lease, also reproduced in National Consumer Law Center, Consumer Law Pleadings No. 1, Ch. 9 (2003 Cumulative CD-Rom and Index Guide).
- New car lemon law complaints from California and Ohio. The California complaint is also reproduced in National Consumer Law Center, Consumer Law Pleadings No. 2, Ch. 5 (2003 Cumulative CD-Rom and Index Guide) and the Ohio complaint in National Consumer Law Center, Consumer Law Pleadings No. 4, Ch. 15 (2003 Cumulative CD-Rom and Index Guide).
- Two complaints concerning home improvement fraud, which are also reproduced in National Consumer Law Center, Consumer Law Pleadings No. 2, Ch. 4 (2003 Cumulative CD-Rom and Index Guide), and a third complaint, including a claim for cancellation under the state home solicitation sales law, which is also found in National Consumer Law Center, Consumer Law Pleadings No. 6, Ch. 17 (2003 Cumulative CD-Rom and Index Guide).
- A complaint regarding defective construction of prefabricated housing, which is reproduced in National Consumer Law Center, Consumer Law Pleadings No. 5, Ch. 7 (2003 Cumulative CD-Rom and Index Guide).

Discovery, motions, memoranda, sample correspondence, trial papers, and other documents are included on the CD-Rom accompanying many of these complaints.

K.1.3 *How to Use the Pleadings Found in This Appendix*

Page 840

K.1.3.3 Truth in Lending Counts Found in the Home Improvement Complaint

Replace NCLC citation in subsection's last sentence with:

National Consumer Law Center, Truth in Lending (5th ed. 2003)

Page 844

K.3 Sample Complaint for Used Car Sale

Replace note 34 with:

34   Undisclosed wreck damage raises many potential issues and can lead to other claims that are not addressed by this pleading. *See* National Consumer Law Center, Automobile Fraud (2d ed. 2003).

Page 845

Addition to notes 42, 43, 50.

42   *Replace NCLC citation with*: Unfair and Deceptive Acts and Practices § 6.6 (5th ed. 2001 and Supp.).
43   *Replace second paragraph of note with*:
        Additional statutory or common law grounds for liability should probably be pleaded separately and specifically. For a full discussion of the FTC Holder Rule and other bases for lender liability, see National Consumer Law Center, Unfair and Deceptive Acts and Practices § 6.6 (5th ed. 2001 and Supp.) and National Consumer Law Center, The Cost of Credit: Regulation and Legal Challenges § 10.6, Ch. 11 (2d ed. 2000 and Supp.). For assignee liability under a Truth in Lending claim additional facts may need to be alleged. *See* National Consumer Law Center, Truth in Lending §§ 2.3, 7.3 (5th ed. 2003). If Truth in Lending rescission is sought, see *id.* § 6.9.

Page 846

50   *Replace NCLC citation with*: Unfair and Deceptive Acts and Practices § 6.6.3 (5th ed. 2001 and Supp.).

Page 847

Replace note 61 with:

61   *See* National Consumer Law Center, Unfair and Deceptive Acts and Practices (5th ed. 2001 and Supp.).

Page 848

Replace note 62 with:	62	Undisclosed wreck damage raises many potential issues and can lead to other claims that are not addressed by this pleading. *See* National Consumer Law Center, Automobile Fraud (2d ed. 2003).

Page 849

Replace parenthetical below Count VIII heading with:

[*Plead here your facts and claims under the Truth-in-Lending Act. See National Consumer Law Center, Truth in Lending (5th ed. 2003) at Appendix E for sample pleadings.*]

Replace note 71 with:	71	*See* National Consumer Law Center, The Cost of Credit: Regulation and Legal Challenges Appx. E.1 (2d ed. 2000 and Supp.) (sample pleadings).

Page 850

K.4 Sample Complaint for Home Improvement Case

Addition to notes 79, 82, 92.

79 *Replace second paragraph of note with*:
For a full discussion of the FTC Holder Rule and other bases for lender liability, see National Consumer Law Center, Unfair and Deceptive Acts and Practices § 6.6 (5th ed. 2001 and Supp.) and National Consumer Law Center, The Cost of Credit: Regulation and Legal Challenges § 10.6, Ch. 11 (2d ed. 2000 and Supp.). For assignee liability under a Truth in Lending claim additional facts may need to be alleged. *See* National Consumer Law Center, Truth in Lending §§ 2.3, 7.3 (5th ed. 2003). If Truth in Lending rescission is sought, see *id.* § 6.9.

Page 851   82 *Replace NCLC citation with*: Unfair and Deceptive Acts and Practices Ch. 6 (5th ed. 2001 and Supp.).
Page 852   92 *Replace NCLC citation with*: National Consumer Law Center, Truth in Lending § 8.5.3 (5th ed. 2003).

Page 853

Replace note 94 with:

94 TILA applies solely to consumer credit transactions. National Consumer Law Center, Truth in Lending § 2.2 (5th ed. 2003).

Replace note 95 with:

95 For a definition of "regularly," see Regulation Z, § 226.2(a)(17) n.3; National Consumer Law Center, Truth in Lending § 2.3.3 (5th ed. 2003).

Replace note 96 with:

96 The complaint must allege all facts necessary to bring the transaction and the parties within the scope of TIL. *See generally* National Consumer Law Center, Truth in Lending Ch. 2 (5th ed. 2003). If the credit extended was not subject to a finance charge, then it must be alleged that it was payable by written agreement in more than four installments. *See* National Consumer Law Center, Truth in Lending § 2.3.4 (5th ed. 2003).
A rescission action may also be brought against an assignee, regardless of whether the assignee is a "creditor" or whether the violation was apparent on the face of the disclosure statement. TILA § 131(c), 15 U.S.C. § 1641(c); *see* National Consumer Law Center, Truth in Lending § 6.9.2 (5th ed. 2003).

Addition to notes 98–100, 102.

98 *Replace second paragraph of note with*:
Although only some disclosure violations create civil liability for statutory damages, all of the "material" disclosure violations do create such liability. *See* National Consumer Law Center, Truth in Lending § 8.6.5 (5th ed. 2003). Actual damages should be available for all disclosure violations. *Id.* at § 8.5.

99 *Replace first sentence of note with*: *See* National Consumer Law Center, Truth in Lending Appx. D (5th ed. 2003) (sample TIL rescission notice).

Page 854

100 *Replace last sentence of note with*: *See* National Consumer Law Center, Truth in Lending §§ 2.3.5.2, 3.10, 6.9.2, 7.3, 8.6.3.3 (5th ed. 2003).

102 *Replace last sentence of note with*: *See* National Consumer Law Center, Truth in Lending § 6.9.5 (5th ed. 2003).

Appendix L Sample Discovery

L.1 Introduction

Page 865

L.1.1 *Sample Discovery in the Appendices and on the Companion CD-Rom*

Replace note 1 with:

1   These documents are also included in National Consumer Law Center, Consumer Law Pleadings No. 1, § 3.2 (2003 Cumulative CD-Rom and Index Guide).

Replace note 2 with:

2   These documents are also included in National Consumer Law Center, Consumer Law Pleadings No. 1, §§ 4.5, 4.6 (2003 Cumulative CD-Rom and Index Guide).

Replace note 3 with:

3   This document is also included in National Consumer Law Center, Consumer Law Pleadings No. 1, § 9.2 (2003 Cumulative CD-Rom and Index Guide).

Replace note 4 with:

4   These documents are also included in National Consumer Law Center, Consumer Law Pleadings No. 2, §§ 5.2–5.7 (2003 Cumulative CD-Rom and Index Guide).

Replace note 5 with:

5   These documents are also included in National Consumer Law Center, Consumer Law Pleadings No. 2, Ch. 6 (2003 Cumulative CD-Rom and Index Guide).

Add to text after bulleted item containing note 5:

• Interrogatories and document requests in a case involving sale of a defective mobile home.

Replace note 6 with:

6   These interrogatories are also included in National Consumer Law Center, Consumer Law Pleadings No. 5, § 7.2 (2003 Cumulative CD-Rom and Index Guide).

Replace note 7 with:

7   These documents are also included in National Consumer Law Center, Consumer Law Pleadings (2003 Cumulative CD-Rom and Index Guide).

Addition to note 8.

8   *Replace first sentence of note with*: These documents are also included in National Consumer Law Center, Consumer Law Pleadings (2003 Cumulative CD-Rom and Index Guide).

Page 872

L.2 Sample Interrogatories to the Seller

Addition to note 23.

23   *Replace NCLC citation with*: Unfair and Deceptive Acts and Practices Ch. 6 (5th ed. 2001 and Supp.).

Page 873

L.3 Sample Document Requests

Replace note 25 with:

25   If there was a repossession, you will want to add "after the relevant period" to the time frame of this request. *See* National Consumer Law Center, Repossessions and Foreclosures Appx. E (5th ed. 2002 and Supp.).

L.7 Sample Document Request to Mobile Home Manufacturer

31   *Replace NCLC citation with*: National Consumer Law Center, Consumer Law Pleadings No. 5 (2003 Cumulative CD-Rom and Index Guide); *add at end of note*: Another sample document request, prepared by Attorney T. Michael Flinn, a consumer specialist in Carrollton, Georgia, may be found on the CD-Rom accompanying this volume, along with a set of interrogatories.

Sample Trial Documents

Page 883

Replace Appx. M.1 with:

M.1 Introduction

This Appendix contains a series of sample trial documents from three different jurisdictions: plaintiff's pretrial statement, trial brief in a new car case, *voir dire*, opening statement before a jury, outline of direct examination of consumer's expert, closing argument before a jury and excerpt of a rebuttal, jury instructions, verdict forms from both a used car case and a new car case, and a motion to treble a damage award. These documents are also included on the CD-Rom accompanying this volume. In addition, the CD-Rom contains the following pretrial and trial documents that are not reproduced in this Appendix:

- Class certification, summary judgment, and settlement papers in several cases, one involving odometer rollbacks, UDAP violations and warranty claims, a second involving claims against a bank that financed sales of defective cars without including the FTC Holder Notice, and a third involving disclaimers of warranties in auto leases. These documents are also reproduced in National Consumer Law Center, Consumer Law Pleadings No. 1, Chs. 3, 4, 9 (2003 Cumulative CD-Rom and Index Guide).
- An expert report, pretrial disclosure statement, trial brief and jury instructions in a case involving sale of a vehicle with undisclosed wreck damage. These documents are also reproduced in National Consumer Law Center, Consumer Law Pleadings No. 2, § 6.2 (2003 Cumulative CD-Rom and Index Guide).
- Sample correspondence, a request for judicial notice, a 54(C) demand, a pretrial statement and a motion to bifurcate the attorney fee issue from the other issues in an Ohio lemon law case. These documents are also reproduced in National Consumer Law Center, Consumer Law Pleadings No. 4, Ch. 15 (2003 Cumulative CD-Rom and Index Guide).
- Jury instructions on a Magnuson-Moss claim, which also are reproduced in National Consumer Law Center, Consumer Law Pleadings No. 5, § 6.3 (2003 Cumulative CD-Rom and Index Guide).

All of these documents, along with pleadings from all the other NCLC books, are also found on the comprehensive CD-Rom *Consumer Law in a Box*.

Page 896

Add new section to text after Appx. M.6.

M.6a Sample Outline of Direct Examination of Buyer in Case Involving Breach of Warranty and Fraud[5.1]

PRELIMINARY INFORMATION

Identify Self:

Please tell the Court your name, where you live, what you do for a living.

Are you married?

Any children?

Identify Exhibits:

We need to identify the exhibits for this case, so would you please tell the Court what each of these documents is?

Exhibit #1?
  (Etc.)

Specific Representations at Sale:

What did dealer say about the vehicle that made you decide to buy it?

Your Story:

Tell the Court what happened:

What was the primary purpose of vehicle?

> [**Possible answer:** *Go to work, out to dinner, movies, doctor's office, grocery store, the usual sort of things that a person uses a car or truck for.*]

Did you know you were getting a Warranty?

Was that important to you?

> [**Possible answer:** *Yes, otherwise I might as well have bought a used car out of the Trading Post or the newspaper. I wanted a car that would run right and not have problems.*]

LEMON LAW QUESTION 1

PROBLEM:

Did you give an authorized dealer at least three chances to fix this?

About how many chances total did you give them?

Did it get fixed by the end of the third attempt?

LEMON LAW QUESTION 2

Was your vehicle tied up in the shop for more than thirty days *during the warranty period* for repair work that was covered by warranty?

About how many days *total* do you think it was?

LEMON LAW QUESTION 3

Did you go to an authorized dealer more than eight times for the correction of defects that were covered by the manufacturer's warranty?

About how many times total do you think it was?

LEMON LAW QUESTION 4

Did you have more than eight different defective parts or problems that were covered by the manufacturer's warranty?

About how many *different defects* were there total?

LEMON LAW QUESTION 5

Did you ever have a problem that you considered dangerous enough that it could cause an accident or for someone to get hurt?

What was it?

Why did you consider it serious?

How many different times did an authorized dealer work on that problem?

When did they finally and completely get it fixed?

BREACH OF CONTRACT/WARRANTY

What kind of warranty or service contract did you think you were getting when you bought this vehicle?

[***Possible answer:*** *A good one; one that would cover everything.*]

Why did you think that?

[***Possible answer:*** *That's what their advertisements say, that they sell/build a good vehicle and their warranty backs it.*]

Did you think you were getting a good quality vehicle?

[***Possible answer:*** *Sure, or I would not have bought it.*]

Why did you think that?

[***Possible answer:*** *That's what they told me.*]

What did the dealer say about this vehicle, when you were first looking at it, that made you decide it would be a good deal, and to go ahead and get it?

What did the dealer say about the service contract that made you decide that it was worth getting, and to go ahead and get it?

[***Possible answer:*** *That it would cover everything.*]

As the owner, do you think that this vehicle is fit for the ordinary use that people make of this kind of vehicle? Why not?

[***Possible answer:*** *You can not trust it.*]

Did you tell the dealer what you were going to be using the vehicle for or who was going to be using it?

What did the dealer say about that?

Did the dealer say anything to you about the prior use of this vehicle before you bought it?

Did the dealer tell you where the miles came from that were on this vehicle before you bought it?

FEDERAL WARRANTY ACT

What did you understand the manufacturer's warranty would do for you if you had problems with your vehicle?

[***Possible answer:*** *That it would cover anything that went wrong. That they would fix things right and not take repeated trips to get the job done.*]

Did you have problems with your vehicle that you thought should have been covered by warranty but were not fixed?

What were they?

CONSUMER ACT (GENERIC)

Do you think that the manufacturer lived up to its warranty with you?

[***Possible answer:*** *No.*]

Why do you say they did not?

[*Possible answer:* *You should not have to keep going back again and again to fix the same thing or to fix new things all the time.*]

Did the manufacturer or dealer live up to their service contract with you?

Why do you say they did not?

Did you ever get the feeling that you were getting the run around or any deliberate stalling was taking place by the dealer in your repairs or answering your complaints?

Did you ever get the feeling that the manufacturer was stalling you or giving you the run around in answering your questions or seeing that the dealer took care of your problems?

What made you feel that way?

MOTOR VEHICLE SALES RULE

What was the impression that you had of the quality of this vehicle from your conversations with the dealer before you bought it?

Did that turn out to be accurate?

What was the impression you had of the value of this vehicle from your conversations with the dealer before you bought it?

Did that turn out to be accurate?

What was the impression you had of the useability of this vehicle from your conversations with the dealer before you bought it?

Did that turn out to be accurate?

What was the impression you had of the prior use of this vehicle from your conversations with the dealer before you got it?

Did that turn out to be accurate?

Did the dealer create any impression about any aspect of this motor vehicle, during the time that you were talking with them, before you bought the vehicle, which later on turned out not to be true?

What was it?

REPAIR RULE

Did the dealer:

—ever have you sign a repair order document and *not* give you a copy at the time you signed it?

—ever give you back your vehicle at the end of a repair job and *not* give you a document showing what they did to it?

—ever offer the old, replaced parts back to you at the end of a repair job?

—ever identify for you the individual performing the repairs to your vehicle at any given date?

Did you ever see a sign at the dealer's service department area that said you weren't getting the replaced parts back?

FRAUD

What did the dealer say to you in selling this vehicle to you, that you think was not the truth?

Why do you think it was not the truth?

Was it important to you that what they said to you *was* true?

How have you lost money from the dealer *not* telling you the whole truth?

If you had been told the whole truth about this vehicle, would you have paid the same amount of money for it?

WINDOW STICKER RULE

Did you understand that you were buying a new or a used car?

At any time before you signed on the dotted line to buy this vehicle, did you ever see any sort of window sticker on the vehicle that talked about either the price of it or the miles per gallon or whether you were buying it as is or with a warranty, or anything like that?

At the time that they delivered the vehicle to you, was there any sort of window sticker on the vehicle that talked about your warranty rights or if the vehicle was being sold as is or the price of the car or the miles per gallon it would get or anything like that?

PRICE GOUGING

Was there anything here that you bought from the dealer that later on you found out that you might have paid too much money for when you got it from them?

What was that? Cost of car? Service contract?

Did you ever refuse to bring the vehicle in for repairs?

Did you ever abuse the vehicle?

Did you maintain the vehicle?

Did you ever do anything to the vehicle except normal operation of vehicle?

Do you think this vehicle is not fit for its ordinary purpose?

DAMAGES

You have bought and sold vehicles before?

You have been with others who did that?

Have you seen magazine, newspaper, TV, or radio ads that talked about vehicles and prices?

So, you have a general knowledge of vehicle prices and values, right?

Do you have an opinion on the value of this vehicle on date of delivery *if* it had been as it was represented to be?

   [***Possible answer:*** *Yes, if it ran right, it would have been worth the price I paid.*]

Do you have an opinion on what was the value of this vehicle on date of delivery *in the condition* that it actually was in?

   [***Possible answer:*** *Yes. I would not have paid over $_____ for it. I did not want a lot of trouble, just a vehicle that would run right.*]

Have you made all your loan payments to date?

   [***Possible answer:*** *Yes.*]

Have you continued to use the vehicle while this dispute was going on?

   [***Possible answer:*** *Yes.*]

Why?

   [***Possible answer:*** *I had to. I could not afford to park it and go get another one and have two payments to make each month.*]

Do you have any faith in the reliability of this vehicle?

[***Possible answer:*** *No. I never know what it is going to happen next or how long it will run or where it will break down next.*]

Why did you file this lawsuit?

[***Possible answer:*** *I had to, they left me no choice. They would not take it back and cancel the deal.*]

What do you want to Court/Jury to do here?

Is there any one problem or complaint that was really "the straw that broke the camel's back"?

> 5.1 The following is an outline of the direct examination of the buyer in a case involving breach of warranty and fraud. It includes, when appropriate, the expected responses of the buyer for whose case it was prepared. This outline is based on one prepared by Ronald L. Burdge, an attorney in Dayton, Ohio, who specializes in consumer law.

M.8 Sample Jury Instructions

Page 901

M.8.1 *Express Warranty, Merchantability, Revocation and Magnuson-Moss Warranty Act*

Add note 7.1 at end of PROOF OF NONCONFOR-MITY *instruction.*

> 7.1 It may be appropriate to add a final sentence to this instruction: "Neither is it necessary that plaintiff provide expert testimony to establish an impairment, defect, or nonconformity, but rather these may be established by the consumer's own testimony."

Page 905

M.8.2 *Rejection, Revocation, Merchantability, Fitness for a Particular Purpose and Disclaimer*

Add note 8.1 at end of second paragraph of UCC—REVOCATION—NONCONFORMITY SUBSTANTIALLY IMPAIRING VALUE *instruction.*

> 8.1 An alternative, expanded version of this paragraph lists the circumstances the jury is to consider as follows:
>
> 1) the use to which the plaintiff put or intended to put the goods;
> 2) the nature or severity of the defects in the goods;
> 3) the number of defects in the goods;
> 4) the price paid;
> 5) the length of time the goods were in the shop as found by you;
> 6) the number of times the goods were in the shop;
> 7) whether repair attempts were made which were unsuccessful;
> 8) whether the nonconformities and the attempts to repair them were a breach of a warranty applicable to the goods; and
> 9) any other fact or circumstance in the totality of circumstances surrounding the transaction.

Add new subsections to text after Appx. M.8.2.

M.8.3 *Substantial Impairment, Shaken Faith Doctrine, and Continued Use*[8.2]

SUBSTANTIAL IMPAIRMENT

In determining whether the plaintiffs rightfully revoked their acceptance of the vehicle, you must decide whether the nonconformity "substantially impaired" the use or value of the vehicle to the plaintiffs.

"Substantial impairment" means that there is a nonconformity with respect to the vehicle which diminishes its value or interferes with its use to a substantial degree. This is a subjective test, which means that the issue of impairment of use or value must be determined from the point of view of the actual buyer (in this case, plaintiffs) rather than what may impair the use or value of the vehicle to any other buyer. Plaintiffs have the burden of proving that the nonconformity substantially impaired the use or value of the vehicle to them and of proving that their assessment had some basis in fact. In this regard, you should consider the purpose for which the plaintiffs purchased the vehicle and whether the nonconformities substantially impaired their ability to use the vehicle for the purposes intended.

SHAKEN FAITH DOCTRINE

In some instances, a defect or nonconformity which occurs shortly after delivery of a new vehicle may be serious enough to reasonably destroy the consumer's faith in the integrity and reliability of the vehicle. This is known as the "shaken faith doctrine."

If you determine that the plaintiffs' faith was reasonably shaken with respect to the vehicle, then the defendants have no right to cure and plaintiffs may justifiably revoke their acceptance of the vehicle.

CONTINUED USE

The law permits the plaintiff to continue to use the vehicle in an effort to mitigate his damages even after he has notified the defendant of his claims. Thus, the fact that the plaintiff continued to use the vehicle is not a defense to the plaintiff's claims.

M.8.4 Lemon Law Instructions[8.3]

VIOLATION OF LEMON LAW

I charge you that the Georgia Motor Vehicle Warranty Rights Act provides that a new motor vehicle purchase is a major purchase and that a defective motor vehicle is likely to create hardship to the consumer.

I charge you that the knowing failure of a manufacturer or its agents to honor any express warranty issued by that manufacturer or agent constitutes an unfair or deceptive act for which the manufacturer or its agent may be liable. In determining whether there is a deceptive act or practice, you may consider the number of attempts to repair and the number of repair attempts provided for in the Motor Vehicle Warranty Rights Act.

I charge you that the Warranty Rights Act presumes that a manufacturer or its agent has had a reasonable number of attempts to repair any nonconformity in a vehicle when the nonconformity in the vehicle has been subject to repair three or more times and the nonconformity continues to exist; or, if the vehicle is out of service to the consumer by reason of repair of one or more nonconformities for a period of thirty days in any twenty-four month period.

A nonconformity is a defect or condition which substantially impairs the use, value, or safety of the vehicle to the consumer.

If the manufacturer or its agent is unable to repair the new motor vehicle after a reasonable number of repair attempts, the consumer shall notify the manufacturer by certified mail, return receipt requested. The manufacturer shall, within seven days after receipt of such notification, notify the consumer to take the vehicle to a designated repair facility where the manufacturer will be given another repair attempt. If the manufacturer is unable to repair the nonconformity, the manufacturer shall, within thirty days of written notification, certified mail, return receipt requested, at the option of the consumer, replace or repurchase the motor vehicle.

O.C.G.A. § 10-1-781
O.C.G.A. § 10-1-790
O.C.G.A. § 10-1-784(b)
O.C.G.A. § 10-1-782(13)
O.C.G.A. § 10-1-784(a)(20)

8.2   These sample instructions are based on ones prepared by Michigan attorney Dani Liblang and Georgia attorney T. Michael Flinn, both of whom handle a substantial number of lemon law and consumer warranty cases.

8.3   The following jury instruction relates to a claim under the Georgia lemon law. As the elements of a lemon law claim differ, sometimes subtly, from jurisdiction to jurisdiction, advocates will have to take particular care to adapt these instructions to their jurisdiction. These instructions are based on instructions prepared by T. Michael Flinn, an attorney in Carrollton, Georgia, who specializes in consumer law. [*Editor's note:* Citations as in the original.]

Car Manufacturers

Appendix N
replacement appendix

The following is reprinted with permission from the 2003 Consumer Action Handbook, originally published by the United States General Services Administration, Consumer Information Center.

Acura
Customer Relations Department
Acura
1919 Torrance Blvd. 500-2N-7E
Torrance, CA 90501-2746
Toll free: 800-382-2238
Toll free: 800-594-8500 (roadside assist)
Fax: 310-783-3535
Website: www.acura.com

Alfa-Romeo Distributors of North America, Inc.
7454 Brokerage
Orlando, FL 32809
407-856-5000
Fax: 407-856-5000

American Honda Motor Co., Inc.
Corporate Office:
American Honda Motor Co., Inc.
Consumer Affairs Department
1919 Torrance Blvd.
Torrance, CA 90501-2746
310-783-2000
Toll free: 800-999-1009
Fax: 310-783-3273
Website: www.honda.com

American Isuzu Motors, Inc.
Owner Relations Department
American Isuzu Motors, Inc.
13340 183rd St.
Cerritos, CA 90702-6007
Toll free: 800-255-6727
Fax: 562-229-5455
Website: www.isuzu.com

American Motors Corp.
see **Daimler Chrysler Motors Corp.**

American Suzuki Motor Corp.
Customer Relations Department
American Suzuki Motor Corp.

P.O. Box 1100
3251 East Imperial Hwy.
Brea, CA 92822-1100
714-996-7040, ext. 380 (motorcycles)
714-572-1490
Toll free: 800-934-0934 (automotive only)
Fax: 714-524-2512
Website: www.suzuki.com

Aston Martin, Jaguar Landrover Premier Auto Group
Customer Relations Department
Aston Martin, Jaguar Landrover Premier Auto Group
U.S. National Headquarters
1 Premier Place
Irvine, CA 92618
949-341-6100
Toll free: 800-452-4827
Fax: 949-341-6152
Website: www.jaguar.com

Audi of America, Inc.
Client Relations
Audi of America, Inc.
3499 West Hamlin Rd.
Rochester Hills, MI 48309
Toll free: 800-822-2834
Fax: 248-754-6504
Website: www.audiusa.com

BMW of North America, Inc.
Corporate Office:
BMW of North America, Inc.
300 Chestnut Ridge Rd.
Woodcliff Lake, NJ 07675
201-307-4000
Toll free: 800-831-1117 (BMW Customer Service Center)
Fax: 201-930-8362
Website: www.bmwusa.com

Chrysler
see **Daimler Chrysler Motors Corp.**

Daihatsu America, Inc.
Consumer Affairs Department
Daihatsu America, Inc.
28 Centerpointe Dr., Ste. 120
La Palma, CA 90623

714-690-4700
Toll free: 800-777-7070
Fax: 714-690-4720
Website: www.daihatsu.com

Daimler Chrysler Motors Corp.
Daimler Chrysler Customer Center
P.O. Box 21-8004
Auburn Hills, MI 48321-8004
Toll free: 800-992-1997
Fax: 248-512-8084
Website: www.chrysler.com

Dodge
see **Daimler Chrysler Motors Corp.**

Ferrari North America Inc.
Corporate Office:
Ferrari North America Inc.
250 Sylvan Ave.
Englewood Cliffs, NJ 07632
201-816-2600
Fax: 201-816-2626
E-mail: administrative@ferrari.com
Website: www.ferrari.com

Ford Motor Co.
Ford Dispute Settlement Board
P.O. Box 5120
Southfield, MI 48086-5120
Toll free: 800-428-3718

Customer Relationship Center
Ford Motor Co.
16800 Executive Plaza Dr.
P.O. Box 6248
Dearborn, MI 48121
Toll free: 800-392-3673
Website: www.ford.com

General Motors Corp.
Corporate Affairs/Community Relations:
General Motors Corporation
100 Renaissance Center
Detroit, MI 48265
313-667-3800
313-556-5000

Customer Assistance Center
Buick Division
General Motors Corp.
P.O. Box 33136
Detroit, MI 48232-5136
313-556-5000
Toll free: 800-521-7300
Toll free: 800-252-1112 (roadside assistance)
TDD toll free: 800-832-8425
Website: www.buick.com

Customer Assistance Center
Cadillac Motor Car Division
General Motors Corp.
P.O. Box 33169
Detroit, MI 48232-5169
Toll free: 800-458-8006
Toll free: 800-882-1112 (roadside assistance)
TDD toll free: 800-833-2622
Website: www.cadillac.com

Customer Assistance Center
Chevrolet Motor Division
General Motors Corp.
P.O. Box 33170
Detroit, MI 48232-5170
Toll free: 800-222-1020
Toll free: 800-243-8872 (roadside assistance)
TDD toll free: 800-833-2438
Fax: 313-556-5108
Website: www.chevrolet.com

Customer Assistance Center
GMC Division
General Motors Corp.
P.O. Box 33172
Detroit, MI 48232-5172
Toll free: 800-462-8782
Toll free: 800-223-7799 (roadside assistance)
TDD toll free: 800-462-8583
Website: www.gmc.com

Customer Assistance Network
Oldsmobile Division
General Motors Corp.
P.O. Box 33171
Detroit, MI 48232-5171
Toll free: 800-442-6537
Toll free: 800-535-6537 (roadside assistance)
TDD toll free: 800-833-6537
Website: www.oldsmobile.com

Customer Assistance Center
Pontiac Division
General Motors Corp.
P.O. Box 33172
Detroit, MI 48232-5172
Toll free: 800-762-2737 (800-PM-CARES)
Toll free: 800-762-3743 (1-800-ROADSIDE)
TDD toll free: 800-833-7668
Website: www.gm.com

Saturn Customer Assistance Center
Saturn Corp.
Division of General Motors Corp.
100 Saturn Parkway
Spring Hill, TN 37174
931-486-5050

Toll free: 800-553-6000
TDD toll free: 800-833-6000
Fax: 931-486-5059
Website: www.saturn.com

Honda
see **American Honda Motor Co., Inc.**

Hyundai Motor America
Consumer Affairs
Hyundai Motor America
10550 Talbert Ave.
P.O. Box 20850
Fountain Valley, CA 92728-0850
714-965-3000
Toll free: 800-633-5151
Fax: 714-965-3861
E-mail: cmd@hma.service.com
Website: www.hyundai.usa.com

Isuzu
see **American Isuzu Motors, Inc.**

Jeep/Eagle Division of Chrysler Corp.
see **Daimler Chrysler Motors Corp.**

Kia Motors America, Inc.
Consumer Assistance Center
Kia Motors America, Inc.
P.O. Box 52410
Irvine, CA 92619-2410
Toll free: 800-333-4KIA
Fax: 949-470-2812
Website: www.kia.com

Lexus
see **Toyota Motor Sales USA, Inc.**

Mazda Motor of America, Inc.
Corporate Office:
Customer Relations Manager
Mazda N. American Operations
Jamboree Plaza
4 Park Plaza, Suite 1250
Irvine, CA 92614
Toll free: 800-222-5500
Website: www.mazdausa.com

Mercedes Benz of North America, Inc.
Customer Assistance Center
Mercedes Benz USA, Inc.
3 Paragon Dr.
Montvale, NJ 07645
Toll free: 800-222-0100
Toll free: 800-367-6372 (800-FOR-MERC)
Fax: 201-476-6213
Website: www.mbusa.com

Mitsubishi Motor Sales of America, Inc.
Customer Relations
Mitsubishi Motor Sales of America
6400 Katella Ave.
Cypress, CA 90630-0064
Toll free: 800-MITSU-2000
Website: www.mitsubishimotors.com

Nissan Motor Corp. in USA
Consumer Affairs Group
Nissan North America, Inc.
P.O. Box 191
Gardena, CA 90248-0191
310-532-3111
Toll free: 800-647-7261 (all consumer inquiries)
Fax: 310-771-2025
Website: www.nissan-usa.com

Peugeot Motors of America, Inc.
Consumer Relations
Peugeot Motors of America, Inc.
Overlook at Great Notch
150 Clove Rd.
Little Falls, NJ 07424
973-812-4444
Toll free: 800-345-5545
Fax: 973-812-2148
E-mail: peugeot2@bellatlantic.net
Website: www.peugeot.com

Plymouth
see **Daimler Chrysler Motors Corp.**

Porsche Cars North America, Inc.
Owner Relations
Porsche Cars North America, Inc.
980 Hammond Dr., Suite 1000
Atlanta, GA 30328
770-290-3500
Toll free: 800-545-8039
Fax: 770-360-3711
Website: www.porsche.com

Saab Cars USA, Inc.
Customer Assistance Center
Saab Cars USA, Inc.
4405-A International Blvd.
Norcross, GA 30093
770-279-0100
Toll free: 800-955-9007
Fax: 770-279-6499
Website: www.saabusa.com

Subaru of America, Inc.
National Customer Service Center
Subaru of America, Inc.
Subaru Plaza
P.O. Box 6000

Cherry Hill, NJ 08002
856-488-8500
Toll free: 800-782-2783
Fax: 856-488-0485
Website: www.subaru.com

Hawaii
Schuman Carriage Subaru
1234 S. Beretania St.
P.O. Box 2420
Honolulu, HI 96804
808-592-4464
Fax: 808-592-4494

Suzuki
see **American Suzuki Motor Corp.**

Toyota Motor Sales USA, Inc.
Customer Assistance Center
Toyota Motor Sales USA, Inc.
Department H200
19001 S. Western Ave.
Torrance, CA 90509
310-468-4000
Toll free: 800-331-4331
TDD toll free: 800-443-4999
Fax: 310-468-7800
Website: www.toyota.com

Customer Satisfaction Department
Lexus, a Division of Toyota Motor Sales USA, Inc.
Mail Drop L203, 19001 South Western Ave.
Torrance, CA 90509-2732
Toll free: 800-25-LEXUS
Fax: 310-468-2992
Website: www.lexus.com

Volkswagen of America
Customer Relations
Volkswagen of America
Hills Corporate Center
3499 West Hamlin Rd.
Rochester Hills, MI 48309
Toll free: 800-DRIVE VW
Toll free: 800-822-8987
Fax: 248-340-4660
Website: www.vw.com

Volvo Cars of North America
Customer Service
Volvo Cars of North America
P.O. Box 914
7 Volvo Drive, Bldg. A
Rockleigh, NJ 07647-0915
Toll free: 800-458-1552
Fax: 201-768-8695
Website: www.volvocars.com

Useful Warranty Law Websites

Live web links can be found on the CD-Rom accompanying this volume.

Governmental Websites

Secretaries of State: www.nass.org, www.residentagentinfo.com, and www.statelocalgov.net

Federal Rules: www.uscourts.gov/rules/approved.htm

National Highway Traffic and Safety Administration: www.nhtsa.dot.gov

Federal Trade Commission: www.ftc.gov

U.S. House: www.house.gov

Federal legislative information: http://thomas.loc.gov

Securities and Exchange Commission's EDGAR database: www.sec.gov (use "filings and forms" web link)

National Conference of Commissioners on Uniform State Laws: www.nccusl.org

Consumer Advocacy Organizations

Center for Auto Safety: www.autosafety.org (posts insider documents, technical service bulletins, other information)

Consumers for Auto Reliability and Safety: www.carconsumers.com (lemon law index, links to websites that rate auto safety, other information)

National Consumer Law Center: www.consumerlaw.org

National Association of Consumer Advocates: www.naca.net

Consumers Union: www.consumersunion.org

Trial Lawyers for Public Justice: www.tlpj.org

American Trial Lawyers Association: www.atlanet.org

General Consumer Information

www.consumerworld.com (non-commercial website that catalogs over 1500 useful consumer resources)

www.consumeraffairs.com (links to consumer-related websites)

Federal Consumer Information Center: www.pueblo.gsa.gov

International Association of Lemon Law Administrators: www.ialla.net (links to every state's lemon law website as well as to Canada's)

www.camvap.ca (information about Canada's lemon law)

Investigating Vehicle Safety and Defects

National Highway Traffic and Safety Administration: www.nhtsa.dot.gov (allows searches for recall notices, technical service bulletins, defect investigations, and consumer complaints)

Center for Auto Safety: www.autosafety.org (insider documents, technical service bulletins, publications, other information)

www.alldata.com (allows on-line searches for technical service bulletins and recall notices; also has a comprehensive set of links)

www.crashtest.com (provides crash test results; retrieves recall information)

Vehicle Pricing Guides

NADA Guides: www.nadaguides.com

Kelly Blue Book: www.kbb.com

National Auto Research publications: www.blackbookguides.com

Other Vehicle Pricing Information

www.carprice.com

www.edmunds.com

www.autoweb.com

Quick Title Searches

www.carfaxreport.com

www.autocheck.com

Vehicle Financing

www.FinanCenter.com

www.TValue.com

www.auto-loan.com

General Information about Dealers and Creditors

www.stoneage.com

www.spotdelivery.com

www.creditcompliance.com

www.pimall.com/nais/n.repo.html

www.consumerreports.org

Other Vehicle, Dealer, and Manufacturer Information

www.autopedia.com (names and locations of dealers, links to state attorney general lemon law websites, text of state lemon laws, other web links)

www.dr.bbb.org/autoline (rules and information about Better Business Bureau dispute resolution programs)

www.automotivenews.com (Detroit weekly trade publication; information about mergers, acquisitions, lawsuits, other automotive topics)

www.cartalk.cars.com (website of weekly radio show about cars; includes car owners' comments about their vehicles)

www.rv.org (non-profit organization for RV owners, including information about buying, repairing and trouble-shooting)

www.blueovalnews.com (news about Ford Motor Co.)

www.hud.gov/offices/hsg/sfh/mhs/mfrlst.cfm (list of mobile home manufacturers)

http://web.archive.org/collections/web.html (archives of old webpages)

www.tmcpubl.com (source for owner's manuals for vehicles)

www.nonoise.org (Noise Pollution Clearinghouse)

www.jlwarranty.com (website of J & L Warranty Pros, which publishes an annual Official Warranty Guide)

www.AA1Car.com (sources of information on manufacturers' warranties; click on "Links")

Cumulative Index

This is a cumulative index. Only use this index, not the one in the main volume which is now superseded. When a section is referenced in this index, turn to that section in both the main volume and this Supplement. Section references followed by "S" are found only in the Supplement.

References are to sections; references followed by "S" appear only in this Supplement

References are to sections; references followed by "S" appear only in this Supplement

BREACH OF WARRANTY (*cont.*)
mobile homes
    federal standards breach, 15.3.6
    litigating, 15.8
model or sample warranty, 7.3.4.1.3
new cars, 13.2.4, 13.3.2
new homes
    common law warranties, 16.3.5
    litigating, 16.7
    notice of defects, 16.4.1, 16.6.2
    pleading, 16.8
    statutory warranties, 16.4.1
nonconformities not involving, 8.3.2.6
notice of breach, *see* NOTICE OF BREACH
perfect tender rule, application, 7.3.1
picture warranties, 7.3.4.1.3
pleading, 10.1.3.4
    sample complaints, Appx. K
present characteristic warranties
    breach of statement, 3.2.2.4
    defective condition at delivery, 7.5
    generally, 7.3.4.1
    overview, 7.3.2
privity issues, 2.3.5, 2.3.6, 6.1
promise of future performance, 3.2.2.4
proof, *see* BURDEN OF PROOF; EVIDENCE
proper use and maintenance, 7.5.2
publicity efforts as litigation alternative, 10.1.2.7
questions of fact, 10.1.7.1
remedies, overview, 1.7.4
repair or replace remedy
    contractual provisions, 9.1, 9.4.2
    failure of essential purpose, 9.5.2
    purpose, 9.5.2
right to cure, *see* RIGHT TO CURE
self-help remedies, *see* SELF-HELP REMEDIES
statement of present condition, 3.2.2.4
statute of limitations, 10.3
strict liability, 7.3.1
substantial impairment, test, 8.3.2.1–8.3.2.3
UDAP application, 11.1.1
UDAP violations, 11.1.3
written warranties, 2.3.4

BREAKDOWN INSURANCE
see MECHANICAL BREAKDOWN INSURANCE; SERVICE
    CONTRACTS

BROCHURES
affirmation of fact or promise, 3.2.2.5
description of goods warranty, 3.3
disclaimers appearing in, validity, 5.8.5
express warranties, manufacturer's liability, 6.2.3
written warranty status, 6.2.2

BUILDERS
new home warranties
    application, 16.3.3, 16.4.1
    disclaimers, 16.6.1
    notification of breach, 16.4.1, 16.6.2

BUILDING CODES
breach of statutory duty, 12.2.5
home improvement contracts, relevance, 17.7.3
new home warranties, application, 16.3.5.2

BUILDING MATERIALS
see also CONSTRUCTION; HOME IMPROVEMENTS
consumer product status, 2.2.2.3

BUILDINGS
see also HOUSE SALES
strict liability doctrine, application, 12.3.3

BURDEN OF PROOF
see also EVIDENCE
breach of warranty, 1.7.3, 7.4.1, 13.2.4.1
buyer's conduct as affirmative defense, 7.6.2.1
consequential damages, 10.6.4
cover, improperly obtained, 10.4.3.3, 10.4.4
cure after performance date, acceptability, 8.2.7.6.1
damage, causation-in-fact, 7.4.1
damages for breach, existence and extent, 10.4.4
defects, 13.2.4
    practice tips, 10.1.7.3
    responsibility for defect, 6.2.7, 7.5.1.3
definition, 7.4.1
expert evidence, admissibility, 10.1.7.5.4
express warranties
    creation, 5.2
    statements not part of bargain, 3.2.5.3, 3.2.5.5
good faith, 11.3.6
indirect seller's breach of warranty, 6.2.7
lemon law arbitration appeals, 13.2.9.2
misuse or neglect, 2.5.7.4, 13.2.4.3
new home warranties, waiver, 16.6.1
offset for use by cancelling buyer, 10.4.6, 13.2.8.7
original ownership, 2.5.7.5
parol evidence, exclusion, 3.7.1, 3.7.2
particular purpose warranty, 4.3.4, 7.3.6
proof of purchase, 2.5.7.5
rejection of goods, 8.1
repair attempts, reasonable number, 13.2.6.3
revocation of acceptance, 8.1, 8.3.2.1
sample or model warranty, 3.4.2
substantial impairment of value, 8.3.2.2, 13.2.4.4
UCC self-help remedies, 8.1
unconscionability, 9.6.1, 11.2.7, 10.1.7.1
unreasonable use, 2.5.7.4, 13.2.4.3
waste doctrine, 16.7.2.5

BURGLAR ALARM SYSTEMS
see HOME IMPROVEMENTS

BUYERS
see also CONSUMERS; NONBUYERS
commercial buyers, *see* COMMERCIAL BUYERS
conduct as cause of damage, 7.6.2
    assumption of risk, 7.6.2.3
    characterization, 7.6.2.1
    failure to abide by directions, 7.6.2.5
    misuse of product, 7.6.2.4
    negligence, 7.6.2.2
definition, 1.4.7
good faith obligation, application, 11.3.6, 14.4.3
individual circumstances, relevance, 10.1.1.4
knowledge, effect, 3.2.5.4
new home warranties, availability, 16.3.2
prospective buyer, door-to-door sales definition, 2.6.5.4
reasonable conduct, 10.1.7.8.2
remedies, *see* BUYER'S REMEDIES
special relationship, determination, 12.2.5

References are to sections; references followed by "S" appear only in this Supplement

References are to sections; references followed by "S" appear only in this Supplement

HEATING AND AIR CONDITIONING EQUIPMENT
see HOME IMPROVEMENTS

HERBICIDES
FIFRA regulation, 1.4.9

HIDDEN DEFECTS
see LATENT DEFECTS

HOLDER RULE (FTC)
cancellation of sales, application, 8.4.5.5, 8.4.5.6, 8.5.3, 8.5.5, 8.5.6
leases, application, 19.5, 19.7.5
Magnuson-Moss derivative liability, 2.2.7.4
mobile homes, application, 15.8.1.5

HOLDERS-IN-DUE COURSE
FTC rule, *see* HOLDER RULE (FTC)

HOME IMPROVEMENTS
see also HOME SOLICITATION SALES; SERVICE
        TRANSACTIONS
building codes, 17.7.3
cancellation of contract, 17.6, 17.7.1
complaints
    government investigations, 7.5.7
    pleading, 17.7.9.2
    sample client interview sheet, Appx. I.3
    sample complaint, Appx. K.4
    TIL, 17.7.1.2, Appx. K.1.3.3
completion certificates, 17.7.2
consumer product status, 2.2.2.3
cooling-off periods, 17.6, 17.7.1
failure to complete work, 17.7.2
HOEPA coverage, 17.7.1.2
insolvent contractors, 17.7.5
litigation tips, 17.7.9
mortgages and liens, 17.7.7
permits, 17.7.2, 17.7.3
punitive damages, lender liability, 17.7.8
refusal to pay as remedy, 17.7.6
sample complaint, Appx. K.4
sample discovery, Appx. L
state statutes and regulations, 17.7.4
unmerchantable, examples, 7.3.5.1

**HOME OWNERSHIP AND EQUITY PROTECTION ACT
        (HOEPA)**
mobile homes, application, 15.8.1.4
home improvement violations, TIL rescission, 17.7.1.2

HOME SOLICITATION SALES
see also HOME IMPROVEMENTS
cooling-off periods
    effective remedy, 17.6
    FTC rule, 17.7.1.3
    state law, 17.7.1.4
prospective buyer, definition, 2.6.5.4
used car sales, 14.3.7
warranty disclosures, presale requirements, 2.6.5.4

HOMES
mobile homes, *see* MOBILE HOMES
new home warranties, *see* NEW HOME WARRANTIES
prefabricated homes, *see* PREFABRICATED HOMES
sales, *see* HOUSE SALES; REAL ESTATE TRANSACTIONS

HORIZONTAL PRIVITY
see also PRIVITY OF CONTRACT
Magnuson-Moss claims, 2.3.5
nonbuyer claims, 6.3

HOUSE SALES
see also REAL ESTATE TRANSACTIONS
caveat emptor, 16.1, 16.3.1
defects, overview, 16.1
disclosure requirements, 11.4.4.3
federally insured loans, 16.4.3
Magnuson-Moss Warranty Act, application, 16.2.3
new home warranties, *see* NEW HOME WARRANTIES
prefabricated homes, *see* PREFABRICATED HOMES
scope issues, 1.4.3
strict liability doctrine, application, 12.3.3
UCC, application, 16.2.1

HOUSEHOLD PRODUCTS
see CONSUMER PRODUCTS

HOUSING
substitute housing, consequential damages, 10.6.3.1.2

HUD LABEL
express warranty creation, 15.4.1

HUD WARRANTY
see also DEPARTMENT OF HOUSING AND URBAN
        DEVELOPMENT (HUD)
mobile homes
    circumstances, 15.4.1
    dealer responsibilities, 15.4.3, 15.7.4, 15.8.1.5
    lender responsibilities, 15.4.3, 15.8.1.5
    manufacturer responsibilities, 15.4.3
new homes, 16.4.3

IMPLIED WARRANTIES
see also WARRANTIES; WARRANTIES (UCC)
arbitration clauses, validity, 10.2.4.7S
"as is" or "with all faults" disclaimers
    alternative language, 5.5
    effect, 5.2
    used car sales, 14.3.3, 14.3.4
    validity, circumstances, 5.11.1
breach, *see* BREACH OF WARRANTY
buyer's expectations, 3.6.2
characterization
    advantageous, 10.1.1.5
    performance warranty, 7.2.2, 7.3.3, 7.3.6, 10.3.3.4
common law warranties, 17.4.3
component suppliers, application, 2.2.7.2
condominiums, 16.4.2
creation, 1.7.1.3, 1.7.1.4
cumulation, 3.8.1
definition, 2.3.1, 2.3.6.2
disclaimer or modification restrictions
    conspicuousness requirement, 5.8.1, 14.3.4, 14.3.5
    FTC Used Car Rule, 14.3.5
    leases, 19.3.3, 19.6.2
    Magnuson-Moss restrictions, 2.3.2, 2.5.4, 5.3
    state law restrictions, 5.4, 14.3.6
    UCC restrictions, 5.5, 14.3.4
    used car sales, 14.3.3, 14.3.4
duration
    disclosure, 2.6.4.8
    limits on, 2.3.2.3, 2.5.4, 5.3

References are to sections; references followed by "S" appear only in this Supplement

LIMITED REMEDY CLAUSES (*cont.*)
disclaimers distinguished, 1.7.2.3, 5.1, 9.1
disclosure requirements, 2.3.3, 2.6.4.9, 9.7
effect, 5.12
express warranties, application, 9.4.2
failure of essential purpose, 9.5
implied warranties, application, 9.4.3
incidental or consequential damages, 9.5.3, 9.5.4
lemon law claims, application, 13.2.10.2, 13.4.2.3
Magnuson-Moss restrictions, 2.3.3
nonbuyers, validity, 6.3.7
overview, 1.7.2.3, 9.1
personal injury damages, validity, 5.12
plain language laws, 9.7.3
postsale conduct of seller as waiver, 9.8
repair or replace remedy, 9.1, 9.4.2
  failure of essential purpose, 9.5.2, 13.4.2.3
scope, 9.4
state restrictions, 9.9
tort claims, validity, 12.1
UDAP claims, effect on, 11.1.1.2
UDAP violations, 9.11
unconscionability, 9.6, 11.2.6
  burden of proof, 9.6.1, 11.2.7, 10.1.7.1

LIMITED WARRANTIES
see also WARRANTIES
designation requirements, 2.6.3
full warranties distinguished, 2.5.1
implied warranties, duration, 2.3.2.3, 2.5.4
registration card conditions, disclosure, 2.4.3
used cars, Buyers Guide requirement, 5.7

LIQUIDATED DAMAGES CLAUSES
unconscionability, 11.2.4.4.3

LITIGATION AIDS
see PRACTICE TIPS; RESEARCH AIDS

LOAN STATUTES
see CREDIT STATUTES

LODESTAR FORMULA
lemon law claims, application, 13.2.10.3

LOSS
see DAMAGES

LOST WAGES
consequential damages, 10.6.3.1.2

LOW-MILEAGE VEHICLES
see DEMONSTRATOR CARS

MAGNUSON-MOSS CLAIMS
see also MAGNUSON-MOSS WARRANTY ACT
attorney fees and costs, 2.7.6
binding arbitration, 2.7.2, 2.8.1, 10.2.4S, 10.2.5S
circumstances, 2.7.1
class actions, 2.7.7
damage requirement, 2.2.6
derivative liability, 2.2.7.4
FTC Used Car Rule violations, 14.7.8
individuals, liability of, 2.2.7.5S
informal dispute resolution, 2.8
jurisdiction, 2.7.3
limitations, 2.7.8
mandatory arbitration clauses, validity, 2.7.2, 10.2.4.1S

mobile homes
  breach of federal standards, 15.3.6
  pleading, 15.8.1.1
new cars, 13.4.4, 13.5.2
notice of breach, 2.3.7, 2.5.7.3, 7.2.2
pleading, 2.2.6, 10.1.3.1
postsale warranty disclaimers, 5.7
preconditions, 2.3.7, 2.7.4, 2.8.1
privity considerations
  horizontal privity, 2.3.5, 6.3.2
  vertical privity, 2.3.6, 6.2.2
relief available, 2.7.5
right to cure not necessary, 2.3.7
sample complaints, Appx. K.4–K.7
sample jury instructions, Appx. M.8.1
service contracts, 2.3.8.2, 18.4.3, 18.5.3

MAGNUSON-MOSS WARRANTY ACT
actions under, *see* MAGNUSON-MOSS CLAIMS
arbitration case law, 10.2.4.5S, 10.2.4.6S
auto repairs, application, 17.8.2
basis of the bargain, 2.2.5.4
commercial use, 2.2.2, 2.2.6
common law, relationship, 1.5.3
conditions precedent, restrictions, 7.6.3
Consumer Product Safety Act, relationship, 2.2.2.2
consumer products, application, 1.4.1, 1.4.3, 2.2.2
consumer use, 2.2.2, 2.2.6
damages under, 2.7.5
date of application, 2.2.3
disclaimer restrictions, 2.3.2
disclosure requirements, 2.6, 9.7.1
  violations as UDAP violation, 11.1.6
equitable relief, 2.7.5.4
federal enforcement, 2.7.9
federal preemption, 2.2.4
FTC rules, *see under* FTC RULES
full warranties, requirements, 2.5
implementing regulations, 10.2.4.4S
implied warranties
  duration limitation, 2.3.2.3, 2.5.4, 2.6.4.8
  restrictions on disclaimers, 2.3.2, 2.5.4, 2.6.4.8, 5.3
interpretation, resources, 2.1.2
leases, application, 19.2.3
legislative history, 10.2.4.3S
liable parties, 2.2.7
liberal construction, 1.6.1
limited remedy clauses, requirements, 9.7.1
medical devices, application, 2.2.2.2
mobile homes, application, 15.2.2
new home sales, application, 16.2.3
overview, 1.2.1, 2.1.1, 2.2.1
preemption by other federal laws, 2.2.4
preemption of other laws, 1.5.1, 2.9
prefabricated houses, application, 15.2.2, 16.2.3
research and resource aids, 1.3.5
return of defective goods, application, 8.2.7.8.2
right to cure, 2.3.7
rules, *see under* FTC RULES
scope, 1.4, 2.2
seed exemption, 2.2.2.1
service contracts, application, 1.7.1.6, 2.3.8, 18.5.3
service transactions, application, 17.2.1
state law preemption, 2.9

References are to sections; references followed by "S" appear only in this Supplement

References are to sections; references followed by "S" appear only in this Supplement

References are to sections; references followed by "S" appear only in this Supplement

SERVICE CONTRACTS (*cont.*)
shoddy repair work, 18.6
state law, *see* SERVICE CONTRACT LAWS (STATE)
subsequent owners, 18.9
third party liability, 18.7
    bonds, 18.7.4
    contract administrators, 18.7.2
    creditors and lessors, 18.7.5
    dealer, 18.7.3
    insurance guaranty funds, 18.7.4
UCC, application, 1.2.7
UDAP statutes, application, 18.5.4
UDAP violations, 11.1.3
used car sales, effect, 14.3.3
warranties distinguished, 2.3.8.1, 18.2

SERVICE TRANSACTIONS
auto repairs, *see* AUTOMOBILE REPAIRS
common law warranties, 17.4
cooling-off periods, 17.6, 17.7.1
economic loss damages, 12.2.4
fraud claims, 17.6
home improvement contracts, *see* HOME IMPROVEMENTS
Magnuson-Moss Warranty Act, application, 2.2.2.4, 17.2.1
mixed goods and services transactions, *see* MIXED
      TRANSACTIONS
negligence claims, 12.4.1.1, 17.5
nonconformity with contract obligations, 7.3.1
overview, 1.2.6
rescission, 17.6, 17.7.1
scope issues, 1.4.2
strict liability doctrine, application, 12.1, 12.3.3
tort claims, economic loss damages, 12.2.4
UCC Article 2, application, 17.2.2, 17.2.3, 17.7.1.1
UCC unconscionability, application, 11.2.1, 17.7.1.1
UDAP claims, 17.6

SERVICES
see SERVICE TRANSACTIONS

SET-OFFS
cancelled sales, use of goods, 2.5.3.1, 8.4.6.6, 10.4.1, 10.4.6
    mobile homes, 15.6.3
cover, expenses saved, 10.4.3.5
lemon law claims as defense, 13.2.7
lemon law refunds, allowance for use, 13.2.4.5, 13.2.8.7

SETTLEMENT
lemon law claims, 10.1.6
Magnuson-Moss claims
    attorney fees, 2.7.6.2, 2.7.6.5
    outside dispute mechanism, 2.8.2
mediation, 10.1.6.4S
other parties, effect on, 10.1.6.5S
terms, 10.1.6.2S
UCC claims, 10.1.6

SHAKEN FAITH DOCTRINE
lemon laws, application, 13.2.6.1
major defects, 8.2.7.4

SIDING
see BUILDING MATERIALS; HOME IMPROVEMENTS

SIGNS
see also NOTICE
auto repair shops, notice of statutory rights, 17.8.3.2.3

SPECIAL RELATIONSHIP
determination, 12.2.5

SPECIFIC PERFORMANCE
new home warranty breach, 16.4.1, 16.7.2.6

SPECIFIC PERFORMANCE WARRANTIES
see FUTURE PERFORMANCE WARRANTIES

SPOLIATION
evidence, 10.1.2.5

STANDARD FORM CONTRACTS
see also CONTRACTS
parol evidence rule, application, 3.7.4
unconscionability, 11.2.4.3.3

STANDARD OF CARE
see DUTY OF CARE

STANDARDS
auto repair shops, 17.8.3.3
conspicuousness, determination, 5.8.8
consumer buyers, flexibility, 1.6.2.3, 1.6.3
deception, 11.1.2
evidence, admission into, 10.1.7.4.4
merchantable, 4.2.3, 7.3.5.1, 14.3.2
merchants, good faith, 11.3.2
mobile homes
    construction and safety, 15.3
    federal quality assurance and inspection, 15.3.4
    HUD label, 15.4.1
    HUD standards, 15.3, 15.4.1
    setup, 15.3.1, 15.7.6
negligent conduct, 12.4.1, 12.4.2
new homes, habitability, 16.3.5.1
nonconformity, 7.3
reasonable person standard, 5.8.8
safety, *see* SAFETY STANDARDS
UCC unconscionability, 11.2.4
unfairness, 11.1.2
used cars, 14.3.2, 14.8–14.11
    failure to meet, 14.3.7
warranty, *see* WARRANTIES

STATE LAW
arbitration clauses
    contract law application, 10.2.2S
    validity, 10.2.2S
credit repair, *see* CREDIT REPAIR ORGANIZATION
      STATUTES (STATE)
disclosure duty, 11.4.4.5
federal preemption, *see* FEDERAL PREEMPTION
home improvement contracts, 17.7.4
home solicitations, 17.7.1.4
horizontal privity, 6.3.3
implied warranty disclaimer restrictions, 5.4, 14.3.6
lemon car laws, *see* LEMON LAWS (STATE)
limited remedy clauses, restrictions, 9.9
loans, *see* CREDIT STATUTES
Magnuson-Moss claims, application
    class actions, 2.7.7
    damages, 2.7.5.1
    limitations, 2.7.8
Magnuson-Moss Warranty Act, preemption, 2.9
manufacturer's liability (vertical privity)
    express warranties, 6.2.3
    implied warranties, 6.2.4.2

References are to sections; references followed by "S" appear only in this Supplement

References are to sections; references followed by "S" appear only in this Supplement

Quick Reference to the Consumer Credit and Sales Legal Practice Series

References are to sections in *all* manuals in NCLC's Consumer Credit and Sales Legal Practice Series. References followed by "S" appear only in a supplement.

This Quick Reference pinpoints where to find specific consumer law topics analyzed in the NCLC manuals. References are to individual manual or supplement sections from NCLC's Consumer Credit and Sales Legal Practice Series. For more information on other volumes, see *What Your Library Should Contain* at the beginning of this volume.

This Quick Reference is a speedy means to locate key terms in the appropriate NCLC Manual. More detailed indexes are found at the end of the individual NCLC volumes. The detailed contents pages at the beginning of each volume provide further elaboration once the appropriate manual is identified by use of this Quick Reference. Both the detailed contents pages and the detailed indexes are also available at www.consumerlaw.org.

Pleadings, statutes, regulations, agency interpretations, legislative history, and other appendix material are also found on the CD-Roms that are included with the specified volume. In addition, everything found on the sixteen individual CD-Roms is also included on NCLC's *Consumer Law in a Box* CD-Rom. **NCLC strongly recommends that those searching for pleadings refer to the *Index Guide* that accompanies *Consumer Law Pleadings on CD-Rom*, and not to this *Quick Reference*.**

Another search option can be found on our web site at **www.consumerlaw.org/keyword**. There, users can search all sixteen of NCLC's manuals for a case name, party name, statutory or regulatory citation, or any other word or phrase. The search engine provides the title and page number of every occurrence of that word or phrase within all of our manuals. Further instructions and tips are provided on the web site.

Abbreviations		
AUS	=	Access to Utility Service (2d ed. 2001 and 2003 Supp.)
Auto	=	Automobile Fraud (2d ed. 2003 and 2004 Supp.)
Arbit	=	Consumer Arbitration Agreements (3d ed. 2003)
CBPL	=	Consumer Banking and Payments Law (2d ed. 2002 and 2004 Supp.)
Bankr	=	Consumer Bankruptcy Law and Practice (6th ed. 2000 and 2003 Supp.)

CCA	=	Consumer Class Actions: A Practical Litigation Guide (5th ed. 2002 and 2004 Supp.)
CLP9	=	Consumer Law Pleadings Number Nine (2003)
CLP8	=	Consumer Law Pleadings Number Eight (2002)
CLP7	=	Consumer Law Pleadings Number Seven (2001)
CLP6	=	Consumer Law Pleadings Number Six (2000)
CLP5	=	Consumer Law Pleadings Number Five (1999)
CLP4	=	Consumer Law Pleadings Number Four (1998)
CLP3	=	Consumer Law Pleadings Number Three (1997)
CLP2	=	Consumer Law Pleadings Number Two (1995)
CLP1	=	Consumer Law Pleadings Number One (1994)
COC	=	The Cost of Credit (2d ed. 2000 and 2004 Supp.)
CD	=	Credit Discrimination (3d ed. 2002 and 2004 Supp.)
FCR	=	Fair Credit Reporting (5th ed. 2002 and 2004 Supp.)
FDC	=	Fair Debt Collection (5th ed. 2004)
Repo	=	Repossessions and Foreclosures (5th ed. 2002 and 2003 Supp.)
Stud	=	Student Loan Law (2d ed. 2002 and 2003 Supp.)
TIL	=	Truth in Lending (5th ed. 2003)
UDAP	=	Unfair and Deceptive Acts and Practices (5th ed. 2001 and 2003 Supp.)
Warr	=	Consumer Warranty Law (2d ed. 2001 and 2004 Supp.)

Abandonment of Apartment Building in Bankruptcy—Bankr § 17.8.2
Abbreviations Commonly Used by Debt Collectors—FDC App G.4
Abuse of Process—UDAP § 5.1.4; FDC § 10.6
Acceleration—COC §§ 5.6.2, 5.7.1; Repo § 4.1
Accessions—Repo § 3.5.3.2
Accord and Satisfaction—CBPL § 1.7.3
Account Aggregation—CBPL § 4.10
Accountants—UDAP § 5.12.8
Accrediting Agencies, Student Loans—Stud § 9.4.1.2
Accurate Information in Consumer Reports—FCR § 7.8
ACH—*See* NACHA

References are to sections in *all* manuals in NCLC's Consumer Credit and Sales Legal Practice Series

References are to sections in *all* manuals in NCLC's Consumer Credit and Sales Legal Practice Series

References are to sections in *all* manuals in NCLC's Consumer Credit and Sales Legal Practice Series

References are to sections in *all* manuals in NCLC's Consumer Credit and Sales Legal Practice Series

References are to sections in *all* manuals in NCLC's Consumer Credit and Sales Legal Practice Series

References are to sections in *all* manuals in NCLC's Consumer Credit and Sales Legal Practice Series

References are to sections in *all* manuals in NCLC's Consumer Credit and Sales Legal Practice Series

References are to sections in *all* manuals in NCLC's Consumer Credit and Sales Legal Practice Series

NOTES

NOTES

NOTES

NOTES

NOTES

452

NOTES

453

NOTES

NOTES

NOTES

NOTES